George Eliot's notebooks ... contain memoranda of her reading ... ing *Daniel Deronda*, together with ... notes she recorded in the year foll... e all, the notebooks reveal her ac... about Judaism, and provide insigl... ing that learning into *Daniel Derond*...

One of these notebooks is published here for the first time; others are offered in new transcriptions. They are presented in a form which demonstrates the intellectual coherence underlying the diversity of the memoranda: translations are provided for the notes in German, French, Latin, Greek, and Hebrew; explanatory headnotes are offered, and interpretative links are made to the novel; primary sources are traced and the chronology of George Eliot's reading outlined.

With love
Christmas 2008
x

George Eliot's

Daniel Deronda notebooks

GEORGE ELIOT'S
Daniel Deronda notebooks

Edited by Jane Irwin

CAMBRIDGE
UNIVERSITY PRESS

CAMBRIDGE UNIVERSITY PRESS
Cambridge, New York, Melbourne, Madrid, Cape Town, Singapore, São Paulo, Delhi

Cambridge University Press
The Edinburgh Building, Cambridge CB2 8RU, UK

Published in the United States of America by Cambridge University Press, New York

www.cambridge.org
Information on this title: www.cambridge.org/9780521460644

First published 1996
This digitally printed version 2008

A catalogue record for this publication is available from the British Library

Library of Congress Cataloguing in Publication data

Eliot, George, 1819–1880
[Daniel Deronda notebooks]
George Eliot's Daniel Deronda notebooks/edited by Jane Irwin.
p. cm.
Includes bibliographical references and index.
ISBN 0 521 46064 6 (hardback)
1. Eliot, George, 1819-1880. Daniel Deronda – Criticism, Textual.
2. Eliot, George, 1819–1880 – Notebooks, sketchbooks, etc.
I. Irwin, Jane, 1941– . II. Title.
PR4658.E45D353 1996
823'.8–dc20 96–10391 CIP

ISBN 978-0-521-46064-4 hardback
ISBN 978-0-521-08797-1 paperback

It may be doubted, whether a mind which has no susceptibility to the pleasure of changing its point of view, of mastering a remote form of thought, of perceiving identity of nature under variety of manifestation – a perception which resembles an expansion of one's own being, a pre-existence in the past – can possess the flexibility, the ready sympathy, or the tolerance, which characterizes a truly philosophic culture. Now and then, however, we meet with a nature which combines the faculty for amassing minute erudition with the largeness of view necessary to give it a practical bearing; a high appreciation of the genius of antiquity, with a profound belief in the progressive character of human development ... a wonderful intuition of the mental conditions of past ages with an ardent participation in the most advanced ideas and most hopeful efforts of the present ...

From the first contribution to the *Westminster Review* by Marian Evans: her review of Robert William Mackay's *Progress of the Intellect, as Exemplified in the Religious Development of the Greeks and Hebrews*

Some of his pages read like extracts from his common-place book, which must be, as Southey said of his own, an urn under the arm of a river-god ... Only a devotedness of research such as his own, can give interest and significance to the mass of allusions and particulars ...

Ibid.

Contents

Contents

Contents

PART TWO: THE PFORZHEIMER NOTEBOOKS

Contents

Contents

List of abbreviations

[ ]	Matter supplied by the editor
AC	GE's abbreviation for 'after Christ', equivalent to AD or CE
AD	*Anno Domini,* Latin for 'year of our Lord' according to the Christian calendar, equivalent to CE
AV	Authorized Version of the Bible, also known as the King James Version. Unless otherwise indicated, all references are to this translation.
b.	GE's abbreviation for either 'born' (with birthdate) or 'ben', 'son of'
B	Berg Notebook in the Henry W. and Albert A. Berg Collection of the New York Public Library
Baker I, III, IV	William Baker, ed. *Some George Eliot Notebooks: An Edition of the Carl H. Pforzheimer Library's George Eliot Holograph Notebooks MSS 707, 708, 709, 710, 711.* 4 vols. Salzburg: Institut für Englische Sprache und Literatur, Universität Salzburg, 1976–1985. Volume I - 707, Volume III - 711, Volume IV - 709, 710
BC	Before Christ, according to the Christian calendar, equivalent to BCE
BCE	Before the Common Era, equivalent to BC
Beinecke Notebook	George Eliot MS IV. 6 in the Beinecke Rare Book and Manuscript Library, Yale University. References are to the entry and page numbers in Wiesenfarth.

List of abbreviations

Bennett	Joan Bennett. *George Eliot.* Cambridge: Cambridge University Press, 1948
Carroll	David Carroll, ed. *George Eliot: The Critical Heritage.* London: Routledge and Kegan Paul, 1971
Catalogue	William Baker, ed. *The George Eliot–George Henry Lewes Library: An Annotated Catalogue of Their Books at Dr. Williams's Library, London.* New York: Garland, 1977
ch.	chapter
CE	Common Era, equivalent to the Christian abbreviation AD
Cross	John Walter Cross, ed. *George Eliot's Life as Related in her Letters and Journals.* 3 vols. Edinburgh: Blackwood, 1885
d.	GE's abbreviation for 'died' (with date of death)
DD	George Eliot. *Daniel Deronda.* Edited by Graham Handley. Oxford: Clarendon Press, 1984. Page references are to this edition. Additional references are to the Cabinet Edition, 3 vols. Edinburgh: Blackwood, 1878.
DNB	*Dictionary of National Biography*
DWL	Dr. Williams's Library, London
Felix Holt	George Eliot. *Felix Holt the Radical.* Edited by Fred C. Thomson. Oxford: Clarendon Press, 1980
Folger 13	George Eliot MS M.a.13 in the Folger Shakespeare Library, Washington. The pagination supplied by Pratt and Neufeldt is adopted here.
Folger 14	George Eliot MS M.a.14 in the Folger Shakespeare Library, Washington.
GE	George Eliot
GE Journal	George Eliot MS IV. 3. Journal July 1861 – December 1877 in the Beinecke Rare Book and Manuscript Library, Yale University
GEL	Gordon S. Haight, ed. *The George Eliot Letters.* 9 vols. New Haven: Yale University Press, 1954–1978
GHL	George Henry Lewes
GHL Diary	MS diaries for 1869–1876 in the Beinecke Rare Book and Manuscript Library, Yale University

List of abbreviations

Haight	Gordon S. Haight. *George Eliot: A Biography.* Oxford: Oxford University Press, 1968
Handley	Graham Handley. Introduction and notes to *Daniel Deronda.* Oxford: Clarendon Press, 1984
Hardy	Barbara Hardy. Introduction and notes to *Daniel Deronda.* Harmondsworth: Penguin, 1967
Herodotus	*The History: Herodotus.* Translated by David Grene. Chicago: Chicago University Press, 1987. Passages are identified by book and section numbers.
Impressions	George Eliot. *The Impressions of Theophrastus Such.* Edited by D. J. Enright. London: J. M. Dent, Everyman, 1995
i.q.	*idem quod,* Latin for 'the same as'
Jacobs	Louis Jacobs. *The Jewish Religion: A Companion.* Oxford: Oxford University Press, 1995
Libraries	William Baker, ed. *The Libraries of George Eliot and George Henry Lewes.* Victoria: University of Victoria, English Literary Studies Monograph Series No 24, 1981
Löwy, Bella	Heinrich Graetz, *The History of the Jews.* Abridged and translated by Bella Löwy. 6 vols. Philadelphia: The Jewish Publication Society of America, 1891–1898
McCobb	Anthony McCobb, ed. *George Eliot's Knowledge of German Life and Letters.* Salzburg: Institut für Anglistik und Amerikanistik, Universität Salzburg, 1982
Middlemarch	George Eliot. *Middlemarch.* Edited by David Carroll. Oxford: Clarendon Press, 1986
OED	*Oxford English Dictionary*
Ouvry, Mrs	Mrs E. Carrington Ouvry, granddaughter of GHL. Her inventory of books owned by GE and GHL is published in *Libraries.*
Pinney	Thomas Pinney, ed. *Essays of George Eliot.* New York: Columbia University Press, 1963
Poems	George Eliot. *Collected Poems.* Edited by Lucien Jenkins. London: Skoob, 1989

List of abbreviations

Pratt and Neufeldt
: John Clark Pratt and Victor A. Neufeldt, eds. *George Eliot's 'Middlemarch' Notebooks: A Transcription.* Berkeley: University of California Press, 1979

Pf 707, Pf 708, Pf 709, Pf 710, Pf 711
: Pforzheimer Notebooks MSS 707, 708, 709, 710 and 711 in the Carl H. Pforzheimer Library, New York

R. — GE's abbreviation for Rabbi

Scenes of Clerical Life
: George Eliot. *Scenes of Clerical Life.* Edited by Thomas A. Noble. Oxford: Clarendon Press, 1985

Silas Marner — George Eliot. *Silas Marner: The Weaver of Raveloe.* Edited by Q. D. Leavis. Harmondsworth: Penguin, 1967

sqq. or seqq. — GE's abbreviations for *sequentes,* Latin for '[and] the following [pages]'

u. — GE's abbreviation for the German *und,* in English 'and'

v. — GE's abbreviation for the Latin *vide*, directing herself to 'see, refer to' for further information

V. — GE's abbreviation for Volume

Waley — Daniel Waley, ed. *George Eliot's Blotter: A Commonplace Book.* London: The British Library, 1980

Wiesenfarth — George Eliot. *A Writer's Notebook, 1854–1879, and Uncollected Writings.* Edited by Joseph Wiesenfarth. Charlottesville: University Press of Virginia, 1981

Xtian — GE's abbreviation for Christian

Preface

Like other George Eliot scholars, I am indebted to earlier generations of scholars who have published editions of material essential to our study of her works. Pre-eminent amongst these is Gordon S. Haight's indispensable edition of her letters, which set for later editors the highest standards of accuracy and usefulness.[1] Thomas Pinney's edition of selected essays made many of her periodical articles more readily accessible.[2] The Clarendon edition of the novels now provides critical texts 'based on collation of the manuscripts with all the relevant editions published in George Eliot's lifetime'.[3] It remains to complete the work of publishing critical editions of

1 *The George Eliot Letters*, 9 vols. (New Haven: Yale University Press, 1954–1978), henceforth referred to as GEL.

2 *Essays of George Eliot* (New York: Columbia University Press, 1963). This selection has since been supplemented by Pinney's 'More Leaves from George Eliot's Notebook', *Huntingdon Library Quarterly* 29 (1966): 353–76; Joseph Wiesenfarth's inclusion of uncollected essays in his edition of *A Writer's Notebook, 1854–1879, and Uncollected Writings* (Charlottesville: University of Virginia Press, 1981); *Selected Essays, Poems and Other Writings*, edited by A. S. Byatt and Nicholas Warren (Harmondsworth: Penguin, 1990); and *Selected Critical Writings*, edited by Rosemary Ashton (Oxford: Oxford University Press, 1992).

3 Gordon S. Haight, 'Preface by the General Editor' in George Eliot, *Daniel Deronda*, edited by Graham Handley (Oxford: Clarendon Press, 1984), p. v. All quotations from *Daniel Deronda*, unless otherwise indicated, are from the Clarendon edition. Page references are preceded by chapter numbers, which are provided for reference to other editions.

her notebooks and journals.[1] The task of editing these is challenging. Since George Eliot's memoranda were, of course, addressed only to herself, her handwriting is often hurried and the contents always more elliptical and obscure than in manuscripts intended for other readers. Like other editors, I have experienced the frustrations of failing to trace every note to its source. But the very difficulty of exploring this more private territory has enhanced the satisfaction of discovery and the sense of gaining more insight into the intellectual and imaginative working of her mind. John Livingston Lowes's *The Road to Xanadu* (1927) has made many of us dream that some other 'Gutch Note Book' may serve as a guidebook to 'the Ways of the Imagination' of *our* author. I have not, however, emulated Lowes's method of reporting his heroic journey, as if for armchair travellers, but instead have set forth George Eliot's notes in a form intended to facilitate future scholarship. My models have been Wiesenfarth's edition of her 'Commonplace Book' in the Beinecke Rare Book and Manuscript Library, in *A Writer's Notebook 1854–1879*, and Pratt and Neufeldt's edition of *George Eliot's 'Middlemarch' Notebooks.* The latter includes her book of 'Miscellaneous Quotations' in the Folger Shakespeare Library, and some 130 pages of the Berg Notebook (B 1 to 90v and 175 to 181).[2]

The hitherto unpublished pages of the Berg Notebook partially coincide, in time and in content, with three notebooks in the Carl H. Pforzheimer Collection: Pf 707, Pf 710 and Pf 711. As it was necessary for me to retrace trails marked by William Baker's pioneering work in his editions of the Pforzheimer notebooks, I came to recognize the peculiar difficulties of his

1 Notebooks so far published include the following: Anna Theresa Kitchel, editor, *Quarry for Middlemarch* (Berkeley: University of California Press, 1950); William Baker, editor, *Some George Eliot Notebooks: An Edition of the Carl H. Pforzheimer Library's George Eliot Holograph Notebooks, MSS 707, 708, 709, 710, 711,* 4 vols. (Salzburg: Institut für Englische Sprache und Literatur, Universität Salzburg, 1976–1985); John Clark Pratt and Victor A. Neufeldt, editors, *George Eliot's 'Middlemarch' Notebooks: A Transcription* (Berkeley: University of California Press, 1979); Daniel Waley, editor, *George Eliot's Blotter: A Commonplace Book* (London: The British Library, 1980); and Wiesenfarth's edition of *A Writer's Notebook, 1854–1879.* References to these editions are cited as Baker I, III, and IV, Pratt and Neufeldt, Waley, and Wiesenfarth.

2 Entries on those pages of the Berg Notebook were mostly made before George Eliot changed the colour of her ink from black to violet, 'probably sometime in 1872' (Pratt and Neufeldt, p. xxi). There are also numerous later additions in violet ink.

project.[1] One satisfying aspect of my study of the Berg Notebook sources was to find incidental clarification of a great many entries in the Pforzheimer notebooks. The four notebooks together comprise what may properly be called 'George Eliot's *Daniel Deronda* notebooks'. Their contents form an integral record of her preparatory reading before and during the writing of the novel.[2]

In preparing George Eliot's notes for publication, I have followed the practice established by Haight's edition of the *Letters*. My principal concern, like his, has been the reader's convenience. I have tried to provide an accurate text, but the transcription includes minor alterations.[3] Her customary plus sign (+) is represented by an ampersand (&). Her parentheses and square brackets are both represented by parentheses; square brackets indicate editorial insertions in the text. Quotation marks have been standardized to single inverted commas; double quotation marks are reserved for quotations within quotations. Her ellipses have been standardized to three (…).

No spellings have been altered or standardized: old-style spellings in her transcriptions, such as 'bran new', 'stedfast', 'œconomy', and 'aera', are retained. In German transcriptions, her use of 'ss' for 'ß' has beeen kept. The variant transliterations of Hebrew words and names, reflecting various sources – French, German, and English – have also been retained. 'Mishnah', 'Mishna', and 'Mischna' are easily recognized as transliterations of the same Hebrew word, as are the alternative spellings of 'Cabbala' and 'Kabbalah'. Those of her abbreviations which are retained are listed in the table of abbreviations. Some contractions such as w^{h} and comm^{y} have been silently expanded; others such as 19th are rendered as 19th. Punctuation has been

1 Baker's other publications include *The George Eliot–George Henry Lewes Library: An Annotated Catalogue of Their Books at Dr. Williams's Library, London* (New York: Garland, 1977) and four works related to the Jewish aspect of *Daniel Deronda*: 'George Eliot's Readings in Nineteenth-Century Jewish Historians', *Victorian Studies* 15 (1972): 463–73; 'The Kabbalah, Mordecai, and George Eliot's Religion of Humanity', *Yearbook of English Studies* 3 (1973): 216–21; *George Eliot and Judaism* (Salzburg: Institut für Englische Sprache und Literatur, Universität Salzburg, 1975); and 'George Eliot and Zionism' in Alice Shalvi, editor, *'Daniel Deronda': A Centenary Symposium* (Jerusalem: Jerusalem Academic Press, 1976).

2 Pf 710 and Pf 707 also include notes made following its publication. For a more specific discussion of the contents and formats of the Pforzheimer notebooks, see the Introduction to Part Two, pp. 217–229.

3 GEL I, xxv.

supplied sparingly, for the sake of clarity or consistency. Paired slash marks indicate a note added later above the line; however, the occasional word first overlooked in her transcription or translation and added immediately is inserted in the appropriate place without editorial comment.

George Eliot's pagination of the Berg Notebook has been preserved, with verso numbers supplied by the editor. Page numbers 93, 95, 98 and 113 were omitted by George Eliot; the number 153a was given to a page she first overlooked, and the number 174 to her last numbered page, the verso of 173. Her Index and cross-reference numbers for the Berg Notebook clearly indicate that she intended her numbers to refer to the double-page opening.[1] The page numbered by George Eliot as 174 would have been editorially designated as 173v, and the opposite page, containing the first page of the Positivist Calendar, would have been 174. However, the numbers supplied by Pratt and Neufeldt for the unpaginated Positivist Calendar – 175 to 181 – have been preserved in this edition, and the alphabetized pages of the Index have been numbered 182 to 194. Notebook page numbers, whether George Eliot's originals or supplied by the editor, are indicated within the text between slash marks, in bold type: **/182v/**.

For the greater convenience of the reader, the policy of not reproducing exact transcriptions of the notebooks has been applied to page order and layout. Ends of lines do not imitate the constraints of the notebook page sizes. Running heads are not reproduced so as to break into sentences or paragraphs. The extensive notes which are characteristic of the Berg Notebook often do not fill consecutive pages: George Eliot occasionally began, on a facing verso page, an additional note which then continued, in tandem with her original note, for several pages. Some passages in German, such as the lengthy extracts from Moritz Steinschneider, are interrupted by running translations on six intervening pages. Finally, when no blank pages remained, she began her notes on the Jewish liturgy, intermittently infilling the available spaces beneath Index entries. I have tried to present the continuities of her thought and reading, rather than to reproduce the discontinuities of the Berg Notebook's page layouts.

The coherence of George Eliot's notes, seldom immediately apparent in the manuscript notebooks, is also seldom well represented in the standard publication format, where her notes are set in a single heterogeneous block of text between the introduction and the endnotes. In the Berg Notebook,

1 For example, her Index entry 'Aristobolus, 151' refers to a note on B 150v.

coherence and clarity are most evident when sections of her text – one might borrow her term 'pericopes' – are read as distinct 'lessons'. I have therefore presented her text in thirty-four sections, each comprising between one page and eighteen pages of her manuscript notes, and each having its own introductory headnote. The final section of the Berg Notebook is George Eliot's Index. Wherever possible, the wording of her index reference has been used in the section title. The integrity of each section is grounded in its subject matter, or the author of her source, or a combination of both. This method has two practical benefits: the headnotes address ramifications of the particular topics of each section; and page references to most sources may be bracketed in the text, rather than proliferating as 'Ibid.' footnotes.

The headnote to each section begins with the identification of George Eliot's sources and the records, where known, of her reading these works. Her notes elsewhere, from these sources or on related topics, are indicated as well. My guideline for explanatory introduction of the content of her notes has been to assume that the reader's ignorance of these topics is comparable to my own when I began my study of the notebooks. I have tried not to make a display of every aspect of the source material that has fascinated me in the course of my studies, but to present concisely what is most pertinent to George Eliot's interest in the material. Equally, I have tried not to display continuing ignorance on my part. For editorial comments on Judaism my reference guides have been the *Encyclopedia Judaica*[1] and *The Jewish Religion: A Companion.*[2]

The footnotes for each section include references to occasional sources not identified in the headnote, page references not accommodated in brackets within the text, and translations. The footnotes also make connections to George Eliot's use of her notes in *Daniel Deronda.* The organization of each section thus reflects a process: George Eliot acquires a text, reads it, annotates it, writes excerpts or summaries in her notebook, and incorporates some aspects of it in her novel.

Of course, the process is not so simple. George Eliot's notes and sources are not all equal in their relevance to *Daniel Deronda.* The dangers of over-ingenuity and narrowness in the critical pursuit of specific sources for ideas and images in her novels have been pointed out by W. J. Harvey. As he has

1 Edited by Cecil Roth and Geoffrey Wigoder, 16 vols. (Jerusalem: Keter, 1972).

2 Compiled by Louis Jacobs (Oxford: Oxford University Press, 1995), henceforth referred to as Jacobs.

remarked, 'George Eliot's mind is like the National Gallery; for every canvas on display there are two stored away in the basement'.[1] Sir Hugo Mallinger's metaphor may also be adduced: unless one is occupied in writing 'donnish books', one is never given a cue to spin out 'pages of the Greek dramatists'. A 'cartload of learning in the right place' will occasionally, however, 'tell in politics'[2] and even in art. In the Berg Notebook, notes on the oral transmission of the Homeric epics and on the question 'When was the Mischna written down?' reveal George Eliot's general intellectual curiosity about topics of cultural history; this research is never put on public exhibition. In other sections, anecdotes or 'Motives & Pictures' recorded because they intrigued her are later reproduced in *Daniel Deronda*. Her notes from Leopold Zunz on the sufferings of Israel, in contrast, are deeply involved with her imaginative conception of Mordecai's role.

These variable levels of engagement of George Eliot's intellectual and imaginative energy evoke for me a compelling metaphor for the critical endeavour of editing her notebooks. In charting the ways of her imagination, I aim not to publish a roadmap but to trace some contour lines of her imaginative terrain.[3]

1 The Intellectual Background of the Novel: Casaubon and Lydgate', in Barbara Hardy, editor, *'Middlemarch': Critical Approaches to the Novel* (London: Athlone Press, 1967), p. 37. See also Harvey's 'Idea and Image in the Novels of George Eliot' in Barbara Hardy, editor, *Critical Essays on George Eliot*, 2nd edition (London: Routledge and Kegan Paul, 1979), pp. 151–98.

2 DD ch. 16: 161.

3 Harvey refers to maps and contours in 'The Intellectual Background', p. 25, and in 'Idea and Image' on p. 179. His preferred metaphor, however, is one borrowed from GE: following threads in the 'tangled skein' of her ideas. See 'Idea and Image', pp. 160–98, *passim*.

Acknowledgments

My first thanks are due to Jonathan G. Ouvry, in whom the George Eliot copyright is vested, and to the Henry W. and Albert A. Berg Collection in the Research Libraries of the New York Public Library, the Carl H. Pforzheimer Shelley and his Circle Collection, also housed in the New York Public Library, and the Beinecke Rare Book and Manuscript Library, Yale University, for permissions to publish manuscript material.

In these and other libraries I have incurred many obligations for professional assistance. I am especially grateful to Mihai H. Handrea, former Curator of the Carl H. Pforzheimer Collection, for his gracious and unfailing support of my work, even when my research leaves were timed inopportunely to coincide with structural renovations to the New York Public Library.

In my visits to Dr. Williams's Library, my very numerous requests met ever courteous responses, for which I thank John M. Creasey, Head Assistant Librarian, and his colleague Janet E. Barnes. Their work gives substance to the words of the plaque honouring the memory of the Reverend Daniel Williams (1643–1716), who 'left his library to public use / Without distinction of creed status or vocation', so that 'seekers after / Truth Wisdom and unfettered Religious Fellowship' might find 'their path to solid learning / Easier than he himself had found it'. It is fitting that George Eliot's and George Henry Lewes's books are deposited in the library founded by him.

Efficient staff have facilitated my study of manuscripts and many a book 'nicht so leicht zu bekommen' in the following collections: the Special Collections and the Reading Room of the New York Public Library; the Beinecke Rare Books and Manuscripts Library, Yale University; the British Library; the Bodleian Library; the Folger Shakespeare Library; the Morris L.

Parrish Collection, Princeton University; the University Library, Cambridge; the Girton College Library, Cambridge; the Robarts Library at the University of Toronto; the Library of University College, London, especially the David Mocatta Collection; the Jews' College Library, London; the John Rylands University Library of Manchester, whose rich collection of Judaica includes the library of Dr. A. Marmorstein; and the Manchester Jewish Museum. Closer to home, the Mills Memorial Library of McMaster University has earned my gratitude by preserving many books from its founding years, when it was a Baptist theological college. In an era when too many libraries de-accession old volumes to make room for new acquisitions, it is gratifying to find books, which may have been quite out of request since the 1870s, still kept in storage. Special thanks are due to Carl Spadoni, Research Collections Librarian for the Mills Memorial Library, for expediting my study of microfilms in the early stages of this research.

My work, during my graduate year at McMaster University and doctoral studies at Cambridge University, and in the course of my recent research, has benefited from the criticism and encouragement of other scholars and the generous support of colleagues and friends. I wish to record my warm gratitude to them: Matt Adamson, Philip Alexander, Maqbool Aziz, Richard Bachmann, William Baker, Bernard Baskin, Gillian Beer, Alwyn and Jayne Berland, Alvan Bregman, David Carroll, Gerald Chapple, Lucille Cohen, Margaret Ezell, Riemer Faber, John Harvey, James King, Elizabeth Legge, Norma Lundberg, Victor Neufeldt, Michael Ross, Shannon Smith, Paul Vigneux, Joseph Wiesenfarth, and David Womersley. The anonymous external readers of my manuscript also deserve my sincere thanks. The remnant imperfections of this work are my own.

I am grateful to Cambridge University Press, and in particular to Andrew Brown, Kevin Taylor, and Josie Dixon for their patient encouragement.

For financial assistance which made this work possible, I wish to thank the Social Sciences and Humanities Research Council of Canada for a Research Grant – awarded when independent scholars were still permitted to enter competitions for these grants – which supported one year's research in 1989–1990, and for the earlier award of a Doctoral Fellowship (1978–1983); and Girton College, Cambridge, for a Graduate Scholarship (The Pfeiffer). Trent University provided intermittent unemployment leaves and three short-term Faculty Research Grants.

Finally, this work is dedicated to R. M. B. in remembrance of happy times.

Introduction

In the summer and autumn of 1872, while George Eliot was finishing the writing of *Middlemarch,* she was also making notes in the small portable book now known as Pforzheimer MS 711. This is the first of several books which include notes related to the novel she was to begin in 1874 and complete in 1876, *Daniel Deronda.* She finished the Finale to *Middlemarch* on October 2; a fortnight earlier, she and Lewes crossed the Channel to take the waters at Homburg, where on 26 September they saw amongst the roulette players 'Miss Leigh (Byron's granddaughter) having lost 500 £, looking feverishly excited. Painful sight' (GHL 1872 Diary). George Eliot also mentioned this scene, in a letter to John Blackwood, as 'the saddest thing to be witnessed'. Despite her comment to Blackwood that 'there is very little dramatic "Stoff" to be picked up by watching or listening' in the Kursaal, the source of the dramatic opening paragraphs of *Daniel Deronda* was the painful sight of Miss Leigh's play 'in the grasp of this mean, money-raking demon' (GEL V 314). But the written record of this 'Stoff' is to be found only in Lewes's Diary and George Eliot's letter to Blackwood. Her notebook recorded no observations from life, but was reserved for notes from her reading. For instance, her notes on gambling superstitions (Pf 711 40, 41) date from April 1874, when she looked up an article on the topic in the June 1872 *Cornhill Magazine.* By that time, having made 'sketches towards Daniel Deronda, [in] Jan. & Feb. 1874', she must have formed an intention to make gambling a dramatic scene and thematic motif in her novel.[1] Yet there is only one indirect allusion in *Daniel Deronda* to 'the "axioms of a professional gambler and cheat", as narrated by Houdin'. If we turn to the *Cornhill* article, we do not find there the source

1 'Order of Writings' in the GE Journal.

of certain glimpses, in the novel's first chapter, of an impassive Italian with an infallible system, or a worn-out libertine inspired by 'some dream of white crows'. In this instance little is gained by indefatigable searching into written sources. The matter that engages the reader in the opening chapter had its source in the painful impressions made during George Eliot's visit to the Kursaal in September 1872. For memories of that experience she needed no memoranda.[1]

As an introduction to an edition of George Eliot's memoranda, this *exemplum* is perhaps unduly sceptical. *Caveat lector,* if you will. On the other hand, George Eliot's distinction as a novelist lies in her power to locate vivid impressions and dramatized experience within a considered and comprehensive intellectual framework of reference. The intelligence which sustains her fiction is nourished by extensive preparatory reading. Her written records of that reading provide insight into a process of mental argument which may remain latent or scarcely manifest in the novel itself. In this regard, the *Daniel Deronda* Notebooks – the second part of the Berg Notebook, together with the Pforzheimer notebooks Pf 711, Pf 710 and Pf 707 – have peculiar significance. The predominantly Jewish content of George Eliot's notes must be pertinent to the critical problem of the disparity of reader response to the Jewish content of the novel. The disagreement among readers is summed up in Henry James's well-known 'Conversation': Constantius complains that 'all the Jewish burden of the story tended to weary me'; Theodora's rejoinder is that she thinks 'the Jewish element in *Deronda* ... a very fine idea; it's a noble subject'. But then, she says, she has 'never disliked the Jews, as some people do'. That is, she had no initial prejudice against Jews which the novel had to overcome. Pulcheria, in contrast, has an imagination which supplies each Jewish character, including Deronda, with 'a horrid big Jewish nose', even though the author makes no mention of it. Pulcheria has known some Jews, 'clever, but not charming'; clever or not, they kept themselves 'so dirty'. Clearly, any number of ablutions performed by fictional

1 For Joan Bennett, the witnessing of this scene is 'the originating impulse' of one central theme of the novel; she admires the success of its realization, citing the passage which begins, 'suddenly he felt the moment become dramatic' (DD ch. 1: 5). But, she argues, 'the widely separated origins of the two themes ... create a fissure between them of which most readers have been conscious in spite of the bridges the author has built across it' (Bennett, pp. 181, 183). Her argument about the fissure between the dramatic theme and the Zionist theme will be discussed later in this Introduction.

Jewish characters would not alter her opinion of real Jews known – or not known – to her.[1] James's 'Conversation' dramatizes an implicit truth that must be acknowledged: *Daniel Deronda* has no power to convert readers to philosemitism, or even to diminish the strength of any aversion to Jews.

In a letter written to Harriet Beecher Stowe in October 1876, George Eliot admitted the impossibility of overcoming the usual English attitude towards Jews and other 'oriental peoples', a narrow-minded 'spirit of arrogance and contemptuous dictatorialness':

> There is nothing I should care more to do, *if it were possible*, than to rouse the imagination of men and women to a vision of human claims in those races of their fellow-men who most differ from them in customs and beliefs. [Emphasis added.]

But in view of 'the intellectual narrowness – in plain English, the stupidity, which is still the average mark of our culture', she had only expected that 'the Jewish element in "Deronda" would [have created] much stronger resistance and even repulsion than it [had] actually met with'. Of her Christian readers, she had expected not to influence the conversion of opinion, but only to provoke 'more aversion' than, in the event, she found.[2]

Responses from her Jewish readers indicated a greater influence amongst them. In her journal entry for 1 December 1876, she notes: 'Words of gratitude have come from Jews & Jewesses, & there are certain signs that I may have contributed my mite to a good result'. That the result was not better Jewish–Christian fellowship is evident from the preceding statement that she had 'been made aware of much repugnance or else indifference towards the Jewish part of Deronda, & of some hostile as well as adverse reviewing'. A fortnight later she referred to an American Jew's assurance that *Deronda* had 'already had an elevating effect on the minds of some among his people', and to the editor of the *Jewish Chronicle* (Abraham Benisch), who had used 'strong words as to the effect the book [was] producing' among his readers. Four months later, she noted that she had had 'some delightful evidence of the great effect wrought by "Deronda", especially among Jews'.[3]

1 'Daniel Deronda: A Conversation', *Atlantic Monthly* 38 (1876): 684–94. Reprinted in Carroll, pp. 417–33; see pp. 422–3 and 417.

2 GEL VI 301–2; also reprinted in Carroll, pp. 405–6.

3 GE Journal, 1 and 15 December 1876 and 22 April 1877.

Jewish readers of the novel were amazed by the authenticity of the Jewish part of the novel. Lewes's diary entry for 6 June 1876 notes that he was told of 'an old Rabbi who marvelled how a Christian could so enter into the spirit of Judaism as G. Eliot'. The marvel was not that George Eliot could identify 'the *talith* or white blue-fringed kind of blanket which is the garment of prayer' (DD ch. 32: 338), or that she had acquainted herself with Jewish ceremonies, customs, and traditions, but that she had acquired so inward a comprehension of 'the spirit of Judaism'. As Sigmund Freud was to remark, George Eliot knew of things 'we [Jews] speak of only among ourselves'.[1]

Her familiarity with Judaism was acquired in various ways, each having its fictional parallel in Daniel Deronda's education. Her visits to the Juden-gasse and Orthodox synagogue in Frankfurt produced a mixture of impressions; in the same settings Deronda experiences similarly powerful and resistant feelings.[2] Like Deronda, she was acquainted with Jewish musicians and knew a young, petite and impoverished 'little Jewess'.[3] George Eliot's friendship with Emanuel Deutsch, who taught her Hebrew, has its fictional complement in Mordecai's friendly instruction of Deronda: '(for somehow, in deference to Mordecai, he had begun to study Hebrew)' (DD ch. 35: 384). Personal acquaintance with these and many other Jews certainly contributed to her sympathetic interest, as James surmises when he makes Theodora remark, 'George Eliot must have known some delightful Jews!'[4] But such acquaintance does not account for her knowing what they spoke of only amongst themselves.

1 Ernest Jones, *The Life and Work of Sigmund Freud,* edited and abridged in one volume by Lionel Trilling and Stephen Marcus (Harmondsworth: Pelican, 1964), p. 166.

2 DD ch. 32. Compare GHL 1873 Diary entries for August 1, 8, 15, and 16, published in part in GEL V 425 and 427.

3 DD ch. 36: 405. On 10 March 1874 GE and GHL attended a private concert after an elegant dinner party, where Agnes Zimmerman performed, and they attended another concert by her on 28 November (GHL Diary). GE became acquainted with 'Hertha' Marks, a young and impoverished 'little Jewess' in September 1874, through Barbara Bodichon, and in 1875 and 1876 contributed to assist her study at Girton College; see GEL VI 83, and many later references. On 26 March 1875 'Barbara & Miss Marks [came] to dinner; after dinner Miss M. sang Hebrew Hymns'. On 4 April, a Sunday, 'Miss Marks sang' again at the Priory (GHL Diary).

4 Carroll, p. 423.

Emanuel Deutsch, as both friend and author, had a key role in the genesis of the novel. He has been identified as 'the probable model' for Mordecai and also as a source for Mirah.[1] Readers of the *Daniel Deronda* Notebooks will come to see that in the novel's conception, his life was less influential than his literary remains. George Eliot's familiarity with his prolonged suffering from cancer and his wish to commit suicide no doubt informed her presentation of Mordecai's endurance and Mirah's suicide attempt.[2] But without her inward understanding of Judaism, these characters might have been only vessels of pathos, comparable to Riah in *Our Mutual Friend.* After the death of Deutsch in Alexandria in May 1873, George Eliot corresponded with and visited Lady Strangford, the editor of the posthumous collection of his writings.[3] The notes from Deutsch in Pf 711 are taken from this collection, which was published early in 1874. The Berg Notebook extracts from Deutsch were also made at this time, and not during the period from 1866 to 1869, when he was a regular visitor to the Priory. His essays are brief introductions to large topics – the Talmud, the Midrash – written for non-Jewish readers. George Eliot's notes from Deutsch are also brief; but she takes up his writings as if they were letters of introduction to a new world of literature, and sets out on her own kind of journey to the Orient.

A fortnight after receiving news of his death, George Eliot and Lewes visited Oxford, where on 7 June they met David Mocatta (GHL Diary). A wealthy philanthropist, of the seventh generation of a family which had settled in England in 1670, 'Mocatta did all he could to promote education, especially of the Jewish poor, and he encouraged Jewish literature and research' (*DNB*). Amongst other works, he funded the publication of books by Leopold Zunz and an English translation (in 1891) of Heinrich Graetz's *History of the Jews.* Mocatta's valuable collection of books on Judaism may have been that referred to by Oscar Browning: 'George Eliot obtained access to a large library of Jewish literature in London, and the books

1 Baker, in *George Eliot and Judaism,* p. 131, cites Deutsch as 'the probable model' for Mordecai. George Grove wrote to GE on 27 March 1876: 'You must have thought of our dear Deutsch when you conceived [Mirah's] character' (GEL IX 173).

2 Haight, p. 471, and GEL V 160–1.

3 *Literary Remains of the Late Emanuel Deutsch* (London: John Murray, 1874), edited anonymously by Emily Anne Beaufort, Viscountess Strangford. See the headnote to the 'Mohammed, the Hebrews in Egypt, and the colonization of Jerusalem' section, Pf 711 43–46, 50, 51.

preserved still show traces of her untiring labours'.[1] Alternatively, Browning's reference may be to her own acquired library; the books now preserved in Dr. Williams's Library still show those traces of her 'untiring labours'. Her acquisitions began in earnest that summer: Lewes's 1873 Diary records 'Books on Jewish subjects for Polly's novel' (in Frankfurt, 30 July), and on 27 August, after their return to London, he 'went into town & saw Haas about books for Polly on Judaism'.[2]

George Eliot's 'Books Wanted' note on Pf 711 21 lists eighteen books, the primary reading for an intensive study of Jewish subjects. She immediately began reading and making notes. On 6 September 'Polly read Stanley's Palestine & Sinai aloud' (GHL Diary); her note from *Sinai and Palestine* on Pf 711 25 records the peculiar 'confluence of associations' in a land where 'side by side are to be seen the hieroglyphics of the great Ramses, the cunieform inscriptions of Sennacherib, the Latin inscriptions of the Emperor Antoninus'. But she soon turned her attention from the land of Palestine to the people whose national and religious history may be said to inscribe an even greater confluence of associations.[3] 'Grätz Geschichte der Juden' was read daily from 14 September to 3 October, and on 4 October she began 'Milman's History of the Jews' (GHL Diary). Notes from her reading on Jewish subjects began to fill the small pages of Pf 711, beginning with two short notes from Milman on Pf 711 8. Her first Jewish note in the Berg Notebook combines material from Milman, Graetz, and Deutsch's essay on 'The Talmud'. Subsequent entries in the Berg Notebook are records of a concentrated programme of reading which preceded the writing of the novel's opening chapters: during the period from September 1873, through 'Sketches towards Daniel Deronda, Jan. & Feb. 1874', to Lewes's Diary entry for 11 June 1874: 'Polly read opening chapters of her new novel'.[4]

1 *Life of George Eliot* (London: Walter Scott, 1890), p. 123. The Mocatta Collection was bequeathed to University College, London; however, much of the collection was destroyed by enemy action during the Second World War. The present Mocatta Collection in the University College Library is a partial restoration.

2 Nicholas Trübner was another source; see Pf 711 114: 'Books retained from T'. Also, some of Deutsch's books were given or bequeathed to GE and are now in DWL.

3 In 'The Modern Hep! Hep! Hep!' GE refers to 'a small nation – "the smallest of the nations" – whose territory lay on the highway between three continents' (*Impressions*, p. 141).

4 This period almost coincides with the calendar for the Jewish year 5634, which began on 22 September 1873 (B 173).

Her intimacy with Jewish life has its source in this preparatory reading, which extended far beyond what might have been useful for colour in her novel and gave her an entry to the inner life of Judaism. It is this intimacy – not merely the visitor's view of the Juden-gasse, the service at the synagogue, or the family Sabbath meal – which was recognized by Jewish readers. Deronda shares some of this reading: Leopold Zunz's *Die Synagogale Poesie des Mittelalters* and *Salomon Maimons Lebensgeschichte* are mentioned. But these two texts are merely a visible portion of the novel's vast subtext and infrastructure of Jewish literature, which is occluded or scarcely noticed by non-Jewish readers. A. S. Byatt has commented that written language, addressed to someone unknown, is 'a matter of what used to be called the inner life':

> reading lets us into someone else's privacy while we retain our own. It is in this sense that I can say that I know George Eliot better than I know my husband. I have shared her inner life.[1]

This comment by a fellow-novelist is suggestive, for the intimacy of this matter of addressing someone unknown is central to the imaginative conception of Deronda's character. He grows up longing for news of his unknown mother. When he finally meets her, there is no reunion, only a formal audience, the purpose of which is to deliver to him the address of his grandfather's literary remains. These written memorials are nevertheless necessary to restore to Deronda his life as a Jew.

The Berg Notebook extracts reveal that the inner life of Judaism is peculiarly constituted by two forms of communication: the transmission of the written word to future generations unknown, and oral disputes about the interpretation of the written word. That Deronda's grandfather loved disputation is significant, for addressing an opponent, whether known or unknown, is the most inward theme of Jewish literature.

What Jews speak of only among themselves is often difference of opinion, controversy. In the study of the Talmud, 'what is truly Talmudic' is 'the thrust and parry, the give and take of argument'.[2] The inner conflict among Jews has frequently been self-destructive, but it has not destroyed Judaism. Indeed it might be argued that what has enabled Judaism to survive its long history

1 *Guardian Weekly*, 15 March 1992, p. 26.

2 Jacob Neusner, *Invitation to the Talmud: A Teaching Book*, revised edition (San Francisco: Harper and Row, 1984), p. xv.

of martyrdom and persecution, from outside and inside its own community, is Jewish skill in the thrust and parry of argument. That such an inner struggle could stimulate the development of survival techniques for the evolution and growth of Judaism was of great interest to George Eliot.[1] For instance, she noted that in the tenth-century controversy over Menahem's Hebrew Lexicon, hot-blooded contention and virulent satire served to enrich the Hebrew language (B 139v); the witty lampoons hurled by the opposing camps produced its renewed power and resiliency.

Contention is a very common topic of the Berg Notebook extracts. A few instances are the period of civil war between the Sadducees and Pharisees (B 110v, B 153), the battle between the adherents of Hyrcanus and Aristobulus (B 154v), the dispute between the schools of Hillel and Schammai (B 107v), and the Maimonidean controversy (B 193). In the nineteenth-century conflict between Orthodox and Reform views (B 110 to 111 and 124 to 128v), many of these historical struggles were incorporated into contemporary argument. Even apostates such as Salomon Maimon (B 136) and Hyam Isaacs (B 129v to 135v) carry a Jewish habit of argument into their writings as non-believers or Christians.

In the novel, this history of Jewish controversies is almost concealed. When Deronda asks the exact time of service at the synagogue in Frankfurt, he is directed by a youth 'who entered cordially into his wanting not the fine new building of the Reformed but the old Rabbinical school of the orthodox' (DD ch. 32: 338); but this preference might seem, to non-Jews, to be based on an interest in architectural history. Non-Jews might also be puzzled by Mordecai's reference to a tenth-century schism: 'Our religion united us before it divided us – it made us a people before it made Rabbanites and Karaites' (DD ch. 63: 698). Its relevance to nineteenth-century divisions is obscure to most readers who are not of that united-but-divided people. Jewish sectarianism is not dramatized in *Daniel Deronda*. Instead, the discussion in the *Hand and Banner* is presented as a reasoned communication of various differences of opinion.

1 In 'The Modern Hep! Hep! Hep!' she comments:

> Such internal conflict naturally tightened the bands of conservatism, which needed to be strong if it were to rescue the ... vital spirit of a small nation ... But all that need be noticed here is the continuity of that national education (by outward and inward circumstance) which created in the Jews a feeling of race, a sense of corporate existence, unique in its intensity. (*Impressions*, p. 141)

This vigorous exchange of views is in strong contrast to sectarian disputes between Christian opponents in George Eliot's other works. From *Scenes of Clerical Life* onwards, such disputes are mostly forms of non-communication. Perhaps the least memorable of these is Amos Barton's 'extremely argumentative [sermon] on the Incarnation ... preached to a congregation not one of whom had any doubt of that doctrine, and to whom the Socinians therein confuted were as unknown as the Arimaspians'.[1] Perhaps the most memorable is a great non-debate between the Dissenting challenger, the Rev. Rufus Lyon, and the defender of the Church, a curate who runs away without attempting to read his prepared speech. The subsequent private printing of the text of the curate's non-speech (with a motto from the golden-mouthed orator St. Chrysostom) aptly re-enacts the Rector's strictly rhetorical question: 'You don't suppose I'm going to hold a public debate with a schismatic of that sort?' There is no hint that public controversy might strengthen a religious tradition. On the contrary, it is Baruch Nolan's opinion that 'this debating is an atheistical sort of thing; the Atheists are very fond of it'.[2] Nolan, a Churchman whose extraction is never questioned – despite his Hebrew name and his 'remarkable hooked nose'[3] – seems to be unaware that for 'the rabbis of the Talmud ... their chief rite was *argument*'.[4]

For George Eliot, the great schism between Judaism and Christianity must be set in the historical context of their separately schismatic development. No doubt she hoped, despite her later disclaimers to Stowe and others, that her novel would help some readers, 'western people who have been reared in Christianity', to acknowledge their 'peculiar debt' to 'the Hebrews'. She may also have thought that making Christians aware of neglected 'oriental' aspects of the history of their faith would contribute to the evolutionary development of Western tradition.[5] Henry Hart Milman had proposed that

> the philosophy of the Talmud [be considered] without the apologetic reserve and prudent suppression of the modern Jewish writers, or without the remorseless literalness of most Christian expositors; without receiving it as altogether a mystery of esoteric wisdom ... only really intelligible to

1 'The Sad Fortunes of the Reverend Amos Barton', in *Scenes of Clerical Life*, ch. 3: 35.

2 *Felix Holt*, ch. 23 and 24: 198–210.

3 *Felix Holt*, ch. 20: 178.

4 Neusner, pp. xix–xx.

5 'They hardly know that Christ was a Jew. And I find men educated at Rugby supposing that Christ spoke Greek.' (GEL VI 301–2).

> the initiate, but as the growth of the human mind in a very peculiar condition ... and a mysticism of half-European, half-Asiatic cast.

Such a project, as Milman acknowledged, required uncommon gifts:

> a perfect mastery of Rabbinical Hebrew ... as well as a calm and subtle, and penetrating, I would almost say, ... a reverential judgement – the gift of few men, of still fewer who are likely to devote their minds to what after all might prove but a barren study ... A religious mind would be above all indispensable; but the combination of religious zeal with respect for the religion of others is the last and tardiest growth in the inexhaustible soil of Christian virtue.

'So alone should we know', he concludes, 'what the Jews have been, what they may be; and fully understand their writings, and their later history.'[1]

As Milman observed, few Christian men had the qualifications for such a project. His estimate of the scarcity of such a combination of gifts reveals, however, a mind a little spotted with commonness; he unconsciously excluded certain candidates. If a woman, a lapsed Christian, whose mastery of Rabbinical Hebrew was far from perfect, nevertheless came to understand the Jews' writings and their later history, it was because she looked for that uncommon mixture of scrupulous scholarship and reverential judgement in the nineteenth-century *Wissenschaft des Judentums* movement. She was peculiarly well-fitted to know that the German Jews had taken the lead in such historical inquiries. Zunz, Graetz, and Steinschneider were closely studied by her in the original German; she did not need to wait for, or depend upon, translations of these critical studies of Judaism.

When she came to read the English translation of Abraham Geiger's *Das Judenthum und seine Geschichte*, she found in the Appendix these opening words: 'Nearly thirty years ago, Strauss performed the great deed of writing a critical work of the Life of Jesus ...'[2] Nearly thirty years had passed since the publication of her translation of David Friedrich Strauss's *Das Leben Jesu*. To trace the full history of her lifelong fascination with the varieties of religious experience is beyond the scope of this Introduction. Even to explore the relation between the Religion of Humanity and Judaeo-Christian

1 *The History of the Jews from the Earliest Period Down to Modern Times*, 4th edition, 3 vols. (London: John Murray, 1866), III, 42.

2 *Judaism and its History*, translated by Maurice Mayer (New York: Thalmessinger, 1865), p. 299.

tradition, a relation which is most pertinent to *Daniel Deronda,* cannot be undertaken here.[1] It must merely be observed that she did not study religion as a life form that had become, or was about to become, extinct. The forms of religion would continue to adapt to a changing environment, and evolve new patterns of survival.[2] Neither did she have any ecumenical motivation for her comparative study of sectarian variations of Judaism and Christianity. Ecumenicism, insofar as it combines proselytizing with the reduction of different beliefs to common denominators, may improve religious tolerance and may be a short-term strategy for survival; but the smoothing over of differences does not, in the long term, encourage new development and growth. Schisms are not to be resolved by conversion or mended by reunion of the severed parties. A diversity of views is essential for 'separateness with communication' (DD ch. 60: 673), a reforming process which leads to ever more diversity. When Deronda says that Mordecai has 'raised the image of such a task ... to bind our race together in spite of heresy' (DD ch. 63: 698), what does he mean? What could *heresy* mean to the unorthodox, nay atheist, George Eliot?[3] For her, heresy was not meant to be hunted out and suppressed by the dominant orthodoxy; it meant 'sect', retaining the original senses of the Greek root αἵρεσις: choosing, choice, course taken, course of action or thought, philosophical or religious sect.[4] Deronda must be speaking

1 GE's relation to Positivism and the Religion of Humanity is discussed by T. R. Wright in 'George Eliot and Positivism', *Modern Language Review* 76 (1981): 257–72; U. C. Knoepflmacher, *Religious Humanism and the Victorian Novel* (Princeton University Press, 1965); and William Myers, *The Teaching of George Eliot* (Leicester University Press, 1984). Connections between *Daniel Deronda* and John Stuart Mill's *Three Essays on Religion* are discussed in Chapter IV of my unpublished doctoral dissertation,
'"A Process and an Unfolding": Character-Formation in the Fiction of George Eliot' (Cambridge University, 1982).

2 Compare GHL's view, that the old religions must be transformed or perish, in his *Problems of Life and Mind. First Series, The Foundations of a Creed*, Vol. I (London: Trübner, 1873). See also the headnotes to 'Physical science' (B 97v to 101v) and 'Science and religion' (Pf 711 62 to 67 and 70).

3 In his review of Cross's *Life* in *Nineteenth Century* xvii (1885): 464–85, Lord Acton paid this tribute to GE: 'her teaching was the highest within the resources to which Atheism is restricted.' Reprinted in Carroll, pp. 463–4.

4 According to the *OED* entry for *heresy*, 'The earlier sense-development from "religious sect, party or faction" to "doctrine at variance with the catholic faith", lies outside

of a racial bond which does not inhibit this freedom of choice. Indeed, Mordecai's impassioned discussion of the development of the Jewish people culminates in his declaration that 'the strongest principle of growth lies in human choice' (DD ch. 42: 499).

If heresy is viewed negatively as a problem, one kind of solution is that recorded in Mocatta's history, *The Jews of Spain and Portugal and the Inquisition* (1877): the heretics must be eliminated before the problem multiplies.[1] Another kind of answer involves an effort to reason with those who differ. But in most argument there is really no 'great gulph', as William Hazlitt points out, between reason and prejudice.[2] Prejudice can be found even in men whose conscious intentions are to communicate good will towards men of other faiths: men such as Milman and Deutsch.

Milman's philosemitism was so offensive to his fellow Christians that the first edition of his *History of the Jews* was withdrawn from public sale. Yet his Jewish sympathies are worded in noticeably prejudicial terms, when he writes of 'the miserable Jews' being goaded

> to the only vengeance in which, besides overreaching in trade, they could indulge, – writings in their own secret unintelligible language, such as the Toldoth Jesu, and the other 'fiery weapons of Satan', published later, to the horror and detestation of Christian Europe, by Wagenseil.[3]

Deutsch's essay on the Talmud, addressed to Christian readers and intended 'to bridge over one of the ghastliest gulfs in History', had drawn upon its author the torment of 'buzzing and stinging' attacks from both sides.[4] But Deutsch himself was capable, in private conversation, of repellant references to the Slavonic peasants of his native region; these references are recalled in Lady Strangford's prefatory Memoir in the *Literary Remains*:

1 GE's copy of Mocatta's self-published book is in DWL.

2 From a passage in *The Atlas,* 18 April 1830, chosen by Christopher Ricks as an epigraph for his indispensable study of prejudices, arguments, and convictions, *T. S. Eliot and Prejudice* (London: Faber and Faber, 1988), p. vii.

3 Milman II, 41. For the reception of the first edition of Milman's *History of the Jews* , see the *DNB* and the headnote to B 106. For notes on the Toldoth Jesu, see Pf 710 36 and Pf 711 98. Milman's reference is to Johann Christoph Wagenseil, *Tela Ignea Satanae* (Altdorf: Schönnerstaedt, 1681). GE refers to Wagenseil on B 183 and 193v, Pf 711 54, and Pf 710 41.

4 See Haight, p. 47, and GEL IV, 409.

> The contrasts that struck him day by day yet early in his youth, between the wit and wisdom he found in his Hebrew literature, and these 'stupid' people made an impression upon him that he often referred to in after life; his sole amusement seems to have been watching the 'rough, narrow-brained peasantry' bringing in provisions on most primitive carts to supply the garrison in the 'much-respected fortress'. (pp. vi–vii)

This reminiscence is offensive; most readers will think that Jews might better speak of such a source of amusement only amongst themselves. George Eliot's version, in a letter to Lady Strangford, construes instead the boy's animated interest in observing a different way of life:

> It would be safe for you to mention how the flat amidst which the fortified town rises had an animated interest for the boy, who came away from his Talmudic studies to watch the strange rough peasantry bringing in provisions ... in a primitive sort of cart.[1]

In her version, the focus shifts from a besieged fortress mentality to a more engaging fascination with the strange peasants who supply necessary provisions.

George Eliot was well aware that, in a field of prejudice on both sides, the publication of Jewish material for Christian readers ran the risk of supplying additional weapons for further conflict – as Wagenseil's *Telae ignea Satanae* had done. That the Jewish part of *Daniel Deronda* provoked not just indifference, but hostility – resistance, repulsion, repugnance – did not surprise its author. Nevertheless, being 'happily independent in material things', she did what seemed to her most needful to be done (GEL VI 302). From Jews she received not only 'words of gratitude' but also signs that she had contributed her mite towards a good result amongst them (GEL VI 314).

This Jewish response has been belittled or patronized by non-Jews, such as Leslie Stephen: 'George Eliot's sympathy for the Jews, her aversion to Anti-Semitism, was thoroughly generous, and naturally welcomed by its objects.' Stephen's concluding sentences put Jewish readers in their place: 'but in spite of the approval of learned Jews, it is impossible to feel any enthusiastic regard for Deronda in his surroundings'. Since 'the restoration of the Jewish nationality' is a 'chimerical' scheme, a hero who devotes himself 'to an unreal

1 GEL V 455 and 455n. In transcribing the passage from the Memoir, Haight inserts 'Slavonic' in brackets after Deutsch's word 'stupid'. The offensive racial antagonism is echoed in a 'Polack' joke copied by GE on Pf 711 98a.

and dreamy object' must be 'composed of more moonshine than solid flesh and blood'.[1] F. R. Leavis's argument that 'the Zionist inspiration' of the novel tempts George Eliot into 'modes of self-indulgence' resembles Stephen's argument in tone and even in some details.[2]

Joan Bennett, writing at the time of formation of the modern state of Israel, was more specifically dissatisfied with the Zionist 'propaganda', as she called it,[3] and argued that 'intellect and conscience usurp the place of creative

1 See Chapter XIII in *George Eliot*, second edition (London: Macmillan, English Men of Letters, 1903), pp. 185–91. See pp. 189, 191, and 188. The verbal reminiscences of *The Merchant of Venice* are probably unconscious.

2 *The Great Tradition*, 2nd edition (Harmondsworth: Penguin, 1962), pp. 93–9. See pp. 94 and 96. For an echo of Stephen's argument on p. 189, see Leavis, pp. 98–9. Leavis's proposal that the Gwendolen Harleth part be severed from the Zionist part is poignant when considered in the light of his wife's experience: the severing of all relations with her family on her marriage to a non-Jew. It is said that the Roth family mourned her loss with the ritual *Shivah*. See M. C. Bradbrook, 'Queenie Leavis: the Dynamics of Rejection', *The Cambridge Review* (20 November 1981), reprinted in her *Collected Papers*, Vol II (1982), and also her essay, '"Nor Shall my Sword": the Leavises' mythology', in Denys Thompson, editor, *The Leavises: Recollections and Impressions* (Cambridge: Cambridge University Press, 1984), pp. 31–2.

3 Bennett first states that 'the conception of Daniel's character and story arises out of a conscious – *almost* a propagandist – intention' (emphasis added), but goes on to refer to GE's 'occasional lapses' from art into propaganda:

> The accident that this scheme for a national Jewish home in Palestine has become a desperately difficult political issue serves to emphasize the danger of incorporating propaganda in a fiction. No modern reader can accept Deronda's mission unquestioningly as a valuable service to mankind, but to George Eliot herself it seemed to offer a more promising field than politics for his altruistic energies.
>
> (pp. 182, 195, 187–8)

But she has just quoted Deronda's statement that he wants to restore 'a political existence to my people'. In his own mind, and to GE herself, he is taking up the field of politics just as much as if he were at Sir Hugo's elbow (DD ch. 69: 747 and ch. 16: 161). According to Bradbrook, Bennett – who like Q. D. Leavis married a non-Jewish member of the Cambridge English faculty – was 'née Frankau ... from a more liberal Jewish family than Queenie's' (*The Leavises*, p. 32). It is remarkable that Bennett refers especially to 'Daniel's mother ... who repudiated the restricting claims of race and religion to follow her own taste and talent as an opera-singer' (p. 189). In fact, the Alcharisi tells her son that she was baptized only just before her temporary 'fit' of singing out of tune drove her to marry a second time – that this repudiation of her Jewishness was a preparation for the enforced *loss* of her career (DD ch. 51: 592, 596).

power' (p. 185). Her argument rests in part on the novelist's faulty choice of doctrine:

> The Zionist Movement was founded in 1900, twenty-four years after the novel was published. George Eliot knew nothing, and apparently foresaw nothing, of the international problems that would follow in its train. The claims of the Arabs in Palestine did not enter her head. (p. 186)

That George Eliot failed to foresee the terrible magnitude of twentieth-century problems such as refugee camps (or death camps) is, in Bennett's view, linked with 'the central flaw' in the novel and the failure of creative power (p. 189). Indeed, the phrasing suggests that 'the place of creative power' has been *usurped* by 'intellect and conscience', just as Palestine has been usurped by Zionist Jews. According to Bennett, George Eliot's 'course of serious study ... of Jewish history and Jewish thought' is to blame. 'The favourable impression made on learned Jews in her own time bears witness to the thoroughness of her researches.' But those 'learned Jews' were no judges of Jewish characterization, for unlike Bennett they failed to notice that Mordecai is unconvincing, unreal, the result of conscientious construction – in contrast to the 'little cockney Jew, Cohen', who 'endears himself to the reader' (pp. 184–5). Although Bennett quotes part of a letter to Barbara Bodichon, mentioning that 'part of the scene at the club is translated into Hebrew in a German-Jewish newspaper', she does not notice that Mordecai was in this scene convincingly real to Jewish readers (p. 182). As for Deronda, for most non-Jewish readers, *he* is just the same as if he were not a Jew (DD ch. 69: 746). Few have noticed the remarkable fact that George Eliot could so enter into the spirit of Judaism that Jews have accepted Deronda as one of themselves.

The arguments of Stephen, Leavis, and Bennett may have been compelling in their own terms and within their own historical contexts, but they fail to communicate with the different context of Judaism. When Bennett refers to 'learned Jews', she does not consciously echo Stephens's particular words, but rather signals a common field of reference which owes rather more to prejudice than to reason. In such a cause, even her phrase 'intellect and conscience' may take on prejudicial connotations. Is it possible that non-Jewish readers might have something to learn from the Jews? George Eliot thought so. Before concluding that her Jewish learning made her an advocate for the Zionist cause, so that 'she deserted her own vocation and spoilt her novel',[1] readers of *Daniel Deronda* might well inform themselves about her acquisition of that learning. Her researches into 'Jewish history and Jewish thought' are now accessible to all readers: her notes on 'Hebrew Matters' in the Berg Notebook will reveal 'the place of creative power' in an area of the novel which lies outside the experience of most of us who have not been, or are not, Jews. We might begin with Gwendolen's question, 'Can I understand the ideas, or am I too ignorant?' (DD ch. 69: 747) – bearing in mind that acknowledged ignorance is no barrier to understanding, that it is not equivalent to 'the intellectual narrowness – in plain English, the stupidity, which is still the average mark of our culture'.

George Eliot's Jewish reading did not make her a proselyte; she did not, like Deronda, depart for the East.[2] Rather, her comprehensive intelligence, sustained by her learning, freed her from unconscious prejudice. She was able to bridge 'one of the ghastliest gulfs in History' because her study of Christian sectarianism and Jewish controversies let her see the great schism between Judaism and Christianity in the historical context proper to them both. Heresy – choosing to differ – is one of the traditions they have in common. The 'modern reader' has no need to look for irony in George Eliot's inability to foresee 'the accident that [the] scheme for a national Jewish home in Palestine [would] become a desperately difficult political issue'.[3] George Eliot was well aware that the history of relations between Jews and non-Jews bears a heavy burden of irony. She had no need of second-sight to foresee that their relations would continue to be disputed ground. Nevertheless, one of the most strikingly ironic images in her novel presents a sign of her hope, if not her confident belief, that historical development may yet bring more intelligent forms of communication with heresy.[4] Mordecai, who waits and yearns for the deliverer of his message to the next generation of his people, is supported by a structure which is a complexly ironic image of how a gulf may be bridged: Blackfriars Bridge commemorates the Dominicans who worked with such missionary zeal to exterminate Judaism.

1 Bennett, p. 188.

2 A journey was thought of, but not deemed practicable; see GEL VI 319.

3 Bennett, p. 187.

4 The words 'second-sight', 'disputed ground', 'hope' and 'confident belief' are taken, out of context, from GE's commentary on the image of Mordecai on Blackfriars Bridge, at sunset (DD ch. 38: 439–40). In Jewish tradition, sunset marks the beginning of the new day (B 125v). The entry for 18 November in GHL's 1875 Diary records that GE and GHL 'walked on Blackfriars Bridge watching sunset'.

Part One

The Berg Notebook

B 91 to B 194

Homer (Paley) and quotations from Pindar

B 91, 92, 102, 102v, 103, 103v, 104, 104v, 105, 105v, 92v, 94, 96, 97

In the autumn of 1873, GE returned to the Berg Notebook, resuming a topic that had occupied some of its earlier pages: Homeric studies. Between July 1869 and October 1872 she had transcribed, in black ink, passages from the Iliad and the Odyssey (B 12, 22, 67, 71, 72, and 84). In violet ink she later added the heading 'Iliad' (B 72) and a note on an image in the Odyssey (B 66v). Her study of Homeric scholarship began in December 1870, when her reading of Friedrich August Wolf's *Prolegomena ad Homerum* (1795) was recorded in the GE Journal and reflected in her notes from Wolf on B 72 and Folger 13 83. A 'list of books on the Homeric Question' (Pf 711 15, 16) was copied in the summer of 1873. Her notes below are from two articles by Frederick Apthorp Paley: 'The Odyssey of Homer' in the *British Quarterly Review* 58 (October 1873): 414–45; and 'On the Comparatively Late Date and Composite Character of our Iliad and Odyssey' in *Transactions of the Cambridge Philosophical Society* 11, Part II (1871): 360–86. GHL's Diary records his reading of the *British Quarterly Review* on 16 October 1873. It is probable that GE's reading of the 1873 article prompted her to look up the 1871 article; her copious notes suggest the use of a borrowed copy of the *Transactions.* For an account of her discussion of the Homeric question on 23 November 1873 with John Fiske, who found her 'a strong Wolfian!', see the headnote to Pf 711 15 and 16.

Paley presents a 'Wolfian' account of Cyclic ballads and poems orally transmitted by Rhapsodists and later collected as the written epics we call Homeric. Pindar figures largely in his Homeric argument, not only in the *Transactions* article (B 102, 102v, 103, and 104v), but also in his preface to his translations of *The Odes of Pindar* (London: Williams and Norgate, 1868). GE's copy is in DWL. In the preface Paley argues that

> There is not the slightest proof that the Odes of Pindar were originally *written.* On the contrary, there are several strong arguments to prove that they were orally taught, and conveyed to their destination by ἄγγελοι, i.e. by persons instructed by Pindar himself both in the words and the music, and commissioned to teach them to the local choruses by whom they were to be publicly performed. (p. x)

His conviction that '*a written literature was entirely unknown to the Greeks even in the time of Pindar*' (p. xi) makes him

> anxious to call attention to the 'Homeric' question, and to invite those equally interested in it with myself to study it with, and test it by, Pindar and the Greek vases, as our earliest representatives of Grecian literature and Grecian art. (p. xxviii)

He concludes that the evidence

> ought to make us pause in giving full credit to the prevalent opinion that our Homer is the genuine and original Homer of the very remote antiquity of BC 850 or 900! (p. xxx)

Paley's concern with cultural transmission to 'our' time from 'very remote antiquity' and his argument for oral, as opposed to written, transmission suggest that in GE's mind there was a link between studies of the literature of ancient Greece and Judaic matters – in particular, the oral tradition of the Mishnah (B 107v, 108v).

In this respect she is part of a characteristically Victorian appropriation of the Homeric epics to nineteenth-century preoccupations. Frank M. Turner's chapter on 'The Reading of Homer' in *The Greek Heritage in Victorian Britain* (New Haven: Yale University Press, 1981) explores an intellectural milieu whose significance for GE is suggested by Turner's statement that 'the most significant contemporary issue upon which Homeric scholarship touched was the implication of Wolfian or skeptical approaches to Homer for the reading, study, and appreciation of the Bible' (p. 140). Against the assertion of the 'archconservative churchman' E. B. Pusey that 'the scepticism as to Homer ushered in the scepticism on the Old Testament', Turner sets the observation of T. H. Huxley that 'criticism of Homer was a manifestation of the scientific spirit that examined the previously unexamined idols of the day' (p. 146). GE's sceptical inquiry into the *Wissenschaft des Judentums,* or 'Science of Judaism', is close to the spirit of Huxley's pursuit of the truths of physical science.

GE's source for the quotations from Pindar's Olympian victory odes is *Poetae Lyrici Graeci,* edited by Wilhelm Theodor Bergk (Lipsiae: Reichenbach, 1843); her copy is in DWL. In her transcription there are minor discrepancies, some of which are emendations suggested by Bergk's notes. Bergk is also the source for the 'Fragments of Sappho' and 'Mimnermus, Frag.' noted in her list of works 'read since September [1872]' (Pf 711 11).

Homer (Paley) and quotations from Pindar

The passage copied on B 96 is that indicated by an earlier note on Folger 13 89, 'v. Pindar, Olymp. II, v. 123 sqq or 68 sqq'. The verse '123' citation refers to verse numbers at the right margins of the Bergk text, verse '68' to numbers at the left. In the Berg Notebook excerpts, GE's references are to the approximate right margin verse numbers; exact left margin verse numbers are cited within square brackets and in the editorial notes. GE's heading for this passage, 'Retributive Future', is perhaps an echo of Paley's statement in his Preface that there is

> only one great theological passage ... in Pindar, and that is the remarkable and very explicit statement in Ol. ii. 55–75, of a final judgment and of the happier lot of the good than of the bad hereafter. (p. xxi)

GE's abiding interest in relationships between ethical questions and various theological doctrines of a life 'hereafter' is reflected in her long extract from this 'great theological passage'. The souls who 'remain stedfast thrice in each life' (ll 68 ff, the lines referred to on Folger 13 89) are perhaps superficially reminiscent of the Kabbalic doctrine that souls are allowed three terms to develop the germs of perfection implanted in them; see B 169 and 174 and Pf 707 20. Translations provided in the notes below are from Paley. His translations are of interest because contemporary with, and known to, GE. Her readings of Pindar, however, do not necessarily conform to his; see the editorial note to Olympian IX, 48–9. Readers may wish to compare the translations by Frank J. Nisetich in *Pindar's Victory Songs* (Baltimore: Johns Hopkins University Press, 1980).[1]

In Richard Jenkyns's chapter on 'George Eliot and the Greeks' in *The Victorians and Ancient Greece* (Cambridge, Massachusetts: Harvard University Press, 1980), there is no hint that GE's reading of Pindar and Homer contributes anything to *Daniel Deronda.* This particular 'cartload of learning' (in Sir Hugo's phrase) is not called for; but there is no reason to suppose that *her* 'Greek has all evaporated', like his (DD ch. 16: 161, 162). Jenkyns sees her use of Greek literature in this novel as often sentimental and self-indulgent; other readers may hear satirical and ironical tones.[2]

1 For a valuable introduction to the strange world of the Pindaric epinician ode, for the non-specialist modern reader, see D. S. Carne-Ross, *Pindar* (New Haven: Yale University Press, 1985).

2 See, for example, the report of the *ennui* of Ulysses and Calypso (DD ch. 22: 221–2).

It was, incidentally, Paley's grandfather William Paley, the author of *Evidences of Christianity and Natural Theology,* whose future greatness was predicted by his father, as Rex Gascoigne's father recalls (DD ch. 58: 657).

/91/ *In re* Homeric poems

'By far the greatest number (of the Romaic ballads) owe their preservation to a class of men who here, as among the Montenegrins & the Greeks of the heroic age, are the great depositories of the national poetry, *the blind wandering minstrels.* Throughout the country it is an established custom that the blind man should obtain his livelihood by composing & reciting ballads, *of which some of them are said to know an incredible number by heart;* & in his character of rhapsodist he passes from village to village, selecting especially for the time of his visit some local festival, when a large audience will be gathered together, from whom he never fails to obtain an enthusiastic hearing & bountiful contributions. He is at the same time the author of the music to which each ballad is sung, & accompanies himself during his recitation on a small guitar.'

Tozer's Researches in the Highlands of Turkey[1]
quoted by Paley, Brit. Quarterly [58], Oct. 1873 [434–5]

'To the same class (of ballads) may be referred a number of poems highly characteristic of the condition of the people; those, for instance, which describe *the recognition of husbands* by faithful wives after many *years' absence.* In these the unexpected visitor, whose appearance has been changed by time or other causes, ... finds his wife washing clothes at the fountain, & after testing her fidelity is put to a searching cross-examination by the lady.'

Ibid. [435]

/92/ νεκυιὰ [2] (Odyssey)

The Greeks, in quite late ages, offered libations & sacrifices to their heroes, with the view of propitiating by offerings of food the malignant spirits, or at least the 'daemons' powerful for harm. If the dead were not thus fed &

1 This and the following excerpts are from Henry Fanshawe Tozer, *Researches in the Highlands of Turkey*, 2 vols. (London: John Murray, 1869), II, 229–30 and 239–40. GE has reproduced Paley's italics.

2 Transliterated as 'Nekuia' in GE's Index (B 188v or N): 'sacrifice'.

propitiated, the survivors lived in constant dread that pestilences & sudden deaths would carry off victims to satiate them. These sacrifices were of two kinds: blood-offerings, with the idea of animating & strengthening the enfeebled ghost by that which they regarded as the life; & the milder drinks of wine, water, oil, honey, flour &c. This was done from a notion that *meiligmata*, or soothing emulsions, would calm the angry spirit ... These (in the Odyssey) are essentially the same as those offered in the age of the Tragic poets, e.g. to the Furies in the 'Oedipus at Colonus' (wine excepted), & to the daemon of Darius in the 'Persians' ... It may be said that all Greek rites paid to the dead turn primarily on this point, the *feeding* of the spirit; & it is to be feared that many indications may be traced of remote cannibal offerings. The offering of milk, honey, &c., is followed by the promise of blood-offerings at Ithaca; but a burnt sacrifice of sheep is at once performed, the fire being supposed to transmit the cooked food to the ghosts below, & not present at the rite, as the Earth transmitted the wine.

Paley, à propos of the question whether the ideas about the state of the dead are evidences of antiquity in Homer [pp. 424–5]

/102/ *Homer.* Paley

'On the comparatively late date & composite character of our Iliad & Odyssey. By F. A. Paley, M.A.'

(From the Transactions of the Cam. Philosophical Soc. vol. XI. Pt. II)

The Iliad & Odyssey not original works of the 9th cent. BC but compilations from other, earlier epics, probably those which we find so constantly referred to in Pindar & the Tragics: nay, put together in a continuous form not very long before the time of Plato – that being the age in which they begin first to be uniformly quoted as 'Homer', & to which a large part of the language, though mixed up with very archaic forms, can with the greatest probability be referred. [p. 360]

Pindar & the Tragics knew these earlier epics, not through writing, but as to the subject matter traditionally, & probably many of the verses from the recitations of the rhapsodes. These epics were gradually parcelled out in separate subjects under distinct titles, were then first assigned to different authors & were ultimately worked in with our present poems, so as to form a continuous narrative or rather narratives, of the Troica & the Thebaica, & thus the whole collection eventually took the name of the 'Epic Cyclus'.

Homer (Paley) and quotations from Pindar B 102 102v 103

Herodotus mentions by name the Iliad, Odyssey, Cypria & Epigoni, vide book III. 117 & IV. 32. [p. 362]

Altered treatment of like or identical Homeric subjects **/102v/** indicating a diffused plasma of myth & legend.

The author of our Iliad & Odyssey beyond question an Asiatic who knew little of Greece proper. The catalogue shows such knowledge as a European Greek would have. [p. 363]

Wolf rested his doubts on the improbability of oral transmission of lengthy poems as wholes; on the uncritical character of the early Greeks; on the internal evidence of various ballads having been put together to form our Homer; & on the comparative lateness of the art of writing. But still he seems to entertain no doubt that our I. & O. did exist in the time of Pisistratus, as related in the Platonic dialogue *Hipparchus*, & repeated by Cicero, Pausanias & others. [p. 364]

Paley does not believe this: thinks rather that the I. & O. were compiled by an Ionian of the school & age of Herodotus & Antimachus, & he ranges the evidence for this opinion under the following heads:

1. The negative argument, from the absence of direct reference to our poems in the older writers, & even in Pindar & the Tragics.

2. The general absence of Homeric *scenes* (not always of *characters*) in early Greek art, especially the Greek vases, prior to BC 450.

3. The fact (which is undeniable & extremely suggestive) that the Iliad & the Odyssey are first largely quoted **/103/** & appealed to as 'Homer' by Plato & Aristotle.

4. The comparatively modern style of the diction, intermixed with numerous archaic forms, which must be considered to belong to a wholly different & very much earlier period of the language.

5. The fact that in general the dialect & forms of inflexion very closely resemble the style of Herodotus; & that there are even some allusions (e.g. to the wealth of Delphi, the greatness of Egyptian Thebes, the 'just' Scythians or Abii (see Herod. I. 50 seqq. IV. 23–6 & Iliad XIII. 6), that seem referable to his writings.

6. The strongly-marked & frequent references in our Homer to earlier epics, which Pindar & the Tragics throughout make large use of, while they rarely if ever contain passages that can be shown to have been directly derived from our Homer.

7. The artificial & thoroughly dramatic nature of our poems, indicating an advanced period in Greek thought & literature when they were composed.

8. The fact that our poems form but a small part of the ancient Homeric themes, being primarily incidents culled from the adventures of two principal Homeric heroes.

9. That throughout our Homer a knowledge is presupposed of all the incidents & characters, as well as of the general **/103v/** motives & events, of the Trojan war, up to quite a late period in its history.

10. That the Homeric characters (with some inconsistencies) are almost uniformly virtuous, often even amiable; whereas we have good reasons for thinking that treachery, brutality & debauchery marked to a great extent the same characters in the ancient epics.

11. The strong probability that this general ethical goodness is due to the age of philosophy rather than to a remote & semi-barbarous one.

12. The details of the armour being generally those of a late age.

13. The laws of organic change to which all languages are liable, & which make it incredible that the genuine Greek of BC 800 or 900 (archaic forms, apparently adapted, being excepted) co-exist with the Attic & Ionic dialects of BC 400.

14. The constant repetition even of many verses together; the great irregularities in the use of the article & the digamma; & lastly, the strong indications, from internal evidence, of whole episodes having been adapted & annexed from other ballads.

15. Instances of anticipation in the narrative, as in Iliad II. 874 of Iliad XXI & Odyssey II. 20 of IX. [pp. 364–5]

Homer (Paley) and quotations from Pindar B 104 104v

/104/

'What I contend for is, that the cyclic epics had, generally speaking, more of genuine antiquity in them than our Homer, i.e. that they were primary rather than secondary: & I infer this from the undeniable & most significant fact, already mentioned, that it is from them & not from our Homer, that early Greek poetry & Greek art uniformly borrowed their themes.' [p. 369]

'The fact is ... that the so-called "Cyclic" poetry was Homer to the ancients – the only Homer they had.'

v. Odyssey I. 10 τῶν ἁμόθεν γε, θεά, θύγατερ Διός, εἰπὲ καὶ ἡμῖν.[1]
ἁμόθεν is a word of the Platonic age: the digamma in εἰπὲ is violated, contrary to the general usage in the I. & O.: thirdly, καὶ ἡμῖν, 'to us too', shows that other poems addressed to other audiences did exist. [p. 370]

'It is simply impossible (& I speak as one who has worked at it for many years) to reduce the Homeric digamma to any fixed rules or principles. It is used just as a compiler would use it in times when it had become obsolete.' [p. 375]

It is in Herodotus that we first read of the Iliad & Odyssey by name, II. 116–7 & IV. 21. [p. 377]

Herodotus refers to Homer or Homeric subjects ten or eleven times, & these references leave a presumption that the Iliad as we have it was not the same poem that he had, whether under this name or under several. E.g. when he tells us II. 53 that 'Homer & Hesiod were the first to compose Theogonies for the **/104v/** Greeks, to give the gods their names &c. & to indicate their forms,' he must be speaking of some then existing poems, attributed to Homer, but totally different in their nature from our Iliad & Odyssey.

Pindar refers to persons & subjects in the Troica not less than sixty times. Only four or five of these touch upon scenes in our Iliad not, as I contend, *from* it, but from a common source.[2] The name, *Homer,* is mentioned three times by Pindar, & the Homeridae, as rhapsodes, once. [p. 378]

1 Translation, by Robert Fitzgerald: 'Of these adventures, Muse, daughter of Zeus, / tell us in our time, lift the great song again.'

2 In her synopsis of Paley, GE at first omitted his reference to a common source ('not ... source'), then added it as a footnote at the bottom of the page.

Homer (Paley) and quotations from Pindar B 104v 105 105v

Thucydides has eight passages in which he either mentions Homer, or has some reference to the Troica. He quotes a verse from the second book of the Iliad as we now have it, but seems to give that part of the poem the title of Σκήπτρου Παράδοσις.[1] He twice speaks of οἱ παλαιοὶ τῶν ποιητῶν & ποιηταὶ[2] (I, 5 & VI, 2).

Aristophanes has six passages which refer or may refer to our Iliad & Odyssey; but he has five others, in two of which Homer is mentioned by name, that do not pertain to our poems, but to others then current under the comprehensive name of 'Homer'.

Xenophon alludes to our Homer four or five times, & Mem[orabilia] I. 2, 58 quotes nine verses from Iliad II. 188 seqq. though not exactly as we have them. Also, he refers to an incident not in our **/105/** Homer, the death of Palamedes, as a well known theme – πάντες ὑμνοῦσι. It is in Plato that our Homer suddenly bursts as it were into full recognition. [p. 379]

The accounts of making the trench & palisade in B. VII & XII are precisely similar to like works as described in Thucydides. [p. 383]

We know that a so-called recension or διόρθωσις of Homer was made in the time of Pericles by Antimachus, the celebrated poet of Colophon; though beyond this we know nothing of what he did to the text. Did he import into it the verses which must be counted by hundreds, representing so closely the Ionic dialect of Herodotus? If not he, some other Ionic poet not very long before Plato's time. [p. 384]

The details of the Homeric armour & war-chariots generally identical with the vase paintings of BC 400. [p. 385]

/105v/

The name 'Homerus' can hardly mean anything but 'fitted together', 'harmonious'; & this is an epithet as applicable to the verse of the ancient minstrel as 'daedal' to the contrivance of the mechanician.

1 The reference in Thucydides' *Peloponnesian War,* I, 9 is to the bequeathing of the hereditary sceptre borne by kings and chiefs – 'a title', Paley suggests, 'which may have pertained to a more ancient arrangement' of the stories of the Troica.

2 Translation: 'some of the ancient poets' and 'the poets'. Paley continues: 'as if [Thucydides] recognized the authority of more than one composer of these ancient epics'.

If so, the Homerids, instead of being the descendants of a person Homer, are in truth united by being the 'sons of verse', & Homer, like Eumolpus or Daedalus, is the personification of an art & the eponymous ancestor of an hereditary guild. D. B. Monro, Quarterly review, 1868 [1]

The name 'Homerus' is sometimes explained as a compiler or arranger (from ὁμοῦ & ἀραρεῖν or ἀραρίσκειν).[2]

Apion pretended that the shade of Homer had appeared to him & told him in which city he was born – *only he was not to repeat it*.[3]

/92v/ Pindar Olymp.

χαρις δ' ἅπερ ἅπαντα τευχει τα μείλιχα θνατοις,
ἐπιφέρουσα τιμαν καὶ ἄπιστον εμήσατο πιστὸν
εμμεναι το πολλάκις·
ἁμεραι δ' ἐπίλοιποι
μαρτυρες σοφωτατοι. I. 46 [I, 30–34][4]

θανειν δ' οἷσιν ἀναγκα, τί κέ τις ἀνώνυμον
γῆρας ἐν σκότῳ καθήμενος ἕψοι μάταν
ἁπάντων καλῶν ἄμμορος; [I, 82–84][5]

ἀναξιφόρμιγγες ὕμνοι [II, 1][6]

1 David Binning Monro, 'The Homeric Question', *Quarterly Review* 125: 444–5.

2 Paley, *British Quarterly Review* 58: 434: 'one derivation ... for the name *Homerus* is founded upon this very principle of fitting and adapting'. Translation: 'to fit together'.

3 This note, added later, is repeated from Pf 711 23. Source: Graetz 3, 257.

4 Parenthetical page references in these notes are to Paley's translations in *The Odes of Pindar.* Olympia I, verses 30–4:

> But Poesy, which is the author of all that affords pleasure to mortals, by giving [to these myths] acceptance, ofttimes makes what is incredible to be credible; but succeeding time gives the most certain evidence of truth. (p. 3)

5 I, 82–84:

> When men must die, why should one sit in the dark and spend to no purpose a sodden, nameless life, unsharing in any noble deeds? (p. 6)

6 II, 1: 'Ye hymns that control the tones of the lute' (p. 8).

τοι βροτῶν [γε] κέκριται
πεῖρας οὔτι θανάτου
ουδ' ἀσυχιμον ἀμεραν ὁπότε παῖδ' ἀλίου
ἀτειρεῖ συν αγαθῷ τελευτάσομεν· ῥοαὶ δ' αλλοτ' ἄλλαι
εὐθυμιᾶν τε μετὰ καὶ πόνων ἐς ἄνδρας ἔβαν. [II, 30–34][1]

/94/ Retributive Future. Pindar Ol. II

(ἀστὴρ ἀρίζηλος ἐτὴτυμον
ἀνδρὶ φεγγος) εὖ δέ μιν ἔχων τις οἶδεν τὸ μελλον,
ὅτι φόνων τῶν μὲν ἐνθάδ' αὐτικ' απαλαμνοι φρένες
ποινὰς ἔτισαν, τὰ δ' ἐν τᾶδε Διὸς ἀρχᾶ
ἀλιτρὰ κατὰ γᾶς δικάζει τις ἐχθρὰ
λόγον θράσαισ' ἀνάγκα.

ἶσον δὲ νυκτεσσιν αἰεὶ
οἶον ἐν ἀμέραις ἅλιον ἔχοντες ἀπονεστερον
ἐσλοι δεδορκαντι βίον, οὐ χθονα ταράσσοντες ἐν χερὸς ἀκμᾶ
οὐδὲ πόντιον ὕδωρ
κεινὰν παρὰ δίαιταν· ἀλλὰ παρὰ τιμαόροις[2]
θεῶν, οἵτινες ἔχαιρον εὐορκίαις,[3] ἄδακρυν νέμονται
αιῶνα· τοὶ δ' ἀπροσόρατον ὀκχέοντι πόνον.

/96/

ὅσοι δ' ἐτολμασαν ἐστρὶς
εκατέρωθι μείναντες ἀπὸ πάμπαν ἀδίκων ἔχειν
ψυχάν, ἔτειλαν Διὸς ὁδὸν παρὰ Κρόνου τύρσιν· ἔνθα μακάρων
νᾶσον ὠκεανίδες
αὔραι περιπνεοισιν, ἄνθεμα δὲ κρυσοῦ φλεγει,

1 II, 30–34:
'Tis true indeed that in *men* there is no fixed term for their death, nor know we when we shall pass through a quiet day, the child of the sun, with unfailing good; for currents run now this way, now that, bearing both delights and trials to men. (p. 10)

2 Bergk has μὲν τιμίοις.

3 GE underlined the words ἔχαιρον εὐορκίαις, 'took delight in keeping their fidelity to their oath'.

τὰ μὲν χερσόθεν ἀπ' ἀγλαῶν δενδρέων, ὕδωρ δ' ἄλλα φερβει,
ὅρμοισι τῶν κάρα ἀναπλέκοντι καὶ στεφάνοις. [II, 55–74][1]

τῶν δὲ πεπραγμένον
ἐν δίκα καὶ παρὰ δίκαν αποιήτον οὐδ' ἄν
χρόνος ὁ παντων πατὴρ δύναιτο θέμεν ἔργων τέλος.
Olymp. II [15–17][2]

ἴων ξανθαισι καὶ παμπυρφύροις ακταῖσι βεβρεγμένος.
Olymp. III [VI, 55][3]

/97/

γλυκὺν καρπὸν φρενός VII. 14 [VII, 8][4]

1 II, 55–74. This includes the passage indicated in Folger 13 as verse '68 sqq.':
... a conspicuous star, the truest light to a man. But he who has it is well aware of what is in store for him, – that the guilty souls of those who die here have to pay the penalty in another life, – for there is one beneath the earth who judges the crimes committed in this empire of Zeus, delivering sentence by a hateful constraint. But the good, enjoying ever sunshine as much in the nights as in the days, succeed to a less laborious life, not stirring the ground by strength of hand nor the water of the sea in that blest abode; but with the honoured of the gods all such as took delight in keeping their plighted faith pass a tearless existence, while the bad have to endure toils too horrible to look upon. And those who have had the courage to remain stedfast thrice in each life, and to keep their souls altogether from wrong, pursue the road of Zeus to the castle of Cronus, where o'er the isles of the blest, ocean breezes blow, and flowers gleam with gold, some from the land on glistering trees, while others the water feeds; and with bracelets of these they entwine their hands and make crowns for their heads. (pp. 11–12)
Bergk has 'κεφαλας' for GE's 'στεφάνοις'.

2 II, 15–17:
Now of deeds which have been done, whether rightly or wrongly, not even Time, the Father of all things, can make the accomplishment undone. (p. 9)

3 VI, 55: '[And in truth] he had been hidden by her in a reed-bed and an impenetrable brake' (p. 27). GE transcribed III for VI.

4 VII, 8: 'the sweet fruit of my mind' (p. 32).

Homer (Paley) and quotations from Pindar B 97

δαεντι δὲ και σοφία μείζων ἀδόλον τελεθει. VII [53][1]

αἴνει δὲ παλαιὸν μὲν οἶνον, ανθεα δ' ὕμνων
νεωτέρων. IX [48–49][2]

τὸ δὲ φυᾶ κράτιστον ἅπαν. [IX, 100][3]

τὸ γὰρ
ἐμφυὲς οὔτ' αἴθων ἀλωπηξ
οὔτ' ἐριβρομοι λεοντες διαλλάξαιντ' ἄν ἦωος. X [19–21][4]

ἅπαν δ' εὑρόντος ἔργον. XIII. 24 [17][5]

αἵ γε μεν ἀνδρῶν
πολλ' ἄνω, τα δ' ἀυ κάτω, ψευδη μεταμώνια τάμνοισαι
κυλινδοντ' ἐλπιδες·
συμβολον δ' οὔ πώ τις ἐπιχθωνίων
πιοτὸν ἀμφὶ πράξιος ἐσσομένας εὗρεν θεόθεν·
τῶν δὲ μελλόντων τετύφωνται φραδαί. XIII [XII, 5–9][6]

1 VII, 53: 'For in a skilled artist his craft appears even greater when it is without fraud.' (p. 35)

2 IX, 48–49: 'Be your theme old wine and the flowers of newer hymns.' (pp. 48–9) Paley's note to these lines reads: 'If you must praise old things, let your theme be a harmless and convivial one, but not one concerning the gods' (p. 47). A pencilled note in the margin, apparently in GE's hand, corrects Paley's interpretation: 'rather, Let your subject be old but your treatment new'. This comment accords with the newer translation of Frank J. Nisetich: 'But we praise wine for its age, and songs / for the fresh bloom upon them.' (*Pindar's Victory Songs*, p. 126)

3 IX, 100: 'that which comes by nature' (p. 50).

4 X (or XI), 19–21: 'For in their in-born character neither tawney fox nor roaring lions are likely to change.' (p. 52)

5 XIII, 17: 'To the inventor belongs the credit of everything that is done.' (p. 62)

6 XII, 5–9:

> But the expectations of men too oft toss to and fro in a vain voyage through a sea of disappointment; and no man on earth has ever yet found any sure token from heaven about his future success. (p. 60)

Physical science

B 97v, 99, 99v, 100, 100v, 101, 101v

The 'Physical Science' section, so designated by GE's Index entry and running heads, occupies space between the excerpts from Pindar and her notes from Paley (B 102 to 105v), which were apparently copied as a sequel to the Paley notes made in October 1873 (B 91–92). This collection of notes on scientific topics therefore postdates GE's study of Jewish history, begun in mid-September. Having defined a science section, GE added notes in its available spaces at later times. Some of these scientific notes, indeed, are from much earlier reading: three brief entries on B 97v are recopied from earlier notes on Pf 711 8 and Folger 13 115,[1] and the note from Saigey's *Les Sciences au XVIIIe siècle,* read in December 1872, is copied from Pf 711 9.

The notes on geometry on B 101v may date from 1875, when Trübner published a second edition of *The Positive Philosophy of Auguste Comte,* 'freely translated and condensed' in two volumes by Harriet Martineau. It was first published by John Chapman in 1853. In November of that year Marian Evans, then still working for Chapman, wrote to Sara Hennell, 'I have not seen H. M.'s Comte yet – she is going to give me a copy [2] – but Mr. Lewes tells me it seems to him *admirably well* done' (GEL II, 127). Her notes some twenty years later suggest that she continued to think well of Martineau's work.

The extracts from John Tyndall were copied in February 1874. His *Six Lectures on Light, Delivered in America in 1872–1873* (London: Longmans, Green, 1873) was read from 1 to 6 and 13 to 21 February. His lecture 'On the Scientific Use of the Imagination' was reprinted in *Fragments of Science for Unscientific People* (London: Longmans, Green, 1871). 'Polly read Tyndall's *Fragments of Science*' on 3 May 1871, and reread it from 22 to 24 February 1874, just after reading 'Tyndall on Light' (GHL Diaries).

Tyndall's lectures are of particular interest to any reader concerned with the role of the imagination in scientific inquiry, experiment, or deduction. They also bear upon a topic dear to GE and GHL in 1874: the relation

1 The latter note was made in June 1871; see Pratt and Neufeldt, pp. 144–5.

2 There is no GE–GHL copy of either edition in DWL.

between modern science and religion. His most controversial lecture was his inaugural address as President of the British Association for the Advancement of Science, delivered on 19 August 1874, and published the next day in *Nature.* '"Nature" – Tyndall's Address' was read by GE and GHL on 23 August (GHL Diary). GE's single note from this lecture records the pious prayer of Alhazen, the mediaeval Arabian scientist, 'that in the day of judgment the All-Merciful will take pity on the soul of Abur-Raihan, because he was the first of the race of men to construct a table of specific gravities' (Pf711 63).

Can one expect a table of specific gravities to weigh in the balance on the Day of Judgment? This choice of excerpt is not as eccentric as it may at first seem, for Alhazen's prayer epitomizes the central controversy raised by Tyndall's inaugural address: whether religion would be superseded by the advancement of scientific knowledge. Science – always with an upper-case S in these discussions – was seen as competing in areas conventionally thought to be the preserve of religion. This controversy was pursued in various public and private forums, including GE's correspondence with Mary Ponsonby in December 1874 on whether 'the consideration of molecular physics' may negate 'the idea of God, so far as it has been a high spiritual influence'.[1] The redefinition of metaphysics as 'the Science of the most general conceptions', to be pursued solely by the method of Science, had been a starting point for GHL in the first volume of his *Problems of Life and Mind,* published in September 1873 by Trübner, after Blackwood withdrew from publishing a work that affronted his feelings about 'the extinction of religion'.[2]

James Clerk Maxwell's address to the British Association for the Advancement of Science in 1870 is the source of GE's notes referring to the formation of theories representing 'the actual properties of molecules', as opposed to arbitrarily invented 'theories of molecular action' (B 100 to 101). GE and GHL read Maxwell's address when it was first published in *Nature,* and reread it when GHL was revising the second volume of *Problems of Life and Mind,* in which Helmholtz's theorem of ring-vortices – 'if a whirling ring be once generated in such a perfect fluid, it will go on forever, always

1 See GEL VI, 97–100.

2 *Problems of Life and Mind, First Series: The Foundations of a Creed,* I, 2–5. See GEL V, 400–1, 410–11, 413–16. For further discussion of GE's interest in the question of antagonism or reconciliation between 'Science and Religion', see the headnote for that section (Pf711 62 to 67 and 70).

consisting of the same portion of fluid first set going' – is incorporated into GHL's argument about 'two great systems ... Atomism and Dynamism'.[1]

In the epigraph and first paragraph of DD, the startlingly novel use of a scientific term to describe the 'dynamic quality' of Gwendolen Harleth's glance follows upon the observation that 'even Science, the strict measurer, is obliged to start with a make-believe unit': the sidereal clock is set to begin with an arbitrarily chosen, or pretend, moment (DD ch. 1: 3). Unsettling questions explicitly raised in the opening paragraph are set against implicitly revolutionary concepts of the new science. The epigraph seems to overturn the concept, apparently indispensable to science and fiction, of 'once upon a time', although GE is careful to point out that starting *in medias res* is a narrative method adhering to an established convention of temporal continuity.[2] Nevertheless, the narrative opening is as challenging to received ideas of time, dynamism, and the power of natural causes as are the implications of Helmhotz's theorem that a ring vortex, 'if once generated, would go on whirling forever' (B 100v).

No great gulf divided the two cultures of science and literature amongst the acquaintance of GE and GHL. It was listening to Paley address the Cambridge Philosophical Society 'on Solar Myths, Odusseus as the Setting Sun, etc.' in February 1873 that inspired Maxwell's brilliant impromptu analysis of the elaborately conscious 'astronomical or meteorological' significance of the characters in *Middlemarch*: 'The whole thing is, and is intended to be, a solar myth from beginning to end.'[3]

---

1 *Problems of Life and Mind, First Series: The Foundations of a Creed,* II (London: Trübner, 1875), 316–21. This volume was revised in the summer and autumn of 1874; see GEL VI, 72, 79, and 83. The excerpt on ring-vortices on B 100 and 100v is repeated in abbreviated form on Pf 711 67.

2 For an alternative reading, assuming a modern 'conception of relativity', see Sally Shuttleworth, *George Eliot and Nineteenth-Century Science: The Make-Believe of a Beginning* (Cambridge: Cambridge University Press, 1984), pp. 175–7.

3 See the letter from Maxwell to Lewis Campbell on 3 April 1873 in *The Scientific Letters and Papers of James Clerk Maxwell,* edited by P. M. Harman, 2 vols. (to be complete in 3 vols.) (Cambridge: Cambridge University Press, 1990, 1995 –), II, 840–1.

/97v/

Epact – ἡμεραι επακται – Mercury playing at dice with the moon & winning from her the twentieth part of all her illuminations. [Pf 711 9][1]

The papyrus now unknown in Egypt & only found in the Anapo in Sicily & in a small stream two miles N. of Jaffa. [Pf 711 8][2]

The leaves of the Cacalia Ficoides are sour in the morning, tasteless at noon & bitter in the evening.[3]

Transparency & opacity which seem opposites are really only differences of degree. [Tyndall, *Light,* p. 35]

/99/ Physical Science

'Many believed that metals grew like vegetables; indeed it was customary to close mines for a time to allow them to grow again.'[4]

Also, that pearls would multiply if grains of rice were put with them. Rice is put with gold & precious stones to this end.

Vide Tylor, Early Hist. of Mankind[5]

Also Mandeville's Travels, about the breeding of diamonds.[6]

1 This fanciful astronomical note is copied from that on Pf 711 9; 'seventieth' there is here copied as 'twentieth'. Source not traced.

2 John Gardner Wilkinson, *A Popular Account of the Ancient Egyptians,* 2 vols. (London: John Murray, 1854), II, 97.

3 Copied from Folger 13 115. Source: John Ayrton Paris, *Pharmacologia,* 9th edition (London: Samuel Highley, 1843), p. 119. GE also made notes from Paris in August 1861 and the summer of 1865; see the Beinecke Notebook, entries 131–134 and 271–275, and Wiesenfarth, pp. 184 and 209–10.

4 Source not traced. The following note was inserted later, with references to Tylor and Mandeville added at the foot of the page.

5 Edward Burnett Tylor, *Researches into the Early History of Mankind and the Development of Civilization* (London: John Murray, 1865), p. 278. 'Tylor's Early Hist of Mankind', read from 30 July to 18 August 1874 (GHL Diary), was also the source of notes on Pf 711 62 and 63.

6 The Book of Sir John Maundeville', perhaps read by GE in *Early Travels in Palestine,* edited by Thomas Wright (London: Bohn, 1848), pp. 207–8.

Physical science B 99 99v

'The life of all men is nothing else but an astral balsam, a balsamic impression & a celestial invisible fire, an included air & a tingling spirit of salt.'

Paracelsus [1]

'The temperature of the comet could not be inferred from its nearness to the sun. If its power of absorption were low enough, the comet might carry into the sun's neighbourhood the temperature of stellar space.'

Tyndall, *Light* [p. 171]

The astronomer Messier, during the time of the Terror, shut up in his observatory in the hotel de Cluny, discovered a comet. Not being good at calculation, he was embarrassed to determine the orbit of the wandering star: he thought of the president Bochart de Saron, an able calculator who loved to aid astronomers in their labours. The president, already condemned by the revolutionary tribunal, had only a few hours to live. He employed them in determining by Messier's observations the orbit of the new comet.

(Les Sciences au XVIIIe Siècle, Emile Saigey) [Pf 711 9] [2]

/99v/

Light. Its effect on chemical compounds affords us a striking instance of the extent to which a force, ever active, may be ignored through successive ages of philosophy. If the walls of a large room were covered with photographic apparatus, the small amount of light reflected from the face of a person situated in its centre would simultaneously imprint his portrait on a multitude of recipient surfaces. Were the cameras absent, but the room covered with photographic paper, a change would equally take place in every portion of it, though not a reproduction of form & figure. As other substances not commonly called photographic are known to be affected by light ... every portion of light may be supposed to write its own history by a change more or less permanent in ponderable matter.

1 GE's copy of Paracelsus, *Nach seinem Leben und seinen Lehren dargestellt aus seinen eignen Schriften* (Sulzbach, 1819) is in DWL; the page reference has not been traced. See *The Hermetic and Alchemical Writings of Aureolus Philippus Theophrastus Bombast of Hohenheim,* translated by Arthur Edward Waite, 2 vols. (London: James Elliot, 1894; reprinted Berkeley, California: Shambhala, 1976), I, 136. For GE's references to Robert Browning's *Paracelsus,* see Pf 707 33.

2 Emile Saigey, *Les Sciences au XVIIIe siècle, la physique de Voltaire* (Paris: G. Baillière, 1873), p. 182. 'Saigey La Physique de Voltaire', read from 14 to 22 December 1872 (GHL Diary), is in DWL.

Radiant impulses which falling on certain bodies, give no effect of light, become luminous when falling on other bodies. That which is, or becomes light, when it falls on one body, is not light when it falls on another.

Sound can decompose substances which are held together by feeble affinities. E.g. Iodide of nitrogen.[1]

/100/ Physical Science

Irreversible processes, i.e. which always tend towards & never away from, a certain limiting state. If two gases be put into the same vessel, they become mixed, & the mixture tends continually to become more uniform. If two unequally heated solids be placed in contact, they continually approximate to an intermediate temperature. J. Clerk Maxwell, Brit. Assoc. 1870 [p. 421][2]

'Even in our ordinary experiments on very finely divided matter we find that the substance is beginning to lose the properties which it exhibits when in a large mass, & that effects depending on the individual action of molecules are beginning to be prominent.' Ibid. [p. 420]

Ring-vortices

A theory which Sir W. Thomson has founded on Helmholtz's splendid hydro-dynamical theorems, seeks for the properties of molecules in the ring-vortices of a uniform, frictionless, incompressible fluid. Such whirling rings may be seen when a dexterous smoker sends out a puff of smoke into the still air, but a more evanescent phenomenon it is difficult to conceive. This evanescence is owing to the viscosity of the air; but Helmholtz has shown that in a perfect fluid **/100v/** such a whirling ring, if once generated, would go on whirling forever, would always consist of the very same portion of the fluid which was first set whirling, & would never be cut in two by any natural cause. The generation of a ring vortex is of course equally beyond the power of natural causes, but once generated, it has the properties of individuality, permanence in quantity & indestructibility. It is also the recipient of impulse & of energy, which is all we can affirm of matter: & these ring-vortices are capable of such varied connections & knotted involutions, that the properties of differently knotted vortices must be as different as those of different kinds of molecules can be.

1 The source of these notes on properties of light and sound has not been traced. They may have been added later.

2 Maxwell's address was reprinted in *Nature* 2 (22 September 1870): 419–22.

If a theory of this kind should be found, after conquering the enormous mathematical difficulties of the subject, to represent in any degree[1] the actual properties of molecules, it will stand in a very different scientific position from those theories of molecular action which are formed by investing the molecule with an arbitrary system of central forces invented expressly to account for the observed phenomena. In the vortex theory we have nothing arbitrary, no central forces or occult properties of any **/101/** other kind. We have nothing but matter & motion, & when the vortex is once started its properties are all determined from the original impetus, & no further assumptions are possible.' Ibid. [p. 421]

'A molecule, say of hydrogen, if either its mass or its rate of vibration were to be altered in the least, would no longer be a molecule of hydrogen.'
Ibid. [p. 421]

'From their perviousness to stellar light & other considerations, Sir John Herschel drew some startling conclusions concerning the density & weight of comets. You know these extraordinary & mysterious bodies sometimes throw out tails 100,000,000 miles in length, & 50,000 miles in diameter ... Now suppose the whole of this stuff to be swept together & suitably compressed, what do you suppose its volume would be? Sir John Herschel would probably tell you that the whole mass might be carted away at a single effort by one of your dray-horses.' Tyndall, Brit. Ass. 1870[2]

'A sky as vast as ours & as good in appearance, could be formed from a quantity of matter which might be held in the hollow of the hand.'
Ibid. [p. 152]

/101v/ Physical Science

'There appears to be no connection between the determination of the direction of a curve at each of its points & that of the velocity of a body at each moment of its variable motion; but to the eyes of a geometer these questions are but one.' Comte, Phil. pos. [I, 42]

1 GE first wrote 'way', then corrected her transcription by adding 'degree' above the line.
2 *Fragments of Science for Unscientific People,* pp. 151–2.

'By the infinitesimal calculus it becomes possible in geometry to treat curved lines as composed of an infinity of rectilinear elements, & curved surfaces as formed of plane elements; & in mechanics, varied motions as an infinite series of uniform motions, succeeding each other at infinitely small intervals of time.' Ibid. [I, 61][1]

'The study of the properties of the same figure is so extensive, that the labours of geometers for twenty centuries have not exhausted the study of conic sections.' Ibid. [I, 90]

'When Torricelli showed that air & gas (geist) could be weighed, he showed that substances which had been deemed spiritual & essentially different from ponderable matter were possessed of its attributes.'[2]

Phlogiston, according to Stahl, was a spiritual substance endowed with positive levity.[3]

1 GE unintentionally repeated 'small': 'at infinitely small small intervals'.

2 Source not traced. Evangelista Torricelli (1608–47) was a physicist and geometer, a younger contemporary of Galileo, and discoverer of the principle of the barometer.

3 Source not traced. According to the *OED*, Georg Ernst Stahl introduced the use of the term 'Phlogiston' in 1702 in his edition of Joachim Beccher's *Physica Subterranea* of 1669. An offprint of an unidentified article, 'Phlogiston and Lavoisier', in DWL (*Catalogue,* p. 223), has not been seen by the present editor.

The Mishnah, the Talmud, and the Rabbins

B 106, 107, 108, 107v, 108v, 109, 109v

The section of the Berg Notebook devoted to Jewish history and religious practices begins with these notes on the Mishnah. The first major codification of Jewish law, the Mishnah collected together the orally transmitted teachings of scribes, Pharisees, and scholars, from the period of the Second Temple (the return from the Babylonian captivity, the period of Ezra and Nehemiah), down to the time of Rabbi Jehuda (or Juda), the *Nasi* or President under whose auspices the redaction was completed, c. 200 CE. GE's heading, 'When was the Mischna written down?' (B 107v and 108v), shows the link between the 'Homeric Question' and the scholarship of Samuel David Luzzatto, who determined that the Mishnah was preserved by oral tradition alone until the sixth century CE.

Mishnah means 'learning' or 'teaching'. It is fitting that GE's first notes from her learning about Judaism should be drawn from an article by Emanuel Oscar Menahem Deutsch (1829–73), who had given her lessons in Hebrew. 'The Talmud', his most famous essay, was first published in the *Quarterly Review* and caused such a stir that the issue went into six editions.[1] Within a year the essay was translated into German, French, Swedish, Russian, Danish, and Dutch.[2] Deutsch sent GE a proof copy in October 1867, and in December 1869 sent her a copy of the German reprint, *Der Talmud.*[3] The *Quarterly Review* copy is the source of her notes on B 106 and also on Pf 708 98 to 101.

These notes from Deutsch are combined with information from books acquired in the summer and autumn of 1873. Her list on Pf 711 21 of 'Books Wanted' includes two sources for these notes on the Mishnah and Talmud: 'Milman, History of the Jews' and 'Grätz, Geschichte der Juden'.

1 *Quarterly Review* 123 (1867): 417–64. It was later reprinted in *Literary Remains of the Late Emanuel Deutsch,* edited anonymously by Lady Strangford (London: John Murray, 1874). See the headnote to 'Mohammed, the Hebrews in Egypt, and the colonization of Jerusalem' (Pf 711 43–46, 50–51).

2 *Literary Remains*, p. x.

3 See GEL IV, 384–5, 409–10, and V, 73.

The Mishnah, the Talmud, and the Rabbins

The reference on B 106 to *The History of the Jews from the Earliest Period Down to Modern Times*, the fourth revised edition of a three-volume work by Henry Hart Milman (London: John Murray, 1866), is to a passage marked by a marginal line in GE's copy in DWL. 'Milman's History of the Jews' was read on 4 October 1873 (GHL Diary). Milman presents a sympathetic view of Jewish history, while not concealing his opinion that in modern times Judaism has little to offer. Nevertheless, the publication of the first edition in 1830 caused such consternation amongst his fellow Christians that the sale of the book was stopped. According to the *DNB*,

> In this unpretending book for the first time an English clergyman treated the Jews as an oriental tribe, recognised sheiks and emirs in the Old Testament, sifted and classified documentary evidence, and evaded or minimised the miraculous.

A more authoritative historian of the Jews was Heinrich (Hirsch) Graetz, whose eleven-volume *Geschichte der Juden von den ältesten Zeiten bis auf die Gegenwart* (Leipzig: Oskar Leiner, 1863–76) greatly surpassed and superseded the earlier scholarly history by Isaac Marcus Jost, *Geschichte der Israeliten* (Berlin: Schlesinger, 1820–47). Although Jost's ten-volume work is listed amongst the 'Books Wanted' on Pf 711 21 and again on Pf 710 1, there is no evidence that GE read it. Jost's later three-volume work – influenced by Graetz – *Geschichte des Judenthums und seiner Secten* (Leipzig: Dorffling, 1857–9) is included in book lists on Pf 711 21, Pf 710 1, and Folger 13 56, but also appears to have remained unread by GE. Graetz, in contrast, was central to her study of Jewish history. GHL's Diary notes the reading of Graetz from 14 September to 3 October 1873. GE frequently returned to it later. Her volumes of *Geschichte der Juden*, now in DWL, are extensively marked and annotated, and notes from Graetz fill many pages of the Berg notebook and Pf 711.[1]

GE made no notes from volume 1, which includes the period of the Pentateuch, and only one note from volume 2; and her copies of these volumes have few annotations and markings. Although Graetz followed the critical approach of biblical scholarship with regard to Rabbinic literature and the rest of the Bible, he 'adopted a completely traditional view on the authorship of the Pentateuch'.[2] For this period, GE preferred to consult the

1 See the entries for Graetz in the Bibliographical Index.

2 Jacobs, p. 199.

untraditional account of Abraham Kuenen, the source of many notes in Pf 710. Her extensive note-taking from Graetz began with volume 4, the first published volume,[1] which covers the period from the destruction of the Second Temple and the conquest of Judaea by Titus in 70–72 CE, to the completion of the Talmud in 550 CE. This epoch marks the great transformation of Judaism: its lost political identity in the land of Israel was replaced by the jurisdiction of the leaders of the Jewish community, the Sanhedrin, and the great Jewish academies in Babylonia (B 107, 108). The lost ritual of Temple worship was replaced by a complex form of cultural transmission culminating in the Mishnah and Talmud. Instead of the Levites and the priestly caste of Cohens performing the Temple rites, the essential practices of religious life were henceforth transmitted by scholars or Rabbis. Their exemplary teachings are illustrated by anecdotes drawn from Graetz about the Rabbis of the Talmudic period (B 109, 109v).

Occasionally GE copied Graetz's German text almost verbatim – for example, on B 157, 162v, 163, 166v, 171v, and 193 – but more often she translated and condensed it. His neo-Orthodox perspective provided a context for the more Reform-minded sources also consulted by her. His nationalist fervour, which found some echoes in parts of her novel, offended the sensibilities of German nationalists and provoked an anti-Jewish backlash in 1879. In response to attacks upon his history, Graetz anonymously published *Briefwechsel einer englischen Dame uber Judenthum und Semitismus* (Stuttgart, 1883), which included warmly appreciative references to *Daniel Deronda.*[2]

---

1 In 1853; her copy in DWL is the second edition, 1863.

2 For a translation of *The Correspondence of an English Lady on Judaism and Semitism*, see *The Structure of Jewish History and Other Essays* by Graetz, edited and translated by Ismar Schorsch (New York: The Jewish Theological Seminary of America, 1975), pp. 191–258.

/106/ *Talmud : Mischna*

Mischna, from *shanah (tana)* to learn, repeat, of old translated δευτεροσις or second law. But this derivation, correct as it seems literally, is incorrect in the first instance. It simply means 'learning' (Steinschneider says, discussion – as Midrasch is exegesis),[1] like *Gemara*, which besides indicates 'complement' to the Mishnah. [Deutsch, p. 430; Steinschneider, p. 367]

The abstract of about 800 years' legal production [Deutsch, p. 448] (i.e. from the Return till AC 200; Milman quotes Jost as saying that no 'part' of the Mishna except a few sayings from the Asmonean time, is older than the time of Herod, but Jost's word is *Lehrsätze,* & surely does not refer to the laws). [Milman II, 479n]

Jehuda, the 'Redactor', had excluded all but the best authenticated traditions, as well as all discussion & exegesis, unless particularly necessary. This redaction took place about 200 AD. A few generations after this official Mishnah, the mass of materials excluded by Jehuda were also collected, as a sort of apocryphal oral code. First a so-called external Mishnah – *Boraitha*; further, the discussions & additions, called *Tosefta*, supplement; finally the exegesis or methodology of the Halacha, *Sifri, Sifra*, *Mechilta*, much of which was afterwards embodied in the Talmud. [Deutsch, pp. 448–9][2]

(Talmud more than 3000 f. pages) [Deutsch, p. 449][3]

What is called the Talmudic period (as distinguished from the rabbinical periods) numbered 970 years; the epoch of the Tanaim, from the foundation of the school of Jamnia to completion of Mischna, from 70–200, forming its

1 This parenthetical note, also copied on Pf 711 60, was added when GE was making copious notes from Moritz Steinschneider's 'Jüdische Literatur'; see B 141 to 150.

2 For 'called' GE inadvertently wrote 'call'. In pencil, she later added 'Book' above *Sifri*, and 'measure, order' above *Mechilta*. As her note on Pf 710 40 indicates, *Zifri* and *Zifra* are both derived from *Sepher,* or 'book'; however, the note on Pf 710 40 confuses the two. *Zifra* refers to the Commentary on Leviticus, *Zifri* to the Commentary on Numbers and Deuteronomy. Notes on B 125 and Pf 711 98a give correct references, and also identify *Mechilta* as the Commentary on Exodus. The latter note, translating *Mechilta* as 'Mass, Form, Ordnung', and *Zifra* as 'das Buch', appears to be related to the pencilled additions here. Compare notes from Steinschneider on B 144.

3 Deutsch has 'exactly 2947 folio leaves'. Above this note GE pencilled in 'Babli'. In DD ch. 62, there is a reference to '*Babli* – by which affectionate-sounding diminutive is meant the vast volume of the Babylonian Talmud' (691).

first division.[1] The founder of the school was R. Jochanan b. Sakkai, who got himself **/107/** carried out of Jerusalem in a coffin, & obtained leave from Vespasian thus to save alive the soul of Judaism. He maintained that the religion was not lost because the Temple service was extinct, & insisted on the passage, 'I have loved mercy better than sacrifice' [Hosea vi, 6]. He re-established the Sanhedrin at Jamnia, & thus gave an organic existence to Judaism apart from the Temple service. Jamnia now became the religious & national centre. Thence were issued the ordinances concerning the new moon & festival-times. The trumpet was blown on new year's day (Rosch-ha-schana), & some other memorial observances were retained, but ordinances having relation to the Temple-services were for the most part revoked.

[Graetz 4, 11–15]

The first founder of Talmudic Judaism was Hillel. He laid down *seven rules* of interpretation, which had both given a secure basis to the already existent Sopheric deductions & had also made a standing-ground for future extensions & developments. At about the same time the subjection of the national life under the Herodian or Idumean princes had generated another form of exegesis – the allusive or homiletic, in which present circumstances were regarded as the kernel of ancient texts, & Edom or Esau was taken as the symbol either of the Romanizing Jewish princes, or of Rome itself.[2] This form of interpretation was called *Agada*, as the legal doctrine was called – **/108/** in so far as it was elicited according to rule from the Mosaic text – Mischna.

[Graetz 4, 16–17][3]

1 For GE's note on the three epochs of the Talmudic period – the Tannaim, the Amoraim, and the Saboraim – see B 114 and 114v.

2 Joseph Kalonymos expresses his disgust at Daniel Charisi's grandson having been raised in ignorance of his Jewish ancestry by exclaiming, 'A robbery of our people – as when our youths and maidens were reared for the Roman Edom' (DD ch. 60: 670).

3 For a note on Hillel and the seven rules of interpretation, see B 153v and 153av. For more on the *Sopherim* or scribes of the Second Temple period, see B 140, 141, 142, and 146v.

The content of the Mischna was presented in three ways, constituting three methods of teaching which were nevertheless in close connection with each other & mutually influential.

1. The first method was to communicate the traditional enactments quite simply & briefly in the name of an ancient authority or decision of the Sanhedrin, in order that the law should not be forgotten for want of written documents. Such definite, brief sentences were called *Halacha*, which may equally imply tradition, custom, or practice.
2. The second method was to gather the traditional material from the written text according to certain rules, either from the contents & context, or from some hint or indication supposed to be contained in a particle or word. This mode of inference was called *Midrasch*: the material of tradition no longer rested on personal authority, but on the text.
3. The third method, was the application of rules to new cases. This was called Talmud (in the narrower sense). Grätz IV, 17[-18] [1]

'Die Halacha bildete den Grundstamm der Lehre, der Midrasch die Saugwurzeln, die aus dem Schriftworte Lebenselement sogen, der Talmud die weitverzweigten Aeste, & die Agada war die Blüthe.'

Sachs, d. Poesie d. Juden [Graetz 4, 19][2]

1 As Graetz indicates, the teaching methods outlined here and in the previous note are interconnected and mutually influential. David J. Goldberg and John D. Rayner clarify the connections in *The Jewish People: Their History and Their Religion* (London: Penguin, 1989): *Halacha* (law) and *Aggada* (lore) form 'a twofold strand in Rabbinic thought':

> While literature based on the Midrash method is generally aggadic, it may also be halachic, namely when the Scripture verse being interpreted is of the legislative kind ... Conversely, although literature based on the Mishnah method is primarily concerned with *Halachah*, it often digresses into aggadic topics. (pp. 90, 211)

For more on the Midrash, see B 115 to 117v and 141, 142, and 143.

2 Graetz refers to Michael Jehiel Sachs, *Die religiöse Poesie der Juden in Spanien* (Berlin: Veit, 1845), p. 148. This work is also referred to on Pf 711 21 and Pf 710 20. Translation:

> The Halacha formed the central stem of the teaching, the Midrash the shoots, which sucked the life-element from the written word, the Talmud the many-branched limbs, and the Agada was the blossom.

The Mishnah, the Talmud, and the Rabbins B 107v 108v

/107v/

'When was the Mischna written down?'

The collection of the Mischna bore originally the sub-title 'of R. Juda' (under whose presidency it was completed, about 180–200); by degrees this addition was dropped & it began to be regarded as the sole authoritative collection. R. Juda's scholars disseminated it in distant lands & used it as a text of their discourses & judicial codex. But this Mischna was *not*, any more than the previous collections, committed to writing; it remained for *several* centuries in charge of oral Tradition alone. Indeed, it was held a religious offence & a degradation of the material to write down the Tradition. Only Hagadas were here & there put in writing, & even this was just as severely blamed by many Teachers. Some indeed, as R. Chija, carried rare or striking Halachas in a roll, but so secretly that they were called *Megillat Setarim*, Secret Rolls.

Grätz IV, 221

When R. Gamaliel was deposed (circa 90) witnesses were called before the Sanhedrin to testify concerning the traditions of the schools of Hillel & Schammai which had been matter of dispute. Among them two poor weavers. Apparently a protocol was drawn up, & this collection was the beginning of the Mischna arrangement, though without any connection other than an occasional number. It was called *Adojot* (Testimony) & *Bechirta* (selection).

[Graetz 4, 38][1]

/108v/ 'When was the Mischna written down?'

'To Luzzato[2] belongs the merit of having corrected the old & general error of supposing that the Mischna & Talmud were written down immediately after they were collected & arranged. With abundant acumen he adduced proof that on the contrary Mischna & Talmud afterwards as well as before were preserved orally alone until in the period of the Saboraim during the lives of Rabbi Gisa & R. Simona (550), a half-century before the appearance of Mohammed, they were committed to writing.' (According to testimony in the Midrasch) 'at the time when the Septuagint was read in the churches, & Christian Rome gave itself out as the true Israel, the Mischna was not yet

1 Disputes between opposing schools of thought remain a strong characteristic of the Talmud. For a major difference of opinion between Hillelites and Schammaites, see B 194 and Pf 711 58.

2 For another reference to the scholarship of Samuel David Luzzatto, see B 125.

written down. As there are still some who are incredulous – ' let these proofs be mentioned from the Talmud. In one place it is presupposed that the historical calendar alone is in writing, & no Halacha. In another, it is debated what shall be done with copies of the sacred writings (Thora); but no word about rolls of Halachas. It is time that the mention of a Hagada-book occurs, & Josua b. Levi declares that he had never looked more than once in such a book, because he held it unlawful to write down Hagadas. There is a curse of Chija ben Abba's against the writing down of Agadas. But no trace in the Talmud of a complete MS. of the Mischna. Some fragmentary records of Halachas are however mentioned. [Graetz 4, 494–5]

/109/ Rabbins

R. Jochanan b. Sakkai once gave this question to his disciples for study: What should a man most desire to possess? One answered: 'A benevolent disposition'; another, 'a noble friend'; a third, 'a worthy neighbour'; the fourth, 'the gift of calculating beforehand the consequences of his acts'. But Eleasar b. Arach said: 'A man should most desire to have a noble heart.' This last answer pleased R. Jochanan, because everything else is included in it. [Graetz 4, 16][1]

R. Jochanan was the leader of the elder Tanaim. He was carried out of Jerusalem in a coffin, & obtaining an interview with Vespasian, got leave to found a school at Jamnia. He was followed by Gamaliel II, whose presidency was characterized by a stringent effort to keep unity among the teachers & transmitters of the law. v. Grätz IV, [ch] 2 [11–13]

R. Josua b. Chananja, one of the younger Tanaim, was a needle maker, very poor & ugly, of gentle, conciliatory disposition. *As a young Levite of the Singer clan he had seen the glories of the Temple worship.* He disapproved of the decision by the *Bat-Kol*, saying that the law was not for heaven but for men, who should decide by majorities. [Graetz 4, 50, 52; Pf 711 24][2]

R. Akiba took to study that he might win his master's daughter. After they were married they were so poor that she sold her hair to get him bread.

1 On the first leaf of Graetz 4, GE noted 'Edel Herz 16'.

2 In DD ch. 40, Mordecai compares his lot to that of Joshua ben Chananja:

> 'after the last destruction he earned his bread by making needles, but in his youth he had been a singer on the steps of the Temple, and had a memory of what was, before the glory departed' (464).

He exerted himself on behalf of Bar-Cochba, & afterwards fell a martyr to his patriotism. [Graetz 4, 53–4, 177]

/109v/ Rabbins

R. Juda I, called by pre-eminence simply 'Rabbi', who finished the arrangement of the Mischna, being remonstrated with for having relaxed the severity of the laws concerning tribute, replied, 'Our forefathers bequeathed this deed to me to execute.'
('Our fathers did not do this.' 'No, they left it for me to do.') [Graetz 4, 219] [1]

R. Josua b. Levi (one of the earlier Amoraim) when in Rome observed a fine statue enveloped in carpets, to protect it from the heat & cold, & not far from it a beggar sitting with scarcely rags to cover his nakedness. R. Josua thought that the Messiah would come out of Rome; that he waited there in the form of a slave among the beggars & sick at the gate. [Graetz 4, 264] [2]

Of the sufferings endured by the Jews in Palestine after a desperate insurrection of theirs under Constantius, R. Huna narrates, 'When we took refuge in the subterranean passages we had torches with us: when they burned dimly we knew that it was day, if they burned brightly we knew that it was night.' [Graetz 4, 342] [3]

1 An indication of the Rabbins' revisionary contribution to inherited tradition. GE's parenthetical explication suggests its pertinence to Deronda's deliberate response to Kalonymos: 'But I will not say that I shall profess to believe exactly as my fathers have believed' (DD ch. 60: 673).

2 In DD ch. 41, Deronda thinks of 'that Rabbi who stood waiting at the gate of Rome in confidence that the Messiah would be found among the destitute who entered there' (477).

3 Mordecai recalls this story in the *Hand and Banner* (DD ch. 42: 494).

Extracts from the Mishnah

B 110, 110v, 111

'Eighteen Treatises from the Mischna translated by Sola & Raphall' is included in the 'Books Wanted' list compiled in the summer of 1873 (Pf 711 21), but is not in DWL. GE's rather extensive notes suggest that she read a borrowed copy of *Eighteen Treatises from the Mishna*, translated by David Aaron de Sola and Morris J. Raphall, second edition (London: Sherwood, Gilbert, and Piper, 1845). De Sola also translated both the Portuguese (or Sephardi) Prayers and the German (or Ashkenazi) Festival Prayers into English.[1] With Dr Raphall, he began a new edition of *The Sacred Scriptures in Hebrew and English*. Only the first volume was published (London: Samuel Bagster, 1844); this translation of Genesis, given to GE by Nicholas Trübner, is now in DWL. Unlike those publications, the partial translation of some treatises of the Mishnah into English provoked bitter controversy.

The translation was commissioned in 1839 by the Reform-minded Moses Mocatta and others, who in 1841 seceded from the Orthodox congregation to found the West London Synagogue in Bloomsbury. Subsequently, after the schism, it was published by a prominent member of the Reform congregation, Benjamin Elkin, who neglected first to consult the translators. De Sola and Raphall, in a notice in *The Times* of 23 December 1842, repudiated responsibility for the publication and especially the preface, which was unsigned and therefore seemed to be attributable to them, although it was in fact written by Elkin. In their *Times* advertisement, de Sola and Raphall objected to 'the Anti-Judaic principles expressed in the preface', including, in their view, 'a covert attempt to bring the Mishna into contempt, as well as the Oral Law, which it contains'.[2] The offending part of Elkin's preface refers to the origin of the translation project in a public discussion

1 James Picciotto, *Sketches of Anglo-Jewish History* (London: Trübner, 1875), p. 360. GE's copy, a gift from the publisher, is in DWL. See 'The Jewish Liturgy' and the headnote (B 184 to 190).

2 See Benjamin Elkin (identified only as B. E., 'The Writer of the Preface to the lately published Mishna'), *Letters Addressed to the Editor of 'The Voice of Jacob'* (London: J. Wertheimer, 1843), pp. 9–10.

'on the subject of revising the liturgy used in that synagogue and improving its Public Worship':

> the opponents to alteration took shelter under the authority of the Mishna; and this led the advocates of improvement to express their long entertained doubts as to the divinity of the Oral Law.

Elkin pointed out that the German Reform movement had produced a German translation of the complete Mishnah, declared that 'free access should be given to pages containing so large a portion of the Oral Law, for which a Divine origin is claimed', and expressed his hope that the whole Mishnah would be 'rendered into English for the enlightenment of the British Jew, who will thereby be enabled to read a book said to contain God's explanation of the Written Law' (pp. 5–6).

The authority of the Oral Law, challenged by the nineteenth-century Reform movement, had been disputed earlier. Even in the time of Jehuda the Redactor of the Mishnah, the pre-eminent 'Rabbi' was 'remonstrated with for having relaxed the severity of the laws': 'Our fathers did not do this.' 'No, they left it for me to do.' (B 109v). Insofar as the challenge may reflect an 'Anti-Judaic' viewpoint, it is an anti-Judaism peculiar to those raised within the teachings of the Oral Law, like the apostate Salomon Maimon (see B 136). Deronda's mother may be seen as personalizing this challenge to the laws of 'our fathers' in her revolt against the severity of the laws of her father:

> 'I hated living under the shadow of my father's strictness. Teaching, teaching for everlasting – "this you must be," "that you must not be" – pressed on me like a frame that got tighter and tighter as I grew.'
>
> (DD ch. 51: 587–8)

If Judaism is to continue to be a living faith, it must grow and develop: such is the basic Reform argument. As Deronda tells Joseph Kalonymos, the friend of his grandfather,

> 'But I will not say that I shall profess to believe exactly as my fathers have believed. Our fathers themselves changed the horizon of their belief and learned of other races.' (DD ch. 60: 673)

The Mishnah focuses on minute details of the practical observance of divine law. Do plaits of hair become a question of conscience, or is such a question the mere hair-splitting for which Talmudic dispute has been blamed and ridiculed? (See B 110 and 145v.) GE's note on 'Talmudic Questions' from

'Salomon Maimon's Life' on Folger 13 123 suggests that she may share some of Maimon's scepticism:

> How many white hairs a cow can have and still be red?
> Whether one may kill a louse or a flea on the Sabbath?
> Answer, a louse may be killed, but to kill a flea is mortal sin.

On the other hand, GE's fascination with fine discriminations of casuistry, and her awareness of the role of taboos in the preservation of cultural and national distinctness, make it most unlikely that her 'Extracts from the Mishnah' reflect a dismissive or 'Anti-Judaic' attitude. The organic development of religion, including Judaism, was of great interest to her; but understanding the laws which framed that development was also essential. That is, she saw that the framework might both constrict and support growth, and that authority might combine authoritarian and legitimate powers. The complexities of this double viewpoint are suggested by GE's epigraph about 'human progress', a witty play upon the Rabbinical prohibition: 'no man ... may turn the bones of his father and mother into spoons' (DD ch. 33: 351).

Benjamin Elkin, unlike the apostates Salomon Maimon or the Princess Halm-Eberstein, considered himself to be an observant Jew, and denied that his principles were 'Anti-Judaic'. Nonetheless, his bones were refused burial in the Jewish cemetery, in the space reserved next to those of his wife.[1] The Reform-movement Jews of the nineteenth century are sometimes said to be 'assimilationist'.[2] But that label has been applied to a very broad spectrum of viewpoints and often reflects an exclusionist definition of what is Jewish and what is anti-Judaic. Thus it is significant that Deronda prefaces his assertion that Jews have learned of other races – an assertion that might by some be labelled assimilationist – with his inclusive self-definition: 'I shall call myself a Jew' (DD ch. 60: 673).

---

1 The intricacies of the dispute over *Eighteen Treatises from the Mishna* are outlined in *Bibliotheca Anglo-Judaica: A Bibliographical Guide to Anglo-Jewish History*, compiled by Joseph Jacobs and Lucien Wolf (London: Office of the *Jewish Chronicle*, 1888), p. 113. For more on conflicts between Reform and Orthodox Jews in England, see GE's notes from R. Hirschfeld (B 123v to 129). See also the revised edition of Picciotto's *Sketches of Anglo-Jewish History*, edited by Israel Finestein (London: Soncino, 1956), pp. 481–6.

2 For example, by Baker in *George Eliot and Judaism*, pp. 143–6.

/110/ Extracts from the Mishnah

From what time is the שׁמע (Schma'h) to be said in the morning? From the time a man can distinguish between blue & white. R. Eleazar saith, 'between blue & leek-green'. [p. 2] [1]

'It is lawful for a man to set two rows of cucumbers, two rows of pumpkins, & two of Egyptian beans; but a single row of cucumbers, one of pumpkins, & one of Egyptian beans is prohibited.' [p. 19] [2]

(*Kilaim* or mixture – in garments of linen & woollen &c.) [p. 30] [3]

'A woman may go out (on the Sabbath) with plaits of hair, whether of her own hair or of another woman's, or of an animal ... with false ringlets into the courtyard ... A false tooth, or a gilt tooth, Rabbi -- [4] permits, but the sages prohibit.' [p. 46] [5]

A man may verbally count the number of his guests (on the Sabbath) & also of his additional *hors d'oeuvres*, but he must not do it from a written list. [p. 67]

'A wife is acquired in three ways, & may recover her liberty in two ways: by money, by a marriage contract, & through natural connection. (That is, when he says, "Behold thou art wedded to me with this connection &c.") Although such a marriage is a legal one, & cannot be dissolved, except by a *get* (divorce) or the death of the parties, yet the man who thus marries is, as a transgressor against morality & decency, punishable by the tribunal with the infliction of stripes for rebellion. **/110v/** She regains her liberty by a divorce or by the death of her husband.' [pp. 306, 306n, 307] [6]

1 The Shema, the essential prayer of Judaism, uttered twice daily, morning and evening, is traditionally the first and last word spoken by every pious Jew. Thus in DD ch. 70, the dying Ezra 'raised himself and uttered in Hebrew the confession of the divine Unity' (754). See also B 133v and 148v and Pf 711 22 and 57. This excerpt is from Treatise Berachoth, containing laws for regulating the daily prayers.

2 Reference is made to Deuteronomy xxii, 9: 'Thou shalt not sow thy vineyard with divers seeds.' This and the following note are from Treatise Kilaim.

3 'The word "Kilaim" denotes the commixture of things differing in kind, species, or nature' (p. 14n). Deuteronomy xxii, 11 is cited on p. 31: 'Thou shalt not wear ... a garment of divers sorts.'

4 'Rabbi --' is R. Jehuda; see B 114v.

5 This and the following note are from Treatise Sabbath.

6 From Treatise Kedushin 'of Betrothing'.

Extracts from the Mishnah B 110v 111

Ketubah, Letter or writing of divorce by which the husband engaged to pay a sum of money to the divorced wife towards her maintenance. This was instituted by Simon ben Shetach & Juda ben Tabbai, under Alexander Jannaeus, 105–79. They wished by it to restrain the abuse of divorce.

v. Grätz V. III [Graetz 3, 119–20] [1]

The Sadducees said, 'We blame (object to) you Pharisees because you say, "Sacred scriptures make the hands unclean, but the books Hameram (perhaps the books against revealed religion – perhaps Homer) do not make the hands unclean."' R. Jochanan ben Zachai said (ironically), 'And have we nothing else to object to the Pharisees but this? They also assert the bones of an ass are clean, but the bones of Jochanan the High Priest are unclean.' The Sadducees replied, 'According to their love (the estimation in which they / the bones / are held) is their uncleanness, *so that no one may turn the bones of his father & mother into spoons*.' He answered them, 'In like manner, the Sacred Scriptures: according to their love is their uncleanness; whereas the books Hameram which are not beloved do not make the hands unclean.'

[pp. 366–7] [2]

In the Treatise Rosch Hashanah are the rules about giving evidence that the New Moon has been seen. The Sabbath may be profaned by journeying in order to give this important testimony; & those who are afraid of robbers may carry sticks. [pp. 156–8] [3]

The following are held incompetent witnesses: gamblers with dice, pigeon-breeders (for gambling purposes), [4] those who trade in the produce of the new year, & also slaves. **/111/** The rule is, that all evidence which cannot be received from a woman cannot be received from any of these. [p. 158]

1 This note was added later, on B 111, with a cross-reference, 'v. note', inserted on B 110v.

2 This passage, from Treatise Yadaim, is given an ironic twist in the epigraph for DD ch. 33:

> 'No man,' says a Rabbi, by way of indisputable instance, 'may turn the bones of his father and mother into spoons'... The market for spoons has never expanded enough for anyone to say, 'Why not?' and to argue that human progress lies in such an application of material. (351)

3 Here GE added, in pencil, a cross-reference to her note on Sabbath prohibitions: 'v. 127' (i.e., B 126v).

4 'This includes all games of hazard; usurers and gamblers being considered as reputed thieves' (p. 158n).

Extracts from the Mishnah B 111

Formerly fires were lighted on the tops of mountains (to announce the new moon); but when the Samaritans led the nation into error, it was ordained that messengers should be sent out.
(Language of torches) [p. 159][1]

In the sentences of the Rabbis it is emphasized, that it is a duty to 'report everything in the name of the person who predicated it'.[2]

Eighteen Treatises from the Mishna, translated by Sola & Raphall

1 In DD ch. 42 Mordecai's metaphor seems to allude to this former custom: 'Let the torch of visible community be lit!' (497).

2 Source not traced in the extracts from the Mishnah. This is one of the maxims in *Avot* or *Pirke Avot* (6. 6), the Teachings of the Fathers. In DD ch. 63, Mordecai speaks for joint authorship and his own anonymity, even though 'our Masters delivered rightly that everything should be quoted in the name of him that said it' (698).

Maimonides and the name of Jahveh

B 112, 112v, 168, 193

Moses ben Maimon, or Maimonides (also known as Rambam, as GE notes on Pf 711 103 and Pf 710 33), the great mediaeval Jewish philosopher, produced a most influential commentary on the Mishnah, from which the Thirteen Articles of Belief have been extracted (B 168), and was also the author of the great Code of the Law, the *Mishneh Torah*. GE's copy of Hermann Hedwig Bernard's translation, *The Main Principles of the Creed and Ethics of the Jews, exhibited in Selections from the Yad Hachazakah of Maimonides* (Cambridge: Cambridge University Press, 1832), is in DWL.

The notes on the name Jahveh are drawn from Maimonides' philosophical treatise, *More Nebuchim* or *The Guide for the Perplexed*, which is not in DWL, although 'More Nebuchim, Guide des Egarés' is included in GE's 'Books Wanted' list (Pf 711 21). Her source is Moïse ben Maimoun 'dit Maïmonide', *Le Guide des égarés*, translated with a commentary by Salomon Munk, 3 vols. (Paris: A. Franck, 1856–66). Almost equal in length to her notes from Maimonides are her extracts from Munk's commentary, which are marked in her MS by being enclosed within brackets. Munk's scholarly expertise was well known to her: his *Mélanges de philosopie juive et arabe*, which she had read for the first time in 1868, and his *Palestine* are sources of many notes in Pf 711, Pf 710, and Pf 707.

Among the scriptural references for the discussion of the ineffable name of JHVH, the best known is Exodus iii, 13–14:

> And Moses said unto God, Behold, when I come unto the children of Israel, and shall say unto them, The God of your fathers hath sent me unto you; and they shall say to me, What is his name? what shall I say unto them?
>
> And God said unto Moses, I AM THAT I AM …

Munk's commentary may be compared to GE's note on 'Allah':

> The Çufis who developed Mohammed's idea, fell on the same sort of expression as the Jehovists. 'Wenn du uns fragst, wer Gott ist, so antworten wir: Howa, howa, i.e. *er ist er*.' (Howayya = Ipseität)

['When you ask us who God is, we reply thus: Howa, howa, that is, he is that he is.' (Howayya = being one's self)] (Pf 710 2)

The account of 'the remorse of Jonah Gerundi' (B 193) – the last extended note in the Berg Notebook – refers to the bitter Maimonidean controversy, which divided the Jewish people and betrayed them to the more powerful hostility of the Gentile world. The writings of Maimonides were to become greatly influential and highly regarded, but at the time of their publication they met severe opposition. His discussion of Aristotle's proof of the eternity of the universe and his hope that faith and science could be reconciled were seen as heretical. According to GE's note from 'R. Hirschfeld',

> Maimonides published his Mishna Thora, in which he omitted all Talmudic disputations & on his own authority declared what was the explanation of the Law, where the Talmud had not done so. During subsequent centuries he was regarded as the pillar of rabbinism, but not so by his contemporaries, who attacked him as having no right to decide where the Talmudic authorities had failed to do so. (B 126)

Aided by Rabbi Jonah Gerundi, the Dominicans burned Maimonides' works at Montpellier and Paris in 1233. In 1242 the Talmud itself was burnt at Paris. GE's source for this note is Graetz; unusually, she copies the German text rather than making a summary translation. Her extract omits Graetz's mention of the reconciliation of the two Jewish factions, who cast aside their rancour 'and treated each other as brethren'.

Maimonides' life and works are summed up in the Chronology on B 171:

> Maimonides, b. 1135
> finished Comm. on Mischna, 1168
> finished Mischna Thora or Religious Codex, 1180
> Moreh Nebuchim, 1190
> died & was buried at Tiberias, 1204

/112/ The name *Jahveh*
(From Maimonides, *More Nebuchim*)[1]

Tout Hébreu sait que le nom d'Elohim est homonyme, s'appliquant à Dieu, aux anges et aux gouvernants régissants les états. Déjà Onkelos, le prosélyte, a expliqué – et son explication est vraie – que par les mots: 'Et vous serez comme des Elohim connaissant le bien et le mal,' on a en vue le dernier sens; car il dit (dans sa traduction chaldaïque), 'Et vous serez comme des grands personnages'. [I, 37][2]

Tous les noms de Dieu qu'on trouve dans les livres (sacrés) sont généralement dérivés des actions, ce qui n'est point inconnu. Un seul nom doit être excepté, c'est celui qui s'ecrit par *yod*, *hé*, *waw*, *hé* (le nom tétragrammate) ... appelé *schem mephorasch.* [3] [I, 267]

Note, by Munk. Notre auteur entend ... que ce nom désigne l'*essence* de Dieu, et n'est point un homonyme, c'est à dire, qu'il ne s'applique pas à la fois à Dieu et à d'autres êtres. On sait que dès les temps les plus anciens[4] les Juifs par un pieux respect pour le nom propre de Dieu n'osaient pas prononcer ce nom, et lisaient toujours אדני (Adonai) à la place de יהוה (JHVH).[5]

1 In this transcription, the first and second excerpts have been transposed, and also the final two excerpts, to their original sequence in Munk's edition.

2 Translation:

Every Hebrew knows that the name Elohim is a homonym, applying to God, angels, and rulers governing states. Onkelos, the proselyte, explained previously – and correctly – that in the words, 'And ye shall be as [Elohim], knowing good and evil' [Genesis iii, 5], the latter sense is meant, for in his Chaldaic translation he says, 'And you shall be like persons of high rank.' [The AV translation is 'gods'.]

3 Translation:

As is well known, all the names of God found in the scriptures derive from His actions. The only exception is the name written as *yod, hé, waw, hé* (the tetragrammatic name) ... called *schem mephorasch.*

4 GE, having mistakenly written 'dans' for 'dès', later added a query mark here.

5 Translation:

Our author means that this name designates the essence of God, and is not a homonym, that is, that it does not apply both to God and to other beings. We know that since very ancient times the Jews, through a pious respect for the proper name of God, have not dared to pronounce this name, and always read אדני Adonai (Lord) in place of יהוה JHVH.

C'est pourquoi déjà les Septante mettent pour ce dernier nom ὁ κύριος. Les Masorèthes lui ont donné pour la même raison, les voyelles du mot *Adonai*, de sorte qu'on lit Jehovah, ce qui n'est pas la vraie prononciation du nom יהוה. [I, 267n–268n] [1]

Note, Munk. Le nom *yod, hé, waw, hé,* renferme le sens d'être. L'auteur, à l'exemple d'autres théologiens, **/112v/** croit devoir isoler le nom tétragrammate de tous les autres noms de Dieu, et y voir un nom propre sans étymologie connue. [I, 269n] [2]

Il n'est pas douteux que ce nom glorieux, qui ne devait être prononcé que dans le sanctuaire, et particulièrement par les prêtres sanctifiés à l'Eternel, dans la bénédiction sacerdotale, et par le grand prêtre au jour de jeûne, n'indique une certaine idée à l'égard de laquelle il n'y a rien de commun entre Dieu et ce qui est en dehors de lui; peut-être indique-t-il – selon la langue hébraïque *dont il ne nous reste aujourd'hui que très peu de chose,*[3] et selon la manière dont il était prononcé – l'idée de l'existence nécessaire.

Maimonides [1, 269–70][4]

1 Translation:

This is why the Septuagint translators put for this name *Kyrie.* The Masoretic punctators for the same reason gave it the vowels of the word *Adonai,* so that we read Jehovah, which is not the true pronunciation of the name יהוה.

2 Translation:

The name *yod, hé, waw, hé,* includes the sense of being. Following the example of other theologians, the author thinks he ought to isolate the tetragrammatic name from the other names of God, and to see it as a proper name with no known etymology.

3 GE's added emphasis.

4 Translation:

There is no doubt that the glorious name – which should be pronounced only in the sanctuary, and particularly by the priests consecrated to the Eternal, in the sacerdotal blessing, and by the high priest on the Day of Atonement – denotes some idea of something peculiar to God and not associated with anything other than him. Perhaps according to the way it was pronounced in the Hebrew language, *very little of which remains to us today,* the tetragrammaton conveys the idea of absolute existence.

Maimonides and the name of Jahveh B 112v 168

Ehye ascher ehye = je suis celui qui suis – c'est là un nom dérivé de *haya* היה – *il fut*. De même, le nom de Yah יה implique l'idée de l'existence éternelle. *Schaddai* שׁדי est dérivé de *day* די, qui signifie suffisance. [I, 282, 285–6][1]

The glorious name is by Eisenmenger spelt Schem hammphorasch. The waters turned back at the sound of it.[2]

It is the name which the Jew is fabled to have uttered in the ear of a bull at Rome in the presence of the emperor; whereupon the bull fell down dead.

[Milman III, 10]

/168/ Maimonides

In his commentary on the Mischna Maimouni lays down Thirteen Articles of Belief:[3]

1. The existence of God
2. His Unity
3. His incorporeality & unchangeableness
4. His eternity
5. That he alone is to be worshipped & prayed to
6. The inspiration of the prophets
7. The supremacy of Moses as a prophet
8. The divine authority of the Thora
9. Its finality
10. The providential government of God
11. The future rewards & punishments of the righteous & the wicked
12. The coming of Messiah
13. The resurrection of the dead

1 Translation:

'I am that I am' – is a name derived from *haya* היה, *he was*. The name *Yah* יה implies, likewise, the idea of eternal existence. *Schaddai* שׁדי is derived from *day* די, which signifies sufficiency.

2 *Entdecktes Judenthum*, I, 159; see B 118 to 121. GE added this note later.

3 Maimonides' Thirteen Articles of Belief are included in the prayer books, such as GE's copy, in DWL, of *Daily, Festival and Occasional Prayers* (London: Ann Abrahams and Son, 5634/1874). GE's source here may be Graetz 6, 303.

/193/ Die Reue des Jonah Gerundi

Als nun Jona die Gehässigkeit des inquisitorischen Mönchsordens gegen den von ihm hochgeehrten Talmud gewahrte, bereute er es aus tiefstem Herzen sie zu Werkzeugen seines Hasses gegen Maimuni gebraucht zu haben, und sah in dem Brande des Talmud eine göttliche Strafe für das von ihm veranlasste Verbrennen der maimunischen Schriften. Er war so sehr von seinem Unrechte durchdrungen, dass er seine Reue öffentlich in der Synagoge aussprach und seinen Entschluss zu erkennen gab, zu Maimuni's Grab zu wallfahrten, dort sich trauerverhüllt niederzuwerfen und den Schatten des grossen, frommen Mannes in Gegenwart von zehn Personen um Verzeihung zu bitten. Zu diesem Zwecke trat er sofort die Reise an, verliess Paris und berührte Montpellier, wo er ebenfalls in der Synagoge seine Reue wegen seines Verfahrens gegen Maimuni öffentlich aussprach ... Er konnte aber seinen Plan nicht ausführen, da er auf seiner Reise nach Palästina zuerst von der Barceloner Gemeinde und dann von der Toledaner inständigst angegangen wurde, in ihrer Mitte zu weilen und den Talmud in Spanien zu lehren. Er blieb. In seinen Vorträgen nannte er geflissentlich Maimuni's Namen stets mit Ehrfurcht, wie den eines Heiligen. [Graetz 7, 107–8][1]

1 The following translation by Bella Löwy (3, 580) includes the reconciliation not included in GE's extract, but omits the sentences within brackets:

> As soon as Jonah became aware of the bitter hostility of the monkish orders of the Inquisition to the Talmud, which was so highly revered by him, he very deeply regretted that he had employed them as the instruments of his hate against Maimuni, and beheld in the burning of the Talmud a divine punishment for his having allowed the writings of Maimuni to be consumed by fire. He was so overwhelmed by the sense of his injustice that he publicly, in the synagogue, confessed his sincere repentance, and announced his intention of making a pilgrimage to the grave of Maimuni, there, veiled in mourning, to prostrate himself and, in the presence of ten persons, to implore the pardon of this great and pious man. For this purpose he set out on a journey, left Paris, and stopped at Montpellier, where he also made public confession of his remorse for his procedure against Maimuni. This act reconciled the two parties. The opponents cast aside all feelings of rancor, and treated each other as brethren. [But he could not carry out his plan, since he was most urgently drawn away from his pilgrimage to Palestine, first by the Jewish community of Barcelona and then by the Toledo community, to stay in their midst and teach the Talmud in Spain. He remained.] In his discourses, he repeatedly mentions the name of Maimuni with the respect due to that of a holy man.

The Tanaim, Amoraim, and Saboraim

B 114, 114v

This note on the three rabbinical schools or epochs of the Talmudic period is summarized from Graetz.

/114/ Jewish Schools

1. The Tanaim, or *transmitters* [Graetz 4, 17][1]
   The first of these was R. Jochanan b. Zakkai, who founded the School of Jamnia, about 70 AC. [Graetz 4,13]
   The last was R. Jehuda, called by eminence 'Rabbi', who completed the redaction of the Mischna. [Graetz 4, 219; B 109v]
2. The Amoraim, or *interpreters* / (Deutsch says, Speakers)[2] /
   The first was R. Chanina b. Chama, 180–260. [Graetz 4, 253, 254]
   Chief among the later R. Aschi, 352–427
   When the barbarians were breaking over the Roman empire, when old nations were falling & new nations arising, Jewish thinkers were impressed with a conviction that their own nation was everlasting: 'One people passeth away & another cometh, but Israel remains forever.' In this iron period, when the next morning was uncertain, the leaders of Judaism were inwardly moved to place in security that treasure which had been committed to their hands. The traditional matter which had grown to enormous bulk in the course of generations, which had been enriched & illuminated by a variety of schools, must now be arranged. The representative of this effort to collect & put in order is R. Aschi.
   [Graetz 4, 377–8]

1 In the margin of Graetz 4, 17, GE wrote 'Transmitters?' beside the reference to the Tanaim. These are 'the great Transmitters' referred to by Mordecai: 'the Masters who handed down the thought of our race' after the destruction of the Second Temple, 'who laboured with their hands for scant bread, but preserved and enlarged for us the heritage of memory' (DD ch. 42: 484).

2 The Talmud', p. 450.

3. The Saboraim, 500–640 / or 400–550? Settlers of opinions, *Sebara* +/
   + Another says, Guessers – Vermuther[1]
   The enormous material of the Talmud, which discussions & controversies had deprived of decisiveness, required rendering practically useful. The judges needed a stable rule, by which to decide cases as they arose, & every man needed an undoubted prescription by which he could regulate his religious life. From this side of their labours, namely, the fixing of religious & judicial praxis according to **/114v/** an estimate of the *pro* & *con*, the post-Amoraic teachers received the name of Saboraim, because they arrived at an effective decision by an estimate of the various opinions (*Sebara*). Their aim was practical rather than theoretical: they ascribed no authority to themselves in points of theory. The Saboraic masters R. Giza & R. Simuna in the first half of the 6th century made it their task to reduce the Talmud to writing. [Graetz 5, 8–9]

Rabbi κατ᾽ἐξοχὴν is R. Jehuda, said to have completed the canon of the Mischna. *Rab*, abba Aricha, his pupil. Rab is Babylonish, Rabi, Palestinian. [Pf711 60; Pf710 33][2]

The Laying on of Hands was a ceremony which conferred rabbinical authority on the learned, & was forbidden by Rome after the insurrection under Bar Cochba. [Pf711 60; Pf710 30][3]

1 This note was added later at the foot of the page.
2 This note and the next were added later. Their source is Steinschneider's 'Jüdische Literatur', pp. 366–7; see the 'Extracts from Steinschneider' section, B 141 to 150.
3 The ceremony is 'das Recht der Promotion' or 'the right of promotion' which was 'withdrawn from the schools'; see B 145 and GE's translation on B 144v. In the margin of Graetz 4, 68, next to his account of the ordination or promotion ceremony, GE wrote 'Laying on of hands'.

Midrash

B 115, 115v, 116, 116v, 117, 117v

The source of the following extract is Emanuel Deutsch, 'Ein Stück jüdischer Volkspoesie, aus dem Midrasch der Klagelieder' in *Westermann's illustrirte deutsche Monatshefte fur das gesammte geistige Leben der Gegenwart* 6, No 35 (1859): 540–6.[1] Just as Deutsch's essay on the Talmud was GE's first source for her notes on the Mishnah (B 106); her first extended note on Midrash is also drawn from an essay by him, and includes his translation into German of an exemplary *Märchen* or legend from Midrash Rabbah, 'the Great Midrash'. Thus two complementary methods of rabbinical teaching are introduced by extracts from her former tutor in Hebrew. As GE notes (B 106, 108), the Mishnah method was a formulation or discussion of the Oral Law, topic by topic, whereas the Midrash method was the interpretation of the Scripture, either as running commentaries, verse by verse, or as anthologies of homilies.[2] The homiletic origin of Aggadic Midrash accounts for the predominance of Aggada or 'narration' – including history, legend, and parable – over Halacha.[3] On Pf 710 4 GE records an anecdote illustrating the greater popular accessibility of the Aggada:

> [Rabbi Abbahu] preaching with another in the same town – he Agada, the other Halacha – consoled the mortification of his colleague at having fewer hearers while Abbahu had many, by comparing his own Agadistic teaching to a basket of cheap trumpery which everybody could buy, whereas his friend's resembled jewels of high price that get few purchasers.

---

1 Some of the introductory material reappears in an article by Deutsch in William Smith's *Dictionary of the Bible*, 3 vols. (London: John Murray, 1863), reprinted as 'On the Targums' in *Literary Remains*.

2 For more on the history of the Midrash, see GE's notes from Steinschneider (B 141, 142 to 143, and 149v) and Pf 707 25. For a recent discussion of the Midrash method of rabbinical exegesis, see the collection of essays edited by Geoffrey H. Hartman and Sanford Budick, *Midrash and Literature* (New Haven: Yale University Press, 1986).

3 But see B 108 for interconnections between these teaching and interpretative methods.

/115/ Midrasch: Post-Talmudic collections

Natürlich, dass diese Auslegungshagada, der Midrasch κατ' ἐξοχὴν des Volkes, in einer mehr als tausendjährigen ununterbrochenen Strömung zu riesigen Dimensionen anwuchs und sehr früh schon getrennte Sammlungen nöthig machte. Man folgte dabei entweder der Ordnung der Schrift und benannte den Midrasch nach dem Buche das er speciell behandelte, oder der Ordnung der Sabbat- und Fest-perikopen und benannte ihn nach diesen. Die Auslegungen gruppirten sich um die einzelnen Verse, und deren Wiederholungen ...[1]

Die bedeutendsten der auf uns gekommenen, ursprünglich aus Fragmenten zusammengesetzten, Sammlungen sind Midrasch Rabba (begonnen um 700, abgeschlossen um 1100 n. Chr.), den Pentateuch und die fünf Megilloth umfassend, und die Pesikta (um 700 n. Chr.), die den vollständigsten Cyclus der Perikopen enthält.* Diese Sammlungen wurden in Auszügen, Bearbeitungen, Uebersetzungen, gar bald die beliebteste Volkslectüre der Juden ...[2]

*Seltsam genug war diese letztere selbst, über gewissen früh aus ihr veranstalteten Auszügen (Jalkut, Pesikta Rabbathi, Sutarta) seit dem 15.

1 Translation:

It stands to reason that this Aggadic exegesis, the Midrash *par excellence* of the people, had grown to immense proportions in its more than thousand years of uninterrupted flow, and very early on made selected compilations necessary. Either the Midrash followed the order of the Scripture and was named after the particular book that it dealt with, or it followed the order of the pericopes [*parashen* or portions, or, Anglicized, lessons] read on the Sabbath and Holy Days and was named after them. The exegesis became clustered around individual verses and their repetitions ...

Compare 'On the Targums', *Literary Remains*, pp. 333 and 335.

2 Translation:

The most significant collections that have come to us, composed originally from fragments, are Midrash Rabbah (begun about 700, completed about 1100 AD) – including the Pentateuch and the five Megilloth [scrolls, i.e. Song of Songs, Ruth, Lamentations, Ecclesiastes and Esther] – and the Pesikta (about 700 AD), which contains the most complete cycle of pericopes. These collections, in extracts, reworkings, and translations, quite soon became the best-loved popular reading of the Jews ...

Compare GE's partial translation on B 123.

Jahrhundert fast vollständig in Vergessenheit gerathen bis Zunz, der Humboldt jüdischer Wissenschaft, in seinem Buche 'Die gottesdienstlichen Vorträge der Juden', Berlin 1832, nicht nur ihre Existenz bis zur Evidenz nachwies, sondern sie selbst aus eben diesen Auszügen und andern **/115v/** Parallelstellen auf wunderbare Weise wiederherstellte - und fast um dieselbe Zeit fand Steinschneider in Oxford das alte Manuscript, das mit Zunz' Angaben bis in's Einzelnste uebereinstimmte.[1]

Einer der ältesten und unsers Bedünkens der eigenthümlichste und grossartigste aller Midraschim ist der welcher die Klagelieder Jeremia's umrankt. Hier musste sich ja auch Alles zusammenpressen, was von Schmerz und Hoffnung in den Dulderherzen bebte, hier wie nirgends liess sich in die qualvolle Vergangenheit die nicht minder qualvolle Gegenwart hineintragen, jeder Buchstabe erzählte die neue wie die alte Schmerzensmähr und jeder Buchstabe gemahnte, wie an die Schuld der Väter, so an die eigene - aber das Buch erschloss zugleich eine Fülle reichsten Trostes. Einmal schon, nachdem diese Lieder erklungen, waren sie heimgekehrt, da die Zeit sich erfüllt hatte, und die zweite Heimkehr sollte eine schönere, eine Heimkehr für immer sein.[2]

1 For more on Leopold Zunz, see B 164v to 165v. Translation:

Strangely enough the latter [the Pesikta], known earlier only through the extracts made from it - Jalkut, Pesikta Rabbathi, Sutarta - had since the fifteenth century almost completely sunk into oblivion, until Zunz, the Humboldt of Jewish scholarship, in his book *Die gottesdienstlichen Vorträge der Juden* (Berlin, 1832), not only proved its existence from the evidence, but moreover restored it in an amazing manner, unaided, from just these extracts and other literary parallels. And almost at the same time Steinschneider found in Oxford the old manuscript that corresponded in every detail with Zunz's restoration.

2 Translation:

One of the oldest, and in our opinion the most characteristic and most magnificent, of all the Midrash is the one that grew around the Lamentations of Jeremiah. All that trembles with pain and hope in the long-suffering heart cannot help but be crowded together here. Here, as nowhere else, the agonizing past has been borne through to the no less agonizing present. Each letter narrates the new, like the old, tale of affliction, and admonishes one of the guilt of the fathers, as of one's own guilt - but at the same time the book opened up a wealth of most abundant comfort. These songs rang out once before and were carried back home, when the promised time had come, and the second homecoming was to be more splendid, a homecoming for ever.

Und so drängten sich denn alle Zeiten und Gestalten hier zusammen im engsten Raume - Egypten, Jerusalem, Babilon, Rom, Athen - Palast und Tempel, Theater und Forum, Imperatoren und Philosophen, Feldherren und Senatoren, Frauen und Kinder, Lebende und Todte, Geschichte u. Märchen, u. Lied u. Räthsel. [pp. 541-2][1]

/116/ Midrash: Lamentations of Jeremiah

Es steht geschrieben: - 'Und es rief Jehova, Gott der Heereschaaren, auf an jenem Tag zur Thräne und zur Klage'... Jes. 22, 12.[2]

Zur Stunde, da der Heilige - hochgepriesen[3] - das Haus des Heiligthums, gedachte zu zerstören, sprach er: So lange ich darinnen weile, rühren alle Weltenvölker nicht daran - meine Augen will ich davon abthun u. will schwören dass ich nimmer bis zur Zeit des Endes ihm will nahen. Mögen denn die Feinde kommen, es zerstören ... Alsbald hat der Heilige einen Schwur gethan bei seiner Rechten und hat sie rückwärts abgewandt (Klagelied 2, 3).Und in derselben Stunde sind die Feinde eingegangen in dem Tempel und haben ihn verbrannt. Und da er war verbrannt, sprach der Allheilige: Nun hab' ich keinen Wohnsitz mehr auf Erden ... Und da hat der Allheilige - hochgepriesen - geweint u. hat gesprochen: Weh mir, was hab' ich gethan, ich habe meine Majestät auf Erden ruhen lassen wegen Israels, und nun, da sie gesündigt, bin ich zurückgekehrt zu meinem Ort - Das sei verhütet, dass ich werde zum Gespött den Volkern und zum Hohne den Geschöpfen.[4]

1 Translation:
And so all times and characters mill together here in a narrow space - Egypt, Jerusalem, Babylon, Rome, Athens - palace and temple, theatre and forum, emperors and philosophers, generals and senators, women and children, the quick and the dead, history and folk-tale, song and riddle.

2 Translation:
It is written: 'And in that day did the Lord God of hosts call to weeping, and to mourning ...' Isaiah xxii, 12.

3 In her transcription from Deutsch, GE omitted numerous instances of 'hoch - gepriesen', or 'blessed be He'. They are retained in the following translation by A. Cohen, from pp. 40-3 and 48-9 of *Lamentations* (London: Soncino Press, 1939), one of the ten volumes of the Soncino Press *Midrash Rabbah,* under the general editorship of H. Freedman and Maurice Simon.

4 Translation:
At the time when the Holy One, blessed be He, sought to destroy the Temple, He said, 'So long as I am in its midst, the nations of the world will not touch it; but

Zur Stunde kam der Engelfürst Metatron, fiel auf sein Angesicht und sprach: O Herr der Welt, - ich, ich will weinen, aber Du - Du weine nicht ... Doch jener sprach: Wenn Du mich [nicht] willst jetzo weinen lassen, so will ich gehen an einen Ort, den Du nicht darfst betreten u. will dort weinen ... Dann sprach der Heil'ge - hochgepriesen - zur Engeldienerschaar: kommt **/116v/** und lasst uns gehen, ich und ihr, und lasst uns sehn in meinem Hause, was die Feinde dran geübt ...[1]

Und wieder hat der Heil'ge geweint und hat geredet: Weh mir um mein Haus! ... Dann sprach der Heil'ge zu Jeremia: Ich gleiche heute einem Manne, der einen einzigen Sohn besessen und ihn zur Trauung [hat] geführt, und mitten in der Trauung ist er ihm gestorben - und hast du gar keine Wehe - nicht um mich und nicht um meinen Sohn? - Geh hin u. rufe Abraham u. rufe Ischzak, Jacob, Mosche auf aus ihren Gräbern - die verstehn zu weinen ... Geh hin an's Jordanufer, erhebe laut die Stimme u. rufe: Sohn Amram's, Amram's Sohn, steh' auf und schaue deine Heerde, wie sie der Feind verschlungen ...

Alsbald ging Jeremia an die Höhle zu Machpelah, und rief den Welturvätern: Steht auf, steht auf, es ist die Zeit gekommen, da ihr gefordert werdet vor den Höchsten. Sie aber fragten ihn: Warum? - Und er entgegnete: Ich weiss es

I will close My eyes so as not to see it, and swear that I will not attach Myself to it until the time of the end [the Messianic era] arrives.' Then came the enemy and destroyed it. Forthwith the Holy One, blessed be He, swore by His right hand and placed it behind Him. So it is written, He hath drawn back His right hand from before the enemy (Lamentations ii, 3). At that time the enemy entered the Temple and burnt it. When it was burnt, the Holy One, blessed be He, said, 'I no longer have a dwelling-place in this land ... ' At that time the Holy One, blessed be He, wept and said, 'Woe is me! What have I done? I caused My *Schechinah* [Presence - in Deutsch's German translation, Majesty] to dwell below on earth for the sake of Israel; but now that they have sinned, I have returned to My former habitation. Heaven forfend that I become a laughter [laughing-stock] to the nations and a byword to human beings!'

1 Translation:

At that time Metatron [the Prince of Angels, in Deutsch's German translation], came, fell upon his face, and spake before the Holy One, blessed be He: 'Sovereign of the Universe, let me weep, but do Thou not weep' ... He replied to him, 'If thou lettest Me not weep now, I will repair to a place which thou hast not permission to enter, and will weep there' [Jeremiah xiii, 17] ... The Holy One, blessed be He, said to the Ministering Angels, 'Come, let us go together and see what the enemy has done in My house' ...

nicht. Er fürchtete, sie möchten mahnend sagen: *In Deinen Tagen ist unsern Kindern das geschehn.* [1]

(Jeremiah then goes to call Moses, who also asks why? and Jeremiah again answers, 'Ich weiss [es] nicht.') [2]

Da liess ihn Moscheh und ging zu den Dienerengeln, die er kannte vor der Stunde der Gesetzesübergabe und redete zu ihnen: Höchste Diener, ihr, wisst ihr es nicht warum **/117/** ich bin gefordert vor den Heiligen – hochgepreisen – ? Und sie entgegnete[n]: Sohn Amram's, Du – Du weisst es nicht, dass das Haus des Heiligthums ist zerstört und Israel vertrieben? – Da schrie er auf und weinte laut, bis er die Welturväter traf. Und allsogleich zerrissen auch sie Alle die Gewänder, schlugen ihre Hände über'm Haupt zusammen und sie schrieen und sie weinten, bis sie kamen zu des Heiligthumes Thoren ... [3]

1 Translation:

At that time the Holy One, blessed be He, wept and said, 'Woe is Me for My house!'... The Holy One, blessed be He, said to Jeremiah, 'I am now like a man who had an only son, for whom he prepared a marriage-canopy, but he died under it. Feelest thou no anguish for Me and My children? Go, summon Abraham, Isaac and Jacob, and Moses from their sepulchres, for they know how to weep ... Go, stand by the bank of the Jordan, and raise thy voice and call out, "Son of Amram, Son of Amram, arise and behold thy flock which enemies have devoured."' There and then Jeremiah went to the cave of Machpelah and said to the patriarchs of the world: 'Arise, for the time has come when your presence is required before the Holy One, blessed be He.' They said to him, 'For what purpose?' He answered, 'I know not,' because he was afraid lest they say, *'In thy lifetime has such a thing happened to our children!'* [GE underlined this last sentence.]

2 Translation: 'I know not.'

3 Translation:

Moses left him and proceeded to the Ministering Angels whom he recognised from the time of the giving of the Torah. [According to legend, when Moses ascended Mount Sinai he had to contend with those angels who wished God to withhold the Torah.] He said to them, 'O celestial ministers, know ye why my presence is required before the Holy One, blessed be He?' They replied, 'Son of Amram, knowest thou not that the Temple is destroyed and Israel gone into exile?' He cried aloud and wept until he reached the patriarchs. They immediately also rent their garments, placed their hands upon their heads, and cried out and wept until they arrived at the gates of the Temple.

Und wie sie der Allheilige nun erschaute, da – 'rief Jehovah, Herr der Heeresschaaren, auf an jenem Tag zur Thräne und zur Klage' ... So weinten sie und gingen von diesem Thor zu jenem Thor, gleichwie ein Mensch, vor dem die Leiche dessen liegt, was ihm das Liebste ist gewesen ... [pp. 543–4][1]

(The patriarchs & Moses in turn plead with Jehovah, but in vain – Israel has sinned.) [pp. 544–6]

Da – urplötzlich – sprang Rachel, uns're Mutter, vor den Heiligen – hochgepriesen – : Herr der Welt, Dir ist's bewusst, wie Dein Knecht Jacob übermächtig mich geliebt, wie er um meinetwillen sieben Jahre meinem Vater hat gedient. Und da die sieben Jahre endlich hingeschwunden, gedachte mich mein Vater mit der Schwester zu verwechseln, – und gar hart traf mich der Anschlag, den ich ausgespäht. Jacob kündet' ich's, gab ihm geheime Zeichen, dran er mich erkennen sollte vor der Schwester und meines **/117v/** Vaters Plan vereiteln. – Doch bald bereut' ich's, der Schwester mich erbarmend, das sie der Beschämung nicht verfalle, kämpft' ich nieder meiner Liebe Gluth, und da am Abend sie statt meiner Jacob zugeführt ward, gab ich ihr all die heimlichen Erkennungszeichen, daran er Rachel kennen sollte.[2]

1 Translation:

When the Holy One, blessed be He, saw them, immediately 'In that day did the Lord, the God of hosts, call to weeping, and to lamentation'... They went weeping from one gate to another like a man whose dead is lying before him ...

2 Translation:

At that moment, the matriarch Rachel broke forth into speech before the Holy One, blessed be He, and said, 'Sovereign of the Universe, it is revealed before Thee that Thy servant Jacob loved me exceedingly and toiled for my father on my behalf seven years. When those seven years were completed and the time arrived for my marriage with my husband, my father planned to substitute another for me to wed my husband for the sake of my sister. It was very hard for me, because the plot was known to me and I disclosed it to my husband; and I gave him a sign whereby he could distinguish between me and my sister, so that my father should not be able to make the substitution. After that I relented, suppressed my desire, and had pity upon my sister that she should not be exposed to shame. In the evening they substituted my sister for me with my husband, and I delivered over to my sister all the signs that I had arranged with my husband so that he should think that she was Rachel.

Midrash B 117v

- Und nicht das allein - ich selber war im Brautgemach - dem Paare nah - und wenn er mit der Schwester sprach, habe ich ihm drauf erwiedert, dass er an ihrer Stimme Lea nicht erkenne. - Und ich - ein Weib, Fleisch und Blut, Staub und Asche, habe nicht geeifert gegen meine Nebenbuhlerin - Du, O Gott, der Allgewaltige, Ewiglebende, Erbarmungsvolle - warum hast Du geeifert gegen Götzenbilder, Holz und Stein, nicht'gen Tand - hast vertrieben meine Kinder - sie durch's Schwert getödtet - der Feinde Willkühr preisgegeben.

Da ward erregt des Höchsten Allbarmherzigkeit - und also sprach er: Um Deinetwillen, Rachel, Rachel, führ ich Israel zurück in ihre Heimath.[1]

Translated by Emanuel Deutsch
in the Illustrirte Deutsche Monatshefte B. vi. Nro 35. - Aug. 1859

1 Translation:

More than that, I went beneath the bed upon which he lay with my sister; and when he spoke to her she remained silent and I made all the replies in order that he should not recognise my sister's voice ... And if I, a creature of flesh and blood, formed of dust and ashes, was not envious of my rival and did not expose her to shame and contempt, why shouldest Thou, a King Who liveth eternally and art merciful, be jealous of idolatry in which there is no reality, and exile my children and let them be slain by the sword, and their enemies have done with them as they wished!'

Forthwith the mercy of the Holy One, blessed be He, was stirred, and He said, 'For thy sake Rachel, I will restore Israel to their place.'

The final reference is to Jeremiah xxxi, 15–17.

Eisenmenger

B 118, 118v, 119v, 121, 119

'Eisenmenger, Entdecktes Judenthum' is another work included in GE's 'Books Wanted' list (Pf 711 21), but not in DWL. Her extensive notes from Johann Andreas Eisenmenger's *Entdecktes Judenthum*, 2 vols. (Königsberg, 1711), suggest that she read a copy not her own, perhaps the copy in the British Library. The anti-Judaism expressed in the German title, whose literal translation is 'Judaism Exposed', is somewhat concealed in the title of an eighteenth-century English translation which is in DWL, but not from the GE–GHL library: *The Traditions of the Jews: With the Expositions and Doctrines of the Rabbins, Contained in the Talmud and Other Rabbinical Writings: Translated from the Heigh Dutch,* 2 vols. (London: John Brotherton, 1732, 1734). This anonymous translation[1] is the source for the translation of the Lilith legend in the footnotes below.

The legend of Lilith, the first woman and first insubordinate wife, is not repeated in GE's other notebooks, although Folger 13 90 includes a brief allusion: 'Lilith = Ilythia'. GE added the three-page note on Adam's first marriage as an afterthought, after having completed her other notes from Eisenmenger and begun her extracts from Persius on B 120. In a discussion of Gwendolen Harleth in her '*ensemble du serpent*' (DD ch. 1: 8), A. S. Byatt comments,

> ... I'm quite sure George Eliot is thinking also of Lilith, the first wife of Adam in the Garden, and other daemons. These were serpent beings, serpent angels, in Hebrew mythology.[2]

Lilith's daring to utter the ineffable name, 'the Shem-hamphorasch', puts her in interesting company; see the discussion by Maimonides of the tetragrammaton and GE's subsequent note from Eisenmenger (B 112, 112v).

1 The Preface is signed G. M.

2 A. S. Byatt and Ignês Sodré, *Imagining Characters: Six Conversations about Women Writers,* edited by Rebecca Swift (London: Chatto and Windus, 1995) p. 86. See also GE's note on 'Seraphim+, fire angels / +Said now to come from a root meaning Serpent' (Pf 710 5).

Eisenmenger

GE's note on Pf 711 57, repeated on B 149v and Pf 710 39, reflects her awareness of the dubious reliability of Eisenmenger:

> Yalkut Rubeni, so often quoted by Eisenmenger, is, says Geiger, the work of an addle-brained Cabbalist, Ruben Hoeske.[1]

Franz Delitzsch, a Lutheran, disparaged '*Eisenmengerschen* Judenthum' as 'schädlicher als nützlich', more harmful than useful.[2] In *The History of the Jews*, Milman suggests that the fault lies in Eisenmenger's viewpoint, rather than his scholarship:

> Eisenmenger undertook the hateful task of disclosing all the mysteries of Rabbinical learning, only to make the Jews more detestable to the Christian world, and to expose them to more merciless persecution ... Odious as was the spirit and intention of Eisenmenger, his reading was vast, his industry indefatigable (two enormously thick quarto volumes are crowded with citations in the original, and with translations). I have never heard his accuracy seriously impeached. But the grave defect of the book is, that passages from the Talmud are heaped together indiscriminately with passages from modern writings, writings of times when cruel persecution, as well as contempt, had goaded the miserable Jews to the only vengeance in which, besides overreaching in trade, they could indulge, – writings in their own secret unintelligible language ...
>
> [The] extracts in Eisenmenger, read with this caution and in the more generous spirit of our times, form certainly a most curious and instructive collection. Take the strange, monstrous Oriental hyperboles, in which the barbarized Jews endeavoured to describe the Undescribable, to represent under imagery the Inconceivable Godhead and His attributes; the wild, sometimes profound, and almost sublime allegories, which Eisenmenger, and probably the more ignorant Jews themselves, understood literally, as they did the strange apologues and parables. [III, 40–2]

1 The source of this note is Abraham Geiger's *Judaism and its History*, p. 341.

2 *Zur Geschichte der jüdischen Poesie* (Leipzig: Karl Tauchnitz, 1836), p. 14. For GE's notes from Delitzsch, see B 123, 140, and 193v, and Pf 711 59.

Eisenmenger B 118

Some of these strange parables and 'monstrous Oriental hyperboles'[1] recur in GE's extracts from the Festival prayer books (B 184 to 190): the Pentecost service includes an account of the dance in Paradise in the Messianic time, when the righteous will feast upon Leviathan and Behemoth (B 188v, 189v; compare B 119). Another note on Leviathan is copied on Pf 711 102–103 and translated on Pf 710 25. The notes on the angelology of the Talmud (B 118, 118v) may be compared with GE's notes from Ginsburg's *Kabbalah* (Pf 707 19 and 21) and Hamburger's *Real-Encyclopädie des Judenthums* (Pf 710 5).

/118/

Eisenmenger
(1711) Entdecktes Judenthum

Names of Angels in the Talmud

Kemuel, the doorkeeper, who is set above twelve thousand angels of destruction who stand at the gates of the Firmament

Hadarniel, of whom it is said that he is six hundred thousand miles higher than his fellow angel, & that with each word that goes out of his mouth come twelve thousand lightnings [I, 308]

Sandalfon – apparently still more fiery

(Rigion, the river of fire in which the angels bathe)

Galizur, the same as Raphael [I, 309]

1 The comment made by Miller, the bookseller, may hint at GE's viewpoint:
'There's been a good deal of fun made of rabbinical fables, but in point of fables my opinion is, that all over the world it's six of one and half-a-dozen of the other.' (DD ch. 42: 492)

Jesifja, the angel of the Law, who teaches it to Moses again after his encounter with *the terrible angel of Fear, of Sweat, & of Trembling, had driven it clean out of his mind*
(*Moses was 40 days learning the Law & forgot it all in one.*) [I, 310][1]

Metatron – 'den Fürsten des Angesichts'. Chief of the Angels [I, 311][2]

Sammaël, the Angel of Death. But there are two angels of Death: the other being Gabriel who takes charge of those that die within the promised land, Sammaël only of those that die outside it. Each has a host of subordinate angels, every soul having its own angel, of rank according to the worth of the soul. [I, 854–5][3]

Sammaël is also the fallen Seraph, the Tempter. When he with his followers was cast out of heaven, he tried to save himself by clinging to the wings of Michael; but God rescued Michael. [I, 831]

Jorkemo, the angel of hail (as Gabriel, of fire) [II, 378]

'The angel Ipiphith, the prince of the law'
Service for the Feast of Tabernacles[4]

1 Eisenmenger has Moses forgetting his forty-day lesson in only one hour. In DD ch. 16, Hans Meyrick likens this memory lapse to the effects of cramming for Cambridge University examinations:

> 'With your mathematical cram one may be like Moses or Mahomet or somebody of that sort who had to cram, and forgot in one day what it had taken him forty to learn.' (166)

Meyrick's acquaintance with Jewish legend is to become a little more precise under Mirah's influence.

2 Translation: 'the Prince of the Countenance', that is, the angel who beholds the face of the Lord. Compare the reference to 'der Englefürst Metatron' (B 116).

3 In DD ch. 42, the 'rational Gideon' protests that the Jewish connection with Palestine 'has been perverted by superstition till it's as demoralizing as the old poor-law. The raff and scum go there ... to be taken special care of by the angel Gabriel when they die' (495). For more on Gabriel, see the headnote to 'Parables from the Talmud' (B 158 and 159).

4 *The Festival Prayers, According to the Ritual of the German and Polish Jews,* translated by David Levi, 6 vols. (London: Abrahams and Son, 5620/1859 – 5633/1873), IV, 183: 'The angel יפיפית the prince of the law, who taketh a handful of black fire to form a crown for the letters of the law'. This note was added later, when GE was making notes on B 184 to 194 and Pf 711 105–104.

Eisenmenger B 118v 119v

/118v/

Rasiel taught Adam; *Jophiel*, Shem; *Zidkiel*, Abraham; *Segansagel*, Moses; *Malthiel*, Elijah. [II, 375][1]

Lilith, Adam's first wife, came to him against his will, & they were always wretched together, in sorrow & sighing & there was no joy between them. Of her in 130 years Adam begat the giants, devils, genii, witches. She was called the crooked snake. Was chased away (or dissolved herself?) into the air by the Shem-hamphorasch. She is one of the four mothers of devils, who have a host under their command. These were subject to Solomon. They are the wives of Schammael, prince of devils. [I, 165, 374, 461, 822–3; II, 416]

Als der heilige gebenedeyte Gott den ersten Menschen allein erschaffen hatte, sprach er, es ist nicht gut dass der Mensch allein sey, und schuf ihm ein Weib aus der Erden, wie er ihn erschaffen hatte und nennete sie Lilith oder Lilis. Hierauf fingen sie beyde alsobald an zu zanken: Sie sprach, ich will nicht unten liegen (und dir unterthänig seyn), er aber sagte, ich will nicht unten sondern oben liegen, denn dir gebühret es unten mir aber oben zu seyn (und mir zu gehorchen). Da sagte sie, wir beyde sind einander gleich, denn wir sind beide aus der Erde[n] erschaffen; u. wollte keines dem andern gehorchen. **/119v/** Als nun die Lilis solches gesehen hatte, sprach sie den Schem hamphorasch, und flog in die Luft der Welt.[2]

1 These are mentor angels.

2 Translation, from the anonymous *The Traditions of the Jews*, II, 110–13:

> When the Holy and Blessed God had created the First Man by himself, he said, *It is not good that the Man should be alone*; and he made him a Wife of the Earth, in the Manner as he had made him (*Adam*) and he called her *Lilith* or *Lilis.* Hereupon they both began, and quarreled with each other. She said, I will not lay under, nor be subject unto thee; and he said, I will not lay Under, but be above, for it behoveth thee to be Undermost, and me Uppermost, and for thee to obey. Then said she, we both are equal one to the other; for we were both created out of the Earth: but the one would not obey the other. When the *Lilis* saw this, she pronounced the *Shem Hamphorasch* and flew into the Air of the World.

Eisenmenger B 119v 121

Der Adam aber stund mit einem Gebet vor seinem Schöpfer und sprach, O du Herr der Welt! das Weib das du mir gegeben hast ist von mir weggeflohn. Da schickte der h. g. Gott stracks diese drey Engel, Senoi, Sansenoi, und Sammangelof, nach ihr, sie wieder zurück zu bringen; und sprach Gott zu ihnen, wenn sie wieder zurück gehet, so ist es gut; wo aber nicht, so soll sie es auf sich nehmen (zur Strafe) dass alle Tage ...[1]

Hierauf gingen sie ihr nach und trafen sie mitten in dem Meer, in dem mächtigen Wasser an, in welchem die Aegyptier umkommen sollten; und erzähleten ihr Gottes Befehl, aber sie wollte nicht zurück gehen. Und als sie zu ihr sagten, wir wollen dich im Meer ersäuffen wenn du nicht folgest, sprach sie zu ihnen, lasset mich gehen, denn ich bin zu nichts anders erschaffen als die jungen Kinder zu schwächen und umzubringen, und habe ich Gewalt über ein Knablein von dem Tage da es gebohren wird, bis an den achten Tag: wenn es aber ein Weiblein ist, von dem Tage seiner Geburt bis zu dem zwanzigsten Tage. Als sie nun ihre Worte gehöret hatten drungen sie drauf sie wegzunehmen; sie aber **/121/** schwur bei dem Nahmen des lebendigen und ewigen Gottes und sprach, allezeit wann ich euch, oder euren Namen oder eurer Bildniss an einem Zettel oder Pergament so einem Kinde angehenket wird, sehen werde, will ich selbigem Kinde keine Gewalt und nichts leides thun; und sie nahm es an dass alle Tage hundert von ihren Kindern sterben sollten deswegen sterben alle Tage hundert Teufel. Um solcher Ursach halben schreiben wir selbige Nahmen (der gedachten dreien Engel) auf einen Zettel der kleinen Knaben. [II, 417–18][2]

1 Translation:

But *Adam* stood before his Creator with a Prayer, and said, O thou Lord of the World! The Wife which thou gavest me is flown from hence. Then did God immediately send Three Angels, namely, *Senui*, *Sansenoi*, and *Sammangelof* after her, to bring her back, to whom God thus spake; If she returns again, it will be well; but if not, she shall draw this Punishment upon her self, that every Day [she shall have 100 of her Children die.]

2 Translation:

Hereupon they pursu'd her, and catch'd her in the Midst of the Ocean, in the mighty Waters, wherein the *Egyptians* should be destroy'd, and they told her the Command of God; but she would not return back again. And when they had made Answer, we will drown thee in the Sea if thou dost not follow us; she said, Let me go; for I am created for no other End but to weaken the little Children, and to destroy them; and I have Power over the Male Children, from the Day they are born until the Eighth Day; but if it be a Female, from the Day of its Birth until

When the little children laugh (babies smile)[1] it is because Lilith is playing with them: it is then good that Father or Mother should strike it on the nose & three times say, 'Get thee gone, thou accursed one, for thou hast no dwelling here.' [II, 419]

v. also Kalisch[2]

/119/

The Rabbins teach that there is not a thing on the earth, not even the smallest herb, which has not an angel set over it; hence the prohibiting to mix the seed of plants, which confuses the angelic œconomy.

[II, 376-7][3]

A wall between Hell & Paradise: some say, only a space the breadth of two fingers; some, *only a thread's breadth.* [II, 334]

Even the righteous must abide in Hell for a time, as a purgatory.[4]

There are times of rest & solace for the damned in hell – at the times of prayer, on the Sabbath & New Moon. (Fridays?) [II, 348–53][5]

> the Tenth [i.e., twentieth, 'zwanzigsten'] Day. Now, when they had utter'd [i.e., heard] these Words they insisted upon taking her away: But she swore by the Name of the Living and Eternal God, and said, at all Times, whenever I see either you, or your Names, or your Pictures, upon a [*Kamea,* that is a] Slip of Parchment hung round a Child's Neck, I shall use no Violence to it. To this they agreed, and that there should daily die One Hundred of her own Children; wherefore, die every Day One Hundred Devils. For this Reason, we write the Names of the forementioned Angels upon a Slip, for the little Boys [that in Case she happens to see them, she may remember her Oath, and save the Child].

1 In their sleep.

2 Ludwig Kalisch, *Bilder aus meiner Knabenzeit* (Leipzig: Ernst Keil, 1872), p. 94. Added later, when Kalisch was read from 4 to 7 August 1875 (GHL Diary).

3 In DD ch. 40, Mordecai interprets this teaching: 'It is true – what the Masters said – that each order of things has its angel: that means the full message of each from what is afar' (460–1). The primary sense of 'angel' is 'messenger'; see B 710 5 and Paley's reference to ἄγγελοι ιν the headnote to B 91 ff.

4 Compare the note on purgatory and Kaddish on B 135.

5 Compare the note on Pf 711 102: 'Even the damned get rest on Sunday!'

Eisenmenger B 119

Hell will finally in the time of the Messiah be embraced within the boundaries of Paradise, & the righteous will dance there & the blessed God will lead the dance (II, 368). Hell will be purified & sanctified & all the Israelitish sinners there will be gathered within the borders of paradise (after Leviathan & the wild Ox have been eaten) & they will go from strength to strength & will see God in Zion, & will be numbered with the righteous.[1] And the pious peoples of the earth, who in the times of the Messiah shall sorrow that they had not before served the blessed God, & shall repent of their sins, shall also be held worthy of this great grace (the being included in Paradise).

[II, 368–9][2]

The longest punishment does not last more than 12 years, whence the Jew does not beyond this period perform the *Kaddisch* or prayer for the deliverance of his dead friends. [II, 360–1][3]

1 GE changed her translation from 'elect' to 'righteous', a term whose connotations are perhaps less Christian and more Jewish.

2 In DD ch. 52, Hans Meyrick's letter shows a partial acquaintance with the Leviathan legend: he expects that 'the orthodox Jew' enjoys 'the prospect that the Gentile mouth will water in vain for a slice of the roasted Leviathan, while Israel will be sending up plates for more, *ad libitum*' (598).

3 Eisenmenger has twelve months. Compare GE's note on Kaddish (B 135 and 135v), where she changed the 'eleven months' in her source to 'eleven years'. As she correctly notes on Pf 710 23, Kaddish is performed monthly for eleven months and on Yahrzeit, the anniversary of the death (see DD ch. 34: 369). In the first edition of the novel, Deronda's dying mother wishes to believe that no harm came to her first husband 'because the eleven years went by with no wretched *Kaddish* said for him', but she wants her son to feel for her 'as they feel for the dead whom they say prayers for – you shall long that I may be freed from all suffering – from all punishment'. As Kaddish is a religious observance, requiring a minyan or quorum of ten Jewish men, she makes a great concession by telling him, 'if you think *Kaddish* will help me – say it, say it' (DD ch. 53: 618).

Quotations from Persius

B 120, 120v, 121v, 122, 122v

This collection of excerpts from the six satires of Persius (Aulus Persius Flaccus), which has no apparent relation to the context of GE's notes on Judaism, includes several repetitions of passages in other notebooks. The 'magister artis' excerpt from the Prologue is also found on Folger 13 34 and Pf 708 41; the line beginning 'Scire tuum nihil est', from Satire I, is copied again on Pf 708 55, along with quotations from Martial, Juvenal, Seneca, and Varro; and the dialogue beginning 'Quis populi sermo est?', also from Satire I, is found on Pf 708 31. The last sentence of this excerpt, 'scit tendere versum / Non secus, ac si oculo rubricam dirigat uno', is cited in GE's 1869 essay on 'Versification', to illustrate her observation that 'our English blank verse [has] had the good fortune to be written by poets & not by carpenters'.[1]

In Satire V, a passage excerpted below (lines 66–68) is followed by a line noted on Pf 711 43: 'Quum rota posterior curras et in axe secundo' (line 72). In DD ch. 52, Hans Meyrick quotes from this and supplies a translation: 'Fate, my friend, has made you the hinder wheel ... – run behind, because you can't help it' (600–1).

Although the edition of Persius used by GE has not been traced, her text corresponds closely – except for variant punctuation – to *Opera Omnia Auli Persii Flacci*, edited by G. L. Koenig, bound with Vol. III of Juvenal in the Delphin Classics edition (London: A. J. Valpy, 1820). There is no evidence that GE used the translation, which does not include the Latin texts, in DWL: Lewis Evans, *The Satires of Juvenal, Persius, Sulpicia, and Lucilius* (London, 1852). Her own occasional interlinear translations are here printed in the editorial notes, for comparison with the translations by John Conington in *The Satires of A. Persius Flaccus*, edited by Henry Nettleship (Oxford: Clarendon Press, 1872); the line references in Conington's translations coincide with those of the Koenig edition.

---

1 The essay is reprinted in Wiesenfarth, p. 287.

Quotations from Persius B 120

/120/ Persius

Proem Magister artis ingenique largitor
Venter, negatas artifex sequi voces. Prol[ogue, 10–11] [1]

Sat. I. 'nec te quaesiveris extra.' [I, 7] [2]
Sat I. Lit[erature]

'Scire tuum nihil est, nisi te scire hoc sciat alter.'
At pulchrum est digito monstrari, et dicier, *hic est*! [I, 27–28] [3]

Sed recti finemque extremumque esse recuso
'Euge' tuum et 'Belle'. Nam 'Belle' hoc excute totum:
Quid non intus habet? [I, 48–50] [4]

(You are [a] thief! What says he?) crimina rasis
Librat in antithetis, doctas posuisse figuras
Laudatur: *bellum hoc*. [I, 85–87] [5]

1 Prologue, 10–11, p. 141:
That great teacher of art and bestower of mother-wit the stomach, which has the knack of getting at speech when nature refuses it.

2 I, 7, pp. 9–11: 'don't you be ... asking any opinion but your own'.

3 I, 27–8, p. 15. Conington has the first line as a question. Modified translation:
'This knowing of yours is of no account, unless some one else knows that you are knowing.'
[Friend:] But it is a fine thing for men to point one out and say, 'There he goes!'

4 I, 48–50, pp. 17–19:
But I utterly deny that the be-all and end-all of excellence is your Bravo and Exquisite – for just sift this Exquisite to the bottom, and what do you not find there?

5 I, 85–7, p. 25:
[The accuser tells Pedius point blank, You are a thief. What does Pedius do?] Oh, he balances the charges in polished antitheses – he is deservedly praised for the artfulness of his tropes. Monstrous fine that!

Quotations from Persius B 120 120v

'Calidum scis ponere sumen;
Scis comitem horridulum trita donare lacerna:
Et, verum, inquis, amo; verum mihi dicite de me.' [I, 53–55] [1]

'Quis populi sermo est?'

'– Quis enim, nisi carmina molli
Nunc demum numero fluere, ut per laeve severos
Effundat junctura [unguis]? Scit tendere versum
Non secus, ac si oculo rubricam dirigat uno.' [I, 63–66] [2]

'Quidnam igitur tenerum, et *laxa cervice* legendum? [I, 98] [3]

'Men' moveat quippe, et, cantet si naufragus, assem
Protulerim? [I, 88–89] [4]

/120v/ Sat. II. *Religion*

'aperto vivere voto.' [II, 7][5]

1 I, 53–5, p. 19:

You know how to serve up a sow's paunch smoking hot – you know how to present a poor shivering dependant with a cast-off cloak – and you say, 'Truth is my idol – pray tell me Truth about myself.'

2 I, 63–6, p. 21:

'What does the town say?' What *should* it say – but that now at last we have verses which flow in smooth measure, so that the critical nail runs glibly along even where the parts join. He can make a long straight line, just as if he were ruling it with a ruddle cord, with one eye shut.

In her transcription, GE copied 'severos' again, in place of 'unguis'.

3 I, 98, p. 29:

Well, what should you instance as soft and adapted for being recited with a gentle bend of the neck?

4 I, 88–9, p. 25:

Am I to be touched forsooth and pull out a penny, if a shipwrecked man begins singing me a song?

5 II, 7, p. 39: '[to] live in the use of prayers to which all may listen'.

Quotations from Persius B 120v

Ast ego nutrici non mando vota: negato,
Jupiter, haec illi, quamvis te albata rogarit.
Poscis opem nervis, corpusque fidele senectae:
Esto, age; sed *grandes patinae tucetaque crassa*
Annuere his Superos vetuere, Jovemque morantur. [II, 39–43] [1]

Quid juvat hos templis nostros immittere mores,
Et bona Dis ex hac scelerata ducere pulpa? [II, 62–63] [2]

Quin damus id Superis, de magna quod dare lance
Non possit magni Messalae lippa propago?
Compositum jus, fasque animo, sanctosque recessus
Mentis, et incoctum generoso pectus honesto? [II, 71–74] [3]

1 II, 39–43, p. 43:

But *I* will never trust a nurse to pray for me or mine; good Jupiter, be sure to refuse her, though she may have put on white for the occasion. You ask reinforcement for your physical strength, and a body to stand you in good stead in old age. So far so good – go on; but your great dishes and thick gravies have laid an injunction on the gods not to grant it, and clog the gracious purposes of Jupiter.

Compare GE's interlinear translation:

But I do not trust prayers to a nurse: deny / [Jupiter] them to her though she may have besought thee in white robes. / You desire vigour for your sinews & a frame that will be strong in old age. / Good! But rich dishes & fat sausages / Forbid the gods to grant this prayer & are a hindrance to Jove himself.

2 II, 62–3, p. 47:

How can it answer to introduce the spirit of the age into the temple-service, and infer what the gods like from this sinful pampered flesh of ours?

Compare GE's interlinear translation:

What use to transfer to the gods our own habits
And infer what they will like from our own accursed flesh?

3 II, 71–4, p. 49:

Give *we* rather to the gods such offering as great Messalla's blear-eyed representative has no means of giving even out of his great dish – duty to God and man well blended in the mind, purity in the shrine of the heart, and a racy flavour of nobleness pervading the bosom.

Quotations from Persius B 120v 121v

Sat. III. *Education*

'Sonat vitium percussa, maligne
Respondet viridi non cocta fidelia limo: (the ill-baked jar)
Udum et molle lutum es, nunc nunc properandus, et acri
Fingendus sine fine rota.' [III, 21–24][1]

'Ad populum phaleras! ego te intus et in cute novi.' [III, 30][2]

Magne pater divum, saevos punire tyrannos
Haud alia ratione velis ...
Virtutem videant, intabescantque relicta. [III, 35–36, 38][3]

/121v/

Et tibi, quae Samios diduxit littera ramos, (letter Y)
Surgentem dextro monstravit limite callem. [III, 56–57][4]

Est aliquid quo tendis, et in quod dirigis arcum?
An passim sequeris corvos testaque lutoque,
Securus quo pes ferat, atque ex tempore vivis?
Helleborum frustra, quum jam cutis aegra tumebit,
Poscentes videas: venienti occurrite morbo.
Et quid opus Cratero magnos promittere montes?

1 III, 21–4, p. 55:
The jar rings flawed when one strikes it, and returns a doubtful sound, being made, in fact, of green ill-baked clay. Why, at this moment you are moist soft earth. You ought to be taken instantly, instantly, and fashioned without end by the rapid wheel.

2 III, 30, p. 55: 'Off with your trappings to the mob! I can look under them and see your skin.'

3 III, 35–6, 38, p. 57:
Great Father of the Gods, be it thy pleasure to inflict no other punishment on the monsters of tyranny ... – let them look upon virtue and pine that they have lost her forever!

4 III, 56–7, p. 61:
And the letter which spreads into Pythagorean ramifications has set your face towards the steep path which rises to the right.
The Pythagorean letter is the Greek Y, as GE notes on Folger 14 63v:
Y Pythagorean symbol – Samian letter – the upright stem the difficult ascent of virtue, the left the easier path of vice.

Quotations from Persius B 121v

Disciteque, o miseri, et causas cognoscite rerum:
Quid sumus, et quidnam victuri gignimur; ordo
Quis datus, aut metae quam mollis flexus, et unde;
Quis modus argento; quid fas optare; quid asper
Utile nummus habet; patriae carisque propinquis
Quantum elargiri deceat; quem te Deus esse
Jussit, et humana qua parte locatus es in re. [III, 60–72] [1]

Sat. IV. *Statesmen*

'Ut mavis, da verba, et *decipe nervos*
Si potes.' [IV, 45–46] [2]

'dicenda tacendaque calles.' [IV, 5] [3]

'Tecum habita, et noris, quam sit tibi curta supellex.' [IV, 52] [4]

'Ingemit (miser) Hoc bene sit! tunicatam cum sale mordens
Caepe.' [IV, 30–31] [5]

1 III, 60–72, pp. 61–3:
Have you any goal? any mark at which you aim? or are you on a vague wild-goose chase armed with broken pots and mud, not caring where you go, and living by the rule of the moment? It is too late to ask for hellebore, as you see men doing, when the skin is just getting morbid and bloated. Meet the disease at its first stage, and what occasion is there to promise Craterus gold-mines for a cure? Be instructed, poor creatures, and acquaint yourselves with the causes of things, – what we are, what life we are sent into the world to lead, what is the rank assigned us at starting, where is the smooth turn round the goal and when to take it, what should be the limit to our fortune, what we may lawfully wish for, what is the good of coin fresh from the mint, how much ought to be spent on one's country and one's near and dear friends, what part God has ordained you to bear, and what is your position in the human commonwealth.

2 IV, 45–6, p. 81:
'Well, just as you please, play the sophist and cheat your physical powers, if you can do so.'

3 IV, 5, p. 73: 'You know well what should be said and what not.'

4 IV, 52, p. 81:
Live at home, and learn how slenderly furnished your apartments are.

5 IV, 30–1, p. 79: '[The miser] groans out, May it be for the best! as he munches onions, coats [skins] and all, with salt.'

Quotations from Persius B 122

/122/ Sat. v. *Libertas*

Verba togae sequeris, junctura callidus acri,[1]
Ore teres modico, pallentes radere mores
Doctus, et ingenuo culpam defigere ludo:
Hinc trahe quae dicas; mensamque relinque Mycenis
Cum capite et pedibus, *plebeiaque prandia noris.* [v, 14–18][2]

Quumque iter ambiguum est, et vitae nescius error
Diducit trepidas ramosa in compita mentes. [v, 34–35][3]

Mille hominum species, et rerum discolor usus:
Velle suum cuique est, nec voto vivitur uno. [v, 52–53][4]

–Cras hoc fiet. Idem cras fiet. Quid quasi magnum
Nempe diem donas? – Sed quum lux altera venit,
Jam *cras hesternum* consumpsimus. [v, 66–68][5]

Heu steriles veri, quibus una Quiritem
Vertigo facit! [v, 75–76][6]

1 GE has added here an interlinear translation: 'quick at ingenious combinations'.

2 v, 14–18, pp. 85–7:
Your line is to follow the language of common life, with dexterous nicety in your combinations, and a moderate rounding of the cheek; your skill must be shown in rubbing against the bloated skin of morality, and pinning vice to the ground in sport which will do for gentlemen. Let this be your storehouse of materials; leave Mycenae its feasts with their baskets of extremities, and make yourself at home at the early dinners of common Roman folk.

3 v, 34–5, p. 89:
Just when the way of life begins to be uncertain, and the bewildered mind finds that its ignorant ramblings have brought it to a point where roads branch off.

4 v, 52–3, pp. 91–3:
Men are of a thousand kinds, and the practice of life wears the most different colours. Each has his own desire, and their daily prayers are not the same.

5 v, 66–8, p. 95:
'So I will [do it], tomorrow.' 'Tomorrow will tell the same tale as to-day.' 'What? do you mean to call a day a great present to make to a man?' Aye, but when next day comes, we have spent what was tomorrow yesterday already.

6 v, 75–6, p. 97:
What an unproductive soil for truth, where a single twirl makes a citizen of Rome!

Quotations from Persius B 122 122v

Ne liceat facere id, quod quis vitiabit agendo.
Publica lex hominum naturaque continet hoc fas,
Ut teneat vetitos inscitia debilis actus. [v, 97–99] [1]

sed nullo thure litabis
Haereat in stultis brevis et semuncia recti. [v, 120–121] [2]

/122v/ Sat. vi. *Wealth*

'Discrepet his alius. Geminos, horoscope, varo
Producis genio.' [vi, 18–19] [3]

'Mihi nunc Ligus ora
Intepet, hibernatque meum mare, qua latus ingens
Dant scopuli, et multa littus se valle receptat.' [vi, 6–8] [4]

1 v, 97–9, pp. 99–101:

... that no one be allowed to do what he will spoil in the doing. It is a statute contained in the general code of humanity and nature, that ignorance and imbecility operate as an embargo on a forbidden action.

Compare GE's interlinear translation:

Let none do that which he will spoil in the doing.
The public law of men – and nature herself – contains this principle:
that feeble ignorance should hold all acts forbidden.

2 v, 120–1, p. 103:

But no amount of incense will induce the gods to rule that one small grain of wisdom may get itself lodged in a fool's nature.

Compare GE's interlinear translation:

No incense can win this prayer – / that half an ounce of right should inhere in the breast of fools.

In the margin just below this extract GE has written 'Sat. vi'.

3 vi, 18–19, p. 119:

Another man may take a different view; aye, good horoscope, you sometimes give birth to twins whose star is strangely different.

4 vi, 6–8, pp. 117–19:

As for me, the Ligurian coast is giving me the benefit of its warmth, and the sea is wintering just as I like it to do, where the sides of the cliffs present a vast barrier, and the shore retires into a deep bay.

Quotations from Persius B 122v

(Preparations for a triumph)
'Missa est a Caesare laurus
Insignem ob cladem Germanae pubis, et aris
Frigidus excutitur cinis; ac jam postibus arma,
Jam chlamydes regum, jam lutea gausapa captis,
Essedaque, ingentesque locat Caesonia Rhenos.' [VI, 43–47] [1]

'Progenies terrae! – Quaere ex me, quis mihi quartus
Sit pater: haud prompte, dicam tamen. Adde etiam unum,
Unum etiam: terrae est jam filius; et mihi ritu
Manius hic generis prope major avunculus exit.' [VI, 57–60] [2]

Persius born at Volterra, AD 34

Younger than Horace, older than Juvenal. Died AD 62

1 VI, 43–7, pp. 123–5:
Bays have arrived from the emperor in honour of a signal victory over the Germans; the cold ashes are being shovelled away from the altars; the empress has begun to contract for arms for the temple-gates, and royal mantles, and yellow woollen for the prisoners, and chariots, and Rhines as large as life.

2 VI, 57–60, pp. 125–7:
'What, a [low-born] groundling!' Ask me who is my great-great-grandfather. Give me time and I can tell you. Go back one step more, and one more. I come to a groundling at last; and so in a strict legal descent Manius here turns out to be something like my great-great-uncle.

Hebrew names and phrases

B 123

This page of miscellaneous Hebrew terms and definitions begins with a note on two Midrash collections: Midrash Rabbah and the Pesikta. GE's summary translation of Deutsch's preface to his German translation from the Midrash Rabbah (B 115) ends with her reminder, 'v. supra p. 115'. At the foot of the page is another reminder, 'v. 141', to see her notes from Steinschneider on the Midrash (B 141 to 150).

The brief notes filling the rest of the page are copied from various sources and often duplicate entries in other notebooks. In the small portable notebook she was using during this period, lists of Hebrew terms occupy available spaces on several pages; Pf 711 22, 24, and 63 include words apparently noted from her reading of Graetz. Terms and definitions on Pf 711 53 and 54 are originally drawn from the text by Leopold Stein which accompanies reproductions of paintings by Moritz Oppenheim, illustrating Jewish family life, in *Bilder aus dem altjüdischen Familienleben. Pajtanish* and *Pijuthim*, with their German definitions, are copied from Pf 711 59, where GE noted them from her reading of Delitzsch's *Zur Geschichte der jüdischen Poesie. Nissouin* and *Mikra* – crowded belatedly on this page – appear again on Pf 711 60 and Pf 710 23 and 27; the original source of these notes is obscure. The titles from the Gaonic period in Babylon, also found on Pf 711 60 and again on Pf 710 36, are from Steinschneider's 'Jüdische Literatur'; see B 145v. This list of 'Hebrew names & phrases' (GE's Index entry on B 185v) thus presents a partial compendium of her extensive note-taking on 'Hebrew Matters'. Since her notes are crowded on the page, their order is somewhat altered in the list as printed below.

/123/

Midrasch, chief collections: Midrash Rabbah (begun about 700, ended about 1100 AD), comprising the Pentateuch & the five Megilloth; & the Pesikta (about 700 AD) which contains the most complete cycle of Pericopes, but the very existence of which had until lately been forgotten, through the extracts made from it – Jalkut, Pesikta Rabbathi, Sutarta &c. v. supra p. 115.

Seder Olam Rabba [Steinschneider, p. 372][1]
Seder means ordinance, ritual [Pf 711 54]
Olam, world

Megilloth, volumes, rolls [2]
Sepher, a book

Mikra, writing [Pf 711 80; Pf 710 27]

Ketubim, writings, inscriptions, documents[3]

Olam-ha-Ba, the world to come [Graetz 3, 219; Pf 711 63]

Ruach-ha-Kodesch, the Holy Spirit [Graetz 4, 40; Pf 711 24, 63][4]

Kodesch-ha-Kodeschim, Holy of Holies [Pf 711 24]

Kiddusch, consecration, blessing, hence *fiançailles* [Pf 711 54, 80][5]

Nissouin, marriage [Pf 711 80; Pf 710 29]

1 *Seder Olam Rabbah*, the Great Seder Olam or the 'Order of the World', is a Midrashic chronology which numbers the years from the Creation. Attributed to one of the Tanaim in the second century CE, it is 'the historical calendar' mentioned on B 108v. Since the eleventh century CE, the dates used in Jewish communities derive from the calculations of the *Seder Olam Rabbah* that the world was created 3828 years before the destruction of the Second Temple. Compare GE's note (B 193v): '3761 years to be subtracted from a Jewish date after Christ, to find out its correspondence with our own'.

2 That is, scrolls. The five Megilloth are the Song of Songs, Ruth, Lamentations, Ecclesiastes, and Esther.

3 Compare *Ketubah*, B 111.

4 In DD ch. 40, Mordecai offers a variant translation of 'the Ruach-ha-kodesh – the breath of divine thought' (466).

5 See also 'Kidduschin', Pf 710 23.

Hebrew names and places B 123

Pajtanish, gottesdienstlich
Pijuthim, synagogalen Poësie [Delitzsch, p. 49; Pf 711 59][1]

Almemor, raised platform in the Synagogue [Pf 711 22][2]

Aron-ha-Kodesch, the sacred ark or chest containing the Thorah
Ez-chajim, tree of life: silver pinnacles of the Thora roll so called
[Oppenheim, Plates II and III; Pf 711 53]

Hazan, precentor[3]
Schochet, slayer of animals
Bodek, searcher [Pf 711 22]

Chuppa, canopy held over the bride & bridegroom
[Oppenheim, Plate VI; Pf 711 53][4]

Nasi & *Ab-beth-din*, first appointed by John Hyrcanus, 135–106
Resh Metibta, president of the school
Resh Galuta, president of the exile
Gaon, excellency [Steinschneider, pp. 366–9; Pf 711 60; Pf 710 36]

Beth-hamidrasch, house of prayer & instruction over & above the Synagogue

Bar-Mizwa (youth of 14[5] – period of confirmation), son of the law
[Oppenheim, Plate V; Pf 711 53]

Derech-Erez, landesbrauch, sitte[6]

1 Translations: 'relating to divine worship' and 'liturgical poetry'.
2 In DD ch. 32, Deronda's visit to the Orthodox synagogue in Frankfurt illustrates the meanings of several Hebrew terms: 'The Reader had mounted to the *almemor* or platform, and the service began' (339). GE and GHL attended evening service in this synagogue on 1 August 1873 (GHL Diary).
3 GE later pencilled in the alternative spelling 'Chazan'. The role of the precentor or cantor in the Orthodox liturgy is demonstrated in the Frankfurt synagogue in DD ch. 32: 'the chant of the *Chazan's* or Reader's grand wide-ranging voice with its passage from monotony to sudden cries' (339).
4 Compare B 134.
5 Actually, thirteen years plus one day.
6 Steinschneider, p. 376, refers to 'Derech erez' as the title of a tractate on ethics and courtesy, but does not use the German words meaning 'customs of the country, manners'.

The inner life of modern Judaism

B 124, 125, 126, 123v, 124v, 125v, 126v, 127, 128, 129, 127v, 128v

The source of these notes from *Das innere Leben des modernum Judenthums*, translated from English into German 'in R. Hirschfeld' (B 129), has not been traced. For convenience, the author is referred to below as 'Hirschfeld'.

Hirschfeld's material demonstrates two separate but related internal divisions in nineteenth-century Judaism: between the Reform movement and Orthodox (or 'ultra-orthodox') practitioners; and between Sephardim (descendants of Jews who lived in Spain or Portugal before the 1492 expulsion) and Ashkenazim (German, French, Polish, and Lithuanian Jews).

The Sephardim accepted Joseph Caro's *Shulchan Aruch*, or 'Prepared Table' (1564), as an authoritative précis of rabbinical law; but the Ashkenazim, who tended to be more fundamentalist and rigorous in religious practices, thought Caro too liberal and permissive and adhered to a work by a Polish Talmudist, Moses Isserles, who provided a *Mappah* or 'Tablecloth' for Caro's 'Table' (B 126). Their stricter practices are reflected in the spelling of *Abos* – indicating the Ashkenazi pronunciation of the Hebrew *Avot* – in GE's notes on the 'heaps of prohibitions' hedging round the Sabbath (B 126v).

In London, cultural and social differences also influenced relations between Sephardim and Ashkenazim. Bevis Marks, the 'richly endowed' Sephardi synagogue, was established in 1701 (B 128v). In the following century, the Sephardim came to be greatly outnumbered by Ashkenazi immigrants. The newcomers were, for the most part, less prosperous in worldly pursuits and less well educated than their Sephardi precursors. According to Hirschfeld, 'in their social position, intelligence & wealth, [the Sephardim] used to be far the superior' (B 128v), whereas many Ashkenazim, in his view, after two 'centuries in deep darkness' were still mediaeval in their garb and 'narrow rabbinical opinions'. 'All scientific study' was held to be heretical, and 'it was decried as un-Jewish to learn the language of the country'. Speaking 'the language of the country' was, in the opinion of these 'the ultra-rabbinical' or Orthodox Jews, the first step towards assimilation to other heathen ways, 'Hukot Hagoyim' (B 124).

Language differences also separated Sephardim from Ashkenazim, who spoke the 'Jew-German dialect' (B 127v), Yiddish, disparaged by Hirschfeld as 'the Jargon or Kauderwälsch spoken by the Jews only' (B 123v). GE's interest in this dialect is evident in her repeated notebook references to 'Wagenseil's Belehrung der Jüdisch-Deutschen Red- und Schreibart (Kauderwälsch)' (B 193v, Pf 711 54, and Pf 710 41), and in her many pages of notes from Tendlau's collection of proverbs in German with a vigorous mixture of Yiddish idioms, *Sprichwörter und Redensarten* (Pf 711 97a, 98a, and 101 to 104). Yiddish, as a vulgar tongue, may seem to be merely a degraded form of German. Deronda's reaction is typical of someone who knows German well, having studied in Germany (DD ch. 34: 369). In the Juden-gasse in Frankfurt, Deronda hears 'a dingy man', and then 'another dingy man of the same pattern', both shouting in the same 'Jew-dialect'; the language of their trading is part of what he finds repellent in 'vulgar Jews' (DD ch. 32: 338). GE's aptly chosen *dingy* ('a recent word of obscure origin ... common in speech, but not in writing')[1] conveys Deronda's mingled disgust for both the dirty aspect of these men and their speech patterns.

The mixing of Jewish-German dialect with English is presented much more appealingly in the next chapter; a degree of sentiment about childish speech softens the realistic mimicry of the young Cohen children's accents. Adelaide Rebekah's use of the familiar Ashkenazi or Yiddish pronunciation, 'Shabbes', for Sabbath, is promptly translated or 'explained' for the English gentleman by her parents:

> 'Shlav'm Shabbes fyock on ... '
>
> 'Her Sabbath frock, she means ... She'll have her Sabbath frock on this evening.' (DD ch. 33: 363)

We might compare Jacob Cohen's 'we'll shwop' with Totty Poyser: 'Munny, *me* want half-a-toun in *my* bots'.[2] The church-going Totty is no less mercenary than the Jewish pawnbroker's son, with his Yiddish-flavoured English, which converts the 's' to 'sh'. Such a 'corrective comparison' may, as GE implies, make us conscious, like Deronda, of 'falling into unfairness' in our judgements or prejudgements (DD ch. 32: 338).

1 *OED*: an 1837 reference is cited.

2 See ch. 18, 'Church', in *Adam Bede*, edited by Stephen Gill (Harmondsworth: Penguin, 1980), p. 238.

The Sephardi equivalent to Yiddish is Ladino, the Judaeo-Spanish dialect. The early Sephardi immigrants to England,

> proud of their descent, used only the Spanish language, which prevailed even to the latest time in public notices even after it had been superseded in the pulpit by English. But the Sephardim now form scarcely the twentieth part of the English Israelites ... (B 128v)

Hirschfeld's references to *English* Israelites, a liturgy in the English language, and a pulpit rather than an *almemor,* all signal his Reform orientation. Reform Jews in London not only adopted 'the language of the country' in daily life and in their liturgy, but also published an English translation of the Mishnah (see the headnote to 'Extracts from the Mishnah', B 110 to 111) and identified their nationality as a mixture of British and Jewish. In this they followed the example set in the ancient Jewish community of Worms, by Jews whose ancestors had migrated there many centuries earlier – according to their legend, 'as early as the Benjamite disgrace' (B 159v) – and who in 1848 declared:

> We must no longer utter prayers for the return to Palestine while we are wholeheartedly attached to the German fatherland ... We must not mourn in sackcloth and ashes the destruction of the Temple when we so long ago came into the possession of a fatherland that has become so dear to us.[1]

In their view, prayers uttered by most German Jews for their personal return to Israel were not sincere. The Orthodox viewed such assimilation as a defection to heathen ways; the Reform proponents were offended by accusations that they were not good practising Jews – that they did not observe the Law. Thus the authority of the Oral Law became a contentious issue.

Hirschfeld's discussion of the 'Origin of the Talmud' (B 124, 125, 126) may be compared to GE's earlier notes on the Mishnah (especially B 106, 107v, 108v); but the tone of his account of the gradual establishment of 'the doctrine of a divine oral law' suggests a connection in GE's mind between these notes and those from the English translation of *Eighteen Treatises from the Mishna.* The reference to '2 synagogues of the reformed or British Israelites in London – Burton St., Margaret St.' (B 128v) strengthens

1 Quoted in the *Encyclopedia Judaica,* 3, 774.

the link, for Benjamin Elkin, the publisher of the Mishnah translation, was a founding member of the West London Synagogue of British Jews in Burton Street. According to Elkin, the idea of translating the Mishnah arose 'during one of the discussions that took place at the vestry board of the Sphardim synagogue' about the proposed 'improvement' of the liturgy. Elkin, by way of conciliation, '[took] this occasion further to observe',

> that so far from there being any *dogma* amongst [the Burton Street Community] as to the Divine authority of the Oral Law, the most ultra believer in that doctrine might become a member of the West London Synagogue of British Jews.[1]

Elkin's term, 'the most ultra believer', is echoed by Hirschfeld's reference to 'the ultra-rabbinical Jew' (compare GE's headings for B 124v, 125v, and 126v). It is this 'strict rabbinical' Jew whose liturgy includes prayers of such 'mountainous extent' that 'the worshipper must utter about 440 words a minute' (B 123v, 124v).

Elkin's appeal to the precedent of a German translation of the Mishnah – his claim that 'the British Jew' should be given 'the same free access' to its pages – is a reminder that the centres of the Reform Movement were in Germany: in Frankfurt, Breslau and Berlin. It is in Frankfurt that Deronda meets a 'Jewish youth, who entered cordially into his wanting not the fine new building of the Reformed but the old Rabbinical school of the orthodox' (DD ch. 32: 338).

Identifying the source of these notes will no doubt bring into more precise focus some connections between 'English Israelites' in London and the German centres of the Reform movement. In *Daniel Deronda,* GE occludes doctrinal issues, presenting without comment a broad range of Jewish observance. The scene of the most subtle complexity in this respect is the Cohen family's celebration of the Sabbath, while accommodating as their guest a gentleman who is both a heathen and a customer (DD ch. 34).

---

1 Elkin's anonymous preface to *Eighteen Treatises from the Mishna* is cited in his *Letters Addressed to the Editor of 'The Voice of Jacob',* pp. 5, 29.

The inner life of modern Judaism B 124 125

United through training in Polish seminaries

/124/ Condition of Jews in 17th & 18th centuries

The Jews in Russia, Poland, Turkey & Germany were during the 17th & 18th centuries in deep darkness. Nothing was studied by them except the Talmud. The Hebrew Bible itself was little studied & the able authors of the 12th century such as Aben Ezra, Kimchi &c. who were familiar with the old classical Hebrew, were entirely neglected.[1] Talmudism had become an oppressive despotism. The Polish seminaries from which all the Rabbis came systematically hindered all scientific study – & even prohibited grammar & philosophy. It was decried as un-Jewish to learn the language of the country. To have any idea at variance with mediaeval opinion, or to pursue a business which did not agree with the narrow rabbinical opinions of the time, nay, to dress in any other garb than the long garment of the Middle Ages, was regarded as an apostacy from the faith, & held up to scorn as 'Hukot Hagoyim', fashions of the heathens.[2] Such Hebrews – many such – are still to be found in the East, Russia, Poland, & perhaps in Alsace. Hirschfeld

Origin of the Talmud[3]

The fundamental idea of the Talmud is that of the Oral or traditional Law supposed to have been given to Moses on Sinai. Probably, it was in the time of Ezra or soon after his death that the attempt to bring the ordinances of the Pentateuch into harmony with the altered political & social conditions of the age originated that traditional interpretation which was the nucleus of the 'oral law'. The mass of the Jews being then ignorant of Hebrew, having lost it during the captivity, were dependent for the interpretation of the sacred text **/125/** on the *Sopherim* or scribes.[4]

The doctrine of a divine oral law gradually established itself as a conviction. Rabbinical schools were founded for its discussion & development, & the political disasters in 70 & 133 AC caused no important interruption of their activity. The rabbins continued their discussions interweaving the subtilties of the age with the rationalism of the Sadducees, the mysticism of the Essenes, & the Cabala – a kind of theological metaphysics in which the spiritual elements

1 Here GE added a cross-reference to the note on the Hebrew prayer book and 'the life of the ultra-rabbinical Jew' (B 123v, 124v, 125v, 126v).

2 See 'Chukot Hagoyim' on Pf 711 91a and the '*Jewish Chronicle*' section headnote.

3 GE's heading for B 125.

4 For a note on the Sopherim, see B 140.

of Judaism with the superstitions of Babylon & the Neo-Platonism of Egypt are blent together.[1] In the beginning of the 3d century all the traditions of the oral law which could be remembered were written down & incorporated as the Mishna.[2] This committal to writing was bitterly condemned by many Rabbis, who held that the authority of the *oral* law ceased in its ceasing to be *oral*. The redactor of the Mishna is constantly stated to have been Rabbi Jehuda, son of the Patriarch Simon ben Gamaliel. But modern critics like Rapoport, Luzzato[3] &c. find in it traces of a later date & believe that Rabbi Jehuda did indeed for his own satisfaction write a Mishna, but not for public use, & that his Mishna cannot be the same as that we possess. Either the Mishna was never perfect or a great part is lost. It is based on the Pentateuch of which it undertakes to explain the ordinances, yet much is omitted. Out of the Mishna & other sources of traditional learning, as Zifra (commentary on Leviticus), Zifri (commentary on 4 & 5 Buch Moses), Mechilta (commentary on Exodus), **/126/** arose the Talmud, also called Gemara – the two words meaning the same thing, the one having a Hebrew, the other an Aramaic, root.[4]

Rabbi Simon of Cairo in the year 741 published a selection from the Talmudic theses: & somewhat later Rabbi Acha gave an extract from the Babylonian Talmud concerning the rules applicable to the weekly portions of the Pentateuch. This latter, called *Schiltos,* is not extant except in mutilated editions. From this time nothing more was done by the Babylonian schools. In 1040 they were closed. In the next century Maimonides published his Mishna Thora, in which he omitted all Talmudic disputations & on his own authority declared what was the explanation of the Law, where the Talmud had not done so. During subsequent centuries he was regarded as the pillar of rabbinism, but not so by his contemporaries, who attacked him as having no right to decide where the Talmudic authorities had failed to do so. His work was variously criticized till in the 14th century it was superseded by a compilation of Rabbi Jacob ben Ascher, *Arba Turim.* This work contains no less than 13,602 religious laws (Dinim), great parts of which are still retained

1 GE later underlined, in pencil, 'superstitions of Babylon'.

2 GE later inserted 'But see 108' (i.e., B 107v), referring to her note, 'When was the Mischna written down?'

3 Solomon Rapoport (1790–1867) and Samuel David Luzzatto (1800–1865).

4 Compare GE's earlier note on B 106. *Buch* for 'book' is a slip confirming that this is a running translation from a German source.

in Barbary & other places where ultra-rabbinism reigns. In the 16th cent. Rabbi Joseph Karo published an improved edition called *Schulchan Aruch*,[1] which became the rabbinical law-book of the Sefardim. But the Polish, German, French & English Jews take as a standard the work of the same name by Rabbi Moses Iserless aus Krakow, 1573. Hirschfeld

/123v/ Hebrew Prayer Book

Before Moses Mendelssohn the Bible was only translated into the Jargon or Kauderwälsch spoken by the Jews only. In this Jargon too the travelling mendicant preachers (called *Maggid* & *Mocheach*) used to preach. To speak a pure dialect would have laid them open to excommunication, *Cherem*.

'Die Liebe zu den Ihrigen war es allein die einen Sonnenblick auf dieses Bild tiefen Schattens warf.'[2]

In this hour of need appeared Mendelssohn, born in Dessau 1729. He translated the Thora into classical German. It was not till after Mendelssohn's death (1786) that a movement took place towards the alteration of the Liturgy.

The history of the Hebrew prayer book is remarkable. *After the destruction of the Temple,* a form of prayer understood to have been framed by Ezra, Haggai & other members of the Great Synagogue took the place of the sacrifices & offerings. For *1000 years* additions were made to this formulary, partly in prayers written by individual pious men, partly in such as were made for special occasions & subsequently retained. Then there were whole chapters from the Mishna, a complete list of hermeneutical rules (from the Talmud) for the interpretation of the Bible, various treatises of a cabbalistic & esoteric character, hyper-poetic hymns, about Angels, Demons, magic, adjurations &c. A modern, not unfriendly, critick said that the Jews 'sang Logic & prayed metaphysics'. The prayers were of mountainous **/124v/** extent. The daily morning devotions fill 40 close pages; those for the Sabbath morning 62. In all orthodox synagogues the worship still takes place in this form, & with this task before him the worshipper must utter about 440 words a minute.

1 GE added above the line 'betreiterer Tisch' ('prepared table').

2 Translation: 'It was the love for their own that cast the only ray of sunlight on this picture of deep shadow.'

The inner life of modern Judaism B 124v 125v

The life of the ultra-rabbinical Jews[1]

Jacobson built a synagogue for reformed worship in Berlin but it was not allowed to remain open. Then in 1819 one was built in Hamburg.

In general the Jews are divided into 3 classes: the strict rabbinical, the progressists, & the ultra-reformers. The great temple built 2 years ago in Berlin belongs to the second.

The ultra-orthodox or rabbinical Jew goes to the synagogue soon after daybreak, where the service lasts 2 hours on Mondays & Thursdays & 1½ on the other days. Till lately it was the custom (& still in Poland, Russia, & parts of Austria) for the officer of the Synagogue to go round to the houses & knock at the door before daybreak, & call to prayer. Then he must utter certain forms of blessing or praise to the number of a hundred daily – when it thunders, or he sees a rainbow, when a great personage passes by, when he eats or drinks &c. He must visit the sick, wash the dead, attend funerals. And except on Fridays & Sundays pass 2 hours of the evening in the Bes Hammedrasch – the place where the Talmud is read & discussed. He observes five entire fasts besides the one instituted by Moses (Yom Kippur) & 30 half fasts (till midday). On the first evening of every **/125v/** New Moon[2] he must assemble in an open place with not fewer than nine others to pray that the light of the moon may be increased. On the Eve of Pesach he goes round the house with a spoon & a feather to gather any crumb of leavened bread (some being purposely deposited in order to be gathered up). At the feast of Purim he takes a small hammer into the Synagogue, to beat loudly on his seat at the mention of Haman, the enemy of the Jews. The women are not concerned in the chief part of these ceremonies. On them it is incumbent to attend to the ritual of *cookery*, & avoid the fatal contact of butter & flesh, for which two sets of utensils are kept.[3]

1 This is GE's heading on B 124v. B 125v is headed '*The ultra-rabbinical Jew*' and B 126v 'Ultra-rabbinical Judaism'.

2 GE added in pencil above the line, 'v. p. 131', i. e., B 130v, a reference to her notes from Hyam Isaacs on the 'time of praying for the New Moon'. For notes on the *Minyan*, or quorum of ten Jewish men, see Pf 711 95 and 103–4. The latter is translated on Pf 710 27.

3 Deronda's mother, decades afterwards, resents her father's attempt to force her 'to be what he called "the Jewish woman" under pain of his curse ... [She] was ... to dread lest a bit of butter should touch a bit of meat' (DD ch. 51: 587).

The inner life of modern Judaism B 125v

When the Sabbath comes at sunset[1] (Princess Sabbath, as Heine calls it)[2] while the Father & sons are gone to the synagogue, the mother spreads the evening table, & places on it the two long flat loaves strewn with poppy-seed (Challas) in memory of the manna. When the Father comes home again the children all go in turn according to their ages to receive the blessing of each parent. Then the family sings the *Scholem Nigelechim,*[3] the refrain of which is the welcoming to the hearth of the ministering angels. Afterwards the Father & children sing in honour of the mother the 31 ch. of Proverbs beginning at verse 10.[4]

1 The beginning of the new day, in Jewish tradition, at sundown rather than sunrise is significant for the imagery of the novel. See, especially, Mordecai's expectant meditations on Blackfriars Bridge (DD ch. 40: 459–61): the 'golden sky' in the West is, as Barbara Hardy points out, 'an appropriate image for a beginning' (Hardy, p. 896).

2 Lines from Heine's 'Prinzessin Sabbath' form an epigraph for DD ch. 34: 365.

His name is
Israel. He has been changed
by an eldrich spell, into a dog.
...
But every Friday night,
as dusk falls, suddenly
the spell is lifted, and the dog
turns, once again, into a human being.

This translation is by S. S. Prawer, in his *Heine's Jewish Comedy* (Oxford: Clarendon Press, 1983), pp. 554–5. Although Prawer does not mention GE, his 'Study of [Heine's] Portraits of Jews and Judaism' provides a significant context for considering not only her essays about Heine's work, but also *her* portraits of Jews and Judaism. Heine's acquaintance with Rahel Varnhagen von Ense, whose husband was a friend of both Goethe and GHL, and with many authors cited in the Pforzheimer and Berg notebooks (Zunz , Delitzsch, Jost, Kalisch, Karpeles, and Munk), illustrates the particular web of multiple interconnections in nineteenth-century German and Jewish culture and society. Although Heine is mentioned just once in the Berg Notebook, GE's extensive familiarity with his writing is confirmed by McCobb, pp. 193–201.

3 Thus in GE's note; the correct form is *Scholem Aleichem.*

4 'Who can find a virtuous woman? for her price is far above rubies ... Her children rise up and call her blessed; her husband also, and he praiseth her' (Proverbs xxxi, 10 – 28). Mordecai quotes this in praise of his mother: 'Her children arise up and call her blessed' (DD ch. 43: 503). Her husband, however, does not much care whether she is dead or alive (DD ch. 52: 687).

At the Sabbath meal poor guests are received. No cooking done. Between services & meals works of charity are done or a walk taken within the rabbinical limits – namely 2000 amos or steps. With the first star, either worship is attended in synagogue, or at home the **/126v/** 'Havdole' or domestic devotion is performed. Before the Havdole a hymn is sung to Elias, of which the refrain is, 'O prophet Elias (thrice repreated), come quickly with the Messiah the Son of David.' After the Havdole the prophet Elias is again in a mysterious or cabbalistic way called upon, the 5 Hebrew letters of his name being 109 times transposed. No work allowed except the making of a coffin for one to be buried the next morning. The Sabbath is hedged round with heaps of prohibitions – *Abos* or greater & *Toldos*, or lesser. Of the latter – no man may carry a stick or umbrella – or a pocket-handkerchief, unless it is wound round his waist – or an amulet unless it be from a famous sage. *That Rabbi Meir, in opposition to R. José, allowed a cripple to use his wooden leg is regarded as a great indulgence.*

/127/ The Jews in Holland

The great Sephardim Synagogue in Amsterdam built 1675. Before this three others had been built. In the course of the 18th century there was such a stream of Polish & German Israelites into Holland that they soon outnumbered the Spanish & Portuguese Jews who had formerly constituted the elite or aristocracy of the race. The old Portuguese were worthy of all respect. Their wealth was employed for the noblest objects: they built & endowed synagogues, schools, hospitals & asylums, & showed the highest patriotism towards the country that protected them. They willingly taxed themselves to support the Netherlands against Louis XIV, gave thousands of gulden on behalf of the Huguenot refugees, & aided William III in his famous expedition in 1688. In the memorable crisis of 1784, they saved the state – as is acknowledged in a letter still preserved in the archives of the Synagogue, addressed to Isak de Pinto. There are more than 86,000 Jews in Holland – men of the highest reputation in all branches. Among the chief names are Lipman, van Mesrith, Godefroi, Mulder, Goudsmid and Hartogh.

In Russia there are 200,000 Jews. In Poland 780,000, or more than $1/8$ of the whole population.[1] In these countries they are still dreadfully oppressed.

1 For other notes on Jewish population numbers, see B 194, Pf 711 22, Pf 707 1, and the newspaper article on the 'Jewish Population of the World' for 1878, attached to the inside front cover of Pf 710.

Their worst endurance is the conscription – twenty-five years of service without hope of advancement.

/128/ The Jews in England

From the expulsion of the Jews under Edward I, nothing was heard of them in England till 1655 when Menasse ben Israel was sent as an envoy to Cromwell from the Jews in Holland to ask for the repeal of Edward's edict of banishment. It seems that a synagogue in King Street, Duke's Place was built in 1656, but by & by there were petitions for the maintenance of the edict, & the Jews were so maltreated by the mob that they entreated protection from Charles II & received it. But persecutions were nevertheless continued. Not till 1723 did the Jews get themselves recognized as British subjects, & were allowed to take the oath of Abjuration.

By their spirited monetary aid in 1745 they rescued the country from bankruptcy, & the government was able to get a bill of naturalization for Jews born in England. But a storm was raised in consequence & the government was actually compelled to revoke the bill. Thus checked, the Jews contented themselves with an obscure life in Cripplegate, Bishopsgate, Aldgate & Whitechapel. But from a correspondence of Joshua van Oven with Colquhoun, secretary of state, it appears that at the beginning of this century their condition was changed for the worse & that they were in poverty – van Oven desiring that they should be freed from the payment of the ordinary Poor rate, they having their own poor to maintain. Abraham Goldsmid came to their aid, built a great hospital at Mile End, since **/129/** removed to Lower Norwood. In 1824, the Jews were made admissible to the London Gilds. The emancipation of the Catholics in 1829 induced Isaac Lyon Goldsmid to hope that the same citizenship would be granted to the Jews. In 1830 the motion was made by Sir Robert Grant & passed the first reading by a majority of 80, but was thrown out on the second by a majority of 63. In 1835 David Solomon was made Sheriff of London & Middlesex. In 1847 Sir Robert Peel moved for the removal of the disabilities which hindered Alderman Solomon in the discharge of his functions – which was granted by both houses. In 1846 Baron Rothschild was elected member for the city, but not till July 26 1858 could he take his place in Parliament. In the present Parliament there are seven Jews – members for London, Greenwich, Reading, Dover, Hithe, Aylesbury & Dewesbury. As there are only 60,000 Jews in England, they are more fully represented than any religious body except the Church of England.

The inner life of modern Judaism B 129 127v

There is a strong contrast in the educational condition of the Jews now from what it was at the beginning of the century. There is the Jewish Free School in Ebenezer Square founded in 1816, now removed to Bell Lane Spitalfields, in a building which receives 2000 children. Other schools are that in Greek Street, Soho, & the West Metropolitan in Red Lion Square.

(Das innere Leben des modernum Judenthums aus dem Englischen übertragen, in R. Hirschfeld)

/127v/

In the beginning of this century the Jews in England had a miserable position. Their numbers had increased out of proportion to their gains. There were very few rich among them – still fewer who could rank with our middle class. The children were only during a few hours in the week under an old ignorant Rabbi, with a cane in his hand, who for small pay taught them to read the Hebrew prayers, & to translate some chapters of the Pentateuch into Jew-German dialect which was as unintelligible to them as Hebrew itself. Even the elements of English remained utterly unknown to them. There were no Free Schools in which English was taught, only a few schools for the poor Spanish & Portuguese exclusively.[1]

1 In DD ch. 40, Mr Ram illustrates the effects of their 'miserable position':

> He was an elderly son of Abraham, whose childhood had fallen on the evil times at the beginning of this century, and who remained amid this smart and instructed generation as a preserved specimen, soaked through and through with the effect of the poverty and contempt which were the common heritage of most English Jews seventy years ago ... Mr Ram dealt ably in books in the same way that he would have dealt in tins of meat and other commodities – without knowledge or responsibility as to the proportion of rottenness or nourishment they might contain. (470)

GE's allusions to improvements in education often employ double-edged irony. Her reference to 'this smart and instructed generation' may be compared with her ironic comment that 'Deronda's undergraduateship occurred fifteen years ago, when the perfection of our university methods was not yet indisputable' (DD ch. 16: 164). Nevertheless, her chosen simile for Mr Ram's wares, in that era of unreliable canning processes, implies a greater proportion of rottenness than nutrition in his second-hand copies of esoteric treatises. His ignorance of the contents of his books also serves as an analogue to the consequences of the schooling common in his childhood, when 'an old ignorant Rabbi' taught children to translate chapters of the Pentateuch 'into Jew-German dialect ... as unintelligible to them as Hebrew itself'.

/128v/ London Synagogues

The first synagogue in London was built by Sephardim in 1656. Their ritual differs somewhat from that of the Aschkenasim or Polish & German Jews. In their social position, intelligence & wealth the former used to be far the superior, & proud of their descent, used only the Spanish language, which prevailed even to the latest time in public notices even after it had been superseded in the pulpit by English. But the Sephardim now form scarcely the twentieth part of the English Israelites, & by their narrowness they have gradually alienated the best families so that at present they consist chiefly of emigrants from Barbary, Morocco, & Gibraltar. Their synagogue in Bevis Marks, City, is richly endowed, & there is a branch synagogue in Bryanston Square.

The synagogue in Duke's Place was the first erected by the German & Polish Jews. During the last 25 years synagogues have been built in almost all parts of London & the provinces. The Portuguese Synagogue is nominally under the control of a Chacham, whose power however is very limited since the supreme authority is in the hands of a corporation called Mahamad. The German & Polish synagogues are under the direction of a Head Rabbi. There are 2 synagogues of the reformed or British Israelites in London – Burton St., Margaret St., Cavendish Sq. (another being built near Portman Sq.). These are under Prof. Marks. There is one in Manchester under Dr. Gottheil.

Ceremonies, customs, rites, and traditions of the Jews

B 129v, 130v, 131v, 132v, 130, 131, 132, 133, 133v, 134, 134v, 135, 135v

'"Ceremonies, customs, rites & traditions of the Jews", by Hyam Isaacs, a converted Jew (Exeter)', listed with other books on Pf 710 1, is the source of brief notes on Pf 711 55 and 56, as well as these thirteen pages in the Berg Notebook. GE probably read a borrowed copy of this book; references below are to the second edition (London: William Buck, [1830]), in the British Library. The full title-page reads:

Ceremonies, Customs, Rites, and Traditions of the Jews,
Interspersed with Gleanings from the Jerusalem and Babylonish Talmud
and the Targums, Mishna, Gemara, Maimonides, Abarbanel, Zohar,
Aben-Ezra, Oral Law, etc. etc.
In a manner never before published.
Also, a Copious Selection from some of their prayers,
as translated and used by the Polish and German Jews,
at the present time, in their different synagogues.

By Hyam Isaacs, A Converted Jew

As GE comments, 'this writer ... seems in spite of his conversion still to love the Jews better than the Xtians' (B 135). Indeed, unlike some converts to Christianity who have published tracts designed to persuade other Jews to join them in their new faith, Isaacs directs this publication towards those Gentiles who may be curious about Jewish religious practices. In his preface, addressed to 'Christian Readers', he even exhorts them to practise what they profess and preach: 'I have oftentimes prayed to God, that those who call themselves Christians, would be as strict in the gospel of Jesus Christ as the Jews are in the law' (p. 18). The preface is signed 'Hyam Isaacs, from the seed of Abraham'. The conversion of this 'Converted Jew' has not altered his love for his people: the substantive 'Jew' outweighs the epithet 'Converted' in his self-definition. He has neither taken a new baptismal name nor discarded his inheritance as a son of Abraham. Isaacs' motive for publication seems to be a desire for his fellows in his newly adopted faith to understand where he has come from. Even his later work, *The Awakening of the Jews from their Slumbers* (London: Ward, 1842), with its greater emphasis on conversion – or apostasy, in the view of '[his] brethren the Jews' (p. iv) – merely encourages his Christian readers to be 'more urgent in prayer for the speedy conversion of the Jews' (p. v).

That the ceremonies, customs, rites, and traditions of Christianity itself have a significant Jewish inheritance is of little concern to Isaacs. He makes no link between the Passover feast, celebrating the deliverance from bondage in Egypt, and the Last Supper of Jesus and his disciples; neither does he observe that the bread and wine of Christian ritual derive from the symbols of Pesach.[1] Perhaps he was converted in Exeter by a non-ritualistic sect, such as the Plymouth Brethren. One may be confident that the links between the traditional Christian Year and the Jewish Year were not lost on GE, although she does not explicitly refer to them. Her notes from Isaacs on the Feasts and Fasts of the Jewish calendar (B 129v to 133) may be compared with the brief calendars on B 172v–173 and Pf711 19–20.

---

1 For a reference work comparing the ceremonies, rites, customs, and traditions of Judaism and Christianity, see Dan Cohn-Sherbok, *A Dictionary of Judaism and Christianity* (Philadelphia: Trinity Press, 1991), in which may be traced the history of the development, derivation, and discarding of components of an inheritance that was once shared.

/129v/

Rosch Haschana

For 28 days before the first of Tisri the ram's horn is blown either by the chief rabbi or by a worthy member of the synagogue – generally after the service. On the new-year's day none break their fast until the horn has been blown. This is the 'feast of trumpets', Numbers 29, 1. Immediately after the portion of the law & the prophets has been read & the prayer said for the prosperity of the government under which they dwell, they blow the ram's horn – Schofar. As the synagogues in London will not hold the tenth part of the Jewesses & none of them dare break their fast unless they hear the sound of the trumpet, it is customary for the Jews to open their houses for the accommodation of the Jewesses (in the vicinity of the synagogue). On the second day, they go to the synagogue again & after nearly the same prayer as before, the portion of Genesis is read treating of Abraham offering up Isaac, & of God blessing him & his seed for ever – which portion is read to five persons called to the law for that purpose. If the first or second day is a Sabbath, the trumpet is not blown. [pp. 12, 38–40, 51–2] [1]

Apple & Honey on the table at this festival? Kompert[2] [p. 32]

The days between new year's day & the day of atonement are reckoned the ten days of repentance. On New Year's day God forgives sins, & decrees who shall die in the following year. [pp. 53, 17][3]

'Ye shall afflict your souls.' [Leviticus xxiii, 27; Numbers xxix, 7]

1 DD ch. 42 ends with a metaphorical *shofar*. 'Mordecai's high-pitched solemnity' brings to an end the evening's talk and makes 'the tone of phlegmatic discussion ... unseasonable': 'It was as if they had come together to hear the blowing of the *shophar*, and had nothing to do now but to disperse.' His speech is a new-year's summons, delivered in the *Hand and Banner* in lieu of a synagogue; and the club members hear a revised version of the traditional biblical readings for Rosch Haschana: 'The sons of Judah have to choose that God may again choose them' (500, 499).

No editorial explanation is given in the Clarendon edition for the substitution of 'unreasonable' for 'unseasonable' (Cabinet edition II, 397). The complex metaphoric cluster of seed and fruit in this discussion is more likely to have prompted GE to choose 'seasonable'.

2 The Leopold Kompert reference has not been traced. GE read many of his short stories in 1872 and 1873; see McCobb, pp. 213–15.

3 GE marked this note with a marginal pencil line.

/130v/

Day of Atonement *Iom Kippur,* 10 Tishri – Sept. (New Moon)

The day before the day of expiation many Jews have a fowl killed, swing it nine times over their heads & pray to God that their sins may enter into this fowl. On the ninth day, before (the eve of) the atonement, an hour before the synagogue service, they have a feast, before going to the synagogue, where on this day the free will offering is made. Every half year the synagogue dues are paid. [Pf 711 55]

'It is awful & grand to see the reader & the chief Rabbi & many of the congregation in prayer upwards of three hours clad with a shroud in which they are to be buried.'[1] There are many who stand on the same spot from the ninth day at even to the tenth day at even.

The *Mophter*, from Numbers 29, 7–11.
The *Musoph*, or addition, Numb. 29, 7[2]
The fasts are total, & not mere abstinence from meat. [pp. 54–8]

Time of praying for the New Moon:[3] They stand in groups of 40 or 50, one in the midst holding a candle that they may see to read their prayers. It is surprising to see with what earnestness they bow & leap toward the moon. 'May it be thy pleasure, O God, & the God of our Fathers! to continue to fill up the deficiencies of the moon; & that the light of the moon be as the light of the sun, as during the six days of the creation, before her diminution; as it is said, "the two great lights"' [pp. 60–1]

1 GE added a marginal note, 'vide p.', meaning to refer to B 137v. The custom of wearing one's shroud during the Yom Kippur service may explain Kalonymos's declaration: 'I am a wanderer, carrying my shroud with me' (DD ch. 60: 671). Klesmer also declares that he 'had better put [his] burial-clothes in [his] portmanteau and set off at once' (DD ch. 22: 225). His words seem to echo the phrase GE copied on Folger 13 120, from the *Arabian Nights:* 'He put his burial clothes in his portmanteau.' Travelling with one's own shroud is a Jewish and oriental practice, quite different from packing a 'suit of mourning', as Raffles does in *his* portmanteau in *Middlemarch* (ch 53: 517). The slip made by Pratt and Neufeldt (p. 148) illustrates just how foreign such customs may be to western readers. Isaacs observes that 'it is not uncommon for some [Jews] to have their shrouds twenty or thirty years by them' (p. 56).

2 Originally, the additional sacrifice offered on festivals; now the additional service recited to replace the *musoph* sacrifice of Temple times.

3 GE marginally noted a cross-reference to B 125v: 'v. p. 126'.

/131v/

Soukoth. The feast of Tabernacles. 15 Tishri – September

Every Jew who has a yard or garden is obliged to make a booth. It must be at least 8 feet high & ten ft square – of boards, roofed with laths which are covered with ornamental shrubs. The ceiling on the inside is hung with fruits – pumpkins, apples, pears, partly gilded. During the 8 days, they take all their meals in the tabernacle. The first night the master takes a glass of wine in his hand & says the Kiddusch, or sanctification.

In the morning they go to the Synagogue as on the Sabbath, where after the prayers, they take the citron, a palm branch, myrtles & willow, which being fastened together they wave uttering words of praise. (But if the day happens to be a Sabbath, this is omitted, it not being lawful to carry anything.) All Jews who can afford it have now a goodly bough of almond, another of willow well-leaved & which has grown beside a brook, & a third of myrtle with neither more nor less than three leaves on the top; the two latter are bound round the former, & decorated with ribbons. Also they have preserved citrons. And there is great particularity in choosing the faultless citrons which are brought for this purpose to the Rabbi.

The seventh day of the Feast is called Hosanna the Great, because on this day everyone has a branch of a willow tree. It is the custom of the clerks of the congregations **/132v/** to buy willow branches according to the numbers of the congregation & afterwards go from house to house to distribute them. [pp. 68–73] [1]

Kislev /November/ the third month, twenty-sixth[2] day, is the Feast of Hanucah, or the dedication – the cleansing of the temple by the Maccabees. This lasts eight days & is kept with lighted lamps, in memory of the miracle by which the oil left unpolluted in quantity only enough for one night was made to last for eight. The first night one lamp is lit, the second two, & so on to the eighth. [pp. 81–2]

1 On Pf 711 56 GE notes, from the same source, 'Willow branches at the Feast of Tabernacles, done up in small bundles to give to each family.'

2 GE later added the query, 'fifth?', in accord with her note on Pf 711 20: '*Hanouka*, Feast of Lights, 25 Kislev, the Purification & restoration of the temple-worship under Judas Maccabeus.'

Purim /In Feb. or March/ There is more feasting on the Purim than on any other festival. The rabbinical writings teach that when the Messiah comes all feasts will be abolished except that of *Purim*. *Adar* the thirteenth, being the day before, is kept as a fast, called the fast of Esther, in commemoration of her fasting three days & nights before going to supplicate for the deliverance of the Jews. On the fourteenth is the feast, when they keep open house & go about giving to the poor. [pp. 87–90]

15 *Nissan.* The Passover. The sabbath immediately preceding the Passover is called the great sabbath. The chief Rabbi spends about six hours every day in the synagogue. [pp. 91–2]

/130/ Mode of celebrating the Passover[1]

On the 14th day Nisan at even the feast begins, when they go to synagogue & then return to their feast. The table is covered with a white cloth: in the midst is a dish on which 3 passover cakes are laid, each covered with a white napkin. At the top are three vessels of gold, silver, or china: one is filled with salt water, one with a kind of sweetmeat made from apples, nuts, sugar &c to the consistency of paste; the other holds a small lamb-bone about 2 inches long which has been roasted, & on the top of it are strewed bitter herbs. When the master of the family comes in from the Synagogue he washes his hands, & the rest do likewise. The servants sit down at table (in commemoration of their all having been bondsmen), & the plate, valuables & jewels are laid on the table or in the room, as a memorial. At supper, the master takes a glass of wine in his hand & utters a blessing. Each person on this night is to drink four glasses of wine. The blessing is repeated by each. Then the master chants with a loud voice & all the males follow, repeating psalms & thanksgivings to God; in the course of which when they come to mention the ten plagues of Egypt, every time of mention each in quick succession dips his finger in the salt water, in commemoration of their forefathers going through the salt sea in safety. Then, in rotation they take one of the cakes from between the napkins, & break it into pieces about the size of an olive, & give each some of the bitter herbs. Afterwards they take another cake from between the napkins **/131/** & break it as the former, & with it eat some of the sweetmeat (which has the appearance of clay). The bitters represent the bondage, the sweetmeat the release. At a certain moment they all rise from their seats & touch the lamb's bone.

1 GE's heading for B 131 is 'The Passover / Pesach'.

After this, they take their supper. Then the service begins again & lasts till midnight. They say the usual grace after meat, & the solemnities are begun again by each drinking a glass of wine (in addition to the four). Then the youngest child rises from his seat & opens the door, & all at the table rise too under the idea that Elijah the prophet makes his appearance in every Jew's house in the world. The additional glasses of wine are for Elijah.
(One glass left for Elijah?)

After this the master takes the other cake from between the napkins, & breaks it as the former, except one quarter of it, which is left whole. Then he gives to each round the table two pieces, one to eat & the other to save. This they do all the year round in memory of the Passover, & in the quarter which is not broken a hole is bored & it is hung up in some conspicuous place in the dwelling. The 2d night of the Passover they go through the same ceremony as the 1st.

It is usual for them on their festivals & chief sabbaths to go to the synagogue three times a day, but at other times only twice. The passover continues 8 days. The first two & last two, no servile work is done. The four intermediate days **/132/** works of necessity may be done. On the last day of the feast when the time of stars is come they go to synagogue & as soon as this evening service is done the feast is over, & they may eat leaven as usual. [pp. 104–12]

Pentecost &c

6 *Sivan.* (May) *Schabouoth.* The Feast of weeks, also of First Fruits. On this day they believe the law was delivered on Sinai. The synagogues are decorated with choice flowers. The second day each person reads the whole book of Ruth. [p. 112]

9 *Ab.* (July) *On the ninth day of the month* is a strict fast,[1] commemorating the burning of Jerusalem by Nebuchadnezzar (on the same day the second temple was burnt by Titus). On beginning the service, after the evening prayer, the reader in a low mournful voice reads the Book of Lamentations & some other prayers, all expressive of their misfortunes. In the morning & afternoon they go to synagogue again, not putting on veils or frontlets. When the time of stars is come they may break their fast which has lasted from the evening before, not even a drop of fair water being tasted. During the service on the eve of this fast the whole congregation sits on the ground without shoes,

1 Here GE added an asterisk to a footnote: 'called the "black fast"'.

& whereas on other nights they have not less than 300 lights, on this they have not more than 12 distributed here & there. One holds in his hand a slight wax taper & by rotation some chant mournfully different lamentations.

[pp. 114–16]

/133/ Passover Cakes &c

The corn is bought by the elders of every synagogue. They have got stated mills & millers who, though not Jews, follow their prescriptions; two Jews being provided by the rulers of the synagogue to be overlookers. Every year they provide new boulting cloths, as the meal is to be boulted in the presence of these overlookers. To provide for the poorer brethren each of the rulers of the synagogue makes a purchase of large quantities of wheat – eight pounds being calculated for each person. [p. 97]

Redemption of the First born son, when he is a month old by five shekels,[1] if not performed by the Father, must be performed by the son himself when he arrives at age. [p. 123]

Burial

Every synagogue has two Kabronim i.e. societies of Buriers, one for the men, the other for the women. Their business is to watch by the sick, to wash the dead, & dig the grave, & they draw lots which is to serve: they account it the most meritorious of services to serve the dead. The sepulchre is sacred; no corpse or grave is to be disturbed & when space is wanting fresh earth is brought & heaped over the former graves to make a new layer.

In sign of mourning they rend the upper garment a hand's breadth. As soon as the burial is over the *Shivoc* or *seven* days of mourning begin. They sit on the ground barefoot, & are visited by condoling friends. The first meal they eat must not be of their own providing, and is sent by friends.

[pp. 124, 128–32]

1 GE added the equivalent in Sterling currency: 'about 10/6'.

/133v/ Prayers[1]

Of the daily prayers morning, noon & night, the most solemn are those called Kiriath Shema, & Shemoneh Efreh. The first consists in reading Deut. vi, 4–9; xi, 13–21; Numb. xv, 37 to the end of the chapter. Because the first of these passages begins with *Shema, Hear,* all three are called *Kiriath Shema,* the reading of the *Shema.*[2] The *Shemoneh Efreh,* i.e. eighteen prayers, were composed by Ezra & the men of the Great Synagogue. But in the days of Rabbi Gamaliel (a little before the destruction of the second temple), because the heretics had increased, he & his Sanhedrim agreed to compose another prayer for the annihilation of the heretics, & placed it among these eighteen, so that they are in reality nineteen. These to be said thrice a day either in public or private. [pp. 134, 135]

When they say their prayers in the morning they make use of the garment *Talith* with the *Fringes* called Zitzzis /Tzitzith/ & also of the Tephillin or phylacteries. The former is made of two square pieces & two bands which hang over the shoulders, one square piece before, the other behind. At the four corners are fastened the fringes by means of 5 knots, which with the eight threads of the fringes make 13; & the numerical letters of the Hebrew Zitzzis are 600, making 613, exactly the number of precepts contained in the law. This garment is called the 'small veil', & is worn under **/134/** the clothes; the large veil being the fringed garment worn in the synagogue. [pp. 135, 137–9][3]

The name for these is *Talîth,* lesser & greater. The 4 corners are called Arba Canphoth, & this is now the name for the small Talith, the greater only being called Talith. [pp. 346–7]

1 GE added a cross-reference, 'v. 149', to B 148v. See also B 140.

2 The Shema, the prayer of divine unity, begins, 'Hear, O Israel: The Lord our God is one Lord' (Deuteronomy vi, 4), see B 110 and Pf 711 22

3 By way of distinguishing Joseph Kalonymos, who is a 'total stranger', GE has Deronda notice his *talith,* or 'white blue-fringed kind of blanket which is the garment of prayer', as she explains (DD ch. 32: 340, 338). This is a moment of recognition, whose full impact, much delayed, leads to the discovery of Deronda's parentage. Before the reunion of mother and son as 'unknown persons', Deronda attends an evening service in the synagogue at Genoa. There the 'sparse *taliths*' signify to him the exceptional rarity of 'ardent zeal' like his father's amongst Italian Jews whose 'easy familiarity ... might be called Hebrew dyed Italian' (DD ch. 55: 637). GE perhaps knew that the exact colour of the dye required for the sky-blue fringe has been a topic of debate.

The Tephillin are made for the head & arm, & besides the inscription confessing the divine unity, must have the letter Shin, the initial of Shaddai: one of the incommunicable names on one side in relievo, in the other in sunken letters. These are to be put on at least once – in the morning when saying the *Shema.* Maimonides gives strict directions in his Hilcott Tephillin. The afternoon prayers, called Mincha Kytone, little mincha, begin from ½ past 3 to sundown, or if on Friday the 14th Nisan from ½ past 12 till ½ past 3. Mincha Gedoulah i.e. Great Mincha – the time of beginning having relation to the time of evening sacrifice. [pp. 140–4]

The Mezuzza is placed over every door. It consists of the *shema* written on vellum, with Shaddai also inscribed. This is rolled up & put in a leaden cylinder & placed over the door, with nails. [pp. 151–2][1]

Marriage & Funerals

Every Jew is obliged to marry. The proper age is eighteen. A man who lives single till he is twenty is looked on as a profligate unless he can make it appear that he cannot find a wife to suit his disposition. Marriage is valid, though not approved, if it consist merely in a statement in the presence of others, 'with this ring I wed thee.' The betrothal is public, usually 6 months before marriage. At the wedding, the velvet canopy or Chuppah is held over the bride & bridegroon, she being veiled. The Rabbi or Reader takes a glass of **/134v/** wine in his hand before beginning the service – this the bride & bridegroom drink of before the latter makes his declaration & puts the ring on her finger. The marriage contract is read. Then the reader drinks a glass of wine, & after a prayer the bride & bridegroom again taste the wine, the glass is laid on the ground & the bridegroom stamps on it – as a reminder of the fragility of mortal things (said otherwise to be in memory of the destruction of the Temple). [pp. 156–61][2]

1 The young Leonora Charisi bore a particular resentment for the mezuza and tephillin, inscribed with the *shema* and *Shaddai*:

> 'I was to feel everything I did not feel, and believe everything I did not believe. I was to feel awe for the bit of parchment in the *mezuza* over the door; to dread lest a bit of butter should touch a bit of meat; to think it beautiful that men should bind the *tephillin* on them, and women not, – ... I was to love the long prayers in the ugly synagogue, and the howling, and the gabbling, and the dreadful fasts, and the tiresome feasts ...' (DD ch. 51: 587)

2 Compare B 123 and Pf 711 53. In DD ch. 66, Lapidoth exploits the sentimental associations of the Chuppah (723).

Giving *Chalitsa*, is giving a brother's wife leave to marry again. The *ghet* or writing of divorcement can (or could before the Jews were included in the national marriage laws of the country in which they are resident) be delivered by a messenger. [pp. 163, 165]

A death is announced in two ways – one, by the clerk in the synagogue with a loud voice mentioning the name, the spot where the corpse lies & the place of interment. The other by one of the synagogue going to a place of resort & shaking a copper money-box, with a niche in it – shaped like a half-gallon cask. The Jews flock round, make inquiries, & drop in what sum they please. This is always done unless the departed be an illegitimate child, a person of impure life, or one grossly negligent of Jewish forms. It is an extreme opprobrium, sometimes flung out in quarrels, 'When your great grandfather or fourth cousin died, no box was carried round for him.'

Women hardly ever attend funerals. They sit on the floor & mourn for seven days. The light placed beside the corpse is kept in **/135/** for seven days, Aaron having been mourned for that time. It is called the light of the departed spirit, & its dimness or clearness is an augury. Every morning the water & napkins must be changed under the idea that the spirit comes & purifies himself with them. Every anniversary a light must burn in the same way for 24 hours; a fast must also be kept & the synagogue visited night & morning to say Kaddish on its behalf. [pp. 169–70][1]

'Ceremonies, customs, rites, & traditions of the Jews'
by Hyam Isaacs, a converted Jew

This writer, who gives the address, Cowick Street, Exeter, seems in spite of his conversion still to love the Jews better than the Xtians. Unhappily there is no date to the book, but he speaks of Hirschell, the predecessor of Adler, as the Chief Rabbi.[2]

1 GE first wrote '*Kodesh* (prayers)', but later crossed this out and wrote 'Kaddish' above.
2 Solomon Herschell or Hirschel, Chief Rabbi in London from 1802 to 1842, is mentioned by Isaacs on p. 92.

Kaddish

If a Jew or Jewess has no children, or if single, adopted children are provided for, or a society is joined, in order that when they die *Kaddish* may be said for them.[1] Kaddish is said by children for parents, but not by parents for children. When the soul leaves the body, it enters purgatory. As soon as the body is laid in the grave & covered over, the angel wakes it up & so long as the soul is in purgatory, so long does the body remain alive in the grave & feel the gnawing of the worms – the period being long or short according to the sins committed. Kaddish [is said] **/135v/** for eleven years.[2] Every time it is said, the departed soul for whom it is uttered rises one degree out of purgatory, & when the torment is ended, the soul lies dormant for a time.

[pp. 255–6]

The Rabbis resident in Jerusalem are supported by a collection in every synagogue at *Purim*: a bowl is placed on the desk & those who think proper cast in 4d ¼ = a shekel of Jerusalem. This money is then remitted. Collectors come making a tour to the various parts of the world where there are synagogues, & to every one of these they consign a certain quantity of Jerusalem earth. When a Jew dies as much of this earth as will lie on a shilling is placed on each eye. (Some is placed under his head as a pillow.)[3]

[pp. 260–1]

1 Mirah, acknowledging that her mother may be dead, says,

> 'If she were, I should long to know ... whether my brother lives to say Kaddish in memory of her.' (DD ch. 32: 342)

Throughout this note, GE later replaced her original *Kodesh* with *Kaddish*. At the end of B 135, 'Kodesh is a prayer' is crossed out and replaced with only 'Kaddish' above the line.

2 GE changed 'eleven months' to 'eleven years'. Compare the notes on B 119 and Pf 710 23. In the first edition of DD, Deronda's mother asks, 'Is any harm come to [her first husband] because the eleven years went by with no wretched *Kaddish* said for him?' (DD ch. 53: 618). Joseph Jacobs was one of the Jews who pointed out that 'the Kaddish, the prayer in honour of the dead, is only said for eleven months, not eleven years ... and then only by a son'. See 'Mordecai: A Protest against the Critics', in *Macmillan's Magazine* (June 1877), reprinted in *Jewish Ideals and Other Essays* (London: David Nutt, 1896), pp. 64–5. In the second edition GE altered the words to 'Will any harm come to me because I broke his trust in the daylight after he was gone into darkness?' (DD ch. 53: 618n).

3 GE's source for her parenthetical note has not been traced.

Story of the *Shameer* or insect which God created to cut the law in stone, & to cut the stones out of the quarry for the building of the temple, & which Satan was obliged to produce from its hiding-place under the throne of God, at Solomon's commmand. [pp. 286–7]

v. Levy. (According to another legend Schamir is a stone.)[1]

There is a belief that the 10 tribes exist in a body & perform the ceremonies, in a city with walls so high they cannot see the summit of them – surrounded by the river Sambadion. [p. 291][2]

Connected with a fiction due to Eldad the Danite in the 9th century, Sefer-ha-Dani – a book welcomed by the suffering Jews as giving them a consolatory sense of brethren in security.
(The pendant to Prester John & his realm)[3]

Story told of Elijah & a rabbi his companion in pilgrimage – the original of 'Zadig'. Hyam Isaacs [pp. 359–65][4]

1 The note 'v. Levy' was added later. Giuseppi Raffaele Levi, *Parabeln, Legenden und Gedanken aus Thalmud und Midrasch,* translated into German by Ludwig Seligmann (Leipzig, 1863), includes the legend of the Schamir on p. 86. For other notes from Levi, see B 158 and 159, and Pf 707 28, 29, and 32. The note in parenthesis was added still later. For other legends on the Schamir, see Sabine Baring-Gould, *Legends of Old Testament Characters from the Talmud and Other Sources,* 2 vols. (London: Macmillan, 1871), II, 184–5. For other notes from Baring-Gould, see B 183v, Pf 710 14 and 20, and Pf 711 92a and 93a.

2 In DD ch. 32, Mirah's imagery is suggestive of Sambadion:

> 'I thought none but our people would feel that. I thought it was all shut away like a river in a deep valley, where only heaven saw – I mean –' she hesitated, feeling that she could not disentangle her thought from its imagery. (346)

3 The source may be Graetz 5, 256–7; he does not give the name Sefer-ha-Dani. GE added this note later as a footnote and contributed the reference to Prester John. For her note on Prester John, see Pf 707 39–40.

4 The moral of the story of Elijah and Rabbi Benjamin is, 'Whatever happens is for the best, according to God's decree.' Voltaire's *Zadig, ou la Destinée* (1748) records a philosophical response to comparable vicissitudes. The comparison is suggested by Baring-Gould, II, 117: 'Voltaire has taken this legend [of Moses and El Khoudr] as the basis of his story of Zadig.' According to Baring-Gould, 'El Khoudr, identified by the Jews with Elias, is the original of the Wandering Jew' (II, 115).

Kabbalah (from Salomon Maimon's *Life)*

B 136

The source of the following notes on the Kabbalah and its basic text, the Zohar, is the very book which turns up in Mr Ram's second-hand bookshop in DD ch. 33: 'that wonderful bit of autobiography, the life of the Polish Jew, Salomon Maimon' (356). GE's heavily annotated copy is in DWL: *Salomon Maimons Lebensgeschichte von ihm selbst geschrieben*, edited by K. P. Moritz (Berlin: Friedrich Vieweg, 1792). It too was purchased second-hand, perhaps by GHL; he was familiar with Maimon as a philosopher whose critique of Kant influenced post-Kantian thinkers. According to his diary, he read 'Maimon's Leben' and 'Finished Maimon's Leben' on 6 and 7 November 1871. GE's note on 'Talmudic Questions' from 'Salomon Maimon's Life', on Folger 13 123, also dates from November 1871. On 10 July 1874, GHL 'looked into Maimon Erkenntnissvermögen' but his diaries do not mention Maimon's *Life* again.

Nevertheless, GE must have reread it when her preparatory studies for her novel were under way; her marginal annotations, often challenging Maimon's assertions, indicate her familiarity with more authoritative and scholarly sources. She corrects his errors of chronology: 'Sabbatai Zewi lived long after the production of the Sohar. He was a contemporary of Spinoza' (p. 215). Or she comments on his presumption: 'But this is simply what the Cabbala teaches – not his [Maimon's] own ingenious explanation' (p. 40). This is the only text to which she adds a prefatory warning on the first page: 'This Book might mislead many readers, not acquainted with other parts of Jewish History'.

The Kabbalistic material incorporated into *Daniel Deronda* is drawn, not from Maimon, but from Christian David Ginsburg's *Kabbalah* (1863); see GE's extensive notes on Pf 707 17 to 25. One may wonder why, then, Deronda in the East End bookshop makes the rather unlikely discovery of Maimon, rather than Ginsburg's *Kabbalah*. The answer to this (rather Talmudically hypothetical) question lies in the occult significance of Maimon's *Life* in GE's narrative of Deronda's life.

Salomon Maimon was, like Hyam Isaacs, an apostate from the Jewish faith; unlike Isaacs, however, he retained no affectionate remembrance of the customs of his people. In J. Clark Murray's preface to his translation, *Solomon Maimon: An Autobiography* (London: Alexander Gardner, 1888), Maimon's alienation is treated as a form of objectivity:

> the sketches, which this book contains, of Jewish speculation and life were made at a time when the author had severed all vital connection with his own people and creed; and they are therefore drawn from a point of view outside of Jewish prejudices. (p. xii)

In view of GE's marginal corrections of the many misleading tendencies and outright errors in Maimon's representations of Jewish life, however, Maimon appears to be an unreliable, rather than an unprejudiced, witness. His having 'severed all vital connection with his own people and creed' is the link between Maimon and two separatists in her novel: Daniel's mother, Leonora Charisi, and Mordecai's and Mirah's father, Lapidoth.

The *Bildungsroman* elements of Maimon's autobiography include an episode of influential friendship not approved by his family. The title of Maimon's Chapter 27, devoted to this episode, might also apply to the chapter of 'Freundschaft und Schwärmerei' opened by Deronda's purchase of Maimon's book, for a half-crown, from Mordecai. In the friendship between Deronda and Mordecai, 'Schwärmerei' would be translated as 'enthusiasm'; Maimon's friendship, in contrast, inclines more towards the alternative translation of 'revelry, riotous behaviour'.

Maimon and his 'Busenfreund' stroll on the wall round their town, during the usual hours of prayer: given the Sabbath prohibitions against travel (see B125v), their perambulation is a clearly symbolic representation of their desire to break the bounds of their Jewish community. Conscious of their difference from 'the common herd, upon whom [they look] down with a sort of noble pride and contempt' (Murray, p. 139), they are like the Princess Halm-Eberstein, née Leonora Charisi, who has also not felt 'like a brute, obliged to go with [her] own herd'. Having heard more than enough about 'Our People', she has gone her own way (DD ch. 51: 592, 587). But can she ultimately escape being a Jewish daughter, or even a Jewish mother? Maimon's book is an account of how and why he severed his affiliation with Polish Jewry; yet he is still, after all, in GE's carefully worded identification, 'the Polish Jew, Salomon Maimon'.

GE has marked with a marginal '+' a paragraph in which Maimon ruefully contemplates his own and his friend's idleness. Is their so-called 'contemplative life' really superior to the occupations they find contemptible?

Denouncing 'the vanity of all things', do they nevertheless secretly hanker after things they cannot purchase?

> In conversations of this kind we two cynics spent our pleasantest hours, while we made ourselves merry sometimes at the expense of the world, sometimes at our own. (Murray, pp. 139 and 142–3)

This youthful friendship, although it soon lapses, confirms Maimon in a course of life that ends in selfish indolence and alcoholism.[1]

The mocking spirit of Maimon and his friend is echoed in that of Mirah's father. As she recalls,

> 'He would even ridicule our own people ... imitating their movements and their tones in praying, only to make others laugh ... I said, "Father, you ought not to mimic our own people before Christians who mock them ..."' (DD ch. 20: 200)

As Mirah perceives, such mimicry only reinforces his audience's identification of Lapidoth as 'one of those clever Jews'. His mocking separation of himself from 'those' Jews is imperceptible to a non-Jewish audience (DD ch. 20: 199).

Lapidoth / Cohen, Deronda / Charisi: Daniel learns that Jewish surnames are not reliable identifiers, for, as his mother comments, 'the Jews have always been changing their names'; one surname is 'as real as another' (DD ch. 51: 594). GE's readers never learn whether Daniel reads in his copy of Salomon Maimon's Life as far as the opening sentence of Chapter 27, 'Freundschaft und Schwärmerei': 'Ich hatte in meinem Wohnorte einem Busenfreund, mit Nahmen Moses Lapidoth' (p. 194). The book is not mentioned again after its epoch-making purchase; the coincidence that Maimon's bosom friend shares the surname adopted by Mirah's and Mordecai's father is never revealed to the reader of *Daniel Deronda.* After all, the occult significance lies not in Lapidoth's name, but in the pattern of Maimon's life story. Maimon may be a misleading witness about some aspects of Jewish history, but he is a quite exemplary source concerning the experience of breaking one's affiliation with Jewish customs, rites, and traditions, or prejudices.

In such a severance of 'all vital connection' with one's people or creed, it is sometimes difficult to distinguish between the pressure of external circumstances and the force of individual difference, or genius – or to

1 Murray, p. x.

distinguish between the insufficiency of the discarded creed and the maladaptation of the individual misfit. Here the life history of George Eliot, née Mary Anne Evans, intersects with the matter of her novel.

Her own rejection of 'the system of [Christian] doctrines' – as distinct from 'the moral teachings of Jesus himself'– put her, in her own mind, 'in unison with some of the finest minds of Christendom'; yet in order to compel her apparent conformity to orthodox views, heavy social pressure had been brought to bear upon her, including the threatened expulsion from her father's house (Haight, pp. 38–44). Her own 'Holy War', as Haight calls it, ended in a face-saving compromise. In her later reading about the Jewish excommunication ceremony, in which the *Shofar* is blown, she could see uncompromising principles result in ignominy – in the case of the expulsion of Spinoza – or farce. Heine's story about Salomon Maimon heightens the ridiculousness of a confrontation that might have been perceived as tragic:

> ... the rabbi of Altona once sought to lead this disciple of Kant back to the old faith; when Maimon obstinately insisted on his philosophical heresies, the rabbi resorted to threats and showed him the shofar, saying in gloomy tones: 'Do you know what this is?' When the disciple of Kant calmly answered: 'It is the horn of a ram,' the rabbi was so horrified that he fell over backwards.[1]

GE would have known that Salomon Maimon's own surname was adopted by him, as a tribute to Moses Maimon, or Maimonides (see B 112, 112v, 168, 193). The Maimon he honoured was the author whose books were deemed heretical by his fellow Jews and were burned publicly in Paris in 1233.

A brief essay by Israel Abrahams on 'George Eliot and Solomon Maimon' provides an informed summary of GE's annotations to her copy of Maimon's autobiography.[2] Abrahams also declares his pleasure in finding 'a fresh confirmation, that George Eliot's favorable impression of Judaism was based on a very adequate acquaintance with its history' (p. 246).

---

1 Translation by S. S. Prawer, in *Heine's Jewish Comedy,* p. 248.

2 See his *Book of Delight and Other Papers* (Philadelphia: Jewish Publication Society of America, 1912), pp. 242–6 and 310–11.

Kabbalah (from Salomon Maimon's *Life*) B 136

/136/ The Kabbala

The Kabbala is understood to have been delivered to Moses on the Mount, over & above the oral law. 'Das Hauptwerk um daraus die Kabbala zu studiren, ist der Sohar, der in einem sehr erhabenen Stil in syrischer (?) Sprache geschrieben ist. Alle andere kabbalistiche Schriften sind bloss als Kommentare oder Auszüge desselben zu betrachten.' (Maimoun) [p. 128][1]

The Zohar is in the form of a midrasch to the Pentateuch; probably the work of Moses de Leon; at any rate of some 13th century erudite. It was 80 years from the rise of the Kabbala to the production of the Sohar. It was according to the Sohar that the Polish Jews expected the Messiah, 1648.

[Graetz 7, 220 and 10, 209][2]

'Diese wird in *theoretische* und *praktische* getheilt. *Jene* begreift in sich die Lehre von Gott, seinen Eigenschaften, die durch seine mannigfaltigen Nahmen ausgedrückt werden, die Entstehung der Welt durch eine stufenweise Einschränkung seiner unendlichen Vollkommenheit, und das Verhältniss aller Dinge zu seinem höchsten Wesen. *Diese* ist die Lehre, durch die mannigfaltigen Nahmen Gottes die besondere Wirkungsarten und Beziehungen auf die Gegenstände der Natur vorstellen, nach Belieben auf sie zu wirken. Diese heiligen Nahmen werden, nicht als bloss willkürliche, sondern als *natürliche* Zeichen betrachtet, so dass alles was mit diesen Zeichen vorgenommen wird, auf die Gegenstände selbst, die sie vorstellen, Einfluss haben muss.' (Maimon) [pp. 126–7][3]

1 Translation:

> The principal work for the study of the Cabbalah is the *Zohar*, which is written in a very lofty style in the Syrian language. All other Cabbalistic writings are to be regarded as merely commentaries on this, or extracts from it. (Murray, p. 95)

2 This correction of Maimon's account was added later at the foot of the page.

3 Translation:

> This is divided into *theoretical* and *practical* Cabbalah. The former comprehends the doctrines of God, of His attributes which are expressed by means of His manifold names, of the origin of the world through a gradual limitation of His infinite perfection, and of the relation of all things to His supreme essence. The latter is the doctrine which teaches how to work upon nature at pleasure by means of those manifold names of God, which represent various modes of working upon, and relations to, natural objects. These sacred names are regarded, not as merely arbitrary, but as *natural* signs, so that all that is done with these signs must have an influence on the objects which they represent. (Murray, pp. 94–5)

German Jews in the Middle Ages

B 137, 138

'Aus dem inneren Leben der deutschen Juden im Mittelalter, Dr. A. Berliner' is one of several 'Books retained from T[rübner]' listed on Pf 711 114. GE's annotated copy of Abraham Adolf Berliner's work (Berlin: Julius Benzian, 1871) is in DWL. Her marginal comments – 'Honeyed teaching' on p. 4 and 'Sacredness of Education' on p. 5 – express the essence of her note on the child's introduction to primary schooling (B 137). Deronda, who goes to Eton as 'a gentleman's son must do' (DD ch. 16: 157), misses the sweetness of this fatherly introduction to learning. His father died when he was much too young to be carried to school in his father's mantle. But in retrospect, readers may realize that his 'dim sense of having been kissed very much, and surrounded by thin, cloudy, scented drapery, till his fingers caught in something hard, which hurt him, and he began to cry' must be a pre-verbal memory of his *father* – Talith, Tephillin, scent, and parental affection – rather than his mother, as he supposes (DD ch. 16: 150).

His mother's side of the story is revealed in the next page of notes (B 138), concerning the restriction of intellectual education to boys only. The Torah or 'doctrine' is a man's occupation; women are 'to sew, spin, knit'. This persistence of mediaeval ideas about women is disabling, and might even impair the survival of the Jewish faith. If a woman's prayers, as the elder Rabbis say, have 'no effect either for evil or for good', the piety of a woman like Mirah's mother would seem to be nullified. GE's novel, however, revises this view, so that Mrs Cohen's prayers are shown to be not utterly futile: 'What was prayed for has come to pass: Mirah has been delivered from evil' (DD ch. 46: 531). The recurrent visions of her mother, which comfort and sustain the lost daughter, seem to prove that women's prayers may indeed have some efficacy (DD ch. 20: 194–6). Furthermore, as Mirah says, it is the religious observances of a *Jewess* that effect the closer companionship between mother and daughter, despite their separation:

> 'But because my mother used to take me to the synagogue, and I remembered sitting on her knee and looking through the railing and hearing the chanting and singing, I longed to go ... our landlady was a

> Jewess and observed her religion. I asked her to take me with her to the synagogue; and I read in her prayer-books and Bible, and ... asked her to buy me books of my own, for these books seemed a closer companionship with my mother: I knew that she must have looked at the very words and said them.' (DD ch. 20: 197–8)

Thus the written word provides for Mirah, as for Deronda, filial links with a previous generation.

For other Jewish daughters, however, the limits placed upon women are intolerable. Their place is at home, in the kitchen. They are 'to dread lest a bit of butter should touch a bit of meat; to think it beautiful that men should bind the *tephillin* on them, and women not' (DD ch. 51: 587). GE's marginal note on p. 7 of her copy of Berliner underlines this division: 'What is good for boys / what for girls'. Trouble will inevitably arise when a daughter refuses to be a 'good' girl; but in GE's novel the source of this trouble is the father's need for a *son* to carry on his work – even though he may be a scholar rather than a Dombey. The crux of the conflict between Daniel Charisi, 'a learned man', and his only child, is the traditional exemption of Jewish women from 'doctrine' or the study of the Torah. As his daughter recalls,

> 'I was to be what he called "the Jewish woman" under pain of his curse ...To have a pattern cut out – "this is the Jewish woman; this is what you must be ..." That was what my father wanted. He wished I had been a son ...' (DD ch. 51: 587, 588–9)

The last sentence tells what he really wanted. For him, a daughter's learning has no meaning. When his wife's sister teaches his daughter music and singing, he thinks nothing of it (DD ch. 51: 590).

GE's notes on B 138 give evidence for an alternate tradition, which encouraged learning for Jewish women. In the fifteenth century, Miriam, wife of Jochanan Luria, was a learned teacher of the Talmud. The two grandmothers of Ludwig Kalisch illustrate complementary forms of learning: one was literate in Hebrew, the other knew a wealth of Haggadic and other oral lore. Other Jewesses have headed great financial enterprises. GE's heading for this page was first 'Instructed women among the Jews'; as an afterthought she inserted 'Uninstructed & '. The alternate, learned, tradition for Jewish women is excluded from her novel; amongst the Jewish women she shows a single apostate rebel and others who are content with domestic roles.

It is, however, possible that GE planted an allusion for the few amongst her readers who were sufficiently familiar with scriptural texts to appreciate her hidden irony. Lapidoth is not the best-known of biblical characters, but his name is mentioned once, as the husband of one of the most powerful (and undomestic) of Jewish women:

> And Deborah, a prophetess, the wife of Lapidoth, she judged Israel at that time.
> And she dwelt under the palm tree of Deborah ... and the children of Israel came up to her for judgement.

Calling the Israelites to battle, she tells Barak that Sisera and his army will be delivered into his hand, or, more precisely, 'into the hand of a woman' (Judges iv, 4–9).

GE's second source for notes on these pages is a memoir by Ludwig Kalisch, *Bilder aus meiner Knabenzeit* (Leipzig: Ernst Keil, 1872), which she read from 4 to 7 August 1875 (GHL Diary). Her notes from Kalisch are brief and tend to be added later to notes from other sources; see B 121. In the margin of Maimon's account of his schooldays, she adds a corrective reference on p. 45 to 'Kalisch', that is, to his description of his own schooling.

/137/ Education of German Jews 'im Mittelalter'

Usually at the fifth year the regular schooling begins. At the Feast of Weeks, the little one was brought at daybreak into the Synagogue or to the Teacher's house. On the way thither the Father covered him with his mantle. The Teacher took him on his arm, & showed him a tablet of parchment or wood on which the Hebrew alphabet, each 4 letters combined in a word, together with Deut. 33, 4 & Lev. 1, 1 & the words 'Die Lehre sei meine Beschäftigung' were inscribed. The alphabet & the texts are repeated to the child backwards & forwards, whereupon the letters are smeared with honey for him to lick off them. Then there is a sweet cake inscribed with texts & an Egg covered with 8 verses from the 119 Psalm.[1] These all are read to the child; & there is a

1 The texts of the inscriptions are 'Moses commanded us a law, even the inheritance of the congregation of Jacob' (Deuteronomy xxxiii, 4); 'And the Lord called unto Moses, and spake unto him out of the tabernacle of the congregation, saying ...' (Leviticus i, 1); 'Let the Torah [the teaching] be my occupation.' Psalm 119 is composed of 22 sections, headed by the letters of the Hebrew alphabet (Aleph, Beth, Gimel, etc.); each section has eight verses.

cabbalistic conjuration of the spirit that protects against forgetfulness; whereupon the cake & egg are shared among the little scholars present. After this solemnization of the entrance into school the child was taken to the water as a symbol of the Divine doctrine, the source of all knowledge. To further the education of the young was held more meritorious than to maintain the synagogue. The slip of wood which was used in pointing to the alphabet was not to be used for profane purposes, e.g. as a tooth-pick. 'Even when the building of the temple is in question,' says the Talmud, 'there must be no less strict attendance of school.' [pp. 3–5]

(See in Kalisch, Bilder aus meiner Knabenzeit, a description of the first school.) [pp. 17–70]

/138/ Uninstructed & Instructed women among the Jews

'Mirjam, die Tochter des Salomo Spiro, Gattin des Jochanan Loria, trug mehrere Jahre hindurch, hinter einem Gitter sitzend, der studirenden Jugend Talmud vor.' 'Ueber die Vorsängerin Urania in Worms', vide Lewysohn, Epitaphien, p. 85[1] v. also, for women, Steinschneider, hebr. Bibliographie; Karpeles, die Frauen der jüdischen Literatur; Weinhold, die Frauen in dem deutschen Mittelalter[2]

It is characteristic that on a flyleaf of an old book after the record of the boys' birthdays, follows the wish: God grant, that I may bring them up for doctrine, marriage & good deeds. But after the girls': God grant that I may bring them up to sew, spin, knit – & to doing good deeds. Nevertheless there were Jewesses, heads of great banking-houses. [p. 7]

1 Translation: 'For several years, Miriam, the daughter of Salomo Spiro and wife of Jochanan Loria, sitting behind a lattice, lectured on the Talmud to young students.' Salomon Spiro was a Rabbi in Worms, c. 1500. For 'On Urania, the leader of the choir in Worms', Berliner cites Ludwig Lewysohn, *Sechzig Epitaphien von Grabsteinen des israelitischen Friedhofes zu Worms* (Frankfurt: J. Baer, 1855). This and the following notes are from Berliner's endnotes on p. 51, referring to his text on p. 6. There is no evidence that GE read the works listed here.

2 Moritz Steinschneider, *Catalogus Librorum Hebraeorum in Bibliotheca Bodleiana* (Berolini: Friedlaender, 1852–60); Gustav Karpeles, *Die Frauen der jüdischen Literatur* (Berlin, 1871); and Karl Weinhold, *Die deutschen Frauen in dem Mittelalter* (Vienna: C. Gerold, 1851).

German Jews in the Middle Ages B 138

Kalisch gives an account of his two grandmothers: the one who knew & wrote Hebrew well, the other who was full of legends & sayings. [pp. 147, 171, 179]

The elder Rabbis enjoined a daily thanksgiving to be uttered by every man, that God had not made him a woman!

This is part of the Liturgy.[1]

When a woman prays, say the Rabbis, it has no effect either for evil or for good.[2]

1 Precise source untraced. This seems to be GE's first acquaintance with this negative thanksgiving, part of the prayers for which the Jewish man binds on the *tephillin*. As her later note indicates, it is also part of the liturgy. For the liturgical form, see B 188v; see also B 184, where GE at first inadvertently omitted the essential 'not'.

In the first and second edition of DD, Ezra Cohen explains, 'A man is bound to thank God, as we do every Sabbath, that he was not made a woman' (46: 535). But as this note indicates, thanks are due daily. David Kaufmann pointed out this mistake in *George Eliot and Judaism*, translated by John W. Ferrier (Edinburgh: Blackwood, 1877), p. 83; GE's annotated copy is in DWL. She therefore altered the text of the 1878 Cabinet Edition to read:

> 'A Jewish man is bound to thank God, day by day, that he was not made a woman; but a woman has to thank God that He has made her according to His will.'
>
> (III, 46)

2 This note, added later, repeats that on Pf 711 55. Source: Isaacs, *Ceremonies, Customs, Rites, and Traditions of the Jews,* p. 39. For other notes from Isaacs, see B 129v to 135v.

Extracts from Abraham Geiger

B 136v, 137v, 138v, 139

Abraham Geiger's summation of the Reform view of Jewish history, *Das Judenthum und seine Geschichte* (Breslau: H. Skutsch, 1865–71), is included twice in a book list on Pf 710 1: first as 'Abr. Geiger's Gesch. des Judenthums', and later as 'A. Geiger, Das Judenthum u. seine Geschichte, 1864 & 5'. GE's source for the notes below and on Pf 711 56 to 59, however, is the translation by Maurice Mayer, *Judaism and its History* (New York: Thalmessinger, 1865), distributed in London by Trübner. Mayer's translation includes an appendix which had particular interest for the English translator of David Friedrich Strauss's *Leben Jesu.* In 1846 her anonymous translation, *The Life of Jesus, Critically Examined,* had been published by Chapman. Almost thirty years later, she could read, in translation, Geiger's opening paragraph on 'Renan and Strauss':

> Nearly thirty years ago, Strauss performed the great deed of writing a critical work on the Life of Jesus, and showed that the records of this Life, being contradictory in themselves and in conflict with each other, contained no real history, but merely myths sprung into existence among the first Christian Congregation with regard to the person of Jesus; but that these very myths resulted from the Messianic belief, and were based upon expectations which were brought into connection with the coming Messiah, or with events in the lives of other divine men, which were either distinctly foretold in the Bible or interpreted into it. And all that remained as truly historical was very doubtful, except the existence of the person himself. (p. 299)

In this appendix, Geiger is concerned with Christianity's 'Ignorance of Judaism' (pp. 333–43), especially its ignorance of the Jewish Messianic tradition, from which, in his view, Christianity is one form of evolutionary development. This appendix is the source of GE's notes about Eisenmenger's citations from 'an addle-brained cabbalist, Ruben Hoeske' (B 149v, Pf 711 57, and Pf 710 39). Strauss's uncritical use of Eisenmenger, according to Geiger, is one of the forms of ignorance which 'betray the sad relapse of the historian into the character of a prejudiced apologist' (p. 341).

Critical as Geiger is of the sad relapses of Strauss and other historians of 'the so-called *Tuebingen School*', his purpose is not unlike theirs: in his view, modern Judaism, like early Christianity, must also be an evolutionary development from Orthodox Rabbinical traditions. His 'life-long conviction was that *Wissenschaft* would enable Judaism to reshape its theology on an orderly, scientific basis'.[1] In tracing the process of historical evolution in Judaism, the historian plays a critical role: the public lectures comprising *Judaism and its History* were meant to inform and reform contemporary Jewish history.

GE's 'Miscellaneous Notes' on B 136v are copied from a larger miscellany; see the 'Notes from Abraham Geiger and others' section (Pf 711 53 to 61, especially Pf 711 54 to 59). Geiger's reference to the Septuagint, the first instance in history of the translation of a book, is relevant to his programme of Reform. Controversies over translations of the prayer books and the role of Hebrew in the liturgy were central topics in the Reform conferences of the 1840s in Brunswick and Breslau, in which Geiger was a leading figure. Here he cites a significant precedent for use of the vernacular – the translation, circa 250 BCE, of the holy scriptures into Greek, for the benefit of the many non-Hebrew-speaking Jews and converts to Judaism in Egypt and Greece.

In the Reform context, GE's extended note about the isolated sect of Judaism in Samaria, which history has passed by, has a certain poignancy (B 138v). On B 193v and Pf 711 59, she repeats notes about 'races looking forward to annihilation – the remaining one hundred families of the Samaritans'. Although the heathen philosophers of Harran were also doomed to extinction, they at least left to their successors the fruits of their scientific, engineering, medical, and philosophical studies (B 139).

The blank space on B 137v is partly filled by a reference to *Sippurim*, a repetition of a note on Pf 711 68. '*Sippurim*' is included in a list of 'Books retained from T[rübner]' on Pf 711 114. GE's copy of the third volume of the collection edited by Wolf Pascheles, *Sippurim, eine Sammlung jüdischer Volkssagen, Erzählungen, Mythen, Chroniken, Denkwürdigkeiten und Biographien berühmter Juden aller Jahrhunderte, insbesondere des Mittelalters* (Prague: Pascheles, 1854), is in DWL. There is a marginal check mark beside the title of this story by M. Jastrow, 'Der Besuch in der Synagoge'

1 David J. Goldberg and John D. Rayner, *The Jewish People. Their History and Their Religion* (London: Penguin, 1989), p. 148.

('The Visitor in the Synagogue'). On B 130v, GE has a note about the custom of wearing shrouds at the Yom Kippur service:

> It is awful & grand to see the reader & the chief Rabbi & many of the congregation in prayer upwards of three hours clad with a shroud in which they are to be buried.

In DD ch. 46, Mordecai makes an indirect allusion to this custom:

> 'But now I am as one who had clad himself beforehand in his shroud, and used himself to making the grave his bed, and the divine command sounded in his ears, "Arise, and go forth; the night is not yet come."'[1]

/136v/ Miscellaneous Notes

Relic said to have been carried away with them by the Jews when they were driven out of Ratisbon in 1519: Part of the stone tables which Moses threw down & broke. [Pf711 54][2]

Savasorda, a mathematician = Abraham b. Chija, a Spaniard who lived in Provence. He was surnamed Zahib Alshorta, meaning 'Chief of the Police', as a large landed proprietor was then named, or as we should say, Nassi, in Hebrew. By his name Savasorda he is known through the Middle Ages. He would perhaps not have been mentioned so often, says A. Geiger, if it had been known he was a Jew. [p. 290; B 194; Pf711 56–57]

The Septuagint, Geiger says, was the first instance in history of the translation of a book. [p. 146; Pf711 57]

1 This passage is quoted here from the Cabinet Edition, III, 47. In the Clarendon edition, 'making' is altered to 'make', without an editorial explanation (536). For references to the custom of travelling with one's shroud, see the footnote for the passage on B 130v.

2 Source not traced.

Extracts from Abraham Geiger B 137v 138v

/137v/

Steinschneider, 'Volksliteratur der Juden'[1]

Iom Kippur. The dead for whom the lights are burning appearing in the Synagogue in their shrouds: the living also wearing shrouds. The Rabbi orders all to lay off their shrouds. The dead do not obey – & thus he recognizes them.
v. *Sippurim* [pp. 173–5; Pf 711 68]

/138v/ Samaria

The Kingdom of Israel was destroyed by the Assyrians & its inhabitants carried into captivity; a portion however remained in their native country. These were joined by a class of settlers sent thither by the conqueror. And here intellectual culture proved its power; the conquerors yielded to the spirit of the conquered, & became Israelites – Ephraimites. Henceforth they took their name from *Shomron,* the ancient capital of the Kingdom, & called themselves Shomronites, Samaritans. They had only the law of Moses, & had kept off with jealousy & hostility the prophets of Judah. They clung with tenacity to their ancient Holy places. Sichem continued to be their holy city; Mount Garizim, at the foot of which Sichem is situated, was venerated as the place of revelation; there to offer their sacrifices was regarded by them as an act of the loftiest piety. The Samaritans of later times adopted many parts of the Jewish Doctrine – but very partially so as not to endanger their own peculiarities. They remained a sickly religious community. Through all changes they clung to their native city: there they live even to this day, dwindled down to about 100 families – & there they look forward to annihilation. (Geiger) [pp. 120–4]

1 Moritz Steinschneider, *Ueber die Volksliteratur der Juden* (Berlin, 1870). This twenty-one-page work is bound with other short publications in a one-volume 'Steinschneider Collected Works' now in the Mocatta Library, University College, London. There is no evidence that GE read this work.

/139/ *Harran*

Even in the 9th century the dispersed philosophers, who had saved themselves in the East, the Harranenses, asserted with full self-consciousness, that they stood far higher than the Christians. *Thabet ben Koran*, a Harranensian Syrian heathen – for even into the 10th century philosophical Hellenism had preserved its existence in those regions, until the combined fury of Xtianity & Mohammedanism succeeded in destroying also those small remnants – Thabet ben Koran says, in one of his writings: 'When many were subjugated by violence under the new error, our fathers persevered with the help of God, & escaped through their heroism, & this blessed city (Harran) has never been defiled by the errors of Nazareth. We indeed are the heirs & devisees of heathenism which shone so brilliantly in this world. Happy is he who, with unshaken trust, endures sufferings for the sake of heathenism. Pray, who rendered the world inhabitable – who converted the cities into places of abode for families – who else than the nobles & kings of heathenism? Who builded havens, made rivers navigable, who unlocked hidden sciences? Only the renowned among the heathen have fathomed this, have caused healing to shine forth unto the souls, shown the means for their redemption, have also discovered & taught the healing of the flesh; they alone have filled the world with well-ordered morals, with wisdom, which is the fountain-head of excellency. Without these fruits of heathenism the world would be void, poor, clad in deficiency & barrenness.'

(Geiger) [pp. 262–3]

Hebrew language

B 139v, 156v

These notes, drawn from Graetz's *Geschichte der Juden*, refer to three periods of revival of Hebrew as a living language. The development of Hebrew as the 'popular tongue' (B 139v) occurred during the Hasmonean dynasty, also called the Maccabean Period, beginning with the reign of Simon, the youngest of the Maccabee brothers, from 166 BCE, and ending with the conquest by Herod in 37 BCE (see GE's 'Chronology', B 169v).

This was 'a sort of resurrection' (B 139v), but by the eighth century, reading Hebrew again presented difficulties to the layperson. The twenty-two letters of the Hebrew alphabet are consonants. GE's note on the introduction of vowel points or Masoretic points 'to vivify the dead consonants' (B 156v) shows her interest in the processes by which scholarship may open new fields of knowledge to the layperson as well as the learned.

GE's third note refers to a later revival of the language, in tenth-century Spain; under the patronage of Chasdai (or Chisdai), Menachem produced the first Hebrew dictionary (see B 159v and 160 and Pf 711 75). The outspoken critics of this dictionary, by provoking verbal battles in Hebrew, contributed to the enrichment of the language. In this way, this controversy perhaps contributed to the 'Rise of New Hebrew poetry' (see GE's 'Chronology', B 170v). Although Graetz characterizes the New Hebrew as 'inferior in depth and poetry' to the Old Hebrew, poets may work with any living language, giving voice to its hidden depths and richness. For GE's notes on two New Hebrew poets of eleventh-century Spain, Ibn Gebirol and Jehuda Halevy, see B 165v, 166, and 166v.

When Deronda first sees Mordecai, the thought glances through him 'that precisely such a physiognomy as that might possibly have been seen … in some New Hebrew poet of the mediæval time' (DD ch. 33: 356). In fact, Mordecai does compose 'New Hebrew poetry after the model of Jehuda ha-Levi' and endeavours to imprint his words on the memory of young Jacob Cohen, in the hope that 'their meaning may flash out on him' some day (DD ch. 38: 444–5). One might think that little Jacob would be more impressed if 'the coins had Hebrew stamped upon them', as in the Hasmonean times. He seems an unlikely vessel to bear onwards to another age the treasure of the Hebrew language. But Mordecai's predicament as a poet lacking a responsive audience does not, perhaps, differ much from that of other Victorian poets, writing in English. For GE, the significant point would be that the language of Mordecai's poetry is not merely an archaic liturgical vehicle (to be compared to Latin, perhaps), but a language which had again and again proved capable of renaissance as a vernacular tongue.

/139v/ Hebrew Language

Under the Asmonaeans, in the glorious time, the Hebrew tongue which had been almost driven out by contact with the Asiatic mores & given place to the Aramaean, had a sort of resurrection, renewed its youth & with a certain difference of form became again the popular tongue. The coins had Hebrew stamped upon them, public documents were drawn up in Hebrew, popular songs were sung in Hebrew – which last shows that the language was again current amongst the people. It is true that this Hebrew retained Aramaic & Greek elements but it showed a living development, enriched its store of words with new formations & gave the foreign elements its own peculiar stamp. This form of Hebrew or rather the form which the language held from this time is called New Hebrew, which is distinguished from the Old Hebrew by clearness & ease, if inferior in depth & poetry. [Graetz 3, 70]

Die Erforschung & Ergründung der hebräischen Sprache wurde in Spanien mit leidenschaftlichem Kampf, mit heissem Blute, mit galliger Satyre betrieben. Vide Grätz, on Menahem who produced the Hebrew Lexicon & Dunasch who criticized it, under the patronage of Chasdai, Xth century. [Graetz 5, 342–3][1]

1 Translation: 'The study of the Hebrew language was carried on in Spain by means of severe contention, hot blood, and virulent satire.' Bella Löwy's translation (which omits the heated blood) continues:

> The followers of Menachem and Dunash hurled witty lampoons at each other, which fact contributed largely towards making the Hebrew language at once pliant and rich. (3, 227)

/156v/ Vowel-points

When Hebrew studies revived (in the 8th century) the need was felt for vowel points to vivify the dead consonants. Only the experts & the public readers understood these consonants; to the people they were dead letters. Who first introduced the signs of the vowels & at what period, is not decided. One source states that Moses *the Punctator* was the originator of them, as well as of the diacritic signs. Syntactical & tonal signs were also needful. It appears that the inventor availed himself of the vowel system of the Syrian language as a model, & indeed the Arabians had borrowed from the same quarter. But the earliest vowel-points were quite different from our actual ones - standing, with the exception of the *U*-sound, *over* the letters. This is called the Assyrian or Babylonian system of points - still extant in a few copies in Caucasus & Krimm.

In the vocalising of the biblical text, in such passages as were not familiar through public reading, grammatical tact was necessarily the guide. The Punctators (assuredly more than one) must have followed partly tradition & partly 'Sprachegefühl'.[1] In this way two departments of knowledge were opened: conscious rules of the Hebrew tongue, & traditional knowledge of the orthography & exceptions.

These lectional signs made openings in the wall of separation between the *Chacham* or learned man & the *Am-ha-Arez* or layman.

[Graetz 5, 153–5]

1 *Sprachegefühl*: 'a feeling for the language'.

The Great Synagogue

B 140

The source of this note is Franz Julius Delitzsch, *Zur Geschichte der jüdischen Poësie vom Abschluss der heiligen Schriften Alten Bundes bis auf die neueste Zeit* (Leipzig: Karl Tauchnitz, 1836), a work included in GE's list of 'Books Wanted' on Pf 711 21. GE's annotated copy, in DWL, is also the source of brief notes on Pf 711 59, and two terms in the list of 'Hebrew Names & Phrases' on B 123: *Pajtanish* (relating to the divine service) and *Pijuthim* (liturgical poetry).

Several liturgical references are included in the note below. The period of the Second Temple is significant not only for the restoration of the *avodah* or temple cult, but also for the founding of rituals for synagogue worship, which were to continue long after the second destruction of the Temple. The custom of reading a portion or *parashah* of the Law or Torah is referred to again on Pf 710 19: 'The origin of the Thora-readings in the public services is dated from Ezra & Nehemiah'. During the same period originated 'probably the oldest portions of the Tefila or *eighteen prayers*'; compare GE's notes from Isaacs on 'the *Shemoneh Efreh*, i.e. eighteen prayers ... composed by Ezra & the men of the Great Synagogue' (B 133v). Finally, Delitzsch refers to the collection of ethical epigrams of 'the Fathers' in the Mishnah tractate called *Abot* or *Avot*. These also form part of the liturgy; many of them are marked in GE's one-volume prayer book in DWL. In the liturgy they are called *Pirke Avot*, or Sayings of the Fathers. GE's copy of Delitzsch has her marginal query, 'Pirke Abot?', next to his reference to the Mishnah *Avot* (p. 22).

Another liturgical innovation is the introduction of a *Meturgeman*, who translated the Torah readings orally, verse by verse, into the Aramaic vernacular. His office was superseded by the publication of an Aramaic translation of the Pentateuch, known as the *Targum* or Translation of Onkelos the Proselyte. This is the translation to which Maimonides refers (B 112). Since this is the period of the *Sopherim* or scribes, GE's note emphasizes authorship and scripture: the founding of the *masorah*, or scribal discipline; the transcription of the Torah in an improved script; and the writing of several texts now part of the canon. The Great Synagogue or Synod, the 'ecclesiastico-political college', was the predecessor of the Sanhedrin, the later legislative assembly, which was a forum for both Sadducees or priests and Pharisees. On Pf 710 18, GE has a longer note on the 'Great Synagogue ... which began under Esra'.

The attribution to Ezra of so many changes in Judaism during this period suggests the reason for Mordecai Cohen's change of name in GE's novel. The scriptural Mordecai had been carried away to captivity in Babylon, where he foiled a Persian plot to exterminate the Jews, and ended as a powerful advisor to King Ahasuerus, protecting the well-being of his people in that foreign land (see the Book of Esther). The scriptural Ezra, in contrast, is the leader of the return from Babylon to the land of Israel: the leader, that is, of those Israelites who chose to return to the hardships of reconstructing their material, intellectual and religious life.

Deronda regrets finding a pawnbroker's shop owned by an Ezra Cohen, and is 'half-inclined to decide that he [will] not increase his knowledge about that modern Ezra, who [is] certainly not a leader among his people' (DD ch. 33: 355). But, as Mrs Meyrick remarks, 'there are Ezras and Ezras in the world' (DD ch. 46: 528). Her comment applies not only to varieties of modern Ezras, but also to differing views of the original namesake who led the rebuilding of Judaism after the Babylonian captivity. This Ezra's edict against foreign wives and his dissolution of mixed marriages has been seen as based on an offensively exclusive definition of Jewish identity, as if restoring the covenant meant reviving the worship of a merely tribal god. Alternatively, Ezra's programme of developing a college of lay interpreters of the law (the *Sopherim*) and promulgating the law to the people may be seen as extending an invitation to proselytes of any racial origin. Definition of a Jew would henceforth depend upon fidelity to the Torah, rather than birth or mere adherence to the Temple ritual. These two views of Ezra put him at the centre of a peculiarly Jewish theological tension, between particularism and universalism. GE perhaps tried to occlude that tension in her novel by showing Deronda as responding almost as a potential proselyte might, before learning that his parentage is unmixed: that he *is* a Jew by birth. However, this plot resolution has provoked many troubled readings or misreadings, from Leslie Stephen to the present day.

/140/ Great Synagogue

The first great period of our history extends from the rebuilding of the Temple under the Persian protectorate to the destruction of the Holy City. We call this the period of the *Sopherim*, because through it stretches the unbroken succession of the Sopherim or chiefs of the Synagogue, first in the men of the Great Synagogue, then since the foundation of the Sanhedrin (142 BC) in the chiefs (or members) of the Sanhedrin; & with the dissolution of the Synagogue a new æra in Jewish history begins. [p. 18]

Ezra was not alone the restorer of the legal cultus (the *Aboda*); he was the first organizer who succeeded in making it a permanent institution. Tradition ascribes to him: the founding of the ecclesiastico-political college called the Great Synagogue; the transcription of the law in the *Ashurit-Schrift* (square characters); the foundation of the Masora; the custom of reading the law according to *Parashen* on Sunday, Monday & Thursday; the introduction of the *Meturgeman* who stood beside the reader of the law & rendered the original into the speech of the people; nay, even the authorship of the book of Malachi (with whom Ezra is identified), a part of the Chronicles & some Psalms. [pp. 18–19]

From the members of the Great Synagogue came probably the oldest portions of the Tefila or *eighteen prayers*, namely the three first & the three last *eulogia*, which already in the Mishna are mentioned with specific titles. Also in the Mishna *Abot* are preserved their sayings – with the exception of Zadok & Bajtos who founded Sadduceeism. Delitzsch [pp. 19–20, 23]

Extracts from Steinschneider

B 141, 142, 143, 142v, 143v, 144v, 145v, 146v, 147v,

143, 144, 145, 146, 147, 148, 149, 150, 148v, 149v

The primary source for these notes is Moritz Steinschneider, 'Jüdische Literatur', in *Allgemeine Encyklopädie der Wissenschaften und Kunste*, edited by Johann Samuel Ersch and Johann Gottfried Gruber, 3 sections, 167 vols. (Leipzig: Brockhaus, 1818–89), Section II (H–N), Volume 27, 'Juden – Jüdische Literatur' (1850), 357–471. Volumes of this encyclopaedia could be purchased singly; Volume 27, for instance, is in the Mocatta Library. A revised English translation by William Spottiswoode, *Jewish Literature from the Eighth to the Eighteenth Century, With an Introduction to the Talmud and Midrasch* (London, 1857), which includes author's emendations absent from the Ersch and Gruber text, has been reprinted (Hildesheim: Georg Olms, 1967) and is still a valuable reference work. GE's source, however, is the German text and not the English translation. Her brief notes on Pf 711 60 also indicate the German source: 'v. Steinschneider, Ersch u. Gruber'. 'Ersch und Gruber', Volume 82, is also the source of GE's notes from the 'Griechenlands' article on Folger 13 90–96. The extensiveness of the following notes suggests that GE was working with a borrowed text. After two and a half pages of running translation, GE filled the next six recto pages with German notes; her later translations occupy the facing verso pages. In this transcription, her English version precedes the German.

The next four pages, mostly in English, include material from other sources: Graetz, Abraham Geiger's *Judaism and its History*, and two works not previously noted in the Berg Notebook. Salomon Munk's *Palestine: Description géographique, historique et archéologique* (Paris: Firmin-Didot, 1845) is one of the works on the 'Books Wanted' list on Pf 711 21: 'Munk's Palestine'. GE's annotated copy, in DWL, is the source of her note below on the Yeçira and the Zohar, 'the great storehouses of the Kabbala' (B 150). The note on 'the Epithet Kabbala' (B 150) is from Ludwig Geiger, *Johann Reuchlin, sein Leben und seine Werke* (Leipzig: Duncker amd Humblot, 1871), also the source of several pages of notes on Pf 711 95 to 98 about the fifteenth-century philosopher who defended the study of Jewish literature.

Extracts from Steinschneider B 141

Steinschneider's comprehensive work interconnects with material in many entries elsewhere in the Berg notebook. Next to the heading 'Liturgy' for her note on Blessings and Prayers (B 148v), GE adds a reference, 'v. 134', to her notes from Isaacs on the Shema and daily prayers (B 133v). To the notes on the Kabbala (B 150), she adds a reference, 'v. 136', to her note from Solomon Maimon. The notes on the Mishnah (B 142v to 144) should be compared with those from Deutsch and other sources (B 106), and the notes on Midrash (B 141 to 143, 149v) with those from Deutsch (B 115 and 115v). The material on the Sopherim or scribes (B 142) complements that from Delitzsch (B 140). The account of the Babylonian Amoraim, governed by their *Resch Metibta* or Chiefs of Schools and *Resch Galuta* or Princes of the Exile (B 145v to 147v), includes topics to be found throughout the notebooks; see especially the long note from Graetz on the 'Prince of the Captivity & Judaic Community in Babylon' (B 162v, 163), and various notes on Babylonian titles (B 123, Pf 711 60, and Pf 710 36).

/141/ *Midrash* Steinschneider

A characteristic mark of the Jewish literature as distinguished from all others, is its relation to the Scriptural Canon, which rendered it less freely subjective. But the period of the Midrash is especially distinguished not merely by the greater amount of that order of intellectual activity, but rather by the almost exclusive authority of the Bible so that no Science could have a value independently of its relation to the Scriptures.

The Institution which gave to this activity a practical fulcrum was the public teaching, the history of which stands in the closest connection with the literature, being indeed its principal source. Lectures or readings out of the Law, of very ancient origin, were established & enlarged by Ezra & the Sopherim. Along with these, the Prophets formed in the schools exercised a freer activity, but one which had always reference to the Law. Those public teachings must early have had various stages from mere reading & explanation to homily. As the biblical writings were necessarily unintelligible to a people speaking Aramaean, the reading & explanation must take the character of a translation or paraphrase, & hence gradually arose the literatures of the Targums, Chaldaic, Greek & Syriac, which just like the Midrash for a long time were developed simply by oral means on the lips of the readers & interpreters, before they were collected & written down – & even in their intrinsic character do not stand far off the Midrash. Even the Arabic translation **/142/** of R. Saadja still carries the stamp of the paraphrase, nay Mendelssohn's German translation of the Pentateuch coheres in legal points to the traditional interpretation. This reading in public & exposition of the Scriptures on feast days & assemblies already during the existence of the second temple took the nature of a sort of divine service,[1] & became finally an integral part of the Cultus. In the place of the priests & Levites as teachers came now the learned in the law, the Sopherim or scribes – viz the head of the school (רבן), the graduated Rabbins (רב) & the members of the college who called themselves modestly the disciples of the Wise. As earlier there had been schools of the priests & prophets, so now of the Learned in which the discussion & investigation of the Law was the chief business. Here were held in the first place lectures & discussions for scholars & experts; but also freer, more popular discourses & homilies (דרוש darush) to the assembled congregation, who also prayed in the place of assembly (synagogue). Also such public & domestic solemnities as circumcision, marriage, & burial were occasions for discourse. These various discoursings, which had usually the Scriptures for their nucleus, are therefore called Midrash, an Aramaic infinitive from *darash* (דרש), properly the investigation & interpretation of the sacred writings, & later, a cyclus of such interpretations. On the occasions of these discourses hung their matter & form. The cyclus of extracts **/143/** or passages from Scripture was accompanied by a corresponding cyclus of paraphrases & homilies: the stricter doctrinal or legal teaching formed a text or nucleus in the scriptural cyclus; on the other hand, the freer discourses ranged unrestricted through the whole Bible, & it was according to the will of the subsequent redactor or collector, from what point of view he should arrange his material. Now since the Bible itself contains the most diverse elements, the *midrash* in its starting points, oral transmission, superposed series of explanations, & varieties of method in collection, must necessarily issue in the most variegated mass of literary material. (Jüdische Literatur, Ersch u. Gruber) [pp. 360–1][2]

1 GE altered her translation from 'a sort of' to 'the nature of a sort of', and from 'public worship' to 'divine service'.

2 The following notes are GE's translations, on facing pages, of B 143 to 148.

Extracts from Steinschneider B 142v 143v 144v

/142v/

The Mischna of R. Jehuda had excluded not only theoretically false or critically suspicious traditions but also for the most part discussion (Talmud) & exegesis (Midrasch), which already about that time had considerable growth & to some extent had the prestige of antiquity & (in relation to the Midrasch) even of Tradition, & also was much favoured by individual teachers. Though the Mischna through internal & external causes gradually attained the authority of a canon, it nevertheless could not be otherwise than that individual teachers preserved older Halachas either single or in collections so that outside **/143v/** the official collection there could still be an external or apocryphal one founded; & this was accomplished by Abba Aricha, his younger contemporary R. Chija, & in the next generation R. Oschaja, called 'Father of the Mishna'. The Halacha assembled by the latter are called External Mischna – (*Matnito, Boraito*). Also R. Chija & R. Oschaja collected the discussion & other additions to the Halacha omitted from the Mischna, according to the method of R. Nehemiah, the so-called *Tosefta.* Yet more urgent was the demand for collections which embraced the exegesis & methodology of the Halacha, as they were pursued by the elder teachers. Such are the works called *Sifra, Sifri*, (redacted in the school of Rab) & *Mechilta.*

All these & some other collections are extant either as separate works in a later form or as fragments only in other works, especially in the Talmud & chiefly in the language of the Mischna.

Such wealth of material preserved with pious care from the past, & the additions constantly made by current life, gave the schools accumulated in Palestine & Babylon matter enough to carry on to a pyramidal height the superstructure previously wrought.

/144v/

The succeeding generations occupied themselves yet more with the critical treatment of their Halachian texts; but as already a part of discussion & exegesis had penetrated into the Mischna & were completed in special collections which claimed authority, so these also, like the simple Halacha, & like the Bible, in their turn became matter of oral interpretation & discussion in connection with the Bible; whence the biblical interpretation became more intricate & finally the traditional element of the Halachas was overshadowed by speculation.

Extracts from Steinschneider B 144v 145v 146v

The further the study of the Halacha was developed the more pressing was the need for sifting & arrangement of the new & old materials – subordination of the new to the old; & after the ancient Halachas & their explanation had been fixed in writing & made a canon, the subsequent discussions followed periodically, not without the co-operation of some external causes along the same path of redaction in writing, which must be regarded as more & more the work of a school under the stimulus of a prominent individual. In Palestine such a redaction was accomplished about 370–380, after the right of promotion had been withdrawn from the schools there. **/145v/** And thus arose at Tiberias the so-called Jerusalem Talmud (more properly Gemara) falsely ascribed to R. Jochanan who died 279.

In Babylon flourished the schools of Syra, Pumbeditha, Nehardea, Mahusa, Neresch, under *Resch Metibta* or chiefs of schools & *Resch Galuta* or princes of the exile. Their more subtle & hair-splitting method was blamed & ridiculed by many Palestinian teachers. The Babylonian Amoraim number seven generations after the heads of schools – Rab and Samuel, Huna [& Jehuda, Rabbah & Josef, Abbaje] [1] & Rabba, Ashe & his son, Mar, & Rabina. To Rab Asche, Chief of the School at Syra, it was granted during a long duration of office (said to be 60 years) & after a long period of external calm to get the whole Halachean material collected & arranged by his numerous disciples; but he died 427 before the close of the work. Hence he or his son (d. 467) is cited as the last Talmudic authority. The redaction of the Babylonian Gemara was finally effected by R. José of Syra (d. 475); but this so-called Babylonian Talmud appears as a finally complete work only in the time of the Saboraim. The persecutions under Jezdegerd, Firuz & Kobad in the latter half of the 5th century – under whom **/146v/** among other things the office of Resch Galuta had been degraded into a marketable title – had brought about the ruin of the Babylonian schools & had conspicuously interrupted the direct & immediate reception of the doctrinal store; hence the succeeding teachers could not claim any authority against the traditional deliverances, & limited their teaching & judgments or decisions to the conciliation of what was already delivered, to interpretation & opinion, whence they are called Saboraim. By them however certain additions, viz the methodological & mnemonic signs, were introduced into the Babylonian Gemara. But the latest of the Saboraim must have had these writings (a few later additions & variants excepted) in the form presented by the oldest

1 GE overlooked the bracketed names.

manuscripts & printed editions. Inasmuch as the Gemara - or Talmud in the narrower sense - was subordinated to the Mischna (according to the Babylonian recension) the word Talmud received the wider significance of Mischna & Gemara combined. Thus the Saboraim are related to the Babylonian Talmud as the Sopherim or Scribes are related to the Sacred Scriptures. It lay before them as a written text, as a subject for interpretation & discussion. To them **/147v/** or rather to itself - its own character - as the last result of a (so-called) uninterrupted tradition, amidst a universal mental subjection & belief in authority, the Talmud owes its credit with later generations (as also do its earlier elements in relation to the later); not at all to any Individual or College which had exalted it into a canon. Thus it came to pass that Mischna & Talmud as a living Commentary of the Scriptures, were regarded as the foundation of all subsequent development; which is the more comprehensible because the Talmud is almost the sole literature of more than 500 years, since - excepting the few above-mentioned Midrashim in part scattered through the Talmud - all other collections of Halacha made during that period (probably in consequence of its predominant authority) were lost.

/143/

Die Mischna des R. Jehuda hatte nicht bloss theoretisch falsche oder kritisch verdächtige Ueberlieferungen, sondern auch grosstentheils die Discussion (Talmud) und Exegese (Midrasch) ausgeschlossen, die selber um diese Zeit weit gediehen waren und zum Theil das Ansehen des Alterthums und (den Midrasch betreffend) sogar der Tradition genossen, auch von einzelnen Lehrern mit Vorliebe gepflegt wurden. Gelangten nun die Mischnijjot (unsere Mischna) des R. Jehuda durch innere u. äussere Ursachen allmälig zum Ansehen eines Kanons ... so konnte es doch, besonders in erster Zeit, nicht fehlen, dass einzelne Lehrer auch anderweitige vereinzelte oder gesammelte ältere Halachas aufbewahrten, sodass ausserhalb **/144/** der officiellen Sammlung noch eine externe oder apokryphische veranstaltet werden konnte, & dies thaten der erwähnten Abba Aricha, sein jüngerer Zeitgenosse R. Chijja & der um eine Generation jüngere R. Oschaja, genannt 'Vater der Mischna'. Die von Letzeren gesammelte Halacha heisst: Externe Mischna (*Matnito*, *Boraito*). Ebenso sammelten schon R. Chijja und R. Oschaja die Discussion und sonstige in der Mischna weggelassene Zusätze der Halacha nach der Methode des R. Nehemiah, die sogenannte *Tosefta*. Noch dringender war das Bedürfniss nach Sammlungen, welche die Exegese u. Methodologie der Halacha umfassten, wie sie von älteren Lehrern gepflegt ward. Solche sind die Werke *Sifra, Sifri*, (in der Schule Rab's redigirt) und *Mechilta*. Alle diese und einzelne andere Sammlungen sind zum Theil noch als gesonderte Werke in späterer Bearbeitung, theils nur fragmentarisch in anderen Werken, namentlich im Talmud, vorhanden, und meist in der Mischnasprache abgefasst.

Ein so reiches, mit frommer Sorgfalt gehütetes Material der Vergangenheit, und das stets hinzufügende Leben, gaben den in Palästina u. Babylon sich häufenden Schulen Stoff genug, um den bisher stätig fortgeführten Ueberbau **/145/** in ähnlicher Weise noch weiter thurmhoch aufzuführen. Die nächsten Generationen befassten sich noch mehr mit kritischer Behandlung ihrer halachischen Quellen; allein war schon ein Theil der Discussion u. Exegese in die Mischna eingedrungen und in eigenen Sammlungen zu einem Fertigen geworden, welches an sich Geltung beanspruchte, so musste auch dieses, gleich der alten einfachen Halacha, also gleich der Bibel, neuerdings Gegenstand mündlicher Auslegung u. Discussion und auch an die Bibel angeknüpft, daher die Schriftdeutung immer willkührlicher, die Methodologie immer verwickelter, und endlich das traditionelle Element der Halacha von der Speculation ueberschattet werden ... Je weiter das Studium der Halacha sich entwickelte, oder vielmehr verwickelte, desto näher rückte das Bedürfnis nach Sichtung u. Unterordnung des neuen Materials unter das alte, u. nachdem einmal die alte Halacha und selbst ihre Erläuterung durch die Schrift fixirt u. zum Kanon erhoben war, folgten die nachfolgenden Discussionen periodisch, nicht ohne äussere Mitursachen, auf demselben Wege der schriftlichen Redaction, die man sich stets mehr als Werk einer Schule unter Anspornung eines hervorragenden Individuums zu denken hat. In Palästina fand eine solche um 370–380 statt, nachdem das Recht der Promotion den dortigen Schulen genommen ... und so entstand zu Tiberias der **/146/** sogenannte Jerusalemische Talmud (richtiger Gemara) welcher fälschlich dem R. Jochanan (st. 279) zugeschrieben wird ... In Babylon erblüheten die Schulen zu Syra, Pumbedita, Nehardea, Mahusa, Neresch unter Schulhäuptern – *Resch Metibta*, u. sogenannten Princes of the Exile – *Resch Galuta* – deren subtilere u. spitzfindigere Lehrmethode bei manchem palästinische Lehrer Spott und Tadel fand. Die Babylonischen Amoraïm zählen sechs bis sieben Geschlechte[r] nach den Schulhäuptern: Rab u. Samuel, Huna und [...] Rabba, Asche u. sohn Mar und Rabina. Dem Rab Asche, Schulhaupt zu Syra, war es vergönnt, bei einer (angeblich 60 Jahre) langen Amtsdauer und nach einer langen Periode äusserer Ruhe, seine zahlreichen Schüler den gesammten halachischen Stoff sammeln u. ordnen zu lassen; doch starb er vor Beendigung (427). Daher wird er oder sein Sohn (gest. 467) als die letzte talmudische Autorität bezeichnet. Die Redaction der Babylonischen Gemara geschah durch R. Jose, Vorsteher zu Syra (st. 475); doch erscheint auch dieser sogenannte babylonische Talmud als ein abgeschlossenes Ganzes erst zur Zeit der Saboraïm.

Es hatten nämlich in der letzten Hälfte der 5ten Jahrh. die Verfolgungen durch Jezdegerd, Firuz, und Kobad, die unter Anderm das Amt des **/147/** Resch Galuta zu einer käuflichen Titulatur der Reichen herabgewürdigt, den Untergang der Babylonischen Schulen herbeigeführt und die Unmittelbarkeit der Reception auf eclatante Weise unterbrochen; daher trauten sich die nachfolgenden Lehrer nicht mehr eine Autorität gegen die Ueberlieferung zu, und beschränkten ihre Lehren und Gutachten blos auf Ausgleichung der vorhandenen Relationen, auf Deutung & Meinung, weswegen sie Saboraïm heissen. Durch sie sind noch einige Zusätze, namentlich die methodologischen und mnemonitechnischen Zeichen, in die babylonische Gemara geflossen. Die letzten Saboraïm müssen aber letztere (wenige noch spätere Zusätze und Varianten abgerechnet) schon in der Gestalt gehabt haben, in der die alten Handschriften und ersten Drucke vorliegen. Da nun die Gemara (Talmud im engeren Sinne) der Mischna (nach ihrer babylonischen Recension) untergeordnet ward, so erhielt das Wort Talmud die weitere Bedeutung nach welcher es Mischna u. Gemara umfasst. – Es verhalten sich demnach die Saboraïm bereits zum babylonischen Talmud, wie die Sopherim zur heiligen Schrift. Er lag ihnen als ein fertiges Schriftliches, als Gegenstand der Auslegung, Erorterung und Discussion vor; ihnen, **/148/** oder vielmehr sich selber als letztem Ausfluss der als ununterbrochen betrachteten Ueberlieferung, unter allgemeinen Geistesdruck und Autoritätsglauben, verdankt der Talmud sein Ansehen den Spätern (so wie dessen ältere Bestandtheile den jüngeren) gegenüber; keineswegs einem Individuum oder Collegium, welches ihn zum Kanon erhoben hätte, was schon seiner Beschaffenheit nach unmöglich war. So kam es dass man Mischna und Talmud als lebendige Commentare der Schrift, gleich dieser, allen späteren Entwickelungen zu Grunde legte, was um so begreiflicher, da der Talmud fast die alleinige Literatur von mehr als einem halben Jahrtausend bildet, indem die wenigen oben erwähnten halachischen Midrashim zum Theil im Talmud zerstreut aufgenommen, – alle sonstigen halachischen Sammlungen aus jener Zeit, vermuthlich in Folge des Ansehens der recipirten, verloren gegangen sind.

(Steinschneider, Ersch u. Gruber) [pp. 367–8]

/149/

Haggada - legend - saying[1]

Midrash, in its narrower sense, means 'haggadische Midrasch'.

'Die Haggadische Behandlung war entweder vorherrschend subjectiv oder objectiv, ihr Zweck entweder einfaches Wort- und Sachverständniss: *Peschat*, oder homiletische Verwendung welche die ganze äussere Gegenwart mit ihren Erscheinungen im Spiegel der Prophezeiung verklärte, wo also das Bibelwort und der subjective Gedanke einander das Gleichgewicht hielten, ebenso viel hinein- als herausgedeutet wurde: *Darusch* im engern Sinne; endlich gab es auch einzelne, auf engere Schulkreise beschränkte Themen, *Sod*, Geheimniss.' [Steinschneider, pp. 370–1][2]

Even in the Mischna, spite of its strictly halachistic character, the Haggada is found - in separate tractates as *Abot*, *Middot*; in the concluding passages of various tractates, containing comfort & blessing in the prophetic manner; & in single Halachoth which, partaking of the nature of Haggada, are associated with it. [Steinschneider, p. 372]

1 Deutsch, 'The Talmud', p. 430.

2 Translation:

The Haggada mode of treatment was either mainly subjective or mainly objective; its end was either the simple understanding of words and things, *Peshat*, or else a homiletical application, reflecting the present condition of things in the mirror of Prophecy, where the words of the Bible and subjective thought were evenly balanced, as much being brought into the Bible as was taken out of it, *Darush* in a restricted sense; and, finally, there were some themes confined to a narrower circle of students, *Sod*, mystery. (Spottiswoode, p. 30)

Extracts from Steinschneider B 149 150

1. The Ethical Haggada is called *Maschal.* The simplest form is the Gnome; a more artificial form, the riddle & apologue, the fable & parable. In the Talmud *there is mention* of a collection of Fox-fables & 'Dattelfabeln oder Wäschergespräche'.[1]

2. Then there is the historical Haggada – which corresponds to Legend in its fullest sense; &

3. *the secret doctrine* which **/150/** under the influence & form of the Midrash, was viewed in two groups which embraced the two spheres of being, Heaven & Earth, under the names of 'Doctrine of the Divine Chariot', & Doctrine of Creation. Herein were included teachings concerning the attributes, activities (names) & revelations of God & of the heavenly court, stars & angels, also concerning the first & continuous production & nature of created beings (as expositions of Gen. I, Ezekiel, Jacob's dream & the Mosaic theophany). To this were added materials from the Persian lore about demons, astrology, cheiromancy, sympathetic cures, also views as to the hidden meaning & end of the law. The combination of these various themes into a systematic whole was precisely what constituted the later Cabbala.

All these forms belong to the *General* Haggada, or that in which the matter predominates over the direct aim of exposition. The *Special* Haggada is strictly expository. (Steinschneider) [pp. 373–6, 380]

The great storehouses of the Kabbala, says Munk, are the Yeçira & the Zohar. The former was already considered ancient in the 10th century. The latter was compiled in the 13th century, & contains probably much matter of an earlier date.[2]

The Yeçira, Grätz thinks, probably originated in Tiberias, but [he] does not know when to place it in time. [Graetz 7, 71]
It was commented by Saadia.[3]

1 Translation: 'Fables of the Dates or of the Washers' (Spottiswoode, p. 39). For another note on Fox-fables, see B 184v.

2 Solomon Munk, *Palestine*, p. 519.

3 The last sentence was added later as a footnote. See the note on 'Sefer Jezirah' on B 149v.

Extracts from Steinschneider B 150 148v

The Epithet Kabbala first became current in the end of the 12th century. (L. Geiger, Reuchlin) The Cabbalistic Literature dates in the 2d half of the Gaonitic epoch (from 780).[1]

/148v/

Liturgy[2]

1. Blessings (berachott) on certain occasions, as eating, ceremonies &c
2. Daily Prayers: the *Schema* or confession of the divine unity, & remembrance of what God had wrought for Israel

   The *Tefilla*, or eighteen prayers (Schemoneh Efreh)

   The *Schema* was probably introduced as a morning & evening prayer in or about the time of the Syrian war.[3]

The language of the more ancient prayers is Hebrew; only a few are Aramaic, e.g. the Kaddisch, originally a concluding formula of haggadistic discourses.

Steinschneider [pp. 382–3]

1 Ludwig Geiger, *Johann Reuchlin*, p. 166.

2 For other notes on prayers, see B 133v and 140.

3 GE added in parentheses, from another source, the Hebrew words *berachott* and *Schemoneh Efreh*, and added a marginal query beside the note about the introduction of the Shema. For her other notes on the Shema, see B 110 and Pf 711 22 and 57. In DD ch. 42 Mordecai declares that 'the soul of Judaism is not dead', even in 'the multitudes of the ignorant on three continents', so long as they 'observe our rites and make the confession of the divine Unity' (494). In DD ch. 61 he reminds Mirah that 'the *Shemah*, wherein we briefly confess the divine Unity, is the chief devotional exercise of the Hebrew'. His subsequent interpretation of this prayer is universalist, rather than particularist, and expresses GE's view of Judaism as an original form of the Religion of Humanity:

> '... and this made our religion the fundamental religion for the whole world; for the divine Unity embraced as its consequence the ultimate unity of mankind. See, then – the nation which has been scoffed at for its separateness, has given a binding theory to the human race. Now, in complete unity, a part possesses the whole as the whole possesses every part: and in this way human life is tending toward the image of the Supreme Unity ...' (683)

/149v/ *Midraschim* &c [1]

Midrasch Rabba – 10 Midraschim on the Pentateuch & 5 Megillot, the oldest in the 6th century, the latest in the XIIth

Pesikta, 700. Pesikta rabbati, 845

Midrasch Tanchuma, 9th century

Midrasch Bajoscha, contains the first formation of the Armillus (Romulus) saga, after the analogy of the Arabian Deddschal. [2]

Midrasch Jalkut, of R. Simon Kara of Le Mans, 11th century [Steinschneider, p. 381]

Jalkut Rubeni, the work of an addlebrained Cabbalist, Ruben Hoeske [Pf 711 57; Pf 710 39] [3]

Sefer Jezirah (Buch der Schöpfung) commented by Saadia, but its origin not known [Graetz 7, 7] [4]

Bereschit Rabba, Haggadistic collection by R. Moses of Narbonne (11th century) [Graetz 6, 57]

Tachkemoni, by Salomon b. Sakbel, a sort of satirical romance in which the hero, Ascher b. Jehuda is exposed to wanderings & deceptions. The hero himself narrates his adventures in rhymed prose, interspersed with verses – how he formerly spent a long while in a forest solitude, accompanied by his beloved alone, longed for company & conviviality. He is invited in an enigmatic letter to an assignation, taken into a harem, & finds himself threatened by the master &c. but the whole turns out to be a practical joke of friends. [Graetz 6, 122–3]

There is another Tachkemoni by Jehuda Alcharisi in the 13th century – one of three satirical romances of that period. v. Grätz v. VII [Graetz 7, 83–4]

1 Compare B 115 and 123.
2 For Armillus, see Pf 710 6 and Pf 711 60.
3 Abraham Geiger, *Judaism and its History*, p. 341.
4 Above 'Jezirah', GE later wrote 'Yeçira' See B 150. In the margin of Graetz 7, 7, GE noted 'Jeçira' next to a reference to 'das alte Buch der Schöpfung', or 'the old Book of the Creation'.

Biblical interpretation

B 150v

GE's heading and index entry for this page, 'Biblical Interpretation', refers particularly to the explanation by Aristobulus concerning the signification of the seven days of the Creation story. This first note is drawn from Graetz's history of the period between the end of the Hasmonean dynasty and the destruction of the Second Temple. The other notes have no readily apparent hermeneutical significance. They are all closely linked to notes in Pf 711, or copied again there.

/150v/ *Biblical Interpretation*

1. *Aristobulus* in his dedicatory introduction to the Septuagint, addressed to Ptolemy Philometor, explains that the Creation in six days signifies that order & succession reign in the universe. The resting on the seventh day signifies the continued preservation of that which is created. This is the first appearance of a mode of interpretation which sacrifices the plain meaning of the text in accommodation to opinions. [Graetz 3, 43]

2. The Rabbis say that when the Jews borrowed of the Egyptians God wrought this miracle, that what each Jew borrowed was exactly the price of his unpaid labour. [Pf 711 56] [1]

3. The Talmudic doctrine that each day of the creation symbolized a thousand years of the world's duration & that the seventh Chiliad (the day of rest) would be the Messianic time. [Graetz 5, 140; Pf 711 76] [2]

1 Source: Isaacs, p. 106.

2 A chiliad is a 'cycle of a thousand years, counting from the creation of the world' (Bella Löwy translation, 3, 107). Compare the note on Pf 711 76:

> The Talmudic doctrine that the Messianic Time would be the seventh Chiliad made much of by the Jews of Spain in their persecutions under the Goths ...

4. Zadokites – Sadducees: descendants of the priestly estate, with the families of rank allied to them. Their opponents were called Pharisees, i.e. Separatists, by an Aramaic name. [Pf 711 58][1]

5. 'Seven' & six are the only numerals which the Hebrew has in common with the Indo-European languages. [Pf 711 29][2]

6. The very term signifying to swear literally means 'to do seven times' (Gen. xxi. 28; comp. Herod. III. 8, for a like custom among the Arabians). [Pf 711 29]

7. Same Hebrew word for forty & a great number [Pf 711 29][3]

1 Source: Abraham Geiger, *Judaism and its History*, p. 163.

2 The source of this and the following notes is the article, 'Seven', by William Latham Bevan, in Smith's *Dictionary of the Bible*, III, 1218–19. Genesis xxi, 27–32 gives an account of Abraham setting seven ewe lambs as symbolic witnesses to his oath with Abimelech. According to Herodotus 3, 8, Arabians make a pledge by marking seven stones with the blood of the contracting persons.

3 Source not traced. GE's note on Pf 711 29 expresses more uncertainty:

> The same Hebrew word, or the same with a slight variation, stands for forty & a great number.

According to her later parenthetical note,

> This is doubtful ... If true, it comes from a time when the Hebrews said – one, two, three, many ...

Rabbis' sayings (Pirke Abot)

B 152, 152v, 153v, 153av, 154

Avot is a tractate of the Mishnah comprising ethical sayings and maxims of the 'Fathers' of Rabbinic Judaism. GE became familiar with several English translations. Her copy of *Daily, Sabbath, Festival and Occasional Prayers, According to the Ritual of the German and Polish Jews* (London: Ann Abrahams and Son, 5634/1874), in DWL, has many pencilled marginal markings in the 'Ethics of the Fathers' section (pp. 239–64). She also knew the translation in Isaacs, *Ceremonies, Customs, Rites, and Traditions of the Jews* (pp. 216–23). 'Rabbinical sayings' from 'Pirke Aboth', gleaned from Deutsch's essay on the Talmud are noted on Pf 708 98–99, and others from 'P. Aboth', drawn from Giuseppe Levi, are copied on Pf 707 28. Finally, her annotated copy of Charles Taylor's *Sayings of the Jewish Fathers, comprising Pirqe Aboth and Pereq R. Meir, in Hebrew and English* (Cambridge: Cambridge University Press, 1877), is in DWL. Her source for the notes below is Graetz.

/152/ Rabbis *Sayings* (*Pirke Abot*) [1]

1. *José ben Jochanan,* head of the Great Council in the time immediately following Judas Maccabaeus: 'Let thy house be always open & treat the poor as part of thy own family.' [Graetz 3, 7][2]

2. *José ben Joeser,* his contemporary: 'Dein Haus sei ein Versammlungsort für die gesetzesbeflissenen Weisen, setze dich in den Staub zu ihren Füssen und trinke durstig ihre Worte.' [Graetz 3, 7][3]

1 This page begins with a note in parentheses: '(John Hyrcanus, 135–106)'. See B 151v, 153, 154v.

2 GE omits the third part of his saying: 'and do not converse with women' (Bella Löwy translation, 1, 436).

3 Let your house be a place of assembly for the wise men, allow yourself to be covered with the dust of their feet [or, more simply, 'sit at their feet'], drink in their words greedily' (Bella Löwy translation, 1, 436).

3. *Josua b. Perachia*[1]
'Richte jede That nach der Seite der Unschuld' or more fully, 'Suche dir ein Lehrer, erwirb dir ein Freund, und beurtheile jeden Menschen nach dem Maassstabe der Unschuld.' [Graetz 3, 89][2]

4. *Simon ben Shetach,* leader of the Pharisees under Alexander Jannaeus 105–79: 'Wisdom, whom I serve, entitles me to a place among kings.' [Graetz 3, 110–11]

5. *Juda ben Tabbai,* fled to Egypt on the outbreak of Alexander's ferocity against the Sadducees. After Alexander's death Simon, instead of accepting the presidency of the Sanhedrim for himself, called Juda ben Tabbai out of Egypt to take it. The letter ran, 'From me Jerusalem, the holy city, to thee Alexandria: my spouse dwells with thee & I am forsaken.' Juda came & with Simon reorganized the Sanhedrim, improved the observances, & restored the shaken dignity of religion – increasing the means of instruction & in general introducing regulations suited to the time. They were a new Ezra & Nehemiah. With them began the dominance of legal Judaism on the Pharisaic model. Hence they are called the restorers of the law, giving it anew its ancient splendour. [Graetz 3, 118–19][3]

/152v/

α One of their acts was to abolish the book of penal laws which the Sadducees had introduced as supplementary to the biblical laws, & to bring again into usage the traditional norm, which was milder. This was satisfactory to the people, who hated the Sadducean severity.

β They established the Ketubah, to restrain divorce.[4]

γ They founded schools – one in every large town a high school for youths of 16 & more.

1 GE's first note was on Joshua ben Perachia. She later numbered the rabbis to indicate their chronological sequence, which has been followed in this transcription.

2 The source of the first saying has not been traced. Translation: 'Judge every deed according to the presumption of innocence.' Or more fully, 'Take a teacher, win a friend, and judge every man from the presumption of innocence' (Bella Löwy translation, 2, 20).

3 GE first wrote, 'With them began the authority of legal Judaism', and then added above the line an alternative translation, 'dominance'.

4 For GE's note on the Ketubah, see B 111.

δ They gave new emphasis & splendour to many of the festivals, as the *Wasser-gussopfer* & the Holzfeste.[1]

ε They established the temple tribute: each Israelite above 20 to pay yearly at least a half-shekel (12 Sgr).

It is a fine trait in Juda ben Tabbai that when as Nassi he had wrongly punished with death a false witness (one witness not being properly punishable because incapable of establishing an accusation) he, smitten with repentance, resigned his dignity, & openly declared his contrition. He stretched himself on the grave of the victim & intreated for his own death. His saying was, 'Regard the accused as a transgressor only so long as he is before the judges; at large again, regard him as innocent.'

[Graetz 3, 125–6]

The son of Simon ben Shetach being falsely accused & condemned, & the witnesses smitten with pity having declared their testimony false, the judges were about to absolve the prisoner who was condemned to death. But he himself pointed out the illegality of their procedure, the laws **/153v/** not allowing belief in the retractions of witnesses, & he intreated his father to regard him *as the door-sill on which men tread pitilessly*, rather than injure Israel by a breach of the law. [Graetz 3, 126]

6. *Schemaja* (Sameas) & *Abtalion* (Pollion), chiefs of the Synagogue after Simon & Juda, in the melancholy time of early subjection to the Romans after the expedition of Pompey. Schemaja said, to the disciples: 'Love handicraft, flee from command & hold no friendship with the powers of this world.' Abtalion said to the teachers: 'Be cautious in your words, that you may not be sent into exile: where your disciples would then follow you into a land of perverting influences (pernicious water) & would drink it in, so that the name of God would be desecrated.' They retained their posts 25 years (60–35) & in the political depression of the Sanhedrim laboured in the investigation & definition of the law. [Graetz 3, 145–6]

1 *Wasser-gussopfer*: the celebration of drawing water from the spring for the Sukkoth water libation. *Holzfeste*: a festival for young women, with singing and dancing, for the wood-offering.

7. *Hillel,* made president of the Sanhedrim under Herod (30 BC). He was born 75 BC & died 5 AC. He gave as the whole law, while his hearer was standing on one leg, 'What thou wouldst not that another should do to thee, that do not to him.' He is regarded as a great restorer of doctrine. He brought old traditions **/153av/** with him from Babylonia. He laid down seven rules according to which an oral law might be derived from the Scriptures, & have equal authority.

    1. By a conclusion from smaller to greater & vice versa
    2. By analogy with another legal decision
    3. By a principle expressed in a single passage
    4. By a principle expressed in two or more passages
    5. By opposition of the general & particular
    6. By internal (intrinsic) similarity to another decision
    7. By the connexion (or sequence) of the text

[Graetz 3, 172, 173, 175]

8. *Manahem* the Essene was Ab-Beth-Din under the presidency of Hillel, but he held the post only a short time & was succeeded by

9. *Schammai,* whose severity made the traditional antithesis to the mildness of Hillel. His saying was: 'Let learning be thy principal business, speak little but perform much, & receive every man with a friendly countenance.'

[Graetz 3, 178–9]

The school of Schammai was the exaggeration of all Pharisaic strictness & separatism. Zaddok, one of the immediate disciples of Schammai, is in all probability he of whom it is narrated that filled with fanatical hatred of the Romans he formed along with Judas the Galilean a religious republican party who called themselves Zealots – Kannaim – also, after their founder, Galileans.

/154/

The motto & flag which Judas gave to the Zealots & which was eagerly espoused by Zaddok was, that it was a breach of the law to obey the Roman ruler: God alone was the ruler of the Jews. [Graetz 3, 206–8][1]

1 In the margin of Graetz 3, 208, GE notes, 'God the only ruler of the Jews'.

10. *Gamaliel I* or the Elder (ha-Saken), president of the Sanhedrim under Agrippa (40), the grandson of Hillel. Under him the presidency became more monarchical. The settling of an intercalary year depended on his decree. Epistles to near & distant communities went in his name. The formulary of such Epistles has been preserved. v. Grätz III, 274[1]

Gamaliel originated many beneficent ordinances, many in the mild spirit of Hillel: e.g. that the heathen should not be hindered from gleaning in the fields, but should be treated as the Jewish poor were, & that the greeting of Peace should be given to the heathens also on their days of solemnity &c. Possibly these ordinances of friendliness towards pagans were due to the beneficence of Agrippa's four years' rule. And the favourable disposition of the Emperor Claudius towards the Jews extended the period of truce between Romans & Jews. [Graetz 3, 275–6]

A Josua ben Gamala, whose rich wife is said to have bought the high priesthood for him from Agrippa the Second – about 60 or 64 – instituted the schools for boys of 5 years old. Before that, there were only schools for youths of 16 & upwards founded by Simon ben Shetach. [Graetz 3, 333][2]

1 GE's marginal note on Graetz 3, 274 is 'Encyclical Letters'.

2 Her marginal note on Graetz 3, 333 is 'Schools for 5 year old children'. For a story of Joshua ben Gamala's rich wife, Martha, see B 155.

Motives and pictures from the Maccabean and Roman periods

B 151v, 153, 151, 153a, 155, 154v, 161v

In these notes drawn from Graetz and Milman, GE turns again to 'the glorious time' (B 139v) of the Hasmonean dynasty or Maccabean period, beginning with the reign of Simon Maccabee (166 BCE), and ending with Herod's conquest (37 BCE). She also refers briefly to the preceding period, 'that great gap in Jewish History of 210 years, from Ezra & Nehemiah to Antiochus Epiphanes' (B 151). The 'blank' period 'from Nehemiah to Judas Maccabaeus', in her 'Chronology' (B 169v) and on B 182v, is said to be '280 years'. Finally, on B 155 she notes four vignettes or 'Motives and Pictures' from the 'Romanizing Period', from Herod's reign to the destruction of the Second Temple (70 CE).

From the time of Ezra and Nehemiah, the Jews who chose to return from the Babylonian captivity were allowed to live in the land of Israel, to worship in the rebuilt Temple, and to administer their own judicial system, through the Great Sanhedrin and the lesser courts (B 151v, 153). Jewish history, however, whether blank or recorded, was determined by events in the greater world. Judaea remained a minor province of first the Persian Empire, then the Hellenistic Empire, and finally the Roman Empire. GE's notes on the 'Vessels of the Temple' (B 154v and 161v), recording successive stages of their history as loot or relics of military triumph, before their return as 'sacred remnants' to a Christian church in Jerusalem, intimate their accretion of symbolic significance.

Jews living outside Palestine, including proselytes, far out-numbered those in Judaea. In Israel and elsewhere, Jews were troubled not only by the side-blows of external power struggles and by numerous states of siege (B 154v), but also by bitter division of opinion amongst themselves concerning assimilation to the dominant culture of the imperial powers. The repeated desecrations of the Temple, although imposed by foreign tyrants, were focal points for those internal differences (B 153a, 151). Conflicts between Sadducees and Pharisees (B 153) or between the followers of Hyrcanus and of Aristobulus (B 154v) were sometimes even more destructive than foreign tyrants to Jewish well-being.

The Book of Daniel was composed in response to 'the desecration [in 167 BCE] by Antiochus Epiphanes when a great sow was sacrificed on the altar of burnt offerings' (B 153a). The story of Daniel and his companions, Shadrach, Meshach, and Abed-nego, who refused to eat unclean food and walked unscathed in the fiery furnace, was meant to encourage the Jews to a less half-hearted and more effective resistance against the Seleucid tyranny. There seems to be no very clear connection between this story and that of the Daniel in GE's novel. It is true that Deronda rejects many of the values of the dominant culture. But there is a great difference between the hospitality of Quetcham Hall and the feast of Belshazzar, and GE's social satire does not encourage us to see Victoria's Britain and Belshazzar's Babylon as equally impious tyrannies. Neither does the apocalyptic vision which ends the Book of Daniel find a parallel in GE's picture of mid-Victorian society.

/151v/ Sanhedrim

The *Nassi*, or president of the Sanhedrim, & the *Ab-beth-din,* were first appointed by John Hyrcanus.[1]

With penal justice the Great Sanhedrim had nothing to do: this was administered by courts of three & twenty members each – small Sanhedrims – in every great town; which how-ever were apparently chosen or confirmed by the Greater Sanhedrim. This last was the legal organ of Judaism, the interpreter of the law, which consulted on the *general* religious questions, gave forth ordinances & even embraced political interests within its domain. Thus Bezetha was included in Jerusalem by a decree of the Sanhedrim. It could even summon High priests & princes before its bar. The calendar was under its management. Also genealogical tables. It was the interpreter both of the written & traditional law. It had to decide doubtful cases; but for this purpose two committees were appointed who sat in the fore-court of the Temple, & only in case of their disagreement was the case referred to the entire assembly. The sittings were daily except on Sabbaths & festivals, when the Synhedrists gave lectures in the Lehrhaus of the Temple. The qualifications for membership & criminal judgeship were, together with

1 For other references to the Nasi and Ab-beth-din, see B 123, Pf 711 60, and Pf 710 36. John Hyrcanus, son of Simon the Just (B 151), was High Priest and Ethnarch from 135 to 106 BCE.

knowledge of the law, descent from Jewish parents in legal marriage, favour with the people, & humility. [Graetz 3, 88–91]

/153/ Cases of cruelty

Though crucifixion was not a death sanctioned by the Jewish law (which admitted only beheading, stoning, burning & strangling) it was practised by Jewish rulers, e.g. Alexander Jannaeus crucified 800 Pharisees, prisoners – men of his own nation! – And this was the grandson of a Maccabee!

[Graetz 3, 114]

A Sadducee was stoned to death for riding a horse on a Sunday – this under the Pharisaic reform of Simon ben Shetach & Juda ben Tabbai. – At the same period 80 witches were crucified in Askalon. [Graetz 3, 125–6][1]

With regard to spiritual tyranny, it must be remembered that John Hyrcanus compelled the Idumaeans to become proselytes to Judaism. [Graetz 3, 64–5]

The punishment for blasphemy according to the law was first stoning by which death was inflicted, & *then* crucifixion of the dead body. This must have been the punishment inflicted on Jesus, who was condemned for blasphemy. Thus it seems that the punishment of crucifixion had been adopted by the Jews. [Graetz 3, 245]

/151/

Simon the Just (der Fromme) is associated with the striking episode of Caligula's attempt to have his own statue placed in the Temple. He comforted the terrified outraged people & exhorted them to keep the Feast of Tabernacles joyfully, for that the threatened evils would not take place. Grätz remarks how the unanimity & intensity of feeling among the Jews, who declared themselves ready to die rather than suffer the desecration of their temple, proves the strong hold which Judaism had taken through the exertions of the Pharisees. Two hundred years before, when Antiochus Epiphanes made a like attempt, the members of the high-priestly family had themselves lent their hand to the desecration, & been traitors to the Law.

[Graetz 3, 268–9]

1 For another note on the crucifixion of witches in Askalon, see Pf 711 22.

There appear to have been two previous Simons, named the Just: the First, high priest from BC 300 to 292; the second (who repelled Ptolemy Philopator from the Temple), from 219 to 195. [Milman I, 450n][1]

These lived during that great gap in Jewish History of 210 years, from Ezra & Nehemiah to Antiochus Epiphanes – nearly as long, observes Milman, as from the death of Elizabeth to Victoria, or from the reign of Henry IV to Louis Napoleon. [Milman I, 443][2]

/153a/ Temple-desecration

Entrance of Pompey into the Temple in the year 63. It was on a Sabbath in June that, a tower of the temple falling before the besiegers, the Roman soldiery entered the court of the Temple & killed the priests along with the sacrificial animals: the priests halted not an instant in their duties, but faced death calmly. Pompey after entering the Holy of Holies, left the Temple treasure untouched. (He had had before the present of the golden vine.)
[Graetz 3, 140–1, 137]

The other occasion (less certainly historical in its details) of a heathen ruler showing curiosity about the Holy of Holies is that of Ptolemy Philopator entering Jerusalem after defeating Antiochus the Great at the battle of Raphia. After making sumptuous presents to the Temple, he pressed forward to enter the Sanctuary, but was repelled by Simon, the high priest. As he persisted, there was a tumult & wailing through the whole city as if the walls & pavement shrieked with the shrieking people. Ptolemy is said to have been seized with a supernatural awe & horror; he trembled like a reed before the wind & fell speechless to the earth. From that time he entertained implacable animosity against the Jews. [Milman I, 452–3]

After this came the desecration by Antiochus Epiphanes when a great sow was sacrificed on the altar of burnt offerings. And finally the inrush into the Sanctuary under Titus. [Milman I, 461, and II, 368]

1 After making this note, GE added a marginal 'A 3d' to her note about 'Simon the Just', above.

2 GE's copy of Milman in DWL has a marginal line beside this passage. Compare her note on B 182v: '280 years, from Nehemiah to Judas Maccabaeus blank. Imagine what it would be if our history were blank from Edward the First to Elizabeth – or, to take a time of less rapid advance from Edward the Confessor's days to Chaucer's.'

(Apion's story of the fattened Greek) [Graetz 3, 258][1]

/155/ Motives & Pictures

1. King Agrippa mixing himself with the people when in the Feast of Weeks they carried the first fruits of the trees & fields with solemn songs to the Temple, & himself carrying the basket of fruit.[2] Reading the Book of Deuteronomy aloud in the Court of the Temple at the end of the Sabbatical year, & at the passage 'From the midst of thy brethren shalt thou choose thee a King',[3] bursting into tears remembering his half-Idumaean origin: whereupon the people cried, 'Thou art our brother!' [Graetz 3, 272][4]

2. In the siege under Titus, the rich Martha, the wife of Josua ben Gammala, who had bought the high priesthood for her husband, & who had been wont to walk on carpets from her house to the Temple, wandered in the streets with the poorest in search of some disgusting food to still the pangs of hunger. [Graetz 3, 401]

3. After the Destruction a youth & maiden of a noble house were given or sold as slaves to two masters, & as the slaves were of extreme beauty the owners resolved to marry them to each other. Led into one chamber at night, they wept in silence over their sad lot, that they as nobly born Jews should be doomed to a slaves' marriage. When the morning light came they recognized each other as brother & sister rushed into each other's arms & died! This story occurs in the Talmud. [Graetz 3, 406]

Simon Bar Giora, after attempting to work a subterranean way of escape from the passages under the temple, appearing suddenly above ground in his linen & purple, in the midst of the Roman soldiers. [Milman II, 376–7]

1 Antiochus Epiphanes was said to have found in the Temple an imprisoned Greek who was being fattened up for ritual slaughter by the Jews. For another of Apion's stories, see B 105v and Pf 711 23. Josephus' apologia, *Contra Apionem,* was written as a defence against Apion's anti-semitic oratory.

2 For the Feast of Weeks (Pentecost), see B 132 and 189 to 190.

3 Deuteronomy xvii, 15: 'one from among thy brethren shalt thou set king over thee; thou mayest not set a stranger over thee, which is not thy brother'.

4 For the half-Jewish King Agrippa's sister Berenice, and her liaison with Titus, the Roman conqueror, see Pf 711 66.

/154v/

The vessels of the Temple, the golden candlesticks, the golden table & the Thora-roll, were deposited by Vespasian in the Temple of Peace. Afterwards when Rome had been sacked they were carried to Africa.

v. Gibbon c. xli. Ref. Milman 2, 382[1]

When Eleazar, the Zealot leader who had held the fortress of Masada, despaired of any longer resisting the besieging Romans, he prevailed on his companions to agree to kill themselves rather than fall into the hands of the enemy. They first slew their wives & children, then themselves. The Romans on entering found the stillness of death. Only an old woman & five children came in answer to their call. [Milman II, 387–9][2]

Onias's Prayer. When the adherents of Hyrcanus & Aristobulus had fortified themselves, the one party in the temple, the other outside besieging, Onias was applied to as one whose prayers were efficacious. He knelt down publicly & prayed that, as those in the temple were the sons of the people & those outside the sons of the people, God would hear the prayers of neither against the other. The people stoned him to death. [Pf 711 58][3]

1 Milman refers to chapter xli of *The Decline and Fall of the Roman Empire,* where Gibbon mentions 'the holy vessels of the Jewish temple, which, after their long peregrination, were respectfully deposited in the Christian church of Jerusalem'. For GE's notes from Milman's edition of Gibbon, see Pf 710 22, 28, 36, and 40, and Pf 707 41 and 46 to 48.

2 The Zealots' actions – 'They first slew their wives & children, then themselves' – are echoed in Mainz during the first Crusade, when 'the men ... killed first the women & children & then themselves' (B 164v).

3 Abraham Geiger, *Judaism and its History,* pp. 180–1.

/161v/ Vessels of the Temple

The Jews of Byzantium sorrowfully beheld the sacred vessels of the Temple, which had been carried to Carthage by Genseric when he plundered Rome, brought (nearly a century later) by Belisarius the Conqueror of the Vandals to Constantinople (534) & carried in triumph along with Gelimer grandson of Genseric & the treasures of this unhappy king. A Jew remarked to a courtier that it was not advisable to deposit them in the palace: they might bring misfortune there, as they had done to Rome & to the descendant of Genseric. It would be safer to restore the sacred remnants to the place where King Solomon had had them made. The Emperor Justinian, hearing of this, felt a superstitious fear & had them carried to Jerusalem & placed in a church there.

[Graetz 5, 32–3][1]

Fiscus judaicus: the 2 drachmas formerly paid by each Jew to the temple at Jerusalem, paid by order of Vespasian to the Capitoline Jupiter

[Graetz 3, 410; B 193v and Pf 711 65]

1 Here GE added a cross-reference, 'See also 155' (for B 154v).

Alexandrian Jewish literature and the Canon

B 155v, 156, 157

These notes on the 'Alexandrian-Jewish Apocryphal Writings' and the fixing of the Canon are drawn from Graetz's comprehensive endnotes for the period at the end of the Hasmonean dynasty, just preceding the destruction of the Second Temple. Extracts from books of the Apocrypha were copied on Pf 708 31, 100, and 101, and her Blotter (see Waley, p. 11).

/155v/ Canon

In the last four years before the destruction of the Temple there were carried 18 decrees against commerce with the pagans;[1] & also there was an editing of the calendar of victories, or Megillat Ta'anit, with a redaction of the history of the Asmonaeans /Megillat Bet-Chasch monaim/, in order to intensify the national spirit. At the head of these measures was Eleasar ben Anania b. Chiskia, probably to be identified with the Zealot Eleasar who was active during the siege. Along with the 18 decrees there went also two ordinances as to uncleanness of hands – one of which was that the Holy Scriptures being touched caused uncleanness, which R. Jochanan b. Sakkai thus accounts for: 'In order that men should not use the H. S. as saddles & coverings for beasts'. Here arose the question, 'What exactly are these Scriptures which, being Holy, make the hands unclean'; & thus the Canon came to be more rigorously defined. Ecclesiastes & Solomon's Song were disputed, also the prophet Ezekiel, as being in contradiction with the Pentateuch. It is certain that the Hillelites & Schammaites, i.e. the Pharisaic leaders, fixed the Canon some years before the destruction of the Temple. It is possible that the superscriptions assigning the authorship of the several books were then prefixed. [Graetz 3, 355–6]

1 In the margin of Graetz 3, 355, GE wrote '18 Rules against the heathens'.

/156/ Alexandrian-Jewish Apocryphal Writings

The Sibylline books written by a Jew not earlier than the time of Cleopatra – during the second triumvirate, about 35 BC[1]

2d pt Esther also proceeded from the Jewish-Alexandrian school, with the pregnant purpose of making pagan potentates pronounce in favour of Judaism. This date refers only to the additions to the Book of Esther in our Apocrypha. The other part of the Book had a much earlier origin, & was included in the Canon.

2d & 3d Book of Maccabees; the latter about the year 40 under Caligula – after the terrible oppression of the Jews under Flaccus & during the continuance of the struggle [Pf 711 64]

The Letter of Aristeas, de lege divina, containing the romance of the origin of the Septuagint, seems to stand next in age to the Sybilline Books. The *Book of Wisdom* is vaguely assigned to the Ptolemaic period. Only thus much is certain concerning the fragments & complete writings called apocryphal – that they were all later than the Septuagint, for they all show signs of its use. Thus according to Grätz's notion of the date of the Septuagint they are all later than 160 BC.

Apoc. Writings:
Book of Wisdom, Baruch, Letter of Jeremiah,
Song of the Three Children, Susanna, Bel & the Dragon

Poetical & historical Fragments
Pseudepigraphic poems: pseudorphica, Jewish Sibylline Books &c.
Legendary narratives concerning historical events: Aristeas' Letters & the so-called 4th Book of Maccabees falsely attributed to Josephus

[Graetz 3, 438–45]

1 For another note on the Sybilline books, see Pf 710 35.

/157/

Josephus gives 22 sacred Books: 5 Books of Moses, 13 historical books giving the Jewish history from the death of Moses to Artaxerxes, i.e. the book of Esther. These 13 include:

1, Joshua; 2, Judges; 3, Ruth; 4, Samuel in one book; 5, Kings;
6, Chronicles in one book; 7, Ezra & Nehemiah in one book;
8, Daniel; 9, Esther; 10, Isaiah; 11, Jeremiah; 12, Ezekiel;
13, the minor prophets in one book – as the Talmud gives them.

Finally, he gives 4 Books which include Hymns & Rules of life. Which books he means under these 4 is doubtful, since there were 6: Psalms, Proverbs, Job, Lamentations, Canticles & Ecclesiastes. Did Josephus reject the two last?

At this period of discussing the Canon the Book of Wisdom (Sirach) with others (unnamed) was rejected.

The Schammaites placed a guard outside armed, as a compulsory means of getting the 18 statutes passed in the house of Eleazar.

'So weit auf historischem Gebiete Gewissheit möglich ist, hat sich aus der Untersuchung herausgestellt dass die Schammaiten mit den Beschlüssen der tumultuarischen Synode in dem Hause des Zelotenführers Eleasar b. Anania Repressalien gegen die Feind-seligkeit der Heiden in den Nachbarländern Judäa's erzielt haben, und, um den religiösen Patriotismus oder den Zelotismus auf der Höhe der Gefahr zu erhalten, wurden nationale Schriften gesammelt und unter das Volk vertheilt.' [Graetz 3, 501–2][1]

1 Translation:

Through investigation it has been established, so far as certainty in historical matters is possible, that in accordance with the decrees of the riotous Synod in the house of the leader of the Zealots, Eleasar ben Anania, the Schammaites made reprisals against the hostility of the gentiles in the neighbouring countries of Judaea, and in order to preserve religious patriotism or fanatic zeal at the height of the danger, national writings were collected and distributed amongst the people.

GE's mistaken transcription of 'Feindseligkeiten' for 'Feindseligkeit' has been corrected above.

Parables from the Talmud

B 158, 159

The source of these stories is Giuseppi Raffael Levi, *Parabeln, Legenden und Gedanken aus Thalmud und Midrasch,* translated from the Italian by Ludwig Seligmann (Leipzig, 1863). GE's annotated copy is in DWL. GHL's Diary records that 'Polly read ... Levi Parable from the Talmud' on 2 July 1874. Several apothegms from Levi, including some from 'P[irke] Aboth', are noted on Pf 707 28, 29, and 32. GE used one passage from Levi in her poem, 'The Death of Moses':

> God spake to Gabriel, the messenger
> Of mildest death that draws the parting life
> Gently, as when a little rosy child
> Lifts up its lips from off the bowl of milk
> And so draws forth a curl that dipped its gold
> In the soft white – thus Gabriel draws the soul.[1]

Her simile elaborates upon the mysterious, evocative image in the extract from Levi (Pf 707 32): 'Die Seele löst sich vom Körper, wie man ein Haar aus der Milch zieht.' ('The soul is freed from the body, just as one draws out a hair from the milk.')

The first parable below provided the story for a projected poem included in a list on GE's Blotter: '"Antico amor" – the divorced wife', (Waley, p. 6). The Italian part of this title echoes the Italian heading below, with its emphasis on the great power of old love: 'Dell antico amor – la gran potenza'. In Levi's title, however, the rejected wife takes precedence over the old feeling: 'Die Verstoßene, oder die alten Gefühle' is a direct translation of 'La Ripudiata, ossia gli antichi affetti', in the original *Parabole, leggende e pensieri raccolti dai libri talmudici dei primi cinque secoli dell' E. V.* (Florence, 1861).

Levi's stories often refer – directly or indirectly – to Jewish–Gentile relations. They were intended for a wide popular readership, and meant to promote better understanding between Jews and non-Jews.

---

1 *Poems,* p. 196, ll. 17–22.

/158/ *'Dell antico amor – la gran potenza'* Legend

Rabbi José had a bad wife, who besides other scandals insulted him in the presence of his disciples. These called on him to separate from her, but he excused himself, the fact being that he was poor & unable to restitute her dowry. The disciples collected to enable him to pay the money, & he was induced to separate from his wife. She found a wealthy match in the governor of the city & for some time lived sumptuously. But the governor fell into disgrace, lost all his wealth, was reduced to great misery, & finally became blind. He was obliged to beg in the streets, & every day the wife led him through the principal parts of the city. The blind man knew the ways, & after some days he observed that his wife never conducted him to a certain place which was very populous. He rebuked her for this, & ordered her to take him there because the Jews who lived there would have given him liberal alms. 'The Jews?' said the wife, trembling. 'Don't you know that one of them was my former husband? No, I will never expose myself to that shame.' The blind man again insisted, but the wife declared that she would never comply. In one of their usual rounds the blind man, secretly aware when they were near the piazza in question, raised his voice & with threats demanded to be **/159/** conducted thither. The wife refuses, the blind man curses, throws himself at her, holds her by the hair & beats her furiously. At her cries the crowd gathers, & with it comes the former husband. He recognizes the wife & feels his soul stirred by painful memories. He quiets the blind man, comforts the wife, gives them shelter & always afterwards provides for their sustenance.

(Rabot) [pp. 138–9]

Eliezer, the servant of Abraham, had to pass through Sodom. He had scarcely arrived when an inhabitant of the city attacked & gave him a blow that drew blood. In this condition Eliezer went straight to complain to a magistrate, who after hearing the complaint said, 'Ungrateful man! my fellow-citizen gave thee a blow for thy good: it is thy part now to repay him the benefit.' At this unjust sentence Eliezer infuriated rushed at the judge & gave him a blow that drew blood. The judge cried: 'Scoundrel! How dare you ...' 'I dare nothing,' answered Eliezer; 'I have given a blow to you for your good; & I beg you yourself to pay my debt to the fellow who struck me: you have the value.'

Talmud. Sanhedrin [p. 348]

Chisdai and the title of Gaon

B 159v, 160, 160v, 161, 162, 162v, 163

For a chronology of the 'Period of the Gaonim, 658–997', see B 170v, 171v, and 172, and Pf 711 28. In the first centuries of Islamic rule, leadership of the dispersed Jews remained in the hands of the Babylonian Exilarch, or Resch Galuta.[1] In time, the prestige and authority of the Gaonim (or *geonim*), the presidents of the two great academies at Pumbedita and Sura, came to surpass that of the Exilarchs (B 160).

The primary source for GE's notes on Chisdai Ben Isaac, the *Nasi* or Patriarch of the Jews in Cordova towards the end of the Gaonic period, is David Cassel's biographical sketch of 'Chisdai, the Son of Isaac' in *Miscellany of Hebrew Literature.*[2] Pf 711 contains brief notes from Cassel's article, including two references to matters noted more fully below:

> Chisdai, contemp. Abderrahman III. 911–961
> Also Menachem b. Jacob, author of the oldest Hebrew dictionary
> (Pf 711 75)

> Vessel captured in the Aegean Sea containing Jewish scholars:
> these sold for slaves & redeemed by their brethren became
> Rabbis in Cairo, Greece & Cordova (Pf 711 76)

Chisdai is the patron of Hebrew studies referred to as Chasdai in the note on the New Hebrew poetry and 'Chasdai, in Spain, 915–970' in the Chronology (B 139v, 170v, and 172).

---

1 For GE's notes on the origin of this title, see B 123, Pf 710 30 and Pf 711 60.

2 Edited by Albert Löwy, vol. I (London: Trübner for the Society of Hebrew Literature, 1872), pp. 73–91. GE's copy of this volume of the *Miscellany* is in DWL.

/159v/ Legend

'Chisdai ben Isaac (911–976) remembered a saying which he had heard from his father in his youth, viz, that a great number of Jews, driven from their ancestral dwellings, had gone to a country where, in order to escape from the persecutions of the Chaldaeans, they had hidden their scrolls of the law & other sacred books in a cave, & were therefore obliged to perform their religious services in the cave. This custom was continued through many generations so that after a long time nothing remained of the religion of their fathers but the habit of praying morning & evening in the cave, without their even knowing why they did it there. But after a lapse of some time a strange Jew came to the cave, who examined it closely & found the concealed books which had long been forgotten; & from these they were again instructed in their primitive religion.' Misc. Heb. Lit. I, 86

Jews in Cologne. There is certain testimony to the presence of Jews in Cologne in the 4th century. [Graetz 4, 333]

Fables concocted by the Jews in Worms, Ulm &c as to their migration thither as early as the Benjamite disgrace, in order to justify them against the accusation of being concerned in the crucifixion.[1]

/160/ Spain

The Byzantine Emperor sent to Abderrahman III as a present a copy of Dioscorides. But as no one in Cordova was master of the Greek language, Abderrahman asked the emperor to send him someone acquainted with both Latin & Greek, that his learned men might learn the latter tongue through the former. He sent a monk Nicolaus with whom the Jew Chisdai soon entered into friendly terms & was successful in discovering the significance of various medicaments in Dioscorides – previously unknown.

Ibid. [*Miscellany*, p. 77]

1 Source not traced. The Benjamite disgrace occurred during that barbaric era when 'there was no king in Israel: every man did that which was right in his own eyes'; see the Book of Judges, xix–xxi. GE noted two other legendary early migrations from Judaea: one from Cassel, 'Legend of Jewish immigration into Spain in the time of King David' (Pf 711 75), and another tradition that Jews first settled in Medina 'as early as Joshua' (Pf 711 76).

Chisdai stood to his brethren in the relation of Nasi, or temporal head of the Jewish congregations of the land. He sought in every way to advance Jewish studies; assembled scholars & poets about him, supported needy orphans & provided copies of religious books. His best known scholar is Menachem b. Jacob, who was the author of the oldest Hebrew dictionary.

[*Miscellany*, pp. 81–2]

At that time a thorough knowledge of the Talmud could only be got at the high schools of the Gaonim in Sura & Pumbedita. Hence young men were sent there, & European Jews were dependent on the Gaonim in religious matters generally. Without doubt a lively intercourse had taken place between Spain & Babylonia in the 9th & 10th centuries; questions on difficult points were sent to the Gaonim, generally accompanied with rich presents. In the time of Chisdai, the chief rabbi at Cordova was Nathan, **/160v/** not very learned, but estimable, who according to the universal custom at that time acted both as instructor & as judge in civil processes. Now the Caliph's admiral Romahis, cruising through the Mediterranean in pursuit of Christian ships, captured a vessel in the Aegean sea, in which were several Jewish scholars. These with the other prisoners were sold as slaves: one in Alexandria, where he was redeemed by his brethren & became Chief Rabbi; another in Cyrene, who had the like fortune; a third, Moses, was taken to Cordova, his beautiful wife throwing herself into the sea on the way to escape the persecutions of the Admiral. He & his son Chanoch were also redeemed by the Jews, not so much because he was a learned man as because there was a special fund for the redemption of Jewish slaves. Moses in the garb of a slave went to the house of instruction where R. Nathan was discoursing on the section Joma, & sat listening in a corner unobserved till the Rabbi came to a difficult passage which he could not well explain, when Moses stepped forward & by a few words on this theme drew the general attention. Soon the listeners & Nathan himself saw that the stranger far excelled them in knowledge, & question after question was put **/161/** to him which he answered to the satisfaction of all. When the discourse was ended, Nathan left his place & said, 'I am no longer judge; that stranger is my teacher.' And he induced the community of Cordova to elect Moses as their chief Rabbi. This event was welcome to the Caliph because he saw that the dependence of his Jews on the Persian colleges would cease, & the large sums of money which were sent to Persia every year would remain in his country.

Ibid. [*Miscellany*, pp. 83–5]

/162/ Title of Gaon

The Babylonian Jews having declared for Ali (against Moawija) as the successor to the Khalifate,[1] & having assembled themselves, it is said, to the number of 90,000 under a School-president named Mar-Isaak, to do him homage (658), Ali warmly accepted this homage & it may be well believed granted privileges to Mar-Isaak. It is apparently from this time & this cause that we must trace the custom that the Head of the Academy of Sura should hold a certain dignity & bear the title of Gaon - a word which seems to be not of Hebrew but of Arabic or Persian origin (excellency, Würdenträger). With the Gaonat were combined certain rights which even the Exilarch or Resch-Galuta must not infringe. Hence a peculiar relation arose between these two dignities which led to misunderstandings. With Bostanai, confirmed & honoured as Resch-Galuta by Omar, & with the aforesaid Mar-Isaak, begins a new division of Jewish history, the epoch of the Gaonim. [Graetz 5, 121]

About the beginning of the eighth century was developed the three-fold authority in the Jewish Babylonian community. The Resch-Galuta held the political supervision, with a certain show of princely dignity & splendour; the Gaon of Sura the religious authority; while the judicial power was divided between the Resch-Galuta & the Head of the School of Pumbadita.

[Graetz 5, 125]

1 For notes on Ali, Moawiyah, and the Mohammedan Empire, see Pf 710 26.

/162v/ Central point of Jewish affection & religion
Prince of the Captivity & Judaic Community in Babylon

Das jüdische Gemeinwesen, der exilarchatische Staat in Babylonien so abhängig er auch von den Launen der islamitischen Statthalter und der Willkühr der eigenen Träger war, erglänzte in der Ferne mit dem Glorienscheine von Macht und Grösse. In dem Exilsfürsten erschien den Juden auf dem ganzen Erdenrund, so weit sie dunkle Kunde davon hatten, das davidische Scepter wieder erstanden, & in den Gaonen der beiden Hochschulen sahen sie die lebendigen Träger und Fortpflanzer der idealen talmudischen Zeit ... Jede Eroberung der mohammedanischen Feldherren erweiterte die Grenzen für die Herr-schaft des Exilsfürsten und der Gaonen. Selbst Palästina ordnete sich Babylonien unter, da es des Mittelpunktes beraubt war. Die Herzen aller Juden schlugen den Machtinhabern entgegen, und ihre Spenden strömten ihnen freiwillig zu, damit das Haus David's würdig auftreten & die talmudischen Hochschulen in Glanz fortbestehen könnten. Sich dem Mittelpunkt in Babylonien unterzuordnen, gebot eben so sehr die religiöse Pflicht, wie das patriotische Gefühl. Der Schmerz des Zerstreutseins in alle Winkel der Erde war durch das Bewusstsein gelindert, dass da an den Strömen Babel's, wo die Blüthe des jüdischen Volkes sich in seiner Vollkraft /163/ niedergelassen, wo die grossen Amoras gelebt und gewirkt, ein jüdischer Staat bestehe.[1]

1 Translation:

The Jewish commonwealth of Babylonia, notwithstanding its dependence on the humors of a Mahometan governor and the caprice of its own leaders, seemed nevertheless to those at a distance surrounded with a halo of power and greatness. The Prince of the Captivity appeared to the Jews of distant lands, who heard only confused rumors, to have regained the sceptre of David; for them the Geonim of the two colleges were the living upholders and the representatives of the ideal times of the Talmud ... Every conquest of the Mahometan generals enlarged the boundaries of the dominion under the rule of the Prince of the Captivity and the Geonim. Even Palestine, deprived of its center, subordinated itself to Babylonia. The hearts of all Jews turned towards the potentates on the Euphrates, and their presents flowed in freely, to enable the house of David to make a worthy appearance, and the Talmudical colleges to continue to exist in splendor. The grief for their dispersion to all corners of the earth was mitigated by the knowledge that by the rivers of Babylon, where the flower of the Jewish nation in its full vigor had settled, and where the great Amoraim had lived and worked, a Jewish commonwealth still existed. (Bella Löwy 3, 100)

Dort in dem Ursitze jüdischer Grösse strömte, so wurde im jüdischen Kreise allerwärts geglaubte, der Urquell altjüdischer Weisheit. 'Gott habe die Hochschulen von Sura und Pumbadita zwölf Jahre vor der Einäscherung des Tempels durch Nebukadnezar entstehen lassen und sie besonders geschützt. Sie haben nie Verfolgungen durch Rom und Byzanz erlitten, keinen Zwang und keine Knechtung gekannt. Von dort aus werde die Erlösung Israels ausgehen und die Bewohner dieses glücklichen Erdpunktes werden auch von den Leiden der messianischen Zeit verschont bleiben.' Das war die Auschauung derer, welche das Exilarchat und Gaonat nicht mit eigenen Augen gesehen hatten. Es galt für eine Ehre, nach dem Tode in einer Trauerfeierlichkeit an den Hochschulen erwähnt zu werden. Dazu wurde ein Tag an jedem Versammlungsmonat bestimmt. Die Thätigkeit der Lehrhäuser ruhte an demselben, die Collegien-Mitglieder trauerten um die verstorbenen Wohlthäter der Hochschulen innerhalb eines Jahres und beteten für deren Seelenruhe. Selbst von Frankreich und Spanien sendete man später eine Liste der Verstorbenen ein, um sie der Ehre theilhaftig werden zu lassen.

Grätz V, [133-]134[1]

1 Translation:

It was universally believed by the Jews that in the original seat of Jewish greatness the primitive spring of ancient Jewish wisdom was still flowing. 'God permitted the colleges of Sora and Pumbeditha to come into existence twelve years before the destruction of the Temple by Nebuchadnezzar, and vouchsafed them His special protection. They never suffered persecution at the hands of the Romans or the Byzantines, and have known neither coercion nor bondage. From thence will proceed the deliverance of Israel, and the dwellers in this happy corner of the earth will be spared the sufferings that are to usher in the age of the Messiah.' Such was the view held by all who had not seen the Babylonian settlement with their own eyes. It was accounted an honor for a dead person to be mentioned at a memorial service at the colleges. For this purpose a special day was set apart in each month of assembly, during which no business was transacted by the colleges; the members mourned for the benefactors of the colleges that had died during the past year and prayed for the peace of their souls (Ashkabá). Later on it became the custom to forward lists of the dead, even from France and Spain, in order that they might also be thus honored. (Bella Löwy 3, 100-1)

Simon ben Jochai and Abraham Ibn Esra

B 163v, 164, 167, 167v

Rabbi Simon ben Jochai lived during the 'Period of the Tanaim, 70–200', following Rabbi Akiba and preceding the 'Close of Mischna – R. Jehuda'.[1] Abraham Ibn Esra (1088–1167 CE) and Rabbi Jacob Tam, the grandson of 'Rashi (Rabbi Shelomah b. Yitzschak)', lived during the third Rabbinical Period (B 170v). Ibn Esra not only had a romantic life story, but also contributed significantly to the development of biblical interpretation and historical criticism.

/163v/ R. Simon b. Jochai

Rabbi Simon b. Jochai of Galilee has been falsely stamped by the later legend as a miracle-worker, a mystic & the creator of the Kabbala. Though only a few traits of his life are known, thus much is to be inferred from them, namely, that he was rather of a sober than a fantastical, mystic, nature. After his return from exile during Hadrian's persecution his individual activity is merged in the corporate activity of the Sanhedrim of Uscha. He was an inveterate enemy of the Romans. The incidents of his hiding from their persecution in a cave, & of his pointing out by the experiment of planting the wolf's bane which were the unclean (burial) places in Tiberias have been incrusted with legend.

Instead of an inclination to mysticism, a thoroughly rational principle of interpretation marks his decisions. In distinctive advance on R. Akiba's procedure of developing the law[2] from pleonastic words, syllables & letters, Simon b. Jochai inquired into the motive of a given law in order to conclude as to its applications.

1 For more on the Tanaim, see B 114 and the 'Jewish chronology', B 170.
2 GE emended her translation from 'eliciting the law' to 'developing the law'.

He said that the exact fulfilment of the law was only possible to those who lived on Manna or Tithes. He was the only man of his time whose entire profession was study. He lived at Tekoa[1] in Galilee, & had a circle **/164/** of disciples around him. Like his colleagues he gave a Mischna collection under the name of *Midot*,[2] which contains a compressed selection from R. Akiba's.[3] He gave the preference to the subtle mode of teaching which had come into practice since R. Akiba & which bore the special name of Talmud, over the merely traditive. He outlived all his colleagues & was hence the sole authority for the succeeding age. In his later life he made a journey to Rome, in order to hinder the renewal of Hadrian's edicts. [Graetz 4, 196–200]

/167/ Abr. Ibn Esra

Ibn Esra's life (1088–1167) makes a romantic picture. At fifty he had not written anything & had no fame in his city, Toledo. Unfortunate in all his undertakings & very poor, he set off with his son on travel & saw Africa, Egypt, Palestine, Babylon, Bagdad. At last he settled for a time in Rome & drew attention among its people, then under the unsung influence of Arnold of Brescia. He commented here the five Megilloth; & of Solomon's Song ridiculed the idea of its being in the first instance other than a poem of young love. Nevertheless he interpreted it in the edifying manner of the elder exegetists. He also wrote on the grammar of Hebrew. Then he went to Salerno, but seems to have been ill-contented there. Next at Mantua, he wrote a grammatical work on the refinements of the Hebrew language, which is a sample of his diffuse desultory style. There was this antithesis in him that he denounced the least questioning of the masoretic text as heresy, & yet was himself very daring in his sceptical suggestions about the biblical writings. In Lucca he occupied himself with astronomy & wrote several books on astrology. According to him the influence of the stars on the human destiny is unalterable, but he allows so much of energy to the human soul, that it can in some degree weaken the evil influence.[4]

When he was sixty-four, after recovery from an illness, he vowed to undertake the explanation of the Thorah. His **/167v/** method is that of strict grammatical interpretation, in opposition to the mystical & the haggadistic.

1 GE added a reference mark indicating a later footnote: '*ölreiche*' ('oil-rich').

2 GE later pencilled in an interlinear translation 'Rules'.

3 For another note on Rabbi Akiba, see B 109.

4 GE added a marginal line beside the last sentence.

But along with all his severity about the text, he threw out hints that many verses in the Thora were later interpolations, nay, that the whole had originated at a later period. Only he leaves his reader in doubt as to his earnestness either way.

In Lucca also he produced a luminous commentary on Isaiah (1154–55) in which he expresses a doubt whether the last three & twenty chapters are from the same hand as the earlier ones.[1]

When he had finished his commentary he left Italy & went to Provence, & afterwards when he was seventy he visited London (Henry II regnant). In 1160 he returned to Narbonne & revised his commentary in his advanced old age. He died at Calahorra, apparently on his way back to Spain, in 1167.

Grätz, VI [186–96]

Of *R. Jacob Tam*, grandson of Raschi, Grätz says that 'although a private person & carrying on a business' he was regarded as the most authoritative Rabbi of his time, not only in France but in Spain & Italy. There is only one stain on his high character – that he took usury from Xtians, & from Jews through the medium of Xtians, *while from baptized Jews* he took it *directly* – thus setting aside the strict laws of the Talmud concerning usury.

[Graetz 6, 197][2]

1 GE has marked, with a marginal ink line, the sentence on the 'luminous commentary on Isaiah' which expressed a doubt (shared by later scholars) that the Book of Isaiah was written by a single author. The later, anonymous, hand is that of the Second Isaiah, also known as 'The Great Unknown'. This is the (unexplained) joke made in the *Hand and Banner*:

> 'Is the gentleman anonymous? Is he a Great Unknown?' said the broad-chested quoter of Shelley, with a humorous air.
> 'My name is Daniel Deronda. I am unknown, but not in any sense great.'
> (DD ch. 42: 485)

As GE knew, the same joking allusion was made about Sir Walter Scott – who was not at all unknown, but only anonymous – by the publisher of his novels.

The 'suffering servant' passage of Isaiah liii is attributed to the Second Isaiah. See B 166 and 166v.

2 For GE's query, 'The Talmudic laws about usury?', see Pf 711 101.

Leopold Zunz

B 165, 164v, 165v

GE's list of 'Books Retained from T[rübner]' (Pf 711 114) includes 'Zunz, Synagl. Poesie, & Ritual', a reference to two volumes by Leopold Zunz: *Die synagogale Poesie des Mittelalters* (Berlin: Julius Springer, 1855) and the second part of that work, *Der Ritus des synagogalen Gottesdienstes, geschichtlich entwickelt* (Berlin: Julius Springer, 1859). Both parts, bound together, are in DWL, as are GE's copies of two other works by Zunz: *Die gottesdienstlichen Vorträge der Juden, historisch entwickelt* (Berlin, 1832), and *Gesammelte Schriften*, vol. I (Berlin, 1875). Zunz was a major figure in the 'Wissenschaft des Judentums', or scientific study of Judaism. He was the first to outline the principles of the new science, and edited the journal *Zeitschrift für die Wissenschaft des Judenthums* (Berlin, 1822–3). GE would have known of his friendship with Heinrich Heine; see the footnote to B 125v.

The source of the notes on 'Music in the Synagogue' (B 165) and on 'Sufferings' (B 164v) is *Die synagogale Poesie des Mittelalters.* Zunz's second chapter, 'Leiden', a summary of Jewish sufferings in the Middle Ages, is prefatory to his anthology of the '*Piut Selichah*' or penitential poems. The *selichot* are supplications for divine forgiveness, recited during the ten days of repentance at the beginning of the new year. For GE's note from Zunz on *Selicha,* see Pf 711 94, copied again in part on B 190 and 194. Zunz's historical study of the *selichot* brought to light the early poets who were forerunners of the great New Hebrew poets, such as Ibn Gebirol, Jehuda Halevy, Kalonymos ben Jehuda, and Alcharisi.

GE knew Albert Löwy's translation of the second chapter, published in the *Miscellany of Hebrew Literature* as 'Zunz on the Sufferings of the Jews during the Middle Ages' (I, 167–218); she also read Löwy's introductory survey of Zunz's scholarship (I, 151–66; see B 193v and Pf 711 76). The opening sentence of Löwy's translation is marked by a marginal pencil line in GE's copy, but the Berg notebook translations are her own. Unusually, she drafted two translations, and then supplied a third in DD ch. 42, following the epigraph in German:

> 'If there are ranks in suffering, Israel takes precedence of all the nations – if the duration of sorrows and the patience with which they are borne ennoble, the Jews are among the aristocracy of every land – if a literature is called rich in the possession of a few classic tragedies, what shall we say to a National Tragedy lasting for fifteen hundred years, in which the poets and actors were also the heroes?' (480)

According to Graham Handley, the qualifying 'among', not in the MS, was added before the first printing (480n).

The elevated aristocratic rank and tragic heroism of the Zunz passage contrast with the petit-bourgeois prosperity of 'the Cohens', who in turn serve as a foil for the 'poor dear creature' they have taken into their home, to be 'nested in ... self-gratulating ignorant prosperity'. This double contrast signals the ambivalence of the comparison: inherent likeness may coexist with apparent dissimilarity. Thus, when Cohen speaks 'apologetically', his speech is both excuse and a vindication of principle:

> '... [We] wouldn't part with him if he was a still worse encumbrance. It isn't that we don't know the long and short of matters, but it's our principle. There's fools do business at a loss and don't know it. I'm not one of 'em.' (DD ch. 42: 480–1)

GE's control of tone in this speech is very fine: the pawnbroker as patron is patronizing and even self-gratulating, but not so ignorant that he does not know the difference between principal and principle.

The title of Book VI is 'Revelations'. In this book, GE has set herself the daunting task of bringing the revelations of Old Testament visionary prophecy into conjunction with the mundane world of contemporary London – in a context where the prophetic mode of William Blake's *Jerusalem* would be inappropriate. Here a double contrast between ignorant prosperity and heroically borne sorrows is mediated through Deronda's consciousness. As his thoughts pass, in the opening pages of this chapter, from Zunz to the Cohen family, GE adumbrates complexities of likeness and difference to be found in a tragedy 'in which the poets the actors the heroes were all one' (B 164v):

> Deronda had lately been reading that passage of Zunz, and it occurred to him by way of contrast when he was going to the Cohens, who certainly bore no obvious stamp of distinction in sorrow or in any other form

of aristocracy. Ezra Cohen was not clad in the sublime pathos of the martyr ... (DD ch. 42: 480)

But the negations of this mediating passage – 'bore no *obvious* stamp of distinction' and 'not *clad* in the sublime pathos of the martyr' – are so worded as to imply that apparent contrasts may be illusory. These denials are meant to heighten our awareness of the pathos and suffering of Mordecai, who will soon be revealed to be the other Ezra Cohen.

/165/ Music in the Synagogue

A fine voice was demanded in the 'Vorbeter' of the Synagogue. The prayers & songs / hymns / were not simply read but chanted or delivered melodically. Nay, gentile melodies were sought after – this being mentioned with disapproval about the end of the eleventh century ... Abenezra says that on the MSS. of hymns the melody was notified & explains in this way the superscriptions of some of the Psalms. Benjamin of Tudela knew in Bagdad an able singer of the psalms in use in the divine service. Nearly about the same time it is prescribed in Germany that pains should be taken to find suitable melodies for the prayers, & to deliver each portion in an appropriate manner; towards the end of the 13th century a French Rabbi enumerates it among the qualifications of a Vorbeter to have an agreeable voice & artistic delivery. At that time there were professed singers who supported the Vorbeter, especially on festival days, & from that time the singing of a great part of the service is mentioned by authors & testified by MSS ... With many portions it is noted that they are to be sung according to the melody of this or that hymn: in the ritual of Avignon & Carpentras the number of these model melodies is nearly 150, consisting of every species of synagogal poetry ...

'Manche der noch heute in den Synagogen gehörten Melodien, namentlich der Bussezeit, sind wohl nicht viel jünger als die Stücke, die nach ihnen vorgetragen werden.' Zunz [pp. 113–16][1]

1 Translation:

Many of the melodies heard even to this day in the Synagogue, particularly in the time of repentance [preceding the Day of Atonement], are probably not much more recent than the portions that are sung to them.

/164v/ Sufferings

When in the first Crusade the Jews in Mainz were threatened with death, if they would not be baptized, the men assembled together, killed first the women & children & then themselves. (Zunz) [p. 16][1]

'If there are ranks in suffering, Israel takes precedence of all the nations; if the duration of sorrows & the patience with which they are borne, ennoble, the Jews are the aristocracy of every land: if a literature is called rich because it possesses a few classic tragedies, what place is due to a national tragedy which lasts more than a thousand years, in which the poets & the actors were also the heroes?' (Zunz) [p. 9]

(If a literature is rich because it possesses a few classic tragedies on a few mythical themes, what shall we say to a tragedy which lasted for fifteen hundred years in which the poets the actors the heroes were all one?)[2]

For the poet's personification of Israel see the poems of Ibn G'ebirol.
Grätz, VI, 54 [-55][3] & Geiger, Life of Ibn G.[4]

/165v/ Death of Ibn Gebirol

The legend relates that an Arabian poet murdered him out of envy & buried his body under a fig-tree. This fig-tree consequently bore an extraordinary show of blossoms which drew the attention of the passers-by till the crime was detected.

Israel was the fig-tree which Ibn Gebirol fed with the sap of his poetry & made it bear a glorious burthen of blossoms. [Graetz 6, 55]

1 Mirah twice refers to this and other similar events as precedents for her suicide attempt – not having a father who will kill her to save her from apostasy:

'I know our fathers slew their children and then slew themselves, to keep their souls pure.' (DD ch. 17: 176)

'And in the wars and troubles when Christians were cruellest, our fathers had sometimes slain their children and afterwards themselves; it was to save them from being false apostates.' (DD ch. 20: 205)

2 GE's alternate translation.

3 This reference leads to GE's notes from Graetz on B 165v.

4 Abraham Geiger, *Salomo Gabirol und seine Dichtungen* (Leipzig: Oskar Leiner, 1867).

Leopold Zunz B 165v

XIth century

It is remarkable how in the XIth century it was the clergy who began to protect the Jews from the hatred of the multitude; whereas previously, it was the clergy who hounded on the persecutors.[1]

A mystic had reckoned that the Messiah would appear towards the end of the 256th lunar cycle between the years 1096–1166. But instead of the trumpet of deliverance the dispersed sons of Juda heard the wild cry of the crusaders: 'The Jews crucified our Lord; they must be converted or die.' [Graetz 6, 84]

1 Perhaps GE's own comment; compare her note on Pf 711 95, from Graetz 6, 83.

Jehuda Halevy

B 166, 166v

Jehuda Halevy was the great twelfth-century Sephardic author whose New Hebrew poetry is a model for Mordecai's (DD ch. 38: 445). 'Jehuda Halevi, 1086. Great poet: author of Chozari' is included in GE's 'Chronology' (B 172) and in her other chronology on Pf 711 28: 'Jehuda ha Levi, wrote 1140'. GE was familiar with translated passages from the *Chozari* in the *Miscellany of Hebrew Literature*, pp. 63–72. On Pf 707 23 she also cites a reference to 'Cassel's German version of Khozari with learned annotations'. Her source for the following notes, as for B 165v, is volume 6 of Graetz.

She begins with a brief summary of Halevy's 'system': the Israelitish people, having inherited a particular virtue or spiritual fortune, form 'the heart & kernel of mankind, exclusively capable of the prophetic function' (B 166). On the last page of this notebook, she writes, 'That Israel is the heart of Humanity & therefore feels more keenly occurs first in *Chozari*, by Jehuda Halevy' (B 194). The same image is cited by Sephardo in *The Spanish Gypsy:*

> 'Israel
> Is to the nations as the body's heart:
> Thus writes our poet Jehuda.'[1]

Halevy's heart imagery was not new to GE, then; but it has more essential significance in *Daniel Deronda* than in *The Spanish Gypsy.* Mordecai makes this commentary:

> 'But it is true, as Jehuda-ha-Levi first said, that Israel is the heart of mankind, if we mean by heart the core of affection which binds a race and its families in dutiful love, and the reverence for the human body which lifts the needs of our animal life into religion, and the tenderness which is merciful to the poor and weak and to the dumb creature that wears the yoke for us.' (DD ch. 42: 492)

Mordecai undoubtedly speaks here for GE. A full consideration of the meaning of this passage might begin with her translator's note on

1 Book III, in *Poems*, p. 344.

'the *psychological* distinction' between *Herz* and *Gemüth* in Feuerbach.[1] But in this novel she moves away from Christian hermeneutical tradition to a more inclusive viewpoint.

The passage quoted in German from Graetz (B 166v) shows the developing of greater significance in Halevy's imagery of the sensitive heart:

> The greatest sufferer, however, is Israel, since he is among men what the heart is in the human organism ... The words which the great prophet represents the nations of the world as saying apply to Israel: 'He hath borne our griefs, and carried our sorrows.' (Bella Löwy translation, 3, 335)

The quotation within this passage directs us to Isaiah liii, on the suffering servant:

> He is despised and rejected of men; a man of sorrows, and acquainted with grief ... He was despised, and we esteemed him not. Surely he hath borne our griefs, and carried our sorrows: yet we did esteem him stricken, smitten of God, and afflicted. (Isaiah liii, 3–4)

In Christian hermeneutics, this passage is taken to refer to the atonement of the crucified Messiah, Jesus. Gentiles may be aware of this interpretation's derivation from Jewish tradition, which identifies the suffering servant as the people of Israel, all the people who are part of the Covenant. GE's revised interpretation owes more to those Jewish origins than to their Christian evolution.

Mirah voices the Jewish reading of the passage when she refers her suffering to the affliction of Israel:

> '... it comforted me to believe that my suffering was part of the affliction of my people ... that has been going on through ages and ages. For if many of my race were wicked and made merry in their wickedness – what was that but part of the affliction borne by the just among them, who were despised for the sins of their brethren?'

Remembering Isaiah liii, 3 ('despised and rejected of men'), she says to Mrs Meyrick, 'you have not despised me', and later, 'But you have not rejected me' (DD ch. 20: 193, 199).

1 Ludwig Feuerbach, *The Essence of Christianity* (London: John Chapman, 1854), reprinted with an introduction by Karl Barth and a foreword by H. Richard Niebuhr (New York: Harper and Row, 1956), p. 287n.

After being reunited with her brother, she sees him as a suffering servant:

> '... when I am with Ezra he makes me feel that his life is a great good, though he has suffered so much; not like me, who wanted to die because I had suffered a little, and only for a little while.'

Later in the same chapter, when she foresees 'bad people, wrong things, misery' coming to touch their lives, he advises her,

> 'We must take our portion, Mirah. It is there. On whose shoulder would we lay it, that we might be free?' (DD ch. 52: 604, 613)

Here GE reworks the problem of how to bear suffering, in a context foreign to that of *The Mill on the Floss*. There is no 'Imitation of Christ', for the suffering servant in Isaiah liii is not, as in the Christian tradition, the figure of Christ. No saviour will bear our griefs for us. In Mordecai's terms, 'our portion' of suffering is part of a larger economy of gain and loss – a closed economy. Material aspects of such a closed economy figure largely in this novel: inheritances, share speculation, gambling salons, pawn-shops. But readers who conclude prematurely, in DD ch. 2, that Deronda is a Redeemer figure, must beware of employing too exclusively Christian hermeneutics.

It may have been in part for the purpose of averting such Christian readings that GE in her revisions for the third edition of this novel altered 'redeemed' to 'repurchased' (DD ch. 2: 16), replaced 'redeem' with 'repurchase' (DD ch. 28: 297), and changed 'redemption' to 'repurchase' (DD ch. 32: 333).[1] Deronda does indeed act as a redeemer of pawned goods, but the Christian connotations of that title are modified by these revisions.

---

1 Graham Handley characterizes these changes as 'second thoughts rather than corrections'; see his introduction to the Clarendon edition, p. xxvi.

/166/ Chozari, by Jehuda Halevy

Jehuda Halevy's system in his 'Chozari' is briefly: that Judaism in opposition to all philosophies & religious systems rests on *eye-witness* & *facts* e.g. the existence of God is more firmly proved by the revelation on Sinai than by the arguments of reason. So far of Judaism in general. As to its special content - starting from the creation he lays down that as Adam came from the hand of God without intervention of earthly parentage, he presented both corporeally & spiritually the Ideal Man. All truths accessible to the human intellect were known to Adam without labour, by intuition; so that he had to a certain degree a prophetic nature & was therefore called the Son of God. This spiritual fortune he bequeathed to such of his descendants as by their mental organization were susceptible of it. Through the long chain of generations, not without interruption, this inborn virtue passed to Abraham & the fathers of the 12 tribes. The Israelitish people hence forms the heart & kernel of mankind, exclusively capable of the prophetic function. This ideal nature is the middle step between men & angels. To cherish it was needed a theatre - a land with favourable climate - the middlepoint of the earth. There the divine government was visibly manifest in a succession of Prophets & by blessings & curses of a preternatural order. Also the commands & prohibitions of Judaism are means intended to cherish the divining-prophetic nature in the Israelites. To this end **/166v/** the house of Aaron was chosen for the priesthood, the temple built & the whole cultus prescribed. God alone knows how they subserve this end: human ingenuity must not meddle with them. Not moral duties, not rational laws constituted the speciality of Judaism - these are necessary conditions to social life. The pith of Judaism is its *religious duties*, which are adapted to preserve the Divine light & mercy & the continual arousing of the prophetic gift ... [Graetz 6, 138–41]

Der grösste Dulder ist aber Israel, weil er im Menschengeschlechte das ist, was das Herz im menschlichen Organismus' ... Von Israel gelte das Wort ... 'Es trägt unsere Krankheit und unsere Schmerzen sind ihm aufgeladen.'

Grätz VI [143][1]

1 For a translation, see the headnote to this section.

Kabbalah (from Graetz)

B 168, 168v, 169, 174

These notes from Graetz on the Kabbalah may be compared with those from Maimon (B 136) and Ginsburg's *Kabbalah: Its Doctrines, Development and Literature* (Pf 707 17 to 25). Mordecai's articulation of the Kabbalistic doctrine of the pre-existence of human souls, and of their rebirth in new bodies for the complete development of their germs of perfection, owes much to GE's reading of Ginsburg and these notes from Graetz: compare Pf 707 20 and 21 with B 169 and 174, below. The uniting of souls which may accomplish conjointly what they were too feeble to do separately is, in Mordecai's view, a 'parable' of the continuation of his soul's work, after his death, by Deronda, who is a 'companion soul of better fortune or more strength' (Pf 707 21). As he tells Deronda,

> 'In the doctrine of the Cabbala, souls are born again and again in new bodies till they are perfected and purified, and a soul liberated from a worn-out body may join the fellow-soul that needs it, that they may be perfected together, and their earthly work accomplished. Then they will depart from the mortal region, and leave place for new souls to be born out of the store in the eternal bosom. It is the lingering imperfection of the souls already born into the mortal region that hinders the birth of new souls and the preparation of the Messianic time: – thus the mind has given shape to what is hidden, as the shadow of what is known, and has spoken truth, though it were only in parable. When my long-wandering soul is liberated from this weary body, it will join yours, and its work will be perfected.' (DD ch. 43: 501–2)

A cancelled epigraph for chapter 43[1] was an excerpt from Browning's *Easter Day*, xviii:

> 'truth by means
> Of fable, showing while it screens
> Since highest truth man e'er supplied
> Was ever fable on outside.'

1 Handley, p. 501n.

The sense of Browning's rhymes is expressed by Mordecai's exposition of Kabbalistic doctrine: 'thus the mind has given shape to what is hidden ... and has spoken truth, though it were only in parable.' However, the 'Messianic time' Mordecai refers to is not the Easter resurrection or the second coming of the Christian Messiah, as in Browning's poem, but the end of time, 'the great Jubilee' (B 174). In Kabbalistic doctrine, as GE notes, the suffering and perfection of each soul leads towards not merely individual liberation but also the 'great deliverance' of the world (B 169, 174). She also notes that the doctrines of the Kabbalah are not 'ancient Jewish', but originate in 'Alexandrian neo-platonic philosophy' (B 174; see also Pf 707 18).

GE's notes from Salomon Maimon concern the twofold division of the Kabbalah into 'theoretical' and 'practical', the latter being a mode of conjuring natural forces (B 136). Her project as a novelist is to fit the theory or fable of Kabbalistic doctrine into the practical, naturalistic world of her narrative. Thus she introduces 'the notion of the Cabbalists' in her narrative commentary about Mordecai's psychological need for 'the more beautiful, the stronger, the more executive self' projected in his own mind, before he meets Deronda:

> his imagination had constructed another man who would be something more ample than the second soul bestowed, according to the notion of the Cabbalists, to help out the insufficient first ... His inward need for the conception of this expanded, prolonged self was reflected as an outward necessity. (DD ch. 38: 441)

Her balancing of this 'inward need ... reflected as an outward neccessity' has a psychological acuity which prepares for the natural aspect of the deathbed scene in the final chapter – a scene which might otherwise, with the quasi-biblical archaism of Mordecai's language, have slipped into semi-mystical apotheosis.

In several studies of connections between Ginsburg's book and *Daniel Deronda*,[1] William Baker refers, not merely to 'the non-rational', but also to 'the non-real parts of *Daniel Deronda*' and 'this very non-reality'. In his view GE failed to transform the mysticism of Kabbalistic doctrine into a fully

1 'The Kabbalah, Mordecai, and George Eliot's Religion of Humanity', *Yearbook of English Studies* 3 (1973): 216–21; *George Eliot and Judaism* (Salzburg: Institut für Englische Sprache und Literatur, Universität Salzburg, 1975), pp. 159–66; and Baker I, 43–50.

natural and psychologically truthful characterization of Mordecai.[1] She has, nonetheless, taken pains to show the philosophical concept of souls and their transmigration as a product of human need, and consequently a real part of the larger life of humanity.

/168/ *Kabbala*[2]

The original Kabbala presented the following doctrines: The Godhead is exalted above all, even above Existence[3] & Thought. It must not therefore be said of it that it has speech or action, thought, will, or design. All these attributes which adorn man imply limitation, & the Godhead is without limit, being perfect. It has properly only this one attribute of illimitability. The Kabbala therefore called God the unlimited (absolute) or Infinite, in Hebrew the *En-Soph*; & this was its first novelty. In this his incomprehensible generality, God or the En-Soph is impenetrably hidden, veiled, & *non-existent*. For that which the thinking mind cannot conceive is not existent for it. Hence undetermined Being, the En-Soph = das Nichts (Ajin).[4] Thus to announce his existence he must manifest himself; he must become active & create, that his Being may become cognizable. But not directly. The En-Soph **/168v/** in virtue of his infinite fullness of light has a spiritual *Substance* or *Force* rayed out from him, partaking of his perfection & infinity. But this cannot in all respects equal its producer: it is derivative not original – *like* but not equal. This is the first Sefira; & from this streams forth a second force, & so again a third, & so on until the tenth spiritual substance or force or medium / intermediate existence/ or organ has manifested itself. These are the ten Sefiroth, which form among each other & with the En-Soph a strict unity & only exhibit various sides or phases of one & the same Being. They create the spiritual & corporeal world in their image ... All things have been created through the Sephiroth. All things, not merely species but individuals in the lower world, have their types in the higher, so that nothing here is trivial, but

1 *George Eliot and Judaism*, p. 159.

2 The first note on B 168, listing 'Thirteen Articles of Belief' laid down by 'Maimouni', has been relocated to the 'Maimonides' section.

3 GE originally translated *Sein* as 'Being', then crossed it out and wrote 'Existence' above the line. This passage in her copy of Graetz is marked with a marginal line.

4 *Das Nichts*: 'nothingness, the void'.

all has a higher significance. All things are bound together in an endless chain. Especially is the human soul a complete citizen of the higher world & stands in immediate connection with all the Sephiroth. Hence it is able to act on them & on the Godhead itself.

By means of its moral & religious bearing the soul can further or hinder the outflow of blessing. Especially is Israel called to further the fullness of grace & the preservation of the world. To this end it has received the law & the 613 religious precepts, that by religious activity it may work on the Sephiroth & in a certain **/169/** way force them to flow forth. The ritual has therefore a deep mystical significance & imperishable value: it is the magical means of preserving & blessing the world. 'The righteous is the pillar of the world.' After the destruction of the Temple, prayer took the place of offerings, & has therefore a mystic efficacy.

Starting from the doctrine that all souls have been pre-existent from the beginning in the Spiritual world, the Kabbala taught that they are all destined to an earthly career in a corporeal form. The problem of the soul is to preserve its purity in spite of its union with the body – whence it will ascend at death into the spiritual realm & have part in[1] the world of the Sefiroth. But if the soul becomes stained it must once & again, but at most only thrice, return into corporeal life, till by these repeated trials it can ascend in purity. On this transmigration of souls was founded the theory of retribution. The sufferings of the righteous serve simply to purify them. Seth's soul passed into Moses. The Kabbala found a confirmation of the transmigration theory in the command that the brother of a man who died childless should marry his widow – the object being that the soul of the deceased should be born again in her child & finish his course. Marriage in general was a mystical institution, being the means of bringing souls into corporeality. Now as most souls are stained by their union with the body, forget their heavenly origin, & are subjected[2] **/174/** to repeated transmigrations, it is chiefly old souls, i.e. such as have already been on earth, that come into physical existence, & only seldom does a *new soul* come on earth. Through the sinfulness of men which causes the same souls continually to re-enter earthly bodies, the great deliverance is delayed. For the new souls cannot come into existence because the world is almost entirely peopled with old souls. And the time of Grace, the

1 GE first translated 'have part in' as 'partake of'.

2 Here GE added a note, 'v. 174.

spiritual perfection of the world cannot come until all fore-created souls have had an earthly incorporation. The Soul of the Messiah which like the others in the spiritual world of the Sephiroth waits in its state of pre-existence, cannot appear until all other souls are incorporated. Thus the Messiah will appear at the End of the Days. Then the great Jubilee - Jobel ha-Gadol - will begin, when all souls will be restored purified to heaven. Thus the furtherance & hastening of this Time depends on the acts of the righteous.

The doctrines of the Cabbala are neither ancient Jewish, nor new-philosophical. The ideal potencies, the spiritual intermediators between the Divine fullness of light & the dim world - the pre-existence of the soul - the transmigration of souls - the magical operation of human actions on the higher world - all belong to the Alexandrian neo-platonic philosophy. It is true that the doctrine of transmigration was received in some Jewish circles in the Gaonitic period; but Saadia rejected it with indignation.

Grätz VII [69–77]

Jewish chronology

B 169v, 170, 170v, 171, 171v, 172

This chronology began as a fair copy of GE's earlier chronological table on Pf 711 27–28. In both notebooks the chronologies contain later additions and modifications. Her source for the 'Biblical Period' has not been traced. Other entries are drawn from the relevant volumes of Graetz or his 'Chronologische Tabelle' (Graetz 8, 482–96). The list for the 'Maccabaean period' is almost identical to GE's pencilled note on the front papers of Graetz 3. On B 171 GE began, but did not complete, a rather cramped schema by centuries, from the thirteenth to the nineteenth. 'Epoch of the Gaonim, 658' (B 171v, 172) expands upon her briefer note, 'Period of the Gaonim, 658–997' (B 170v).

/169v/ Chronology

Biblical Period

Exodus, 1314–21 [sic], acc. to Lepsius & Bunsen
Solomon, 1008
Hezekiah, 726
Josiah (Book of the Law recovered), 640
First Temple destroyed, 587
Zerubbabel & Ezra, 536
Nehemiah, 446

280 years blank till the
Maccabaean period

Judas Maccabaeus, 166
Jonathan, 160–143
Simon, 143–135
John Hyrcanus, 135–106
Pharisees & Sadducees marked
Aristobulus, 106
Alexander Jannaeus, 105
Salome, 79

Aristobulus II, 70
Septuagint
Hyrcanus, 63
Pompey at Jerusalem
Antigonus
Juda b. Tabbai
Simon b. Shetach

Romanizing period

Herod king, 37
Schemaja & Abtalion
Hillel & Schammai
Hillel president of the Sanhedrim

/170/ AC

Philo, aged 40, heads the embassy to Rome, 40
Agrippa (Herod)
King Agrippa
Second Temple destroyed

Period of the Tanaim, 70–200

R. Jochanan b. Zakkai
First insurrection under Hadrian, 118 (Book of Judith)
Bar-Cochba, 132–135 (Book of Tobit)
Rabbi Akiba.
R. Simon b. Jochai
R. Meir
R. Gamaliel II
Close of Mischna – R. Jehuda

Period of the Amoraim, 200–400

R. Chananja b. Chama, first of the Amoraim
Patriarch rises in dignity, has a bodyguard
Babylonian schools: Rab, 175–247
Downfall of schools of Tiberias under Constantius, 337–338
Sepphoris razed to the ground
Jerusalem Talmud written down

Jewish chronology B 170 170v

Period of the Saboraim, 500–550 [1]

B[abylonian] Talmud written down under R. Giza & R. Simuna
[Graetz 5, 8–9]

* Vowel points introduced by Moses, surnamed 'the Punctator' – this is the tradition; but the exact origin of the vowel points is not known.
[Graetz 5, 153; B 156v]

* This did not take place till far in the next century & the 8th, when the activity of Musselmans as to the Koran roused the Jews to a like zeal about their own Scriptures. [2]

/170v/

Period of the Gaonim, 658–997

First Gaon, Mar Isaak, head of the school of Sura
Resch Galuta (exilarch) at Pumbadita; also a Resch Metibta
Karaites (anti-Talmudic movement), 761
Conversion of the Chazari or Cozari
Josippon, 900 (Italian Jew)
Saad, 892–942
Masoretic text founded by Ben Ascher of Tiberias
Chasdai, in Spain, 915–970
Rise of New-Hebrew poetry
Fall of the Gaonate, after Hai, d. about 1038

1 Rabbinical Period

Samuel Halevi Ibn Nagrela, prime minister, b. 993
Ibn G'anach, Hebraist, 995–1050
Ibn Giat, poet
Ibn Gebirol, 1021–1070
First Crusade & its horrors of persecution

1 GE's notes on the Saboraim reflect uncertainty about dating. On B 114, she began with the dates '500–640', then added 'or 400–550?' On Pf 711 28 the date is '400–550'. Here she began with those dates, then added 'or 630', then replaced them with 500–550'. Graetz's dates are 500 to 630.

2 This later addition corrects another questionable date from Pf 711 28, 'Vowel points 6 - -(?)'.

Jewish chronology B 170v 171

2 Rabbinical Period

Rashi (R. Shelomah b. Yitzschak) b. 1039 at Troyes, d. 1105
Emperor Henry IV protects the Jews
Pope Gregory VII is hard on them
Alfassi, Talmudist, d. 1103

3 Rabbinical Period

Ibn Migasch, Talmudist, d. 1141
Jehuda Halevy, 1086
Second Crusade & persecutions
Ibn Ezra, 1088–1167
Almohad persecution, 1147
Ibn Daud, philosophical commentator, b. 1110, d. 1180
Alcharisi, last New Hebrew poet in Spain, 1170–1230
Benjamin of Tudela travelled, 1165–1173
Pilgrimages to the tombs of Ezekiel & Ezra
Revival of Exilarchate at Mosul

/171/

Maimonides, b. 1135
finished Comm. on Mischna, 1168
finished Mischna Thora or Religious Codex, 1180
Moreh Nebuchim, 1190
died & was buried at Tiberias, 1204

In the first quarter of the XIIIth C. rise & development of the Cabbala
Mose de Leon, author of Sohar, 1250–1305

XIIIth Century

Persecution of Jews in France under Louis IX
Talmud burnt at Paris
David Kimchi & Nachmani
Jews driven out of France under Philip the Fair
The (16,500) Jews banished from England under Edw. I
The Black Death
Flagellants

Jewish chronology B 171 171v

XIVth Cent.

XVth Cent.

XVIth Cent.

XVIIth Cent.

Great settlement at Amsterdam: synagogues
Greatest synagogues in Germany – Frankfort, Worms, Prag & Wien
Troubles of Polish Jews
Manasse ben Israel
Uriel da Costa
Leon de Modena
Spinoza
Sabbatai Zewi
Jacob Frank

XVIIIth Cent.

XIXth Cent.

/171v/

Epoch of the Gaonim, 658

Serenus, Messianic pretender, 720
Kaliri, poet
Persecution under Leo the Isaurian, 721,
causing emigration (Chazaren)
Abu 'Isa, another messianic pretender of Isfahan, 750
Scheeltot (Questions), arrangement & practical application of
Talmudic material, 760
Karaites (Anan b. David), 761
Conversion of the Chazars or Cozari

Charles the Great patronizes the Jews & calls the Kalonymos from Lucca to Mainz, to spread knowledge among them, 787.
'Eine regelmässige Gemeindeverfassung haben die deutschen Juden erst durch die aus Lucca verpflanzte Kolonie der Familie Kalonymos erhalten.' [Graetz 5, 195–6][1]

Haroun Alraschid sends R. Machir, a learned Jew from Babylonia, at the request of Charlemagne, who placed him at the head of the School of Narbonne, 797. [Graetz 5, 196]
Golden time for the Jews under Lewis the Pious & Judith, 814–840

Conversion of Bodo (confessor of Lewis) to Judaism, 838. He made a journey to Rome & got a disgust there for Xty; then went to Spain & was known as Eleazar. [Graetz 5, 233–4]

First royal protectorate over the Jews. Hence, in after reigns they were regarded as a sort of royal serfs, & one king 'gave' them to the Church. [Graetz 5, 235][2]

Exilarchate began to sink, 849
Jews ill-treated in Babylonia
Josippon, about 900
Israeli (Isaak), physician. Wrote on fevers
Exaltation of the school of Pumbadita, by Mar-Kohn Zedek, 917–936

1 Translation:
The German Jews have one regular enactment of community only as a result of the colony, transplanted from Lucca, of the Kalonymos family.
Joseph Kalonymos tells Deronda,
'The days are changed for us in Mainz since our people were slaughtered wholesale if they wouldn't be baptized wholesale: they are changed for us since Karl the Great fetched my ancestors from Italy to bring some tincture of knowledge to our rough German brethren.' (DD ch. 60: 671)
In April 1876, GE wrote to John Blackwood,
The printers have sadly spoiled the beautiful Greek name Kalonymos, which was the name of a celebrated family of scholarly Jews transplanted from Italy into Germany in mediaeval times. But my writing was in fault. (GEL VI, 242)
2 GE wrote in the margin of Graetz 5, 235, beside this passage, 'King's Jews'.

/172/

Saad, 892–942
Ben-Ascher of Tiberias, father & son, give copies of the biblical text, on which the now accepted masoretic text is chiefly founded 890–950.
[Graetz 5, 281]
Donnolo, writer of Commentary on Creation (Tachkemoni) & *St Nilus*
Low condition of Jewish culture in Italy (Xth century)
Chasdai, b. 915, d. 970
Beginning of Rabbinical period
Dunasch b. Labrat, poet
New Hebrew poetry
Ibn Abitur, translated the Mischna into Arabic
Rabbi Gerschom, 960–1028
Hai Gaon, 969–1038.
Fall of Gaonat

Samuel Halevi Ibn Nagrela, prime minister, b. 993
Ibn G'anach, great Hebraist, 995–1050
Bachja wrote 'Anleitung zu den inneren Pflichten', 1050–60[1]
Ibn G'ebirol, 1021–1070, author of Fons Vitae. Poet
Rashi – R. Shelomah Yitzchak. b. 1039, at Troyes
Gregory VIIth against the Jews, 1078
Jehuda Halevi, 1086. Great poet: author of Chozari
Ibn Daud, b. 1110, martyred 1180
Abraham b. Meir Ibn Esra, 1088–1167
Jehuda b. Salomon Alcharisi, the last representative
of the New Hebrew poetry in Spain, 1170–1230
Maimonides, b. 1135, d. 1204
Cabbala, 1st quarter of 13th century
Mose de Leon, author of Sohar, 1250–1304

1 Translation: 'Guide to the Duties of the Heart'. For another reference to 'Duties of the Heart, by R. Ba'hya', see Pf 710 41.

The Jewish year

B 172v, 173

Despite minor spelling variants in the names of the months, the notes on these two pages may come from a single source, which has not been traced. Various calendars for the Jewish year were, of course, published annually. In copying the calendar for 1873/74 (the Jewish year 5634), GE at first copied the name of the seventh month, Veadar, then crossed it out and noted that it would occur in 1874/75. The Jewish calendar is lunar; each month runs from new moon to new moon. To keep in phase with the solar year, an intercalary month, Veadar, is added to the third, sixth, eighth, eleventh, fourteenth, seventeenth, and nineteenth year of every nineteen-year cycle.

This liturgical calendar of Feasts and Fasts may be compared with that of 'Jewish Festivals' and Fasts on Pf 711 19–20, whose dates also refer to 1873/74. The Feasts include the five which form the separate volumes of the Festival prayer books (see B 184 to 190): Passover, Weeks (Pentecost), New Year, Yom Kippur, and Tabernacles. Yom Kippur, the Day of Atonement, a day of complete fasting, is the culmination of the penitential season that begins with the New Year, or Rosh Hashanah. Nevertheless, it is listed on B 172v not with the lesser fast days, but with the Feasts: it forms two of the six volumes of Festival prayers. The spiritual elation of this most solemn day results from not merely the confession and forgiveness of sins, but also the turning away from evil-doing ways. According to the Mishnah,

> For transgressions between man and God, the Day of Atonement atones; but for transgressions between a man and his fellow man, the Day of Atonement does not atone unless he has first reconciled his fellow man.[1]

Compare GE's note on 'Kol Nidri which appears to be an absolution from all vows' (B 185).

---

1 Cited in David J. Goldberg and John D. Rayner, *The Jewish People: Their History and Their Religion* (London: Penguin, 1989), pp. 357–8.

/172v/ *Feasts*

Pesach: the Passover
15 Nisan

Schabouoth: Feast of Weeks, or Feast of harvest or of First fruits;
or, anniversary of the promulgation of the Law. (Pentecost)
The fiftieth day from the 16 Nisan; the day of offering the Omer
6 Siwan

Rosch Haschana, New Year. Day of the Trumpet
1 Tisri

Iom Kippur: Day of pardon or reconciliation
9 Tishri

Soukoth: Feast of Tabernacles
15 Tishri

Hanucah: Feast of Lights
Purification of the Temple service under Judas Maccabaeus
25 Kislev

Purim: Deliverance by Esther
14 & 15 Adar

Fasts

3 Tishri
to commemorate the murder of Gedaliah. 2 Kings xxv. Jer. 41

10 Tebeth
first day of the siege under Nebuchadnezzar

13 Adar
the fast of Esther

17 Tammuz
various calamities: the cessation of the worship the day before the destruction;
overthrow of the chief wall of the city in the Roman siege;
breaking of the tables of the Law by Moses

9 Ab
the destruction of the two temples

Wailing at the Wall (?)

/173/

Jewish months 1873

1	Tishri	30 days	begins September 22	Rosch Haschanah
				9 Iom Kippur 10
2	Heshvan	29 days	October 22	Tabernacles 15
3	Kislev	29 "	November 21	25 Hanucah
4	Tebeth	29 "	December 21	
5	Shebat	30 "	January 19	
6	Adar	30 "	February 18	14 Purim & 15
7	Veadar,	29 "	March 19[1]	
8	Nissan	30 "	March 19	15 Passover
9	Iyor	29 "	April 18	
10	Sivan	30 "	May 17	6 Pentecost
11	Tamuz	29 "	June 16	17 Fast Tables of the Law broken &c
12	Ab	30 "	July 15	9 Great Fast Destruction of Temple
13	Ellul	29 "	August 14	

In 1874 comes the intercalary month Veadar of 29 days.

Names of the months Persian:
in Hebrew they are spoken of as first, second, third &c.[2]

1 This line was cancelled by GE, since Veadar was not to come until the following year.
2 GE's source for this later note may have been Salomon Munk's *Palestine*, p. 180.

The Positivist Calendar

B 175, 175v, 176,176v, 177, 177v, 178, 178v, 179, 179v, 180, 180v, 181

In these pages GE transcribed Auguste Comte's 'Positivist Calendar', a lunar calendar of thirteen months, each comprising four seven-day weeks: the names of the Sundays are underlined. Each day honours a great man or woman who has contributed to 'the preparatory period of man's history'.[1] As Christian calendars have their saints' days, the Positivist Calendar celebrates Comte's choice of mostly secular saints. The names listed on the right are those 'who, in Leap-years, take the place of their principals'. Thus, every four years, Mme de Sévigné gives way to Lady Mary Wortley Montagu, and Fielding yields to Richardson. The additional day in Leap Year is the 'Festival of Holy Women'; and every year has a 'Complementary Day', the 'Festival of the Dead'. The months are named after representative figures of thirteen aspects of human progress, from Moses, 'The Initial Theocracy', to Bichat, 'Modern Science'. It may be observed that the progress is not only temporal, but geographical: the Middle East, Greece, and the Orient contribute to the Initial Theocracy and to Ancient Poetry, Ancient Philosophy, and Ancient Science, but are virtually absent after the middle of the fifth month, or – as one may say – the Ides of Caesar.

These notes are in black ink, like most of the entries from B 1 to 90v, made between August 1868 and 'sometime in 1872',[2] and were first published in *George Eliot's 'Middlemarch' Notebooks*, accompanied by the editorial comment that

1 From the full title of the Calendar, as reprinted in Comte's *System of Positive Polity, or Treatise on Sociology, Instituting the Religion of HUMANITY*, 4 vols, Volume I, *Containing the General View of Positivism and Introductory Principles*, translated by John Henry Bridges (London: Longmans, Green, 1875), table facing p. 384. The source of this calendar was identified by Christopher Kent, Professor of History at the University of Saskatoon. Kent's communication was kindly passed on by Victor Neufeldt to the present editor.

2 See the discussion of dating by Pratt and Neufeldt in the introduction to *George Eliot's 'Middlemarch' Notebooks*, p. xxi.

> GE seems to be compiling her own survey of Western civilization, but we have not the slightest idea why she used these particular thirteen groupings, or why each page consists of four groups of seven. (pp. 276–7)

Now that it is known that she found it worth while to copy Comte's calendar, her own views about his positivist programme remain somewhat difficult to determine. The Calendar's full subtitle sums up Comte's programme for a new accounting of history:

> Positivist Calendar: Adapted to all Years Equally; or, Concrete View of the Preparatory Period of Man's History: Especially intended for the transition through which the Western Republic has to pass; the Republic which, since Charlemagne, has been formed by the free cohesion of the five leading populations – the French, Italian, Spanish, British, and German

Is Comte's reference to the republic formed 'since Charlemagne' by the free cohesion of five Western European nations congruent – or not? – with GE's note in the Chronology which precedes this Calendar in the Berg Notebook, but was copied four or five years later:

> Haroun Alraschid sends R. Machir, a learned Jew from Babylonia, at the request of Charlemagne, who placed him at the head of the School of Narbonne, 797. (B 171v)

In Comte's calendrical scheme, Charlemagne provides the name for the seventh month, at the annual half-way point of the 'Preparatory Period of Man's History', whereas Haroun-al-Raschid – his contemporary – is honoured only as the twenty-seventh day of the first month. There, in the 'Initial Theocracy', he keeps company with Prometheus, the Druids, the Theocrats of Thibet, Hercules, and Abraham. In GE's note from Graetz, in contrast, he moves into a more recent historical era, and Middle-Eastern learning is seen to play a central, rather than a marginal, role in the intellectual culture of the Carolingian empire.[1]

---

1 The nature of GE's interest in Comte's doctrines may be explored by study of the twenty-two pages of notes drawn from her reading in 1877 of his *System of Positive Polity* (Pf 707 73 to 98).

The Positivist Calendar B 175 175v

/175/

I. **Moses**: Initial Theocracy

1	Prometheus	
2	Hercules	Theseus
3	Orpheus	
4	Ulysses	
5	Lycurgus	
6	Romulus	
7	**Numa**	
8	Belus	
9	Sesostris	
10	Manu	
11	Cyrus	
12	Zoroaster	
13	The Druids	
14	**Buddha**	
15	Fo-Hi	
16	Lao-Tseu	
17	Meng-Tseu	
18	The Theocrats of Thibet	
19	The Theocrats of Japan	
20	Manco-Capac	Taméhaméa
21	**Confucius**	
22	Abraham	Joseph
23	Samuel	
24	Solomon	David
25	Isaiah	
26	St John Baptist	
27	Haroun-al-Raschid	Abderrahman III
28	**Mahomet**	

/175v/

II. **Homer**: Ancient Poetry

1	Hesiod	
2	Tyrtaeus, 685 fl.	Sappho, fl. 610
3	Anacreon, 631	
4	Pindar, 522 b.	
5	Sophocles, 496 b.	Euripides, b. 486
6	Theocritus, 280	Longus, 4th or 5th cent
7	**Aeschylus**, 525 b.	
8	Scopas, fl. 350	
9	Zeuxis, 424	
10	Ictinus, cont. Pericles	
11	Praxiteles, 448–404	
12	Lysippus, cont. Alex.	
13	Apelles, cont. Alex.	
14	**Phidias, cont. Pericles**	
15	Aesop, about 570	Pilpay
16	Plautus, d. 184	
17	Terence, d. 159 BC	Menander, fl. 321
18	Phaedrus, Augustan period	
19	Juvenal, fl. 80	
20	Lucian, Antonines	
21	**Aristophanes**, Pelop. War	
22	Ennius, b. 239	
23	Lucretius, b. 95 BC	
24	Horace, d. 8	
25	Tibullus, d. 18	
26	Ovid, d. 18	
27	Lucan, d. 65 AC	
28	**Virgil**, d. 19 BC	

The Positivist Calendar B 176 176v

/176/

III. **Aristotle**: Ancient Philosophy

1	Anaximander	
2	Anaximenes	
3	Heraclitus	
4	Anaxagoras	
5	Democritus	Leucippus
6	Herodotus	
7	**Thales**	
8	Solon	
9	Xenophanes	
10	Empedocles	
11	Thucydides	
12	Archytas	Philolaus
13	Apollonius of Tyana	
14	**Pythagoras**	
15	Aristippus	
16	Antisthenes	
17	Zeno	
18	Cicero	The younger Pliny
19	Epictetus	Arrian
20	Tacitus	
21	**Socrates**	
22	Xenocrates	
23	Philo of Alexandria	
24	Saint John Evangelist	
25	Saint Justin	Saint Irenaeus
26	Saint Clement of Alexandria	
27	Origen	Tertullian
28	**Plato**	

/176v/

IV. **Archimedes** : Ancient Science

1	Theophrastus	
2	Herophilus	
3	Erasistratus	
4	Celsus	
5	Galen	
6	Avicenna	Averrhoes
7	**Hippocrates**	
8	Euclid	
9	Aristaeus	
10	Theodosius of Bythinia	
11	Hiero	Ctesibius
12	Pappus	
13	Diophantes	
14	**Apollonius**	
15	Eudoxus	Aratus
16	Pytheas	Nearchus
17	Aristarchus	Berosus
18	Eratosthenes	Sosisgenes
19	Ptolemy	
20	Albategnius	Nassir-Eddin
21	**Hipparchus**	
22	Varro	
23	Columella	
24	Vitruvius	
25	Strabo	
26	Frontinus	
27	Plutarch	
28	**Pliny the Elder**	

The Positivist Calendar B 177 177v

/177/

V. **Caesar**: Military Civilization

1	Miltiades	
2	Leonidas	
3	Aristides	
4	Cimon	
5	Xenophon	
6	Phocion	Epaminondas
7	**Themistocles**	
8	Pericles	
9	Philip of Macedon	
10	Demosthenes	
11	Ptolemy Lagus	
12	Philopoemen	
13	Polybius	
14	**Alexander**	
15	Junius Brutus	
16	Camillus	Cincinnatus
17	Fabricius	Regulus
18	Hannibal	
19	Paulus Aemilius	
20	Marius	The Gracchi
21	**Scipio**	
22	Augustus	Maecenus
23	Vespasian	Titus
24	Adrian	Nerva
25	Antoninus	Marcus Aurelius
26	Papinian	
27	Alexander Severus	
28	**Trajan**	

/177v/

VI. **Saint Paul**: Catholicism

1	St Luke	St James
2	St Cyprian	
3	St Athanasius	
4	St Jerome	
5	St Ambrose	
6	St Monica	
7	**St Augustin**	
8	Constantine	
9	Theodosius	
10	St Chrysostom	St Basil
11	St Pulcheria	Marcian
12	St Genevieve of Paris	
13	St Gregory the Great	
14	**Hildebrand**	
15	St Benedict	St Anthony
16	St Boniface	St Austin
17	St Isidore of Seville	St Bruno
18	Lanfranc	St Anselm
19	Heloise	Beatrice
20	Les architectes du Moyen Age	St Benezet
21	**Saint Bernard**	
22	St Francis Xavier	Ignatius Loyola
23	St Carlo Borromeo	Frederigo Borromeo
24	St Theresa	St Catherine of Siena
25	St Vincent de Paul	L' Abbé de l'Epée
26	Bourdaloue	Claude Fleury
27	William Penn	George Fox
28	**Bossuet**	

The Positivist Calendar B 178 178v

/178/

VII. **Charlemagne**: Feudal Civilization

1	Theodoric the Great	
2	Pelagius	
3	Otho the Great	Heinrich der Vogler
4	St Henry	
5	Villiers	La Valette
6	D. Juan of Lepanto	John Sobieski
7	**Alfred**	
8	Charles Martel	
9	The Cid	Tancred
10	Richard Coeur de Lion	
11	Joan of Arc	
12	Albuquerque	Walter Raleigh
13	Bayard	
14	**Godfrey**	
15	St Leo the Great	Leo IV
16	Gerbert	Pierre Damian
17	Peter the Hermit	
18	St Eloi	Suger
19	Alexander III	Thomas Becket
20	St Francis of Assisi	St Dominic
21	**Innocent III**	
22	Saint Clotilda	
23	Saint Bathilda	Saint Mathilda of Tuscany
24	St Stephen of Hungary	Matthias Corvinus
25	St Elizabeth of Hungary	
26	Blanche of Castile	
27	St Ferdinand III	Alfonso X
28	**St Louis**	

/178v/

VIII. **Dante**: The Modern Epic

1	The Troubadours	
2	Boccaccio	Chaucer
3	Rabelais	
4	Cervantes	
5	La Fontaine	
6	De Foe	Goldsmith
7	**Ariosto**	
8	Leonardo da Vinci	Titian
9	Michael Angelo	Paolo Veronese
10	Holbein	Rembrandt
11	Poussin	Lesueur
12	Velasquez	Alonzo Cano
13	Teniers	Rubens
14	**Raphael**	
15	Froissart	Joinville
16	Camoens	
17	The Spanish Romancists	
18	Chateaubriand	
19	Walter Scott	Cooper
20	Manzoni	
21	**Tasso**	
22	Petrarch	
23	Thomas à Kempis	Lewis of Granada
24	Mde de Lafayette	Mde de Stael
25	Fenelon	François de Sales
26	Klopstock	Gessner
27	Byron	Elisa Mercoeur
28	**Milton**	

/179/

IX. **Gutemberg**: Modern Industry

1	Marco Polo	Chardin
2	Jacques Coeur	Gresham
3	Gama	Magellan
4	Napier	Briggs
5	Lacaille	Delambre
6	Cook	Tasman
7	**Columbus**	
8	Benvenuto Cellini	
9	Amontons	Wheatstone
10	Harrison	Pierre Leroy
11	Dollond	Graham
12	Arkwright	Jacquard
13	Conté	
14	**Vaucanson**	
15	Stevinus	Torricelli
16	Mariotte	Boyle
17	Papin	Worcester
18	Black	
19	Jouffroy	Fulton
20	Dalton	Thilorier
21	**Watt**	
22	Bernard de Palissy	
23	Guglielmini	Riquet
24	Duhamel (du Monceau)	
25	Saussure	Bouguer
26	Coulomb	Borda
27	Carnot	Vauban
28	**Montgolfier**	

/179v/

X. **Shakespeare**: Modern Drama

1	Lope de Vega	Montalvan
2	Moreto	Guillem de Castro
3	Rojas	Guevara
4	Otway	
5	Lessing	
6	Goethe	
7	**Calderon**	
8	Tirso	
9	Vondel	
10	Racine	
11	Voltaire	
12	Alfieri	Metastasio
13	Schiller	
14	**Corneille**	
15	Alarcon	
16	Mde de Motteville	Mde Roland
17	Madame de Sévigné	Lady M. W. Montagu
18	Lesage	Sterne
19	Mde de Staal	Miss Edgeworth
20	Fielding	Richardson
21	**Molière**	
22	Pergolesi	Palestrina
23	Sacchini	Grétry
24	Gluck	Lully
25	Beethoven	Handel
26	Rossini	Weber
27	Bellini	Donizetti
28	**Mozart**	

The Positivist Calendar B 180 180v

/180/

XI. **Descartes**: Modern Philosophy

1	Albertus Magnus	John of Salisbury
2	Roger Bacon	Raymond Lully
3	St Bonaventura	Joachim
4	Ramus	Cardinal de Cusa
5	Montaigne	Erasmus
6	Campanella	More
7	**St Thomas Aquinas**	
8	Hobbes	Spinoza
9	Pascal	Giordano Bruno
10	Locke	Malebranche
11	Vauvenargues	Mde de Lambert
12	Diderot	Tracy
13	Cabanis	Georges Leroy
14	**Francis Bacon**	
15	Grotius	Cujas
16	Fontenelle	Maupertuis
17	Vico	Herder
18	Fréret	Winckelmann
19	Montesquieu	d'Aguesseau
20	Buffo	Oken
21	**Leibnitz**	
22	Robertson	Gibbon
23	Adam Smith	Dunoyer
24	Kant	Fichte
25	Condorcet	Ferguson
26	Joseph de Maistre	Bonald
27	Hegel	Sophie Germain
28	**Hume**	

/180v/

XII. **Frederick**: Modern Policy

1	Molina	
2	Cosmo de Medici	
3	Philippe de Comines	Guicciardini
4	Isabella of Castile	
5	Charles V	Sixtus the Fifth
6	Henri IV	
7	**Louis XI**	
8	Coligny	L'Hôpital
9	Barneveldt	
10	Gustavus Adolphus	
11	De Witt	
12	Ruyter	
13	William III	
14	**William the Silent**	
15	Ximines	
16	Sully	Oxenstiern
17	Colbert	Louis XIV
18	Walpole	Mazarin
19	D'Aranda	Pombol
20	Turgot	Campomanes
21	**Richelieu**	
22	Sidney	Lambert
23	Franklin	
24	Washington	Kosciusko
25	Jefferson	
26	Bolivar	Toussaint l'Ouverture
27	Francia	
28	**Cromwell**	

The Positivist Calendar B 181

/181/

XIII. **Bichat:** Modern Science

1	Copernicus	Tycho Brahe
2	Kepler	Haller [Halley]
3	Huyghens	Varignon
4	Jacques Bernouilli	Jean Bernouilli
5	Bradley	Roëmer
6	Volta	Sauveur
7	**Galileo**	
8	Vieta	Harriott
9	Wallis	Fermat
10	Clairaut	Poinsot
11	Euler	Monge
12	D'Alembert	Daniel Bernouilli
13	Lagrange	Joseph Fourier
14	**Newton**	
15	Bergmann	Scheele
16	Priestley	Davy
17	Cavendish	
18	Guyton Morveau	Geoffroy
19	Berthollet	
20	Berzelius	Ritter
21	**Lavoisier**	
22	Harvey	Charles Bell
23	Boërhaave	Stahl
24	Linnaeus	Bernard de Jussieu
25	Haller	Vicq-d'Azyr
26	Lamarck	Blainville
27	Broussais	Morgagni
28	**Gall**	

The Jewish liturgy

B 182, 184, 185, 185v, 186v, 187, 187v, 188, 188v, 189, 189v, 190

The Hebrew prayer book, as GE observes in her notes from Hirschfeld, has a remarkable history. After the destruction of the Second Temple, the liturgy replaced the sacrificial rites formerly practised by the priests of the Temple. The prayer books comprise not only prayers composed over a thousand-year period, but also

> whole chapters from the Mishna, a complete list of hermeneutical rules (from the Talmud) for the interpretation of the Bible, various treatises of a cabbalistic & esoteric character, hyper-poetic hymns, about Angels, Demons, magic, adjurations &c. A modern, not unfriendly, critick said that the Jews 'sang Logic & prayed metaphysics'. The prayers were of mountainous extent. The daily morning devotions fill 40 close pages; those for the Sabbath morning 62. In all orthodox synagogues the worship still takes place in this form ... (B 123v, 124v)

According to Hirschfeld - who wrote from a Reform viewpoint - the Orthodox worshipper, to get through a complete service, 'must utter about 440 words a minute' (B 124v). The nineteenth-century 'movement ... towards the alteration of the Liturgy' followed upon Moses Mendelssohn's translation of 'the Thora into classical German' (B 123v). Vernacular translations of the liturgy, with the Hebrew text on the facing page, proliferated during the century. In England, various printers, in connection with various congregations, published prayer books comprising both minor and substantial differences in the English text. There was no single authorized version.

GE's copy of the single-volume *Daily, Sabbath, Festival and Occasional Prayers, According to the Ritual of the German and Polish Jews, with a carefully revised translation* (London: Ann Abrahams and Son, 5634/1874) is in DWL. The translator is not named, but may be David Levi. Her source for the following notes from B 184 to 190 is *The Festival Prayers, According to the Ritual of the German and Polish Jews,* translated by David Levi, 6 vols. (London: Abrahams and Son, 5620/1859 to 5633/1873).

Each volume of the festival prayer books includes, in addition to special services peculiar to it, daily services which are constant throughout the year. In her first extract on B 184, GE seems to mistake a part of the daily morning service to be part only of the New Year service. Again, on B 188v, she seems to attribute the daily thanksgiving of the Jewish man – blessing God for not making him a heathen, a slave, or a woman – only to the Pentecost service. But, as she correctly notes on B 138, the rabbis enjoined this as a *daily* thanksgiving. In the first edition of her novel, she had Ezra Cohen say that it is uttered 'every Sabbath' (DD ch. 46: 535). The confusion apparently generated by this thanksgiving, copied three times in the Berg Notebook, produced an interesting slip in GE's second copy on B 184: she at first wrote, 'Blessed art thou, O Lord, our God! King of the universe, who hast made me a woman.'

Deronda's first experience of the liturgy in the Orthodox synagogue in Frankfurt probably reflects GE's and GHL's impressions during their German travels in the summer of 1873. On 8 August, a Friday, they 'walked thro' the moonlighted streets' to the evening service in the Frankfurt synagogue. On 16 August, a Saturday, they attended a morning service in Mainz and 'were delighted with the singing' (GHL Diary). Deronda responds to the music of the service, wondering 'at the strength of his own feeling; it seemed beyond the occasion'.

> Deronda, having looked enough at the German translation of the Hebrew in the book before him to know that he was chiefly hearing Psalms and Old Testament passages or phrases, gave himself up to that strongest effect of chanted liturgies which is independent of detailed verbal meaning – like the effect of an Allegri's *Miserere* or a Palestrina's *Magnificat.* The most powerful movement of feeling with a liturgy is the prayer which seeks for nothing special, but is a yearning to escape from the limitations of our own weakness ... or else a self-oblivious lifting up of gladness ... The Hebrew liturgy, like others, has its transitions of litany, lyric, proclamation, dry statement and blessing; but this evening all were one for Deronda: the chant of the *Chazan's* or Reader's grand wide-ranging voice with its passage from monotony to sudden cries, the outburst of sweet boys' voices from the little quire, the devotional swaying of men's bodies backwards and forwards ... – all were blent for him as one expression of a binding history, tragic and yet glorious. (DD ch. 32: 339)

The reader of the Berg Notebook will see traces of Zunz (B 165) in this passage. Its blending of strong impressions and the analysis of feeling is characteristic of GE, as is her linking of the familiar with the foreign. Equally characteristic is her juxtaposition of this yielding to religious yearnings, with Deronda's subsequent attack of doubt:

> But with the cessation of the devotional sounds and the movement of many indifferent faces and vulgar figures before him there darted into his mind the frigid idea that he had probably been alone in his feeling, and perhaps the only person in the congregation for whom the service was more than a dull routine. (DD ch. 32: 340)

/182/ A [1] Feast of Tabernacles

God regulates the weather for the year.[2] Early to Synagogue, the candles remaining from the day of Reconciliation being lit. Seven men advance to the sacred ark, take each a roll of the Law & hold them upright on the reading-desk. Meanwhile all – the precentor at their head – dance round, shaking & swinging their willow boughs. Finally, these are beaten against the benches & walls, until they are stripped of their leaves; but thus naked they are carefully preserved, in case they are wanted to be burnt in the oven to purify the bread when necessity compels the use of a Xtian oven for baking Jewish food. (v. Kalisch)[3]

Religionsgebräuche &c. Anon.[4]

The blessing of the wine is called 'Kiddusch', the blessing of the bread 'Mauze'. 'Kosher', pure; 'trefah', impure

1 These notes are fitted into spaces below GE's alphabetical Index.
2 GE adds in the left margin '7th day of'.
3 Ludwig Kalisch, *Bilder aus meiner Knabenzeit.* See B 137, 138.
4 The source reference is to an anonymous work, which has not been seen by the present editor, on 'customary religious observances': *Religionsgebräuche, die abergläubischen und sehr beshwerlichen, den talmudischen Juden von ihren Rabbinen vorgeschrieben ...* (Bern: Jenni, 1874).

/184/ E Liturgy

In the morning service for New Year's Day, among the thanksgivings offered by the men is this: 'Blessed art thou, O Lord, our God! King of the universe, who hast /not/ made me a woman.' [Levi I, 17]

Ibid: 'These are the things which have no fixed limitation by the law; viz. the corner of the field; the first-fruits; the offering on appearing at the temple during the festivals; acts of beneficence; & the study of the law of God. These are the commandments whereof the man that performeth them enjoys the fruits in this world, whilst the principal remaineth for the future one: viz. honouring father & mother; acts of beneficence; early attendance at the colleges both morning & evening; entertaining strangers; visiting the sick; portioning dowerless brides; attending the dead to the grave; devotion at prayers; & making peace between man & man; but the study of the law of God is equivalent to them all.' [Levi I, 16]

There is a poem in the morning service for the new year every clause or division of which ends in the word Fire. [Levi I, 66–8]

Also a Hymn of which the burthen is, The Lord reigneth. [Levi I, 60–1]

/185/ G

On the day of Atonement there is a form כל נדרי /Kol Nidri/ which appears to be an absolution from all vows, obligations, oaths or anathemas, made during the ensuing year – an absolution beforehand. An explanatory note states that this form refers solely to religious vows which operate solely on the individual, without relation to other human beings. 'Nothing in this formula can operate on any oath between man & man; on the contrary, it is an expressed sentiment in the Talmud that "oaths can only be dissolved, which a man may make to bind his own person; but those which exist between him & his neighbour cannot be dissolved without the concurrence of the other party."' [Levi II, 1 and unpaginated note]

In various services are read the 13 rules of interpretation laid down by the Rabbi Ishmael. [e.g., Levi I, 21-2; II, 72–3]

Iom Kippur

'We will express the mighty holiness of this day, for it is tremendous & awful; on which thy kingdom is **/185v/ H** exalted, & thy throne established in grace; whereupon thou art seated in truth. Verily it is thou who art Judge &

Arbitrator, who knowest all, & art witness, writer, sigillator, recorder & teller; thou callest to mind all things long forgotten, & dost open the book of records, so that it may be read of itself; every man's signature is in it. The great trumpet is sounded, a dull murmuring noise is heard, the angels shudder, fear & trembling seize them. "Ha! (they cry) it is the day of judgment, the heavenly choir are to be visited in judgment," for in justice, even they are not found faultless before thee. All who are about to enter into the world now pass before thee, as a herd of sheep; as a shepherd mustereth his flock, & passeth them under his crook, so dost thou cause to pass, number, appoint, & visit every living soul, fixing the limitations of all creatures, & prescribing **/186v/ J** their destiny.' [Levi I, 110]

'On the First day of the year it is inscribed, & on the Fast Day of Atonement it is sealed & determined, how many shall pass by, & how many be born; who shall live & who die, who shall finish his allotted time, & who not; who is to perish by fire, who by water, who by the sword & who by wild beasts, who by hunger, or who by thirst; who by an earthquake or who by the plague; who by strangling or who by lapidation; who shall be at rest & who shall be wandering; who to remain tranquil, & who to be disturbed; who shall reap enjoyment & who be painfully afflicted; who grow rich, & who become poor; who shall be cast down, & who exalted.' [Levi I, 110]

In the service for this day occurs also the story of the ten martyrs put to death by 'a certain emperor' because their ancestors had sold Joseph.[1] It is narrated with very preposterous details. Appeal is made by Rabbi **/187/ K** Ishmael by uttering the name, the ineffable name of God, whether the decree of their

1 In the second epigraph for DD ch. 60, GE makes a parable of this story:

> The Roman Emperor in the legend put to death ten learned Israelites to avenge the sale of Joseph by his brethren. And there have always been enough of his kidney, whose piety lies in punishing, who can see the justice of grudges but not of gratitude. (669)

Being interpreted, the parable may refer to those Christians whose piety has historically been expressed in the punishment of the Jews for their ancestors' compliance in the crucifixion, rather than in gratitude or even recognition that Judaism produced and nurtured the Christian Messiah and religion. It also has a personal reference for Deronda, who has grounds for both grudges against and gratitude towards preceding generations. The story of the ten martyrs is also found in Zunz, *Die synagogale Poesie des Mittelalters*, pp. 139–51; on the last page of GE's copy in DWL is her note, '10 Martyrs, 139'.

bearing the iniquity of their fathers was from God – 'he inquired of the angel clothed in white linen; who answered, "Submit, my beloved & righteous sages, for I heard that God hast thus decreed it."' &c &c. [Levi III, 86–7]

In the Service for the Feast of Tabernacles, after the most passionate lyrism of prayer & praise comes all on a sudden a prosaic paragraph, half a page long, stating the ingredients of the incense, as 'the mixture of the perfume of incense was composed of balm, onycha, galbanum, frankincense, of each an equal weight &c.' [Levi IV, 94] [1]

In the same service is a long half-mystical account of the blessings reserved for those who 'kept the precept of the tabernacles' when God shall reign again in Jerusalem: 'in the tabernacle of the tree of life shall they be founded, under it shall they be feasted ... in its streets shall they adorn themselves & measure **/187v/ L** the dimensions of its height, to which it is a journey of five hundred years; & the circumference of its root is of the same dimensions; but the number of its branches are not to be estimated &c ... & seven companies of angels will rejoice under the shadow of its branches ... & above them are sixty degrees, rising one above another, till they reach the throne of glory & with a melodious voice chant the song of degrees. And every one according to his merit will receive glory, honour, & excellence ... Some will be a hundred cubits high, according to the embroidered temple, others will be from 2 to 300, & thus to the height of 900 cubits; thus also will they differ in their walk on the earth; some will go through the world from end to end; others will have the dominion of sixteen worlds; some will bear rule over **/188/ M** 310 &c ... Yet is there great peace among them; no hatred is in their camps, no contention in their dwellings; no enmity in their walks, no divisions in their canopies, no jealousy in their tabernacles, no sleep in their extent, no slumber in their resting-place, no accident in their dwellings, no tears in their eyelids, trouble is not in their imagination, distress is not in their thoughts; there is no evil imagination in their hearts ... They ... rejoice in God; & he walketh in the midst of them, to draw them with him to his tabernacle, to attract them with the cords of love, to shield them under his wings, to cover them in his secret tent, to place them between him & his ministring angels' &c &c.

[Levi IV, 114–16]

1 The recipe comes from Exodus xxx, 34.

Again, in the service for the Sabbath of the same Feast, in a rather heterogeneous account of what is the 'precept of the tabernacle', **/188v/ N** it is said, 'When he who is a perfect Unity created his world, he adorned it with pairs, as he said, two & two. When he formed Leviathan & his mate, he also made the wild beast of the field & its companion, who together feed on a thousand hills. In derision the males were rendered barren, the females were slain, cut in pieces, & salted for the righteous in futurity.' [Levi IV, 122]

In this service there are very lengthy elaborate prayers & poems entreating rain & dwelling on its good influences, – the litany of a parched country. [Levi IV, 164–73]

Passover

Additional service for *Dew* [Levi V, 81–94]

In this & almost every service there is a long hymn of which every sentence or clause ends with the same word – 'dew', 'fire' &c.

Pentecost

> 'Blessed art thou, O Lord our God! King of the universe who givest to the cock knowledge, to distinguish between day & night.'
> 'Blessed art thou &c, who hast not made me a heathen.'
> 'Blessed art thou &c who hast not made me a slave.'
> 'Blessed art thou &c *who hast not made me a woman.*'
>
> *The Women say*
> 'Blessed art thou, O Lord our God! King of the universe, who hast made me *according to thy will.*' [Levi VI, 17]

/189/ O *Service for Pentecost*

'In the Assyrian character, the Hebrew language, & the Egyptian dialect, didst thou cause the Hebrew daughter (the nation) to inherit thy law. Thou didst cause the Beth to precede the Aleph in the beginning of the creation; because the Aleph was ordained from all antiquity, for the delivery of the purchase of the first created thing. The world was established with the second letter, to inform us that there is a second world; but אנכי (I am) begins with the first letter; to shew that he is one & that there is not a second. He explained it (the law) to his people face to face; & on every point there are ninety-eight explanations.' [Levi VI, 56]

From a hymn of praise. 'At the beginning of these sentences before I utter them, I will first crave permission & approbation; with a few words I will rehearse aloud, & speak of the sanctity of the Creator, who upholdeth the world to eternity; his strength is eternal, & which it is impossible to describe, although the heavens were parchment, & all the reeds were pens, [the seas and all the waters were ink] & all the inhabitants of the earth were scribes & writers ... [Levi VI, 80]

'No eye hath seen the delight which they will enjoy in paradise, dancing in the divine presence. To him they will point with reverential awe, saying, this is he in whom **/189v/ P** we hoped in our captivity, in whom we firmly believed. He will ever lead us as a damsel to the dance, & certainly bestow on us the portion which he hath promised us of old. The sporting of leviathan with the ox of the high mountain, when they shall approach each other & engage in battle. With his horns he thrust at the mightiest beasts, but the leviathan will leap towards him with his fins & great strength. His Creator will then approach him with his great sword, & will prepare him for an entertainment for the righteous; who will be seated at a table formed of jasper & carbuncle, with a river of balm flowing before them. When they will delight themselves, & be satiated with the Bowls of wine prepared at the creation, & reserved in the wine-press. As ye have been happy to hear the praise of this poem, so shall ye **/190/ Q** be seated in the society of the righteous.' [Levi VI, 82]

He is called by seventy names & chose his people from seventy nations, & his name is exalted above the seventy ministering angels.' [Levi VI, 161] [1]

13 *Middot der Gnade*, Exod. xxxiv, 6, 7 [B 194; Pf711 94 [2]

1 Levi has 'ministring'.

2 Zunz, *Die synagogale Poesie des Mittelalters*, p. 76. Translation: 'thirteen measures of mercy'. The passage from Exodus xxxiv, 6–7, follows:

> And the LORD passed by before him [Moses], and proclaimed, The LORD, The LORD God, merciful and gracious, longsuffering, and abundant in goodness and truth,
>
> Keeping mercy for thousands, forgiving iniquity and transgression and sin, and that will by no means clear the guilty; visiting the iniquity of the fathers upon the children, and upon the children's children, unto the third and to the fourth generation.

References and notes

B 182v, 183, 183v, 184v, 186, 193v, 194

These brief notes, like the notes on the Jewish liturgy, are fitted into spaces at the bottom of the pages of GE's alphabetical Index. Some of these pages, in which the content is related to the Index letter – 'blank' and 'Bahir' under B, 'Fables' and 'Falasyan' under F, and 'Iaschar' under I – anticipate the method GE was to use throughout Pf 710.

The 'Had Gadya' (B 183) is traditionally sung by Ashkenazi Jews at the end of the Passover Seder. Her source may be *Johann Christof Wagenseils Belehrung der Jüdisch-Teutschen Red- und Schreibart* (Königsberg: P. F. Rhode, 1699).[1] Its subtitle specifies its contents, including 'unter andern jüdischen Büchern (Drey Lieder, welche die Juden ... an dem Oster-Fest zu singen pflegen ...)'. 'Had Gadya' serves to keep the children interested to the end of the lengthy service and has also been subject to various allegorical interpretations. In *Primitive Culture,* Edward Burnett Tylor notes that the song is sometimes looked upon 'as a parable concerning the past and future of the Holy Land. The solemnity of the ending may incline us to think that it was written to convey a mystic meaning.'[2] In 'Der Rabbi von Bacherach'[3] Heinrich Heine includes a version of this song; but he omits the last stanza, in which the Holy One destroys the angel of death.

---

1 This source is suggested by Françoise Bolton in her dissertation, *Les Romans de George Eliot et ses carnets,* 2 vols. (Université de Lille III, 1983), I, 536. The present editor has not seen Wagenseil's *Belehrung,* which is mentioned by GE on B 193v, Pf 7111 54, and Pf 710 41.

2 *Primitive Culture,* 2 vols. (London: John Murray, 1871), I, 78. GE read Tylor's work in July 1872 and again in 1874 and 1875 (GHL Diaries). For other notes from Tylor, see Pf 711 64, 65, and 70, and Pf 707 2.

3 Read on 13 and 14 February 1870 (GHL Diary).

/182v/ B

280 years, from Nehemiah to Judas Maccabaeus blank. Imagine what it would be if our history were blank from Edward the First to Elizabeth – or, to take a time of less rapid advance – from Edward the Confessor's days to Chaucer's.[1]

Bahir (splendour) a cabbalistic book, called otherwise the Midrasch of Nechunja b. Hakana: introduced in the 13th century as having come originally from Palestine – then in old time delivered into the hands of the faithful in Germany, & from them to the rabbinical authorities in Provence. Its contents were pretended to have been delivered in a long chain from Gaon to Gaon: this fable found credence even with Nachmani, who applied himself to the study of the Kabbala – though he was one of the keenest Talmudic critics & sharp to detect in the religious philosophy of Maimonides or Ibn Esra whatever was unjewish. [Graetz 7, 78–9]

/183/ C

At the pascal meal on the 15 Nisan 3 hymns are sung at the close. The third is to the following effect:

1. Ein Zickelein, ein Zickelein das hat gekauft mein Väterlein um zwei Pfenniglein.
2. Da kam ein Kätzelein & frass das Zickelein, das hatte gekauft mein Väterlein um zwei Pfenniglein.
3. Da kam ein Hündelein und biss das Kätzelein, das da hatte gefressen das Zickelein, das hatte gekaufte mein Väterlein &c.
4. Da kam das Stöckelein und schlug das Hündelein, das da biss &c.
5. Da kam ein Feuerlein und verzehrte das Stöckelein &c.
6. Da kam ein Wässerlein, das da loscht das Feuerlein &c.
7. Ein Oechselein, das da sauft das Wässerlein &c.
8. Ein Schochet der da schüchet den Oechselein &c.

1 This period of 280 years is noted in the tables on Pf 711 27 and B 169v. Compare B 151: 'that great gap in Jewish History of 210 years'. The historical comparison seems to be GE's own; no source has been traced.

9. Der Malach Hammowess (i.e. the angel of death) der da schüchet den Schochet &c.

10. Und zuletzt der liebe Herr Gott, der schächet den Malach Hammowess.[1]

/183v/ D

When the Queen of Sheba presented two wreaths to Solomon, one natural the other artificial, but indistinguishable for beauty, Solomon opened the window, observed which of the two the bees settled on & chose that. When she sent him a diamond to thread pierced with a winding hole, he took a worm, put one end of the thread in its mouth & inserted it in the diamond. The worm crawled down the winding passage & appeared at the other opening with the silk.[2]

/184v/ F

Fables. In the 13th century, Berachja, or Crispia, a Southern French Jew, brought out a collection of fables, few of them original – chiefly from Bidpai, Aesop, Lokman, & the Talmud. Of the hundred & seven *Fox-fables* which he gives, only a few are his own invention. [Graetz 7, 85–7][3]

1 Translation, shortened from *The Union Haggadah Home Service for the Passover* (Central Conference of American Rabbis, 1923), pp. 94–100:

1. An only kid! / An only kid / My father bought / For two zuzim [pieces of money]
2. Then came the cat / And ate the kid / My father bought / For two zuzim
3. Then came the dog / And bit the cat / That ate the kid &c.
4. Then came the stick / And beat the dog / That bit &c.
5. Then came the fire / And burned the stick &c.
6. Then came the water / And quenched the fire &c.
7. Then came the ox / And drank the water &c.
8. Then came the butcher / And killed the ox &c.
9. Then came the angel of death / And slew the butcher &c.
10. Then came the Holy One, blest be he! / And destroyed the angel of death &c.

2 Sabine Baring-Gould, *Legends of Old Testament Characters from the Talmud and Other Sources,* 2 vols. (London: Macmillan, 1871), II, 196–8. For more notes from this work, including another on the two wreaths, see Pf 711 92a and 93a and Pf 710 14 and 20.

3 For another mention of fox fables, see B 149, and for Lokman, see Pf 710 24.

Falasyan, Jews of Abyssinia, possessing neither the Hebrew text of the Bible nor the Talmud, supposed to have passed into Abyssinia before the Christian era. The greater part of them, however, are not originally Jews but *converted* Abyssinians.[1]

/186/ I

For want of invention an unknown author, probably a Spaniard in the thirteenth century, imitated the biblical narrative, in the book of *Iaschar* – a history from Adam to the period of the Judges adorned with stories from the Haggada, the Koran & other writings (especially the fictitious Chronicle of Moses). The book of Iaschar (called also Toldot Adam) has no other value than that of a felicitous imitation of the biblical style. [Graetz 7, 87]

/193v/ X References & Notes

Targums a nursery of *Agada*
v. Delitzsch [pp. 27, 50, 135–6, 136n–137n; Pf 711 59]

Saga of *Asnat & Josef* v. Jerome, Ep. 7 (Book III) [Pf 711 59][2]

Races looking forward to annihilation: 100 *Samaritan* families
[B 138v; Pf 711 59][3]

According to Scaliger, 3761 years to be subtracted from a Jewish date after Christ, to find out its correspondence with our own. [Pf 711 59–60][4]

1 This note is copied from 'Notes for *Felix Holt* & other', George Eliot MS IV. 10 in the Beinecke Rare Book and Manuscript Library, Yale University. Source: Ernest Renan, *Histoire générale et système comparé des langues sémitiques,* 3rd edition (Paris: Michel Lévy frères, 1863), p. 332. GE's annotated copy in DWL was read, or reread, on 5 October 1873 (GHL Diary). Since the *Felix Holt* notebook dates from 1861, the note there may be from an earlier edition.

2 *Zur Geschichte der jüdischen Poesie,* p. 24. Delitzsch cites Epistle 127 of Jerome. In GE's annotated copy of *Les Lettres de S. Jérôme* (Paris, 1679), in DWL, the reference to this saga is on p. 519. Asenath was Joseph's wife; see Genesis xli.

3 Abraham Geiger, *Judaism and its History,* p. 124.

4 *The Chronicles of Rabbi Joseph ben Joshua ben Meir, the Sphardi,* translated and edited by Christoph Heinrich Friedrich Bialloblotzky, 2 vols. (London: Richard Bentley for the Oriental Translation Fund of Great Britain and Ireland, 1835–6), I, xv–xvi. Repeated again below.

Kauderwälsch, Jew-German dialect
Wagenseil Belehrung der Jüdisch deutschen Red- und Schreibart contains the Jewish version of King Arthur.[1]

Fiscus judaicus, the 2 drachmas paid by each Jew to the Temple at Jerusalem, paid by order of Vespasian to the Capitoline Jupiter
[Graetz 3, 410; B 161v and Pf 711 65]

Rashi, the biblical & talmudical commentator Rabbi Shelomah ben Yitzschak – commonly known by the initials Rashi, on whom the elder Buxtorf has erroneously fastened the ineradicable misnomer Yarchi. Born 1039, at Troyes.
[Pf 711 76][2]

Mutakallimun, interpreters of the Koran whose rationalizing explanations were held heretical by believers in the Letter

Mutazila, i.e. the separated (or dissident), a school founded by Wassil Ibn Ata (750), whose theology was rationalizing. (Mohammedan Culture)
[Graetz 3, 199–200][3]

Starr, the bonds or contracts between Jews & Christians were so called, supposed to be from the Chaldaic Shtarot. *Star* Chamber – where these Starrs were kept[4]

First Hebrew Bible printed in Italy in 1488
Talmud first printed at Venice, 1520[5]

1 The reference is to *Johann Christof Wagenseils Belehrung der Jüdisch-Teutschen Red- und Schreibart* (Königsberg: P. F. Rhode, 1699). Its subtitle indicates that its contents include 'Jüdischer Geschichte-Roman von dem grossen König Arturo in Engelland und dem tapffern Helden Wieduwilt ...' Wagenseil's *Belehrung* is also mentioned on Pf 711 54 and Pf 710 41, and may be the source for the version of 'Had Gadya' in 'Jew-German dialect' on B 183.

2 Albert Löwy, in his 'Translator's Introduction to the Writings of Dr Zunz', in the *Miscellany of Hebrew Literature,* p. 155, gives Rashi's birthdate as 4800/1040 (as on Pf 711 76); he does not indicate his birthplace. See also Pf 710 33.

3 GE's copy of Graetz 3 in DWL has her marginal lines on p. 200; her index notes on Graetz 3, 512 include 'Course of religious philosophy among Mohammedans'. For GE's notes from Munk's *Mélanges de philosophie juive et arabe* on Motécallemin and Motazalites, see Pf 710 28 and Pf 707 12 and 32.

4 James Picciotto, Introduction to 'Sketches of Anglo-Jewish History', in the *Jewish Chronicle* n.s. 6 (5635/1874–5): 638.

5 Source not traced.

According to Scaliger, 3761 years to be subtracted from a Jewish date (AC) to find our own, & added to our own to find the Jewish[1]

/194/ Y Z

That Israel is the heart of Humanity & therefore feels more keenly occurs first in *Chozari*, by Jehuda Halevy, & is repeated in the *Sohar*. [Geiger, p. 64][2]

'Forsake doctrine (or study) one day & it will forsake thee two days.'
Saying of the Essenes [Graetz 3, 87–8; Pf 711 23; Pf 708 98]

The followers of Schammai said, 'It is better not to be born.'
The followers of Hillel said, 'Well, we are born; therefore let us be active & examine well our actions.' [Geiger, pp. 191–2; Pf 711 58]

'Die Krone der Lehre ueberragt die des Priester u. des Königthums.'
[Pf 711 60][3]

'I sleep but my heart is awake.' Canticles [Geiger, p. 84; Pf 711 57][4]

Tekehá, Teruhá, Shevorim, Gedoulah[5]

1 In repeating this note (see above), GE also repeated 'to find' ('to find to find the Jewish').

2 For other notes from Abraham Geiger's *Judaism and its History*, see the 'Extracts from Abraham Geiger' section (B 136v to 139) and the 'Notes from Abraham Geiger and others' section (Pf 711 56 to 59). For notes on Halevy, see B 166 and 166v.

3 This Talmudic saying is cited by Steinschneider in 'Jüdische Literatur', p. 359. Translation: 'The crown of the Torah surpasses that of the Priesthood, and of Royalty' (Spottiswoode, p. 3).

4 For a discussion of GE's use of this excerpt from the Song of Solomon v, 2, see the footnote for Pf 711 57.

5 These represent the sounds of the shofar or ram's horn trumpet call on the second day of the New Year's Service. See *The Festival Prayers, According to the Ritual of the German and Polish Jews,* translated by David Levi, 6 volumes (London: Abraham and Son, 5620/1859 to 5633/1873), I, 87–8. The call of the shofar is shown as follows:

Tekehá	Shevorim	Teruhá	Tekehá	[thrice]
Tekehá	Shevorim	Tekehá		[thrice]
Tekehá	Teruhá	Tekehá		[twice]
Tekehá	Teruhá	Tekehá	Gedoulah.	

See also GE's notes on the Jewish liturgy (B 182 to 190) and the excerpt from the 'Liturgy for Iom Kippur' on Pf 711 105–104.

'Was dem Gemüthe der Menschen zusagt, sagt auch dem Gemüthe Gottes zu: und was dem menschlichen Gemüthe nicht zusagt, sagt auch dem göttlichen nicht zu.'[1]

13 Middot der Gnade wie sie Exod. xxxiv. 6, 7, gelerht wird.
Selicha, from סלח to pardon. [B 190; Pf 711 94][2]

Savasorda = Abraham ben Chija, a Spaniard who lived in Provence was surnamed Zahib Alshorta i.e. Chief of the Police. Henri Savasorda. A mathematician of eminence [Geiger, p. 290; B 136v; Pf 711 56–57][3]

Auch in der Hagada wird die Schechina = Heiliger Geist, unter dem Bilde einer Taube personificirt. [Graetz 3, 226n][4]

7,000,000 Jews – half only in Europe. 1,300,000 in Russia, Austria 900,000, Prussia 254,000, Rest of Germany 192,000, France 800,000, Great Britain 42,000, Switzerland 3200. [Pf 711 22][5]

1 Source not traced. Translation:

> Whatever pleases the spirit of mankind also pleases the spirit of God; and whatever is not pleasing to the human spirit, neither is it pleasing to the divine spirit.

2 Zunz, p. 76. Translation: 'thirteen measures of grace or mercy as they are taught in Exodus xxxiv, 6, 7'.

3 Geiger does not provide Savasorda's first (Christian) name.

4 In GE's copy of Graetz 3, this passage is marked by a marginal pencil line. Translation: 'Likewise in the Hagada, the Shekhinah [the Divine Presence], equivalent to the Holy Ghost, is embodied in the image of a dove.' Graetz compares this image to the account of the baptism of Jesus in Matthew iii, 13.

5 Source not traced. A similar record of Jewish population numbers (in 1878) is in the newspaper article attached to the inside front cover of Pf 710:

> The total number of the Hebrew race to-day is what it was in the days of King David – between six and seven millions.

Pf 707 1 also notes a total of 7,000,000 Jews. See also B 127.

George Eliot's Index

B 182 to 194

The entries reprinted here include only those for notes from B 91 onwards. GE's page numbers include the facing pages: her 'Gebirol, death of, 166' is a reference to B 165v, and 'Aristobolus, 151' refers to B 150v.

Part Two

The Pforzheimer notebooks

Introduction

In 1976 the notebook known as Pforzheimer MS 707 was published in an edition by William Baker. Thanks to his pioneering efforts, scholars could discover that Gwendolen's name bore several latent meanings, which might be found in George Eliot's memoranda from her reading of Charlotte Yonge's *History of Christian Names.* Readers could also trace the symbolism of Kabbalistic doctrine in the relation between Ezra / Mordecai and Daniel to its source in excerpts from Christian David Ginsburg's *Kabbalah.* For both editor and readers, however, the notebook presented a number of puzzles and frustrations. Baker compared 'George Eliot's notebook of disjointed items' to 'the work of a pointillist painter such as Seurat',[1] but the looked-for effects of chromatic luminosity reflected from her pages were too often lost in obscurity. Sympathetic scholars could only surmise the difficulties inherent in Baker's project.

Although Anna Kitchel had edited the *Quarry for Middlemarch* more than twenty-five years earlier, no other notebooks from the rich hoard of memoranda of George Eliot's reading were then in print. The subsequent publications of *George Eliot's 'Middlemarch' Notebooks,* edited by Pratt and Neufeldt (1979), *George Eliot's Blotter,* edited by Waley (1980), Wiesenfarth's edition of *A Writer's Notebook* (1981), and McCobb's study, *George Eliot's Knowledge of German Life and Letters* (1982), demonstrated that painstaking scholarship could illuminate her patterns of reading: as more notebooks were published, the intelligibility of her memoranda increased. These publications came too late, however, to contribute to Baker's edition of

1 Baker I, 221.

Volume II – MS 711, published in 1980.[1] Although Volume IV – MSS 709 and 710, published in 1985, included 'Additions and Corrigenda' for the previous three volumes, editorial practice followed that of Volume I.[2] The green paperbacks from Salzburg provided a significant starting-point for scholarship, and I acknowledge my debt of gratitude to Baker's publications. Any reader acquainted with his editions, however, will notice several points of difference between them and this edition. These differences may be summarized in a few paragraphs.

George Eliot's notes are newly transcribed from the original manuscripts.[3] No attempt is made to reproduce all the data included in Baker's 'Omitted Textual Details'.[4] A scholar who needs to know, for instance, that in her running translation from a German source, 'George Eliot seems to have written "Great" which she has erased and replaced with the more precise "first pillared"'[5] is perhaps best advised to obtain first-hand acquaintance with the original manuscript. Baker also records minor variants between George Eliot's transcriptions and her sources. The purpose of the present edition is a more comprehensive intelligibility. More significant than the 'T.m.v.' details supplied by Baker are contextual matters, which are indicated – if not expounded fully – in the headnotes and footnotes of this edition.

Endorsing the view that 'changes, no matter how trivial, take the reader one remove from the author',[6] Baker's editions typographically imitate the line divisions and word divisions of George Eliot's notes. As our experience as readers of *Daniel Deronda* sufficiently demonstrates, our comprehension

1 Pratt's unpublished dissertation on Folger 13, 'A "Middlemarch" Miscellany: An Edition with Introduction and Notes of George Eliot's 1868–1871 Notebook', was acknowledged in Baker II, 3, 250, 252, etc.

2 Pf 709, not included in the present edition, comprises 4 pages of Hebrew language notes on vowel points, verb paradigms, and vocabulary from the opening books of Genesis; a transcription, transliteration, and translation of an inscription on a signature seal; and a copy of Wilhelm Freund and Marx, *Präparation zum Alten Testament,* Vol. I, *Präparation zum Pentateuch* (Leipzig, 1847). The latter may have been a source for GE's Hebrew notes on Pf 707 123 to 117, also not reproduced in this edition.

3 For an account of general editorial principles of this edition, see the Preface.

4 Baker I, 216–20; III, 131–8; IV, 78–80. Significant textual revisions are indicated in the footnotes of the present edition.

5 Baker IV, 79, concerning his 'Item 1' on Pf 710 16.

6 Baker I, 91; III, 6 ; IV, xviii–xix.

is more often enhanced than diminished by the substitution of the conventional printed page for the author's holograph manuscript. Through the reading process, the writer's intelligence, perception, and wit are communicated by means and effects such as tones of the spoken word and visual imagery, which are scarcely to be reproduced on the page either audibly or visibly, and yet are carried vividly into our imaginative experience. Details like line endings – in prose – have little impact on our understanding. What is required for effective reading is the potential for shared experience.

Putting the *Daniel Deronda* notebooks into print opens up entry-points to the author's intellectual and imaginative process. Full access to these processes requires precise identification of sources, so that they may be explored by the curious reader. Anyone who is intrigued by George Eliot's interest in war, for example, will not be satisfied simply to discover in her notebooks various references to the Crimean and Peloponnesian Wars, but will want to read further, to explore the original contexts of her extracts. Those contexts may guide our speculation about how her expressed admiration for military discipline as a 'contribution to the sentiment of duty' may be related to her notes on military atrocities, such as Tamerlane's triumphal pyramid of ninety thousand heads in the ruins of Baghdad.[1]

Precise identification of sources is not easily established. Although Baker found many, he felt constrained to declare that

> attention must be drawn to the eclectic nature of George Eliot's reading. This has led to inexorable difficulties in locating the sources of her references.[2]

The more successful overcoming of such difficulties in the present edition is due in part to the editor's familiarity with the *Daniel Deronda* portion of the Berg Notebook. Five pages there of excerpts from Eisenmenger, for instance, make quite superfluous the following speculation:

> ... her reference to Johann Andreas Eisenmenger's *Entdecktes Judenthum* on folio 39 of Ms. 710 is probably to Geiger's reference to it in his *Johann Reuchlin*, rather than to George Eliot's actual consultation of Eisenmenger.[3]

1 See Pf 711 94 and Pf 707 48.

2 Baker III, 139.

3 Baker IV, v.

The grounds for probability in such a statement are weak enough without the unfortunate confusion of Abraham Geiger with Ludwig Geiger. But such confusion is likely to follow from a dearth of precisely identified sources. The puzzle of placing sources is intricate, but more readily solved when more pieces of the puzzle are gathered together.

The occasional synchronicity of references in the Pforzheimer and Berg notebooks has also often helped to establish the chronology of George Eliot's reading. Baker was cautious about questions of timing. In reply to a scholar's questioning of his tentative dating of Pf 710, he observed that

> the problem of dating a George Eliot holograph notebook is difficult and complicated ... Items may not have been entered at the same time .... Caution must be the key word in dating entries in George Eliot's holograph notebooks.[1]

In truth, however, the intrinsic difficulties of determining sources are exacerbated by editorial avoidance of this problem of dating entries. For this edition of the notebooks, dates for George Eliot's readings have frequently been established by referring to the George Henry Lewes diaries, preserved in the Beinecke Rare Book and Manuscript Library, Yale University.[2] The primary caution needed in reference to these diaries is that Lewes records works read by himself alone, as well as works read by 'Polly' alone, and readings shared by them both. Nonetheless, his diaries have often proved most useful.

For example, Lewes's mention of 'Miss Edwards' 1000 Miles up the Nile' on 15 March 1877 provides adequate reason to look to *Up the Nile* for the source of a note on the 'Egyptian Pantheon' (Pf 707 65–69). One may thereby forego a fruitless detour, searching in the thirteen works investigated by Baker, which 'proved negative',[3] or in dozens of other publications on ancient Egypt available to George Eliot, or read by her at other times. In this instance,

1 Baker IV, v–vi, in reply to Mary Wilson Carpenter, 'The Apocalypse of the Old Testament: *Daniel Deronda* and the Interpretation of Interpretation', *Publications of the Modern Language Association of America* (*PMLA*) 99 (1984): 56–71. As with the biblical Book of Daniel, questions of interpretation may be related to uncertainty about dates. Determining the chronology of GE's reading will contribute to clearer speculation about her imaginative reintegration of her source material.

2 These 'GHL Diary' references have been supplemented by information in Haight's notes in GEL.

3 Baker I, 271–3.

the apparently helpful clue – '(Birch)' – on Pf 707 65 is a misdirection, likely to send the hapless researcher to a great many publications by the prolific Samuel Birch, and even to the dead-end reply to a British Library book application: 'It is regretted that this work was destroyed by bombing in the war, we have not been able to acquire a replacement.' It is satisfactory to discover, with the help of Lewes's Diary, that the information about the Egyptian pantheon is simply taken directly from the appendix to Amelia Edwards's fascinating account of her journey, and that Edwards supplies the reference to Birch – her source, but not George Eliot's. In this search, as in many others, the time clue makes all the difference between finding the source and being lured into a labyrinth of blind passageways.[1]

Relations between George Eliot's notes and her sources are often much less complicated than they may initially appear. An editor must beware the temptation to multiply difficulties. For instance, when George Eliot has identified a group of 'Notes from Abraham Geiger' in her list of 'Chief Contents' on Pf 711 1, and then identified a note from 'Ab. Geiger' on Pf 711 56, one may reasonably expect to find that many of the neighbouring notes, four of which mention 'Geiger', will be from the same work. Searching in vain through 'Lasarus Geiger's *Ursprung und Entwickelung*, 2 vols.', three works by 'A. Geiger,' miscellaneous works by Graetz, Tylor, and Maine, and *Les Lettres de S. Jérôme*,[2] Baker not only failed to locate the sources of thirteen notes taken from Geiger's *Judaism and its History*, but also presented, in his mistaken attributions, a mystifying view of George Eliot's methods of reading and note-taking.

Even when her notes are more scattered than in this instance, it is useful to remember that they are produced by a coherent intelligence – not a scatter-brained brilliance. In the present edition, some notes have been relocated so that the coherence of her reading may be more intelligible. The smaller page-size of the portable notebooks, Pf 711 and Pf 707, has on occasion provoked greater editorial relocation and compromise than were required in the Berg Notebook. Even topics included in her list of 'Chief Contents', such as 'Quotations from Rabelais' or 'Quotations from Bacon's Essays', are to be found on widely separated pages of Pf 711 and interspersed with notes from her other reading. Sometimes the yoking together of heterogeneous matter on the same page may prompt fruitful speculation: the interconnections between

1 As alert readers will have deduced, the present editor did not entirely avoid detours.

2 Baker III, 207–8.

excerpts on Pf 711 62 to 70, for instance, do not appear on the surface. Relocated items have been signposted, therefore, for readers who may wish to reconsider them, as it were, *in situ.*[1]

I first saw the *Daniel Deronda* portion of the Berg Notebook during an interval in my study of the Pforzheimer notebooks, which were located in another room on the same floor of the New York Public Library. In the first wave of enthusiasm over my discovery, I spoke to the late Dr Lola L. Szladits, then Curator of the Berg Collection, about my eagerness to edit it for publication, and was only mildly discouraged by her view that George Eliot's notebooks ought to be published in a standard edition prepared by a large and well-funded team of editors. Since such a project, however desirable, did not appear to be imminent, I began my independent research on the Berg Notebook. The project was subsequently expanded to include the Pforzheimer notebooks related to *Daniel Deronda.* The years since my interview with Dr Szladits have not only increased my conviction that she was right in her esteem for the powerful interconnections characteristic of George Eliot's reading and memoranda, but also confirmed my belief in the urgent need for published editions of all the George Eliot notebooks.

Pforzheimer Notebook 711

Pf 711 is a small portable notebook, 14 cm long and 9 cm wide, bound at the top. It has a black leather cover, with a pencil holder attached to the edge, an inside pocket, and a clasp. The pencil is missing, the pocket is empty, and the clasp no longer functions. The pages of unruled wove paper have marbled edges and the cover lining is a multicoloured paper. There is no indication of the manufacturer's name. The label on the cover, in GE's hand – 'Miscellaneous notes' – is in black ink, although the ink used for the notes themselves is violet. The violet ink in this book is pertinent to considerations

1 GE's lines and double lines between notes in Pf 711 and Pf 707 have been omitted in this edition, except where double lines (=) remain to indicate notes relocated to another section. The alphabetized notebook of 'Oriental Memoranda', Pf 710, presents a particularly orderly dislocation, and the arrangement of its entries has been left undisturbed.

of dating, for GE changed the colour of her ink from black to violet 'some time in 1872'.[1]

Since its earliest notes date from December 1871 or January and May 1872, it must be a sequel to the portable notebook labelled 'Miscellaneous Quotations', now known as Folger Notebook MS 13, the latest entries in which have been assigned 'a rough terminal date' of 'possibly December' 1871.[2] There is an apparent overlap between these successive books, for some early notes in Pf 711 have counterparts in the later pages of Folger 13. '*Kismet*' on Folger 13 115 may be synchronous with '*Kismet*, destiny' on Pf 711 4, and parallel references to 'Benfey's Pantschatantra' occur on Folger 13 116 and Pf 711 10.[3] The contents of Pf 708 also overlap with Folger 13 and Pf 711. In fact, Folger 13, Pf 708, and Pf 711 together are the contemporaneous portable counterparts of the Berg Notebook as a whole. The earlier part of the Berg Notebook has been published together with Folger 13 in *George Eliot's 'Middlemarch' Notebooks.*[4] Common references connect the *Daniel Deronda* portion of the Berg Notebook with Pf 711. Notes from Pf 711 8 and 9 are repeated on B 97v and 99; notes on Jewish festivals on Pf 711 19–20 are copied on B 172v–173; and the Jewish chronology on B 169v and 170 began as a copy of one on Pf 711 27–28.

The 'Chief Contents' listed on Pf 711 1 comprise notes made between December 1872 – 'Darwin on Expression' – and February 1875 – 'Reuchlin' – but some entries were added as late as September 1877 (Pf 711 113). As was her habit, George Eliot entered miscellaneous infill notes, out of sequence, wherever she found a blank space on a page. Also according to her usual custom, she took advantage of the binding at the top of the book to begin her note-taking from both ends. In Folger 13, the notes on pages 1 to 136 are recorded 'mainly from her prose reading'; from the other end, 'she copied favourite quotations from lyric, narrative, and dramatic poetry'.[5] For the

1 Jerome Beaty, *'Middlemarch' from Notebook to Novel* (Urbana: University of Illinois Press, 1960), p. 133. See also Pratt and Neufeldt, p. xxi.

2 Pratt and Neufeldt, pp. xx–xxi and 154; but see also the time table on p. xxiii.

3 Other links between the notebooks are not contemporaneous: a memorandum on Folger 13 115 – 'Look for incidents in the life of Raymond Lully' – finds an answer only years later on Pf 711 96. 'Pan is dead', a note from Rabelais on Pf 711 72, recalls her earlier note on Folger 13 96–98 about the same story as told in Plutarch.

4 Notes on the earlier Berg pages, B 1 to 90v and 175 to 181, are mostly in black ink, but there are also many later additions in violet ink.

5 Pratt and Neufeldt, p. xxiii.

latter section the editors have supplied consecutive pagination, along with the warning that the reader 'should realize that from now on until the end (page 172) he is actually reading the notebook in reverse'.[1] In Pf 711 a section which begins from the back cover includes the transcription of poetic excerpts from Keats, Tennyson, Wordsworth, Khayyám, and Keble. This notebook, however, like Pf 707, was paginated, apparently by GE herself: pages are numbered in the upper right corners of the upper (odd-numbered) pages: 1, 3, 5 ... 113. The even page numbers have been supplied by the editor.[2] Thus the reader of this edition will find that the prose and poetry sections meet part-way through Pf 711 104. In the final section of poetical extracts, the transcription continues from Pf 711 114 in reverse numerical order, returning to Pf 711 104.

Pforzheimer Notebook 710

This notebook, bound in purple leather, has a larger page size than the other *Daniel Deronda* notebooks – 17 cm long and 22 cm wide – and is the only one with marginal alphabetical index tabs. Its inside front cover bears a sticker labelled in black ink, in George Eliot's hand, 'Oriental Memoranda / arranged alphabetically'.

She first began to use this notebook before she changed her ink from black to violet, some time in 1872. On five alphabetized pages – D, F, L, P, and W – she made brief notes in black ink. These she obliterated when later adapting the notebook for re-use. She then recut and relettered the marginal index tabs. The page now lettered D (Pf 710 13) is preceded by a page containing four cancelled lines, in which two underlined words beginning with D may be discerned. The page preceding the extant F notes on Pf 710 17 contains two cancelled lines, of which the first word is underlined and begins with F. The page before Pf 710 24 (L) has one cancelled line, ending with the words, 'Theory of the Beautiful'. The page before Pf 710 30 (O) has a cancelled line beginning with P, perhaps 'Polyglot'. A one-line note at the top of Pf 710 36 (T) is followed by three cancelled lines, the first word of which begins with W.

1 Pratt and Neufeldt, p. 154.

2 Four page numbers, from 91 to 97, were inadventently repeated; these supernumerary pages are here renumbered as 91a – 98a.

After preparing this notebook for its new use, she began to enter her alphabetically arranged oriental memoranda, leaving blank pages for later entries under each letter. By preference, she filled in the right-hand pages first, as she had done in the Berg Notebook. Longer notes, however, such as 'Babylonian Empire', run over through the verso pages (Pf 710 7, 8, 9). Some left-hand pages remain blank; others were filled when space became cramped in certain letter sections, for example the A entries on Pf 710 5.

Her notes vary greatly in length. They may be summaries of quite extensive reading: seventy-five pages of Saint-Hilaire's *Le Bouddha et sa réligion* are condensed into two notes, 'Bouddha' and 'Sakya-Muni'. Kuenen's three-volume *Religion of Israel* is the source of twenty-four notes, distributed throughout the alphabet, and ranging in length from the briefest of definitions ('Hadassa = Esther = myrtle') to the excerpt on 'Origins, the Book of'. Alphabetical arrangement establishes one kind of order, at the cost of impaired coherence. The same page of Kuenen, for example, provides separate notes on 'Mosaic law', and 'Psalms', with no hint of their original contiguity or connection.

The discreteness of the Pf 710 notes, however, had the advantage of allowing George Eliot to make her own connections between her most recent reading and somewhat earlier sources. Although all of her notebooks include excerpts from other notebooks, Pf 710 has the largest number of recopied notes; amongst its major sources are Pf 711 and Pf 707. Her choice of recopied material provides insights to links not visible on the notebook pages. One line of connection, for instance, may be surmised: a copy of Mohammed's family tree (Pf 710 26) has an etymological note added later, from Deutsch's essay on 'Islam', which in turn led her to read Deutsch's copy of Sprenger's *Mohammad,* the subject of his review essay. Sprenger is the source of nine notes on historical connnections between Judaism and Islam. These notes on Jewish–Arabic philosophical and cultural interminglings have occluded links with two from Munk's *Mélanges de philosophie juive et arabe.* Then her note from Sprenger on the Arabic etymology of 'Jinn' may have prompted her to look up the 'Arabian story of the death of Solomon', in which Solomon tricks the Djinns into finishing building the Temple (Pf 711 93a). Although that note is not recopied, two others on that page and the previous page, and from the same source, Baring-Gould's *Legends of Old Testament Characters,* reappear in Pf 710. Thus for present-day readers, her notes and references serve as signposts directing us to a programme of more extensive and intensive reading.

When she had finished writing in this notebook she numbered every page, whether recto or verso, which contained any uncancelled notes; pages with only obliterated black-ink entries were left unnumbered. One page that was overlooked – containing only the brief note, 'Stone-worship = Baetyliendienst' – is here numbered 35a. All other pagination is that found in the notebook, and refers indiscriminately to recto or verso pages.[1] Most pages, however, were left blank. Perhaps the alphabetical arrangement of a bound notebook was found to be too inflexible for continued usefulness. Or perhaps her interest in oriental history, philosophies, and religions, waned somewhat after she began in June 1877 – twelve months after the completion of *Daniel Deronda* – to read and take extensive notes from Comte's *System of Positive Polity.* Her reading from June to October 1877 – listed on Pf 707 83v and 84v – includes almost nothing on oriental topics. From the summer of 1877, her preparatory reading and notetaking was related either to projected novels or to the moral essays later collected in *Impressions of Theophrastus Such* or *Leaves from a Notebook.* Her note-taking in Pf 710 probably ended in 1877.

Her re-use of Pf 710 probably began when the Berg Notebook was completely filled, late in 1874. The last Berg notes were fitted into available spaces below the alphabetical index.[2] A few of them were arranged according to the index letter: B, F, and I, in this respect inaugurating the system of Pf 710. No doubt Hamburger's *Real-Encyclopädie für Bibel und Talmud,* which provided material for twelve notes in Pf 710, also encouraged the adoption of a semi-encyclopaedic or alphabetical format. The 'Lexicon: Real-Encyclopädie', published in 1874–75, is included in a list of 'Books retained from T[rübner]' on the last page of Pf 711.

Another book retained from Trübner, 'Tendlau, Sprichwörter und Redensarten', supplied entries on four of the seven remaining blank pages of Pf 711; five of the entries were translated or copied again in Pf 710. Sandwiched between them on Pf 711 99, 100, and 101 are notes from Graetz, many of them also linked with notes in Pf 710. Finally, a few notes from Ludwig Geiger's *Johann Reuchlin* (Pf 711 95–98), read in January or February 1875, are repeated in Pf 710. Pf 707, the portable sequel to Pf 711, in its turn also became a source for notes dispersed alphabetically in Pf 710: excerpts

1 In Baker's opinion (IV, xiv), the pagination is not in GE's hand.

2 The latest datable notes, from Kalisch, *Bilder aus meiner Knabenzeit,* which was read in May 1875, were added as postscripts to earlier notes.

from Yule, Gibbon, Duncker, and Palgrave. None of the Pf 707 notes later than January 1877 are copied again in the alphabetically arranged notebook. These patterns of note-copying tend to confirm that Pf 710 was used in the period between January 1875 and the spring of 1877.

The dating of George Eliot's Blotter, which includes material derived from Pf 710 – such as the excerpt from the Egyptian Book of the Dead – may now be reconsidered. According to Daniel Waley, 'the blotter-anthology, which appears to have been written all at one time ... must date from the end of 1868 or the beginning of 1869'.[1] The list of themes for projected poems on the Blotter repeats six of the 'Themes for Poems' on Folger 13 138, which probably dates from 1869. Four themes for poems published between 1869 and 1873, however, are listed on Folger 13 138 but excluded from the Blotter,[2] and two new themes on the Blotter must date from no earlier than the autumn of 1873: 'Akiba' (see B 109) and 'Antico amor – the divorced wife' (see B 158 and 159). The 'Ben Abuja' theme is probably even later (see Pf 710 15). The Blotter therefore cannot be earlier than 1873, and perhaps postdates the writing of *Daniel Deronda.* Waley's conclusion that George Eliot 'was, in fact, in her poetical period' and that the Blotter 'bears witness to a time of much poetical reading as well as of plans for poetical writing'[3] is not incorrect; but the period of poetical intentions must be extended to include the 1870s.

Pforzheimer Notebook 707

Pf 707 is similar to Pf 711 in size – 14 cm long and 8 cm wide – and format. It is bound at the top and has a black leather cover, secured by a metal clasp at the bottom. The cover, which is lined in yellow, has a pocket on the inside front and a leather pencil holder attached to the right edge of the back. According to the manufacturer's notice on the front end-paper, this is 'No. 7' of

> Henry Penny's Patent Improved Metallic Books. Best prepared Paper. Warranted if written on with his prepared pencils to be as plain & durable

1 Waley, p. 4.

2 See Pratt and Neufeldt, pp. 154–5.

3 Waley, p. 5.

as ink.[1] They will be found of great advantage to Travellers and all persons who wish to preserve their Writing.

No doubt the pencil used by George Eliot, which is now missing, was one of Penny's prepared pencils. Nevertheless, she was able to erase, at least partially, some of her pencilled notes. Her extract from Demosthenes is written over an earlier pencilled note in Roman script. On the facing page, Hebrew terms and their definitions replace a roughly erased passage. In addition to its imperfect durability, the 'plain' visibility of the pencilled writing was less than satisfactory, and GE followed her customary practice of preserving her notes by writing over them in ink later. Some, however, such as the extracts from Ginsburg's *Kabbalah,* are written solely in ink.

The notebook pages were numbered in the upper right corners of the upper (odd-numbered) pages: 1, 3, 5 ... 123, and the even numbers are supplied here, as in Pf 711. Two unnumbered pages – containing lists of books 'Read from June to Oct. [1877]' and those read '*Aloud*' – were stuck together, apparently by George Eliot, and overlooked or excluded from this sequence; these are referred to here as 83v and 84v. As was her usual practice with the portable notebooks, she worked from both front and back covers. The first page from the back shows a sketch map of Warwickshire, beneath brief notes on Egypt and Bouddhism.[2] On the next page, an excerpt from Wordsworth's 'Ode 1815': 'Commemoration holy, that unites / The living generations with the dead', is followed by seven pages (Pf 707 123 to 117) devoted to Hebrew verb paradigms and vocabulary lists. These may date from July 1876, just after the completion of *Daniel Deronda*, when she had 'taken to instruct [Lewes] in Hebrew' during their mountainside vacation in Ragatz (GEL VI, 274).[3]

The list of contents on Pf 707 1 was made after the book was completely filled, some time after March 1878, when George Eliot read Lecky's *History of England in the Eighteenth Century.* '1875', written in the upper right corner

1 A semi-heraldic device of the lion and unicorn with the motto 'Dieu et mon Droit' intervenes here.

2 These comprise references to two books, Carl Friedrich Koeppen, *Die Religion des Buddha und ihre Entstehun* (also referred to on Pf 711 34 and Pf 707 38) and Heinrich Brugsch-Bey, *Histoire d'Egypte* (also referred to on Pf 711 21 and 44), and a note on the Tibetan Buddhist reformer, 'Tsong Kaba, réformateur Bouddhiste', which may be from Huc's *Souvenir d'un voyage*, II, 52–4; see Pf 707 46, 48.

3 The notes at the back are not reproduced in this edition.

of Pf 707 1, may indicate the starting date for her use of this book, but again there are overlaps in the consecutive portable books. Her notes on 'Celtic Names' (Pf 707 10–16, 26–27) must have been made before she wrote about Gwendolen as the lady of the bow; and she let Blackwood read the first twenty chapters, which includes Gwendolen and the Arrowpoint family, in May 1875. But in that same month she was still making notes, also pertinent to the opening of the novel, on Pf 711 94a to 97a.[1]

Perhaps one-third of Pf 707 contains notes made before or during the writing of *Daniel Deronda*, but the completion date of the novel, 8 June 1876, has not been precisely located in the notebook. The passage from Matthew Arnold's translation of the Hymn of St. Francis may be dated to the end of January 1876, and Leopardi's *Canti* must have been read in February. The reading of Yule's *Book of Ser Marco Polo the Venetian,* several notes from which were recopied in Pf 710, has not been dated. The next datable notes are from Huc's *Souvenirs d'un voyage dans la Tartarie,* read in November and December 1876. In fact, the completion of the *Daniel Deronda* manuscript marks no remarkable epoch in George Eliot's reading. In October, Lewes wrote that she was reading his MS and proofs of his *Problems of Life and Mind, Second Series: The Physical Basis of the Mind* 'when she [was] not absorbed in her Hebrew literature' (GEL VI, 294). Palgrave's *Narrative of a Year's Journey through Central and Eastern Asia,* read in January 1877, is the latest datable source for notes in both Pf 707 and Pf 710. The break in her reading came in the summer of 1877, when she put aside her oriental memoranda and Pf 710, and began filling Pf 707 with extensive notes from Comte's *System of Positive Polity*. Her later entries in this notebook, such as those from Green's *History of the English People*, Lecky's *History of England in the Eighteenth Century*, Best's *Principles of the Laws of Evidence*, and Clode's *Military Forces of the Crown*, are from preparatory reading for a new work of fiction.[2] The pages following Pf 707 73 have no connection with the other *Daniel Deronda* notebooks and are not reproduced here. It is hoped that they will find future publication as part of a study of George Eliot's later writings.

1 The first two volumes were sent to Blackwood for printing in November 1875.

2 See Jerome Beaty, 'George Eliot's Notebook for an Unwritten Novel', *Princeton University Library Chronicle* 18 (1957): 182, 175–8; William Baker, 'A New George Eliot Manuscript', in *George Eliot: Centenary Essays and an Unpublished Fragment,* edited by Anne Smith (London: Vision, 1980), pp. 9–20; and William Baker, 'George Eliot's Projected Napoleonic War Novel: An Unrooted Reading List', *Nineteenth-Century Fiction* 29 (1975): 453-60.

Pforzheimer Notebook 711

Pf 711 1 to 114

Chief contents and miscellaneous notes

Pf 711 1, 2, 3, 4

The 'Chief Contents' list on Pf 711 1 serves as an unpaginated index to those topics of chief interest to GE when she had filled the first 98 pages of this notebook.[1] Two unexplained items, which are preceded by GE's marginal query marks and followed by her brace signs, do not refer to this notebook: 'Period of the Fatrah' and 'Drances'. The contents indexed here include notes made between December 1872 – 'Darwin on Expression' – and January or February 1875 – 'Reuchlin'.

In the following three pages are excerpts from works read between Littré's *Médecine* (read from 17 to 22 May 1872) and Lazarus Geiger on languages (read from 29 March to 12 April and from 6 to 23 August). During this period GE was writing *Middlemarch*: on 28 April she finished Book V. For three months, from 24 May to 28 August, GE and GHL escaped to a comfortable country retreat at Redhill, Surrey, where she finished Books VI and VII and most of Book VIII.[2] There she read Wallace's *Malay Archipelago*; 'May & June 72 Read at Redhill' was pencilled in on Pf 711 4. 'Polly began Wallace Malay Archipelago' on 24 May, their first day at their 'new home at Red Hill', and finished it on 9 June (GHL Diary). As GE wrote to Maria Congreve, it was the first book read aloud by her after they came down: 'It is delightful. The biography of the infant ourang-outang alone is worth getting the book for' (GEL V 288).

Extracts from Keats's 'Isabella; or, the Pot of Basil' (Pf 711 3) may be linked to the Finale of *Middlemarch*, which was completed on 2 October (GHL Diary). Lydgate calls Rosamond 'his basil plant' and explains that 'basil was a plant which had flourished wonderfully on a murdered man's brains'. This ironic allusion to lines 457–60 may indicate a rereading of 'Isabella' in the summer of 1872.

---

1 Page references within square brackets are supplied by the editor.

2 See GE, pp. 442–3.

/1/ *George Eliot's Miscellaneous Notes*[1]

Population now augmented 14 per ct. in 10 years[2]

Chief Contents

1 Not in GE's hand. Perhaps a note by Mrs Ouvry (compare Pratt and Neufeldt, pp. 94 and 244).

2 The source for this note has not been traced, but may be information from the 1871 census, printed in GHL's *Partridge and Cooper's Annual Diary for 1872.* On Folger 13 1, GE's note on the 'Population of England & Wales' according to the 1861 census indicates an 'increase in 10 years [of] 6 per cent.'

	Cambridge		Oxford[1]
Michaelmas Term	Oct. 1 - Dec. 16		Oct. 10 - Dec. 16
Lent Term	Jan. 13 - Mar. 3		Jan. 14 - Ap. 1
Easter Term	Ap. 14 - June 23		Ap. 12 - May 26
		Trinity Term	May 27 - July 8

/2/

οὐδεὶς οὕτω ἀνόητός ἐστι, ὅστις πόλεμον πρὸ εἰρηνης αἱρέεται. ἐν μὲν γὰρ τῇ οἱ παῖδες τοὺς πατέρας θάπτουσι· ἐν δὲ τῷ, οἱ πατέρες τους παῖδας. Herod. Clio, 133[2]

'Ignoscenda quidem, scirent si ignoscere manes.' Georg. IV. 490[3]

Two editions only of Shakspeare in 41 years, from 1623 to 1664, which, says Johnson, did not probably together make more than 1000 copies.[4]

Interpretation of portents. Kettle boiling over without fire at the Olympic sacrifice = not to marry, if married to put away his wife, or if she had a son, to disown him (à propos of Peisistratos).

[Herodotus I, 59]

1 These dates for the 1872–3 terms at Cambridge and Oxford may have been taken from information printed in GHL's diary for 1872 and his *Beeching's Annual Diary for 1873.*

2 Herodotus I, 87, in *Herodotus Graece & Latine ex editionibus Wesselingii et Reizii,* edited by George Dunbar, 7 vols. (Edinburgh: William Laing, 1806), I, 133. In GHL's copy in DWL this passage is underlined and marked by GHL's marginal comment, 'beautiful expression'. Translation: 'No one is, of himself, so foolish as to prefer war to peace; in the one, children bury their fathers; in the other, fathers their children.' In DD ch. 69, GE refers to 'the tread of an invading army or the dire clash of civil war', when 'grey fathers know nothing to seek for but the corpses of their blooming sons' (748).

3 This line from Virgil's Georgics is quoted by Maximilien Paul Emile Littré in *Médecine et médecins* (Paris: Didier, 1872), p. 91. GE's copy of Littré, in DWL, was read on 13 December 1871 and 17 to 22 May 1872 (GHL Diaries), and is also the source of notes on Folger 13 128–32. In the context of a discussion of foreseeing the fatal consequence of disease, Littré alludes to Virgil's comment on Orpheus' backward look, which was fatal to Eurydice: 'Pardonable indeed, if the dead know how to pardon'.

4 Samuel Johnson, 'Life of Milton' in *Lives of the English Poets.* 'Johnson's life of Milton' was read on 26 and 29 January 1872 (GHL Diary).

Cette obscure clarté qui tombe des étoiles[1]

'Pendant de longs siècles, l'homme qui ne pouvait ni faire un pas ni exécuter la moindre opération sans dissocier les deux électricités et les mettre en jeu, cheminait en aveugle au milieu de cette force que ses yeux ne voyaient pas, que ses mains ne touchaient pas.' Littré[2]

/3/

'Half-ignorant, they turn'd an easy wheel
That set sharp racks at work; to pinch & peel.'

'no mad assail
To make old prose in modern rime more sweet.' Keats[3]

J. J. Ampère said of Lamartine personally that you were aware of the harp but only saw the wooden case.[4]

1 This verse from Corneille is cited by Littré in *Médecine*, p. 179, and again in *La Science au point de vue philosophique* (Paris: Didier, 1873), p.18. GE's copy of the latter in DWL is marked with a marginal line. 'Littré La Science' was read from 29 March to 23 April 1873 (GHL Diary). Translation: 'that dim brightness that falls from the stars'.

2 *Médecine*, p. 300. Translation: 'through long centuries, man, who could neither take a step nor make the least move without separating the two electricities and putting them to work, walked blindly in the midst of this force that his eyes could not see, that his hands could not touch.'

3 John Keats, 'Isabella; or, the Pot of Basil'. The first couplet (ll. 119–20) sums up the hidden costs and laborious production of luxuries and privileges enjoyed by the Florentine merchant class. The other lines (ll. 156–7) comment ironically on Keats's adaptation of Boccaccio's lurid tale. Passages from 'Hyperion' at the other end of the notebook (Pf 711 113 to 112) were copied about the same time as the excerpts on this page. The list of works 'Read since September [1872]' on Pf 711 11 includes 'Keats's Hyperion & Minor Poems', probably read in *Lamia, Isabella, The Eve of St. Agnes, and Other Poems* (London: Taylor and Hessey, 1820). GE and GHL knew Richard Monckton Milnes, who was to edit Keats's *Poetical Works* in 1876; they 'went to lunch at Lord Houghton's' on 15 May 1872 (GHL Diary). Their copy of his *Life, Letters, and Literary Remains of John Keats*, 2 vols. (London: Edward Moxon, 1848) was sold at auction in 1923 (*Catalogue*, p. 229).

4 This comment about the poet, historian, and statesman Alphonse de Lamartine may occur in Jean-Jacques Ampère's *Mélanges d'histoire littéraire et de littérature*, 2 vols. (Paris: Michel Lévy frères, 1867), which has not been seen by the present editor.

Dictum de omni et nullo: whatever can be affirmed (or denied) of a class may be affirmed (or denied) of everything included in that class. Principle of Contradiction. Principle of Excluded Middle. Identity [1]

Consider fundamental parallelism between the struggle of the Roman civilization against the Gothic invasions, & the struggle of the privileged classes against the popular mass.[2]

'Heard melodies are sweet, but those unheard
Are sweeter; therefore, ye soft pipes, play on;
Not to the sensual ear, but more endear'd
Pipe to the spirit ditties of no tone:
Fair youth, beneath the trees, thou canst not leave
Thy song, nor ever can those trees be bare;
Bold lover, never, never canst thou kiss,
Though winning near the goal – yet do not grieve,
She cannot fade, though thou hast not thy bliss,
Forever wilt thou love and she be fair.'

Ode on a Grecian Urn: Keats

1 Source: Alexander Bain, *Logic*, 2 vols. (London: Longmans, Green, Reader and Dyer, 1870), I, 155 and 16–17. GHL discusses the 'Principles of Certitude' – identity, contradiction, and excluded middle – in *Problems of Life and Mind, First Series, Foundations of a Creed*, Vol II (London: Trübner, 1875), pp. 90–6. His copy of Bain's *Logic* is in DWL.

2 Apparently GE's own comparison. Her copy of Anton von Tillier, *Geschichte der europäischen Menschheit im Mittelalter*, 4 vols. (Frankfurt: Schmerber, 1829–30), in DWL, contains her marginal comment, I, 20: 'As Rome grew weak the barbarian grew strong.' This passage is indexed by her note on the end papers of volume I: '20 Rome v. Barbarians'.

/4/

'I have elsewhere vowed a duty
Turn away thy tempting eye.' George Wither[1]

'Your reverend mother has grown
A very aged woman in a few hours.'[2]

The Malay Archipelago, by Alfred Russel Wallace. 2 vols. 1869
Biography of an infant Mias
May & June 72 Read at Redhill[3]

Faraday with Sir Humphrey Davy burning diamonds & finding the result 'invisible carbonic acid'.[4]

1 Wither's Sonnet from 'Faire-Virtue: or, The Mistresse of Phil'arete' (first published in 1622), as reprinted in 1871 for the Spenser Society, Manchester, in his three-part *Juvenilia* (iii, 815), has 'dutie', 'Turne' and 'eyes'. Another of his sonnets from 'Faire Virtue' provided the lyrics for Stephen Guest's song in Book 6, ch. 7, of *The Mill on the Floss:* 'Shall I wasting in Dispaire / Dye because a *Womans* faire?'

2 Source not traced.

3 *The Malay Archipelago: The Land of the Orang-utan and the Bird of Paradise, a Narrative of Travel with Studies of Man and Nature,* 2 vols. (London: Macmillan, 1869). 'Mias' is the native name for orang-outan. Wallace independently discovered the principle of natural selection and published in 1858 a joint paper on evolution with Charles Darwin; for notes from Darwin, see Pf711 6.

4 Source: John Hall Gladstone, *Michael Faraday* (London: Macmillan, 1872), p. 15. In addition, from 4 to 11 December 1869 'Polly read Life of Faraday aloud', 'Polly cont'd Faraday', and 'Read Faraday's life or rather skimmed it' (GHL Diary): that is, Henry Bence Jones, *Life and Letters of Michael Faraday,* 2 vols. (London: Longmans, Green, 1870).

Origin of εγω: vide Geiger
Skt. Aham[1]

Greek story of Cinderella connected with Psammetichus (Rhodopis)[2]

Kismet, destiny
Hamskit[3]

Libussa, Königinn von Böhmen, im Anfange des achten Jahrhunderts, nebst ihrem Gemahl Przemysl, Gründerin von Prag, vielfach im Sage gefeiert.[4]

1 The source of this linking of the Greek and Sanskrit forms of the first-person singular pronoun may be Lazarus Geiger, *Ursprung und Entwickelung der menschlichen Sprache und Vernunft*, 2 vols. (Stuttgart: Cotta, 1868–72), read in March and April and again in August, September, and October 1872 (GHL Diary). This is 'Geiger on the Aryans', noted on Pf 711 11 as 'Read since September [1872]'. They are also linked by Friedrich Max Müller in *Lectures on the Science of Language*, 1st series (London: Longman, Green, Longman and Roberts, 1861) pp. 312–13. 'Max Müller's Science of Language' was read on 25 and 26 July 1872 (GHL Diary). Compare GE's note on Folger 13 99: 'Sanskrit ... aham = ego'.

2 Source not traced. Herodotus writes about Psammetichus, a king of Egypt, (see II, 2 and II, 151–7, etc.) The parenthetical reference to Rhodopis, added later, links this to GE's note on the 'Egyptian Cinderella', Pf 707 42.

3 The single word *Kismet*, noted on Folger 13 115, may have been drawn from John Morley's article on Carlyle, *Fortnightly Review* 8 n.s. (July 1870): 16, as suggested by Pratt and Neufeldt, p. 145: '... the final and conclusive *Kismet* of the oriental. It is fate. Man is the creature of his destiny.' The source and meaning of *Hamskit* have not been traced.

4 Source not traced. Translation: 'Libussa, Queen of Bohemia at the beginning of the eighth century, together with her husband Przemysl, the founder of Prague, is often celebrated in legend.'

Read since September 1872

Pf 711 5, 6, 7, 8, 9, 10, 11, 12, 13, 14

On 18 September 1872, GE and GHL set out for Homburg; they travelled in Germany and France until the end of October. The list of books 'Read since September' on Pf 711 11, compiled by the end of June 1873, includes the sources for two topics listed on Pf 711 1 among the 'Chief Contents' of this notebook: 'Beethoven's Life' and 'Topography of Arthurian Legend'. Apart from Leopold Kompert's *Aus dem Ghetto,* the list includes no books on Jewish subjects. Although the gamblers observed in the Kursaal in Homburg provided dramatic 'Stoff' for GE's next novel (GEL V, 314), she was not yet thinking of combining that scene with themes of Jewish life. Nevertheless, the notes in this section include two from Henry Hart Milman's *History of the Jews,* a book included in GE's 'Books Wanted' list in the summer of 1873 (Pf 711 21). These brief notes were added later, however, probably in September 1873, in available space at the foot of Pf 711 8.

GE's reading of Ernst Curtius's *Peloponnesos* links with the classical Greek texts read by her during this period. 'Odyssey B. XI', 'Fragments of Sappho. Mimnermus, Frag.', 'Phaedrus', 'Iliad B. XVIII & XIX', and 'Phaedo' – all listed on Pf 711 11 – are sources of notes in Pf 708 72 to 78, which must be synchronous with the notes in this section of Pf 711. These readings in Greek, together with her notes from Pindar (B 92v, 94, 96, and 97), the 'List of books on the Homeric Question' (Pf 711 15, 16), and her related notes '*in re* Homeric poems' on B 91 to 105v, combine to suggest that GE was immersed in the culture and literature of ancient Greece during the months just prior to her study of ancient Jewish culture. Her notes on orally transmitted tradition – 'When was the Mischna written down?' (B 107v) – indicate that she was intrigued by points of comparison between Hellenic and Hebraic cultural traditions.

/5/

Beethoven's Life (Marx)[1]

Born, 1770. Wrote in deepest gloom about his deafness in 1800. When his 2d. Symphony was brought out, in 1802, after a severe attack of illness, made his will in which he pours forth his sorrow – 'Es fehlte wenig und ich endigte selbst mein Leben. – Nur sie, die Kunst, sie hielt mich zurück. Ach, es dünkte mir unmöglich die Welt eher zu verlassen, bis ich das alles hervorgebracht, wozu ich mich aufgelegt fühlte.'[2]

After his opera Fidelio failed in 1806, Beethoven answered this threat of Fate by writing the Symphony in B.

After many alterations, Fidelio was given again in 1814, & from that time was accepted as a great work. After its first production the critics pronounced it unintelligible & tiresome, & the chorus of prisoners a total failure.

Beethoven died in 1827.

Sonata Op. 81. Les adieux, l'absence et le retour[3]

'Riesensonate'[4]

1 Adolf Bernhard Marx, *Ludwig van Beethoven. Leben und Schaffen*, 2nd edition, 2 vols. (Berlin: Otto Janke, 1863), included in the 'Read since September [1872]' list on Pf 711 11. The following notes are GE's summary of her reading from Marx. In copying over her pencilled notes, GE introduced two errors in punctuation, which have been silently corrected.

2 Marx I, 227. This is an excerpt from the celebrated 'Heiligenstadt Testament' addressed to Beethoven's brothers. Translation:

> It would not have taken much for me to have put an end to my life. But Art held me back. Ah, it seemed to me impossible to leave the world before bringing forth all that I felt laden within me.

3 This is the French subtitle for Beethoven's three-movements piano sonata no. 26 in E-flat, Op. 81a: 'Das Lebewohl, Abwesenheit und Wiedersehen', or 'farewell, absence, and return'.

4 This may be a reference to the four-movement piano sonata no. 29 in B-flat, Op. 106, 'Hammerklavier', published in London by Ferdinand Ries.

/6/

Die Gothische Styl und die Nationalitäten, art. by W. Lübke
The French the true authors of the Gothic[1]

Darwin on Expression (Dec. 4, 1872)[2]

Three principles of expression

1 Serviceable associated habits
2 Antithesis
3 Actions due to the constitution of the Nervous system, independently from the first of the Will, & independently to a certain extent of Habit [p. 28]

Remarkable case of inheritance in three generations, cited from Galton. Trick during sleep of raising the hand to the forehead & letting the wrist fall on the nose [pp. 33–4][3]

Cry of terror across the pampas when the horse is attacked by wolves [p. 84]

Secretary bird & peacock killers of snakes [p. 110]

Pigs employed in N. America to destroy the rattlesnakes [p. 108]

1 This article by Wilhelm Lübke has not been traced. In Lübke's *History of Art*, translated by F. E. Bennett, 2 vols. (London: Smith, Elder, 1868), the Gothic style is said to be the product of 'the strongly awakened national mind yearn[ing] to express itself': 'Paris and its immediate neighbourhood were its cradle, and the territory of north-east France saw the first stages of its development' (I, 7, 17). In *Ecclesiastical Art in Germany during the Middle Ages*, translated by Leonard Abercromby Wheatley (Edinburgh: Thomas C. Jack, 1870), Lübke writes that the Gothic style, 'a style of which the ancient Goths had no share in the development', has been claimed by the English, French, and Germans 'as their "national" one'; but 'the north of France is really the country where this style originated' (p. 66).

2 'Polly began' reading Charles Darwin, *The Expression of the Emotions in Man and Animals* (London: John Murray, 1872) on 4 December 1872 and continued reading it until 23 December (GHL Diary). Her copy was sold at auction in 1923 (*Catalogue*, p. 227).

3 Francis Galton was a cousin of Charles Darwin. The reference is to his work on the inheritance of mental characteristics, *Hereditary Genius: An Inquiry into its Law and Consequences* (London: Macmillan, 1869).

/7/

Topography of Arthurian Legend[1]

Tintagil
Camelot in Somersetshire (Camelodunum)
Estrangoce (?)
Gerlot or Garlothe
Lyonness: Léonnois in Bretagne
But feigned to be sunk under the sea on the coast of Cornwall
Caerleon-upon-Usk, the Isca Silurum of the Romans
Avelyon – Avallon, the isle on which Glastonbury was built

Kinkenadon, by the sea-side: 'for there is a plentiful country':
the scene of Gareth's marriage
Astolat
Broceliande: two forests of this name,
one in Armorica, another in Britain
Galeford, Gafulford, coast of Cornwall
Logres
Orcanie (Orkneys)
Carduel
Bradigan, forest in Northumberland
Caerlyll

/8/

'All rich & rough with carvings of the gods'[2]

'Lone sitting on the shores of old romance'[3]

1 The following place names are extracted from Thomas Malory, *La Mort d'Arthure. The History of King Arthur and of the Knights of the Round Table,* edited by Thomas Wright, 2nd edition, 3 vols. (London: John Russell Smith, 1866). 'Morte d'Arthur' and 'Romans de la Table Ronde' are listed as 'Read since September [1872]' on Pf 711 11. Wright notes that the 'topography of our romance is not very comprehensible' (II, 10). GE's copy in DWL has a marginal mark beside the following passage: 'Then Arthur made great mone when hee understoode that sir Ector was not his father' (I, 12). Deronda's similar discovery is marked by a silence (DD ch. 49: 570).

2 Source not traced.

3 William Wordsworth, in 'A Narrow Girdle of Rough Stones and Crags', wrote 'sole sitting . . . '

Read since September 1872 Pf 711 8

Epitaph on Aeschylus commemorating his valour, but not his poetry[1]

'Fragments of vast nude figures – Telamones from Akragas'[2]

Petalism, the Syracusan analogue of ostracism[3]

'Naked as a needle'[4]

'Covetous fighting'[5]

Chinese bottles found in Egyptian tombs[6]

The Papyrus now unknown in Egypt, & only found in the Anapo in Sicily & in a small stream two miles north of Jaffa. [B 97v][7]

'We lose the right of complaining sometimes by forbearing it.'

Tristram Shandy[8]

1 The essay on Aeschylus in William Smith's *Dictionary of Greek and Roman Biography and Mythology*, 3 vols. (London: Taylor and Walton; John Murray, 1843–49), I, 42, refers to 'an epitaph written by himself': 'In it ... the field of Marathon [is mentioned] as the place of his most glorious achievements; but no mention is made of his poetry.' GE's copy of this dictionary is in DWL.

2 Source not traced. *Telamones* is an architectural term referring to sculpted male figures used as bearing pillars.

3 Source not traced. *Petalon* is the Greek for 'leaf'. In ancient Syracuse, petalism was a method of temporary banishment practised 'in imitation of the ostracism of Athens, but effected by writing the name of the person on an olive-leaf' (*OED*).

4 Malory, III, 2: 'and there Sir Launcelot took the fairest lady by the hand that ever he saw, and she was all naked as a needell'.

5 Source not traced: perhaps Malory. 'Covetous' here may mean 'eager'.

6 John Gardner Wilkinson, *A Popular Account of the Ancient Egyptians*, revised and abridged from the three-volume edition of *The Private Life, Manners and Customs of the Ancient Egyptians* (1847), 2 vols. (London: John Murray, 1854), II, 68. Mrs Ouvry's inventory refers to the abridged edition (*Libraries*, p. 119). 'Wilkinson's Ancient Egyptians' is included in the 'Read since September [1872]' list on Pf 711 11.

7 Wilkinson, II, 97.

8 'Polly began Tristram Shandy aloud' on 13 January and continued reading it until 13 February 1873 (GHL Diary); see also Pf 711 11. The quotation, from Vol II, ch. 4, is also copied on Pf 708 1.

Read since September 1872 Pf 711 8

Story of a Scape-Camel in Bruce, à propos of scape-goat vide Milman I, 156[1]

Egyptian novel translated by Rongè ibid. 135[2]

1 GE's copy of Henry Hart Milman, *History of the Jews*, 4th edition, 3 vols. (London: John Murray, 1866), in DWL, has her marginal line beside his note on this variant on the scape-goat:

> A camel ... was seized and brought without the town; and then, a number of old men having met, they upbraided the camel with everything that had been either said or done. The camel had killed men; he had threatened to set the town on fire ... After having spent great part of the afternoon in upbraiding the camel, whose measure of iniquity it seems was nearly full, each man thrust him through with a lance, devoting him, as it were ... by a kind of prayer and with a thousand curses upon his head. After which the men retired, fully satisfied as to the wrong they had received from the camel. (I, 156n)

Milman's reference is to James Bruce, *Travels to Discover the Source of the Nile, in the Years 1768, 1769, 1770, 1771, 1772 and 1773*, 5 vols. (Edinburgh: J. Ruthven for G. G. J. and J. Robinson, 1790). Neither Milman nor GE remark that the camel, unlike the scape-goat, is not sent out, physically unscathed, into the desert – where it might survive quite well. In the ancient Hebrew practice, according to Milman,

> two goats were to be chosen, lots cast upon them, the one that was assigned to the Lord was to be sacrificed, the other, on whose head the sins of the whole people were heaped by the imprecation of the high priest, was taken beyond the camp and sent into the desert ... (I, 155)

For GE's other notes from Milman's history, which she read in September 1873, see B 106, 112v, 151, 153a, 154v, and 155.

2 'The later Jewish tradition, preserved by the Apostles, of Moses being versed in the wisdom of the Egyptians' is repeatedly cited by Milman, who argues that although the Hebrews in Egypt 'were reduced to a base helotry and employed on the lowest industrial occupations', they benefited from the 'higher state of civilization' of the Egyptians:

> That before the Exodus the Egyptians had written characters, besides hieroglyphics, seems beyond doubt, whether we admit ... even the Egyptian novel translated by M. Rongè. (I, 135n)

Milman's reference, printed with an incorrect accent, is to an untraced publication by Vicomte Emmanuel de Rougé.

For the later Jewish tradition, as preserved by the Apostle Stephen, see the discussion of Kuenen's *Religion of Israel* in the note on sources for Pf 710.

/9/

Epact – ἡμεραι επακται

Mercury playing at dice with the moon & winning from her 'the seventieth part of every one of her illuminations' [B 97v][1]

The astronomer Messier, during the time of the Terror, shut up in his observatory in the hôtel de Cluny, discovered a comet. Not being good at calculation, he was embarrassed to determine the orbit of the wandering star: he thought of the president Bochart de Saron, an able calculator, who loved to aid astronomers in their labours. The president, already condemned by the revolutionary tribunal, had only a few hours to live. He employed them in determining by means of Messier's observations the orbit of the new comet.

Les Sciences au XVIIIe Siècle par Emile Saigey [B 99][2]

'I might as well try to shave a lion.' Plato. Republic[3]

On a Sarcophagus. *Natura non contristatur*[4]

1 Source not traced. On B 97v, 'seventieth' is copied as 'twentieth'. An epact is the number of 'intercalary days' – the translation of ἡμεραι επακται – constituting the excess of the solar year over the lunar year of twelve months. The ancient Egyptians had an epact of five days added to twelve months of thirty days each; they also added the extra quarter day of the leap year, and even calculated the Sothic period of 1,461 years, according to GE's note on Pf 707 100.

2 Emile Saigey, *Les Sciences au XVIIIe siècle, la physique de Voltaire* (Paris: G. Baillière, 1873), p. 182. 'Saigey La Physique de Voltaire' was read from 14 to 22 December 1872 (GHL Diary). It is in DWL.

3 *The Dialogues of Plato,* translated by Benjamin Jowett, 2nd edition, 5 vols. (Oxford: Clarendon Press, 1875), III, 210. GE's copy of this edition is in DWL. This note is repeated on Folger 14 10.

4 Source not traced. Translation: 'Nature does not mourn.' This note is also repeated on Folger 14 10.

/10/

Story of the Baby princess Edburgh (three years old), made by her father Edward the Elder to choose between rings & bracelets on one side & a chalice & gospels on the other. She turned away from the ornaments, & was therefore made a nun.[1]

The Master Thief. Indian, Scand[inavia]n, Cashmer[ia]n
The Giant who had no heart in his body
(Type of complex hidings for souls)[2]

Kelly's Indo-European Folklore[3]

1 Edward Augustus Freeman, *Old English History for Children* (London: Macmillan, 1869), p. 146. This work, which is in Mrs Ouvry's inventory (*Libraries*, p. 71), is also the source of a note on B 66, which may date from 1870 (Pratt and Neufeldt, p. 267). Freeman, in 'A Few Words on Old-English Words and Names' (p. viii), refers to Charlotte Yonge's *History of Christian Names;* see Pf 707 10–16 and 26–27.

2 John Fiske, *Myths and Mythmakers: Old Tales and Superstitions Interpreted by Comparative Mythology* (Boston: James R. Osgood, 1873), pp. 9–13. Also in Mrs Ouvry's inventory (*Libraries*, p. 70). For another note from *Myths and Mythmakers*, probably from the same time, see Pf 711 111. Fiske sent GE a copy in the summer of 1872. She later told him that when his 'Myth-book came to her'

> ... she was sitting on the floor fixing a rug, or something of the sort, and she got so absorbed in [his] book that she sat on the *floor* all afternoon, till Lewes came in and routed [roused ?] her up! (GEL V, 464)

The book was read again on 11 September 1873 (GHL Diary). Fiske's report of his 'hard battle' with GE over their disagreement 'as to the unity of the Homeric poems' during his visit on 23 November 1873 (GEL V, 463–5) may be related to her notes on the 'Homeric Question' on Pf 711 15 and 16 and B 91, 92, and 102 to 105v. Notes on the 'Story of the Master Thief', 'the wandering soul losing its body', and 'the Giant who has no heart in his body' are also found on Folger 14 83, 83v, 84, and 86; there the source is George Webbe Dasent's translation, *Popular Tales from the Norse* (Edinburgh: Douglas, 1859).

3 Several references to Walter Keating Kelly, *Curiosities of Indo-European Tradition and Folklore* (London: Chapman and Hall, 1863) are found in Fiske, who also refers frequently to Thorpe's *Northern Mythology*, the source of GE's notes on Pf 707 71–73, Tylor's *Primitive Culture* (Pf 711 64, 65, 70) and *Early History of Mankind* (B 99 and Pf 711 62 and 63), and Lane's *Arabian Nights* (Pf 711 107).

Baring Gould's Were-wolves & Swan-maidens[1]

Reduction of legends to about fifty story roots:

- Vide Baring Gould's Appendix to Henderson's Folk-lore
of the Northern Counties of England[2]

& Hahn's (40) Märchen- und Sageformeln in the Introduction
to his Griechischen u. Albanesischen Märchen[3]

Benfey's Pantschatantra[4]

Hahn: 'Vergleichende Blicke auf die hellenischen und germanischen Götter-
Helden- und Weltsagen'[5]

1 Fiske refers on p. 77 to Sabine Baring-Gould, *The Book of Were Wolves* (London: Smith, Elder, 1865). Chapter 3 of Fiske's *Myths and Mythmakers* is titled 'Were-wolves and Swan-maidens'.

2 'In his interesting appendix to Henderson's Folk Lore of the Northern Counties of England, Mr Baring-Gould has made an ingenious and praiseworthy attempt to reduce the entire existing mass of household legends to about fifty story-roots; and his list, although both redundant and defective, is nevertheless, as an empirical classification, very instructive' (Fiske, p. 115n). Fiske makes several other references to William Henderson's *Notes on the Folk Lore of the Northern Counties of England and the Borders* (London: Longmans, Green, 1866).

3 Johann Georg von Hahn's forty formulas for Greek and Albanian tales and sagas are outlined in his Introduction to *Griechische und albanesische Märchen*, 2 vols. (Leipzig: Engelmann, 1864), I, 45–60. Hahn's work is the source of the next notes and a note on Pf711 14.

4 Hahn's list of sources for his collection of 114 tales includes Theodor Benfey, *Pantschatantra: Fünf Bücher indischer Fabeln, Märchen und Erzählungen, Aus den Sanskrit übersetzt*, 2 vols. (Leipzig: Brockhaus, 1859). A note on Folger 13 116 also refers to 'Benfey on the Pantschatantra, for origin of fictions'. Benfey, a Sanskrit scholar and philologist, argues in the introduction to his translation of the *Panchatantra* that a great number of *Märchen* and other folk tales had originated in India.

5 Hahn, I, vii. Translation: 'Comparative views of Greek and Germanic myths, heroic legends, and creation myths'.

/11/

Read since September [1872]

Freitag on Dramatic Art[1]
Kompert's Stories of the Ghetto[2]
Tracts on Science in Virchow & Holzendorff's Series:
on Metamorphoses in the Mineral Kingdom
on the Interpretation of Hieroglyphs
on Modern & Ancient Astrology, &c[3]
Geiger on the Aryans [Pf 711 4]
Wilkinson's Ancient Egyptians [Pf 711 8]
Articles on Egypt in Geographical & Biblical Dictionaries
Burnou f's Science des Religions (aloud)[4]
Herodotus Book II. On Egypt[5]
Morte d'Arthur [Pf 711 7, 8]
Romans de la Table Ronde[6]
Freeman's Old English History [Pf 711 10]
Tristram Shandy (aloud) [Pf 711 8]
Schopenhauer's Welt als Wille u. Vorstellung[7]

1 Gustav Freytag, *Die Technik des Dramas* (Leipzig: S. Hirzel, 1863). 'Polly read Freitag: Technik des Dramas' on 2 and 5 October 1872 (GHL Diary).

2 Leopold Kompert's *Aus dem Ghetto* (Leipzig: Grunow, 1848) was read on 29 and 30 September 1872 (GHL Diary).

3 Rudolf L. C. Virchow and Franz von Holzendorff-Vietmansdorf, editors, *Sammlung gemeinverständlicher wissenschaftlicher Vorträge,* series VI (Berlin, 1871). 'Die Umwandlungsprocess im Mineralreich' (pp. 545–84) was read 'after breakfast' on 15 October and again on 16 October 1872; 'Ueber des hieroglyphische Schriftsystem' (pp. 363–98) was read on 19 October; 'Alte und neue[re] Astrologie' (pp. 710–40) was read 'after breakfast' on 14 October (GHL Diary).

4 Emile Louis Burnouf, *La Science des religions* (Paris: Maisonneuve, 1872), read from 9 to 23 November 1872 (GHL Diary).

5 For a note from Herodotus I, see Pf 711 2. On Pf 708 102 and 103, GE lists 'Stories in Herodotus', Books I and II.

6 *Les Romans de la table ronde mis en nouveau langage,* edited by Paulin Paris, 5 vols. (Paris: Léon Techener, 1868–72). GE's copy is in DWL.

7 Arthur Schopenhauer, *Die Welt als Wille und Vorstellung* (1818), the source of a note on Folger 14 25. GE may have read the 3rd edition (Leipzig: F. A. Brockhaus, 1859). On 8 and 11 October 1872 'Polly read aloud the Vortrag on Schopenhauer' (GHL Diary); this lecture has not been traced.

Read since September 1872 Pf711 11

Keats's Hyperion & Minor Poems	[Pf711 3, 113, 112]
Fawcett's Political Economy[1]	
Portions of Mill's d[itt]o[2]	
Comte's Catechism – 2d & 3d Parts[3]	
Aeneid, B. VI	[Pf711 112]
Odyssey B. XI[4]	
Fragments of Sappho. Mimnermus, Frag.[5]	
Marx' Life of Beethoven	[Pf711 5]
Buckle's Hist. of Civil. (aloud)[6]	
Phaedrus	[Pf708 72, 73, 75, 76, 77, 78][7]
Iliad B. XVIII & XIX	[Pf708 72][8]

1 Henry Fawcett, *Manual of Political Economy*, 3rd edition (London: Macmillan, 1869). GE's copy of the 4th edition (1874) is in DWL.

2 John Stuart Mill, *Principles of Political Economy* (London: J. W. Parker, 1848 and later editions). GE also read this in 1865 (GEL IV, 196).

3 Auguste Comte, *Catéchisme Positiviste, ou Sommaire Exposition de la religion universelle* (Paris: the author, 1852), in DWL.

4 Book XI of the *Odyssey* and Book VI of the *Aeneid* both tell of visits to Hades.

5 Fragments of poetry by Sappho and Mimnermus are in *Poetae Lyrici Graeci*, edited by Wilhelm Theodor Bergk (Lipsiae: Reichenbach, 1843). GE's copy in DWL includes her note on p. 120, after these fragments: 'read 2nd time Feb. 1873'. Bergk is also the source of excerpts from Pindar on B 92v to 97.

6 Henry Thomas Buckle, *History of Civilization in England*, 2 vols. (London: J. W. Parker and Sons, 1857–61), in DWL, was read from 14 February to 24 March 1873 (GHL Diary).

7 GE read Plato's *Phaedrus*, a dialogue on rhetoric, the Muses, and the soul, in the translation by Benjamin Jowett, *The Dialogues of Plato translated into English with Analyses and Introductions*, 4 vols. (Oxford: Clarendon Press, 1868–71). GE's copy of the second edition in 5 volumes (1875) is in DWL. GHL's Diary records reading 'Jowett's translation of Plato – prefaces' on 17 November and 'Jowett's Plato' on 22 and 23 November 1875. But GE also read proof sheets from one volume of the first edition, sent to her by Jowett in August 1870, and commented that 'the translations ... seem to be charmingly done' (GEL V, 112). A passage from Jowett's translation of the *Phaedrus* is cited to illustrate Mab Meyrick's inclination to the opinion of Socrates: 'What motive has a man to live, if not for the pleasures of discourse?' (DD ch. 32: 348). In the second edition, this question, which GE copied on Pf 708 72, is found on II, 136. On 7 June 1873 GE and GHL 'went to Oxford on a visit to Jowett' (GHL Diary).

8 The passage in Pf 708 is in Greek, from Homer, *Ilias, Graece et Latine*, edited by S. Clark, 16th edition, 2 vols. (1810–15). GHL's annotated copy is in DWL.

Read since September 1872 Pf 711 11 12

Phaedo [Pf 708 73][1]
Maine's Village Communities[2]

/12/

So zieht sich unterhalb der Stadt Korinth ein Felsrand mit Grotten hin, welche offenbar vom Meere gestaltet worden sind ... Ueberhaupt ist das westliche Meer vorzugsweise landbildend wie in Klein-Asien, so auch in Hellas, in Aetolien und Akarnanien, wie im Peloponnese.[3]

Seit die Alten (Griechen) anfingen über die Geschichte ihres Landes nachzudenken, kam ihnen die Produktionskraft desselben als eine hinschwindende hervor. Platon hielt die damalige Vegetation für eine entartete und verkümmerte, und betrachtete die nackten Gebirge wie die von

1 The excerpt from the Phaedo dialogue in Greek in Pf 708 is from Plato, *Dialogie Graece et Latine,* 5 vols. (Berolini, 1816–23). GHL's annotated copy is in DWL.

2 Henry James Sumner Maine, *Village Communities in the East and West,* 2nd edition (London: John Murray, 1872) was read from 8 to 14 April and from 26 May to 18 June 1873 (GHL Diary). GE's copy is in DWL.

3 Ernst Curtius, *Peloponnesos: Eine historisch-geographische Beschreibung der Halbinsel,* 2 vols. (Gotha: Justus Perthes, 1851–52), I, 48. Translation:

> Below the city of Corinth extends a rocky ledge, with grottos that obviously have been shaped by the sea ... The western sea has chiefly contributed to forming the land, as in Asia Minor, so also in Hellas, in Aetolia and Acarnania, as in the Peloponnese.

Volume II of *Peloponnesos* is the source for notes on B 37v–40v, 41v, 42v, 43v, 44v. GE's extensive summaries in the Berg Notebook and quotations here suggest that she may have borrowed copies on two occasions. On 16 March 1873 she wrote to thank Oscar Browning

> for the Curtius which came to me the other day. I have already found some nutritive bits in it, and am very glad of the opportunity which your kindness has given me. (GEL IX, 82)

'The Curtius' may have been Volume I of *Peloponnesos.* His *Griechische Geschichte,* now in DWL, had been sent to GHL in March 1870, when GE and GHL attended his lecture in Berlin (GHL Diary; see also McCobb, p. 329, Pf 708 71–72 and B 87–88). Browning may also have sent Adolphus William Ward's English translation, *History of Greece,* 5 vols. (London: Richard Bentley, 1868–73), which GE recommended for Girton students in a letter of March 1873 (GEL IX, 87).

Krankheit abgezehrten Glieder eines einst blühenden Lebens. Flüsse sterben wie Menschen und Städte und der Boden der Erde hat nach Aristoteles wie der Leib der Pflanzen und der Thiere seine Jugend und sein **/13/** Alter ...
[I, 53][1]

Manche Ansiedlungen sind noch neuerdings wegen Wassermangels verlassen worden, nachdem die Einwohner unter Verwünschungen Steine auf die treulose Quelle gewälzt haben. Curtius, Peloponnesus [I, 54][2]

'Ings', meadow-grounds
'Hams', pastures[3]

Types of story. The fatal possession of preternatural power which becomes unmanageable. Example Goethe's ballad of the *Lehrling*. Indian types. Shah Darval grown to be a magician – being the only person near his master who lay dying, he had imparted to him the secret spell by which the two genii were bound to serve him. Hemar Punt (or Hemadri) was obliged to keep his demons employed & set them to build temples with huge stones without mortar, which they finished in one night![4]

1 Translation:

> Ever since the ancients (the ancient Greeks) began to reflect upon the history of their land, its productive power appeared to them to be dwindling away. Plato considered the vegetation of that time to be degenerate and stunted, and the naked mountains to be like limbs, once flourishing with life, but now atrophied by disease. Rivers die like men and cities, and, according to Aristotle, the earth's soil has, like the body of plants and animals, its youth and its old age ...

GE wrote 'Lebens' for Curtius's 'Leibes'.

2 Translation:

> Even recently, many colonies have been abandoned as a result of a lack of water, after the inhabitants, cursing, have rolled a stone over the unreliable spring.

3 These dialect words distinguish between two kinds of meadows. GE's source may be Walter William Skeat, editor, *Reprinted Glossaries* (London: Trübner for the English Dialect Society, 1873–79), Series B, Nos. 1, 5, 6, and 23. GE's copies of these regional glossaries are in DWL. *Ing* is defined as a 'meadow; low mowing ground (B. 2. 32), and *Ham* as 'a stinted common pasture for cows, &c.' (B. 4. 58). GE corresponded with Skeat about Midland dialects, perhaps in 1872 (GEL IX, 39).

4 The source for this note on variations of the theme of Djinns has not been traced. For other notes on Djinns, see Pf 711 93a and Pf 710 21.

/14/

'Unsere gemein-deutsche Heldensage zerfällt bekanntlich in drei Gruppen, nämlich in die nach Siegfried oder den Nibelungen, in die nach Dietrich von Bern oder den Amelungen, und in die nach Gudrun benannte.'[1]

'God is really here, at bottom, a deeply moved way of saying *Conduct* or righteousness.' Matthew Arnold[2]

'When we say that culture is: *To know the best that has been said & thought in the world*, we imply that, for culture, a system directly tending to this end is necessary to our reading ... Our reading being so without purpose as it is, nothing can be truer than what Butler says, that really in general, no part of our time is more idly spent than the time spent in reading.'

Idem [Preface, xxxiii][3]

Herodotus says that Thales was of Phoenician descent.[4]

1 Hahn (see Pf 711 10), I, 29. Translation: 'As everyone knows, our common German heroic legends fall into three groups, that is, those about Siegfried or the Nibelungs, those about Dietrich von Bern or the Amelungs, and those named after Gudrun.' GE inadvertently wrote 'bekannte' for 'benannte'.

2 *Literature and Dogma: An Essay towards a Better Apprehension of the Bible* (London: Smith, Elder, 1873), p. 47. For another note from this source, see Pf 711 65.

3 In this passage GE's underlining of Arnold's definition of culture recalls her comment in a letter to Frederic Harrison, in November 1867, about 'Culture: a Dialogue', a satirical article written by Harrison in response to Arnold:

> I don't know how far my impressions have been warped by reading German, but I have regarded the word 'culture' as a verbal equivalent for the highest mental result of past and present influences. Dictionary meanings are liable rapidly to fall short of usage. But I am not maintaining an opinion – only stating an impression. (GEL IV, 395)

GE's impression of this word's usage was shared by Arnold.

4 'Thales of Miletus (a man of remote Phoenician descent)' (I, 170) predicted the occurrence of a solar eclipse (I, 74), an event indexed by GE on the end papers of her copy of *Herodotus Graece et Latine*: 'Eclipse, 110'.

List of books on the Homeric Question

Pf 711 15, 16

The source of this bibliography is Hermann Bonitz, *Über den Ursprung der homerischen Gedichte,* 3rd edition (Wien: Carl Gerold's Sohn, 1872). The relatively brief text of Bonitz's lecture, originally delivered in March 1860, precedes some 80 pages of notes in fine print, revised in each edition, which comprise a comprehensive critical bibliographical survey of scholarship on the origin of the Homeric poems. GE's list was extracted from these extensive notes. There is no evidence that she read every work listed here; only Lachmann and Bernardy are in DWL.

Her interest in the 'Homeric Question' was of long standing: on 2 December 1870 she noted that she was 'reading Wolf's Prolegomena to Homer' (GE Journal). Copied in the summer of 1873, this list preceded her extensive notes on the 'Homeric Controversy' in the Berg Notebook (B 91, 92, 102–105v) and her disagreement with John Fiske on 23 November 1873 'as to the unity of the Homeric poems'. He was surprised to find that 'she was a strong Wolfian!' According to Fiske, she 'said she was glad of some new considerations that [he] had presented on the subject' – although, on the whole, he did not think that he had converted her. GE's rereading on 11 September 1873 of his *Myths and Mythmakers,* which she thought 'a beautiful book',[1] no doubt prompted the Homeric topic, for it includes a critique of the Wolfian viewpoint expressed by William Ewart Gladstone in *Juventus Mundi: Gods and Men of the Heroic Age* (1869).

Although, as Fiske reminded his wife, he was 'not a fool on the Homer-question', he found GE's knowledge 'quite amazing':

> I found her thoroughly acquainted with the whole literature of the Homeric question ... She showed an amazing knowledge of the subject. (GEL V, 463–5)

---

1 See Pf 711 10 and 111.

/15/

Homeric Question

Die Homerische Kritik von Wolf bis Grote. 1853 *Friedländer* (mainly against Lachmann)[1]

Bernhardy, Gr. Lit.[2]

Lachmann, Betrachtungen ueber die Ilias[3]

On the conservative side against Lachmann,
Nitsch, 'Die Sagenpoesie der Griechen kritisch dargestellt.' 1852 (for admissions)[4]

Minckwitz, Vorschule zum Homer, 1863[5]

Nutzhorn, Die Enstehungsweise der Homerischen Gedichte ... mit einem Vorworte von J. N. Madvig. 1866 or 7.[6] On the conservative side. According to Bonitz, of the rhetorical-arrogant order

J. La Roche, Ueber die Entstehung der Homerischen Gedichte (But this appears in the Zeitschr. f. d. ö. G. 1863)[7]

Sengebusch, Homerica dissertatio prior et posterior (Tradition concerning Homer)[8]

1 The reference is to Ludwig Friedländer's dissertation on 'Homeric Criticism from Wolf to Grote'.
2 Gottfried Bernhardy, *Grundriss der grieschischen Litteratur*, Part II, *Geschichte der grieschischen Poesie* (Halle: E. Anton, 1845), in DWL.
3 Karl Konrad Friedrich Wilhelm Lachmann, *Betrachtungen über Homers Ilias* (Berlin, 1847), in DWL.
4 Gregor Wilhelm Nitzsch, *Die Sagenpoesie der Griechen, kritisch dargestellt*, 2 vols. (Braunschweig: C. A. Schwetschke, 1852).
5 Johannes Minckwitz, *Vorschule zum Homer* (Stuttgart, 1863).
6 Friedrich Nutzhorn, *Die Enstehungsweise der homerischen Gedichte* (Leipzig: Teubner, 1869).
7 Jakob La Roche, 'Über die Enstehung der Homerischen Gedichte', in *Zeitschrift für die österreichischen Gymnasien* (Vienna, 1863), 161–202.
8 Maximilian Sengebusch, *Homerica dissertatio prior et posterior* (Leipzig, 1855–6).

List of books on the Homeric Question Pf 711 15 16

Welcker, der epische Cyclus oder die Homerischen Dichter (stretches the evidence about the cyclic poems)[1]

Kirchhoff, Untersuchungen über die Composition der Odyssee[2]

Bäumlein, Commentatio de Homero ejusque carminibus (vor der Ilias der Tauchnitz'scher Textenausgabe)[3]

B. G. Hermann, de Interpolationibus Homeri, Opusc. V[4]

/16/

A. Jacob, ueber die Enstehung der Ilias u. Odyssee[5]

Fäsi, Einleitung to his Odyssey[6]

Héricault, Charles d', Essai sur l'origine de l'épopée française et sur son histoire au moyen age. Paris, 1859[7]

1 Friedrich Gottlieb Welcker, *Der epische Cyclus oder die homerischen Dichter* (Bonn: E. Weber, 1835).
2 Adolf Kirchhoff, *Die Composition der Odyssee* (Berlin: W. Hertz, 1869).
3 Wilhelm von Bäumlein, *Commentatio de Homero ejusque carminibus* (Leipzig: Tauchnitz, 1854).
4 Johann Gottfried Jakob Hermann, *De Interpolationibus Homeri dissertatio* (Leipzig, 1832).
5 August Jacob, *Ueber die Entstehung der Ilias und der Odyssee* (Berlin: G. Reimer, 1856).
6 Johann Ulrich Fäsi, Introduction to his *Homers Odyssee*, 2 vols. (Leipzig, 1849).
7 Charles de Ricault d'Héricault, *Essai sur l'origine de l'épopée française et sur son histoire au moyen âge* (Paris: A. Franck, 1859).

Fontenelle's *Pluralité des Mondes*

Pf 711 17, 18, 19

In July 1873 GE and GHL were in France, where they read Rousseau's *Contrat Social* on 9 July (GHL Diary). The short excerpt copied on Pf 711 19, just above the list of Jewish Festivals, may be translated: 'The great soul of the legislator is the true miracle which ought to prove his mission'. The context is Rousseau's argument, in Book I, chapter vii, 'Of the Legislator', that the fathers and lawgivers of nations 'honour the gods with their own wisdom', as he ironically comments, and 'put decisions in the mouth of the immortals, to influence by divine authority those that human discretion might not be able to move ...' As Rousseau observes,

> Any man can engrave tablets of stone, or purchase an oracle, or feign a secret communication with some divinity ... or find other gross means of imposing on people ...
>
> Even today, the Judaic law, which still subsists, and the law of the child of Ishmael who, after ten centuries, rules one half of the world [the Islamic world], proclaim the great men who dictated them.

In later notebook entries, GE was to explore the topic of the Judaic law as having been not dictated by one great man, Moses, but formed by discussion amongst many generations of great men: Ezra, the *deuterosis* or second law of the Mishnah, and the exegeses embodied in the Talmud. (See Pf 710 27 and B 140 and 106.)

Fontenelle's *Pluralité des mondes*, a work originally published in 1686, contributed to GE's novel a quotation which serves as an epigraph (DD ch. 6: 46) and an indirect allusion. In a letter to Deronda, Hans Meyrick writes that he has never yet seen a basis for opinion

> ... which is not a world-supporting elephant, more or less powerful and expensive to keep. My means will not allow me to keep a private elephant. (DD ch. 52: 598)

His lightly ironic tone resembles that of Fontenelle's delightful work.

GE's copy of Bernard le Bovier de Fontenelle, *Entretiens sur la pluralité des mondes* (Paris: Dubuisson, 1866), is in DWL. Translations are by Elizabeth Gunning, in *Conversations on the Plurality of Worlds*, edited by Jerome de la Lande (London: T. Hurst and T. Ostell, 1803).

/17/

'Je gage que si les Indiens savaient que la Terre fût le moins du monde en péril de se mouvoir, ils doubleraient les éléphants.'

– Cela le mériterait bien, repris-je en riant de sa pensée; il ne faut pas épargner les éléphants pour dormir en assurance.'

Fontenelle, Pluralité des mondes [p. 42][1]

'Croyez vous m'avoir humilié pour m'avoir appris que la Terre tourne autour du Soleil? Je vous jure que je ne m'en estime pas moins.' ibid. [p. 35][2]

'Assez de gens ont toujours dans la tête un faux merveilleux, enveloppé d'une obscurité qu'ils respectent. Ils n'admirent la nature que parce qu'ils la croient une espèce de magie où l'on n'entend rien; et il est sûr qu'une chose est déshonorée auprès d'eux dès qu'elle peut être conçue.' ibid. [p. 26][3]

1 Copied again on Folger 14 10. Translation:

I dare say if the Indians knew there was the least danger of the earth's being moved, they would double the number of elephants.

– It would be worthwhile, I replied, laughing at the thought, we must not be sparing of elephants if they can enable us to sleep in peace. (Gunning, p. 26)

2 This passage is the epigraph for DD ch. 6. Translation:

Do you suppose I feel humbler for knowing that the earth goes round the sun? I assure you I esteem myself just as highly as I did before. (Gunning, p. 20)

3 Translation:

The generality are affected only by the obscure and the marvellous. They admire nature merely because they consider it a sort of magic; something too occult for the understanding to reach; to them a thing appears contemptible as soon as they find the possibility of explaining its nature. (Gunning, p. 11)

/18/

Pour moi je commence à voir la Terre si effroyablement petite, que je ne crois pas avoir désormais d'empressement pour aucune chose. Assurément, si on a tant d'ardeur de s'agrandir, si on fait desseins sur desseins, si on se donne tant de peine, c'est que l'on ne connaît pas les tourbillons. Je prétends bien que ma paresse profite de mes nouvelles lumières; et quand on me reprochera mon indolence, je répondrai: 'Ah, si vous saviez ce que c'est que les étoiles fixes!'

ibid. [pp. 129–30][1]

'C'est une étrange chose que l'amour, répondit-elle en riant; il se sauve de tout, et il n'y a point de système qui lui puisse faire de mal.' ibid. [p. 130][2]

/19/

'La grande âme du législateur est le vrai miracle qui doit prouver sa mission.'

Rousseau, S. C.[3]

1 Translation:

For my part, the earth begins to diminish into such a speck, that in future I shall hardly consider any object worthy of eager pursuit. Surely people, who form unnumbered schemes of aggrandizement, who are wearing themselves out in following up projects of ambition, are ignorant of the vortices. I think my augmentation of knowledge will increase my idleness, and when I am reproached for being indolent I shall reply, *'Ah! if you knew the history of the fixed stars!'* (Gunning, p. 113)

2 Translation:

Love is a strange thing, said she, laughing; it escapes every corrective; there is no system that can abate its influence. (Gunning, p. 114)

3 Jean-Jacques Rousseau, *Du Contrat social, ou principes du droit politique* (1762), Book I, Chapter vii: 'Du Législateur'. The edition read by GE may have been that published in Paris in 1866, listed in the GHL Library catalogue in DWL, but no longer to be found in the collection. The original text has *seul,* 'only', which is replaced by GE's *vrai,* or 'true'.

Jewish festivals

Pf 711 19, 20

These notes, which immediately precede GE's list of 'Books Wanted', show her focus on preparatory reading for the novel that was to become *Daniel Deronda*. Nisan, Sivan, Tischri, Kislev, Adar, Tebeth, Tammouz, and Ab are months of the Jewish calendar. The non-Jewish dates added in pencil correspond to the Jewish year 5634, beginning 22 September 1873.

/19/ Jewish Festivals[1]

15 Nisan *Pesach*: Passover: Paschal lamb & unleavened bread
2 April

Schabouoth: Feast of Weeks (six *Sivan*) or Feast of harvest, or feast of first fruits – or, anniversary of the promulgation of the law. (Pentecost)
The fiftieth day from the 16 Nisan, the day of offering the *omer*;
Levit. XXIII, 15–16[2] 22d of May

Rosch Haschana: New Year. Levit. XXIII. 24[3] (Trumpet – Schofar)
This festival on the 1st Tischri, is called variously New Year, Day of remembrance, Day of the Trumpet 22 Sept.

1 This calendar was copied again on B 172v and 173. Its source has not been identified. For more notes on Jewish festivals, see the sections on 'Ceremonies, customs, rites, and traditions of the Jews' (B 129v to 135v) and 'Jewish liturgy' (B 182 to 190).

2 Leviticus xxiii, 15–16: 'And ye shall count unto you from the morrow after the sabbath, from the day that ye brought the sheaf of the wave offering; seven sabbaths shall be complete: Even unto the morrow after the seventh sabbath shall ye number fifty days ... '

3 Leviticus xxiii, 24: 'In the seventh month, in the first day of the month, shall ye have a sabbath, a memorial of blowing of trumpets, an holy convocation.' For a note on the sounding of the shofar, see B 194.

Jewish festivals Pf 711 19 20

Yom Kipour, Day of Pardon or Reconciliation. Lev. 16. 30.[1]
'Le jour de Kipour on récite dans nos temples des prières pour les tréspassés.'[2]
10 Tischri 1 Oct.

/20/

Soukoth, Feast of Tabernacles. Exodus 33, 16[3]

Hanouka, Feast of Lights, the 25 Kislev. Purification & restoration of the temple-worship under Judas Maccabeus 15 December

Purim, deliverance of the Israelites by Esther, 14 & 15 Adar
3 & 4 March

Fasts

3 Tischri, to commemorate the murder of Gedaliah (2 Kings XXV, Jer. 41) 24 Sept

10 Tebeth, first day of the siege under Nebuchadnezzar *30 January*

13 Adar, the fast of Esther March 2

17 Tammouz, various calamities:
the cessation of the worship the day before the destruction;
overthrow of the chief wall of the city in the Roman siege;
breaking of the tables of the Law by Moses, at sight of the golden calf
2 July

9 Ab, The destruction of the two temples 23 July

(Wailing at the Wall?)[4]

1 'For on that day shall the priest make an atonement for you, to cleanse you, that ye may be clean from all your sins before the Lord.'

2 Translation: 'On Yom Kippur prayers for transgressions are recited in our temples.'

3 Perhaps miscopied for Exodus xxiii, 16. See also Leviticus xxiii, 34: 'The fifteenth day of the seventh month shall be the feast of tabernacles for seven days unto the Lord.'

4 Part of the wall around the Temple Mount, built by Herod in the first century BCE, has been since the sixteenth century a place of pilgrimage where Jews mourn the destruction of the Temple; see Jacobs, pp. 585–6.

Books on Jewish subjects

Pf 711 21, 22, 23, 24, 25, 26, 27, 28, 29

The 'Books Wanted' list was compiled in July or August of 1873, when GE was beginning her research on Judaism. In June she had met David Mocatta, a philanthropic supporter of Jewish literature and research, and owner of a valuable library of Jewish works. In Frankfurt on 30 July, GE and GHL purchased 'Books on *Jewish subjects* for Polly's novel', on 31 July they 'bought Jewish books & a coat', and on 27 August, after their return to London, GHL 'went into town & saw Haas about books for Polly on Judaism' (GHL Diary).

Some of the books listed are now in DWL. The London Library – 'London Library' was pencilled in on this page and then erased – may have been a source of some others; GHL visited it on 28 August. The British Museum (now the British Library) was a resource for books that could be neither bought nor borrowed: Eisenmenger and the *Eighteen Treatises from the Mishna* may have been read in the Reading Room.

GE began reading 'Stanley's Palestine & Sinai aloud' on 6 September and continued until 9 September. From 14 September to 3 October she read Graetz's *Geschichte der Juden* (GHL Diary). The next eight pages of this notebook are filled with evidence of her daily reading of Graetz's history, which also supplied material for her contemporaneous entries in the Berg Notebook, as well as many subsequent pages of this notebook (see the Bibliographical Index). On 4 October she began reading Milman's *History of the Jews.* References to every other work in this list, except for *Eighteen Treatises from the Mishna,* are included in his *History.* The shared misspelling of 'Delitsch' for Delitzsch suggests that Milman was the primary source of GE's book list.

/21/

Books Wanted

Salvador, Institutions de Moïse[1]

More Nebuchim, Guide des Egarés [B 112, 112v][2]

Munk's Palestine [B 150, 173, Pf 710 33, Pf 707 9][3]

Ewald's Geschichte Israel's [Pf 711 53, 63][4]

Milman, History of the Jews [B 106, 112v, 151, 153a, 154v, 155, Pf 711 8][5]

Moses Mendelssohn's 'Jerusalem'[6]

Eisenmenger, Entdecktes Judenthum [B 112v, 118–119v, 121][7]

Stanley's Syria & Palestine [Pf 711 25][8]

Depping's Les Juifs dans le Moyen Age[9]

Eighteen Treatises from the Mischna translated by Sola & Raphall [B 110–111][10]

1 Joseph Salvador, *Histoire des institutions de Moïse et du peuple hébreu,* 3rd edition, 2 vols. (Paris: Michel Lévy frères, 1862).

2 Moise ben Maimoun (Maimonides), *Le Guide des égarés,* translated with commentary by Salomon Munk, 3 vols. (Paris: A. Franck, 1856).

3 Salomon Munk, *Palestine: description géographique, historique et archéologique* (Paris: Firmin-Didot, 1845), in DWL.

4 Georg Heinrich August von Ewald, *Geschichte des Volkes Israel bis Christus,* 3 vols. (Göttingen: Dieterich, 1843–8). The translation by Russell Martineau and J. E. Carpenter, *The History of Israel,* 2nd edition, 4 vols. (London: Longmans, Green, 1869–71), is in DWL.

5 Henry Hart Milman, *The History of the Jews from the Earliest Period Down to Modern Times,* 4th edition, 3 vols. (London: John Murray, 1866), in DWL.

6 Moses Mendelssohn, *Jerusalem: oder über religiöse Macht und Judenthum,* 2 vols. (Berlin: Friedrich Maurer, 1783).

7 Johann Andreas Eisenmenger, *Entdecktes Judenthum,* 2 vols. (Königsberg, 1711).

8 Arthur Penrhyn Stanley, *Sinai and Palestine in Connection with their History,* new edition (London: John Murray, 1866).

9 Georges Bernard Depping, *Les Juifs dans le moyen âge* (Paris: L'Imprimerie royale, 1834).

10 David Aaron de Sola and Morris J. Raphall, translators, *Eighteen Treatises from the Mishna,* 2nd edition (London: Sherwood, Gilbert, and Piper, 1845).

Books on Jewish subjects Pf 711 21

Salvador's Paris, Rome, Jerusalem[1]

Grätz, Geschichte der Juden[2]

Bleek, Einleitung (Berlin, 1860) [Pf 711 30–33][3]

Brugsch, work on Egyptian antiquities
written for the instruction of the Pasha[4]

Jost, Geschichte des Judenthum[5]

Delitsch, Geschichte der Jüdischen Poesie [B 123, 140, 193v, Pf 711 59][6]

Jost, Geschichte der Israeliten seit der Zeit der Makkabäer[7]

Sachs, Poesie der Juden[8]

1 Joseph Salvador, *Paris, Rome, Jérusalem: ou la question religieuse au XIXe siècle*, 2 vols. (Paris: Michel Lévy frères, 1860). The three cities in Salvador's trilogy are symbols, respectively, of 'revolution', 'the spirit of reaction' and 'rebuilding'.

2 Heinrich Graetz, *Geschichte der Juden*, 11 vols., mixed set of 1st and 2nd editions (Leipzig: Oskar Leiner, 1863–75); in DWL. Read daily from 14 September to 3 October 1873 (GHL Diary), and later.

3 Johannes Friedrich Bleek, *Einleitung in das alte Testament*, 3rd edition (Berlin: Georg Reimer, 1870); in DWL. A note on B 66, added in violet ink, may be from this source, or from *An Introduction to the Old Testament*, edited by Adolf Kamphausen and translated from the 1865 German edition by J. H. Venables, 2 vols. (London: Bell and Daldy, 1869).

4 Heinrich Karl Brugsch-Bey, *Histoire d'Egypte* (Leipzig: J. C. Hinrichs, 1859). Milman refers to this work 'written in French for the instruction of the Pasha of Egypt on the antiquities of his kingdom' (I, 102). 'Brugsch, Histoire d'Egypte' is also listed on Pf 707 124.

5 Isaac Marcus Jost, *Geschichte des Judenthums und seiner Secten*, 3 vols. (Leipzig: Dorffling, 1857–9). Also included in lists on Pf 710 1 and Folger 13 56.

6 Franz Julius Delitzsch, *Zur Geschichte der jüdischen Poesie vom Abschluss der heiligen Schriften Alten Bundes bis auf die neueste Zeit* (Leipzig: Karl Tauchnitz, 1836); in DWL. In his *History of the Jews* (I, xxviii), Milman omits the z in Delitzsch, as GE does here.

7 Isaac Marcus Jost, *Geschichte der Israeliten seit der Zeit der Maccabäer*, 10 vols. (Berlin: Schlesinger, 1820–47). Also included in a list on Pf 710 1.

8 Michael Jehiel Sachs, *Die religiöse Poesie der Juden in Spanien* (Berlin: Veit, 1845). Notes on B 108 and Pf 710 20 include references to this work.

/22/ Number & distribution of the Jews in 1865[1]

Total 7,000,000: half only in Europe

In Russia	1,300,000
Austria	900,000
Prussia	254,000
Rest of Germany	192,000
France	800,000
Switzerland	3,200
Great Britain	42,000

In Frankfurt is reckoned 1 Jew to 16 Xns; in Prussia 1 in 73.
The fewest are in Sweden & Norway, where it is reckoned that there is only 1 in 6000. In Saxony there are only about 1600 Jews, & those mostly in Leipzig & Dresden.

Eighty witches *crucified* in Askalon under the presidency of Simon ben Shetach, about 79 BC [Graetz 3, 126; B 153]

Mesousa, inscription over the house-door[2]

Kadisch, prayer for the departed[3]

Schma'h Isroel, 'Hear O Israel' &c
called the Schemâ (confession of the Unity)[4]

Almemor, raised platform in the synagogue
Hazan, precentor; *Schochet,* slayer of animals; *Bodek*, searcher [B 123]

/23/

Saying of the Essenes: 'Forsake doctrine (or study) one day, & it will forsake thee two days.' [Graetz 3, 87–8; B 194][5]

1 These numbers are the same as those in the note on B 194. The source has not been traced. Compare the total given on Pf 707 1 ('7,000,000 יהודים') and the 1878 numbers printed in the newspaper cutting affixed to the cover of Pf 710: 'The total number of the Hebrew race today is about what it was in the days of King David – between six and seven millions'. See also B 127.

2 See also B 134 on the 'Mezuzza'.

3 For other notes on Kaddish, see B 119 and 135 to135v and Pf 710 23.

4 For other notes on the Shema, see B 110, 133v, and 148v.

5 Compare Pf 708 98: '"Forsake instruction or learning only one day, & it will forsake thee two." An Essene saying'.

'Verumenim vero dubio procul, ita Meus Deus fidius'[1]

καδμεία νίκη. Herod[otus] I, 166[2]

Σπαρτοι θηβαιοι = Sown men[3]

'Qui tria, qui septem, omne qui scibite novit.'[4]

La Musette. Les Pfifferari. By Gounod. Chappell & Co.
Bach's Minuet in E flat arranged by Agnes Zimmerman[5]

Pantheras - Sage - already known to Celsus - that the father of Jesus was a soldier named Pantheras. [Graetz 4, 268; Pf 710 31][6]

Apion pretended that the shade of Homer had appeared to him & told him in which city he was born - *only he was not to tell.* [Graetz 3, 257; B 105v]

After the manner of Caligula - went out to conquer the realms of science & brought back empty shells in triumph. [Graetz 3, 261][7]

Emigration Society for the purchase of land in Palestine[8]

1 Source not traced. Translation: 'But truly, in fact, without a doubt, so help me God'.

2 A 'Cadmean victory' is 'one in which the formal victors lose at least as much as the conquered'.

3 Pindar, Isthmian Ode I, 30, 7 (6), 10. According to Greek mythology, Thebes was founded by Cadmus, who sowed the dragon's teeth, from which sprang the Spartoi, or 'sown-men'. The descendents of these armed warriors formed the aristocracy of Thebes.

4 Source not traced. Translation: 'Who altered three things, seven things, everything that was known'.

5 Chappell and Co. is an English firm of music publishers, established in 1810. GE and GHL may have heard these pieces at a private recital or public concert. The compositions by Charles Gounod (1818–93), the French composer, who took refuge in England in 1870 and did not return to France until 1874, are a piano impromptu (1863) and a 'piano impromptu très facile' (1861). Agnes Zimmerman (1847–1925) was a pianist, arranger and composer. GHL notes 'Concert: Agnes Zimmermann' on 28 November 1874 (Diary). For his notes on other musical evenings in February 1870 and March 1874, see GEL V, 77 and VI, 29.

6 Aurus Cornelius Celsus was a Roman encyclopaedist of the early first century CE.

7 The link between the realms of science and Caligula's soldiers bringing back mollusc shells from British shores is not clear. GE may perhaps have recalled her sea-shore studies with GHL at Ilfracombe in 1856; see GEL II, 238–53.

8 Compare Pf 711 91a.

/24/

Ruach-ha-Kodesch = Holy Ghost [Graetz 4, 40; B 123; Pf 711 63]

Kodesch-ha-Kodeschim, Holy of Holies [B 123]

R. Josua b. Chanania, needlemaker & member of the Sanhedrin, exemplar of Jewish poverty & wisdom (after 70 AD) [Graetz 4, 50] [1]

'Story of Domitian having sent for the relatives of Jesus (as belonging to the house of David) fearing that they might make an insurrection & cast him from power; but he was quieted when he saw *their workmen's hands.*' Hegesippus in Euseb. III. 20 [Graetz 4, 119n] [2]

Coins of Bar-Cochba (& other Jewish periods) stamped over Roman coins. The head of Trajan in some cases clearly discernible. [Graetz 4, 153]

The Schammaites said: It would have been better for men if they had never been born. [Graetz 3, 207] [3]

Auch in der Agada wird die Schechina = heiliger Geist, unter dem Bilde einer Taube personificirt. [Graetz 3, 226n] [4]

First Synagogue in London 1664, founded by Portuguese. The original laws regulating the community were first promulgated in Spanish – afterwards written in Portuguese. [5]

1 Compare B 109 and DD ch. 40, where Mordecai tells Deronda, 'I care not if my lot be as that of Joshua ben Chananja: after the last destruction he earned his bread by making needles' (464).

2 Graetz includes the reference to Hegesippus in *Eusebius Kirchengeschichte.* This note is marked by GE's marginal line in her copy in DWL. Compare the longer note on Pf 710 13. In DD ch. 41, Deronda recalls

> a legend told of the Emperor Domitian, that having heard of a Jewish family, of the house of David, whence the ruler of the world was to spring, he sent for its members in alarm, but quickly released them on observing that they had the hands of work-people ... (477)

3 Compare Pf 711 58 and B 194, from Abraham Geiger.

4 Also copied on B 194. Translation: 'Likewise in the Hagada, the Shekhinah [the Divine Presence], equivalent to the Holy Ghost, is embodied in the image of a dove.'

5 James Picciotto, *Sketches of Anglo-Jewish History* (London: Trübner, 1875), p. 38. GE's copy is in DWL. Picciotto's book is a compilation of articles published earlier in the *Jewish Chronicle*, where GE may have read this in the autumn of 1873.

/25/

Carmel, forest, or holy spot (Forestgarden)[1]

'There is no other country in the world which could exhibit the same confluence of associations as that which is awakened by the rocks which overhang the crystal stream of the Dog River (Nahr-el-Kelb) where it rushes through the ravines of Lebanon into the Mediterranean Sea; where side by side are to be seen the hieroglyphics of the great Ramses, the cuneiform inscriptions of Sennacherib, the Latin inscriptions of the Emperor Antoninus.' Stanley, Sinai & Palestine [p. 117]

Jacob Joseph Frank, a Polish Jew, originally a spirit distiller, went to the Crimea & other Turkish provinces & at 38 years of age returning to his own country, declared himself the Messiah. Afterwards, to avoid persecution, he became a convert to Christianity. But again accused of teaching doctrines contrary to Xty, he was imprisoned. Released by Russian troops he went to Austria, visited several places & everywhere received rich presents. In 1776 under the protection of Maria Theresa he settled at Vienna; but his luxurious living excited the suspicions of the **/26/** police, in consequence of which he went to Brünn in Moravia, where he continued to live in great splendour. In leaving his home daily in the twilight to perform evening service in the open air, his expensive & luxurious carriage was surrounded by a numerous retinue of persons mounted on splendid horses, & attired in glittering raiment of gold. Most of these riders were armed with spears ornamented with eagles, suns & moons. Frank ultimately removed to Offenbach where many of his disciples from Warsaw followed him, taking with them all their property. He died in 1791.[2]

1 Arthur Penrhyn Stanley, *Sinai and Palestine in Connection with their History*, new edition (London: John Murray, 1866), p. 490, translates *Carmel* as 'a park' or 'well-wooded country'. GE read Stanley aloud from 6 to 9 September 1873 (GHL Diary).

2 Source not traced. The account in Milman III, 371–3, lacks some details noted here. Graetz 10, 417 ff, refers to his monograph, *Frank und die Frankisten* (Breslau: Schletter, 1868).

'I myself am indifferent honest but yet I could accuse me of such things that it were better my mother had not borne me. I am very proud, revengeful, ambitious; with more offences at my beck than I have thoughts to put them in, imagination to give them shape or time to act them in? – What should such a fellow as I do, crawling between heaven & earth?'[1]

/27/

Epochs BC[2]

Exodus, 1314–21 [*sic*], acc[ording] to Lepsius & Bunsen
Samuel
Saul
David
Solomon, 1008
Hezekiah, 726
Josiah. Book of the law recovered, 640
First Temple destroyed, 587
Zerubbabel, 536 }
Ezra & Nehemiah, 446 } 370 years &
Judas Maccabaeus, 166 } 280
Jonathan, 160–143
Simon, 143–135
John Hyrcanus, 135–106. Phar[isees] & Sad[ucees] &c

1 Transcribed, perhaps from memory, from Hamlet's speech to Ophelia: 'Get thee to a nunnery ... I am myself indifferent honest ... ' (*Hamlet* III, i). Many editions, following the Second Quarto, have 'earth and heaven'; but the Folio and First Quarto have 'Heaven and Earth'. 'A College Breakfast-Party', written in April 1874 (GEL VI, 388n), begins:

> Young Hamlet, not the hesitating Dane,
> But one named after him, who lately strove
> For honours at our English Wittenberg ... (*Poems*, p. 160)

2 The source for the earliest part of this chronological table has not been traced. GE's pencilled list on the front papers of Graetz 3, from 'Jonathan 160–143' to 'Hyrcanus II (Ethnarch) 63', is almost identical to the list on Pf 711 27. From 63 BCE to the expulsion from Spain in 1492 CE, her source may be the 'Chronologische Tabelle' in Graetz 8, 482–96. GE's table includes her later modifications, such as the change of date for the first Insurrection of Bar Cochba from 132 to 122 CE. The Chronology on B 169v and 170 began as a fair copy of this table, with extra material appended on B 170v to 172.

Aristobulus, 106
Alex[ander] Jan[naeus] 105
Salome, 79
Arist[obulus] II, 70
Hyrcanus, 63
Antigonus
Septuagint
Judah b. Tabbai
Simon b. Shetach
Pompey at Jerusalem, 63
Herod king, 37
Schemaja & Abtalion
Hillel & Schammai
Hillel president of Sanhedrim, 30

AC

Philo, aged 40, heads the embassy to Rome, 40
Second Temple destroyed, 70. R. Jochanan b. Zakkai
First insurrection under Adrian, 118. (B[ook] of Judith)
Insurrection of Bar Cochba, 132[1]–135
Rabbi Akiba. (Book of Tobit)
R. Gamaliel II
Close of Mischna, 200. R. Juda
Alexander Severus favours the Jews, 222
R. Juda II. Beginning of the Amoraïm
The Patriarch rises in dignity, has a body-guard
R. Chananja b. Chama, 1st of Amoraïm, 180–260

/28/

Babylonian Schools
Rab, 175–247
Downfall of the Schools of Tiberias under the oppressions of
Constantius, 337–338
Sepphoris razed to the ground
Saboraim, or settlers of opinions (Sebara) from 400–550
Talmud written. Masora 5 - -

1 GE later added '22' for the alternate date of 122 CE.

Vowel points 6 - - (?) Babylonian system, *over* the letters

Gaonim (Würdenträger) epoch begun about 658[1]
Heads of the School of Sura
Mar Isaak first *Gaon*
Resch-Galuta (Exilarch) at Pumbadita, recognized by Ali
Karaites, 761, anti-Talmudic movement
Rationalism finding its philosophic mediator in
Saadia, b. 892. 942 chief of Academy of Sura, *Gaôn*
Downfall of the Gaonat, 997

Ibn Gebirol, 1021–1070
Ibn Ezra, XIIth Century, 1070–1139
Maimonides, 1139–1204
Jehuda ha Levi, wrote 1140
Benjamin of Tudela, travelled 1160
Kimchi, 1150–70
Charisi, 1170–1230
XIIIth Cent. Zohar collected
Kabbala greatly developed
Spanish persecution begun
Expulsion from Spain, 1482 [*sic* for 1492]
Spinoza, 1632–1677
Israel Baalschem, founder of New Chasidim; b. 1698, d. 1759
with Beer who d. 1772
Moses Mendelssohn, 1729–1786
Maimoun, b. 1753, d. 1800

/29/

'Einige Jahre später (after the Bar-Cochba war) war in dem oelreichen Galiläa ein Oelbaum eine Seltenheit.' [Graetz 4, 164][2]

1 *Würdenträger*: 'dignitary'.

2 Translation: 'A few years later an olive tree was a rarity in Galilee, which had been rich in olive oil.' During the insurrection led by Simon bar Kochba against Rome, agriculture was destroyed, as the population had fled or been killed in the war.

Sebastopol taken 8 Sep. 1855. Peace Congress at Paris assembled Feb. 1, 1856. Peace concluded Mar. 30[1]

On the observance of the 7th day among other nations than the Jews as the Chinese, Egyptians, Arabs, &c. v. Ideler's Chronol. I. 88, 178 – II. 473 'Seven' & 'six' are the only numerals which the Hebrew has in common with the Indo-European languages: seven – *sheba* – six, shish. The very term signifying to *swear* literally means to do *seven times.* (Gen. xxi, 28; comp. Herod. III, 8, for a similar custom among the Arabians)[2]

The same Hebrew word, or the same with a slight variation, stands for forty & a great number. (This is doubtful. The root רָבָה, to be many – If true, it comes from a time when the Hebrews said – one, two, three, many – Because 4 is אַרְבַּע)[3]

1 The source for these notes has not been traced. GE had a long-continuing interest in accounts of the Crimean war. In September 1868 she read Alexander William Kinglake, *The Invasion of the Crimea: Its Origin, and an Account of its Progress, Down to the Death of Lord Raglan,* 2nd edition, 3 vols. (Edinburgh: Blackwood, 1868) (GEL IV, 470). In February 1875 she received a copy of the newly published Volume V of Kinglake: see her note on Pf 711 94. In August 1876 she read César Lecat, Baron de Bazancourt, *L'Expédition de Crimée jusqu' à la prise de Sebastapol: Chroniques de la guerre d'orient* (Paris: Amyot, 1856) (GHL Diary).

2 Also copied on B 150v. Source: William Latham Bevan, 'Seven', in Smith's *Dictionary of the Bible*, III, 1218–19; GE's copy is in DWL. GE later added 'six, shish'. Bevan refers to Ludwig Ideler, *Handbuch der mathematischen und technischen Chronologie,* 2 vols. (Berlin: A. Rücker, 1825, 1826).

GE's copy of Salomon Munk's *Palestine* in DWL has her pencilled marginal line beside Munk's remark on p. 118n that the Hebrew words for *seven, seventy, to swear,* and *oath* derive from the same root:

il est à remarquer que la racine שבע, de laquelle dérivent ces nombres sert aussi en hébreu à former le verbe *jurer* et le mot qui signifie *serment.*

In Genesis xxi, 28–32, Abraham and Abimelech 'sware both of them' at Beer-sheba by 'seven ewe lambs of the flock'. According to Herodotus III, 8,

> The Arabians honor pledges as much as any people in the world, and this is how they make the pledge. Someone, a man other than the two parties to the compact, ... cuts the inside of the hands, near the thumbs, of those who would make the pledge ... Then ... he smears with the blood seven stones that are set between.

3 Source not traced. Also copied again on B 150v. GE's parenthetical comment was added later, in ink.

Semitic languages

Pf 711 30, 31, 32, 33, 34

The source of the following notes on Semitic languages is Johannes Friedrich Bleek, *Einleitung in das alte Testament,* 3rd edition (Berlin: Georg Reimer, 1870). GE's copy of this work, which is included in the 'Books Wanted' list on Pf 711 21, is in DWL.

Comparative philology, the recently developed scientific method of historical investigation into literature and culture, was of continuing interest to GE. On first reading Max Müller's *Lectures on the Science of Language,* first series, in January 1862, she called it a 'great and delightful book' (GEL IV, 8). It is the source of a long note on 'the Semitic family' of languages in the Beinecke Notebook (entries 207–210). Her rereading of the first and second series in July 1871 was the source of many pages of notes (Folger 13 99–100, 106, 108–9 and Berg 76v–77) including a brief reference to the 'Semitic family' of languages on Folger 13 100. 'Max Müller's Science of Language' was read again on 25 and 26 July 1872 (GHL Diary), and between June and October 1877 (Pf 707 84v), and once more in November 1880 (GEL VII, 335).

While preparing her 'Quarry for Felix Holt' GE had read Ernest Renan's *Histoire générale et système comparé des langues sémitiques,* 3rd edition (Paris: Michel Lévy Frères, 1863), now in DWL.[1] It was read again on 5 October 1873 (GHL Diary). As Wiesenfarth observes,

> She absorbed by her reading [of philology] an accurate sense of the methodology of comparative Indo-European grammar, which was to affect the ways that comparative mythology would reach its conclusions. (p. xxxiii)

One key to Mr Casaubon's failure in his mythological pursuits is the fact that he is not 'an Orientalist'.[2] GE's continued study of linguistic scholarship is linked to her indefatigable fascination with the mythologies of many cultures.

---

1 Pratt and Neufeldt, p. 140.

2 *Middlemarch,* ch. 22: 216; see Wiesenfarth, pp. 216–17.

/30/

'This people that knoweth not the law are accursed.'[1]

South Semitic Languages

Arabic - old, or literary. New, or vulgar

South Arabic or Himjaritic
(the speech of the Sabaeans, whom the Greeks call Ὁμηρῖται) Inscriptions. Not extant; in S. Arabia in the 14th century, & there are still kindred idioms spoken there. [pp. 41–5]

Eckhili = New Himjaritic, spoken between Hadramant & Oman.

Ethiopic, a branch of the Himjaritic, simpler than the Arabic & nearer to the Hebrew. Dominant language in Abyssinia till 14th century; called *Ghez* i.e. the speech of the Free.[2]
In this speech there is a complete translation of the Bible. The Book of Enoch, the Ascension of Isaiah, & the 4th Book of Ezra have been preserved in this language.[3] [pp. 45–6]

Amharic, the most general vulgar tongue now in use in Ethiopia or Abyssinia; brought by a new dynasty in the 14th century - before which the Ghez or Ethiopic gave way, though **/31/** it remained the written language till the dissolution of the Ethiopian Kingdom by the Gallas near the end of the 16th century. [p. 47]

North Semitic or Aramaic

Aramaic - Syria, Mesopotamia & Babylonia. (Here comes the question, who were the Chaldees, & was their language Semitic? - the term Chaldaic applied to the Aramaic in Daniel & Ezra being a mistake. Also of the Assyrians it has come to be a question whether they were of Semitic or Medo-Persian stock.

1 John vii, 49. These are the words of the Pharisees to the officers sent to arrest Jesus. The AV has 'cursed'.

2 GE's spelling, *Ghez,* differs from her sources: 'Geez' in Bleek and 'Gees' in Müller (Weisenfarth, p. 196).

3 Compare the note on Pf 711 93a, copied again on Pf 710 20: 'The Book of the Ascension of Isaiah has reached us only in an Ethiopic version ...' GE's copy of *Ascensio Isaiae Aethiopice et Latinae* (Lipsiae: Brockhaus, 1877), is in DWL, not identified as hers, but bound together with pamphlets by Lenormant, Graetz, and others, from her library.

Here has come in the evidence to be drawn from the Cunieform Inscriptions.)
[pp. 47–9]

Three different orders of Cunieform writings at Persepolis. Even now the edicts of a governor of Bagdad are published in Turkish, Arabic & Persian, & it seems that the ancient Kings of Persia addressed people belonging to these three families of speech. By the help of the few trilingual (or bilingual) Achaemenian inscriptions scholars proceeded to decipher the endless unilingual inscriptions of Nineveh and Babylon. These latter are **/32/** called the Third order of inscriptions; & it is now an established result that these belong to the Semitic stem. (The Achaemenian are the first order. Of the Second order are those found at Susa which are maintained to be of the Turkish–Tataric stem.) [p. 50n]

All the writings we possess in Aramaic are either Jewish or Christian. The oldest is the passages in the Bible, next the Aramaic translations of the Old Testament & other Jewish writings. Then came the Christian Aramaic writings, since the 2d century. In this latter form the language is called

Syriac = also *West Aramaean*, (though the correctness of this epithet is disputed) while the so-called Chaldean or language of the Babylonians is called *East Aramaic.* [pp. 53–6]

Syriac still cultivated in the Maronite monasteries of Lebanon, but from the 10th century gave way as a living speech to the Arabic. Written till 3d century.
[pp. 59–60]

Ephraim Syrus & Abulpharagius
(Peshito = *simple*, version of Old Testament in Old Syriac)[1]

/33/

North Semitic continued [pp. 62–5]

Samaritan
Mandaic: language of a mystic theosophic sect on the Euphrates & Tigris
Nabataean. Arabic inscriptions
Palmyrenic
Egyptian – Aramaic

1 Ephraem Syrus or Ephraim the Syrian and Abulpharagius were fourth-century writers in Syriac; see Bleek's note on the Peshito, pp. 806–11.

Semitic languages Pf 711 33 34

Middle Semitic [pp. 65–70]

Hebrew }
Phoenician } Language of Canaan
Punic }

Remains of Phoenician [pp. 68–9]

1 Words used by ancient authors
2 Poenulus in Plautus
3 Coin-inscriptions
4 Inscriptions on stone
5 Opfertafel at Marseilles (1845)
6 Sarcophagus of Eschmunazar (1855)

Moabite stone. Hebrew[1]

/34/ Legenda[2]

Spence Hardy on Bouddhist Legends[3]

Burnouf on Bouddhism[4]

Aristotle's Rhetoric[5]

Köppen, Bouddhismus[6]

1 A reference, added later in pencil, to a stone with a Moabite inscription which was the subject of much discussion. GE heard Emanuel Deutsch lecture on the inscription in May 1870 and 'saw "squeezes"of this stone, with photographs taken from the squeezes', that is rubbings or relief impressions (GEL V 100).
2 Latin for 'being read'.
3 Robert Spence Hardy, *The Legends and Theories of the Buddhists, compared with history and science: with introductory notices of the life and system of Gotama Buddha* (London: Williams and Norgate, 1866).
4 Eugène Burnouf, *Introduction à l'histoire du buddhisme indien,* 2nd edition, with an Introduction by Barthélemy Saint-Hilaire (Paris: Maisonneuve, 1876).
5 Perhaps read in Aristotle's *Werke,* edited by Karl von Prantl et al, 3 vols. (Leipzig, 1854, 1857, 1860); in DWL. Possibly *The Rhetoric of Aristotle* with a commentary by Edward Meredith Cope, revised and edited by John Edwin Sandys, 3 vols. (Cambridge: Cambridge University Press, 1877).
6 Carl Friedrich Koeppen, *Die Religion des Buddha und ihre Entstehung,* 2 vols. (Berlin: Ferdinand Schneider, 1857–9). Also noted on Pf 707 38 and 124 and Folger 13 63.

Ferdinand Lassalle

Pf 711 35, 36, 37

The source for this summary of the last month of the life of Ferdinand Lassalle (1825–64) is Bernhard Becker, *Enthüllungen über das tragische Lebensende Ferdinand Lassalle's: auf Grund authentischer Belege* (Schleiz: Hugo Heyn, 1868). 'L' is Lassalle; 'H' is Hélène von Doenniges, betrothed to 'the Wallachian Janko von Rackowitz'. 'Count K' is Count Kayserling, her sister's fiancé, 'Dr A' is Dr Arndt, her cousin, and 'D' is Doenniges, her father. 'R' is Colonel Rüsto, Lassalle's friend.

There is some irony in Lassalle's 'resolution of becoming a Catholic that he may be married to H by a Cath. priest', beyond his finding out, 'after having made overtures about turning Catholic to the B[isho]p of Mainz, that H is a protestant'. Lassalle was of Jewish birth and upbringing (and a friend of Heine), and Hélène's mother was a Jewess who converted to Christianity just before her marriage; see Elizabeth Edson Evans, *Ferdinand Lassalle and Helene von Dönniges: A Modern Tragedy* (London: Swan Sonnenschein, 1897), pp. 11 and 69.

According to Evans, Countess Hatzfield first tried to commission Karl Marx to write Lassalle's story, and then appointed Becker, who was Lassalle's successor as President of the Working Men's Society (p. 90). The events summarized below inspired George Meredith's novel, *The Tragic Comedians: A Study in a Well-Known Story* (London: Chapman and Hall, 1881).

/35/

L's history. 39 when he met with H – 1864 in Rigi. Had been acquainted with her before in Berlin, & somewhat interested in her as a possible *partie*.

July 26. She writes that she is determined to be his wife.

28. L visits her from Berne, she staying at Wabern close by.

Aug. H returns to her family at Geneva. Finds her younger sister engaged to Count Kayserling. Declares her passion for L to her mother, & resolve to marry him. Mother holds it impossible the Father will consent, since the sister is going to make so brilliant a marriage.

H writes L an ardent letter telling this, he having taken lodgings in Geneva. While he is reading the letter, H enters! In the greatest excitement, says – do with me what you will! L soothes her, trying to persuade her that her father may after all consent. Then leads her back calmed to her mother. (The occasion of her going to L was that her father had returned from a journey with her cousin. A storm had broken out – he had declared that she was no child of his, & had forbidden her to quit the house until she had been betrothed to Rackowitz.)

Same day Count K & Dr Arndt, cousin of H, paid a visit to L. Called on L to renounce H & quit Geneva. **/36/** L declined – insisted on carrying out his intention of visiting the Father, but received no answer to two notes announcing his intention. Sends for Col Rüstow.

Aug. 4. Count K & Dr A pay him a second visit empowered by H. She declares L entirely free, has expressed penitence to her father, & gone away with him from Geneva. L will not abide by that – believes she has acted under coercion. Dr A goes away with Count K saying that they are not hardhearted but must rejoice that the honour of the family is saved.

Aug. 6. L & Rüstow walking out meet H in a carriage; she greets them in a friendly way, being in company with a lady – going to the railway on her departure from Geneva. Letter to Mde Arson in which she says she is forced to go by her friends, & implies that all is over with L – toute résignée.[1] In a previous letter she says how all her family had fallen on their knees before her. Lassalle had caused the Campagne Vaucher where the Doenniges lived

1 Translation: 'entirely resigned'.

to be watched, & had bribed the servants. Hence D applied for police to protect his house. L held himself insulted by A's words (about the honour of the family) & sent R to ask for an explanation.

Aug. 7. R went, but A was denied: Herr D gone a journey; **/37/** Frau D not at home. A in fact gone to Berlin to fetch the Wallachian Janko von Rackowitz, H's betrothed. Then R got Kayserling's address from Gen. Klupker, with whom he made a visit to Kayserling. K also 'verreist'.[1] R left his card begging to know when K returned. L always believing H to be in Geneva writes, Aug. 7, a letter to her full of passion – impossible she can really have renounced him – she is of age. But if really so – good – let him at least have an interview to certify it. 'Seit Mittwoch Nacht, liebe ich dich bis zum Wahnsinn.'[2]

On the 10th he writes again with urgence. Forms the resolution of becoming a Catholic that he may be married to H by a Cath. priest. Learns that she has left Geneva. He also leaves it. Finds out, after having made overtures about turning Catholic to the Bp. of Mainz, that H is a protestant.

Meanwhile he is at München at the Oberpollinger Hof – fancies H at Geneva. Receives, through R, a letter from H formally renouncing him, & declaring her return to Janko v. Rackowitz.

L writes – his letter not delivered. Maddened, he empowers R to carry off H. Meanwhile she has made it up with Janko, & the family has returned to Geneva. Lassalle demands interviews – threatens &c, till he gets the conviction burnt into him that H really wishes to have done with him. Calls for revenge – challenges the father – insults H in letters to him & to Janko. Janko challenges him. They meet & L is shot.

1 Translation: 'Gone away on a journey'.

2 Translation: 'I have been madly in love with you since Wednesday night.' This excerpt from Lassalle's letter is taken from Becker, p. 51.

Catena of novelists and gambling

Pf 711 38, 39, 40, 41, 42, 43

'Catena of Novelists' is GE's entry in her list of 'Chief Contents'. A *catena* is a chain or connected series, from the ecclesiastical Latin *catena patrum,* or 'chain of the Fathers' of the Church (*OED*). The source for this list has not been traced.

The source for her notes on chance is Richard Anthony Proctor, 'Gambling Superstitions, *Cornhill Magazine* 25 (June 1872): 704–17.[1] Proctor was an astronomer and popularizer of science in many publications and lectures. This article was reprinted in *The Borderland of Science* (London: Longmans, Green, 1873), but since GE's reference is to the *Cornhill,* it is likely that she also saw in the same issue (pp. 736–60) an episode of a serialized novel by Robert Edward Francillon, *Pearl and Emerald: A Tale of Gotham*[2] One of its characters is a hunchbacked Jew pawn-broker, whose dirty trade has brought him a precious emerald, once presented by the Queen of Sheba to King Solomon, but of more obscure recent provenance. His speech is rendered as comic dialect, and his most egregious lies are signalled by his repeated oath, ' ... 'elp me Moshesh'. This 'grotesque', as he is called, is featured as a blatant caricature in a full-page illustration (p. 736). It may be that GE turned to this issue of the *Cornhill* to see for herself this extraordinary fictional representation of a contemporary English Jew, and then noticed by chance something she could use in her novel, in Proctor's article on gambling 'axioms'.

In the October 1876 *Gentleman's Magazine,* Francillon gave *Daniel Deronda* a perhaps unexpectedly sympathetic review. Commenting that the novel was 'not likely to extend George Eliot's reputation', because 'the sympathies to which it appeals are not, as in the case of *Adam Bede,* the common sympathies of all the world,' he predicted that *it was* 'likely to *heighten* her reputation' precisely because she had left behind what she had previously 'timidly kept to' – 'the safe ground of probability'.

1 For her observation of a gambling scene as 'the germ' of DD, see Haight, p. 469, and the Introduction to the present work.

2 The novel was published later in 1872 by Smith, Elder.

Catena of novelists Pf 711 38

The following chapter epigraph is cited in Francillon's review:

'This too, is probable, according to that saying of Agathon: "It is a part of probability that many improbable things will happen."'

– ARISTOTLE: *Poetics*[1]

/38/ Boccaccio, b. 1313
Bardello, 1480–1562
Rabelais wrote 1533
Cervantes, *Don Q[uixote]* 1605
Scudéry, 1607–1701
Defoe, b. 1663 d. 1731. *Rob[inson] Crusoe,* 1719
Abbé Prévost, *Manon Lescaut,* 1734
Johnson, *Rasselas*
Miss Burney, *Evelina*
Richardson, b. 1689; wrote 1741–1752
Fielding, b. 1707. *Tom Jones,* 1749
Swift, b. 1667 d. 1745. *Gulliver,* 1704
Smollett, b. 1721 d. 1771
Per[egrine] Pickle, 1751. *H[umphry] Cl[inker],* 1770
Sterne, *Tristram Shandy,* 1759–66
Horace Walpole, *Castle of Otranto,* 1765
Werther, 1774
Voltaire
Diderot
Louvet (*Faublas*)
Moore, *Zeluco,* 1781
Caleb Williams, 1794
Clara Reeve, 1738–1808
Mackenzie, 1745–1831. *Man of Feeling,* 1771
Mrs Inchbald, 1757–1821
Mrs Radcliffe, 1761–1823
Miss Edgeworth, 1771–1817

1 DD ch. 41: 473. This is GE's translation of a passage which is noted in both Greek and Latin on Pf 708 83. Francillon's review is reprinted in Carroll, pp. 382–98. The excerpts quoted are from pp. 382–4.

Miss Austen, 1775–1817
Waverly, 1814. *Pelham*, 1828
Balzac, b. 1798 d. 1850
Hugo, b. 1802
Dumas the Elder, b. 1803
Sand, b. 1804. *Indiana*, 1832

/39/

'The same man may produce a few flashes of volcanic splendour, & a vast monotony of dull extravagance.' Hartley Coleridge[1]

'Classical allusions amalgamated & consubstantiated with his native thought.' Ib. [pp. xxviii–xxix]

'Jonson was not a whit more of a pedant than his contemporaries; he showed more reading because he had more to show.' [p. xxix]

'The fool's coxcomb was the κυρβασια of the Persian King.'[2]

παθήματα μαθήματα Her[odotus] I, 207[3]

The English Bishops. 'Not a voice has been raised by these mitred nullities, either to warn or to vindicate; not a phrase has escaped their lips or their pens, that ever influenced public opinion, touched the heart of nations, or guided the conscience of a perplexed people. If they were ever heard of it was that they had been pelted **/40/** in a riot.' D'Israeli, Tancred[4]

'Having guanoed her mind by reading French novels.' Ibid. [I, 222][5]

1 Hartley Coleridge, Introduction to *The Dramatic Works of Massinger and Ford* (London: Edward Moxon, 1839), p. xiii n. GHL's copy, perhaps presented to him by Leigh Hunt, was sold at auction (*Catalogue*, p. 233).

2 Herodotus twice refers to the Persian bonnet with a peaked crown: 5, 49; 7, 64.

3 Croesus the Lydian tells Cyrus, 'My own sufferings have been a harsh teacher for me.' This passage is also copied on GE's Blotter (Waley, p. 11).

4 Benjamin Disraeli, *Tancred: or The New Crusade*, 3 vols. (London: Henry Colburn, 1847), I, 145.

5 In 1847, GE wrote in a letter to a friend that she had been

> *guanoing* her mind with French novels. (This is the impertinent expression of d'Israeli, who [writes] himself much more detestable stuff than ever came from a French pen ...) (GEL I, 234–5)

It may be noted that her catena of novelists includes many who wrote in French.

Gambling Pf711 40 41

Gambling Superstitions, by Proctor, Cornhill, June 1872.

Quotes Steinmetz, The Gaming Table,[1] for the 'axioms of a professional gambler & cheat' as narrated by Houdin. 'We might expect, that however unsatisfactory to men of honest mind, they would at least savour of a certain sort of wisdom. *Yet these axioms, the fruit of long study directed by self-interest, are all utterly untrustworthy.*'

He distinguishes the chances proper to the game & those depending on the luck of the player. For the former he has two rules: 1° there are limits to the possibility of combinations: e.g. that a certain number may turn up 10 times at roulette, is possible but has never happened; 2° *The maturity of chances* i.e. the oftener the same number has occurred in succession, the nearer we are to the certainty that it will not recur at the next turn up.

[pp. 704–5]

True that results will right themselves but not ever any given number of localized chances. [p. 708]

A captain of a vessel had to bring over a cargo of dollars. He found that the chest had been forced. A large bag of dollars was found in possession of a passenger. By way of evidence, since the dollars were of a large variety of coinage, it occurred to the captain to ascertain the proportions of each kind in the bag & in the chest. The proportions agreed, & thus the evidence seemed clinching. [p. 709]

/41/

If a rod be tossed over a grating of parallel bars, the number of times it will fall through will depend on the length & thickness of the rod, the distance between the bars, & the proportion in which the circumference of a circle exceeds the diameter. [pp. 709–10]

Garcia with his run of luck followed by a crowd who copy his play.

[pp. 713, 716][2]

1 Proctor reviews Andrew Steinmetz, *The Gaming Table: Its Votaries and Victims*, 2 vols. (London: Tinsley Brothers, 1870).

2 Gwendolen 'had begun to believe in her luck, others had begun to believe in it: she had visions of being followed by a *cortège* who would worship her as a goddess of luck and watch her play as a directing augury. Such things have been known of male gamblers; why should a woman not have a like supremacy?' (DD ch. 1: 6).

Old notion of jelly fish being the slough of falling stars[1]

'Till when, this *virtuous plaister* will displease
Your tender sides.' Faithful Shepherdess[2]

In levelling operations allowance is made for the curvature of the earth.[3]

Deus averruncus, an averting deity
'ut deus, qui iis rebus praeest, averruncus.' Varro[4]

/42/

Omar Khayyám, the astronomer-poet of Persia, was born at Naishapur in Khorassan, the latter half of the eleventh, & died within the first quarter of the 12th century. His life entwined with that of Hasan al Sabbáh (founder of the Assassins) & of Nizám ul Mulk, Vizyr to Alp the Lion (Arslan) & Malik Shah, son & grandson of Toghrul Beg the Tartar, who had wrested Persia from the feeble successors of Mahmoud the Great & founded that Seljukian dynasty which finally roused Europe into the Crusades. The three were fellow students under Imám Mowaffak, & agreed that whichever of them attained fortune should share it with the other. When Nizám Mulk became Vizier, he kept the agreement; but Omar Khayyám only wanted ease for the pursuit of science, & to him was given a pension. He was one of the eight learned men who reformed the calender, also author of some astronomical tables, & an Arabic treatise on Algebra. Khayyám signifies tentmaker.[5]

1 Source not traced.

2 Francis Beaumont and John Fletcher, *The Faithful Shepherdess,* IV, ii. GHL's copy of George Darley's edition of *The Works of Beaumont and Fletcher,* 2 vols. (London: Edward Moxon, 1840) was sold at auction in 1923 (*Catalogue*, p. 233).

3 Source not traced.

4 *Averruncus*: a Roman deity who averted evil. The passage from *De Lingua Latina,* vii, 102, is translated by Roland G. Kent in *Varro on the Latin Language,* 2 vols. (London: William Heinemann, The Loeb Classical Library, 1938), I, 355: 'Just as the god who presides over these matters is called Averruncus'.

5 Preface to *Rubáiyát of Omar Kháyyám, the Astronomer Poet of Persia: Translated into English Verse* [by Edward Fitzgerald] (London: Bernard Quaritch, 1859), pp. iii–vii. This first edition is also the source of GE's notes on Pf 711 110–109 and her Blotter (Waley, p. 11), and a verse copied in 1864 in the *Romola* Notebook, Bodleian MS Don. g. 8 (12v). Later editions of the *Rubáiyát* include Fitzgerald's numerous revisions.

/43/

Origines accadiennes, Lenormant[1]

Fate has made you the hinder wheel.
Quum rota posterior curras et in axe secundo. Pers[ius][2]

Greek proverb: ἄνους ὁ μακρὸς[3]

Lat. prov: 'Nihil cum fidibus gracula'[4]

Seneca said that Ovid's pleading or declamation resembled a *solutum carmen*.
Controv[ersiae] ii, iv[5]

Belief in devil or devils – doctrine of despair of the world in all shapes – belief in the preponderance of evil

Systematizers making morality turn on a single hinge – just as in mythology &c.[6]

=[7]

1 François Lenormant, *La Magie chez les chaldéens et les origines accadiennes* (Paris: Maisonneuve, 1874). GE's copy is in DWL. 'Lenormant, La Magie' was read between 21 March and 10 April 1874 (GHL Diary).

2 Persius, Satire V, line 72. In DD ch. 52, Hans Meyrick quotes from this line and provides a translation: 'Fate, my friend, has made you the hinder wheel ... run behind, because you can't help it' (600–601). For other notes from Persius, see B 120 to 122v.

3 Source not traced. Translation: 'not of large understanding'.

4 The source of this Latin proverb has not been traced. Translation: 'A grackle (or jackdaw) has nothing to do with a lyre'.

5 The source of this note is the essay on Ovid in Smith's *Dictionary of Greek and Roman Biography and Mythology*, III, 68:

> When he sat down to write a speech, he wrote a poem instead. The elder Seneca, too, who had heard him declaim, ... tells us that his oratory resembled a *solutum carmen* [fluent song], and that anything in the way of argument was irksome to him.

In *La Magie chez les chaldéens*, Lenormant refers to the Latin *carmen* as the origin of our word charm, in the sense of enchantment by words recited by a sorcerer: 'l'enchantement par des paroles que récite le sorcier, ce que les latins appelaient *carmen*, d'où est venu notre mot, *charme*' (p. 57).

6 Source not traced. Lenormant mentions *maskim*, or evil spirits (p. 57); compare GE's note, '*Mazzikim.* Evil demons', on Pf 710 26.

7 Notes from Deutsch fill the rest of this page; see the next section.

Mohammed, the Hebrews in Egypt, and the colonization of Jerusalem

Pf 711 43, 44, 45, 46, 50, 51

Emanuel Deutsch, GE's friend and tutor in Hebrew, died in Alexandria on 12 May 1873, a few months before GE began her preparatory reading on Judaism for her novel.[1] Many notes in this section are from the posthumous collection of his essays, lectures, and review articles, *Literary Remains of the Late Emanuel Deutsch* (London: John Murray, 1874), edited anonymously by Emily Anne Beaufort, Viscountess Strangford. A presentation copy 'from the Editor' is in DWL. On 3 November 1873, GE 'went to see Lady Strangford'; on 15 December 'Lady Strangford called & stayed till 7'. GE's letter of [6?] November 1873 concerning Lady Strangford's prefatory memoir is discussed in the Introduction. 'Lady Strangford called' on 4 April 1874, and 'Polly went to Lady Strangford' on 10 April (GHL Diaries). This section includes extracts from three reprinted essays by Deutsch: 'Islam', 'Egypt, Ancient and Modern', and 'Hermes Trismegistus'. GE's notes from 'The Talmud' (B 106, 114, and 148; Pf 708 98 and 99), also reprinted in the *Literary Remains*, are from a proof copy sent to her by Deutsch before its publication in the *Quarterly Review* in 1867.

A letter dated 23 April 1874 from Lady Strangford, concerning the development of an agricultural colony at Jaffa, is copied in part on Pf 711 46. This project is related to Deronda's declared purpose of 'going to the East to become acquainted with the condition of [his] race' there, and 'restoring a political existence to [his] people' (DD ch. 69: 747). What he is likely to find in the Holy Land is indicated by 'the genial and rational Gideon' in the *Hand and Banner*:

> 'as to the connection of our race with Palestine, it has been perverted by superstition till it's as demoralizing as the old poor-law. The raff and scum go there to be maintained like able-bodied paupers ... ' (DD ch. 42: 495)

---

1 For a discussion of Deutsch in relation to *Daniel Deronda*, see the headnotes for B 106–109v and 115–117v and the Introduction to the present work.

/43/

When (in the Koran) Mohammed on his heavenly journey with Gabriel stood alone within two bowshots from the Throne, 'there was a great stillness, & nothing was heard except the sound of the reed wherewith the decrees of God are inscribed on the tablets of Fate.' [p. 102][1]

'Pick me out the blackest of those berries' cried Mohammed at Medina when prophet & king he saw some people pass with berries of the wild shrub Arak. 'Pick me out the blackest of those berries for they are sweet – even such as I was wont to gather when I tended the flock at Mecca & Ajyad.' [p. 70]

/44/

Nile at its maximum height about Sep. 30. Nov. 10 its decline perceptible[2]

Aus dem Orient, von Herman Brugsch[3]

Under Ram[e]ses II, who mounted the throne about 1400, were built a line of fortified cities – so say the hieroglyphic sources – from Pelusium to Heliopolis, the two principal being Rameses & Pithom. We even find the name of the Hebrews in the official reports. A papyrus in the museum of Leyden is the following: 'May my Lord find satisfaction in my having complied with the instruction which my Lord gave me, saying, Distribute the rations among the soldiers & likewise among the Hebrews (Aparu) who carry the stones to the great city of King Rameses-Miamun the lover of truth.'

Similar distinct indications of the people & their state of serfdom are found in another Leyden papyrus, & even in the long rock-inscription of Hamamât.

The Exodus took place under Menephthes,[4] the successor of Rameses II. [pp. 176–7]

1 Source: 'Islam', a review article first published in the *Quarterly Review* (October 1869) and reprinted in *Literary Remains*, pp. 59–134. For another reading of GE's notes from Deutsch, see Mary Kay Temple, 'Emanuel Deutsch's *Literary Remains*: A New Source for George Eliot's *Daniel Deronda*', *South Atlantic Review* 54 (1989): 59–73.

2 Source not traced.

3 The source of the following notes is 'Egypt, Ancient and Modern', a review of Heinrich Karl Brugsch-Bey, *Aus dem Orient,* 2 vols. (Berlin: Grosse, 1864), first published in the *Saturday Review* (December 1865), and reprinted in *Literary Remains*, pp. 173–80.

4 GE copied this name twice, the first time rather illegibly.

The name Moses of Egyptian origin: Mas or Massu = child

Confession of the unity of God inscribed on a scroll which the initiated carried with them into the grave. The name of the One God is not mentioned – given only in the circumlocution Nuk pu Nuk – 'I am he who I am.'

[p. 178][1]

/45/

Jerusalem

Jerusalem ... is one of the least commercial or industrial of cities. Its population is estimated at 18,000, of whom about 5000 are Mohammedans, 8 to 9000 Jews & the rest Xtians of various denominations. The chief native industry is the manufacture of soap & what is called 'Jerusalem ware', consisting of chaplets, crucifixes, beads, crosses & the like, made principally of mother-of-pearl & olive-wood, & sold to the pilgrims who annually resort to the Holy City to the number of 6000 to 8000. No mines are worked although it is known that sulphur, bitumen & rock-salt are found on the shores of the Dead Sea; but security & capital are wanting & so long as these are absent, the probable wealth to be abstracted from these regions will remain unavailable. No factories are to be met with. The employment of the people is almost wholly agricultural & pastoral. The road between Jaffa & Jerusalem, never of the best, has been allowed to fall into such disrepair that none but the roughest kind of vehicle could now traverse it. The other roads of the district are of a wretched description. With these improved, more complete **/46/** security established against the predatory Bedouin tribes inhabiting the outskirts of the districts, & certain administrative reforms, whereby encouragement would be given to bring under cultivation the vast & fertile plains now only partially tilled, there can be no doubt that the country could support a population many times larger than its present scanty number of poverty-stricken inhabitants. Academy, April 25, 1874[2]

1 For the translation of 'Nuk pu Nuk', GE first wrote, 'I am that I am'. Compare her note on Pf 710 2.

2 'Notes on Travel', *The Academy* 5 (1874): 460. The anonymous author has not been identified, but may have been Lady Strangford, whose letter follows.

(Letter from Lady S)

Colonization. Since 1863 the Israelitish Alliance chiefly of Paris, shamed by the efforts of Xtians to promote colonies & agricultural occupations in Palestine, have endeavoured to found a colony at Jaffa – & some other feeble efforts have been made of the same kind elsewhere. Till then, nothing of the kind was ever done. The reason was this: since the Jews began to creep back to Palestine, to die in the Holy Land, the Rabbis have lent all their energies to inculcate the doctrine that all who return there are Saints & that therefore they & their descendants shall be entirely supported by the alms of the faithful elsewhere – that the Jews who live there, being Saints, are never to work – only to pray & live idle because holy: they teach that it is irreligious of a Jew in Jerusalem to work. This idea began faintly at the very beginning, with the return under the greatest difficulties, of a few Jews after the repulsion by Ferd[inand] & Isabella. The Rabbis foresaw, *what is now beginning to happen*, that if the Jews in Jerusalem were to work, the faithful would be slower in sending their support thro' the hands of the Rabbis. Efforts have been made of late years to send it through other hands, & the Rabbis excommunicate those who thus receive it, still more those who work for it.[1]

/50/

Islam, peace. Muslim, righteous man [p. 129]

Mohammed, the Praised, περικλυτος [p. 68n][2]

1 The passage transcribed above is an excerpt from a letter dated 23 April 1874 from Lady Strangford, now in the Beinecke Library, Yale University; see Haight, pp. 473–4. A descendent of the Beauforts of the Crusades, she had been given the order of the Holy Sepulchre by the patriarch of Jerusalem before her marriage in 1862 to Percy E. F. W. Smythe, the eighth Viscount Strangford.

2 From Deutsch's 'Islam'. The Greek epithet means 'far-famed, renowned'. On Pf 710 26, the 'Etymology' of Mohammed is given as 'The Praised, or else the Desired', with reference to one of the works reviewed in this article: Aloys Sprenger, *Das Leben und die Lehre des Mohammad,* 3 vols. (Berlin: G. Parthey, 1861–5). GE's copy of Sprenger's work, originally owned by Deutsch, is in DWL. For her notes from Sprenger, see Pf710 2, 12, 19, 21, 23, and 24.

Thoth or Mercury – one of Eight mystic Kabiri, or mighty ones, in Phoenicia. His Phoenician name is Kadmus, the primeval or Eastern; also Taaut.

[pp. 181–2] [1]

When we read Julian the Apostate's bitter & tearful elegy – for this seems the only word for his celebrated pamphlet – when we hear Libanius imploring the 'ragged' priests & votaries of the new faith to spare at least some of the temples, to leave a few gold & silver treasures in the sanctuaries, & not to break every one of the marble statues; when Symmachus in the name of the senate prays that the one altar of Victoria by whose aid they had conquered the world, might be left to the city – we cannot but feel a mournful sympathy with these pleaders for the last remnants of the 'spring-time of humanity'.

[pp. 186–7]

/51/

A chapter in the books of Hermes Trismegistus has this theme: Nothing is lost, & it is only by mistake that changes are called death & destruction.

[p. 188][2]

=[3]

Abdul Wahab, founder of Wahabees, 1725

[Bosworth Smith, p. 241; Pf 710 38][4]

1 This and the two following notes are from 'Hermes Trismegistus', first published in the *Saturday Review* (1867) and reprinted in *Literary Remains,* pp. 181–90. Compare GE's notes on *Kadmon* and *Kabirim* on Pf 710 23, and her note on *qedem* on Pf 710 32.

2 GE refers to '*Thoth-literature*, or writings of Hermes Trismegistus' on Pf 711 74.

3 An excerpt from *Euphues* has been relocated to that section.

4 This and the following notes are from Reginald Bosworth Smith, *Mohammed and Mohammedanism* (London: Smith, Elder, 1874), based on four lectures delivered at the Royal Institution of Great Britain in February and March 1874. In the book, Deutsch's 'Islam' is reprinted as an appendix. The context of these notes is Bosworth Smith's statement that

> it is currently believed that Mohammedism is dying out because it has no such power of revival. But the very reverse of this is, rather, true. Probably no religion has produced, in the various parts of its vast empire, a more continuous succession of reformers, whose aim has been to bring it back to its original simplicity and purity.

The Wahhabis, a reform Muslim sect begun in the eighteenth century, interpreted the Koran literally, practised strict simplicity of life, and attacked superstitious pilgrimages to shrines, the worship of Muslim saints, and the tolerance of other religious beliefs.

Mohammed Pf 711 51

For Bâbyism, the religious movement going on in Persia – ecstatic martydoms & prodigality of tortures submitted to amidst songs of triumph by women & children, the followers of the Bâb[1]

– vide Gobineau, Les Religions & les Philosophies dans l'Asie centrale

[Bosworth Smith, p. 241; Pf 710 7][2]

Also Palgrave, Essays on Eastern Questions [Bosworth Smith, p. 245][3]

Baron von Haxthausen's Tribes of the Caucasus for an account of Schamyl & Muridism [Bosworth Smith, p. 246n][4]

1 Bâbiism was a nineteenth-century Muslim Shiite sect whose revolts against the Shah were suppressed with many deaths and atrocities. After the Bâb was killed, his disciples founded what was to become the international Baha'i sect. The brief version of this note on Pf 710 7 has a later reference to 'an essay by Franck'. 'Franck on le Babisme' was read on 14 July 1876 (GHL Diary).

2 Bosworth Smith refers to Joseph Arthur de Gobineau, *Les Religions et les philosophies dans l'Asie centrale* (Paris: Didier, 1865). There is no evidence that GE read Gobineau, the author of an argument for Aryan superiority. He sent a letter to GHL almost a year after his death; see GEL VII, 217.

3 William Gifford Palgrave, *Essays on Eastern Questions* (London: Macmillan, 1872).

4 Baron August von Haxthausen, *The Tribes of the Caucasus: with an account of Schamyl and the Murids,* translated by John Edward Taylor (London: Chapman and Hall, 1855). Shamil was the spiritual and military leader of the Muslim Caucasian tribes in their guerilla holy war against Russia (1834–59). Bosworth Smith comments on 'the heroic struggle of Schamyl, his personal influence, and his genius for military and political organization':

> Truly while Mohammedanism can throw off geniuses like Schamyl, it may well be able to dispense with such governments as that of the Turks. The Baron's prophecies of a general collapse of Mohammedanism are being signally falsified. (pp. 246n–247n)

Mentions of Shakespeare by contemporaries

Pf 711 47, 48, 49

All but one of the 'mentions of Shakespeare by contemporaries' (Pf 711 1) are from 'Some Account of the Life of Shakespeare' by Alexander Dyce in his *Works of William Shakespeare.* The posthumous third edition (1874), edited by John Forster, has not been seen by the present editor. Page references below are to the fifth edition, 10 vols. (London: Swan Sonnenschein, Le Bas and Lowry, 1886), a reprint 'on superior paper' of the fourth edition, itself 'a careful reprint of the Third Edition, no alterations whatever having been made in the text', except for the replacement of endnotes by footnotes.

/47/

'Many were the wit-combates between him (Shakspeare) & Ben Jonson, which two I behold like a Spanish great galleon & an English man of war: Master Jonson (like the former) was built far higher in learning, solid but slow in his performances; Shakspeare with the English man of war, lesser in bulk, but lighter in sailing, could turn with all tides, tack about & take advantage of all winds, by the quickness of his wit & invention.'

Fuller's Worthies, p. 126 A a a Ed. fol. [I, 90]

(Francis Meres' Palladis Tamia, 1598) [I, 90–1] [1]

'What things have we seen
Done at the Mermaid! heard words that have been
So nimble, & so full of subtle flame,
As if that every one from whom they came
Had meant to put his whole wit in a jest.'[2]

1 A brief excerpt from *Palladis Tamia* is copied on Pf 708 38 and Folger 13 14.
2 Francis Beaumont's 'Letter to Ben Jonson' is not reprinted in Dyce.

/48/

'Thou art a monument without a tomb.'

'And tell how far thou didst our Lyly outshine,
Or sporting Kyd, or Marlowe's mighty line:
And though thou hadst small Latin & less Greek' &c

'He was not of an age, but for all time.'

'For a good poet's made as well as born.'

Ben Jonson on Shakspeare[1]

Greene's Groatsworth of Wit &c, 1592, in which he speaks of one with 'a tiger's heart wrapt in a player's hide, supposes he is able to bombast out a blank verse as well as the best of you; & being an absolute Johannes Factotum, is, in his own conceit, the only Shake-scene in the country.' [I, 74]

Venus & Adonis 1593. Lucrece 1594 [I, 76–7]

Ben Jonson in his *Discoveries*: 'I remember the players have often mentioned it as an honour to Shakspeare, that in his writing (whatsoever he penned) he never blotted a line. My answer hath been, 'Would he had blotted a thousand!' ... I loved the man & do honour his memory, on this side idolatry, as much as any. He was indeed honest, & of an open & free nature; had an excellent fantasy, brave notions & gentle expressions; wherein he flowed with that facility, that sometimes it was necessary he should /49/ be stopped: Sufflaminandus erat, as Augustus said of Haterius.[2] His wit was in his own power; would the rule of it had been so too!' [I, 88]

Sonnets printed, 1609 [I, 116]

New Place bought, 1597. 107 acres, 1602[3] [I, 81]

1 Ben Jonson, 'To the Memory of My Beloved, the Author Mr William Shakespeare: And What He Hath Left Us', ll. 22, 29–31, 43, and 64. Dyce mentions the poem, I, 88, and prints it in full, I, 181–4.

2 Augustus said of Haterius, a rhetorician, that 'he was in want of a brake'.

3 'In 1602 Shakespeare made an important addition to his property by purchasing for three hundred and twenty pounds, a hundred and seven acres of arable land in the parish of Old Stratford.' (Dyce, I, 96)

Chettle, editing the Groat's worth of Wit, says Shakspeare was 'excellent in the quality he professeth'. The rest of the evidence is rather to the effect that his acting was indifferent. [I, 107–9]

Shakspeare on the stage still in 1603 – acted a part in Ben Jonson's Sejanus [I, 104]

'Who, as he was a happy imitator of nature, was a most gentle expressor of it: his mind & hand went together; & what he thought he uttered with that easiness, that we scarce received from him a blot in his papers ... Read him therefore; & again & again: & if you do not like him, surely you are in some manifest danger not to understand him.'

Heminge & Condell: address prefixed to the folio of 1623 [I, 179–80]

Euphues

Pf 711 51, 52

For these excerpts from John Lyly's *Euphues*, page references are to *Euphues, The Anatomy of Wit* (1579) and *Euphues and his England* (1580), edited by Edward Arber (London: Alex Murray, 1868).

/51/

=[1]

'Though the Camomile the more it is troden & pressed down, the more it spreadeth, yet the violet the oftener it is handled & touched, the sooner it withereth & decayeth.' Euphues [p. 46]

=[2]

/52/

'It is a world to see how Englishmen desire to heare finer speech than the language will allow, to eate finer bread than is made of wheat, to wear finer cloth than is wrought of wool.' Euphues [p. 204]

And among all the straunge & beautiful shows, mee thinketh there is none so notable, as the bridge which crosseth the Thames, which is in manner of a continual street, well replenished with large & stately houses on both sides, & situate upon twenty arches, whereof each one is made of excellent freestone squared. Euphues. Glass for Europe, i.e. England [p. 434]

'If I had brought, Ladyes, little dogs from Malta, or strange stones from India, or fine carpets from Turkie, I am sure that either you would have wooed me to have them or wished to see them.' Ibid. [p. 432]

'Let the keyes hang at her girdle & the purse at thine, so shalt thou know what thou dost spend, & how she can spare.' [p. 475]

1 An excerpt from Deutsch has been relocated to a previous section.
2 Notes on Mohammedanism have been relocated to a previous section.

Notes from Abraham Geiger and others

Pf 711 53, 54, 55, 56, 57, 58, 59, 60, 61

These notes on Jewish history and traditions are from various sources, including two from the 'Books Wanted' list on Pf 711 21: 'Ewald's Geschichte Israel's' and 'Delit[z]sch, Geschichte der Jüdischen Poesie'. GE's copies of Delitzsch and an English translation of Ewald are in DWL. Other excerpts come from five works not in her library, all of which were also sources for notes in the Berg Notebook. Comparisons of these notes from works which were probably either borrowed or read in a library, reveal patterns of use for GE's larger-format 'at home' Berg Notebook, where lengthy notes could be entered in ink, and her portable notebook, Pf 711, with its smaller page size and 'prepared' paper and pencil.

The notes from 'Oppenheim's Pictures' on Pf 711 53 and 54 are drawn from Moritz Oppenheim, *Bilder aus dem altjüdischen Familienleben,* with commentary by Leopold Stein (Frankfurt, 1866 and later editions in 1868 and 1872). Oppenheim's paintings are reproduced in full-page plates. Since the book is unpaginated, references to Stein's text are indicated by the plate numbers and titles of Oppenheim's pictures. Most of these notes are copied again on B 123, from GE's original notes in this portable book.

The Chronicles of Rabbi Joseph ben Joshua ben Meir, the Sphardi, translated and edited by Christoph Heinrich Friedrich Bialloblotzky, 2 vols. (London: Richard Bentley for the Oriental Translation Fund of Great Britain and Ireland, 1835–6), is the source of a note on Pf 711 59–60, copied twice on B 193v, and an epigraph on Pf 711 61. This is the Chronicle often cited by Milman, who calls it 'unquestionably the most valuable historic work of the Jews which has been made accessible to the European reader' (III, 454). First published in Venice in 1554, the work chronicles history from Adam to 1520 (Volume I), and from 1520 to 1553 (Volume II). The Genoese focus of the second volume may have an occluded link to the events of the Grandcourt yachting expedition. The chronicler writes of the battles and exploits of the Admiral Andrea Doria and the 'wicked count', his nephew, who was 'cast a second time into the sea': 'the count is drowned, and he is no more who thought to possess dwelling-places that were not his' (II, 430, 432).

Notes from Abraham Geiger and others

Hyam Isaacs, *Ceremonies, Customs, Rites and Traditions of the Jews* (London: William Buck, [1830]), is the source of brief notes on Pf 711 55 and 56 and much more extensive notes in the Berg Notebook. See B 129v to 135v and the headnote to that section.

Abraham Geiger, *Judaism and its History*, translated by Maurice Mayer (New York: Thalmessinger, 1865), is the source of many notes on Pf 711 56 to 59, some of which are repeated in the 'Abraham Geiger' section of the Berg Notebook: see B 136v, 137v, 138v, and 139 and the headnote.

Moritz Steinschneider, 'Jüdische Literatur', in Ersch and Gruber's *Allgemeine Encykopädie der Wissenschaften und Künste*, is the source of very extensive notes in the Berg Notebook; see B 141 to 150 and the headnote to that section. The brief notes from Steinschneider on Pf 711 60 appear to have been copied from notes dispersed over several other pages of the Berg Notebook (B 106, 114v, 123, and 194).

Some notes from Graetz, filling available spaces on Pf 711 63, 64, and 65, are also copied from the Berg Notebook (B 123, 156, and 193v). The longer notes on Pf 711 55 and 66, however, are compilations from Graetz which are original to this notebook.

/53/

Story in the Midrash that Og King of Bashan saved himself in the Deluge by holding on to Noah's Ark. v. Ewald vol 1[1]

The silver pinnacles of the Thora-roll which the year-old infant's hand was made to touch are called Ez-chajim = the Tree of life

(Oppenheim's Pictures) [Plate II][2]

Talith, garment worn in the Synagogue [Plate I][3]

Aron-hakodesch, the sacred ark or chest containing the Thora

[Plate III][4]

The youth of 14 is Bar-Mizwa, son of the law, & this is the period of Jewish confirmation [Plate V][5]

'Mysteriösen pythagoräischen Doppeldreieck' (Shield of David) ✡[6]

'Chuppa' canopy held over the bride & bridegroom [Plate VI][7]

Zeäna ureäna, der allgemeinen weiblichen Sabbath-lectüre in der Gasse, dieser Encyclopädie aller rabbinischen Märchen u. Histörchen diesem Conversations-lexicon populärer Religionswissenschaft und Schriftauslegung

[Plate X][8]

1 Georg Heinrich August von Ewald, *The History of Israel*, translated by Russell Martineau and J. E. Carpenter, 2nd edition, 4 vols. (London: Longmans, Green, 1869–71), I, 228n. This passage is marked in GE's copy in DWL.

2 '*Das Schultragen*', or 'taking the young boy to the Shul or school'.

3 In DD ch. 32, GE defines the *talith* as the 'white blue-fringed kind of blanket which is the garment of prayer' (338). See also B 133v.

4 '*Der Segen der Rabbi*', or 'the Rabbi's blessing'.

5 '*Bar-Mizwa-Vortrag*', or the youth's reading from the Scripture, which is part of his confirmation service.

6 Translation: 'mysterious Pythagorean double triangle'; also called the Star of David. See also Pf 711 92a and Pf 710 14 and 34.

7 This and the previous note are from the commentary for Plate VI, '*Die Hochzeit*', or 'the wedding'. For more on the wedding ceremony, see B 134.

8 Plate X, '*Sabbath-Ruhe*', or 'Sabbath rest'. Translation: '*Zeäna ureäna*, the common Sabbath reading for women in the Juden-gasse, this encyclopaedia of rabbinical folk-tales and anecdotes, this popular encyclopaedia of theology and interpretation of the Scriptures'.

/54/

'*Seder*' heisst Ordnung Rituell [Plate XII][1]

'Kiddusch' consecrating blessing [Plate XIII][2]

Kauderwälsch. Jew-German dialect
Wagenseil's Belehrung der Jüdisch-Deutschen Red- und Schreibart[3]

Relic said to have been carried away with them by the Jews when they were driven out of Ratisbon in 1519: part of the stone tables which Moses threw down & broke [B 136v][4]

A writer in the feuilleton of the Allgemeine Zeitung, writing of the Jews in Venice, says that the name 'Ghetto' came from the fact that there were twelve furnaces for brass manufacture in that quarter. He gives a Latin quotation to this effect, without saying whence. The derivation seems rickety, for getto is not equivalent to Ghetto in Italian. But he says Ghetto was a corruption of Getto. He admits that the learned are in strife on the point.[5]

/55/

The Karaites arose in the beginning of the 8th centy under Anan ben David. Dogmas: adherence solely to the written text, the supremacy of reason, & the right of private judgment. [Graetz 5, 175–8][6]

1 The Passover feast and liturgy is called the *Seder*, which is short for Seder Haggadah, 'order of narration'. For GE's notes on Passover, see B 130 and 131.

2 '*Die Laubhütte*', or 'Feast of Tabernacles'. For GE's longer note on Tabernacles and Kiddush, see B 131v.

3 Defined by *Cassell's German–English Dictionary* as 'gibberish, nonsense, double Dutch', *Kauderwälsch* is a pejorative term for Yiddish. *Johann Christof Wagenseils Behlerhung der Jüdisch-Teutschen Red- und Schreibart* (Königsberg: P. F. Rhode, 1699), a book of instruction in Jewish-German dialect, is referred to again on B 193v and Pf 710 41 and may be the source of the Had Gadya on B 183. For another reference to Yiddish, see the headnote to 'The Inner Life of Modern Judaism' (B 124 to 129).

4 Source not traced.

5 The reference is to the *Allgemeine Zeitung des Judenthums* (Leipzig), but the source has not been traced. One meaning of *getto* refers to bronze-casting.

6 See also Pf 710 23 and Pf 707 33.

Notes from Abraham Geiger and others Pf 711 55 56

Not Richard Simon (Crit. Hist. O. T. 1678), but Saadia, founder of biblical criticism. [Graetz 5, 269][1]

11th century	Rabbi Samuel Nagid
	Isaac ben Baruch
	Alfes. Samuel Halevi
	Rabbi Bechai
1021–1070	Ibn Gabirol
	= Avencebrol, Avicebron (author of the Fons Vitae)[2]
12th	Jehuda Halevi, poet
	Aben Ezra 1070–1139
	Kimchi 1150–?
1139–1204	Maimonides[3]

When a woman prays, say the Rabbis, it has no effect, for evil or for good. [Isaacs, p. 39; B 138][4]

Two guardian angels – one holding the measure of evil deeds, the other of good. Sins forgiven every New Year. Fowl killed, swung over the head with a prayer that the sins may enter into the body of the fowl – the fowl then given to the poor. Manners & Customs of the Jews. [Isaacs, pp. 13, 17, 54; B 130v]

/56/

Willow branches at the Feast of Tabernacles, done up in small bundles to give to each family [Isaacs, p. 73; B 131v–132v]

Jews now everywhere emancipated except in Russia & Roumania[5]

The Rabbis say that when the Israelites borrowed of the Egyptians God wrought this miracle, that what each Jew borrowed was exactly the price of his unpaid labour. [Isaacs, p. 106; B 150v]

1 Graetz refers to Richard Simon, *Histoire critique du Vieux Testament* (Paris: Veuve Billaine, 1678). For another reference to Saadia, see Pf 707 33. For a quotation from him, see Pf 711 80.

2 This note, added later, is from Geiger, pp. 288n–289n. For GE's notes on Ibn Gebirol, see B 165v and Pf 710 20.

3 These names and dates are from Graetz 5.

4 For a discussion of GE's use of this note, see the headnote to B 137 and 138.

5 Source not traced.

Mother singing Hebrew prayers & texts over her sleeping infant.
How a language may sleep & wake again![1]

'Fits as a fist fits the eye.' Wie die Faust auf 's Auge[2]

Of Maimonides, Ab. Geiger says that Albertus Magnus has appropriated his best thoughts & Thomas Aquinas has borrowed much from him.
[Geiger, p. 289]

A Jewish poet, Immanuel, the friend of Dante, intimately connected with him, full of fresh humour. [Geiger, p. 290]

Savasorda (a mathematician) = Abraham ben Chija, a Spaniard who lived in Provence. He **/57/** was surnamed *Zahib Alshorta*, meaning 'Chief of the Police', as a large landed proprietor was then named, or as we should say 'Governor' or Nassi in Hebrew. By his name Savasorda he is known through the Middle Ages: 'he would perhaps not have been mentioned so often if it had been known he was a Jew,' says Geiger.
[Geiger, p. 290; B 136v and 194]

Hillel: '*If I am not for myself who* shall then be for me?'
'If I am for myself alone, what am I then?' [Geiger, pp. 193, 297][3]

Yalkut Rubeni, so often quoted by Eisenmenger is, says Geiger, the work of an addle-brained Cabbalist, Ruben Hoeske. [Geiger, p. 341; B 149v; Pf 710 39][4]

Septuagint, first instance in history of the translation of a book.
Geiger [p. 146; B 136v]

Shemang. A Grecian spirit took possession of the Jews & we are told that at a later period a Teacher of the Talmud heard the people pronounce the Shemang in the Greek language. (corrupt pron[unciatio]n) [Geiger, p. 150][5]

1 Source not traced.

2 Source not traced. In DD ch. 22, Klesmer expresses his annoyance by introducing this German phrase: 'Your Mr Bult's company fits me "wie die Faust ins Auge"' (225).

3 Geiger has two versions of Hillel's saying: 'If I am not for myself, who shall then be for me?' (p. 297) and 'If I work not for myself, who then shall work for me?' (p. 193). GE copied the excerpt from p. 297 and then added 'work ... work' in parentheses above the first line of her note.

4 For GE's notes from Eisenmenger, see B 118 to 121.

5 For other notes on the Shema, see B 110 and 133v and Pf 711 22.

'I sleep but my heart is awake.' Canticles [Geiger, p. 84; B 194][1]

/58/

Onias's prayer: when the adherents of Hyrcanus & Aristobulus had fortified themselves, the one party in the temple, the other outside besieging, Onias was applied to as one whose prayers were efficacious. He knelt down publicly & prayed that as those in the temple were the sons of the people & those outside the sons of the people, God would hear the prayers of neither against the other. The people stoned him to death. [Geiger, pp. 180–1; B 154v]

The followers of Shamai said, It is better to be born than not to be born; the disciples of Hillel said, 'Well, we are born, therefore let us be active & examine well our actions.' [Geiger, pp. 191–2; B 194][2]

The Zadokites = Sadducees, descendants of the priestly estate with the families of rank allied to them. Their opponents were called Separatists, *Pharisees*, by an Aramaic name. [Geiger, p. 163; B 150v]

From what Geiger says it appears that the Separatists signified originally those who wished to keep up the distinctive elements & characteristics of Judaism from solution with the habits of the 'people of the land' found in Judaea after the return from Babylon. [Geiger, p. 160]

/59/

Conception of races looking forward to annihilation – the remaining hundred families of the Samaritans [Geiger, p. 124; B 193v][3]

1 GE later added 'waketh' above Mayer's translation 'is awake', referring to the AV translation of the Song of Solomon v, 2. In DD ch. 38, this quotation is part of the narrative commentary on Mordecai's visionary imagination:

> The visionary form became a companion and auditor; keeping a place not only in the waking imagination, but in those dreams of lighter slumber of which it is truest to say, 'I sleep, but my heart is awake' – when the disturbing trivial story of yesterday is charged with the impassioned purpose of years. (442–3)

For the second and later editions of DD, GE changed 'is awake' to 'waketh'.

2 GE has misplaced the 'not' in her transcription. On B 194, it is copied more briefly and accurately as 'It is better not to be born [than to be born].' For more extensive comparisons between Hillel and Shammai, 'whose severity made the traditional antithesis to the mildness of Hillel', and their followers, see B 107, 153v, and 153av.

3 For a longer note from Geiger on the Samaritans, see B 138v.

The Eskimos call themselves *Innuit.*[1]

Jerome, Ep. 127 for Saga of Asnat & Josef [Delitzsch, p. 24; B 193v][2]

Targums a nursery of Agada
- v. Delitzsch [pp. 27, 50, 135–6, 136n–137n; B 193v][3]

Passage about God calling to the little stars, who are waiting upon him & say 'Here am I.' Where?[4]

Pajtanish – gottesdienstlich
Pijuthim, Synagogalpoësien [Delitzsch, p. 49; B 123][5]

Family of the Kalonymos in Italy & Germany Delitzsch, [p.] 51[6]

Rashi ib. [p.] 52[7]

1 Source not traced. *Innuit* or *Inuit* means 'the people'.

2 Source: Franz Julius Delitzsch, *Zur Geschichte der jüdischen Poesie vom Abschluss der heiligen Schriften Alten Bundes bis auf die neueste Zeit* (Leipzig: Karl Tauchnitz, 1836). GE's copy is in DWL. Delitzsch cites Epistle 127 of Jerome, which is to be found on p. 519 of GE's annotated copy of *Les Lettres de S. Jerome* (Paris, 1679), also in DWL. Asenath was the wife of Joseph; see Genesis xli. This note is copied incorrectly on B 193v.

3 GE's copy of Delitzsch in DWL has an index note on p. 224: 'poetical character of the Targums, 27'; and a marginal note on p. 27: 'Targum[s] cont. Agada'. For her notes on the Hagada, see B 107 and Pf 710 4. For another related note from Delitzsch, see B 140.

4 Source not traced. GE was also apparently unable to trace this passage by 'some oriental poet'. In DD ch. 17, the narrator says that Deronda in his rowboat looks for 'a perfectly solitary spot'

> where he ... could watch out the light of the sunset and the opening of that bead-roll which some oriental poet describes as God's call to the little stars, who each answer, 'Here am I.'

After he discovers Mirah, and she answers his offer of help, the allusion recurs:

> The twilight was deepening ... and the little stars were giving their answer one after another. (173, 176)

5 Copied again in the list of 'Hebrew names and phrases' on B 123. *Pajtanish* is translated as 'relating to divine worship'; *Pijuthim* ('synagogalen Poësie' on B 123) as 'liturgical poetry'.

6 For a note on the Kalonymos family in the time of Charlemagne, see B 171v.

7 For notes on Rashi (Solomon ben Isaac), see B 193v, copied again on Pf 711 76 and Pf 710 33.

According to Scaliger, 3761 years are to be subtracted from a Jewish date after Christ, to find out its correspondence with our own; and of course the same number of years **/60/** must be added to our date in order to find the Jewish. [B 193v][1]

Mirah, sister of Joseph ben Joshua ben Meir[2]

'Die Krone der Lehre überragt die des Priester und des Konigthums.' [Steinschneider, p. 359; B 194][3]

Rabbi κατ' εξοχην is R. Jehuda, who completed the Canon of the Mishna.
Rab, Abba Aricha his pupil. Rab is Babylonish, Rabi Palestinian [Steinschneider, pp. 366–7; B 114v; Pf 710 33][4]

(Talmud, discussion, Midrasch, exegesis)
v. Steinschneider, Ersch u. Gruber [p. 367; B 106]

Armillus (Romulus) Sage ? – Enemy, antagonist of Messiah [Steinschneider, p. 381][5]

The Laying on of hands was a ceremony which conferred rabbinical authority on the learned, & was forbidden by Rome after the insurrection under Bar-Cochba. [Steinschneider, p. 366; B 114v; Pf 710 30]

Nasi
Ab Beth Din } First appointed by John Hyrcanus 135–106
Chacham

Resh Metibta, president of the school
Resh Galuta, prince of the Exile
Gaon, Excellency [Steinschneider, pp. 366–9; B 123; Pf 710 36][6]

1 Source: *The Chronicles of Rabbi Joseph ben Joshua ben Meir, the Sphardi,* translated and edited by C. H. F. Bialloblotzky, I, xv–xvi.

2 The exact reference has not been traced. An aunt Mirah is mentioned as one of those who were 'driven out of Sphard' in the expulsion of 1492 (I, 327). Joseph ben Joshua ben Meir was born in Provence in 1496 and moved with his family in 1501 to Genoa.

3 Translation: 'The crown of the Torah surpasses that of the Priesthood and of Royalty.' This saying from the Talmud is cited by Steinschneider.

4 Translation: 'par excellence' or 'without equal'.

5 Compare notes on B 149v and Pf 710 6. *Sage* is German for 'legend'.

6 See also B 151v. GE 's first translation of Resh Galuta was 'president of the Exile', as on B 123 and Pf 710 36. She then crossed out 'president' and replaced it with 'prince'.

/61/

'These Chronicles are ready for sale at the printer's & bookseller's, the celebrated Rabbi Solomon Proops, the righteous priest (may his rock & his Redeemer guard him!), together with any other sort of books, Pentateuchs, Prayer-books, Liturgies, Absolutions, according to every regulation of each congregation (may their rock & Redeemer guard them!); & sorts of volumes, large & small, either in the holy tongue, or in the strange tongue. He buys & sells also, all sorts of old & new books, Gemaroth, Medrashim (Sermons), & also books of the Cabbalah, Commentaries, Decisions, Questions & Answers, & all other sorts of books whatsoever, as it is known. His dwelling is in the street which is called Broad Street, in the holy community of Amsterdam.'

Epigraph to the Chronicles of R. Joseph ben Joshua ben Meir[1]

1 This epigraph from the 1730 Amsterdam edition of the Chronicles is translated by Bialloblotzky, II, 525–6.

Berenice

Pf 711 63, 64, 65, 66

GE's inclusion of 'Berenice' in the 'Chief Contents' of Pf 711 indicates her intention to use Berenice's story in the novel. On a back leaf of her copy of Graetz 3, GE made a four-point summary of her life:

1. Under Nazarite vow, beseeches Florus, 65–66
2. Appears with Agrippa on the Xystus to warn the people
3. Saves Justus of Tiberius by her entreaties. Liebschaft [liaison] with Titus
4. Expects to be Empress on Vespasian's election

When Hans Meyrick shows Deronda a series of paintings in which he has made Mirah the model for Berenice, he thoughtlessly suggests that his friend is just the model he wants for her half-Jewish, half-Idumaean brother Agrippa (DD ch. 37: 425–7). GE's notes from Graetz present the history of Agrippa and Berenice in an aspect closer to the 'ladies' edition', as Hans calls it, than to the more scandalous and incestuous version that rouses Deronda's indignation.

/63/

It is hateful in David that in his last charge to Solomon, he tells him not to let Joab's grey head go down to the grave in peace, he himself having been afraid to take Joab to account for his murders; & also that he tells him to bring Shimei to the grave with blood for cursing him, he himself having sworn to forgive him.[1]

=[2]

Olam-ha-Ba – the world to come [Graetz 3, 219; B 123]

1 Possibly GE's own comment on I Kings ii, 5–9, based on the account in Ewald, *The History of Israel*, III, 214–15.

2 Notes here and from Pf 711 64 to 65 have been relocated to the 'Science and religion' section.

Ruach-ha-Kodesch – Holy Ghost [Graetz 4, 40; B 123; Pf 711 24][1]

/64/

Reredos[2]

3d Book of Maccabees, about the year 40 under Caligula – after the terrible oppression of the Jews under Flaccus in Alexandria & during the continuance of hostilities. [Graetz 3, 444; B 156]

/65/

Fiscus judaicus – the two drachmas formerly paid by each Jew to the Temple at Jerusalem, paid by order of Vespasian to the Capitoline Jupiter. [Graetz 3, 410; B 161v, 193v]

/66/

Berenice, sister of Agrippa II, born 28 AC. At Jerusalem in 66 to fulfil a Nazarite vow, she pleaded with Florus against the butchery of the people, with peril to herself. In 67 she formed a liaison with Titus, though much older than he. She hoped to become Empress of Rome. After the conquest of Judaea she accompanied Titus to Rome, & lived with him in his palace ten years as if she had been his wife. He was so jealous as to have had a Roman general strangled on suspicion of a liaison with her. But the hatred of the Romans would not allow their Emperor's marriage with a Jewess. Titus was obliged with sorrow to separate from her & even to banish her from Rome (*invitus invitam*, Suet.). Berenice personifies the relation of Rome with Judaea. Whither the last Jewish princess betook herself with her sorrow, & when she died, is not known. [Graetz 3, 319, 338, 375, 396, 410–11][3]

1 Mordecai offers a variant translation. He refers to 'the Ruach-ha-kodesh – the breath of divine thought', in speaking of his writing in Hebrew – a writing set in contrast to his 'stifled breath' in English speech (DD ch. 40: 466, 463).

2 Source not traced. Wilhelm Lübke defines 'Reredos' in his glossary of architectural terms as 'the back wall above the altar' (*Ecclesiastical Art,* p. 282); see Pf 711 6.

3 The back leaf of Graetz 3 includes GE's index references to these pages. The quotation from Suetonius' *Lives of the Caesars* indicates that the order of banishment was against both his will and her will. For GE's note on Berenice's brother Agrippa, see B 155.

Science and religion

Pf 711 62, 63, 64, 65, 67, 70

The excerpts collected here date from July to October 1874, during the time when GHL was working on the revision of the second volume of *Problems of Life and Mind, First Series: Foundations of a Creed* (GEL VI, 72, 79, 83). Like the 'Notes from Abraham Geiger & Others', these notes are closely connected with entries made at the same time in the Berg Notebook. The relevance to GE's own work-in-progress of the notes grouped together under her heading of 'Physical Science' (B 97v and 99 to 101v) may not be immediately apparent. However, a comparison of her entries in the two notebooks suggests interconnecting lines of thought between GHL's project and her own.

A postscript note on B 99, for instance, is drawn from Edward Burnett Tylor's *Researches into the Early History of Mankind and the Development of Civilization* (London: John Murray, 1865), read from 30 July to 18 August 1874 (GHL Diary). From the same source, GE recorded two brief notes on Pf 711 62 and 63, one of which refers to 'Lane's Arabian Nights'. Although the 'story of the ungrateful crocodile' plays no part in her novel, GE went on to read Lane's translation of *The Thousand and One Nights, commonly called, in England, The Arabian Nights' Entertainments.* An excerpt from his translation, about Queen Budoor's 'two delicate feet' (Pf 711 107), is used in a direct quotation in DD ch. 20, which in turn clinches an earlier allusion to Deronda as Prince Camaralzaman in DD ch. 16. Perhaps the connection between the *Early History of Mankind* and GE's novel may seem no less circuitous than the narrative of Scheherazade herself, but there is another more direct link too. Between 3 September and 14 November 1874, GE reread 'Tylor Primitive Culture', and on 15 November 'Polly read over again the early chapters of Daniel De Ronda' (GHL Diary). Tylor's *Primitive Culture: Researches into the Development of Mythology, Philosophy, Religion, Language, Art and Custom*, 2 vols. (London: John Murray, 1871) is the source of notes on Pf 711 64, 65, and 70, including one which is the germ of the following comment by the narrator in DD ch. 19:

> It appears that the Caribs, who know little of theology, regard thieving as a practice peculiarly connected with Christian tenets, and probably they could allege experimental grounds for this opinion. (190)

The allusion in this context contributes to GE's ironic analysis of Deronda's mixed opinions about 'Jewish characteristics and occupations'. Her source, Tylor, merely states:

> The Caribs, when on re-entering their houses, they missed something, used to say, 'A Christian has been here.' (Pf 711 64)

The concepts introduced by GE, of 'Christian tenets' and 'theology', rather than mere practice, and 'experimental grounds' for the Caribs' opinion, connect this note with others in this section, about the controversy over relations between contemporary experimental science and religious belief. The controversy had been provoked by numerous recent publications, including the first volume of GHL's *Foundations of a Creed,* which had been published by Trübner in September 1873. The tenets and foundations of GHL's 'Creed' had so affronted William Blackwood's feelings about 'the extinction of religion' that he had withdrawn from publishing the work (GEL V, 400–1, and 410–16; see also 371 and 431). Reviewers of the first volume had expressed opposition to GHL's declaration that the old religions must be transformed or perish, and criticized his 'new doctrine, which is to reconcile the claims of Religion and Science'.[1]

In the *Contemporary Review* of August 1874, St George Mivart protested against a trend evident in GHL's first volume and John Stuart Mill's *Three Essays on Religion,* which was published posthumously in 1874:

> A population more and more imbued with physical science ... [and] a growing appreciation of science, must favour the already wide-spread belief in a real antagonism between Christianity and Science. (23: 362)

Mivart's own career, as a scientist who converted in his youth to Roman Catholicism, exemplifies the dangers of being caught in the crossfire in the hostilities between Christianity and science. Mivart's sincere efforts in his publications to reconcile the claims of the two antagonists resulted in his being not only discarded by his mentor Thomas Henry Huxley, but also excommunicated by the Church (*DNB*).

Commenting that 'the scientific aspect of Contemporary Evolution appears hostile to the growth and influence of the Church', Mivart looks for a countervailing tendency in modern science – a renewal of interest in religious conceptions once generally current, which have 'gradually passed out of

1 *Nature* 10 (2 May 1874): 1–2.

general consciousness' and been 'forgotten' rather than 'rejected' – and cites the first volume of *Problems of Life and Mind.*[1] His somewhat scornful allusion in this article, to specialist studies of carnivorous beetles and fruit weevils, is copied on Pf 711 62; perhaps GE intended to contribute it to the editors of the *OED*, where it is cited to illustrate the definition of 'Curculionist'. The sequel article in the October issue includes more antagonistic comments on GHL's arguments. Although 'Polly read Contemporary Review after dinner' on 20 October (GHL Diary), she made no further notes from Mivart.

In GE's reference on Pf 711 65 to Matthew Arnold's *Literature and Dogma: An Essay towards a Better Apprehension of the Bible* (London: Smith, Elder, 1873), the conflict between science and religion is examined from another point of view:

> For Science, God is the 'stream of tendency whereby all things fulfil the law of their being' – for Religion ... [God is conceived as] 'the Eternal Power, not ourselves, which makes for righteousness'.

The October and November 1874 issues of the *Contemporary Review* included two parts of Arnold's 'Review of Objections to *Literature and Dogma*', in which he replies to 'those who have attacked' that work 'as anti-Christian and anti-religious' (24: 794–818, 981–1003).

On 1 November 1874, GHL wrote to Elma Stuart,

> Do you see the Contemporary Review ...? If so, you will be interested I think in Mat Arnold's papers in the October and November numbers. Much that he says on Religion we both think very good, and likely to have a *yeasty* effect on that strange fluid Public Opinion. I, myself cannot see how the Bible 'makes for righteousness' though I profoundly agree with him that righteousness is salvation – and is not to be sought in metaphysical refinements about a 'personal God' but is to be found in our idealization of human relations and human needs. (GEL VI, 86–7)

The excerpt on Pf 711 79 indicates that GE was continuing to read Arnold's sequel paper in the January 1875 issue of the *Contemporary Review.*

The prayer of the eleventh-century Arabian scientist Alhazen, 'that in the day of judgment the All-Merciful will take pity on the soul of Abur-Raihan, because he was the first of the race of men to construct a table of specific

1 *Contemporary Review* 23: 363, 363n and 365n.

gravities' is a quotation from the work referred to in the previous note on Pf 711 63, William Draper's *History of the Intellectual Development of Europe.* Alhazen's 'pious prayer' as quoted by Draper was cited by John Tyndall in his Inaugural Address as President of the British Association for the Advancement of Science in Belfast on 19 August 1874. Tyndall's controversial address was published in *Nature* on 20 August and read by GE and GHL on 23 August (GHL Diary). In his Belfast Address, Tyndall declared:

> We fought and won our battle even in the Middle Ages: why should we doubt the issue of a conflict now?
>
> The impregnable position of science may be described in a few words. All religious theories, schemes, and systems, which embrace notions of cosmogony, or which reach otherwise into its domain, must ... submit to the control of science, and relinquish all thought of controlling it.
>
> (*Nature* 10: 318)

The influence of William Draper, who was 'largely responsible for the "warfare" model of the relations between religion and science',[1] is evident in the course of Tyndall's argument and his citations to Draper's work – which consequently was published in a second revised edition in 1875.

GE's note on Helmholtz's theorem of ring vortices (Pf 711 67) repeats part of her note on B 100–100v and is related to GHL's discussion of these phenomena in the second volume of his work-in-progress. For further discussion of GE's excerpts from Tyndall and references to ring vortices, see the headnote to the 'Physical Science' section in the Berg Notebook.

---

1 Tess Cosslett, editor, *Science and Religion in the Ninteenth Century* (Cambridge: Cambridge University Press, 1984), pp. 172, 234. Cosslett reprints an excerpt from the Belfast Address, but unfortunately omits the pages pertinent to GE's notes. See also Frank M. Turner, *Contesting Cultural Authority: Essays in Victorian Intellectual Life* (Cambridge: Cambridge University Press, 1993), pp. 21, 196–7, 270–1, etc.

/62/

=[1]

Tannahill[2]

We hear now of lives being devoted to the study of small sections of natural orders, & that this naturalist is a Carabidist, & that a Curculionist, while a German naturalist has even published a quarto volume, with large plates & numerous tables, the whole being devoted to the anatomy of the lower part of the hindmost bone of the skull of the carp. St. G. Mivart, Conty. Rev.[3]

There may even be words written in ancient hieroglyphics which are still alive in English. Thus h b n followed by two signs, one of which is determinative for wood, is *ebony*. [Tylor, *Early History*, p. 99]

Hic Rhodus, hic salta[4]

/63/

=[5]

Story of the ungrateful crocodile. Lane's Arabian Nights I, 84, 114[6]

1 Notes have been relocated to the 'Quotations from Bacon's *Essays*' section.

2 Reference not traced.

3 St George Mivart, 'Contemporary Evolution', Part IV, in the *Contemporary Review* 23 (1874): 362n.

4 Translation: 'Here is Rhodes, jump here.' This proverb is drawn from an Aesopian fable in which an athlete is requested to re-enact a great jump which he has boasted of performing at Rhodes. GE would have seen it in Deutsch's *Literary Remains*, pp. 70 and 199, and elsewhere.

5 Notes here and at the end of the page have been relocated to the 'Berenice' section.

6 In *Early History*, pp. 10–11, Tylor refers to this story 'which the sage Dûbân declined to tell the king while the executioner was standing ready to cut his head off. It is given by Mr Lane in his Notes to the Arabian Nights'. Tylor cites Edward William Lane, translator, *The Thousand and One Nights, commonly called, in England, The Arabian Nights' Entertainments*, new edition, 3 vols. (London: Charles Knight, 1859). The story, only alluded to on I, 84, is told by Lane in his note on I, 114. For a note from the *Arabian Nights*, see Pf 711 107.

Science and religion Pf 711 63,64 65

Draper, Hist. of Intellectual Developt. in Eur.[1]

Alhazen. Prayer 'that in the day of judgment the All-Merciful will take pity on the soul of Abur-Raihan, because he was the first of the race of men to construct a table of specific gravities.'[2]

> 'If you accept them, then their worth is great.'
> *Taming the Shrew* [II, i, 100]

> 'If this be magic, let it be an art
> Lawful as eating.' *Winter's Tale* [V, iii, 110–11]

/64/

=[3]

The Caribs, when on re-entering their houses, they missed something, used to say, 'A Christian has been here.' [Tylor, *Primitive Culture,* I, 27]

Degeneration of tribes in Africa & among the N. American Indians.
In S.E. Africa: old description of the kingdom of Monomotapa, remarkable ruins of hewn stone fitted without mortar.

'Well might the rude Kamchadal declare that the world is growing worse & worse, that men are becoming fewer & viler & food scarcer, for the hunter & bear & the reindeer are hurrying away from here to the happier life in the regions below.' Tylor, Primitive Culture, I, 42, 43

/65/

For Science, God is the 'stream of tendency whereby all things fulfil the law of their being' – for Religion, i.e. 'Morality heightened by emotion', He may be most adequately conceived as 'the Eternal Power, not ourselves, which makes for righteousness'. *Matt. Arnold. Lit. & Dogma*[4]

1 John William Draper, *A History of the Intellectual Development of Europe* (London: Sampson Low, 1863).

2 Quoted from Draper (p. 359) by John Tyndall in his Belfast Address, reprinted in *Nature* 10: 311.

3 Notes here have been relocated to 'Berenice' section.

4 GE summarizes Arnold's views, presented somewhat repetitively in *Literature and Dogma: An Essay towards a Better Apprehension of the Bible* (London: Smith, Elder, 1873); see pp. 21, 41, 57, 320, 348, 385, etc.

'When a poor man makes a proverb it does not spread.' West African Proverb

He fled from the sword & hid in the scabbard.

He who has only his eyebrow for a crossbow will never kill game.

ibid. [Tylor, *Primitive Culture,* I, 80–1]

=[1]

/67/

Ring vortices – If a whirling ring be once generated in a uniform, frictionless incompressible fluid, it will go on for ever, always consisting of the same portions of the fluid first set going, & because its elasticity causes it to rebound when touched, it could never be divided nor destroyed.[2]

=[3]

/70/

=[4]

Tasmanians: one, two, plenty. The Tasmanian language again shows the man stopping short at the reckoning of himself when he had held up one hand & counted its fingers – 'man' standing for five.

Tylor, Prim. Cult. [I, 220 and 226]

1 A note has been relocated to the 'Berenice' section.

2 James Clerk Maxwell, Presidential Address to the British Association for the Advancement of Science, reprinted in *Nature* 2 (22 September 1870): 421. For other notes from this source, see B 100–101.

3 Notes from Bacon's *Essays* have been relocated to the next section

4 The following extract from Tylor occurs after a note on the 'geology of Wiltshire', relocated in the next section.

Quotations from Bacon's *Essays* and geology of Wiltshire

Pf 711 62, 66, 67, 68, 69, 70, 71

GE was familiar with the essays of Francis Bacon from her youth; in a letter of 1839, she comments that her mind is 'an assemblage' of ingredients including 'morsels of Addison and Bacon' (GEL I, 29). Her copy of Bacon's *Essays* is now in Coventry City Library (Waley, p. 14), and his works were also listed in Mrs Ouvry's inventory (*Libraries*, p. 54). Page references provided below are to *Bacon's Essays and Colours of Good and Evil,* edited by William Aldis Wright (London: Macmillan, 1862). Other excerpts from Bacon are copied on GE's Blotter (Waley, p. 8); one is repeated on Pf 708 1. The morsels collected here have been relocated from their original contexts, where they were interspersed amongst notes on 'Berenice' and 'Science and religion'.

The summary of events in the American Civil War (Pf 711 71) is from *The Annual Register: or, a View of the History and Politics of the Year 1861* (London: J. and R. Rivington, 1862), pp. 220, 224, 237, and 291. In DD ch. 9, the news of Grandcourt's occupation of Diplow Hall is said to excite more interest round Wancester than 'the results of the American war' (81). Gwendolen's personal history during 1865 is set into a global context in DD ch. 11, when the narrator compares the events in her consciousness to some results of the Civil War, just ended: the deaths of Union soldiers and the starvation of Lancashire mill-workers (109).

The sources for the notes on the geological and political structures of Wiltshire have not been traced.[1] GE and GHL visited Salisbury, seeing Old Sarum, and Stonehenge, from 20 to 23 October 1874 (GHL Diary). From 28 to 31 October 1874, they were in Wiltshire, 'driving about looking at ... great houses and parks, probably for details in *Daniel Deronda*' (GEL VI, 86n). The 'geological structure of Wiltshire' plays a role in a scene in DD ch. 14: the 'Whispering Stones' that turn 'their blank grey sides' to Gwendolen, as if to conceal Lydia Glasher, are scattered Sarsen stones (136).

---

1 David Page's *Textbook of Geology, Descriptive and Industrial,* 5th edition (Edinburgh, Blackwood, 1872), requested in January 1874 (GEL IX, 115), is not the source.

Quotations from Bacon's *Essays* Pf 711 62 66 67

/62/

'The river of Lethe runneth as well above ground as below.'
Bacon: Essays ['Of Vicissitude of Things', p. 231]

'This would have done better in poesy, where transcendencies are more allowed.' ['Of Adversitie', p. 16]

=[1]

/66/

=[2]

'Omnium consensu capax imperii nisi imperasset,' saith Tacitus of Galba.
Bacon ['Of Great Place', p. 42][3]

/67/

=[4]

'Sell all thou hast & give it to the poor & follow me; but sell not all thou hast except thou follow me; that is, except thou have a vocation wherein thou mayest do as much with little means as great; for otherwise in feeding the streams, thou driest the fountain.'
Bacon's Essays ['Of Goodness and Goodness of Nature', p. 49][5]

If he be thankful for small benefits it shows that he weighs men's minds, & not their trash. ib. [p. 50]

'Princes are like to heavenly bodies which have much veneration, but no rest.'
['Of Empire', p. 81]

1 Notes have been relocated to the 'Science and religion' section.

2 A note has been relocated to the 'Berenice' section.

3 Translation: 'Everyone thought him capable of exercising authority until he tried it.' (Tacitus, *Histories*, 1, 49). After a distinguished military career, Galba was proclaimed Emperor in 68 CE. His rule – honest, but unsatisfactory – provoked his murder within the year.

4 A note has been relocated to the 'Science and religion' section.

5 Bacon refers to the teaching of Jesus in Mark x, 21.

/68/

'Ashes more generative than dust'[1]

Iom Kippur. The dead for whom the lights are burning, appearing in the synagogue in their shrouds: the living also wearing shrouds. The Rabbi orders all to lay off their shrouds. The dead do not obey – & thus he recognizes them.
Sippurim [B 137v][2]

Buxtorf, Lexicon[3]

Domestic architecture of different periods: a work on the subject to be sought.

The geological structure of Wiltshire is chiefly chalk & oolite, the clays of the Wealden forming but a narrow band around the chalk, & those of the Tertiary beds of Southampton being confined to the vales below Salisbury. The London basin ends at Hungerford, but its former extension to the W. appears probable from the numerous blocks of Bagshot sandstone (Sarsen stones) scattered over the downs. */69/* The cretaceous beds constitute the greater part of S. Wiltshire, forming the central mass of the English chalk, which here attains its greatest elevation in Inkpen Beacon 1011 ft high. The underlying greensand we find exposed in the deep valleys of the chalk, for instance in that of Pewsey ... & also on a ridge skirting the escarpment of the chalk & in some places attaining a considerable elevation, as about Warminster & Stourhead. Below the greensand lies the Wealden clay, which comes to the surface on a narrow tract around the chalk hills, & below the Wealden the oolite, which forms the N. & extreme W. of the county.

1 Source not traced.

2 M. Jastrow, 'Der Besuch in der Synagoge' ('The Visitor in the Synagogue') in Wolf Pascheles, editor, *Sippurim, eine Sammlung jüdischer Volkssagen, Erzählungen, Mythen, Chroniken, Denkwürdigkeiten und Biographien berühmter Juden aller Jahrhunderte, insbesondere des Mittelalters,* Vol. III (Prague: Pascheles, 1854), pp. 173–5. GE's copy is in DWL. See the headnote for B 137v.

3 Johann Buxtorf, editor, *Lexicon chaldaicum, talmudicum et rabbinicum* (1607), new edition, edited by Bernard Fischer (Lipsiae: Schaefer, 1875).

Title & office of Recorder substituted in the place of Town Clerk at Dis by Charles the First. According to this charter the corporation consists of a mayor, recorder, ten **/70/** magistrates, & twenty-four common councilmen, who have the liberty of making what burgesses they please, all of whom have the privilege of voting for members of Parliament, though there are seldom more than thirty voters. The town sent members to all the parliaments of Edw[ard] I.

=[1]

/71/

American Civil War, begun 20 Dec. 1860 by S. Carolina – the state convention sitting at Charleston adopting an ordinance dissolving the connection with the Union. In 1861 this example was followed by the other Southern states. Taking of Fort Sumter. War ended in 1865.

1 A note from Tylor has been relocated to the 'Science and religion' section.

Quotations from Rabelais

Pf 711 72, 85

GE's copy of *Les Oeuvres de François Rabelais*, 5 vols. bound as 2 (Paris: Bibliothèque Nationale Collection, 1870–3), is in DWL. Her pencilled annotations include four index notes which refer to excerpts on Pf 711 85: at the end of Volume II, 'Outré language, 18' and 'Diogenes, 155', and at the end of Volume III, 'Selling the smell of roast, 112', and 'Settling suits by casting lots, 118'.

References within square brackets in the text are to book and chapter numbers. Volume and page references for the edition owned by GE are provided in the footnotes, when not indicated in her own notes. Translations in the footnotes are taken from the historic translation by Sir Thomas Urquhart and Pierre le Motteux (1653–1694), *Gargantua and Pantagruel*, reprinted with an introduction by Terence Cave (New York: Alfred A. Knopf, Everyman's Library, 1994).

/72/ Lace[1]

Cluny
Chantilly
Brussels
Spanish
Irish
Venetian point
Point d'Alençon

Antique lace made by drawing threads out of fine linen, & working in a pattern. Then came pillow-lace, & *appliqué*. Then machine Lace.

1 The source for this note has not been traced. 'Bought lace' is noted in GHL's Diary on 16 October 1874. GE and GHL spent the week of 4 to 11 October in Paris, then stayed in Brussels from 14 to18 October, returning home on 19 October, and starting out immediately for their visit to Wiltshire – Salisbury, Old Sarum, and Stonehenge – from 20 to 23 October (GHL Diary).

Quotations from Rabelais Pf 711 72

Rabelais, born 1483

'Vécut jusqu'à la mort en dépit des envieux.' [I, xxi][1]

'Couvercle digne du chauderon'
(A lid fit for the pot) [I, Prologue][2]

'Mangeant son blé en herbe'
(Turning his asses into the green cornfield) [III, ii][3]

'Pantagruelisme (vous entendez que c'est certaine gaiété d'esprit ... en mépris des choses fortuites)' [IV, Prologue][4]

'Je ne crains rien que les dangers.' Panurge [IV, lv][5]

'Cela, dit Frère Jean, n'est point matière de breviaire.
Je n'en croy sinon ce que vous plaira.' [IV, xxvii][6]

(Story of 'Pan is dead' in Rab. IV, 77) [IV, xxviii][7]

1 I, 66. Translation: 'lived till his dying day in despite of his enemies' (p. 70).

2 I, vii. GE pencilled this translation in the margin of her copy in DWL. Urquhart's translation is 'a lid worthy of such a kettle' (p. 21).

3 II, 164. Urquhart's translation: 'eating his Corn (as it were) whilst it was but Grass' (p. 305).

4 III, 170. Translation: '*Pantagruelism* (which you know is a certain Jollity of Mind pickled in the scorn of Fortune' (p. 516).

5 IV, 154. Translation: 'I dread nothing but Danger' (p. 650).

6 IV, 76. Translation: 'This, said Fryar *Jhon*, is not matter of Breviary; I may believe as little or as much of it as you and I please' (p. 590). Gwendolen's 'daring' comment to Mrs Gascoigne perhaps owes something to Rabelais – as read by GE, not by Gwendolen: '"Why should I waltz if I don't like it, aunt? It is not in the Catechism."' (DD ch. 11: 103)

7 *Thamous* tells '*Tiberius*, who was then Emperor' of the death of Pan:

> For my part, I understand it of that Great Saviour of the Faithfull, who was shamefully put to Death at *Jerusalem*, by the envy and wickedness of the Doctors, Priests, and Monks of the *Mosaic* Law ... for he may lawfully be said in the Greek tongue, to be *Pan*, since he is our *All.* (p. 592)

For GE's note on Plutarch's version of this story, see Folger 13 96 to 98.

'Pleurerai-je? disait-il; car pourquoy? Ma tant bonne femme est morte, qui était la plus cecy, la plus cela qui fut au monde ... Seigneur Dieu, faut-il que je me contriste encore? Cela me fâche; je ne suis plus jeune, je deviens vieux, le temps est dangereux, je pourray prendre quelque fièvre; me voilà affolé.'

[II, iii] [1]

/85/

=[2]

'Mêmement que un quidam des regens disoit souvent en ses lectures qu'il n'y a chose tant contraire à la vue comme est la maladie des yeux.'

Rabelais [II, v] [3]

Outré language, I, 18 [II, vi][4]

Diogenes rolls his tub because he does not like to be idle among people so busy. I, 155 [III, Prologue] [5]

The smell of roast meat paid with the ring of copper. v. III, 112 [III, xxxvii]

Bridoye decides causes by casting lots, nevertheless has bags full of writings before him – for 3 reasons – 'exquises, requises, et authentiques'.[6]

1. For form's sake
2. For gentlemanly & healthy exercise
3. For time's sake, because time ripens all things v. III, 118 [III, xl]

1 II, 7–8. Gargantua mourns for Badabec:

Shall I weep (said he?) Yes, for why? my so good wife is dead, who was the most *this*, the most *that*, that ever was in the world ... Lord God, must I again contrist my self? this grieves me; I am no longer young, I grow old, the weather is dangerous; I may perhaps take an ague, then shall I be foiled, if not quite undone ... (pp. 177–8)

2 Notes on 'Heraldry' fill the first half of this page.

3 II, 16. Translation:

[Pantagruel had an especial care not to study over-much, for fear of spoiling his eyes] ... for that it was told him by one of his Teachers (there called Regents) that the paine of the eyes was the most hurtful thing of any to the sight. (p. 185)

4 II, 18, not I, 18: GE's slip may be due to the binding of five volumes as two.

5 II, 154.

6 His three reasons are 'very exquisite, requisite, and authentical' (p. 456).

Language

Pf 711 73, 74, 75

Principles of Comparative Philology by Archibald Henry Sayce (London: Trübner, 1874) was read from 24 October to 6 November 1874 (GHL Diary). A review article by George Darwin, 'Whitney on the Origin of Language', in the November 1874 issue of the *Contemporary Review*, perhaps prompted the reading on 12 and 24 November of 'Whitney Lectures on Language' (GHL Diary): William Dwight Whitney, *Language and its Study* (London: Trübner, 1874).[1] *Fackelschrift* and *mehrsprachig* (Pf 711 74) suggest that GE's source was German, perhaps Heymann or Hajjim Steinthal's *Die Entwickelung der Schrift* (Berlin: F. Dummler, 1852) to which Whitney refers. Whitney also cites Hensleigh Wedgwood, *On the Origin of Language* (London, 1866), a work owned by GE and GHL and now in DWL. The sources of the following notes on language, however, have not been traced.

/73/

Experiments before the Royal Society by Mr W. H. Barton, by which the concussions & reactions of the air produced in human speech are made to record themselves in diagrams analogous to those which register the beating of the pulse. Such words as 'strength' produce a sharp mountainous elevation. 'Peter Piper picked a peck of pepper' is recorded in a series of sharp angular elevations for the emphatic syllables & rapid falls followed by horizontal lines for the softer tones. The rough R pronounced by Mr Barton begins with a steep elevation, followed by an irregular pattern like the teeth of a small saw.

'One piecy man' in the Pigeon (business) language of Chinese – parallel of 'pezzo di donna'. Hindustanee a camp language, between the Mohammedan invaders & the Hindus: grammar, Hindu; ¾ of the vocabulary, Persian.
Brogue, originally wooden shoe. Pawnee, Skt. paniyi – water?

1 For a note perhaps from Whitney, see Pf 707 14.

/74/

'Chop', Stamp put on bales of tea
Rom Chabo – Gypsy lad, origin of 'Rum Chap'

Dulcarnon, the Pythagorean proposition:
Arabic, Dhu'l Karnan, lord of the two horns[1]

Thoth-literature, or writings of Hermes Trismegistus[2]
Extent of Egyptian literature 1000 papyri, besides the inscriptions [Pf 710 15]

'Fackelschrift' quipu-writing. Wampum (vide Wuttke)[3]

Cunieform discovered by Grotefend, 1803. Greatest cunieform inscription of Darius, 490 BC at Behistun between Bagdad & Hamadan (mehrsprachig)[4] The triple-tongued inscription which Xerxes I had executed in Armenia under the 'Felskammern des Khorkor' stands 60 ft above the plain. Other inscriptions in three tongues by Darius at the foot of the Elwand near Hamadan.

/75/

Effect of words like 'right' 'reasonable' &c = arrangement of iron filings round a magnet[5]

Story of the Rani whose husband was blind, & who tied a handkerchief over her eyes that she might have no advantage over him

Wall built of sculptures smashed up for the purpose on the Esquiline.[6] Many lime-kilns discovered with fragments of sculpture lying round them, proving that hundreds if not thousands of statues, many of them priceless works of Greek art, were burnt into lime to provide mortar for the modern city.

1 For notes from another source on 'Zu'lkarnain', see Pf 710 40 and Pf 707 44.
2 For other notes on Hermes Trismegistus, see Pf 711 50 and 51.
3 Tylor, in *Early History of Mankind*, pp. 154–8, refers to quipu and wampum, but not to 'Fackelschrift' or to Heinrich Wuttke's *Geschichte der Schrift und das Schriftums* (Leipzig: E. Fleischer, 1872), which was read 7 January 1873 (GHL Diary).
4 Compare the note on Pf 710 5. *Mehrsprachig* means 'polyglot'.
5 Perhaps another of Mr Barton's experiments (see Pf 711 73).
6 One of the seven hills of Rome. The Esquiline fortification wall was built during the reign of Servius Tullius, sixth king of Rome.

Hebrew literature

Pf 711 75, 76, 79, 80

These notes, which may be dated by the excerpt from Matthew Arnold to January 1875, are contemporaneous with the notes in the 'Chisdai and the title of Gaon' section (B 159v to 163), which are drawn from the same sources: Graetz and the *Miscellany of Hebrew Literature.*

/75/

Legend of Jewish immigration into Spain in the time of King David
Vide Misc. Heb. Lit. p. 73[1]

Chisdai, contemp. Abderrahman III. 911–961 [*Miscellany*, p. 77; B 160][2]

Also Menachem b. Jacob, author of the oldest Hebrew dictionary
[*Miscellany*, p. 82; B 160]

/76/

Vessel captured in the Aegean Sea containing Jewish scholars: these sold for slaves & redeemed by their brethren became Rabbis in Cairo, Greece & Cordova Vide Misc. Heb. Lit. p. 84 [B 160 v]

The biblical & talmudical commentator, Rabbi Shelomeh ben Yitzschak, commonly known by the initials Rashi, upon whom the elder Buxtorf has erroneously fastened the ineradicable misnomer Yarchi – b. 1040
[*Miscellany*, p. 155; B 193v][3]

1 David Cassel, biographical sketch of 'Chisdai, the Son of Isaac', in *Miscellany of Hebrew Literature,* edited by Albert Löwy, Vol I (London: Trübner for the Society of Hebrew Literature, 1872), 73–91. GE's copy is in DWL. For longer notes from Cassel, see B 159v to 161. Compare the note on Pf 711 76 from Graetz 5, 68.

2 Chisdai is referred to as Chasdai on B 139v, 170v, and 172.

3 Albert Löwy, 'Translator's Introduction to the Writings of Dr Zunz', *Miscellany,* p. 155. See also Pf 710 33.

First settlement of the Jews at Iathrib or Medina & Chaibar n. of Medina, lost in immemorial time: according to one tradition as early as Joshua

[Graetz 5, 68]

The Talmudic doctrine that the Messianic Time would be the seventh Chiliad made much of by the Jews of Spain in their persecutions under the Goths – they writing their antichristian arguments founded on that doctrine

[Graetz 5, 140][1]

/79/

Identical course of religious interpretation founded on documents

Vide Grätz, 5, 200[2]

What culture has won of nature we ought on no account to give up. In the notion of the sacredness of marriage, Christianity has got a culture-conquest of this kind, & of priceless value, although marriage is, properly speaking, unnatural.

Goethe, Letter to Kanzler. v. Müller. Quoted by Matt. Arnold[3]

1 Compare B 150v.

> [A chiliad is a] cycle of a thousand years, counting from the creation of the world; the first six cycles corresponding to the six days of the creation, and the seventh would be the universal sabbath, the reign of the Messiah. (Bella Löwy, 3, 107)

2 On the last page of Graetz 5 is GE's note: 'Course of religious philosophy among Mohammedans'. She marked the passage on Graetz 5, 200 with a marginal line. The Motazalites were a sect of Arabian scholastic rationalists (see GE's notes on Pf 707 12 and 32). 'In order to bring their doctrine into harmony with their religious book [the Koran]', they

> adopted the same method as the Alexandrian–Jewish philosophers of religion had used to reconcile the Bible with Grecian philosophy: they adopted an allegorical interpretation of the text. (Bella Löwy, 3, 150)

3 Quoted by Arnold in 'God and the Bible: A Review of Objections to "Literature and Dogma"', Part III, in the *Contemporary Review* 25 (January 1875): 299. See Pf 711 65.

Judith, wife of Ludwig der Fromme, 9th century

Rhabanus Maurus, Abbot of Fulda at that time, speaks in a letter of the admiration & study given to Josephus & Philo, even more than to the Divine Scriptures. [Graetz 5, 220–1)[1]

Style. 'Another point of the institutional horizon'[2]

/80/

'Der Tod trennt nur auf einige Zeit die Seele vom Leibe. Die Seele umschwebt noch einige Zeit lang ihren Leib und empfindet schmerzlich die Trennung von ihm, wie Jeder von der Zerstörung seines Hauses empfindlich berührt wird. Dieser Schmerz heisse in der Sprache der talmudischen Weisen die Grabesleiden (Chibut-ha-Keber).' Saadia [Graetz 5, 294–5][3]

Mischna – repetition by heart

Mikra – writing [Graetz 5, 178; B 123; Pf 710 27]

Kidouschin, fiançailles [B 123; Pf 710 23]

Nissouin, marriage [B 123; Pf 710 29]

Hagib, Wezier
Katib, secretary of state [4]

1 Marked by a marginal line in GE's copy in DWL. Emperor Louis I ('the Pious') and his wife the Empress Judith were friendly to Judaism; according to Graetz, Rhabanus (or Hrabanus) Maurus stated that the writings of Jewish philosophers were more studied and admired than the writings of the Evangelists. Rhabanus dedicated his commentaries on Judith and Esther to the Empress, comparing her to these heroines.

2 Source not traced.

3 Translation:

> Death only separates the soul from the body for a certain period. The soul still hovers about its body for a time and is painfully aware of the separation from it, just as everyone is affected painfully by the destruction of his house. This pain is called, in the words of the Talmudic sages, the sorrows of the grave.

For other notes on Saadia, see Pf 711 55 and Pf 707 33.

4 The precise source of these Hebrew terms is not known, but may be Graetz 5.

Estates in entail

Pf 711 77, 78

After reading Joshua Williams, *Principles of the Law of Real Property, Intended as a First Book for the Use of Students in Conveyancing*, 7th edition (London: H. Sweet, 1865), in DWL, GE corresponded with Frederic Harrison on 1 January 1875:

> If you are so good as to write to me again after looking through the said lists, will you please tell me whether if A. B. were made legitimate he would as a matter of course inherit the successions or presumptive heirships of C. D. – including even the peerage – or simply the actual family estates? (GEL VI, 105)

On 7 January she wrote again to Harrison, presenting a case which, as Gordon Haight observes, is similar to that of the Mallinger family:[1]

> Pardon my troubling you to give me one more 'response'. I have been looking into Williams on Real Property, but cannot get clear as to the frequency and strict necessity of resettlements of estates in tail. Pray give me a little light on the following case.
>
> Sir A. B. Bart., having resettled the estate (in tail general) on his marriage, has issue, two sons C. and D.
>
> C. remains unmarried till latish in life, while D. marries early and has a son E.
>
> Afterwards, when this son E. is already of age, C. marries and has no other issue than three daughters. What resettlements would probably have taken place? (GEL VI, 110–11)

GE is interested in two related but distinct kinds of family inheritance: estates and titles. Deronda at first seems to be a disinherited, because illegitimate, son. However, death in this narrative brings a disinheritance of a legitimate – in favour of an illegitimate – family. Marriage to Mr Mallinger Grandcourt, 'presumptive heir to the baronetcy', with an additional

1 See also her letters to Harrison from 1 to 18 June 1875 (GEL VI, 147–8 and 149–53). Note that part of GEL VI, 148–9, is to be deleted, according to GEL IX, 355.

'contingency' of becoming 'a baron and peer of this realm', is introduced as a legitimate 'business' prospect:

> and if Mr Mallinger Grandcourt became a baronet or a peer, his wife would share the title – which in addition to his actual fortune was certainly a reason why that wife ... should be thought of ... as a woman sure to be well provided for. (DD ch. 9: 81–2)

The ironies latent in the commentary's indirections, presumptive certainties, and sureties, culminate in the final dialogue between 'the chivalrous Sir Hugo' and Mr Gascoigne, concerning the ultimate terms of Grandcourt's estate. The baronet has to reveal that 'the widow was not so splendidly provided for' and offers this advice on settlements: 'If you marry another niece, though it may be to the Archbishop of Canterbury, bind him down. Your niece can't be married for the first time twice over.' (DD ch. 64: 703–5)

/77/ Suppose an estate in entail general

B only son of A comes of age but does not marry. There is no resettlement of the estate before his father's death. He remains many years unmarried & the next heir is C the son of his brother [*sic*]. When C comes of age would there be a resettlement of the estate?

A has two sons B & C. B the eldest coming of age does not marry; C marries & has a son D. Long after B marries & has four daughters only. D would be the next heir to the estate & title, but if he died without issue & there were no other male in the direct line, the estate would go to the 4 daughters of B.

/78/

A has two sons B & C. B remains unmarried while C marries (Would it be more probable that when B came of age a resettlement of the estates would be made, or might it be deferred till the prospective period of his marriage) & has a son. B coming into possession still unmarried, C is the presumptive heir. Afterwards B marries & has daughters only. What would be the probable resettlement of the estates under these circumstances? And if C died unmarried & there were no other male in the direct line, would the estate go to be divided equally among the four daughters of B? – Would B make a resettlement giving the estate to his daughters?

Heraldry

Pf711 81, 82, 83, 84, 85

The source of the first two notes on Norman and Saxon names has not been traced. According to E. G. Withycombe's *Oxford Dictionary of English Christian Names*, 'Algernon' is Norman-French, meaning 'with whiskers or moustaches':

> William de Percy, companion of William the Conqueror and founder of the Percy family, bore this nickname (most Normans were clean-shaven) ... [As a Christian name Algernon was] commonly used in the Percy family and transmitted by marriage to other families ... It has remained a mainly aristocratic name.[1]

The Mallingers, it is reported in DD ch. 16, 'traced their origin to a certain Hugues le Malingre, who came in with the Conqueror, – and also apparently with a sickly complexion, which had been happily corrected in his descendants' (150). Victorian Algernons might also be happily clean-shaven.

The following notes are from Burke's Peerage.[2] GE's interest in aristocratic heraldry is mixed with a certain sceptical reserve. The marriage of Sir Hugo's younger brother Henleigh to Miss Grandcourt is represented as a form of conquest:

> [Henleigh had] taken her name along with her estates, thus making a junction between two equally old families, impaling the three Saracens' heads proper and three bezants of the one with the tower and falcons *argent* of the other ... (DD ch. 16: 150–1)

Henleigh Mallinger Grandcourt is a product of this marital impaling.

1 (Oxford: Clarendon, 1945), p. 7.

2 Page references supplied within square brackets are to Sir John Bernard Burke, *The General Armory of England, Scotland, Ireland and Wales: Comprising a Registry of Armorial Bearings from the Earliest to the Present Time* (London: Harrison, 1878). The present editor has not seen the earlier edition consulted by GE.

'Maine's Early Institutions' was read from 15 to 26 January 1875 (GHL Diary). GE's copy of Sir Henry James Sumner Maine's *Lectures on the Early History of Institutions* (London: John Murray, 1875) is in DWL.

/81/

Guillaume *algernons* - Will with the whiskers

Gospatrick, Saxon name
Fermor, i.q. Farmer
De la Forterie, de Bouverie

Irish & Hindoo custom: sitting at your debtor's door & starving yourself till he pays. [Maine, p. 40]

The Brehon law could only assert that the unlearned brother who pronounced a false judgment w[oul]d find blotches come on his cheeks, & that the chief who allowed sound usage to be departed from would bring bad weather on his country. Maine [pp. 41–2] [1]

How came the Sclavonians to be bought as slaves? [2]

St. Werburgh[3]

Marrables, Mellent, Arkley [Burke, pp. 660, 677, 24]

1 The Brehons were hereditary judges. According to Maine, the Brehon law - the ancient Irish traditional law which prevailed before the English occupation of Ireland - revealed links between the Hindu and Irish 'races at the eastern and western extremities of the later Aryan world' (pp. 20–1). Maine's *Ancient Law,* read in November 1869, was the source of notes on B 49 to 56.

2 Perhaps GE's query with reference to Maine's comments about 'the enfranchisement of the peasantry' in Sclavonic communities in 'the Russian dominions in Europe' (p. 2).

3 The source of this reference to the seventh-century Mercian royal abbess has not been traced.

/82/

Mottoes:[1] 'Faitz prouverount' ['Deeds will be the proof'] 'Through' 'Cor Immobile' ['Constant heart'] 'Toujours prêt' ['Always ready'] 'Agincourt' 'Per callem collem' ['Eminent through experience'] 'Servate fidem cineri' ['Faith kept to the ashes of my forefathers']
For Vernon: 'Ver non semper viret'
['Spring does not always flourish; or, *Vernon* always flourishes']
Fortescue: 'Forte scutum salus ducum'
['A strong shield is the safety of the commander]

The traditionary origin of 'Lamh dearg Erin', the Red Hand of Ireland, the motto of the O'Neills, is this: – In an ancient expedition of some adventurers to Ireland, their leader declared that whoever first touched the shore should possess the territory which he reached. O'Neil, ancestor of the Princes of Ulster, bent upon obtaining the reward, & seeing another boat likely to land, cut his hand off & threw it upon the coast. [p. xvi]

The earliest heraldic document that has been handed down to us is a Roll of Arms, 1240–1245. It contains the names & arms of the barons & knights of the reign of Henry III. Next, the Siege of Carlaverock, a poem descriptive of the banners of the peers & knights ***/83/*** of the English army at the siege of Carlaverock castle in Scotland, February 1301. The Roll of Arms of Edward II is divided into counties, & comprises the names & arms of about 1160 persons. The Roll of Arms, Edward III, apparently 1337–1350, embraces the arms of all the peers & knights in England.

The earliest writer on Heraldry whose work has reached us is Nicholas Upton, *temp.* Henry V, translated under Henry VI as *The Boke of St. Albans.* Henry V issued a proclamation forbidding heraldic ensigns to all who could not show an original & valid right, except those who had *borne arms at Agincourt.* In the earlier part of 16th century came the *Heralds' Visitations,* documents containing the result of a royal commission of inquiry. They set forth the principal hereditary achievements of the kingdom, & all who can deduce their descent from an ancestor whose enseigns are there acknowledged are entitled to carry those arms by inheritance. Apart from this, the claimant of armorial bearings must ***/84/*** prove his descent from some original grantee, or must

1 Burke, pp. 1126–85. Translations for these family mottoes are supplied within square brackets.

memorialize the Earl Marshal that he may become a grantee himself. This is the English usage. In Ireland Scotland & Wales, it is different. [pp. vi-viii]

Coronets

Ducal: 8 strawberry leaves; 5 visible in Rep[resentatio]n
Marquess: 4 leaves & 4 pearls; 2 pearls 3 leaves [visible]
Earl: 8 points with pearls; 5 visible
Viscount: 6 pearls; 4 visible [pp. xvii-xviii][1]

Helmets

Nobility: steel, 5 bars of gold, profile
Knights & baronets: full-faced steel, vizor thrown back
Esquires: steel, profile, vizor closed [p. xxxiii]

Mantle – in achievements, under the shield

Cap of Maintenance  under crest, formerly a badge of high dignity

[p. xviii][2]

Supporters date from the 14th century. Origin ascribed to the practice at Tournaments of each champion exhibiting his armorial shield on the barriers & pavilions within the lists. Pages & Esquires attended to watch their masters' escutcheons & are said to have assumed the most grotesque fantastic costume – skins of lions & bears. Hence supporters. Several curious **/85/** specimens of these masqueradings may be seen in the illuminated MSS. of Froissart. Brit[ish] Mus[eum] [pp. xviii–xix]

Difference between banner & standard, the latter long & narrow, split at the end. The king's 8 or 9 yds long; duke's, 7; marquess, 6½; earl, 6; viscount 5½; baron 5 &c.

Besides these, guydons (guide hommes) pennons & streamers were used.

[pp. xx–xxi]

=[3]

1 According to Burke, the Viscounts' coronets have 16 pearls with 7 visible, and the Barons' coronets have 6 and 4. GE has conflated the two.

2 GE's sketch of this Cap is copied from p. xxxiv.

3 Quotations from Rabelais' filling the rest of this page have been relocated .

Cambridge 1852

Pf 711 86, 87, 88, 89, 90, 91, 92, 93

The source of these notes on student life at Cambridge is Charles Astor Bristed, *Five Years in an English University,* 2 vols. (New York: Putnam, 1852). GE did not consult the 3rd revised edition, published by Putnam in 1873, for, as the narrator comments, Deronda's undergraduateship at Cambridge 'occurred fifteen years ago', that is, about 1860, 'when the perfection of our university methods was not yet indisputable' (DD ch. 16: 164). GE did not visit Cambridge until February 1868, when many university traditions were under dispute; she had become involved in the founding of Girton College for women.[1] Her notes from Bristed supplement the information and impressions gained during her visits to Cambridge in later years.

In DD ch. 16, Deronda, who has determined 'to try for a mathematical scholarship in the Easter of his second year', fails to win it, having 'relaxed his hold on mathematics' while he was working with Hans Meyrick in classics, to help Meyrick save his chance of gaining 'the much-needed' classical scholarship (164, 166–7). In May 1875 GE consulted Leslie Stephen about a technical problem concerning Cambridge scholarships (GEL VI, 140–1). As Stephen remarks in *George Eliot* (London: Macmillan, 1902), when GE 'sent Deronda to Cambridge' she 'took great care to give an accurate account of the incidents of Cambridge life'. He observes, however, that her account was incomplete:

> In the Cambridge atmosphere of Deronda's days there was, I think, a certain element of rough common sense which might have knocked some of her hero's nonsense out of him. (p. 191)

No doubt the 'moonshine' component of Deronda's character, of which Stephen complains, might have dimmed had GE sent Deronda to join the night climbers of Cambridge. GE's notes from Bristed exclude explorations of the darker aspects of student life.

---

1 See Haight, p. 408, and GEL IV, 399, 401, 425.

Notes on Cambridge 1852 Pf 711 86 87

/86/ *Cambridge 1852* – (Bristed)

Fellow Commoners (young men of fortune & younger sons of noblemen) require 5 or 800 per Annum (1852).[1] Pensioner is the name given to the body of students. [I, 17, 18]

The Fellows, who form the general body from which the college officers are chosen, consist of those 4 or 5 Bachelor Scholars in each year who pass the best examination in Classics, Mathematics & Metaphysics. The 8 oldest Fellows at any time in residence, together with the master, have the government of the college vested in them. [I, 21]

Undergraduates required to keep eight chapels a week: 2 on Sunday & 1 every weekday, morning or evening. Dean, presiding officer in Chapel. Vice Master & Bursar: Lecturers, assistant lecturers & assistant Tutors to the number of 20 (some, however, non-residents, only appearing at examinations) 4 Chaplains & Librarian (Trinity?)[2] [I, 22–3]

Chapel Service, at 7 – ½ hour. At 9, Lectures begin, & continue till 12. For the Freshmen there are 2, classical & mathematical, both which they are required to attend. [I, 20, 23]

/87/

The undergraduate course is 3 years & a third. The students who have completed their 1st year are called Junior Sophs (Sophister) or Second year men; then Senior Sophs or Third year men; & Questionists, or men who are just going out. [I, 24]

It is generally some time before 1 o'clock when the student resorts to his private Tutor – either a Fellow or a Bachelor trying for a Fellow-ship. From 2 to 4, the traditional time for exercise. Dinner at 4. [I, 25]

Bachelors' table next to the Fellows'. Most of them Scholars reading for fellowships & nearly all of them private tutors. Though B.A.'s, they are considered in *statu pupillari* till they are M.A.'s – pay a small sum in fees nominally for tuition & are liable to the authority of the Proctor. [I, 26–7]

1 Deronda has 'a bachelor's income' of 'seven hundred a year' – enough 'to look about with', in Sir Hugo's view, but not to be extravagant (DD ch. 16: 161).

2 Bristed, an American and a graduate of Yale University, was a Fellow Commoner at Trinity College (on an attempted but inadequate budget of £400 per annum).

Foundation Scholars, from whom the future fellows are to be chosen in the proportion of 1 in 3. Their Scholarships are gained by an examination in 2d or 3d year, & entitle them to a pecuniary allowance from the College, & also their commons gratis (these latter subject **/88/** to certain attendance at chapel) – a first choice of rooms & some other privileges. [I, 27]

Chapel 6 p.m. – After chapel the evening reading begins in earnest.
Some students go to their private tutors in the evening. [I, 28]

'Flooring a paper' – answering correctly every question in it
A reading man makes a *spirt* when he crams 12 hours daily before examn. [I, 32]

Entance examn. I Iliad, I Aeneid, easy Greek & Latin prose, Arithmetic, elements of Algebra, 2 Books of Euclid, & Paley's Nat. Theology [I, 15]

Little-go: University Examn in the 2d year, properly *previous* Examn. [I, 13, 33]

Tripos : Any University Examination for honours of Questionists or men who have just taken their B.A. (The University Scholarship Examinations are *not* called Triposes.) [I, 33]

(Tripos or Terrae Filius was originally the name for the author of the Latin verses at the back of the list [of honours]. Hence the list itself was called a Tripos.) [I, 33n]

/89/

Senior wrangler: stands alone – head of 1st class in mathematics. Wranglers, Senior Optimes & Junior Optimes, 1st, 2d & 3d classes of the math. Tripos [I, 34]

Bachelor Scholars, averaging 23 years of age [I, 47]

Examinations: the Freshman has none worth mentioning till the end of his 3d term. [I, 54]

High Steward – represents the University in the House of Lords. The voters in the elections are all the M.A.'s who keep their names on the boards of their respective colleges by paying a small annual sum. [I, 54–5]

Caius = *Keys* College [I, 62][1]

1 The College of Gonville and Caius, pronounced 'keys'.

Chancellor's Medals adjudged for classical proficiency to Bachelors who are at least Senior Optimes or 2d class men in mathematics [I, 84]

The πολλοι – those not candidates for honours [I, 85][1]

The *Easter* is the 3d Collegiate Term, the other two being respectively Michaelmas & Lent. Not more than 22 weeks of real term time in the year. The terms are further divided into **/90/** 2 parts, & after 'division' in the Mich[aelma]s & Lent terms a student who can assign a good plea for absence may go down & take holiday. So, also, a student who is prevented by any accident from coming up at the beginning of either of these terms, may appear just before division, & keep the latter half. The Collegiate year practically ends with the 'division' of the Easter term – the May examn. 'The May' is one of the features that distinguish Cambridge from Oxford: at the latter there are no public College examinations. The Freshman is examined in the Classical authors which have been his lecture-room subjects for the year, & on First year Maths, i.e. Euclid, Algebra & Trigonometry. [I, 86–7]

Number of *Trinity Scholarships* usually vacant at a time from 12 to 20. [I, 118]

The *Little-go* (called at Oxford the *Smalls*) near the end of the Lent term in the student's 2d year. The subjects are partly constant, partly variable. The variable are given **/91/** notice of a year in advance: they are a Greek author, a Latin author, & one of the 4 Gospels; 'author' taken in a limited sense – portion of an author. [I, 126]

Great University Examinations. Math[ematica]l Tripos in January; Class[ica]l in Feb[ruar]y. (Senior Wranglers almost always Johnians) [I, 130]

M.A. degrees conferred at Commencement of Long Vacation – first week in July [I, 152]

The Oxford terms are 4: Mich[aelma]s, Hilary, Easter, & Trinity[2] The two Great University degree Examinations are one at the end of the Mich[aelma]s term, the other at the end of the Easter. The Honour & Poll men all examined together: 5 classes, of which the 5th corresponds to the Cambridge Poll. The examination in mathematics takes place subsequently, being a voluntary after the classical, just as at Cambridge the classical is voluntary after the mathematical. [I, 188, 189]

1 Translation: 'many' or 'mob'; these are the 'Poll men' mentioned on Pf 711 91.

2 See GE's note on dates for the 1872–3 terms at Cambridge and Oxford on Pf 711 1.

('Longs & shorts' is the phrase for Hexameters & Pentameters or Elegiac metre.) [I, 240]

/92/

The M.A. degree can be obtained by any one who has taken a B.A. on paying a certain sum & performing certain trifling ceremonies. [I, 332]

The principal business of a Trinity Bachelor Scholar in residence (no Bachelors except Scholars & Fellow Commoners are allowed to retain their rooms in College beyond the term subsequent to that in which they take their degree) is reading for a Fellowship. [I, 387]

The M.A. *incepts* in about 3 years & two months from the time of taking his first degree, though he does not become a *full* M.A. till July following. 3 years ½ in all. [I, 387]

The average age of taking the B.A. may be set down at 22 & 3 months, so that a Trinity man usually borders on 25 when he attains the dignity of Fellow. The Fellowships are tenable for 7 years from the time of taking **/93/** the M.A. degree to such Fellows as do not go into orders. [I, 390–1]

Cricketing & all games of ball are much practised in the respective seasons. [I, 25]

The Bell scholarships (university) are open to Freshmen who are the sons of clergymen & in moderate circumstances. [I, 85]

The 'Commencement' means the beginning of the Long Vacation. [I, 87]

'May' (Examination) 3d term of Collegian's *first* year. Easter Term [I, 86]

Scholarship Examination [at Trinity] held about the beginning of the Easter term: all 2d & 3d year men eligible candidates [I, 117]

There are five *University Scholarships*, and there are seldom more than one vacant in a year. The examination open to all undergraduates, but the competition chiefly lies among those of the 3d year. (Lent term) [I, 128]

Two Gold Medals (Chancellor's medals) given for classical proficiency to Bachelors who are at least Senior Ops. or 2d class men in mathematics. [I, 133]

Jewish Chronicle

Pf 711 94, 95, 91a

These notes may be dated to January and February 1875. The first reference is to Alexander William Kinglake, *The Invasion of the Crimea: its Origin, and an Account of its Progress down to the Death of Lord Raglan,* Vol. V (Edinburgh: Blackwood, 1875). This volume, *The Battle of Inkerman,* presents an hour-by-hour account of the battle. 'Kinglake: Battle of Inkerman' was read from 27 January to 6 February 1875 (GHL Diary). On 7 February GE wrote to thank John Blackwood for 'the valuable present', which she had 'finished reading aloud to Mr Lewes' on the previous night. She refers to 'the tradition of a Minden yell, the "Men, remember Albuera," and [other] favourite bits' as 'some splendid moments in the story':

> My mind is in this anomalous condition of hating war and loving its discipline, which has been an incalculable contribution to the sentiment of duty. (GEL VI, 122–3)

The tradition of discipline is evident in the 'favourite bits' recorded by GE. The 'inciting apostrophe' uttered by the colonel to the 'Die-hards' of the 57th regiment summons 'the remembrance of that dismal, that valiant command [that] had been cherished in the corps with tenacious affection' (p. 310). And although 'the air was rent by a sound which – unless they be men of the initiated regiment – people speak of as strange and "unearthly"' Kinglake observes that 'it was of course by steady practice in the [20th] regiment that the art and mystery of the 'Minden yell' had been faithfully preserved' (p. 308).

Interrupted by notes from Graetz and Ludwig Geiger on Reuchlin, a sequence of eight brief references to the weekly *Jewish Chronicle* is taken from issues in December, January, and February of 1874–5 (the Jewish year 5635). The reference to Dr Benisch (Pf 711 94) is from a notice in the issue of 1 January for his *Judaism Surveyed; Being a Sketch of the Rise and Development of Judaism from Moses to our Days* (London: Longmans, Green, 1874). According to a review in the same issue,

> The information given in these lectures bridges over many of those gaps in their knowledge of the Jewish people of which persons of average

> education only are generally conscious, and suggests the moral and intellectual value of a deeper understanding of the first principles of Judaism and its later developments. (p. 636)

Abraham Benisch edited the *Jewish Chronicle* from 1854 to 1869 and again from later in 1875 to 1878, the year of his death. GE wrote to him on 16 December 1876, expressing 'heartfelt thanks for [his] kind letter and the copy of the current "Jewish Chronicle"' (GEL VI, 316–17). He may also have supplied these earlier issues (although the editor then was Ludwig Phillipson). A cutting from the *Jewish Chronicle* (9 May 1879) on 'The Late Dr A. Benisch' was attached to the inside front cover of Pf 710 (see the Pf 710 Appendix).

'Anglo-Jewish Sketches, by Picciotto' refers to James Picciotto's introduction, also in the 1 January issue, for his historical articles, previously serialized in the *Jewish Chronicle,* and published in book form by Trübner in 1875. GE's annotated copy of *Sketches of Anglo-Jewish History,* inscribed to 'Mrs Lewes, with N. Trübner's kind regards', is in DWL.[1] For notes from this work, see Pf 711 24 and B 193v. Picciotto's review of *Daniel Deronda,* published in the November 1876 issue of the *Gentleman's Magazine,*[2] presents an alternative or revisionary sequel to Francillon's review in the previous issue; see the headnote to the 'Catena of novelists and gambling' section (Pf 711 38 to 43).

Four brief notes on Pf 711 95, all taken from the issue of 22 January, are quite cryptic when read out of their original context. The first is relevant to Deronda's devotion to the idea of giving 'a national centre' to the Jews, 'such as the English have, though they too are scattered over the face of the globe' (DD ch. 69: 747):

> *Habazaleth* says that there are some large and excellent plots of ground for sale at a very low price, close to the Agricultural School at Jaffa. This opportunity, thinks our contemporary, should be seized by those Jews who are desirous of possessing ground in the holy land of their ancestors. (p. 694)

On the same page, the following item is also reprinted from *Habazaleth,* a journal published in Jerusalem:

1 A revised edition of Picciotto's work, with a prologue, notes and epilogue by Israel Finestein (London: Soncino Press, 1956), is a valuable resource for students of nineteenth-century Anglo-Jewry.

2 Also reprinted in Carroll, pp. 406–17.

> Sad news from Yemen is reported by *Habazaleth*. The Jews there are subject to cruel oppression. They are forbidden from dressing like the other inhabitants of the country. They may only wear black clothes; they must walk bare-footed; they must wear a hideous head-dress, and are not allowed to cut their hair or beards. They are not even permitted to ride when proceeding on a long journey. For the least thing a Jew is beaten and thrown to the ground, and very often seriously injured, and it is he who has to demand pardon from his assailants. We recommend this matter to the attention of the Anglo-Jewish Association. (p. 694)

GE's query, '"Afternoon service with Minyan" (?)', derives from the following anecdote:

> A few days ago ten persons (strangers to each other) were travelling in a railway carriage in Holland, and on its being discovered that all ten were Jews, one of the party proposed to profit by the circumstance by reading the Afternoon Service with minyan. Before, however, the idea could be carried out, the train stopped at a station, at which two of the impromptu congregation had to step out, so that the minyan could not be held. (p. 685)

As GE records in her notes on *minyan* (Pf 711 103–4, translated on Pf 710 27), a quorum of ten adult men is required for the performance of public prayers, whether in morning, afternoon or evening. The anecdote reveals that a community of Jews may be impromptu and may consist of men who are unknown to each other, or not even obviously Jewish. Also on the same page is the announcement of publication of the second volume of Eben Sapher's narrative of his travels:

> Eben Sapher, who is a Pole by birth, was originally engaged by some of his coreligionists at Jerusalem to report upon the social condition and general status of the Jews scattered over the various districts of the Indian Empire and the Australian Colonies ... This volume gives a *resumé* of his personal observations of the condition, habits and usages of the Jews in the different countries which he visited, while the concluding part of his travels is devoted to the consideration of the traditional literature, biblical commentaries and manuscripts in use among them, in regard to which he has made some very interesting and important discoveries. It has been announced that a German and English translation of the original Hebrew will speedily appear. (p. 685)

GE's next note from the *Jewish Chronicle* (Pf 711 91a) is from the issue of 5 February: 'Chukot Hagoyim / Disraeli's Genius of Judaism'. An article called 'The True Aspect of Judaism' includes references to '*Chukot Hagoyim*', or 'customs of the gentiles'. The topic concerns Jewish isolation or assimilation to 'non-Jewish customs'. The author's purpose is to refute the assertion of 'the elder D'Israeli' that 'the "Genius of Judaism" remains immutable'.[1] Under the nom de plume of 'Pam', the author poses and answers the question:

> Who *then* says that Judaism is immutable? I answer ... innovation first took place when Judaism was incrusted with the superstitions of the middle ages. (p. 718)

His argument, that the true genius of Judaism is its ability to change and develop, reflects controversies about orthodox tradition and reform (see B 110–111 and B 123v–129).

Notices for the Moses Montefiore Memorial Fund appeared in several issues of the *Jewish Chronicle.* The urgent wish of Sir Moses that 'the Funds raised should be entirely devoted to the encouragement of those who were anxious to help themselves, & that no part whatever should be applied to alms-giving' reflects Jewish reformers' concern to replace what Gideon calls a demoralizing dependence based on superstition, an outmoded economy where 'the raff and scum' go to Palestine 'to be maintained like able-bodied paupers' (DD ch. 42: 495); see also Pf 711 45–46.

---

1 Isaac D'Israeli (father of Benjamin Disraeli, who was Prime Minister when GE made these notes), *The Genius of Judaism* (London: Edward Moxon, 1833). Nineteenth-century assimilation to 'non-Jewish customs' affected the practice of infant circumcision. GE may have noticed an article in the 15 January issue on a *mohel* of Utrecht who had performed his 500th circumcision in 17 years: 'the number is comparatively large when it is considered that the Jewish community in Utrecht is not a large one' (p. 668). Some twentieth-century readers of *Daniel Deronda,* taking for granted the immutability of this custom, have thought it strange that Deronda did not notice that he was Jewish, and have surmised that GE was ignorant and/or reluctant to write about circumcision, or that Deronda was ignorant and/or unduly imperceptive. In context, however, a more likely conjecture would be that Deronda's mother dictated the non-observance of the practice. Her father had died just after her marriage, and she knew she could 'rule' her husband (DD ch. 51: 589).

/94/

'57th die hard!' – Men, remember Albuera! – vide Kinglake V, 310.
The 'Minden Yell' of the 20th ib. p. 308

'13 Middot der Gnade wie sie Exod. 34, 6, 7, gelehrt wird.'
In den Hagiographen wird die Verzeihung,[1] die Gott gewährt, *Selicha* genannt, und da diess der alleinige Zweck der Gebete jenes Fest-tages ist, so ward die Bezeichnung Selicha-Ordnung bald der üblichere Ausdruck (i.e., instead of Seder Tephilla or order of Prayer).
Selicha from סלח, to pardon [B 190, 194][2]

Dr. Benisch's *Judaism Surveyed* [p. 636]

Anglo-Jewish Sketches, by Picciotto [pp. 637–8]

1 Copying over her pencil transcription, GE wrote *Verzeihung* for *Bezeichnung.*
2 Leopold Zunz, *Die Synagogale Poesie des Mittelalters* (Berlin: J. Springer, 1855), p. 76. GE's copy is in DWL. Translation:

> Thirteen measures of grace or mercy as they are taught in Exodus xxxiv, 6–7.
> In the Hagiographa [the sacred writings or *ketuvim*, the books of the Hebrew Bible not included in the Torah or the Prophets], the forgiveness granted by God is called *Selicha,* and since this is the only purpose of prayer on that Festival [the Day of Atonement], therefore the term 'Selicha-order' soon became the more usual expression.

The passage in Exodus refers to

> The Lord, the Lord God, merciful and gracious, longsuffering, and abundant in goodness and truth,
> Keeping mercy for thousands, forgiving iniquity and transgression and sin ... [but] visiting the iniquity of the fathers upon the children, and upon the children's children, unto the third and to the fourth generation.

GE puts this passage into human terms in DD ch. 42:

> 'It may seem well enough on one side to make so much of our memories and inheritance as you do, Mordecai,' said Gideon; 'but there's another side ... Our people have inherited a good deal of hatred. There's a pretty lot of curses still flying about, and a stiff settled rancour inherited from times of persecution ... There are ugly debts standing on both sides.' (498)

To this, Mordecai replies, 'The Masters have said, an offence against man is worse than an offence against God.' See Pf 707 28.

/95/

In relation to the shutting up of the Jews in ghettos, it is to be remembered that Bishop Rüdiger of Speier granted as a protective regulation to the Jews that they should have their own quarter surrounded with walls which they might fortify & defend. [Graetz 6, 83]

Jewish Chron. Jan. 1875. Large & excellent plots of ground for sale close to the agricultural school at Jaffa [p. 694]

Jews persecuted frightfully in Yemen [p. 694]

'Afternoon service with Minyan' (?) [p. 685]

Eben Sapher's narrative of his travels in Egypt, Arabia, India, Australia – account of condition of Jews Chron. Jan. 1875 [p. 685]

=[1]

/91a/

Chukot Hagoyim
Disraeli's Genius of Judaism [p. 717]

Jewish Chron. Feb. 25. Moses Montefiore Memorial: an undertaking for permanently improving the condition of the Jews in the Holy Land by the promotion of industrial pursuits, the erection of improved dwellings & the acquisition & cultivation of land on a moderate scale. Sir Moses chose this memorial himself, strongly urging that the Funds raised should be entirely devoted to the encouragement of those who were anxious to help themselves, & that no part whatever should be applied to alms-giving.

[pp. 649, etc.][2]

=[3]

1 Notes on Reuchlin (Pf 711 95 to 98) begin here.

2 The 'Feb. 25' date is a mistranscription; this notice appeared in several issues.

3 Subsequent notes on this page are included in the 'Legends of Old Testament characters' section, following the 'Reuchlin' section.

Reuchlin

Pf 711 95, 96, 97, 98

The source of these notes is Ludwig Geiger, *Johann Reuchlin, sein Leben und seine Werke* (Leipzig: Duncker und Humblot, 1871).[1] Johann Reuchlin of Pforzheim (1455–1522) was a German humanist who defended the value of Jewish literature and scholarship during a period of great antagonism towards Jews. His study of Hebrew began in 1492, the year of the expulsion of the Jews from Spain, soon after his meeting with Giovanni Pico, a count of Mirandola and a strong advocate of the study of Hebrew literature by Christian scholars. In 1506 Reuchlin published a Hebrew grammar and dictionary for beginners, *De rudimentis hebraicus*. He defended Hebrew books against confiscation and destruction by arguing that many Jewish books were valuable aids to Christian study: the Old Testament, the Talmud, the Kabbalah, exegetical works such as the commentaries of Rashi, Kimchi, and Ibn Eza, and liturgical works. Only writings which were insulting to Christ, such as the *Toldoth Jesu* and the *Nizachon* (Pf 711 98) were to be burned.[2]

Part of Reuchin's dialogue on the Kabbalah is devoted to a discussion of the precepts of Pythagoras, three of which GE quotes in Latin on Pf 711 97. These gnomic teachings are explicated by 'Philolaus':

> As for what should be our norm for a righteous life, as befits a man, and what the mean between the extremes of excess and deficiency ... the precept runs: 'Do not jump over the balance.' He advises moderation in study and action, but himself says openly, 'Apply the salt,' which relates to our emotions, called 'passions'... In human food [salt] is sprinkled in neither too great nor too little quantity; either extreme, whether over- or

1 Another note from this work is added to B 150:

> The epithet Kabbala first became current in the end of the 12th century. (L. Geiger, Reuchlin) The Cabbalistic literature dates from the 2d half of the Gaonitic epoch (from 780).

2 Reuchlin's *De arte cabbalistica* has been published with a parallel English translation by Martin and Sarah Goodman and introductions by Moshe Idel and G. Lloyd Jones in *On the Art of the Kabbalah* (Lincoln: University of Nebraska Press, 1993). Lloyd Jones (pp. 7–27) is the source of the information summarized above.

> under-salted, is spat out ... The great mass of ordinary and inexperienced people fall so easily into error. It was error of this kind that Pythagoras was anxious to avoid for his disciples: he warned, 'Do not walk in the public way', meaning 'do not follow the errors of the crowd.' (Goodman translation, p. 221)

'Marranus' replies,

> It seems to me that I have emerged from your talk – to which I was in no way deaf or inattentive – a Pythagorean.
>
> Briefly, in passing, you have gone through the whole catalogue of mysteries, apophthegms, allegories, symbols, marks, signs and sacraments of this great man, the first philosopher of all. Now, to commit it all to memory I have made use of Ciceronian devices and rhetorical techniques. Would you like me to prove it? ...
>
> As for individual matters and morality, a scale is a symbol of justice, and salt is moderation; the public way denotes general errors ... (Goodman translation, pp. 225, 227)

/95/

Reuchlin in 1492, when he was nearly 40 years old, began Hebrew, studying under the Emperor's physician Jakob ben Jehiel Loans. [pp. 36–7]

/96/

Again in 1499, in Rome, he found a teacher in the Jew Obadja Sforno, a classically instructed man, physician & philosopher who along with instructing in Hebrew excited his zeal for the Cabbala. [p. 46]

Reuchlin wrote two Latin comedies, the second in imitation of Pathelin which he had seen at Poitiers. In the second, written apparently in '92, he mentions the Zigeuner. [pp. 82, 89]

'Raymond Lully (14th century) hatte sich in das Studium des Geheimwissenschaft der Hebräer versenkt, sie als eine göttliche Wissenschaft betrachtet, als eine wahrhafte Offenbarung, deren Licht der vernünftigen Seele sich zuwendet.' [p. 166][1]

The three Hebrew teachers of Pico di Mirandola were Elia del Medigo (Eliah Cretensis) the Jewish philosopher who taught publicly in Padua & Florence & was once chosen by the Venetian senate as arbitrator in a philosophical contest; /97/ Jehuda or Lev Abarbanel, the author of the Divine Dialogue of Love; & Jochanan Aleman, a Jew who had migrated from Constantinople into Italy. [p. 167][2]

Reuchlin developes the notion of Pico that the doctrine of Pythagoras agrees with the Cabbala – naturally, since Pythagoras was taught by Jews. But Reuchlin rejected the parasitic growths that have almost always clung around the Cabbala: divination, alchymy & astrology. [p. 176]

1 Translation: 'Raymond Lully ... had steeped himself in the study of the occult learning of the Hebrews, and regarded it as a divine science, a true revelation, towards whose light the rational soul turns.' Lully or Ramon Llul (1232–1316), the Neoplatonic philosopher and mystic, was said to be the author of an influential work *De auditu cabbalistico,* which was actually written by an unknown disciple under the influence of Lully and Pico della Mirandola; see Anthony Bonner, translator and editor, *Doctor Illuminatus: A Ramon Llul Reader,* new edition (Princeton: Princeton University Press, 1993), p. 60. Folger 13 115 has GE's earlier note, 'Look for incidents in the life of Raymond Lully'.

2 Copied again in part on Pf 710 15; compare Pf 707 1.

Pythagorean maxims: Stateram ne transilias; salem apponito; per viam publicam ne ambules. [p. 190][1]

'Wieland hat ein schönes Wort über Reuchlin gebraucht: Er sprach (zur Orientalischen Literatur) das Machtwort: 'Stehe auf! Komme herauf Todter!' Der Todte kam wie er war, mit Rabbinischen Grabtüchern umwunden, und sein Haupt mit dem **/98/** Schweisstuch der Cabbalah verhüllet; das zweite Wort war und ist ungleich leichter: Löset ihn auf und lasst ihn gehen! Und das ist das gelobte Verdienst der Folgezeiten Reuchlins gewesen.'

L. Geiger [pp. 195–6][2]

Toldoth Jesu: Jewish book about the story of Xt's Birth [p. 228][3]

Nizachon, a work of the end of the 14th century by Iomtob Lipman.
Nizachon = Sieg i.e. of Judaism. Its object is to go through all the texts of the Bible which have been used as a basis for Xtianity, or have been a ground of ridicule & scorn. [p. 207][4]

Reuchlin b. 1455 d. 1522
He wrote two books on Cabbalistic Philosophy, in dialogue:
De Verbo mirifico & de Arte Cabbalistica [pp. 179, 185]

'Die Reformatoren klagen über den Verfall der Zeiten & sagen den Untergang der Welt voraus; die Humanisten schelten nur die Vergangenheit, schwärmen für die Gegenwart, hoffen auf die Zukunft.'

Johann Reuchlin, von Ludwig Geiger [p. 473][5]

1 'Do not jump over the balance'; 'Apply the salt'; 'Do not walk in the public way' (Goodman translations of Reuchlin on Pythagorean precepts, p. 221).

2 Translation:

Weiland used a splendid saying about Reuchlin: he gave the command (to Oriental Literature): 'Stand up! Arise, o dead thing!' The dead one came as he was, wound about in rabbinical graveclothes, his head shrouded by the sweat-cloth of the Cabbala. The second command was and is a great deal milder: 'Release him and set him free!' And that was the praiseworthy service performed by the ages that came after Reuchlin.

3 For a longer note on *Toldoth Jesu*, see Pf 710 36.

4 This note is copied on Pf 710 29, where *Sieg* is translated by GE as 'victory'.

5 Translation:

The leaders of the reformation deplore the decline of the times and prophesy the end of the world; the humanists only find fault with the past, wax enthusiastic about the present, and look forward to the future.

Legends of Old Testament characters

Pf 711 91a, 92a, 93a

The source of six of these notes is Sabine Baring-Gould, *Legends of Old Testament Characters from the Talmud and Other Sources,* 2 vols. (London: Macmillan, 1871). Three of these are copied again in other notebooks. The sources of other notes on these pages have not been traced.

/91a/

=[1]

'Unkritische Vielwisserei'[2]

Ovid lamenting to his friend Tuticanus the impossibility of bringing him into his verse (because the quantities will not allow it). Ex Pon. Ep. IV, 12[3]

Dispute between two savants

'Purpurei panni'[4]

/92a/

Latin has one word for solemn & recurring.[5]

Jewish school of Gerona (Cabbalistic) [Graetz 7, 77]

1 Notes have been relocated to the '*Jewish Chronicle*' section.
2 Translation: 'indiscriminate collecting of bits of knowledge from everywhere'.
3 The reference is to Ovid's *Ex Ponto Epistola* IV, 12., which GE may have read in *The Metamorphoses ... and minor works of Ovid,* edited and translated by H. T. Riley, 3 vols. (Bohn's Classical Library, 1851–2), I, 464. Her copy is in DWL. Copying over her pencil transcription in ink, GE wrote 'Titicanus'.
4 Translation: 'purple patches'. GE's source may be Bristed, *Five Years in an English University* (see Pf 711 86 to 93). His synopses of variations among Euripides' *Hippolytus* and those of Seneca and Racine include his comment that '[Hippolytus] replies with a beautiful panegyric on rustic felicity, one of those *purpurei panni* which frequently occur in the pseudo-Seneca' (I, 146).
5 The word is *sollemnis.*

'Haut und Haar vertheidigen'[1]

Prof. Chwolson of St Petersburg (Ueber Tammuz &c 1860) quotes from the old Babylonian book called the Agriculture of the Nabathaeans which, he maintains, was written towards the end of the 14th century BC by Qùtami, & was translated into Arabic by a descendant of the ancient Chaldaeans, whose name was Ibn Washiyyah. [Pf 710 32][2]

Some tribes there are even now that regard God as an evil rather than a good – a Being to be destroyed, if possible, but if not to be destroyed, then to be conciliated & bullied.[3]

Balkis, Queen of Sheba, brought two wreaths to Solomon – one real, the other artificial. They were not distinguishable by the eye. But seeing a swarm of bees outside Solomon had the window opened & the bees immediately settled on the wreath made of natural flowers. [Baring-Gould II, 197; B 183v]

The Shield of David is a figure made of two triangles ✡ with the word אגלא & טיר inscribed in the centre & corners. It is said to be a protection against fire. [Baring-Gould II, 176–7; Pf 710 14][4]

1 Translation: 'to defend entirely' – literally 'hide and hair'.

2 The reference is to Daniel Abramovich Chwolson, *Über Tammûz und die Menschenverehung bei den alten Babylonien* (St Petersburg, 1860). Compare the notes on Pf 707 17 and 23 from Ginsburg.

3 In *Silas Marner* the peasantry of Raveloe exhibit 'strange lingering echoes of the old demon-worship', as the narrator observes:

> ... for the rude mind with difficulty associates the ideas of power and benignity. A shadowy conception of power that by much persuasion can be induced from inflicting harm, is the shape most easily taken by the sense of the Invisible in the minds of men who have always been pressed close by primitive wants ... (ch. 1: 53)

4 Compare the notes on Pf 711 53 and Pf 710 34.

/93a/

Belief about Elijah's reappearances the origin of the Legend of the Wandering Jew [Baring-Gould II, 115] [1]

Tendlau's Buch der Sagen u. Legenden jüdischer Vorzeit [Baring-Gould II, 208n][2]

The Book of the Ascension of Isaiah has reached us only in an Ethiopic version which was published along with a translation by Archbishop Laurence, Oxford, 1819 [Baring-Gould II, 210; Pf710 20] [3]

Arabian story of the Death of Solomon

Lest the Djinns should know of his death & leave off building the temple God ordered him to take a staff of a certain tree. Then leaning on this staff & praying Solomon died in the temple, but his soul was taken from him so gently by the Angel of Death that the body remained standing. But an ant ate away the substance of the stick within, till it gave way & Solomon's body fell, & it was evident to the Djinns that he was dead. But meanwhile they had finished building the temple. – Then in order to find out how long Solomon had been dead, an ant was put into a box with a piece of wood, & its eating of this wood was timed. So that by comparison of the quantity with that of the stick, it was known how long before Solomon had been dead. [Baring-Gould II, 205–6] [4]

1 In DD ch. 22, Klesmer indulges in some 'buffoonery' which Mr Bult finds 'rather offensive and Polish'. Gratuitously asserting that his name is Elijah, Klesmer adds, 'I am the Wandering Jew.' (224)

2 Baring-Gould refers to Abraham Moses Tendlau, *Das Buch der Sagen und Legenden jüdischer Vorzeit,* 2nd edition (Stuttgart, 1845).

3 A copy of *Ascensio Isaiae Aethiopice et Latinae,* edited by August Dillmann (Leipzig: Brockhaus, 1877), is bound together with other pamphlets in DWL (16. 8. 6 [7]). Although it is not catalogued as a GHL Library gift, pamphlets bound with it are so catalogued. See also GE's note on '*Falasyan,* Jews of Abyssinia', B 184v.

4 For GE's note on *Jinn,* see Pf710 22.

Nervous mimicry and events of 1865 to 1867

Pf 711 94a, 95a, 96a, 97a

Sir James Paget's 'Nervous Mimicry', first published in *Lancet* 2 (1873), was reprinted in *Clinical Lectures and Essays,* edited by Howard Marsh (London: Longmans, Green, 1875). A presentation copy, inscribed 'G. H. Lewes Esq. / with the Author's kind regards', is in DWL. Sir James attended GE and GHL in their most severe illnesses, including GE's attacks of kidney stone, which recurred at intervals from February 1874 until her death. He examined her on 9 May 1875; on 11 May she wrote to a friend that 'the doctors have decided that there is nothing very grave the matter with me' (GEL VI, 142); 'Paget Clinical Essays' was read on 17 May (GHL Diary).

Paget is careful to distinguish between neuromimesis – the topic of his study – and hysteria. His topic is an 'extreme nervous sensibility', 'hyper-aesthetic or hyperneurotic', which is 'anything but hysteria':

> Nothing can be more mischievous than a belief that mimicry of organic disease is to be found only or chiefly in the silly, selfish girls among whom it is commonly supposed that hysteria is rife or an almost natural state. (pp. 173, 179)

His comments perhaps bear indirectly on the case of Gwendolen, whose 'peculiar sensitiveness' (DD ch. 3: 20), inadvertently displayed in the tableau of Hermione, is recognized and exploited by her sadistic husband.

The list of events in 1865, 1866, and 1867, the years of the action of *Daniel Deronda,* are from *The Annual Register: A Review of Public Events at Home and Abroad* (London: Rivingtons, 1866, 1867, and 1868). Notes on the 'Cattle plague' and 'Jamaica Commission' connect with two topics of conversation in DD ch. 29: 'the talk turned on the rinderpest and Jamaica' (303) – references to 'the cattle-plague of 1865–6 and the rebellion at Morant Bay in Jamaica early in October 1865, ruthlessly put down by Governor Eyre'.[1] 'Commercial panic. May, Overend & Gurney' records a failure like that of 'Grapnell & Co.' whose failure 'for a million' has resulted in the Davilow family's being 'totally ruined' (DD ch. 2: 11).

1 Handley, p. 303n.

Although Gwendolen has 'no notion how her maternal grandfather got the fortune inherited by his two daughters', GE lets the reader know that he was a slave-owner in the West Indies (DD ch. 3: 19 and ch. 29: 304).

/94a/

'Egotism has its keenest life at & about the supposed seat of disease. If the malady be not always uppermost in the thoughts, it seems always in an under-current, rising at every interval between the distractions of work or play.'

Paget, *Nervous Mimicry*

'Few patients with real hip-disease or real spinal disease, for instance, think half so much about their ailments as they do whose nervous systems imitate those diseases. In this egotism they resemble the hypochondriacs: yet ... while the hypochondriacs are in a panic on account of some trivial aching, the neuromimetics will talk of their agonies with calm or smiling faces or with half-closed quivering[1] eyelids; sometimes, even, they seem well-pleased or proud in the immensity of their ailments.' [*Clinical Lectures*, p. 180]

/95a/

Dayanim[2]

Sippree[3]

Luca Signorelli made an anatomical study of the body of his own son. His finest works, the frescoes at Monte Oliveto near Siena, the History of St. Benedict. At Orvieto, *The Last Things* – Antichrist, Resurrection, Judgement & Paradise. He was a pupil of Piero della Francesca, whose chief frescoes are at Arezzo – The Invention of the True Cross.[4]

1 In inking over her pencil transcription, GE altered 'quivering' to 'widening'.

2 *Dayanim* means 'judges'. See GE's note on 'Titles' (Pf 710 36) and the reference to *Dayan* on Pf 707 32.

3 *Sippree* is probably another transliteration of *Zifri*, 'books'; see Pf 711 98a.

4 Sidney Colvin, 'Piero della Francesca' and 'Luca Signorelli' in the *Cornhill Magazine* 31 (February, April, and May 1875): 167–83, 457–66, and 578–96. GE may have read about Signorelli in the May issue and then looked up Colvin's earlier article on Piero della Francesca.

Events of 1865 to 1867 Pf 711 95a 96a 97a

1865

Assassination of Pres. Lincoln April 14, 1875[1]
Cattle disease began to spread in July
Arrest of Fenians, September 14th
2d June, Lord Russell's letter to the Admiralty announcing the termination of the American War
Bill to abolish Tests in connexion with academical degrees brought forward by Mr Goschen, & read a second time, but not proceeded with

/96a/

1866

Cattle plague – bill to prevent its spread. In the last month of 1865 the disease was carrying off from 6 to 8000 a week.
Jamaica Commission – Report delivered Ap. 9
Commission for trial of Fenianism, appointed in the latter part of 1865, still carrying on at the beginning of 1866
Whig Government – had been constructed after the death of Lord Palmerston with Earl Russell at the head, & Gladstone as leader of the Commons
Suspension of the Habeas Corpus twice during the session, in *Ireland* & again later in the year
Government beaten on the question of Parliamentary Reform
Lord Derby formed a new Cabinet
Commercial panic. May, Overend & Gurney
Deficient Harvest
August & September weather unusually wet & stormy
Hyde Park Riots (Reform question). Riots in Hyde Park – July
Cable completed between Europe & America July 27

/97a/

1867

New Reform Bill received the Royal assent August 15
Bad Harvest
Continuance of commercial Depression consequent on Panic in 1866

1 GE's mistranscription for 1865.

Yiddish proverbs from Tendlau and notes from Graetz

Pf 711 97a, 98a, 99, 100, 101, 102, 103, 104

The source of the notes on Yiddish proverbs and idioms is Abraham Moses Tendlau's compendium of Yiddish sayings and stories, *Sprichwörter und Redensarten deutsch-jüdischer Vorzeit. Als Beitrag zur Volks- Sprach- und Sprichwörter- Kunde* (Frankfurt: Heinrich Keller, 1860), which is included in the list of 'Books retained from T[rübner]' on Pf 711 114 and Mrs Ouvry's inventory *(Libraries,* p. 111). Three of the following pages (Pf 711 99, 100, 101) include notes from Graetz. This section fills the last few remaining blank pages in this notebook. The notes and extracts beginning from the back cover had filled the pages beginning from Pf 711 114 to 104, leaving only a little space on the latter page. Many notes from this section are copied again or expanded in Pf 710.

/97a/ Sprichwörter und Redensarten

'In Worten zart, in Werken hart' [p. 6][1]

'He would hang himself for a Kreuzer.' [p. 10][2]

Saul among the prophets! [p. 12][3]

St Never's day [p. 29]

When two Sundays come together [p. 29]

'To thrash straw', 'set fire to a burning house' [p. 31][4]

'Burn candle by daylight' [p. 32]

'No heretic for not believing Mr Nokes' [p. 35]

1 'Gentle in word, harsh in deed'.
2 'A Kreuzer' may be translated as 'a farthing'.
3 The proverb derives from I Samuel x, 10–12.
4 'Thrash straw' is copied again on Folger 14 6.

Die Katze sah einen Topf offen stehen und sagte: 'Da der Topf offen steht, so muss wohl nichts darin seyn!' – 'Nein,' schloss sie wieder, 'es ist was darin, und man hat den Topf eben desshalb offen gelassen damit ich meinen soll, es sei nichts darin.' [p. 38] [1]

/98a/

Zifra, comm[entar]y on Leviticus (das Buch)
Zifri, comm[entaries] on Numbers & Deuteronomy [Pf 710 40]
Mechilta, comm[entar]y on Exodus. Mass, Form, Ordnung [2]

'The thorns as they crackle cry, we too are wood.' [p. 40]

'Polak! Wo is[t] Dein Ohr?' [3] 'The Pole if you ask him where his ear is, puts his right hand over his head to point to his *left* ear.' [p. 48]

'A little pot is soon hot.' [p. 331]

'Nomen fit omen.' [p. 331] [4]

Mendelsohn was fond of sugar. Somebody cited to him the proverb 'Narren essen gern süss!' 'So sagen die Klugen,' answered Mendelsohn, 'that the fools may leave the sugar /sweets/ for them.' [p. 337] [5]

Zertret mir die Würmchen nicht! story v. Sprichwörter, 983 [p. 342–5] [6]

Baal-Schem, Mann des Namens – Beschwörer [p. 361; Pf 710 7] [7]

'*Durch die Finger sehen*' [8]

1 Translation:

The cat saw a pot left open and said, 'Since the pot is open, there is probably nothing in it!' – 'No', she concluded again, 'there is something in it, and someone left the pot open precisely so that I would suppose there was nothing in it.'

2 The note on *Zifra* and *Zifri* is copied incorrectly on Pf 710 40. For other references to *Sifra*, *Sifri*, and *Mechilta*, see B 106 and 143v–144. *Zifra* means 'the book' (in German, 'das Buch'); *Zifri* 'the books', and *Mechilta* 'rules of interpretation'. GE later added the German words meaning 'measure, form, order'.

3 'Polack, where's your ear?'

4 'A name is an omen.'

5 'Fools are fond of eating sweets!'; 'That's what clever people say.'

6 'Don't trample little worms underfoot!' 983 is the number of the story in Tendlau.

7 'Lord of the *name*, conjurer'. Israel ben Eliezer, the Baal Shem Tov, was an eighteenth-century rabbi and the leader of the Hasidic movement; see Pf 710 12.

8 'To see through one's fingers', that is, 'to pretend not to see', 'to turn a blind eye'.

'Hast du gehört, in N. ist ein Jud gehenkt worden?'
'Nun, was wunder? ist der Galge nur für euch gebaut?' [p. 385][1]

/99/

Spinoza 1632–77. Sabbatai Zewi contemp. [Graetz 10, 168–258][2]

Orobio, a contemporary & eyewitness of what he narrates, writes, 'In Spain & Portugal the monasteries & nunneries are full of Jews. Many priests, judges of the Inquisition & Bishops are descended from Jews. Not a few conceal Judaism in their hearts & pretend Christianity from self-interest. Some of these being conscience-bitten, escape when they can. In this city of Amsterdam we have monks, Augustinians, Franciscans, Jesuits, Dominicans, who have thrown off the Catholic idolatry. There are in Spain Bishops & severely devout monks whose parents, brothers or sisters dwell in this & other cities, in order to be able to acknowledge themselves Jews.' [Graetz 10, 173][3]

From 1656 to 1664, when Spinoza was from the age of 24 to 32, he produced the Tractatus Theol. Pol., his first work. [Graetz 10, 178][4]

1 'Have you heard, a Jew has been hanged in N–?' 'So, you're surprised? Is the gallows built only for you?'

2 In GE's copy of Graetz 10, Chapters 7 and 8, both titled 'Spinoza und Sabbataï Zewi' contain many marginal markings. For GE's note on Sabbatai Zewi, see Pf 710 34.

3 Amsterdam was a refuge for Marranos – Jews who after the 1492 expulsion remained in Spain and Portugal, passing as Catholic converts. Marranos who later fled to Amsterdam included Spinoza's parents. Mirah seems to Deronda to be

> a personification of that spirit which impelled men after a long inheritance of professed Catholicism to leave wealth and high place, and risk their lives in flight, that they might join their own people and say, 'I am a Jew'. (DD ch. 32: 347)

Balthasar Orobio de Castro (1620–87), an associate of Spinoza, assumed the first name Isaac after his Marrano parents had been tortured in Spain (c. 1666) and became a bitter opponent of Christianity (Bella Löwy 5, 122, 124). Compare the cryptic note 'Orobio (narrative)' on Pf 710 41.

4 During the five years immediately following his excommunication from the Jewish community in 1656, Baruch Spinoza latinized his name to Benedict and wrote the *Short Treatise on God, on Man, and his Wellbeing.* His *Tractatus theologico-politicus,* published anonymously in 1670, is a defence of freedom of expression for religious thought and belief. GE's note on Sabbatai Zewi (Pf 710 34) includes variations of this note and the following note on Abraham de Herrera's *Porta Coeli.*

Porta Coeli of Abraham de Herrera, a Kabbalistic & quasi-philosophical book that appeared in Amsterdam, 1656, certainly used by Spinoza.
[Graetz 10, 181n]

/100/

To remember – the Marranos in Spain secretly fasting on Iom Kippur[1]

'Der Mittelpunkt der jüngeren Kabbala war die gespannteste Messias-erwartung: Lurja, Vital, ihre Jünger und Nachbeter verkündeten von Neuem: das Himmelreich ist nah.' [Graetz 10, 208][2]

Schulchan Aruch, Lexicon of Talmud [Graetz 10, 58][3]

Das Gebet *Alenu.* v. Schudt [Graetz 10, 303n, 310][4]

Surenhuys translated the Mischna into Latin in Amsterdam, where it was printed 1698–1703. [Graetz 10, 312]

In a poem of Tiedge's, Macht der Gewohnheit, an old peasant whose son has made him a bran new St. Lawrence out of the pear-tree to replace the old image, says, 'How can I pray to a saint that I have known as a pear-tree?' – although he had found no objection to worshipping the old weatherworn one-armed image.[5]

1 GE's note in *The Spanish Gypsy* states that 'multitudes of [Spanish Jews] converted to Christianity at the end of the fourteenth century and beginning of the fifteenth' and defines *Marranos* as

> a term of contempt used for the 'new Christians,' or converted Jews, and their descendents ... Still, many Marranos held the highest secular and ecclesiastical prizes in Spain, and were respected accordingly. (*Poems,* p. 454)

The term, meaning 'swine', was usually applied to forced converts who continued to observe Jewish traditions in secret, thereby becoming vulnerable to the auto-da-fé.

2 Translation: 'At the centre of the later Kabbala was the most intense expectation of the Messiah. [Isaac] Luria, [Chayyim] Vital, their disciples and followers proclaimed once again: the kingdom of heaven is nigh.' GE marked this passage in her copy of Graetz.

3 In her copy of Graetz, GE pencilled in above *Schulchan Aruch,* the German translation, 'bereiteter Tisch' (in English, 'prepared table'); see B 126.

4 For GE's note on the prayer *'Alenu Leschabbeach'*, see Pf 710 2.

5 In Christoph August Tiedge's Force of Habit', the old father, declaring himself to be nothing but a broken ruin, says that he cannot worship a saint who is newer than himself. His question, as translated by GE, ends the poem, which GE may have seen in Tiedge's *Sämmtliche Werke,* 4th edition, 10 vols. in 3 (Leipzig: Renger, 1841), I, 86–9.

Notes from Graetz Pf 711 100 101

Manasseh ben Israel was not a little proud of having married Rahel Soeira, great-granddaughter of Isaac Abravanel, he being firmly persuaded **/101/** that the Abravanels were of the House of David. [Graetz 10, 85]

Uriel da Costa: Selbstbiographie, edited by Jellinek – a translation of Uriel's Exemplar humanae vitae. Gr. V. 10 [132–41; Pf 710 41] [1]

Leon da Modena – ib. [Graetz 10, 141–55; Pf 710 41]

Isaak Lampronti, talmudische Encyclopädie (Hebrew?) [Graetz 10, 144n] [2]

Schudt, Jüdische Merkwürdigkeiten [Graetz 10, 145n] [3]

Frankl's Libanon (again) [Graetz 10, 145n] [4]

Rio, Les quatres martyres
– à propos of the poetess (Venetian-Jewess) Sara Copia Sullam
(another poetess who translated Jewish hymns was Debora Ascarelli)
pub[lishe]d Paris, 1856 [Graetz 10, 146n] [5]

1 Graetz's reference is to Hermann Jellinek, editor, *Uriel Acosta's Leben und Lehre* (Zerbst: Kummer, 1847); in DWL. GE annotated some pages in Uriel da Costa's autobiography, which is subtitled 'Ein Beispiel des menschlichen Lebens' ('an example of human life'). Her marginal comments are 'Breaks the laws'; 'Dissuades converts'; 'Loneliness again'; 'Second penance'; 'Final rancour'; 'Suicide'. When GE copied this reference on Pf 710 41, her use of 'V.' for 'volume' in this note misled her to refer in that note to 'Gr. 5. 10'.

2 Lampronti's Encyclopaedia, first published in 6 vols. (Venice, 1750–1813), was published in a new edition in 10 vols. (Berlin: A. Berliner, 1864–88).

3 Johann Jacob Schudt, *Jüdische Merckwürdigkeiten vorstellende was sich curieuses und denkwürdiges in den neuern Zeiten bei einigen Jahrhunderten mit denen in alle IV Theil der Welt, sonderlich durch Teutschland, zerstreuten Juden zugetragen,* 2 vols. (Frankfurt and Leipzig: S. T. Nocker, 1715–18), is also referred to on Pf 711 100. Schudt's 'Jewish Curiosities' is the work mentioned by Miller in DD ch. 42 as 'a curious old German book ... about the prejudices against the Jews, and the stories used to be told against 'em ... date 1715' (492). GE's copy is in DWL.

4 The reference is to Ludwig August Frankl, *Libanon: Ein Poetisches Familienbuch* (Vienna, 1855 and later editions).

5 Alexis François Rio, *Les Quatre martyrs* (Paris: A. Bray, 1856). GE pencilled an index reference at the back of Graetz 10: 'Jews in Venice, 145'.

The Talmudic laws about usury?[1]

Polygamy, Gershom, 1028 [Graetz 5, 365][2]

Thora, belehrung[3]
Reschaim, wicked
Kahal, Gemeinde [Tendlau, pp. 181, 368, 377][4]

/102/

'If the practice should follow the positions,' was the comment of a thoughtful observer, 'We are not likely *to leave to our successors that freedom we received from our forefathers.'* Green Hist. Eng. p. 466[5]

'Even the damned get rest on Sunday!' [Tendlau, p. 368][6]

1 See B 167v. Deuteronomy xxiii, 19–20, was understood to mean that help to the needy should be given freely without demanding return or interest, (then synonymous with usury); the Talmudic Rabbis held that the borrower did not even owe thanks for the loan. However, both Christians and Jews regarded financial transactions with 'a stranger' as permitting loans 'upon usury'; thus Jews became money-lenders to needy Christians. Amongst Jews, the general principle of the Talmudic tractate on usury was that 'any reward for waiting is forbidden'. See Jacobs, pp. 572–3.

2 Polygamy was forbidden by the Talmudic commentator Gershom ben Jehuda (960–1028).

3 For GE's notes on *Torah* or 'teaching', see B 137–138.

4 *Geeminde*: 'Community'. See the note on 'Minyan', Pf710 27.

5 John Richard Green, *A Short History of the English People* (London: Macmillan, 1874). 'Green's History of England' was read in June, July, and August of 1875 (GHL Diary). In an essay on 'Historic Guidance', not published in her lifetime, GE quotes this passage, substituting 'children' for 'successors' and adds the following comments:

> Pregnant words, those of an observer commenting on the doctrines of James I at the beginning of his reign ... What has been handed down is here regarded as a trust to be preserved intact for the inheritors of our needs.

See Thomas Pinney, editor, 'More Leaves from George Eliot's Notebook', *Huntingdon Library Quarterly* 29 (1966): 372.

6 Tendlau refers to 'die Gottlösen (*reschaim*)', a word copied and translated as 'wicked' on Pf711 101. This note is copied again on Folger 14 6. Compare B 119:

> There are times of rest & solace for the damned in hell – at the times of prayer, on the Sabbath & New Moon. (Fridays?)

'In that day the Lord with his sore & great & strong sword shall punish Leviathan the piercing serpent, even Leviathan that crooked serpent, & he shall slay the dragon that is in the sea.' [Isaiah xxvii, 1]

'Als Gott die Welt erschuf, da schuf er auch zwei gewaltige, langgestreckte und gewundene Meerungeheuer, zwei Leviathane, ein Menschen und ein Weibchen. Aus Besorgnis jedoch, das dieselben sich vermehren und die Welt am Ende zerstören möchten, schlachtete er das Weibchen und salzte dessen Fleisch ein für die Frommen der künftigen Welt, das ihnen einst neben einem in seinen Trauben seit der Schöpfung aufbewahrten Wein als **/103/** paradiesisches Mahl vorgesetzt wird. Das Männchen aber hält noch die Erde umschlungen und wird erst am Ende der Tage in einen Kampfe mit dem eben so ungeheuren Urstier Behemoth – nach Andern mit dem Engel Gabriel – umkommen und dann ebenfalls zum Mahle der Frommen zubereitet werden.' [Tendlau, p. 369; Pf710 25][1]

Dozy, 'die Israeliten zu Mecca' cited by Grätz[2]

Rambam, Maimonides – Rabbi ben Maimoun [Pf710 33][3]

(Kameah, amulet) [Pf710 23]

Selichah	Mechilah	Kapporah	
Vergebung	Verziehung	Versöhnung	[Tendlau, p. 398][4]

1 GE translates this passage on Pf710 25:

> When God created the world he made two powerful enormous & coiling sea-monsters, two leviathans, a male & a female. But lest they should multiply & devour the rest of the living world, he killed the female & salted her flesh for the righteous in the next world to be set before them, with wine which had been in the grape since the creation, as a paradisiac festival. The male however still holds the world in its coils & will not come to an end till its battle with the equally enormous primeval ox Behemoth (or as some say with the angel Gabriel); & then it also will be prepared for the feast of the righteous.

For more on Leviathan, see GE's notes from Eisenmenger (B 119) and the Jewish Liturgy (B 188v and 189v).

2 The untraced citation by Graetz is to Reinhart Pieter Anne Dozy, *Die Israeliten zu Mekka von Davids Zeit bis in's fünfte Jahrhundert unserer Zeitrechnung* (Leipzig: Engelmann, 1864). For a reference to the original Dutch edition, cited by Kuenen, see Pf710 35.

3 For GE's notes on Maimonides, see B 112, 112v, 168, and 193.

4 These are Hebrew and German words for 'pardon, grace, reconciliation'.

Minjen (or Minyan) - Abhaltung des gemeinschaftlichen Abendgebetes mit der erforderlichen Zehn-Zahl, was immer für verdienstlicher gehalten wird als das einzelne Gebet.
Mesuman heisst die nöthige Dreizahl zum öffentlichen Tischgebete.

[Tendlau, p. 393n; Pf710 27][1]

Zur Bildung einer Gemeinde bedurfte es wenigstens zehn Familienväter oder Erwachsene, **/104/** da dieses die zu gewissen Gebeten vorschriftmässig erforderliche *Zahl* von erwachsenen Personen, das sogenannte Minjan ist.

[Tendlau p. 206n; Pf710 27][2]

1 GE translates this passage on Pf710 27:

> *Minjen* or Minyan is the performance of public evening prayer with the requisite presence of ten persons - which is always held more meritorious than private prayer. *Mesuman* is the prayer at table to which the presence of 3 persons is necessary.

A public prayer service at any time of day requires the presence of ten adult men; otherwise, individual prayers are offered. See GE's note, 'Afternoon service with Minyan (?)', Pf711 95, and the headnote for that section.

2 GE paraphrases this passage on Pf710 27:

> Ten is the number of families necessary to the formation of a community or *Kahel* - on the ground of the above-mentioned necessity of ten males for the public prayers.

Extracts, mostly poetical

Pf 711 114, 113, 112, 111, 110, 109, 108, 107, 106, 105, 104

The pagination of this section, in reverse numerical order, reflects GE's practice of beginning a commonplace collection of poetical extracts from the back cover of her portable notebooks. The last page of the notebook, or the first page of this section, Pf 711 114, contains memoranda including a list of 'Books retained from T', that is, Nicholas Trübner, the publisher, scholar, friend of GE and GHL, and source of many of their books. The word 'retained' suggests that he had lent these books to GE 'on approval'. On 27 May 1877, GE returned several books to Trübner:

> I return the precious annotated Hebrew Grammar ... Also the other books you have been so good as to lend me except two, namely: Sola and Raphall's 'Genesis' and Green's 'Hebrew Grammar'. Many thanks for your kind loans. (GEL IX, 193)

GE's copies of the two works mentioned in this letter and all those listed on Pf 711 114, except for Hartmann's *Hebräerin*, are in DWL. All, again except for Hartmann, are sources of many notes in Pf 711 and Pf 710: notebook page references are indicated within square brackets.

The first reference on this page is to *Gesta Romanorum,* subtitled 'or, Entertaining Moral Stories invented by the monks as a fireside recreation, and commonly applied in their discourses from the pulpit: whence the most celebrated of our own poets, and others, from the earliest times, have extracted their plots', and translated 'from the Latin, with preliminary observations and copious notes, by Charles Swan' revised and corrected by Wynnard Hooper (London: George Bell, 1877). GE's copy of this 'new critical edition' is in DWL. Hooper's introduction is not only 'conscientious', as GE observes, but also critical of his predecessor:

> Mr Swan's notes are sometimes erroneous and occasionally pointless .... Notes of the latter class I have sometimes omitted, and those so treated will not, I think, be missed by the reader. (vi)

Hooper's Appendix includes 75 pages (not 35, as GE records) of references to 'parallel stories' in the works of 'most celebrated' poets: Chaucer,

Shakespeare, and others. In reference to the German edition, translated by Hermann Oesterley (Berlin, 1872), Hooper remarks that the library in the British Museum has the first part only:

> ... the authorities apparently not thinking it worth while to obtain the remainder, when it was not spontaneously offered them by the bookseller, perhaps because no one ever asked for the work. The leaves of the first part were not even cut until recently. (vi)

GE's interest in 'parallel stories' is evident in her many references in many notebooks to tales and legends from various cultures. Her note on variations of the William Tell story (Pf 711 111) is from Fiske's *Myths and Mythmakers*, read in September 1873 (see Pf 711 10). A comparable note on Folger 13 82 – 'Legend of Tell; comp Harold Blaatand & Palnatoki: Edgar & Ethelwald, Cambyses & the son of Praixastes' – is from Edward Augustus Freeman's 'Stray Thoughts on Comparative Mythology', read in the *Fortnightly Review* on 2 December 1870 (GEL V, 125).[1]

The excerpts below are from not only those poets who were 'most celebrated' in the 1870s – Shakespeare, Wordsworth, Keats, Tennyson, Browning, Fitzgerald, Keble – but also Joshua Sylvester's translation of *The Divine Weeks and Works of Guillaume de Salluste Sieur du Bartas* (1641). In 1815, Wordsworth had asked,

> Who is there that can now endure to read the 'Creation' of Dubartas? Yet all Europe once resounded with his praise; ... and, when his Poem was translated into our language, the Faery Queen faded before it.[2]

No new edition of his translation of *La Semaine ou Création du monde* (1578) appeared until 1880. GE's source has not been traced.

---

1 Multiple links may be traced between collections of tales such as the *Panchatantra*, *Gesta Romanorum*, and *The Thousand and One Nights;* for an introduction to this topic, see the chapter on 'Oceans of Stories' in Robert Irwin, *The Arabian Nights: A Companion* (London: Allan Lane, Penguin, 1994).

2 'Essay, Supplementary to the Preface to *Poems*' (1815), in *William Wordsworth: The Poems*, edited by John O. Hayden, 2 vols. (New Haven: Yale University Press, 1981), II, 930.

/114/

Gesta Romanorum: a new critical edition of the original text, preceded by a conscientious introduction, & followed by 35 pages of references to parallel stories. *German* edition.

Average yield of wheat per acre in England said by Caird to be 26½ bushels, only in exceptional cases 32; whereas in Jersey, Guernsey & Flanders, 40 is a common yield. (1874)[1]

Books retained from T[rübner]

Tendlau, Sprichwörter u. Redensarten
[Pf 711 97a, 98a, 101–104; Pf 710 7, 25, 27]

Zunz, Synagl Poesie & Ritual [B 164v, 165, 190, 194; Pf 711 94][2]

Sippurim [B 137v; Pf 711 68]

Lexicon: Real-Encyclopädie [Pf 710 2–6, 12, 15, 17–19, 23, 28, 29][3]

Hartmann's Hebräerin, 3 vols[4]

Aus dem inneren Leben der deutschen Juden im Mittelalter
Dr. A. Berliner [B 137, 138][5]

Der Synagogal-Cultus. Dr. Rothschild[6]

1 Reference not traced. Sir James Caird (1816–92), agriculturist and author, who as MP introduced a resolution to provide for the collection of agricultural statistics, wrote books and pamphlets on agricultural production and related social topics (*DNB*).
2 Leopold Zunz, *Die Synagogal Poesie des Mittelalters* (Berlin: Julius Springer, 1855) and volume II: *Der Ritus des synagogalen Gottesdienstes, geschichtlich entwickelt* (Berlin: Julius Springer, 1859). GE's copies, bound in one volume, are in DWL.
3 Jacob Hamburger, *Real-Encyclopädie des Judenthums. Wörterbuch für Gemeinde, Schule und Haus (Strelitz, 1874),* and *Real-Encyclopädie für Bibel und Talmud, Wörterbuch zum Handgebrauch für Bibelfreunde, Theologen, Juristen, Gemeinde- und Schulvorsteher, Lehrer, &c,* Vol. II, *Die Talmudischen Artikel,* parts 1 and 2 (NeuStrelitz, 1874), both in DWL.
4 Anton Theodor Hartmann, *Die Hebräerin am Putztische und als Braut,* 3 vols. (Amsterdam: Kunst- und Industrie Comptoir, 1809–10).
5 Abraham Adolf Berliner, *Aus dem inneren Leben der deutschen Juden im Mittelalter* (Berlin: Julius Benzian, 1871). GE's annotated copy is in DWL.
6 David Rothschild, *Der Synagogal-Cultus in historisch-kritischer Entwickelung populär dargestellt, Vol. I, Die synagogalen Gebete* (Alzey: Joseph Weiss, 1870), in DWL.

Extracts, mostly poetical Pf 711 114 113

To be consulted

Cairnes' Logical Method of Political Economy
'Leading Principles in political economy newly expounded. 1874'[1]

/113/

It is the little rift within the lute
That by & by will make the music mute
And ever widening slowly silence all! *Vivien* [388–90]

'The spires
Pricked with incredible pinnacles into heaven.'
The Holy Grail [422–3][2]

A stream went voiceless by, still deadened more
By reason of his fallen divinity
Spreading a shade. *Hyperion* [I, 11–13][3]

There was a listening fear in her regard
As if calamity had but begun;
As if the vanward clouds of evil days
Had spent their malice, & the sullen rear
Was with its stored thunder labouring up.
['Hyperion', I, 37–41]

1 John Elliott Cairnes, *The Character and Logical Method of Political Economy*, 2nd edition (New York: Harper, 1875), and *Some Leading Principles of Political Economy Newly Expounded* (London: Macmillan, 1874). GE's annotated copy of the latter is in DWL.

2 Alfred Tennyson, 'Merlin and Vivien' and 'The Holy Grail', from *Idylls of the King*, which was read aloud in September 1877 (GHL Diary). 'Idylls of the King' is also listed on Pf 707 84v as read 'Aloud' between June and October 1877. These extracts, however, are probably contemporaneous with the passages from Keats below and the reference to Erinna on Pf 711 112.

3 'Keats's Hyperion & Minor Poems' is included in the list of works 'Read since September [1872]' on Pf 711 11. These extracts were copied about the same time as the lines from 'Isabella; or, the Pot of Basil' on Pf 711 3.

But it is so; & I am smother'd up,
And buried from all god-like exercise
Of influence benign on planets pale,
Of admonitions to the winds & seas,
Of peaceful sway above man's harvesting,
And all those acts which Deity supreme
Doth ease its heart of love in. ['Hyperion', I, 102–12]

'Saturn's voice therefrom
Grew up like organ, that begins anew
Its strain, when other harmonies, stopt short,
Leave the dinn'd air vibrating silverly.'
['Hyperion', II, 125–8]

/112/

'So on our heels a fresh perfection treads,
A power more strong in beauty, born of us
And fated to excel us, as we pass
In glory that old Darkness.' ['Hyperion', II, 212–15][1]

Why should a man desire in any way
To vary from the kindly race of men,
Or pass beyond the goal of ordinance
Where all should pause as is most meet for all?
[Tennyson] *Tithonus* [28–31]

Read rascal in the motions of his back
And scoundrel in the supple sliding knee.
[Tennyson] *Sea-dreams* [163–4]

His saltem accumulem donis, et fungar inani munere (?)[2]

1 This passage is copied again on Pf 708 108 and GE's Blotter (Waley, p. 10).
2 Virgil, *Aeneid,* VI, 885–6. Copied again on Pf 707 79. Translation: 'At least I shall add to the heap these votive offerings, and satisfy myself in making an offering to the void.' Milman quotes this passage in *History of the Jews,* I, xxiv.

Erinna's poem of 'the Spindle' -' Ηλακατη - in which, says O. Müller, she probably expressed the restless & aspiring thoughts which crowded on her youthful mind as she pursued her monotonous work. Erinna died in early youth, when chained by her mother to the spinning wheel.[1]

Paetus & Arria v. Martial I. i. ep. 14[2]

1 Karl Ottfried Müller, *History of the Literature of Ancient Greece* (London: Baldwin and Cradock, 1840), p. 180. GE's copy is in DWL. Müller adds, 'she had as yet known the charm of existence in imagination alone.' In GE's verse epigraph to DD ch. 51, Erinna, the Greek poet of the 4th century BC, sits

> Gazing with a sad surprise
> At surging visions of her destiny -
> To spin the byssus drearily
> In insect-labour, while the throng
> Of gods and men wrought deeds that poets wrought in song. (582)

These are lines 5–12 of 'Erinna', a poem in a notebook now in the Beinecke Rare Book and Manuscript Library (Yale MS Eliot VII, p. 13). The poem is preceded by a more complete quotation from Müller and a transcription of the four extant lines from the original 300 hexameter verses of ' Ηλακατη. See *Poems*, pp. 18, 186–8. The extant verses from Erinna's ' Ηλακατη are included in *Poetae Lyrici Graeci,* edited by Theodorus Bergk (Lipsiae: Reichenbach, 1843). GE's copy of Bergk in DWL, with many pencilled annotations, was 'Read 2nd time Feb. 1873' (her note pencilled in on p. 120). See also Pf 711 11, the list of works 'Read since September [1872]'.

2 In Marcus Valerius Martialis, *Epigrammata,* 2 vols. (London: Valpy, 1823), I, 69–70, this is epigram xiv of Book I, although in other editions it is epigram 13. When Arria's husband was hesitating to kill himself, she stabbed herself with his dagger, to demonstrate to him how to accomplish a noble suicide. Her famous last words - Paete, non dolet - are elaborated in Martial's epigram, which is translated by Peter Howell in his *Commentary on Book One of the Epigrams of Martial* (London: Athlone Press, 1980), as follows:

> While chaste Arria was handing to her Paetus the sword which she had drawn from her own vitals, she said, 'Trust me, the wound which I have made does not hurt, but the wound which you will make, that wound, Paetus, hurts me.' (p. 37; see also pp. 36 and 136–9)

/111/

Earliest mention of William Tell, the Chron. of Melchior Russ, 1482. As the shooting of the apple was supposed to have taken place 1296, the event had slept for 186 years. The charters of Küssenach show that no Gessler ever ruled there. The chroniclers of the XVth. cent. Faber & Hammerlin, who minutely describe the tyrannical acts by which the Duke of Austria goaded the Swiss to rebellion do not once mention Tell's name. In the Zurich chron. of 1479 he is not once alluded to. John of Winterthur, one of the best chroniclers of the Middle Ages, was living at the time of the battle of Morgarten at which his father was present, 1315. He describes with loving minuteness all the incidents of the Swiss revolution, but nowhere says a word of William Tell. The story is substantially found in Saxo Grammaticus, & is told by him of a certain Palnatoki, one of the bodyguard of Harold Bluetooth, 950. It is found besides in England (Will. of Clondeslee), in Norway, Finland, Russia & Persia.[1]

Nor general truths, which are themselves a sort
Of elements & agents, under-powers,
Subordinate helpers of the living mind.
Wordsworth: Prelude [I, 151–3][2]

/110/

'Time, place, & manners do I seek, & these
Are found in plenteous store, but nowhere such
As may be singled out with steady choice;
No little band of yet remembered names
Whom I, in perfect confidence, might hope
To summon back from lonesome banishment
And make them dwellers in the hearts of men
Now living, or to live in future years.' Prelude [I, 158–65]

'How Wallace fought for Scotland; left the name
Of Wallace to be found, like a wild flower
All over his dear country; left the deeds
Of Wallace, like a family of ghosts,

1 John Fiske, *Myths and Mythmakers,* pp. 2–5.
2 GE read the 1850 version of the *Prelude.*

To people the steep rocks & river banks,
Her natural sanctuaries; with a local soul
Of independence & stern liberty. Prelude [I, 214–20]

Come, fill the cup, & in the fire of Spring
The winter garment of Repentance fling:
The Bird of Time has but a little way
To fly – & Lo! the bird is on the wing.[1]

I sometimes think that never blows so red
The Rose as where some buried Caesar bled;
That every Hyacinth the garden wears
Dropt in its lap from some once lovely head. [XVIII]

/109/ While the Rose blows along the River brink,
With old Khayyám the Ruby Vintage drink:
And when the Angel with his darker draught
Draws up to thee – take that, & do not shrink. [XLVIII]

The moving Finger writes, & having writ,
Moves on: nor all thy Piety nor Wit
Shall lure it back to cancel half a line,
Nor all thy tears wash out a word of it. [LI][2]

With Earth's first clay They did the last man's knead,
And then of the last Harvest sow'd the seed:
Yea, the first Morning of Creation wrote
What the last dawn of Reckoning shall read. [LIII]

Oh, Thou, who man of baser Earth didst make,
And who with Eden didst devise the Snake;
For all the Sin wherewith the Face of Man
Is blacken'd, Man's forgiveness give – and take! [LVIII]

1 *Rúbaiyát of Omar Khayyám, the Astronomer Poet of Persia, Translated into English Verse* [by Edward Fitzgerald], 1st edition (London: Bernard Quaritch, 1859), VII. Subsequent stanza numbers are indicated within brackets in the text. For a passage from Fitzgerald's Preface, see Pf 711 42.

2 This stanza is copied again in the Beinecke Notebook, entry 310, and on GE's Blotter (Waley, p. 11).

Alas, that Spring should vanish with the Rose!
That Youth's sweet-scented manuscript should close!
The Nightingale that in the Branches sang,
Ah, whence, & whither flown again, who knows?
Rubáiyát of Omar Khayyám [LXXII]

/108/ When up some woodland dale we catch
The many-twinkling smile of ocean,
Or with pleased eye bewildered watch
His chime of restless motion;
Still as the surging waves retire
They seem to gasp with strong desire,
Such signs of love old Ocean gives
We cannot choose but think he lives. Xtian Year[1]

If, the quiet brooklet leaving
Up the stony vale I wind,
Haply half in fancy grieving,
For the shades I leave behind,
By the dusty wayside drear
Nightingales with joyous cheer
Sing, my sadness to reprove
Gladlier than in cultured grove.

Where the thickest boughs are twining
Of the greenest darkest tree,
There they plunge, the light declining,
All may hear but none may see.
Fearless of the passing hoof
Hardly will they fleet aloof;
So they live in modest ways
Trust entire, & ceaseless praise.[2]

1 John Keble, *The Christian Year: Thoughts in Verse for the Sundays and Holydays throughout the Year* (Oxford, 1827), reprinted in some 109 editions by 1867. This is the second stanza from the verse for the Second Sunday after Trinity. Another excerpt from Keble is copied in the Beinecke Notebook 311.

2 Keble, the last two stanzas from the verse for the First Sunday after Epiphany.

/107/

O gentlemen, the time of life is short;
To spend that shortness basely were too long,
If life did ride upon a dial's point,
Still ending at the arrival of an hour.
Hotspur. Henry IV. [Part I] Act V [ii, 82–5] [1]

For where thou art, there is the world itself,
With every several pleasure in the world;
And where thou art not, desolation.
2 Henry VI. Act 4 [III, ii, 362–4]

I ask, that I might waken reverence,
And bid the cheek be ready with a blush
Modest as morning when she coldly eyes
The youthful Phoebus.
Act I. *Troilus & Cressida* [I, iii, 227–30]

Up & down he paced this London
With no work done & great work undone.
Browning: Waring [26–7]

'Her other charms the describer cannot reckon; but all that I have mentioned, two delicate feet, the work of the protecting & recompensing creator support; & I wondered how they could sustain what was above them.' [2]

1 This passage is the epigraph to DD ch. 12 (110).

2 Edward William Lane, translator, *The Thousand and One Nights, commonly called, in England, The Arabian Nights' Entertainments,* new edition, 3 vols. (London: Charles Knight, 1859), I, 80. This is listed in Mrs Ouvry's inventory (*Libraries*, p. 84). In DD ch. 20, Mab Meyrick exclaims over Mirah's small feet:

> 'Look at the slippers, how beautifully they fit! I declare she is like the Queen Budoor – "two delicate feet, the work of the protecting and all-recompensing Creator, support her; and I wonder how they can sustain what is above them."' (193)

Since Kate Meyrick has already painted Deronda as Prince Camaralzaman (DD ch. 16: 168), readers familiar with Lane's translation of the *Arabian Nights* are encouraged to anticipate their courtship and marriage.

/106/

Songs

Herz, mein Herz (Beethoven)[1]

Wonne der Wehmuth. Beethoven

Trocknet nicht, trocknet nicht,
Thränen der ewigen Liebe!
Getrockneten Auge
Wie öde, wie todt die Welt ihm erschient!
Trocknet nicht, trocknet nicht,
Thränen unglücklicher Liebe!
Trocknet nicht! [2]

Preposterous wits that cannot row at ease
On the smooth channel of our common seas.

Sylvester's *Du Bartas*[3]

O now, forever
Farewell the tranquil mind! farewell content!
Farewell the plumed troop, & the big wars
That make ambition virtue! O farewell!

1 In DD ch. 66, 'Mirah, seated at the piano, was pouring forth "*Herz, mein Herz*".' (720) Goethe's lyric, 'Neue Liebe, neues Leben' ('New Love, New Life'), set to music by Beethoven in Op. 75, Six Songs, begins 'Herz, mein Herz, was soll das geben?' ('Heart! my heart! what means this feeling?').

2 Beethoven's Op. 83, Three Songs, includes the settings of another lyric by Goethe, 'Wonne der Wehmut', or 'The Bliss of Melancholy'. The following translation is from Edgar Alfred Bowring, *The Poems of Goethe* (New York: Hurst, 1853), p. 67:

Never dry, never dry,
Tears that eternal love sheddeth!
How dreary, how dead doth the world still appear,
When only half-dried on the eye is the tear!
Never dry, never dry,
Tears that eternal love sheddeth!

3 These are lines 141–2 of 'The Fourth Day of the First Weeke' in Joshua Sylvester's translation, *The Divine Weeks and Works of Guillaume de Salluste Sieur du Bartas* (1608), edited by Susan Snyder, 2 vols. (Oxford: Clarendon Press, 1979), I, 210.

Farewell the neighing steed, & the shrill trump
The spirit-stirring drum, the ear-piercing fife
The royal banner, & all quality
Pride, pomp & circumstance of glorious war!
[*Othello*, III, iii, 351–8][1]

If it were now to die
'Twere now to be most happy; for I fear
My soul hath her content so absolute
That not another comfort like to this
Succeeds in unknown fate. [*Othello*, II, i, 187–91]

/105/

Had it pleased heaven
To try me with affliction; had he rain'd
All kinds of sores & shames on my bare head;
Steep'd me in poverty to the very lips;
Giv'n to captivity me & my utmost hopes;
I should have found in some place of my soul
A drop of patience: ...
But there where I had garner'd up my heart;
Where either I must live or bear no life;
The fountain from the which my current runs,
Or else dries up; to be discarded thence!
[*Othello*, IV, ii, 48–54 and 58–61]

1 In *On Actors and the Art of Acting* (London: Smith, Elder, 1875), GHL appended a chapter, 'First Impressions of Salvini. 1875', written from 30 May to 6 June 1875 (GHL Diary), which includes dramatic criticism of Tomasso Salvini's Othello:

> This summer I have seen him twice in 'Othello'... The 'farewell the tranquil mind' was not comparable to the deep, manly, and *impersonal* pathos of Kean ... and it seemed to me *over*-acted; the same remark applies to the 'Had it pleased heaven to rain affliction on me'.

Nonetheless, the performances of Salvini reawakened his 'slumbering interest in the stage' and recalled 'the fine raptures of bygone years' (pp. 222, 225, and 5). GE and GHL saw *Othello* on 7 April and again on 19 April, when 'Polly came home in a fever of excitement'. On 26 May she wrote to Alexander Main, 'We have been much interested lately in seeing Salvini, a genuinely great actor, play Othello' (GEL VI, 142, 147).

'Another of his fathom have they none' [*Othello*, I, i, 153][1]

'Defeat thy favour with a usurped beard' [*Othello*, I, iii, 341]

'Happy the eye which saw all these things; but verily, to hear only of them afflicts our soul. Happy the eye that saw our temple, & the joy of our congregation; but, verily, to hear only of them, afflicts our soul. Happy the eye that saw our joy, & the gladness of our soul; but verily, to hear only of it afflicts our soul. Happy the eye that saw the **/104/** fingers, when tuning every kind of song; but verily, to hear only of them afflicts our soul.'

Liturgy for Iom Kippur[2]

Elohenu ve Elohei avothenu

Our God & the God of our fathers – continually recurrent as an independent clause of appeal in the liturgy[3]

1 In 'Mordecai: a Protest against the Critics', first published in *Macmillan's Magazine* in June 1877 and reprinted in *Jewish Ideals and Other Essays* (London: David Nutt, 1896), pp. 61–83, Joseph Jacobs argued that

> the adverse criticism [of] the Mordecai part of 'Daniel Deronda' has been due to lack of sympathy and want of knowledge on the part of the critics, and hence its failure is not (if we must use the word) objective. If a young lady refuses to see the pathos in Othello's fate because she dislikes dark complexions, we blame the young lady, not Shakespeare ... (p. 82)

This implicit reply to Henry James's Pulcheria (see the Introduction, p. xxvi) may reflect an association which had earlier occurred to GE: the Moor's speech, 'Had it pleas'd heaven / To try me with affliction', with its Job-like imagery, is set in the context of Desdemona's definition of herself as 'a Christian' (*Othello* IV, ii, 84).

2 This passage from the Additional Service for the Day of Atonement is taken from *The Festival Prayers, According to the Ritual of the German and Polish Jews,* translated by David Levi, 6 volumes (London: Abrahams and Son, 5620/1859 to 5633/1873), III, 51. For other notes from this source, see the section on 'The Jewish Liturgy' (B 182 to 190). In DD ch. 32, Deronda visits a synagogue – for the service, as it happens, for Yom Kippur. In this chapter the passage excerpted above is introduced by the narrator's comments:

> The whole scene was a coherent strain, its burthen a passionate regret, which, if he had known the liturgy for the Day of Reconciliation, he might have clad in its antithetic burthen: 'Happy the eye ... ' (339).

The sights and sounds of the following 'antithetic burthen' echo the antitheses of this dramatic scene and the thematic content of the musical commentary in this chapter; see the 'Palestrina' section (Pf 707 4 to 9) and the headnote.

3 This phrase recurs, for example in Levi III, 168–93.

'God help thee Ruth! – Such pains she had
That she in half a year was mad
And in a prison housed;
And there, with many a doleful song
Made of wild words, her cup of wrong
She fearfully caroused.' *Wordsworth: Ruth* [194–9]

Upon the margin of that moorish flood
Motionless as a cloud the old man stood,
That heareth not the loud winds when they call;
And moveth altogether if it move at all.
[Resolution & Independence, 74–7]

My former thoughts returned: the fear that kills,
And hope that is unwilling to be fed;
Cold pain & labour, & all fleshly ills;
And mighty Poets in their misery dead.
Resolution & Independence [113–16]

Pforzheimer Notebook 710

Pf 710 1 to 41

Sources

GE's major sources for Pf 710 are introduced here, since the format adopted for the Berg Notebook and the other Pforzheimer notebooks – sections of text with introductory headnotes – is inappropriate for this alphabetically arranged notebook. Her notes are identified by their keywords in bold type, as in the edited transcription of Pf 710.

Duncker

Maximilian Wolfgang Duncker. *Geschichte des Alterthums.* 3rd ed. 4 vols. Berlin: Duncker and Humblot, 1863–76. Volume I, *Aegypter und die Volker Westasiens bis auf die Zeiten des Kyros (550 v. Chr.).*

Duncker is the source of notes on Pf 707 63 and 64, copied again here: **Anna**, **Ashtoreth Karnaim**, **Jubal**, **Kabirim**, **Naama**, and **Tammuz**. These refer to religious cults of the Canaanites, including the cults of Baal and Adonis (or Tammuz), and may therefore be related to Kuenen's argument about the polytheism of the Israelites in Canaan, and in particular to GE's note from Kuenen on **Ashera**. The **Egyptian Chronology** 'adopted by Duncker' on Pf 710 15–16 approximates, but is not exactly equivalent to, that in Chapters 6 and 7. Neither does it conform exactly with the names and dates in the fourth edition of Volume I, published in 1874. It may have been drawn from a secondary source.

Ewald

Georg Heinrich August von Ewald. *Hebräische Sprachlehre für Anfänger.* 2nd ed. Leipzig: Hahn, 1855.

Of the eight Hebrew grammars and lexicons listed on Pf 710 1, this is the only source of a note: '**Q'ri and K'tbi**, spoken and written. Marginal indications of the masorites'. Its cryptic character (further darkened by a mistranscription of *K'tib*) may be clarified by reference to *Ewald's Introductory Hebrew Grammar,* translated by J. Frederick Smith (London: Asher, 1870). The Massoretic 'set of reading signs' or 'so-called *punctuation*' are

> a later addition for establishing the correct reading (Q'rî), and, therefore, carefully distinguished from the ancient text (K'thîb) by means of very fine points and strokes, and was never transferred into the rolls of the synagogues used in public ... Since, therefore, the *Massôra,* or the grammatical doctrine of the schools, could not venture to alter the letters of the text that had been received as sacred, the consonants of the *Q'ri* were written only in the margin, but their points were written in the text where the consonants of the margin should be read. (p. 37)

Compare GE's note on 'Vowel-points' in the section on 'The Hebrew Language' (B 139v, 156v).

After having begun to learn Hebrew with Emanuel Deutsch in 1870 (GEL V, 73), GE continued her studies independently. In July 1876, a month after the completion of *Daniel Deronda,* GHL briefly took up Hebrew lessons with her (GHL Diary and GEL VI, 274, 285). GE continued to study Hebrew from time to time. Between June and October 1877, she read 'Hebrew – Genesis & Grammar' (Pf 707 83v). Her notes on Hebrew vocabulary, vowel-points, and verb forms fill Pf 707 123–117 and three folios of Pf 709; these notes are transcribed in Baker I, 208–14 and Baker IV, 2–6.

Sources for Pforzheimer 710

Graetz

Heinrich (Hirsch) Graetz. *Geschichte der Juden von den ältesten Zeiten bis auf die Gegenwart.* Mixed set of 1st and 2nd ed. 11 vols. Leipzig: Oskar Leiner, 1863–76. In DWL.

GE's much-annotated volumes of Graetz are sources for many pages of notes in the Berg Notebook and Pf 711. Her only reference to Volume II, however, is her note on the **Mesha-Stone**. In GE's copy, the account of the shattering of the stone is marked with her marginal pencil line. Other notes from Graetz in Pf 710 are related to notes in Pf 711. The story of Domitian and the descendents of King David, recounted briefly on Pf 711 24, is retold in **Domitian commands the posterity of David to be slain**, and again in the novel:

> There is a legend told of the Emperor Domitian, that having heard of a Jewish family, of the house of David, whence the ruler of the world was to spring, he sent for its members in alarm, but quickly released them on observing that they had the hands of work-people ...

Deronda objects to the prejudice that a poor workman could not possibly have 'some spiritual force within him that might have a determining effect on a white-handed gentleman' (DD ch. 41: 477).

Notes fitted into the last few empty pages of Pf 711 are linked to notes in Pf 710. Notes on Spinoza and Sabbatai Zewi on Pf 711 99 form part of the **Sabbatai-Zewi** note. References to Uriel da Costa and Leon da Modena on Pf 711 101 recur on Pf 710 41. A mention on Pf 710 41 of 'Orobio (narrative)' refers to the fuller account of Orobio di Castro, another contemporary of Spinoza and eyewitness of Marrano experience in Spain and Portugal (Pf 711 99). The note on **Aruch** enlarges upon the brief mention of 'Schulchan Aruch, Lexicon of the Talmud' on Pf 711 100. The terse reference on the same page of Pf 711 to 'Das Gebet *Alenu*' is expanded in the **Alenu Leschabbeach** note, which tells of the suppression of this prayer by the Prussian Government. Also from Graetz (and mentioned on Pf 711 54) is the reference on Pf 710 41 to Wagenseil. Like Schudt, who is mentioned on Pf 711 100, Wagenseil participated in the acrimonious eighteenth-century controversies between Jews and Christians.

Hamburger, *Bibel*

Jacob Hamburger. *Real-Encyclopädie des Judenthums. Wörterbuch für Gemeinde, Schule und Haus.* Strelitz, 1874. GE's copy, a reprint of *Real-Encyclopädie für Bible und Talmud. Wörterbuch zum Handgebrauch für Bibelfreunde, Theologen, Juristen, Gemeinde- und Schulvorsteher, Lehrer, &c, Vol. I: Die Biblischen Artikel.*(Strelitz: G. Barnewiss, 1870). In DWL.

The first volume of Hamburger's *Real-Encyclopädie*, including articles on biblical topics, is the source of a note on **Angel** deriving from two entries – 'Engel' and 'Klassen und Arten der Engel' – and two shorter notes, **Moon** and **Naara**.

Hamburger, *Talmud*

Jacob Hamburger. *Real-Encyclopädie für Bibel und Talmud ...* Vol. II. *Die Talmudischen Artikel.* Part I (A – Essäer) and Part II (Essäer – Haftarah). (NeuStrelitz, 1874 and 1875). GE's copies of the first two parts are in DWL.

Volume II, 'Articles on the Talmud', was first published in parts. In May 1877 GE wrote with some impatience to Nicholas Trübner, '*When* will another *Lieferung* of Hamburger come out?' (GEL IX, 193). It was not completed until 1892. GE's notes in Pf 710 end with the last entry of the two parts she had received, **Haftara.**

The stories of **Abaji, Abbahu, Armilus,** and **Elisha ben Abuja,** and the notes on **Chassidim, Fable, Great Synagogue,** and **Haftara** are all from the first two sections of Volume II, on the Talmud. Her notes from this work are condensed translations of Hamburger's longer essays, but they are still quite expansive, often extending over more than one page. In this respect they resemble her translations from Steinschneider in the Berg Notebook (B 141 to 150). Even though she could refer to her heavily annotated copy of Hamburger's German original, she prepared her own English version.

Sources for Pforzheimer 710

Kuenen

Abraham Kuenen. *The Religion of Israel to the Fall of the Jewish State.* Translated by Alfred Heath May from the original Dutch edition of 1869–70. 3 vols. London: Williams and Norgate, 1874–5.

'Kuenen's History of Israel' is included in a list on Pf 710 1, along with six other books – by Jost, Bédarride, Geiger, Stern, and Derenbourg – whose titles were taken from Kuenen's 'enumeration of some of the principal works of modern times on the history of Judaism' (III, 326–8). GE had already read Geiger's *Judaism and its History* in English translation. There is no evidence that she read any of the other works recommended by Kuenen. His own history, however, is the source of more than twenty entries in Pf 710. These focus on his discussion of the historical origins and development of the religion of the Israelites, in relation to the religions of their contemporaries. 'Down to the beginning of the Babylonish exile (586 BC)', he argues, 'the religion of Israel was *polytheism*' (I, 223).

GE's first note from Kuenen refers to his distinction between **Ashera,** the tree goddess and consort of Baal, and **Ashtoreth Karnaim,** the moon-goddess (I, 88–92). Kuenen's misspelling of 'Ashteroth-Karnaim' (I, 90–1) seems to be an oversight, since elsewhere he spells the name correctly and states that Ashtaroth is the plural of Ashtoreth. On 3 June 1876, GHL sent to William Blackwood an erratum slip to be inserted in the first edition: '*For* "Ashtaroth" *read* "Ashtoreth"'. The error had occurred in DD ch. 35, where it is surmised that the impromptu conversion 'long ago' of an Abbey choir into stables was made by troopers who took 'a pious satisfaction in insulting the priests of Baal and the images of Ashtoreth, the queen of heaven' (390). The narrator seems here to be rather forcibly yoking together Old Testament conflicts and more recent religious differences between English Protestants and Catholics. To Cromwell's troopers, however, the terms of her comparison might have been familiar. As GE was to comment in 'The Modern Hep! Hep! Hep!', 'the Puritans ... found the Hebrew history closely symbolical of their feelings and purpose'.[1]

But Kuenen's point is precisely that – contrary to the usual reading of the scriptural account – the religious practices of the Israelites were not very different from those of other nations. In I Kings xi, 1–8, Solomon's foreign

1 *Impressions*, p. 142.

wives are said to have 'turned away his heart after other gods', so that 'Solomon went after Ashtoreth the goddess of the Zidonians'. According to Kuenen,

> She does not essentially differ from the 'Queen of heaven', of whose worship the prophet Jeremiah [vii, 18; xliv, 15 seq.] ... informs us that the Israelitish women, with the approval of their husbands, made vows to this goddess ... (I, 91)

GE's note on **Sin**, the moon-god, and other notes concerning planet-worship (**Gad, Kiûn, Saturn**), all derive from Kuenen's long endnote concerning the reminder by the prophet Amos to the Israelites that during the years in the wilderness, the principle deity of their forefathers was the planet Saturn, to whom the seventh day was dedicated (I, 245, 262–7).

Her note on the 'Names of God' in the Book of **Job** is related to the derivation of the name **Eloah** from the root meaning 'Fear'. According to Kuenen, the Book of Job was written 'about the year of [King] Josiah's death' in battle in 608 BCE after his unsuccessful opposition to the Egyptian King Necho (II, 43). The author of Job reflects upon the 'general dejection at Josiah's death ... which seemed to be at variance with Jahveh's justice' (III, 338). In the Book of Job, the name Jahveh is used only once; the god of Israel is named instead El, 'the powerful one', or Eloah: 'its primitive name is "fear," hence "*that* which is feared"'(I, 41).

Kuenen discusses the **Ban or Cherem** as a death-penalty 'originally applied to malefactors and other enemies of Jahveh',[1] a punishment which was a religious act, but distinct from the custom of human sacrifice practised, he writes, among the Israelite tribes in Goshen:

> ... we are not wrong in seeing in Jahveh a severe being, and in maintaining his affinity to the nature-gods, who were considered to be hostile to mankind, and to require propitiation by sacrifices. But ... Jahveh's moral character is brought to light in the *cherem,* for it is applied to those who have transgressed his precepts, or in any way have opposed him. (I, 290–1)

1 In modern Judaism, *cherem* is not the destruction of the malefactor and his property, but excommunication, the most dire penalty imposed by a Kahel, cutting off the accused from contact with fellow Jews. See B 123v and the headnote to B 136.

He connects the history of sacrifice to the origins of the custom of circumcision, which 'was originally a bloody sacrifice to propitiate Jahveh' (I, 238–9).[1]

Kuenen's discussion of Moses in many ways contradicts the customary readings of the scriptural account and the oral tradition. 'The Egyptian origin of Moses' monotheism' forms the context of his quotations from the Book of the Dead (I, 395), which GE copies in her **Papyri** note and again on her Blotter (Waley, p. 9). His account of Moses has much in common with her notes from Deutsch (see Pf 711 44), and is pertinent to her presentation of Deronda as having been prepared, 'as Moses was prepared [by his Egyptian education], to serve [his] people the better' (DD ch. 63: 697). Mordecai's description of Deronda as 'an accomplished Egyptian' (DD ch. 52: 612) is placed between the two parts of the interview in which Deronda meets his mother and discovers that he, like Moses, is a Jew adopted and raised by a Gentile. Mordecai's words reflect a Jewish tradition which is known to some non-Jews through the words of Stephen, the first Christian martyr, who was also a Jew. Stephen retells the story of Moses: 'when he was cast out, Pharoah's daughter took him up ... And Moses was learned in all the wisdom of the Egyptians' (Acts vii, 21–22). GE was familiar with Stephen's reply to his accusers: his calling them 'uncircumcised in heart and ears'; his reminder to his fellow Jews that during the forty years in the wilderness there had been no ritual sacrifice or circumcision; and his equally provocative reminder of Israel's early practice of idol-worship (Acts vii, 51, 42, 43).

This revisionist view of his people's history in some ways adumbrates the nineteenth-century perspective of Kuenen, who examines the evidence that the historical Moses did not decree the abolition of graven images, and that stone-worship was not abolished amongst the Israelites, but exalted, absorbed, and eventually transformed into the image of 'the rock of Israel' (I, 390–95); see GE's notes on **Baitylos, Nehushtan**, and **Stone-worship**. Kuenen compares the much later retroactive attribution to Moses of **Mosaic law** to the predating of the **Psalms** and **Solomon's Song** (I, 273, 373).

His account of 'the priest in Babylonia' who recreated an ahistorical but 'as he thought a truer picture of the past' (II, 157, 173, 245) is recorded in GE's note on the **Book of Origins**. The character of Ezra, the leader of

1 The view of circumcision as 'a barbaric, bloody act' was shared by Abraham Geiger (privately) and other nineteenth-century Reform Jews. See Jacobs, p. 83, and the headnote to the '*Jewish Chronicle*' section (Pf 711 94, 95, 91a).

the return from Babylonia to Jerusalem, is of great interest because of the radical renovations and innovations implicit in the 'restoration' of Zion. Ezra's reforms were based upon 'the *promulgation* and *introduction* of the Mosaic laws' (II, 231). According to the apocryphal fourth book of Ezra, 'he dictated to his assistants the whole of the books of the Old Testament, which had been lost' (II, 232). As Kuenen observes in the passage copied by GE, such a revisionary-minded historian 'certainly possesses the power to reform the future'. Her representation of Ezra Cohen, and in particular his yearning for the transmission of a New Hebrew literature which will blend past and future, incorporates this view of the scriptural Ezra.

In Volume III Kuenen focuses on the numerous connections between Judaism and Parseeism, including the doctrine of angels as messengers and the belief in wicked spirits (III, 37, 39). GE's notes on **Angel** and **Mazzikim**, however, are not drawn from Kuenen. Her excerpts from this volume concern Jewish resistance to alien threats to a distinctly national identity: **Jews in Spain**, **Daniel**, **Hadassah**, **The Jewish community in Rome**, and **Karaites** (III, 95, 111, 151, 166, 304).

The pre-eminence of Kuenen as a source for Pf 710 brings into sharper focus a major topic of this notebook: the historical development of religion as a consequence of international cultural relations. At one extreme is GE's note on the definition of 'strange or foreign worship' as equivalent to 'idolatry' (see **Abodah Zarah**). Contrary to this exclusionary nationalism are her many notes on the development towards intercultural accretion and assimilation of religious concepts – a development which is related to, but not entirely determined by, political dominance. A nineteenth-century instance of this kind of development is linked to Kuenen's earlier publication, *Historisch-kritisch Onderzoek naar het ontstaan en de verzameling van de Boeken des Ouden Verbonds*, 3 vols. (Leiden, 1861–5), listed by GE on Pf 710 1. Sections 1–29 were translated from the Dutch and edited by John William Colenso as *The Pentateuch and Book of Joshua Critically Examined* ... (London: Longman, 1862). According to the *DNB*, 'a state of wild excitement followed' Colenso's publication. GE, however, felt inclined

> ... to be a little impatient at the 'fuss' made about Renan's book, as well as Colenso's doings, by an English public which supposes that these men are finding out new heresies. (GEL IV, 105)

As Bishop of Natal, Colenso had translated Genesis into the Zulu language, and then found that, in response to honest questions from Zulu readers, he could not sincerely affirm that it was 'all true'. Critics in England noted that 'the newly appointed bishop went to convert and was converted himself' and had him canonically deposed. Nevertheless he returned to a warm welcome in his diocese and remained Bishop of Natal until his death in 1883 (*DNB*). GHL's sons called on him in Natal, and Colenso's daughter called at the Priory in 1880 (GEL IX, 158 and VII, 258).

In the context of such unproductive excitement about heresies, the terms of GE's commendation of Kuenen's *The Religion of Israel* may be appreciated: 'Kuenen's "History of Israel" [sic] ... she commended both for its general merit and for its reverential spirit.'[1]

Munk

Salomon Munk. *Mélanges de philosophie juive et arabe.* Paris: A. Franck, 1857.

GE first read *Mélanges de philosophie juive et arabe* in January 1868, when she was writing *The Spanish Gypsy* (GE Journal). In Pf 710 it is the source of a note on **Ibn Gebirol**, who was first identified as Avicebron, the eleventh-century Neoplatonic philosopher and poet, when Munk's research in the Bibliothèque Royale, Paris, was published in 1846. The Hebrew translation and Munk's French translation of extracts of the lost Arabic text of Solomon Ibn Gabirol's philosophical work, *Fons vitae* or 'Source of Life', are included in the *Mélanges.*

Munk's discussion of the scholastic dialecticians called Motecallemin in Arabic and **Medabberim** in Hebrew is also the source of related brief notes in Pf 707. His research into the interconnections and mutual influences between Arabic and Jewish philosopy and theology is also evident in his edition of Maimonides' *Guide for the Perplexed,* the source of notes on B 112 and 112v. GE's understanding of the *Mélanges* is reflected in a comment made by Kalonymos about his friend Daniel Charisi: 'He mingled all sorts of learning; and in that he was like *our Arabic* writers in the golden time' (emphasis added) (DD ch. 60: 672).

1 Wathen Mark Wilks Call, 'George Eliot', *Westminster Review* 60 n. s. (1881): 188. See McCobb, who cites Call, pp. 96–7.

Sources for Pforzheimer 710

Saint-Hilaire

J. Barthélemy Saint-Hilaire. *Le Bouddha et sa religion.* 3rd ed. Paris: Didier, 1866. In DWL.

In DD ch. 46, 'Çakya-Mouni' is said to be one of three men of exemplary greatness – the others are Saint Francis and Oliver Cromwell – whom we might prefer to 'sit up at night to read about', rather than meet them in person (527–8). GE read many books on the Buddha and various forms of his religion. Saint-Hilaire is the source of her note on the meaning of the title **Bouddha** and a summary account of the life of **Sakya-Muni.**

Sprenger

Aloys Sprenger. *Das Leben und die Lehre des Mohammad nach bisher grösstentheils unbenutzten Quellen bearbeitet.* 3 vols. Berlin: G. Parthey, 1861–5. In DWL.

GE's copy of Sprenger's *Mohammad* originally belonged to Deutsch; his signature is on the title page of the first volume. Deutsch's essay 'Islam', reprinted in his *Literary Remains* in 1874, is in part based on his review of Sprenger's work. GE's notes made in April 1874 from 'Islam' include two stories about Mohammed and the etymology of his name (Pf 711 43 and 50). The latter is repeated here in the **Mohammed** note.

Reading Deutsch's reprinted essay may have led GE to take up his copy of Sprenger. Her notes from Sprenger include topics such as the Arabic etymology of the word **Cohen** or **Kohen** and the development of the Muslim idea of **Allah** from that of the pagan Arabs. The influence of **Hanyfs**, a sect of Essene Jews, upon Mohammed's doctrine, is linked to the note on **Çufic writing**, for, according to Sprenger (I, 21) the Sufis were followers of the Essenes. The **Arab saying** about the descendents of Noah's three sons also links Muslim and Jewish tradition.

All of these excerpts are taken from Sprenger I, 245 to 264. In fact, there are no notes from any pages following 264, which is the number pencilled in by GE on the title-page of the first volume of her copy in DWL. She appears to have stopped reading at this page.

Sprenger is also the source of the excerpt about the Arabic etymology and meaning of **Jinn** (I, 221), which may have prompted GE to look up her note on the 'Arabian story of the Death of Solomon' and how he tricked the Djinns into finishing building the temple (Pf 711 93a). GE's acquisition of lore about Djinns makes only a slight appearance in her novel: in DD ch. 38 little Jacob Cohen becomes attached to Mordecai, 'regarding him as an inferior, but liking him none the worse, and taking his helpful cleverness as he might have taken the services of an enslaved Djinn' (443).

GE's note on **Lokman**, the author and collector of fables (I, 101–2), connects with her notes on fables from other sources (B 149 and 184v). Since the Arabian tradition is that Lokman was 'a Jew of the same family with Abraham', but also 'a slave & an Ethiopian', this note may also be linked with those on the Falasyan Jews of Abyssinia (B 184v; see also Pf 711 93a and Pf 710 20).

Pf 711 and Pf 707

Pf 710 includes many notes recopied from Pf 711 and Pf 707. Extracts from Tendlau's *Sprichwörter und Redensarten* (Pf 711 97a, 98a, and 102 to 104) are translated or copied: **Baal Shem**, **Leviathan**, **Mesuman**, and **Minjen** or **Minyan**. Ludwig Geiger's *Reuchlin* (Pf 711 95–98) is the source of notes on **Elia del Medigo**, **Nizachon**, and **Toldoth Jesu**. Two extracts from Baring-Gould's *Legends of Old Testament Characters* (Pf 711 92a and 93a) are sources of notes on the Shield of **David** and **Isaiah.** References to **Babysm** and **Wahabees** are from notes on Pf 711 51 from Bosworth Smith's *Mohammed and Mohammedanism.* Notes from Steinschneider's 'Jüdische Literatur' are recopied from Pf 711 60: **Ordination**, **Rabbi** and **Rab**, and **Titles**. Notes on **Egyptian literature**, **Yalkut Rubeni**, and **Zifra** and **Zifri** are also copied from Pf 711.

Passages from Pf 707 41 to 48 and 63 to 64 are also repeated. Yule's *Book of Ser Marco Polo* is the source of **Bouddha's mystic prayer**, **Babylon**, **Estranghelo**, **Tacwin**, **Uighur**, and **Zu'l Karnain**. Gibbon's *History of the Decline and Fall of the Roman Empire* is the source of notes on **Janizaries**, **Mamluc**, **Timour**, and **Zin-gis**. Notes from Duncker are repeated: **Anna**, **Ashtoreth Karnaim**, **Jubal**, **Kabirim**, **Naama**, and **Tammuz**. **Parness** and **Shekel** are also copied from Pf 707.

Contents

Contents

Pf 710 1

/1/

A Critical Grammar of the Hebrew Language, by Isaac Nordheimer (New York)[1]

Hebräische Sprachlehre für Anfänger von Heinrich Ewald. 1855[2]

Green's Elementary Hebrew Grammar (New York)[3]

Frey's Hebrew Grammar with Dict. & Vocab.[4]

Gibbs' Manual Hebr. & Eng. Lexicon[5]

Döleke's Kleine Hebräische Grammatik (with vocabularies)[6]

Rabbinowicz' Schulgrammatik[7]

d[itt]o. Hebräische Grammatik[8]

'Ceremonies, customs, rites & traditions of the Jews', by Hyam Isaacs, a converted Jew (Exeter)[9]

Oriental Mem [orand] a

1 Isaac Nordheimer, *A Critical Grammar of the Hebrew Language* (New York: Wiley and Putnam, 1842).

2 Georg Heinrich August von Ewald, *Hebräische Sprachlehre für Anfänger*, 2nd edition (Leipzig: Hahn, 1855). Source of a note on Pf 710 32.

3 William Henry Green, *Elementary Hebrew Grammar with Tables, Exercises, and a Vocabulary* (New York: Wiley, 1866). A copy signed 'N. Trübner' is in DWL.

4 Joseph Samuel Frey, *A Hebrew Grammar in the English Language* (London: Gale, Curtis, and Fenner, 1823).

5 Joseph Willard Gibbs, *A Manual Hebrew and English Lexicon including the Biblical Chaldee* (London: J. R. Priestley, 1833). The source of notes on Pf 707 122 and 121.

6 Wilhelm Heinrich Doeleke, *Kleine hebräische Grammatik* (Leipzig: Hahn, 1822).

7 Israel Jehiel Michael Rabbinowicz, *Hebräische Schulgrammatik* (Breslau, 1853).

8 Rabbinowicz, *Hebräische Grammatik* (Grünberg: Levysohn, 1851).

9 This work, published in London by William Buck [1830], is the source of brief notes on Pf 711 55–56 and thirteen pages in the Berg Notebook (B 129v–135v). Isaacs identifies himself on the title page as 'A Converted Jew' and provides his Exeter address in his 'Preface to Christian Readers'.

Abr. Geiger's Gesch. des Judenthums[1]

Haug's Essays (Trübner & Co)[2]

Avesta, translated by C. de Harlez[3]

Kuenen's Religion of Israel[4]

Historisch-kritisch Onderzoek naar het ontstaan en de verzameling van de Boeken des Ouden Verbonds[5]

Renan's Job[6]

Nöldeke, Untersuchungen zur Kritik des Alten Testaments[7]

Jost, Hist. of Israel from Maccabees downwards & Gesch. des Judenthums u. seiner Secten[8]

1 Abraham Geiger, *Das Judenthum und seine Geschichte,* 3 parts (Breslau: H. Skutsch, 1865–71). The English translation of this work by Maurice Mayer, *Judaism and its History* (New York: Thalmessinger and Cohn, 1865), is the source of GE's notes on B 136v, 138v, 139, 150v, 154v, 193v and 194; Pf 711 56 to 60; and Pf 710 39. Trübner was the agent in England for this edition.

2 Martin Haug, *Essays on the Sacred Language, Writings and Religion of the Parsis,* 2nd edition, edited by Edward William West (London: Trübner, 1878). Of the works referred to in Pf 710, this has the latest publication date, but it may have been listed here in advance of its publication by Trübner. It is also listed on Pf 707 1. The first edition, published in Bombay in 1862, is mentioned in GE's 'Quarry for *Felix Holt*' and the Beinecke Notebook; see Weisenfarth, pp. 131 and 216–17.

3 *Avesta: Livre sacré des sectateurs de Zoroastre,* translated and edited by Charles de Harlez, 3 vols. (Paris: Firmin-Didot / Maisonneuve, 1875–7). This title is also listed on Pf 707 1. For a passage from the *Avesta*, see Pf 707 17.

4 Abraham Kuenen, *The Religion of Israel to the Fall of the Jewish State,* translated by Alfred Heath May from the original Dutch edition of 1869–70, 3 vols. (London: Williams and Norgate, 1874–5). Kuenen includes the works by Jost, Bédarride, Geiger, Stern, and Derenbourg, listed below by GE, in an 'enumeration of some of the principal works of modern times on the history of Judaism' (III, 326–8).

5 An earlier work by Kuenen, 3 vols. (Leyden: P. Engels, 1861–5).

6 Ernest Renan, *Le Livre de Job* (Paris: Michel Lévy frères, 1859).

7 Theodor Nöldeke, *Untersuchungen zur Kritik des Alten Testaments* (Kiel: Schwers, 1869).

8 Isaac Marcus Jost, *Geschichte der Israeliten seit der Zeit der Maccabäer,* 10 vols. (Berlin: Schlesinger, 1820–47), listed on Pf 711 21, and *Geschichte des Judenthums und seiner Secten,* 3 vols. (Leipzig: Dorffling, 1857–9), also noted on Pf 711 21 and Folger 13 56.

Bédarride, les Juifs en France, en Italie, et en Espagne. Recherches sur leur état depuis leur dispersion jusqu'à nos jours, sous le rapport de la législation, de la littérature et du commerce. Paris, 1867[1]

A. Geiger, Das Judenthum u. seine Geschichte. 1864 & 5[2]

Stern, Gesch. des Judenthums von Mendelssohn bis auf unsere Zeit[3]

Sayce, Babylonian Literature[4]

Derenbourg, Essai sur l'histoire et la géographie de la Palestine &c. 1867[5]

/2/

עָלֵינוּ לְשַׁבֵּחַ **Alenu Leschabbeach** (pron. by Polish Jews *Olenu*): the prayer so beginning was forbidden by the Prussian Government because there were said to be pronounced in it words meaning, We kneel not & bow not before the hanged Jesus: – whereupon the worshipper spat & moved a little from his place. It was admitted that these words were not printed, but a space was said to be left as an indication where they were to be uttered.

[Graetz 10, 303n; Pf 711 100][6]

Aruch, the lexicon to the Talmud, by Rabbi Nathan ben Jechiel, said, but doubtfully, to have been ruler of the synagogue at Rome in the XIth century (aruch = 'set in order').[7]

1 Jassuda Bédarride, *Les Juifs en France, en Italie et en Espagne,* 3rd edition (Paris: Michel Lévy frères, 1867).

2 A corrected version of the earlier reference to Geiger.

3 Siegmund Stern, *Geschichte des Judenthums von Mendelssohn bis auf die Gegenwart* (Frankfurt am Main: Literarische Anstalt [J. Rutten], 1857).

4 Archibald Henry Sayce, *Babylonian Literature: Lectures Delivered at the Royal Institution* (London: Samuel Bagster, 1877).

5 Joseph Derenbourg, *Essai sur l'histoire et la géographie de la Palestine d'après les Thalmuds et les autres sources rabbiniques* (Paris: L'Imprimerie impériale, 1867).

6 The *Alenu,* a prayer of fervent longing for the coming of the Messianic time, named after its opening words: '*It is our duty* to praise the Lord of all ... ', ends by quoting Zechariah xiv, 9: 'in that day shall there be one Lord, and his name one'. GE's brief note on Pf 711 100, 'Das Gebet *Alenu* ', does not mention the Prussian Government's suppression of the prayer.

7 Source not traced.

Allah. As Jehovah to the Elohim, so, says Sprenger, was Mohammed's Allah to the Allah of the pagan Arabs. At the beginning of his mission, Mohammed did not call God 'Allah' because the name was used by the pagan Arabs of the greatest among their gods. (Also, his first deliverances were in the style of the Kahin or seer, rhymed oracles &c; but later he carefully distinguished himself from that class.) The Çufis who developed Mohammed's idea, fell on the same sort of expression as the Jehovists. 'Wenn du uns fragst, wer Gott ist, so antworten wir: Howa, howa, i.e. *er ist er*.' (Howayya = Ipseität) [1]

[Sprenger I, 253n–254n, 261]

Arab saying – that the children of Shem are prophets, the children of Japhet kings, & the children of Ham, slaves [Sprenger I, 245] [2]

Abaji אביי (my father); also Nachmani נחמני (my consolation): an Amora of the third Babylonian series 280–338: friend & colleague of Raba; in later life president of the school at Pumbadita; of high character, respected among the Gentiles. (The Samaritans restored his lost property without demanding a test.) It was his work, in conjunction with Raba, to give new life to the study of the Talmud by the introduction of a new method. This consisted in choosing certain Halachoth for subtle discussion according to /3/ fixed rules – a procedure known as Havajoth h'Abaji we Raba, a designation which was afterwards extended to the whole Babylonian Talmud. Of his private life it is

1 Translation: '"When you ask us, who God is, we reply thus: Howa, howa, that is, he is that he is." (Howayya = being one's self)'. Compare Exodus iii, 13–14:

> And Moses said unto God, Behold, when I come unto the children of Israel, and shall say unto them, The God of your fathers hath sent me unto you; and they shall say to me, What is his name? what shall I say unto them?
>
> And God said unto Moses, I AM THAT I AM: and he said, Thus shalt thou say unto the children of Israel, I AM hath sent me unto you.

This excerpt from Sprenger is related to GE's note on B 112 from Munk's edition of Maimonides, concerning the Hebrew names of God, and especially the tetragrammatic name (JHWH or Jahveh or Jehovah), as distinct from other names such as Elohim. JHWH is 'a proper name without known etymology': '*Ehye ascher ehye* = I am that I am – it is a name derived from *haya – he was*.' GE's notes from Sprenger outline comparable developments in Islam and Judaism: see also 'Cohen', 'Kohen' and 'Çufic writing' (Pf 710 12, 23).

2 Of the three sons of Noah, Shem was the ancestor of Abram (later Abraham), and Japheth the ancestor of those by whom were 'the isles of the Gentiles divided in their lands'; Ham, 'who saw the nakedness of his father', was cursed by Noah: 'a servant of servants shall he be unto his brethren.' See Genesis ix and x.

told that no wine appeared on his table & that notwithstanding his poverty he accepted no presents except those which fell to him as an Aaronid. His courtesy is extolled as shown even to heathens. He insisted strongly on the learning of some industry together with the study of the law. There is much mysticism - on angels, spirits, &c - in his teaching, yet he is not fairly characterized as a friend of popular superstitions; e.g. when another preacher lauded a man who experienced miracles, Abaji replied, 'What a poor creature must [he] be for whom the laws of nature must be changed!' He denied the possibility of miracles in his own time. He was reproached with refusing to hear the Agadic doctrine of bodily rewards in a future life. With Raba he opposed the interpretation of dreams, & ridiculed a man who interpreted them according to desire in proportion to the price paid. He was in deep poverty & became so feeble in body that he was often unable to utter the priestly blessing in the synagogue, & died when he was scarcely sixty. It was said of him after his death, 'Abaji was a man in whom doctrine went with well-doing.' But he was eclipsed as a subtle expositor by his friend Raba. He sought for the rational ground of the law, & when he failed to find this said: 'I teach the tradition, the ground of it I know not.' He venerated his predecessors & the early teachers greatly; on the other hand, the actual customs & maxims of his people were a sacred book to him. He said: 'The heart, the understanding of our early fathers, was as the great gate of the Temple; that of the later, was as the inner door; but ours is as a chink where a nail will hardly pass.' But also he said, in doubtful cases: 'See what the people practise and think in the matter.' Of his memorable sayings **/4/** one is, 'The world, as bad as it may be, has always the number of just men necessary to the existence of society': another, 'Where there is already a leader, seek not thou to be a leader thyself.' [Hamburger, *Talmud,* pp. 1–4]

Abbahu אבהו, an Amora of Palestine, the friend & colleague of R. Ami & R. Assi, 279–320. He united Greek with Jewish culture, had a fine majestic person, lived in Caesarea, & was much respected by the proconsul there. His occupation was the making of women's veils, he had some wealth & allowed his daughter to be taught Greek. He was early ordained but out of consideration for a poor doctor of the law gave up in his favour the office of president of the school to which he had been chosen. He gave his lectures in the synagogue at Caesarea, but he also visited the south, Bosra, & Alexandria. He disputed much with the Xtians (Minin) & was formidable to them in argument. They are reported to have attempted his life, & it appears that a Jewish-Christian physician attempted to poison him.

Yet there was mutual regard, & in consideration for the Jewish Christians he ordered that the words uttered after the Shema – 'Praised be the glory of his Kingdom for ever & ever' – should be uttered aloud instead of silently, that the Christians might not imagine some blasphemy about the Trinity to follow on the confession of the Unity.[1] When he became a member of the college of judges he introduced several reforms, as that the Meturgeman should not be less than 50 & of good character.[2] He is the Rabbi who preaching with another in the same town – he Agada, the other Halacha – consoled the mortification of his colleague at having fewer hearers while Abbahu had many, by comparing his own Agadistic teaching to a basket of cheap trumpery which everybody could buy, whereas his friend's resembled jewels of high price that get few purchasers. In the traditions concerning him there are many historic indications of the time.

[Hamburger, *Talmud*, pp. 4–8][3]

/5/

The **Achaemenidae** include Cyrus, who died 529; his son Cambyses, d. 522; then (after the interruption of the false Smerdis) Darius, the son of Hystaspes, to whom belongs the inscription at Behistun & who began to reign 521, made an expedition against the Scythians, then into Greece & died 485; Xerxes I, 485–465; Artaxerxes Longimanus, d. 464; Darius Nothus (or Ochus), d. 405; Artaxerxes II (Mnemon), d. 359; Artaxerxes Ochus, d. 338; Arses, d. 336; & Darius Codomannus, d. 330.[4]

1 For GE's notes on the Shema, the confession of the divine unity, see B 110 and 133v. Abbahu's concern that Christians might imagine some anti-Trinitarian blasphemy may be compared to the Prussian suppression, fourteen centuries later, of the 'Alenu' prayer (Pf 710 2).

2 The Meturgeman is the interpreter employed in the Palestinian synagogues to translate the Scripture readings orally from the Hebrew into the Aramaic vernacular; see B 140.

3 For GE's notes on the twofold strand in rabbinic literature, Agada and Halacha, see B 107, 108, 142v, 144v, and 149.

4 William Smith, editor, *Dictionary of Greek and Roman Biography and Mythology*, III, 1401–2 and I, 940–2. For a note on the cunieform inscription of Darius at Behistun, see Pf 711 74.

Angel מלאך = maleach, messenger
Ophanim, wheel-angels
Seraphim,+ fire-angels
+Said now to come from a root meaning Serpent[1]
Chajoth, Thier-engel[2]
Biblical special names: Michael, Gabriel, Raphael, Uriel
Apocrypha: Jeremiel, Salathiel
Talmud: Metatron, Jephephia, Sandalphon, Sagsagel, Achatriel, Sariel, Acharsiel, Samael (Archangel of Egypt)
Ridia, angel of hail; Jurkami, of fire; Duma, of food;
Nakid, of poverty; Nabil, of dreams

[Hamburger, *Bibel,* pp. 305–7 and 649–51][3]

Abodah Zarah, strange or foreign worship = idolatry[4]

/6/

Armilus, the name of the Anti- or Pseudo Messiah, who in the later Jewish legend is the enemy of the Jewish people, their power & doctrine. The word is either derived from the Greek ἐρημέλαος, or is an imitation of Romulus, as representative of the Roman power, the arch enemy of the Jews.

[Hamburger, *Talmud,* p. 72][5]

Ahal, אֹהֶל tent – used in the signification of family, people – & poet. stock[6]

Anna, die *Anmuthige* [Duncker I, 357; Pf 707 63][7]

Ashtoreth Karnaim, the horned Ashtoreth (moon-goddess) [Duncker I, 352; Pf 707 63] [Kuenen I, 91]

1 In *Imagining Characters: Six Conversations about Women Writers,* edited by Rebecca Swift (London: Chatto and Windus, 1995), A. S. Byatt and Ignês Sodré discuss Gwendolen Harleth in her *'ensemble du serpent'* (DD ch. 1: 8). Byatt refers to 'Lilith, the first wife of Adam in the Garden, and other daemons. These were serpent beings, serpent angels, in Hebrew mythology' (p. 86). For GE's notes on Lilith, see B 118v, 119v, and 121.
2 Translation: 'beast-angel'.
3 For notes on angels from Eisenmenger, see B 118 and 118v.
4 Source not traced. Hamburger, *Talmud,* p. 14, has the spelling 'Aboda Sara'.
5 Compare notes on B 149v and Pf 711 60.
6 Source not traced. 'Ahal' occurs in Job xxxi, 31: 'the men of my tabernacle'.
7 Translation: 'the graceful one'.

Ashera. Whenever this word occurs in the O.T. the A.V. has *grove*, i.e. holy wood dedicated to false gods. That the word is here & there the proper name of a goddess is shown by Judges iii, 7 where the Asheras stand next to the Baalim, the images of the goddess next to those of the god; 1 Kings xviii, 19, where besides the 450 prophets of Baal, 400 prophets of Ashera appear; 2 Kings xxi, 7, comp. xxiii, 6, where Manasseh makes a graven image of Ashera & places it in the temple of Jahveh. But *ashera* is used not only as a proper name; it also indicates a holy object, a tree or tree-stem driven into the ground. 2 Kings xxi, 3, 7, the same object is obviously first called *ashera* & then 'the image of Ashera'. If this name be interpreted as 'the fortunate one' or 'bringer of good fortune', or as 'companion' or 'consort' (of Baal), then the proper name of the goddess has actually been transferred to her symbol. But if translated 'the upright one', then it must be held that *ashera* was originally the name of the tree-stem, & that this name of the symbol was afterwards given to the goddess herself. She is not, K. maintains, to be identified with Ashtoreth, the moon-goddess, but does not differ from the Babylonian Mylitta, or from Baaltis who was worshipped at Byblos. (*Kedesha* denotes priestess of Ashera.)

[Kuenen I, 88–92]

/7/

Babysm, religious movement going on in Persia.[1]
V. Gobineau, Les religions & la philosophie dans l'Asie centrale

[Bosworth Smith, p. 241; Pf 711 51][2]

(Also an essay by Franck)[3]

Baal-Shem, Lord of the name, conjurer [Tendlau, p. 361; Pf 711 98a][4]

1 An abbreviated version of a note on Pf 711 51, which adds: '– ecstatic martyrdoms & prodigality of tortures submitted to amidst songs of triumph by women & children'.

2 Bosworth Smith refers to Joseph Arthur de Gobineau, *Les Religions et les philosophies dans l'Asie centrale* (Paris: Didier, 1865). There is no evidence that GE read Gobineau, the author of an argument for Aryan superiority. He sent a letter to GHL almost a year after his death; see GEL VII, 217.

3 Adolphe Franck, *Philosophie et religion,* 2nd edition (Paris: Didier, 1869), chapter 6, 'Une Nouvelle Religion en Perse', pp. 282–340. GE's copy in DWL. 'Franck on le Babisme' was read on 14 July 1876 (GHL Diary). Franck also refers to Gobineau.

4 Israel ben Eliezer, an eighteenth-century rabbi, itinerant preacher, and faith-healer, whose followers were the revivalist Hasidim or 'Chassidim' (see Pf 710 12), was called the Baal Shem Tov.

Bouddha's mystic prayer: Om mani padme houm
= O, the perfection or jewel in the lotus; Amen [Yule II, 560; Pf 707 42]

Babylon: Cairo was commonly so called – Bambellonia d'Egitto, in the middle ages. Babylon of Egypt is mentioned by Diodorus, Strabo, & Ptolemy. [Yule I, 24; Pf 707 43]

Babylonian Empire, first Chaldaean or, was overthrown by Arabs about 1500 BC. Remains partly explored, consisting mainly of tombs, but also of temples, built of sun-dried brick at Mugheir (Ur), Warka (Erech), Niffer (Nipur) & Senkereh (Ellasar). The *Assyrian* Empire probably arose into independence on the subjugation of the old Chaldaean by the Arabs. It finally included Babylonia, embracing the whole of Mesopotamia. At Kileh-Shergat (the ancient Asshur) about 60 miles south of Nineveh, has been found a cylinder showing the earliest historical record yet recovered in Mesopotamia: Tiglath-Pileser I (the Tiger Lord of Assur) celebrates the deeds of his four predecessors. His reign appears to be fixed at the end of the XIIth cent. BC. His son was Asshur-bani-pal I (the Sardanapalus of the Greeks, but not agreeing with the legend of his fate) the greatest conqueror of the upper Assyrian dynasty, & the first known of the Assyrian Kings who left behind him great buildings. He erected the north-west palace of Nimroud, also temples at Colneh & Nineveh. From Nimroud was brought the black obelisk of Shalmanubar or Shalmaneser, the son of Sardanapalus: it has 210 lines of clear writing, recording a series of victories of this king's reign, & presents incidentally the political state of western Asia at the **/8/** beginning of the IXth cent. BC. *Iva-lush,* identified with the biblical *Pul,* is the husband of the more historical Semiramis, as distinguished from the mythical Semiramis (Shem-ram, high name), the wife of Ninus, founder of Nineveh. The Lower Assyrian dynasty begins with *Tiglath-Pileser* II, who figures in Jewish history as the conqueror of Syria & the carrier of some of the eastern & northern Israelites into captivity, BC 740.[1] *Sargon,* 721, built the palace of which the ruins have been found at *Khorsabad* (the choicest remains are in the Louvre). There is a statue of Sargon at Idalium in Cyprus, & the earliest specimen of transparent Assyrian glass bears his name. *Sennacherib,* son of Sargon 702–680, built the palace of which the ruins are found at *Koyunjik.*

1 See I Chronicles v, 26:

> And the God of Israel stirred up the spirit of Pul king of Assyria, and the spirit of Tilgath-pilneser [*sic*] king of Assyria, and he carried them away, even the Reubenites, and the Gadites, and the half tribe of Manasseh ...

A second palace built by him is buried under the mound called Nebbi-Yunus or the Prophet Jonah. *Esar-haddon,* son of Sennacherib, BC 680, the Asshur-abb-iddina of the inscriptions, was also a great builder. Asshur-bani-pal II, son of Esar-haddon, is supposed to have reigned 660–640. His successor, Asshur-emit-ili, is only known as the builder of a palace at Nimrud, the comparative meanness of which is a sign of the monarchy's degradation. Berosus is said to have named Saracus as the king under whom Nineveh was destroyed – who sent Nabopolassar as commander to Babylon, & Nabopolassar rebelling formed an alliance with the Medes, the united armies of the Medes, Chaldaeans & Babylonians marched against Nineveh, & Saracus, after a brief defence, retired to his palace & set fire to it. The era of Nabopolassar, 747, marks the revival of Babylon. Nabopolassar received as his share after the destruction of Nineveh, **/9/** the undisputed possession of Babylonia, 625. Nineveh fell to the share of the Mede who pushed his conquests in Asia Minor; but the region west of the Euphrates as far as Egypt lay open to Babylonian ambition. Nebuchadnezzar, son of Nabopolassar, conquered Pharaoh Necho & took Jerusalem, 605–4.[1]

Babylon, the ruins of: consist of a number of mounds near the Arab village of Hillah; some of enormous size scattered over a vast surface on both sides the river. Three mounds on the left side are Babil, the Kasr (or Castle) & that marked by the tomb of Amram-ibn-'Alb. On the right bank is the Birs Nimroud. Inscriptions found here are supposed to identify it with the temple of Belus, built by Nebuchadnezzar. One great difference between Nineveh & Babylon is that while the former was built almost entirely of crude brick, the latter shows vast masses of burnt brick, cemented by mineral bitumen. Most of the great works ascribed by tradition to Belus & Semiramis, to whom Herodotus adds a Nitocris, are proved by the authority of Berosus & the chroniclers, together with newly discovered inscriptions to have been for the most part executed by Nebuchadnezzar. His name only, occurs on the bricks. Among the ruins at Borsippa (Birs Nimroud) has been discovered a dedicatory inscription thus deciphered by Oppert: a former King built it (they reckon 42 ages), but he did not complete its head. Since a remote time, people had abandoned it without order expressing their words &c. Nimroud is 20 miles south of Nineveh. It is covered with the remains of Calah, a city

1 The sources of this and the next note have not been traced. The contents are similar to articles by George Rawlinson on 'Assyria', 'Babel, Babylon', and 'Present State of the Ruins' in Smith's *Dictionary of the Bible,* I, 129 and 148–58.

which must have rivalled Nineveh. The site of Nineveh is a large enclosure covered with low mounds, surrounded by the ruins of a magnificent wall, 8 miles in circuit, broken on the W. side by the great mounds of Kouyunjik & Nebbi Yunus.

/10/

Bouddha signifies the wise, the enlightened or the awakened, from the root *boudh,* to know. Tathagata, another title of Sakya-Mouni, means: 'he who walks in the paths of his predecessors, the former Bouddhas'.

[Saint-Hilaire, pp. 73–4]

v. Sakya[1]

/11/

Baitylos, name employed by the ancients to designate sacred stones

[Kuenen I, 393]

(Beth-el?)[2]

Ban or Cherem, to be distinguished from human sacrifice proper:
v. Exod. xxii, 19; Lev. xxvii; Deut. vii, 2; xx, 17; xiii, 13–18 [Kuenen I, 290–1]

/12/

Cohen, plu. Cohanim, in Arabic Cahen, signifies originally *diviner.* Afterwards the word was taken in the sense, *minister of God,* & applied to the priests of Jehovah. *Cornarim* was applied only to pagan priests: it comes from a root which signifies to be burnt, blackened, & has been explained by *atrati, pullati,* i.e. *men attired in black.* (Sprenger) [I, 255][3]

1 In GE's annotated copy of Saint-Hilaire in DWL, the definition of 'Tathagata' on p. 74 is marked by a marginal line. For GE's note on 'Sakya-Muni', also from Saint-Hilaire, see Pf710 34.

2 According to Smith's *Dictionary of the Bible,* I, 197, 'Beth-el' was so named after Jacob erected a 'pillar of stone' there; see Genesis xxviii, 19 and xxv, 14, 15.

3 See 'Kohen', Pf 710 23. Service in the ancient Temple was restricted to Kohanim (priests, presumed descendents of Aaron) and Levites. In Orthodox Judaism, a Kohen (Cohen, Cohn, etc.) is forbidden to marry a proselyte. In *Daniel Deronda,* the prohibition seems to be extended to or incorporated by women: Mirah Cohen would not marry a convert to Judaism. Although Deronda does not learn why 'Mrs Cohen, the mother, must not be spoken to about her daughter' (DD ch. 40: 471; see also DD ch 33: 361), a most probable cause of her distress is that her daughter has married a gentile.

Çufic writing: Arabic character from 5th to 10th cent. Koran originally in Çufic characters [Sprenger I, 264]

חקות **Chukot Goyim**, laws of the Gentiles?[1]

Canopus, tablet of, discovered by Lepsius 1866. A Decree[2]

Chassidim, חסדים, 'Ασσιδαῖοι (Assidians). The pious, society of pietists, representing the tendency in Judaism which went beyond the mere observance of the Law – their motto being, not the fulfilment of the letter only, but of the inner as well as outer purport.[3]

[Hamburger, *Talmud*, p. 132]

Covenant, Book of. Exod. xxi–xxiii [Kuenen II, 8][4]

/13/

Domitian commands the posterity of David to be slain. When the same Domitian had issued his orders that the descendants of David should be slain; according to an ancient tradition, some of the heretics accused the descendants of Judas as the brother of our Saviour, according to the flesh, because they were of the family of David, & as such, also, were related to Christ. This is declared by Hegesippus as follows. 'There were yet living of the family of our Lord, the grand-children of Judas, called the brother of our Lord according to the flesh. These were reported as being of the family of David,

1 On B 124, 'Hukot Hagoyim' is translated as 'fashions of the heathens'. GE's cryptic note, 'Chukot Hagoyim', on Pf 711 91a refers to an article in the *Jewish Chronicle* (5 February 1875) on 'The True Aspect of Judaism', in which the author attacks 'that bogy ... of status quo' and 'the practice by us, of what by a misnomer are termed *Jewish customs*'.

2 A trilingual decree (in hieroglyphic, demotic, and Greek) from the reign of Ptolemy Euergetes, concerning the addition of one day to the calendar every fourth year. The tablet was discovered in 1866 by German Egyptologist Carl Richard Lepsius. See Pf 707 42 for a possible excerpt from the tablet.

3 The term 'Hasidim' precedes the revolt of the Maccabees, but now refers primarily to the revivalist movement begun in the eighteenth century by followers of Israel Baal Shem Tov; see Pf 710 7 and Pf 711 98a.

4 Exodus xxi to xxiii, comprising 'Divers laws and ordinances' (AV translation of the running headnote), is, according to Kuenen, 'the oldest collection which we know [which] contains a number of precepts concerning the civil life, of which the majority are obviously taken from existing customs', along with 'purely moral commandments and admonitions'.

& were brought to Domitian by the Evocatus. For this Emperor was as much alarmed at the appearance of Christ as Herod. He put the question whether they were of David's race, & they confessed they were. He then asked them what property they had, & how much money they owed. And both of them answered that they had between them only nine thousand denarii (9½) & this they had not in silver, but in the value of a piece of land containing only thirty-nine acres; from which they raised their taxes & supported themselves by their own labour. Then they also began to show their hands, exhibiting the hardness of their bodies, & the callosity formed by incessant labour on their hands, as evidence of their own labour. When asked also respecting Christ & his Kingdom what was its nature, & when & where it was to appear, they replied 'that it was not a temporal nor an earthly kingdom, but celestial & angelic; that it would appear at the end of the world, when coming in glory he would judge the quick & the dead, & give to everyone according to his works'. Upon which, Domitian despising them, made no reply; but treating them with contempt as simpletons, commanded them to be dismissed, & by a decree ordered the persecution to cease. Thus delivered, they ruled the churches both as witnesses & relatives of the Lord. When peace was established, they continued living even to the time of Trajan.'

Eusebius, Eccles. Hist. B. III. Ch. 19 & 20
[Graetz 4, 119; Pf 711 24][1]

/14/

David, the Shield of, is a figure composed of two triangles ✡ with the words אגלה & טיר inscribed in the centre & corners.

[Baring-Gould II, 176–7; Pf 711 92a][2]

v. Faust. Pythagorean symbol [Pf 711 53; Pf 710 34]

1 See DD ch. 41: 477. Graetz refers to Eusebius of Caesarea's *Kirchengeschichte*, translated by Friedrich Adolph Heinichen in 3 vols., 2nd edition (1868–70).

2 In the note on Pf 711 92a, GE correctly transcribes אגלא (miscopied here), which is the acronym for the beginning of the benediction *Gevurot*, which reflects upon the powers of the Almighty. According to Baring-Gould,

> The ... Shield of David is given in a Hebrew book on the properties and medicaments of things. It is said to be a certain protection against fire. A cake of bread must be made, and on it must be impressed the seal or shield of David, having in the corner the word ט´יר, and in the middle אגלא (Thou art mighty to everlasting, O Jehovah); and it must be cast aside into the fire with the words of Psalm cvi, 30 ... and also Exod. xii, 27.

Daniel, the Book of. 'The unknown teacher to whom we are indebted for the Book of Daniel is entitled to the praise that he was the first who grasped the history of the world, so far as he knew it, as one great whole, as a drama which moves onward at the will of the Eternal One.' [Kuenen III, 111][1]

/15/

Elia del Medigo (Eliah Cretensis) was the Hebrew teacher of Pico di Mirandola. His two other Hebrew teachers were Jehuda or Lev Abarbanel, author of the Divine Dialogue of Love, & Jochanan Aleman, who had migrated from Constantinople to Italy. Elia del Medigo was a philosopher who taught publicly in Padua & Florence & was once chosen by the Senate as arbitrator in a philosophical contest. [Geiger, *Reuchlin*, p. 167; Pf711 96–7][2]

Estranghelo, the character in which Syriac is written. [Yule II, 22; Pf707 2]

Egyptian literature, extent of. Besides the inscriptions, 1000 Papyri [Pf711 74][3]

Eloah or Ilâh. Fleischer traces El, the strong one, back to a root âl, to be thick & dense, to be fleshy & strong; but he takes Eloah or Ilâh for an abstract noun in the sense of fear, derived from a different root, alah, to be agitated, confounded. From meaning Fear, Eloah came to mean the object of fear, God. [Kuenen I, 41][4]

1 The Book of Daniel begins with the story of Daniel and other Judean exiles in the court of King Nebuchadnezzar (and later Belshazzar and Darius), and ends with apocalyptic visions of the rise and fall of the 'four world empires' – 'the Chaldean, the Medean, the Persian, and the Greek' – apparently foreseen in the time of the Great Assembly, but actually a retrospective history written during the Maccabean age, when Jewish identity was threatened by the Seleucid Empire.

> The form of the book, in consequence of which Daniel *foretells* what was already the past or present for the author, gave [his contemporaries] the impression that they had an infallible oracle before them.' (Kuenen III, 110–12)

See also 'Great Synagogue', Pf710 18, 'Jews', Pf710 22, and B 153a.

2 See also Pf710 41. Abarbanel's *Dialoghi di Amore* is mentioned on Pf707 1.

3 Source not traced.

4 This passage also occurs in Friedrich Max Müller, *Introduction to the Science of Religion* (London: Longmans, 1873), pp. 179–80. It is in Mrs Ouvry's inventory (*Libraries*, p. 95).GE read this work from 3 to 9 November 1873 (GHL Diary). See also GE's note on Job, Pf710 21.

Elisha ben Abuja, in the later Midrash spoken of as Acher, i.e. 'another', was born before the destruction of the Temple & lived till after the suppression of the revolt under Bar Cochba 135 AC. His colleagues were R. Akiba, Ben Asai, ben Soma &c. His pupil whom the legendary history connects affectingly with his lot was R. Meir. (vide Encyclopädie [Hamburger, *Talmud,* pp. 168–71], Grätz [Graetz 4, 65, 102–3, 192–3]& Levi) [1]

Egyptian Chronology (adopted by Duncker). Probable beginning – founded on the construction of the calendar – of the Egyptian civilization about 3500 BC. Memphian dynasty. Date of Pyramids about 2800. Thinite dynasty, uniting Upper & Lower Egypt, the capital of the former being Thebes (*Tap,* temple), began with Amenemha I, 2391. Amenemha III, the Moeris of the Greeks, 2221–2178, date of the Lake & Labyrinth. The Tombs of Beni Hassan belong to this period. Hyksos, 2091–1680, when Amosis I drove them to Avaris. Tutmosis III 1599–1560 completely expelled them. Even while this struggle was lasting, began the great structures at Thebes, with the temple at **/16/** Karnac, dedicated by Sesostoris I (before 2300) to the chief god of the Thebans, forming a nucleus or starting point. Tutmosis I, 1642–1621, added the first pillared Hall with its gate & the two obelisks of which one, 69 ft high, still remains. Tutmosis III, 1599–1560 – Temples at Ombo & Esneh, & wall round the temple of Ammon at Karnac, great gate & obelisks. Tutmosis IV, 1557–1520, had the *Sphinx* hewn from the rock (living) – representing probably Horos. Amenophis III, 1520–1484, began the palace at Luxor. Here apparently the avenue of sphinxes numbered 600. This same Amenophis built the Temple-palace on the west bank of the Nile at Medinet-Habu. This is in ruins, but the Pair of colossi placed by Amenophis before the entrance, remain. Horos, 1484–1447, had for successors Ramses I, Sethos I & Ramses II. Of these Sethos reigned 1443–1392. He built the second or Great Hall at Karnac – a temple to Osiris at Abydos, & the rock-temple of Beni-Hassan. His acts are depicted on the outer side of the Great Hall at Karnac. Ramses II, 1392–1326. To him belong the two rock-temples at Abu Simbel, the larger dedicated by Ramses to the god Ra, the smaller by his queen Nefruari to the goddess Athor. Here are painted sculptures exhibiting the deeds of Ramses. He enlarged the palace at Luxor, & he built the huge palace on the west bank, called the Ramesseion, where was the largest of unattached colossal statues

1 'Ben Abuja' appears on a list of topics of projected poems on GE's Blotter (Waley, p. 6). In GE's copy of Giuseppe Levi's *Parabeln, Legenden und Gedanken aus Thalmud und Midrasch,* in DWL, her index notes on the end papers include '208 Acher'.

(probably two such) & again the painted deeds of Ramses II. Began (according to Strabo) the canal to unite the lower Nile & the Red Sea. His son Menephta, 1326–1306. Of him, Josephus cites the famous passage from Manetho, which is a variant of the Exodus narrative. After an interval of three reigns, Ramses III, 1285–1273. He built temples & palaces at Karnac & Medinet-Habu, smaller but not less beautiful than those of Ramses II. His is the only sea-fight recorded on the walls. And he is identified (on the ground of his much glorified wealth) to have been the Rhampsinitus of Herodotus.

[Duncker I, 107–38] [1]

/17/

Fable, משל mashal. Fox-fables, *mishle shualim,* & washer-fables, *mishle kobsim,* are spoken of as cultivated by R. Jochanan b. Sakkai. What were these *mishle kobsim*? There are different opinions. One is, that kobsim is a transcription, the name of a fabulist mentioned by Babrius in the proem to his fables. [Hamburger, *Talmud,* p. 216] [2]

/18/

Great Synagogue כנסת הגדלה (kneseth hagdola) is a New-Hebrew name for the Assembly or *Gemeinde*, for which the biblical word is קהל kahel, or קהלה kehila, or אספה asupha. Under this name is understood the Synod which began under Esra & was dissolved under the Syrian rule, the 'remains of the Gt. Syn[od]' (שיורי) being understood to be the few who provisionally carried on the tradition of its activity. It is remarkable that neither Josephus, Philo, nor the Apocryphal writers have any mention of this 'Great Synod or Synagogue' & even in the Talmudic writings it is not mentioned by any before the teachers of the 3d & 4th century, & then only in general without specification of personalities. Hence many have regarded it as a fiction. The mistake probably lies in the application of the name – the Great Synod or Community meaning (under Esra) the collective people, & the *Men* of the Great Synagogue or Synod meaning the leaders in the popular assembly.

1 See 'Duncker' in the introductory note on 'Pf 710 Sources'. On Pf 707 100 is a briefer synopsis from the same source:

> Sothic periods 275 BC 1780 & 3285. 3 great Pyramids, Chufu, Shafra, Menkeres (2500). Moeris, Lake & Labyrinth. Hyksos 2091. Thutmosis (Thothmes) 1599–1560 (18th dynasty), finally drove out the Hyksos. (Amosis?) 1530? Ramses I. Sethos 1443–1392. Ramses II 1392–1326. Menephtha 1326–1306.

2 For other notes on Jewish fables, see B 149 and B 184v.

Such leaders constituting a sort of board of management are mentioned in the Greek Apocrypha, & implied in Josephus in his statement about the γερυσία. [Hamburger, *Talmud*, pp. 318–20][1]

Gad, name of the planet Jupiter. The comparison of Josh. xi, 17; xii, 7, where the city of Baal-Gad occurs, renders it probable that the worship of that planet was connected with the service of Baal, & that the latter, really a sun-god, & conceived as a beneficent power, was identified with that planet, just as, considered in his destructive action, he was combined with the planet Saturn. [Kuenen I, 253]

/19/

Hanyfs, a sect of Essene Jews settled in Arabia, instructors of Mohammed [Sprenger I, 261]

Haftara, also *Maftir*, the readings from the prophets following on the reading from the Thora in the Jewish liturgy. The word הפטרה is formed from the root פטר to set free, separate, part (in Hiphil). The origin of the Thora-readings in the public services is dated from Ezra & Nehemiah, but there is no hint as to the origin of the Haftara.[2] [Hamburger, *Talmud*, p. 334]

Hadassa = Esther = myrtle [Kuenen III, 151]

/20/

Ibn Gebirol, born at Malaga, educated at Saragossa, where in 1045 he wrote a treatise on Morals. Moses ben Ezra gives him the surname of Al-Kortobi, whence it may be concluded that he lived some time at Cordova. The poem which he himself places first among his hymns is *Kether Malkouth*, The royal Crown. (v. Sachs Poesie der Juden in Spanien.) He is the Avicebron, who wrote the *Fons vitae*, discovered by Munk in the Bibliothèque Royale. [Munk, *Mélanges*, pp. 155, 155n, 162, 151–4][3]

1 For another note on the Great Synagogue, see B 140.

2 'Haftarah' is the 'termination' (Jacobs, p. 208): the final portion of text read during the Sabbath service. Compare the plural 'Haftaroth, readings in the prophets', Pf 707 2. On B 140, GE notes that 'tradition ascribes to [Ezra] ... the custom of reading the law [Torah] according to *parashen* on Sunday, Monday & Thursday.'

3 For other notes on Ibn Gabirol, see B 164v and 165v and Pf 711 55. Michael Jehiel Sachs, *Die religiose Poesie der Juden in Spanien* (Berlin: Veit, 1845), is also referred to on B 108 and Pf 711 21.

Isaiah, Book of the Ascension of, has reached us only in an Ethiopic version.
[Baring-Gould II, 210; Pf 711 93a][1]

/21/

Jinn (Ginn or Djinn) means veil, covering, disguise. 'Man heisst die Nacht in diesem Sinne Ginn, weil sie die Erde bedeckt und gleichsam einhüllt. (So bedeutet auch Ghûl Waldteufel, ein bösartiges Ginngeschlecht, ursprünglich Rausch, Kopfweh, Schwermuth, Delirium.) Ginn bedeutet also Umnebelung, Bedrückung des Geistes, welche freilich in den meisten Fällen einem Wesen ausser uns zugeschrieben wurde. Jedenfalls sind daher die Ginn für die Araber ein Theil der Schöpfung, an deren Existenz sie so wenig zweifeln als an der der Luft.' (Sprenger)[2]
Genius possibly from Ginn, & not from *gignere*[3] [Sprenger I, 221, 221n]

1 A reference to the tenuous links of cultural transmission, in this instance by way of the 'Falasyan, Jews of Abyssinia, possessing neither the Hebrew text of the Bible nor the Talmud' (B 184v). GE's copy of *Ascensio Isaiae Aethiopice et Latine*, edited by August Dillman (Lipsiae: Brockhaus, 1877), is in DWL, not catalogued by Baker, but bound together with other works from the GE–GHL Library. See also Pf 711 30.

2 Translation:

> Night is called Ginn in this sense, since it covers the earth and so to speak enshrouds it. (So too Ghoul signifies forest-demon, a malicious species of Ginn; originally drunkenness, headache, depression, delirium.) Hence Ginn means beclouding or depressing the mind, which indeed in most cases is ascribed to a creature outside ourselves. In any event, for the Arabs the Ginns are therefore a part of creation; their existence is as little doubted as the existence of air.

3 n the *OED* the etymology of *Genius* is said to be adopted from the Latin, from the root of 'gignere, to beget'. Sense 2, however, 'a demon or spiritual being ... now chiefly in pl[ural]. *genii* (the sing[ular] being usually replaced by GENIE)', is 'a rendering of the Arab ... *jinn*, the collective name of a class of spirits ... supposed to interfere powerfully in human affairs'. GE's poem, 'A College Breakfast Party', written in April 1874 (GEL VI, 388n), begins with a 'high debate', of which 'the themes were old': 'Matter, Force, Self, Not-self, Being, Seeming, Space and Time' were 'small words' which took on 'mighty meanings' and

> ... turned to Genii
> And cloudy giants darkening sun and moon.
> Creation was reversed in human talk:
> None said, 'Let Darkness be,' but Darkness was ... (*Poems*, pp. 160–1)

Job xix, 25 [, 26]: (Theoretic translation)[1]

וַאֲנִי יָדַעְתִּי גֹּאֲלִי חָי
liveth /my defender / known have / I &
וְאַחֲרוֹן עַל־עָפָר יָקוּם :
shall arise /the ground / on /at last &
וְאַחַר עוֹרִי נִקְּפוּ־זֹאת
these have enclosed /my skin / after &
וּמִבְּשָׂרִי אֶחֱזֶה אֱלוֹהַּ
Eloah / I shall see / from my flesh /yet

And I know my defender liveth, & at last on the ground shall arise; & tho' after these have enclosed or encircled my skin, yet from my flesh (without the skin?) I shall see Eloah.

The passage translated, '*Though* he slay me, yet will I trust in him', is in the Hebrew, 'Behold, he will slay me. I do not (or will not) hope.' –
הֵן יִקְטְלֵנִי לֹיא אֲיַחֵל [Job xiii, 15]

'As the *sparks fly* upward' Job v, 7

'*sons of lightning*' = birds of prey[2]

Jubal = beauty of Baal [Duncker I, 355; Pf 707 63]

Jews in Spain. Their number increased at the beginning of the 10th century by the destruction of the academy at Pumbeditha; & the Talmud, which the refugees brought with them, was translated into Arabic by order of the Khalif Haschem II. Rabbi Joseph was chosen to perform the stupendous task & brought it to a close towards the end of the 10th cent. At the same period Menachem ben Saruk wrote the first Hebrew dictionary in Spain.[3]

Job, Book of. Date: about the year of Josiah's death 608. (Kuenen)
Names of God, *El, Shaddai, Eloah*; Jahveh only once [Kuenen II, 44, 47, 48]

1 The interlinear translation, like the Hebrew text, reads from right to left. On the original notebook page, the Hebrew text and translation each fit into a single line. In this transcription, the lines break at half verses.

2 The source for GE's notes on Job has not been traced. The last note appears to indicate that the Hebrew word Englished as 'sparks' in the AV translation may be a metaphor for 'birds of prey'. See also 'qedem', Pf 710 32.

3 Source not traced. For notes on Menachem, see B 139v, B 160 and Pf 711 75.

/22/

Janizaries, Yengi cheri, new soldiers. Sclavonian captives converted into troops by the Turks. [Gibbon, viii, 29; ch. lxiv; Pf707 41]

Jews, apparently imminent danger that they would adopt more & more from their Syrian rulers, would lose their individuality & at last become fused with the rest of the nations which formed the empire of the Seleucidae ... Yet, as we know, the result would not answer that expectation: when the first half of the second century BC had passed, Judaism had stood more firmly than it had ever stood before. This was the work of the Maccabees.
(Kuenen) [III, 95][1]

The Jewish community at Rome is a very old one: as early as the year 139 BC the Jews were driven out of Rome & Italy because they had admitted Italian proselytes to the keeping of the Sabbath.
v. Mommsen ii, 429 [Kuenen III, 166][2]

/23/

Kadisch /or **Kaddish** (Deutsch)/ the prayer to be repeated by sons during the eleven months after the death of their parents; also on *Yore-zeit*, i.e. the anniversary of such death. It begins as follows: Let there be magnified & sanctified the Great Name in the world which he has created according to his will, & which he rules as his kingdom, during your life & your days, & the life of the whole house of Israel, speedily & in a near time, & say ye, 'Amen: Be the great name praised for ever & evermore ...' It is in Aramaic – is probably (says Deutsch, 'Targums') of Babylonian origin.[3]

Kameah, amulet [Pf711 103][4]

1 For 'the glorious time' of the Maccabean period, see B 139v.

2 Kuenen, discussing the dispersion of the Jews before the fall of Jerusalem in 70 CE, cites Theodor Mommsen, *Römische Geschichte*, 2 vols. (Berlin: Weidmann, 1854–5).

3 Deutsch, 'On the Targums', *Literary Remains*, p. 323n. Compare B 119, 135, and 135v.

4 Hamburger, *Talmud*, p. 58, has the spelling 'Kamea'.

Pf710 23 24

Kohen, i.q. Arabic *Kahine,* Seer. Hence it came to mean in Hebr. priest. Munk says Kohen means black man, i.e. clothed in black.[1] [Sprenger I, 255n]

Krethi et Plethi, properly, executioners & runners, the body-guard of David; now used to signify the common people[2]

Kadmon. קדמני eastern or earlier – older, former. קדים, קֶדֶם means first the *front*, then the east. Hence Adam Kadmon. Kadmos, the Eastern man. In the same way, שְׂמאלי *left,* sometimes means *north,* because this was on the left of one who faced the East. Thus again, ים meant both the *sea* & the *west.*[3]

Kidduschin, betrothal; espousal, *Nissouin* [B 123; Pf711 80]

Karaites, sect of Jewish puritans, originated in the 8th cent[ury] under the teaching of Anan ben David [Kuenen III, 304][4]

Kabirim (Phoen.) the strong ones [Duncker I, 363; Pf707 64][5]

Kiûn or **Kewan** in Amos v. 26 is variously interpreted: 1. as stand, pillar, or image; 2. as a proper name (pron. Keiwán) & see in it the planet Saturn [Kuenen I, 265, 266]

/24/

Lokman: the oldest Arabian tradition is, that he was a Jew of the same family with Abraham. Wise sayings are given as his but no fables. A bad Arabian translation of Aesopian fables was ascribed to him. Said to have been a slave & an Ethiopian. (But Hammer[6] holds that the Aesopian fables were originally Arabian. v. Sprenger [I, 101–2])

1 Compare 'Cohen', Pf710 12. The Munk reference has not been traced.

2 Ernest Renan, *Histoire générale et système comparé des langues sémitiques,* 3rd edition (Paris: Michel Lévy frères, 1863), p. 55. GE's copy is in DWL.

3 Compare 'qedem', Pf710 32. Souce not traced.

4 Compare Pf711 55, from Graetz 5, 175–8: 'The Karaites arose in the beginning of the 8th cent[ury] under Anan ben David. Dogmas: adherence solely to the written text, the supremacy of reason, & the right of private judgment.'

5 Compare Pf711 50: 'Thoth or Mercury, one of the eight mystic Kabiri, or mighty ones, in Phoenicia. His Phoenician name is Kadmus, the primeval or Eastern ...' The source there is Deutsch, *Literary Remains,* pp. 181–2. Compare 'Kadmon', above, and 'qedem', Pf710 32.

6 Sprenger's reference is to Baron Joseph von Hammer Purgstall. See also Pf 710 41 and Pf707 1

As to this question of origin, we know little. Socrates amused himself in his dungeon by versifying Aesop & 100 years later Demetrius Phalereus made a collection of fables at that time best known & most popular. Perhaps all these & more were accessible to Babrius, who not long before the Augustan age made a Greek collection of μῦθοι or μυθιαμβοι, from which the fables of Phaedrus are closely imitated. The poetical collection of Babrius has not come down to us in a perfect form, & only a few fables out of the whole ten books have been preserved in different MSS of the fables attributed to Aesop. They were written in choliambics – from what source derived is not known. The version of Babrius became the standard edition of these apologues. He found a translator in Phaedrus, a younger contemporary. Syntipas translated his choliambics into Syriac, & Michael Andreopulus retranslated the Syriac into Greek. Ignatius Diaconus (the monk whom Bentley & Blomfield have somehow christened Gabrias) put 53 of his fables into Tetrastichs, & Maximus Ranudes tumbled them into prose so carelessly that the original choliambics may be recognized. It is chiefly from this 'idiot of a monk' that the popular fables of modern Europe are derived.[1]

/25/

Leviathan. Jewish legend. When God created the world he made two powerful enormous & coiling sea-monsters, two leviathans, a male & a female. But lest they should multiply & devour the rest of the living world, he killed the female & salted her flesh for the righteous in the next world to be set before them, with wine which had been in the grape since the creation, as a paradisiac festival. The male however still holds the world in its coils & will not come to an end till its battle with the equally enormous primeval ox Behemoth (or as some say with the angel Gabriel); & then it also will be prepared for the feast of the righteous. [Tendlau, p. 369; Pf711 102–3][2]

/26/

Mazzikim. Evil demons[3]

1 Source not traced. See also GE's note on Jewish fables, B 184v.

2 For more on Leviathan, see GE's notes from Eisenmenger (B 119) and the Jewish liturgy (B 188v and 189v).

3 Source not traced.

Mohammed

Etymology: The Praised, or else the Desired v. Sprenger I, 159[1]

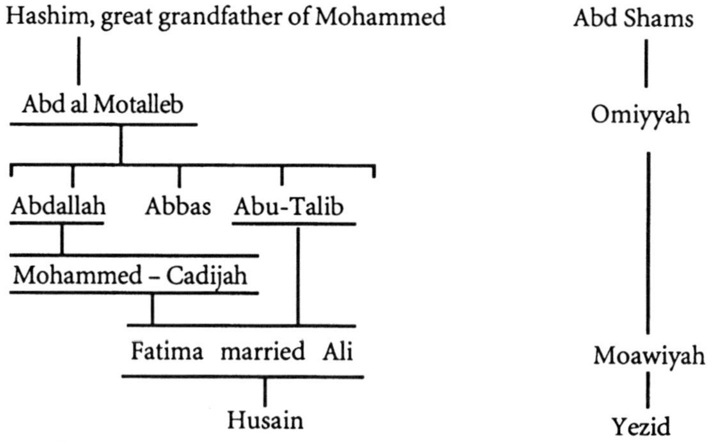

Mohammed b. 569. Hejra, 622. d. 632

Mohajerim, fugitives with Mohammed to Medinah
(Ansars, helpers *in* Medina)[2]

Mohammedan Empire. Syria & Egypt conquered between 632 & 639. Whole of Persia by 651. N. Africa, 709. Spain, 711. Defeated at Tours, 732. Empire divided, 755: one Caliph in Spain & another in Damascus - afterwards at Bagdad. In the course of the Xth century the Eastern Caliphate may be regarded as coming to an end in point of political power. A third Caliph arose in Egypt & the Caliphs of Bagdad fell under the control of their own mercenaries & ministers. 1055 the Caliph Al Kayem asked help of Togrul Beg, chief of the Seljuk Turks. 1071 at the battle of Manzikest the Turks under Alp Arslan beat the Romans & took the Emperor prisoner. 1092 the Seljuk power divided & one line of Sultans reigned in Asia Minor, having Nikaia for their capital & being called Sultans of Roum.[3]

1 Compare Pf 711 50. The biographical charts are similar to two in Theodor Nöldeke's *Sketches from Eastern History,* translated by John Sutherland Black (London: Adam and Charles Black, 1892), pp. 120 and 192, and may have been found by GE in another work by Nöldeke. For other notes on Mohammed, from Deutsch's review of Sprenger, see Pf 711 43.

2 Sprenger, I, 248n, has the spellings Mohâgir and Ançârs.

3 Source not traced.

Mesha-Stone, a stela of black basalt erected by Mesha, King of Moab, mentioned in 2 Kings 3, 4, 1 Chron. 2, 42. When the English, Prussians, & French were trying to get possession of it the Arabs became suspicious & angry, made the stone hot, poured cold water on it & thus shattered it. Clermont Ganneau had previously made a bad cast of it, but this also the Arabs managed to break up. Date 9th century BC. The deciphering is imperfect & uncertain. [Graetz 2, 44 and 430–5][1]

/27/

Mesuman is the prayer at table to which the presence of 3 persons is necessary.

Minjen or **Minyan** is the performance of public evening prayer with the requisite presence of ten persons – which is always held more meritorious than private prayer. Ten is the number of families necessary to the formation of a community or Kahel – on the ground of the above-mentioned necessity of ten males for the public prayers. [Tendlau, pp. 393n, 206n; Pf 711 103-4]

Mishna & Mikra = repetition by heart & writing [Pf 711 80][2]

Memra = Mimra, logos (Kabbala)[3]

Mar = dominus[4]

Mosaic law. Malachi is the first who mentions it. [Kuenen I, 273][5]

Moses. Laws ascribed to him at later periods because it was known that he had laid the foundations of legislation. 'The prophets of the eighth century already knew him in this character: Micah, vi, 4, calls him an envoy of Jahveh; in Hosea xii, 13, he is called a prophet. In the oldest narratives of the Pentateuch he appears in the same light. Nay, in the Egyptian tradition also,

1 GE's copy has a marginal pencil line beside the account of the shattering of the stone.

2 See also B 106 and 123.

3 Deutsch, 'Islam', in *Literary Remains,* p. 130.

4 *Mar* was a title used in the Babylonian Schools, for example, 'Mar Isaak the first *Gaon*' (Pf 711 28). *Dominus* means 'lord' or 'master of the house'.

5 'Remember ye the law of Moses my servant, which I commanded unto him in Horeb for all Israel'. Although Malachi comes at the end of the prophets in the AV Bible, he predates Elijah; see Malachi iv, 5. Kuenen asks,

> Is not the silence of the older prophets as to the Mosaic law … a real obstacle to the supposition that even a very small portion of it originated with him?

the leader of the lepers is a *priest,* who not only gives them freedom but new laws as well.' (Kuenen) [I, 273]

/28/

Moon in Hebrew is יָרֵחַ, the wanderer. v. Job 31, 26
[Hamburger, *Bibel,* pp. 765–6]

Medabberim, Arab. Motécallemin: dialecticians, discoursers
[Munk, *Mélanges,* p. 320; Pf707 32]

Mamluc, pl. Mamalic, defined by Pococke & d'Herbelot, servum emptitium, seu qui pretio numerato in domini possessionem cedit. They frequently occur in the wars with Saladin, & it was only the Bahartic Mamelukes that were first introduced into Egypt by his descendants.
v. note in Gibbon [vii, 252n; ch. lix; Pf707 41][1]

/29/

Naara, i.q. נַעֲרָה, a maiden? [Hamburger, *Bibel,* p. 780]

Nissouin, marriage [Pf711 80][2]

Nizachon, title of a book, end of 14th century by Jomtob Lipman. Nizachon = victory i.e. of Judaism. Its object is to go through all the texts of the Bible which have been used as a basis for Xty.
[Geiger, *Reuchlin,* p. 207; Pf711 98][3]

Naama = die Holde [Duncker I, 357; Pf707 63][4]

Nero-Sage. The popular belief in the preternatural return of Nero, mentioned by Tacitus, Suetonius & Dion Chrysostom. This is developed in a Jewish form in the Sibylline Oracles, & is believed & argumentatively maintained by Neander, to be the governing idea in the presentation of the Apocalyptic Antichrist.[5]

1 Translation: 'a bought slave, or one who goes for a price into the possession of a master'.
2 Compare Pf710 23 and B 123.
3 The note on Pf 711 98 continues, 'or have been a ground of ridicule & scorn'. The original *Sieg* on Pf711 98 is here translated as 'victory'.
4 Translation: 'darling, sweetheart'. 'Naamah an Ammonitess' was one of Solomon's foreign wives and the mother of Rehoboam (I Kings xiv, 21, 31).
5 Source not traced.

Nehushtan = the brass-god. The brazen serpent [Kuenen I, 288][1]

/30/

Ordination, laying on of hands, was a ceremony which conferred rabbinical authority on the learned, & was forbidden after the insurrection of Bar-Cochba. [Steinschneider, 366; B 114v; Pf711 60]

Origins, the Book of [2] ... 'lies before us as an irrefragable proof that the prophetic conception of Israel's early history & of the Mosaic legislation no longer fully satisfied the priest in Babylonia; that in him the necessity arose & the power was present to recreate the past, as it were, & to hold up, as he thought a truer picture of the past to his contemporaries. Even in itself this attempt is interesting, but its significance is increased beyond this both by the result which it has accomplished, & by the presage which it contains. The author of the Book of Origins succeeded in his undertaking: the conception of the past which he advocated gradually became a part of the consciousness of the Jewish nation, & has remained the traditional account down to the present day; we all begin by picturing Israel to ourselves as he has drawn it; it is only with difficulty that historical criticism has freed itself from the prestige which he exercised over his contemporaries & posterity. Such a success may be of no value as evidence for the historical truth of the picture which he designed, yet it must avail as proof of the power of his mind. And therefore I spoke, in the second place, of the presage which the Book of Origins contains. The priesthood which produces such a book is capable of great things. It is ready to pass to practical ground & there to assume the command. He who is able to recreate the past, certainly possesses the power to reform the future. The Book of Origins is an achievement, & the prophecy of other achievements.'

(Kuenen II, 173. Eng. Translation)

1 See II Kings xviii, 4: Hezekiah 'brake in pieces the brasen serpent that Moses had made'. Kuenen argues that the absolute prohibition of 'any graven image' was decreed not by Moses, but at a later period (II, 288–90).

2 The Book of Origins is a system of priestly legislation with historical narratives, written down in the Babylonian exile before Ezra's return to Judaea. It is a forerunner of the reforms introduced by Ezra and Nehemiah (Kuenen II, 157 and 245).

/31/

Porte (Sublime). So-called from the distribution of justice & despatch of business carried on at the gates of a city. (Shaw quoted by Lowth)
Haklyt calls it the Porch.[1]

Parness. Gemeindevorsteher [Pf 707 25][2]

Pantheras-Sage – that the father of Jesus was a soldier named Pantheras. This story was already known in the time of Celsus. [Graetz 4, 268; Pf 711 23][3]

Psalms. 'Probably not one of them is from David's hand; yet in the titles he is named as the author of more than seventy of these songs, & at a later period even the whole of them were attributed to him.' (Kuenen) [I, 273][4]

Papyri. The Prisse papyrus, partly deciphered by Chabas, a work of great antiquity containing moral precepts. 'Le fils qui reçoit la parole de son père deviendra vieux à cause de cela.' 'C'est la coeur qui est maître de l'homme dans l'obéissance et dans la desobéissance.' In the *Book of the Dead* – where the deceased enumerates various sins against which he has guarded, he says 'Je n'ai pas fait molester un esclave par son chef. Je n'ai pas laissé mourir de faim. *Je n'ai pas fait pleurer.*' [Kuenen I, 395–7][5]

1 The Porte was the title of the central office of the Ottoman government. The references to Thomas Shaw's *Travels, or Observations Relating to Several Parts of Barbary and the Levant* (Oxford, 1738) and to Richard Hakluyt, the 16th-century geographer, have not been traced.

2 Translation: 'head of the congregation'. Source not traced.

3 Compare Pf 710 36. Celsus was a Roman encyclopaedist of the early first century CE.

4 Kuenen compares this to the attribution of the Pentateuch to Moses:

> It cannot be proved that a single one of the 'proverbs of Solomon' proceeds from the king in whose name they all stand. Cannot this be the case also with Moses?

5 In his discussion of 'the Egyptian origin of Moses' monotheism' Kuenen refers to François Joseph Chabas, *Le plus ancien livre du monde. Etude sur le papyrus Prisse* (Paris, 1858). The excerpts from the Book of the Dead are drawn from Willem Pleyte, *Etudes égyptologiques* (Leiden: E. J. Brill, 1866–8):

> The son who is receptive to this father's word will become old because of that. The heart is master of the man, in obedience and in disobedience ... I have not let a slave be harmed by his overseer. I have not let anyone die of hunger. *I have not made anyone weep.*

'Je n'ai pas fait pleurer. Egyptian Book of the Dead' recurs, rather cryptically, on GE's Blotter (Waley, p. 9).

/32/

Q'ri and K'tbi, spoken & written. Marginal indications of the masorites [Ewald, pp. viii and 25]

Qutami, supposed author of an old Babylonian Book 14th cent. BC professedly translated into Arabic by Ibn Washiyyah, a descendent of the ancient Chaldaeans. Chwolson believes in the antiquity of the book: others, that it may contain very ancient traditions. [Pf711 92a][1]

קֶדֶם **qedem**, *before*, means secondarily 'on the East' or the East. Hence קַדְמוֹן, eastern. With this is probably connected κάδμος, the eastern man or Phoenician.[2]

/33/

Rosch Hasch-schanah, beginning of the year. It is the rabbinical tradition that this Day of Trumpets, the first of the seventh month, was the anniversary of the creation, & the beginning of the year. But the ancient Hebrews began their year in the spring. It is probable that the rabbinical practice of beginning the year in the autumn was not adopted till after the death of Alexander, under the Syro-Macedonian rule – the Syrians beginning the year at that season. v. Munk, Palestine [p. 184][3]

Rambam is the appellation of Maimonides, formed according to Jewish custom from the initials R. B. M: Rabbi ben Maimoun. [Pf711 103]

Thus, **Rashi** is an abbreviation for Rabbi Shelomah Ben Yitzschak. [Pf711 76]

Rabbi κατ ἐξοχην[4] is R. Jehuda, who completed the canon of the Mishna.
Rab (Abba Aricha) was the pupil of Rabbi. (*Rab* is the Babylonian form.) [Steinschneider, pp. 366–7; Pf711 60 and B 114v]

1 The reference is to Daniel Abramovich Chwolson, *Über Tammûz und die Menschen - verehrung bei den alten Babylonien* (St Petersburg, 1860). Comparable notes on Pf707 17 and 23 are from Ginsburg.

2 Source not traced. Compare *Kadmon*, Pf710 23.

3 Elsewhere in Salomon Munk's *Palestine: Description géographique, historique et archéologique* (Paris: Firmin-Didot, 1845), the spelling 'Rosch-Haschana' is used. GE's copy, in DWL, is included in the 'Books Wanted' list on Pf 711 21 and is the source of notes on B 150 and 173 and Pf 707 9. For notes on the observance and celebration of Rosh Hashanah, see Pf711 19 and B 129v, 172v and 184.

4 Translation: 'par excellence' or 'without equal'.

/34/

Saracen, derivation uncertain – people of the desert or eastern people, the two best guesses [Yule II, 582–3]

Shield of David ✡ (The 'dreieck' over which Mephistopheles could not tread) (Also Pythagorean)[1]

Sabbatai-Zewi, who excited wide-spread belief in himself as the Messiah (subsequently arrested by the Turkish authorities & induced to turn Mussulman to save himself) was the contemporary of Spinoza (1632–77) who evidently refers to him or had him in mind when writing the passage in the Tractatus about the possible restoration of the Jews.[2] The Tractatus was written 1656 to 1664 when Spinoza was 24–32, & was his first work. Abraham de Herrera's *Porta Coeli*, a cabbalistic-philosophic book which certainly influenced Spinoza, was published at Amsterdam 1656. [Graetz 10, 178, 181n; Pf711 99]

Shekel, what is weighed, weight [Pf707 46][3]

Sahhabah, the personal companions of the prophet [Pf707 64][4]

Solomon's Seal

2	7	6
9	5	1
4	3	8

– making 15 each way[5]

1 Compare Pf710 14 and Pf711 53 and 92a.

2 Mordecai alludes to Sabbatai Zewi and other false messiahs when he says, 'the history of our people's trust has been full of illusion' (DD ch. 40: 468), but in DD ch. 42 he also alludes to Spinoza's more positive view of the consequences of messianism:

> 'Baruch Spinoza had not a faithful Jewish heart ... Yet Baruch Spinoza confessed, he saw not why Israel should not again be a chosen nation.' (497–8)

3 Source: Sir John Gardner Wilkinson, *A Popular Account of the Ancient Egyptians*, 2 vols. (London: John Murray, 1854), II, 148.

4 Source: William Gifford Palgrave, *Narrative of a Year's Journey through Central and Eastern Asia (1862–63)*, 2 vols. (London: Macmillan, 1865), I, 384.

5 Source not traced.

Sakya-Muni was born 600 BC (there are differences as to the date) at Kapilavastu. His father Souddhodana was of the family of the Sakyas & the solar race of the Gotamids. His mother Maya Devi. His own name, Siddartha. He was supposed to have the 32 signs of the great man upon him (besides the 20 secondary marks)[1] when presented in the temple as an infant. His bride Gôpa cast aside the veil, saying that the women who conquer their senses & master their thoughts have no need of such covering. Three places in relation to him are especially sacred: Kapilavastu the place of his birth, Ourirevilva[2], of his severe asceticism, & Bodhimanda or the seat of intelligence, where he was revealed as Bouddha. The tree under which he sat to meditate & received the supreme Intelligence (a Fig-tree) is called Bodhidrouma. It was at Varanaçi - Benarès - that **/35/** he first preached or 'turned the wheel of the law'. The 'three Refuges' are: Bouddha, Dharma (the law) & Sangha (the Assembly).[3] 'Soughata' means the welcome; Bhagavat, the blessed, the fortunate (a title often applied in Brahmanism). Bodhisattva is one who has the essence of the Bodhi or the supreme intelligence. Arbat means venerable. [Saint-Hilaire, pp. 3–5, 9, 28, 36, 74–5]

Sibylline Books. XII: the limits of production assigned by the critics to the first eight books are from 200 BC to 350 or 500 AD. A few older polytheistic fragments also hexametrical remain, but the remainder are marked by a monotheism which establishes their Jewish or Christian origin. The third book is evidenced to be the production of a Jew living in the Maccabaean period. Of the ninth book was written by a Jew living in Egypt in the reign of Trajan or Hadrian. In the Tenth Book, written by a Christian, there is a portrait of Nero as the expected Antichrist. The Eleventh Book is Christian, date a little below AD 260. The Twelfth anticipates the restoration of the Jewish monarchy, & was perhaps written by a Jew in the third century.[4]

1 According to Saint-Hilaire, there are 80 ('quatre-vingts') secondary marks.

2 'Ourouvilva' in Saint-Hilaire.

3 Copying the 'Three Refuges of Bouddhism' on her Blotter, GE translated them as 'Human Ideal', 'Doctrine', and 'Social Authority' (Waley, p. 11).

4 Source not traced. Compare the note from Graetz on 'Alexandrian-Jewish Apocryphal Writings' on B 156.

Saturn, the planet. Dozy in *De Israëliten te Mekka* infers from Amos v, 25, 26 & from the Sabbath, that the planet Saturn was originally the principal deity of the Israelites. [Kuenen I, 262][1]

Sin, the Moon-god. Osiander thinks that Sinai, the desert of Sin, & the Sinites were hence derived. [Kuenen I, 267][2]

Solomon's Song. 'There are good reasons for holding that the Song of Solomon is a product of Jeroboam's reign ... It contains a glorification of the power of love, which no treasure can buy & which is proof against all temptation. Where such thoughts are uttered & applauded, there domestic life flourishes & is held in honour, & there consequently the conception of a deeper foundation of religion is not looked for in vain.' (Kuenen) [I, 373]

/35a/

Stone-worship = Baetyliëndienst [Kuenen I, 390][3]

/36/

Tacwin, Arabic name for an Almanach [Yule I, 434; Pf 707 45]
Taccuin remenso is used in *Malmantile.*[4]

Titles, Later Jewish: Nassi, Abbethdin, & Chacham: three principals of the Sanhedrin, all three called the Dayanim דיינם.
Resh-Metibta, president of the School
Resh-Galuta, president of the Exile
Gaon, Excellency [Steinschneider, p. 366–9; Pf 711 60][5]

1 This note is linked to the discussion of *Kiun;* see Pf 710 23. Kuenen's reference is to Reinhart Pieter Anne Dozy, *De Israëliten te Mekka* (Haarlem, 1864); the German translation is cited by Graetz (Pf 711 103).

2 With reference to the Jewish lunar calendar, based on close observation of the new moon (see B 125v and 130v), Kuenen comments that 'It was very natural that the worship of the moon should be introduced among the Israelites during their wanderings in the peninsula of Sinai, if it did not previously exist among them.'

3 Compare the note on *Baitylos*, Pf 710 11.

4 The reference to Malmantile is from a note in the *Romola* Notebook, Bodleian MS. Don. g. 8, 45v: 'Taccuin remenso, an accurate almanach'. To that note GE later added, in pencil, 'Tacwin, Arabic'. GE's copy of *Il Malmantile, racquistato di Perlone Zipoli,* with notes by Puccio Lamoni, 2 vols. (Firenze: Bonducciana, 1788), is in DWL.

5 See also B 123 and 151v.

Toldoth Jesu. Jewish book about the birth of Christ. Toldoth, origins. Here is the story about Pantheras, a soldier, being the father of Jesus.
[Geiger, *Reuchlin*, p. 228; Pf711 98] [1]

Timour or Demir means iron; Beg, lord or prince. By the change of a letter or accent this is turned into lenc (lame) & the two words have been confounded in Tamerlane. [Gibbon, viii, 40n; ch. lxv; Pf707 48]

Tammuz = der Geschiedene [Duncker I, 356; Pf707 63] [2]

Talmud, translation into Arabic of, v. sub **J** [3]

/37/

Uighur. The Uighur *character* was introduced into Turkestan by Nestorian missionaries. The Uighur language is a branch of Oriental Turkish.
[Yule I, 29; Pf707 43]

/38/

Wahabees, founded by Abdul Wahab, 1725 [Pf711 51] [4]

/39/

Yalkut Rubeni, a book often cited by Eisenmenger, said by Geiger to be the work of an addle-brained Ruben Hoeske, a cabbalist [B 149v; Pf711 57] [5]
(Yalkut, leadings or doings?)

/40/

Zifri, (form of Sepher) Commentary on Leviticus
Zifra, (id.) Commentary on Numbers & Deuteronomy [B 125; Pf711 98a] [6]

1 For other references to Pantheras, see Pf710 31 and Pf711 23.
2 Translation: 'the severed or separated'.
3 GE's cross-reference to her note on 'Jews in Spain', Pf710 21.
4 The original source is Reginald Bosworth Smith's *Mohammed and Mohammedanism* (London: Smith, Elder, 1874), p. 241. For other notes from Bosworth Smith, see Pf711 51.
5 Original source: Abraham Geiger, *Judaism and its History,* p. 341. The parenthetical note on Yalkut is added from another source, not traced.
6 The meanings are here transposed. The notes on B 125 and Pf 711 are correct. Compare B 106.

Zin-gis means most great, *zin* being great & *gis* the sign of the superlative.
[Gibbon, viii, 3n; ch. lxiv; Pf 707 46]

Zu'l Karnain, the two-horned, is an Arabic epithet of Alexander, with which legends have been connected, but which probably arose from the horned portrait on his coins. The term appears in Chaucer in the sense of *non plus*: 'At dulcarnon, right at my wittes end'. This use said to have arisen from the Arabic application of the term to the 47th Prop. of Euclid.
[Yule I, 169; Pf 707 44] [1]

/41/

Duties of the Heart, by R. Ba'hya [2] [Munk, *Mélanges*, p. 482]

O Kind by Algazali [Munk, *Mélanges*, p. 368n; Pf 707 1] [3]

Dialoghi di Amore, by Leone Ebreo i.e. Juda Abravanel, son of Isaac Abravanel (b. 1481) [Munk, *Mélanges*, p. 368n; Pf 707 1] [4]

1 Compare the note on 'Dulcarnon, the Pythagorean proposition', Pf 711 74.

2 Rabbi Bahya Ben Joseph Paguda or Pakudah, an eleventh-century Spanish philosopher whose moral and religious treatise, *Duties of the Heart*, influenced by Sufism, was widely read and often quoted in the literature of Jewish piety. Sufism was an Islamic ascetic and mystical movement which may have been been partly influenced by Midrashim. See Jacobs, *Jewish Religion*, pp. 44-5 and 500-1. For GE's note on 'Çufic writing', see Pf 710 12. Bahya was one of a group of notable Jewish philosophers emerging from the tradition of the Ash'arite sect of Muslim philosophers, the most notable of whom was al-Ghazali. The sect opposed the rationalist Mutakallimun who had dominated Jewish and Muslim thought; see 'Medabberim', Pf 710 28. He is the 'Bachja' mentioned on B 172.

3 Pf 707 1 has a more complete reference from Munk to the German translation by Baron Joseph von Hammer-Purgstall, *O Kind! Die berühmte ethische Abhandlung Ghasalis, Arabisch und Deutsch* (Vienna: Strauss, 1838). Al-Ghazali (1058–1111) was an Islamic philosopher and theologian who was appointed to a professorship by the vizier Nizám ul-Mulk, who is mentioned in the note on Omar Khayyám on Pf 711 42. Al-Ghazali's ethical work, *O Child*, is one of 69 works ascribed to him. GHL contributed an article on 'Algazzali's Confessions: Arabian Philosophy' to the *Edinburgh Review* 85 (1847): 340–58.

4 *The Divine Dialogue of Love*, by Juda Abravanel, one of the Hebrew teachers of Pico di Mirandola: see Pf 710 15 and Pf 711 97. His father Isaac (1437–1508) was an eminent philosopher, theologian, scholar, and statesman in Portugal, Spain, and Venice; as minister of state under Ferdinand and Isabella, he was exempted from the 1492 expulsion of the Jews. Munk discusses Leone Ebreo in *Mélanges*, pp. 522–8.

Pf 710 41

Uriel da Costa's Selbstbiographie, edited by Jellinek – a translation of Uriel's Exemplar humanae vitae.[1]

Also Leo da Modena[2] v. Gr. 5. 10 [Graetz 10, 137–55; Pf 711 101][3]

Orobio (narrative) [Graetz 10, 173; Pf 711 99]

Wagenseil's Belehrung der Jüdisch-Deutschen Red- und Schreibart (Kauderwälsch)[4]

1 Graetz's reference is to Hermann Jellinek, editor, *Uriel Acosta's Leben und Lehre* (Zerbst, 1847). GE annotated some pages of her copy in DWL of Uriel da Costa's autobiography, which is subtitled 'Ein Beispiel des Menschlichen Lebens' ('An example of human life'). Her marginal comments are 'Breaks the laws'; 'Dissuades converts'; 'Loneliness again'; 'Second penance'; 'Final rancour'; 'Suicide'.

2 The autobiography of Leone Modena (1571–1648) has been translated in a recent edition by Mark R. Cohen, *The Autobiography of a Seventeenth-Century Venetian Rabbi: Leon Modena's Life of Judah* (Princeton: Princeton University Press, 1988).

3 In copying this note from Pf 711 101, GE misinterpreted the 'V.' for 'Volume' of her first note as the roman numeral for 5.

4 *Johann Christof Wagenseil's Belehrung der Jüdisch-Deutschen Red- und Schreibart* (Königsberg: P. F. Rhode, 1699) is also referred to on Pf 711 54 and B 193v. 'Kauderwälsch' is a derogatory reference to Yiddish.

Articles attached to the inside front cover

In 1879 three newspaper cuttings were attached to the inside front cover of Pf 710. The first is a notice on 'The Late Dr A. Benisch', printed in the *Jewish Chronicle*, 9 May 1879. Abraham Benisch, for many years the editor of the *Jewish Chronicle*, had died in the summer of 1878. In January 1879, while GE was in deepest mourning for GHL, who had died in November, she received a letter from Asher Isaac Myers, then editor of the *Jewish Chronicle*, saying that he found the character of Mordecai to be 'an unconscious photograph' of the late Dr Benisch. Her reply refers to a 'newspaper slip', which was to be the second cutting attached to Pf 710, after being returned to her by Myers:

> What you say of Dr Benisch has reminded me of a brief memoir of another remarkable Jew, which was sent to me long after the publication of 'Daniel Deronda', by a correspondent not otherwise known to me. I feel sure that you will like to read this newpaper slip, which I enclose, and am sorry to be obliged to ask that you will return it. The career it describes is deeply interesting – but it may possibly be already known to you ...

The source of this memoir of 'Abraham Leith' has not been traced, but may be the *Scotsman*. In her letter to Myers, GE mentions 'the mistaken statement' that 'a Jew named Cohn', of whom GHL had published some recollections in the *Fortnightly Review* in 1866,

> bore a resemblance to Mordecai, and was thus a guarantee that the character was not an impossible ideal. Mr Lewes took several opportunities (in conversation) of pointing out that no such resemblance existed .... Such misunderstandings continually arise, and are hardly worth notice. But I mention the subject on this occasion because I believe that my husband would have written this letter for me and would have said nearly what I have said. (GEL VII, 95–6)

The source of the third newspaper cutting, on the 'Jewish Population of the World', has not been traced, but may be the *Jewish Chronicle*, sometime in 1879.

THE LATE DR. A. BENISCH — The following references to the late Dr. Benisch and the Rev. A. Löwy occur in a biographical sketch of Herr Moritz Steinschneider, the well-known bibliographer and Orientalist: 'In Prague, Abraham Benisch, a native of Bohemia, whose commentaries on Ezekiel were published at that time (1836) in the Landau-Bible Edition, studied surgery with the view of preparing himself for a journey to Palestine. Benisch hoped to find in a restoration of a Jewish empire the conditions for the introduction of the necessary reforms amongst the Jews, and was anxious to devote his whole life to the accomplishment of that idea, which then had only been communicated to a privileged few. Among the latter was Steinschneider, who sought to propagate the idea in Vienna (where he was joined by Albert Löwy, from Ausee, at present Preacher at the Reform Synagogue in London) and in Berlin by establishing clubs for Jewish students, in which lectures on scientific subjects were delivered. In connection with those ideas, which, however, had no chance of being realised, neither in Austria nor elsewhere, was the emigration to England in 1840 of Benisch and Löwy, where the former after having for many years edited the *Jewish Chronicle*, died in the summer of 1878.'

[*Jewish Chronicle*, 9 May 1879, p. 12]

ABRAHAM LEITH

Some years ago, we had occasion to record the visit to Sunderland of a very remarkable man, Herr Abraham Leith, of Pesth, a real enthusiast in Rabbinical knowledge, and full of zeal for the temporal and spiritual welfare of the poor Jews in Jerusalem, his kindred according to the flesh. M. Leith, who was a native of Lithuania, settled about forty years since in the capital of Hungary, where he established a flourishing business as a printer and publisher of Hebrew works. In the year 1849, when the Austrian general Kentzi bombed Pesth, M. Leith's premises were seriously damaged, and when the Imperialists some time afterwards entered the city, they were completely wrecked, and the unbound sheets of a large edition of Rashi's Commentary on the Old Testament, - universally recognized as the basis of all Scriptural exegesis, and not yet superseded by any other work, although in the province of philology and antiquities investigation has been much furthered since its author's time, - were used as fuel or otherwise destroyed by the ignorant soldiery, who had been taught to look upon all Jews as rebels, and all Hebrew books as books of magic, sorcery, and sedition. M. Leith was thus reduced to beggary at one fell swoop, and was moreover forced to flee from Hungary to escape from imprisonment or worse. After suffering great hardship, he made his way to this country, in a Hamburg ship bound for the Tyne. Here he found shelter under the roof of another refugee, M. Buerger, ex-citizen of Hamburg, who had been a member of the reformed legislative assembly in that republic in 1848, and had been forced, like M. Leith, to abandon his native country in the following year. M. Buerger, who was a very clever, intelligent, industrious man, was endeavouring to establish a business as a joiner and cabinet-maker in South Shields, but, being unable to speak intelligible English, he had not met with much success. Nearly penniless himself, all he could do for M. Leith was to give him an occasional meal and bedding for the night among the shavings under his joiner's bench. Here the present writer first fell in with him, and a love of kindred pursuits soon made them tolerably well acquainted with each other. He found the poor exile imbued with Talmudic lore, and well versed in the standard works of the great Hebrew doctors, from Maimonides downwards. He was firmly attached to the traditions of the elders, and would sooner have suffered death than infringed one concept of the Mosaic law. He yearned to do something substantial for the good of his beloved Israel, and mourned over the spiritual apathy and gross materialistic worldliness in which, according to his view, too many of the British Jews were steeped. He made repeated journeys to the seats of the universities, in England and Scotland, to try to kindle a spirit of sympathy in the several Hebrew professors there; but, except in the case of the late Dr Duncan, of Edinburgh, of whom he used to speak in the highest terms, he did not meet with much encouragement from these doubtless erudite but to him indifferent gentlemen. He had long had a keen desire to make a pilgrimage to Jerusalem, and, through the kindness of Sir Moses Montefiore, he got free passage thither on board one of the Peninsular and Oriental Company's steamers. Arrived in the Holy Land, he made it his business to inquire closely into the condition of his fellow countrymen there, and finding that the inhabitants of Jerusalem were literally perishing for want of water, of which a supply could be got by laying down pipes from the neighbourhood of Bethlehem, only six miles off, he hastened back to England to lay the case before his friends here, and try to get a fund raised to carry the required waterworks out. That object was in due course happily accomplished, through the liberality of rich Christians as well as Jews, in England and on the Continent, to which M. Leith travelled in prosecution of his scheme.

[Where the newspaper was folded, the brittle paper has broken into two pieces, and a line or two of text has been lost.]

...a ... more important and arduous task in hand, and came back to Sunderland in the summer of 1865, charged with the task of obtaining members to a Palestine Colonization Union, which some of the leading Jews of Prussia, Saxony, and Poland, were then forming, chiefly at his instigation. In the capacity of travelling agent of this society, he had visited, within the preceding three years, nearly every large town from Memel to Dusseldorf; and he had succeeded in getting subscriptions and donations to a considerable amount, as attested by his large folio subscription book, which the present writer had in safe keeping for several months, and which was a perfect curiosity in an autographical point of view, containing, as it did, the signatures and seals of some hundreds of Jewish professors, doctors, rabbis, merchants, litterateurs, and others, in Berlin, Frankfort, Breslau, Elbing, Kalicz, and other places. The Provisional Central Committee of the Union consisted of five Berlin gentlemen, viz, A. N. Haymann, of Haymann and Co., B. Liebermann, Dr J. Bradt, J. Bamberger, and G. Baumann, of N. Heeft and Co. Its object, as set forth in the prospectus, was to purchase land in Palestine, and settle Jewish colonists upon it. Membership was constituted by the payment of at least two dollars yearly, or at least fifty dollars in one sum. The seat of the Union, like that of the Central Committee, was Berlin, with local committees in each of the large towns of North Germany and Poland; and the duties of the Provisional Committee were confined to obtaining members and collecting subscriptions, until the funds of the Union should amount to 50,000 dollars, when the committee, it was arranged, should call a meeting of the members, a definitive statute would be drawn up, and active steps taken to carry out the end in view. Letters and money were directed to be sent to Messrs A. N. Haymann and Co., 23, Unter den Linden, Berlin. After this period, we lost sight of M. Leith. He left Sunderland to go to Edinburgh, and from thence back to the Continent, and what became of him eventually we do not know. The likelihood is that he died shortly after he was there, and that the Colonization Union scheme died with him. However this may have been, he was a remarkable man, and with him must have perished a vast fund of curious information, which, if he had only had taste and time for it, would have made one of the most interesting of autobiographies.

Jewish Population of the World – The 56th annual report for 1878 of the Berlin Society for the Promotion of Christianity Among the Jews has been lately published. There is no concealment of the fact that the visible results do not correspond with the wishes of the society. The receipts during the year amounted to only 16,731 marks (about £836), of which 11,951 marks (about £597) were the proceeds of a simultaneous collection on the Tenth Sunday after Trinity in all the Protestant churches of the kingdom of Prussia.[1] In the appendix some interesting details are given respecting the distribution of Jews all over the world. The total number of the Hebrew race to-day is about what it was in the days of King David – between six and seven millions.[2] There are in Europe, according to the latest statistical information, about five millions; in Asia, 200,000; in Africa, over 80,000; in America, from a million to a million and a half. More than half of the European Jews (2,621,000) reside in Russia; 1,375,000 in Austria (of whom 575,000 in the Polish province of Galicia); 512,00 in Germany (61,000 in the Polish province of Posen); Roumania is credited with 274,000, and Turkey with 100,000. There are 70,000 in Holland, 50,000 in England, 49,000 in France, 35,000 in Italy; Spain and Portugal have between 2,000 and 4,000; 1,800 in Sweden, 25 in Norway. Nothing is said about Denmark or Switzerland. The number of Jewish residents in Berlin is given at 45,000 – nearly as many as in the whole of France and more than in Italy, Spain, Portugal, and the Scandinavian peninsula together. The majority of the African Jews live in the province of Algiers. But they are to be found in Abyssinia and all along the north coast, and even in the Saharan oases, frequently acting as intermediaries between the Mahomedans and Christians. Of the Asiatic Jews, 20,000 are assigned to India and 25,000 to Palestine. The population of Jerusalem is given as 7,000 Mahomedans, 5,000 Christians, and 13,500 Jews; these last are classified as German, Spanish, or Arabic Jews. The report gives no details concerning America, except that in New York there are 30 synagogues.

1 In a letter to Sara Hennell on 19 March 1853, GE wrote:

> So much for bad news. For good, I have nothing better than that the 'Society for the Conversion of the Jews' has converted *one* Jew during the last year and has spent £4400. (GEL II, 102)

2 This total agrees with GE's 1875 note on Pf 707 1: '7,000,000 יהודימ' and her earlier note on Pf 711 22: 'Number & distribution of Jews in 1865 / Total 7,000,000'.

Pforzheimer Notebook 707

Pf 707 1 to 73

Contents and miscellaneous notes

Pf 707 1, 2, 3

The inscription on Pf 707 1 – '"George Eliot's Notes"' – was perhaps added by Mrs Ouvry.[1] '1875', written in the upper right corner of the page, has been thought to represent the starting date for GE's use of this notebook,[2] whose earliest datable entries are from January 1876 – the 'Hymn of St. Francis' and the excerpt from Leopardi's *Canti* (Pf 707 29 and 33). On 13 January 1875, GE began to write 'the part about Deronda' (DD ch. 15), and on 19 May she let John Blackwood have the first twenty chapters.[3] These incorporate information on the settlement of family estates, acquired in January, and on nervous mimicry and the commercial panic of 1866, from her reading in May.[4] Since the GHL Diary records that 'Polly read opening chapters of her new novel' on 11 June 1874, it would seem likely that GE revised those early chapters in the light of her later reading. If she did not read Charlotte Yonge on Christian names (Pf 707 10–16, 26–27) before January 1875, she must even have renamed Gwendolen. Alternatively, entries in this notebook must predate 1875 and overlap with those in Pf 711. A note on Pf 707 9 which may be linked with autumn 1873 tends to support this earlier alternative date.

The list of books on Pf 707 1 includes four also listed in Pf 710. The last four titles were added no earlier than 1876, when Hertzberg's *Geschichte Griechenlands* and Sale's new edition of the *Koran* were published. The final entry is for the second edition of Haug's Essays on the Parsis, published in 1878. GE then fitted on to the page an unpaginated index of 'Contents', after the notebook was filled – some time after January or March 1878, when she read Lecky's *History of England in the Eighteenth Century.* As with GE's 'Chief Contents' list for Pf 711, notebook page references within square brackets have been supplied by the editor.

---

1 Compare Pratt and Neufeldt, pp. 94 and 244.

2 Baker I, 23–8, 224. The date may not be in GE's hand; it appears to differ from the hand of the pagination numbers.

3 GE Journal (GEL VI, 116), and GEL VI, 143.

4 Pf 711 77–78, 94a and 96a; compare DD ch. 15: 143–4, ch. 3: 20, and ch. 2: 11.

/1/ 1875

7,000,000 יהודים In Poland 1 in 7. Ireland 1 in / 17000 or / 18000[1]

Ratich: Comenius[2]

Conv. Lexicon[3]

Dialoghi di Amore, da Leo Ebreo [Pf 710 41]

O Kind! die berühmte ethische Abhandlung Gasalis
(Von Hammer) Vienna 1838 in 12 mo [Pf 710 41][4]

Hertzberg's Geschichte Griechenlands (mediaeval & modern Greece)[5]

Sale's Koran[6]

Avesta trans. by C. de Harlez [Pf 710 1][7]

Haug's Essays (Trübner & Co.) [Pf 710 1][8]

1 The source for the note on population figures for Jews – יהודים or 'Yehudim' – has not been traced; its date is unknown. For similar notes, see B 127 and 194, Pf 711 22, and the newspaper article attached to the inside front cover of Pf 710, on the 'Jewish Population of the World' for 1878 (see p. 431).

2 Johann Amos Comenius or Komensky (1592–1671) and Wolfgang Ratichius (1571–1635) were reforming educationists.

3 GE's copy of *Conversations-Lexicon zum Handgebrauch oder encyklopädisches Realwörterbuch aller Wissenschaften, Künste und Gewerbe,* 4th edition (Leipzig: August Weichardt, 1846), is in DWL.

4 Salomon Munk, *Mélanges de philosophie juive et arabe,* p. 368n, refers to this German translation (in a duodecimo volume) by Baron Joseph von Hammer-Purgstall, *O Kind! Die berühmte ethische Abhandlung Ghasalis, Arabisch und Deutsch* (Vienna: Strauss, 1838).

5 Gustav Friedrich Hertzberg, *Geschichte Griechenlands seit dem Absterben des antiken Lebens bis zur Gegenwart,* 4 vols. (Gotha: F. A. Perthes, 1876–9).

6 George Sale, translator and editor, *The Koran, Commonly called the Alcoran of Mohammed,* new edition (London: Chandos Classics, 1876), in DWL.

7 Charles de Harlez, translator and editor, *Avesta: Livre sacré des sectateurs de Zoroastre,* 3 vols. (Paris: Firmin-Didot / Maisonneuve, 1875–7). The excerpt from the *Avesta* on Pf 707 17 is from another, unidentified, French translation.

8 Martin Haug, *Essays on the Sacred Language, Writings, and Religion of the Parsis,* 2nd edition, edited by Edward William West (London: Trübner, 1878). In Mrs Ouvry's inventory (*Libraries,* p. 76). The first edition was published in Bombay in 1862.

Contents

/2/

Bit of apple with honey on it, on Rosch Haschanah[3]

1 Notes following Pf 707 73 were made after June 1877, the time when GE stopped entering 'Oriental Memoranda' in Pf 710, and are excluded from this edition of GE's *Daniel Deronda* Notebooks. Pf 707 83 and 84, which were stuck together, apparently by GE, include lists of works 'Read from June to Oct. [1877]' (Pf 707 83v) and read '*Aloud*' in the same period (Pf 707 84v). Unlisted notes on Pf 707 99 and 100 include a sketch map of ancient Egypt and brief notes on Egyptian history; see Pf 710 16.

2 Notes beginning from the back cover, not listed here, include a sketch map of Warwickshire and a list of Buddhist books (Pf 707 124), and notes on Hebrew vocabulary and verb forms (Pf 707 123 to 117).

3 See GE's note on 'Rosch Haschana' on B 129v: 'Apple & Honey on the table at this festival? Kompert'.

'Je n'appelle pas gaieté ce qui excite le rire, mais un certain charme, un air agréable qu'on peut donner à toutes sortes de sujets, mesme les plus sérieux.'
La Fontaine[1]

Estranghelo, character in which Syriac is written [Pf 710 15][2]

Haftaroth, readings in the prophets[3]

The day is past like the shadow of a palm tree[4]

Historia [...] scribitur ad narrandum non ad probandum. Quintilian[5]

Drance & upper Rhone valleys[6]

Pulvis veterum renovalitum[7]

1 Jean de la Fontaine, in the Preface to his *Fables*, states that since his stories are 'known to all the world', he must make them new by adding touches of 'novelty and gaiety'. His following words are quoted here and also in 'Story-telling', an essay published posthumously in a collection edited by Charles Lee Lewes, *Essays and Leaves from a Notebook* (Edinburgh: Blackwood, 1884). GE refers to the 'sort of gaiety which plays around the best French novelettes' or novellas, which employ 'spirited narrative, without more than a touch of dialogue here and there':

> Examples of its charm are seen in the short tales in which the French have a mastery never reached by the English, who usually demand coarser flavours than are given by that delightful gaiety which is well described by La Fontaine as not anything that provides fits of laughter, but a certain charm, an agreeable mode of handling which lends attractiveness to all subjects even the most serious. (*Essays*, p. 446)

'Lafontaine' was read from 10 May to 16 June 1871 and again on 6 October 1875 (GHL Diaries). His preface is also the source of a note on Folger 14 56.

2 Henry Yule, *The Book of Ser Marco Polo the Venetian*, II, 22. For other notes from Yule, see Pf 707 34–40 and 42–46; some of these recur in Pf 710.

3 Deutsch, 'On the Targums', *Literary Remains*, p. 320. Compare the note on *Haftara* on Pf 710 19.

4 Source not traced.

5 Marcus Fabius Quintilianus, *De Institutio Oratoria* ('Education of the Orator'), X, 1, 31. Translation: 'History is written to tell a story, not to prove a fact.'

6 The reference to these rivers in Switzerland has not been traced.

7 Translation: 'the ashes of the ancients ploughed again'. Source not traced.

Ayenbite of Inwit, or remorse of conscience. XIVth Century[1]

/3/

Mysticism[2]

Alexandrian philosophy, derived from India
Platonism, Gnosticism
Hesychians in Greek Church
Tauler, 1294–1361
Molinos Guida Spirituale pub. in Rome, 1675
Fénelon, 1651–1715. Mde Guyon died 1717

(There were the Molinists of the 16th century, followers of the Jesuit Molina, b. 1535 died 1601, whose writings showed a bent towards Pelagianism & caused a dispute concerning Grace & Predestination. The mystic Molinists followed *Molinos* in the 17th century.)

Scholasticism deadly enemy of Mysticism
Mediaeval mystics, St. Bernard, Gerson, Tauler, Suss, Heinrich v. Nordlingen, Thomas à Kempis

Gerson is the name of a town near Rheims – hence the name of Jews.[3]

Solon. The Athenians having failed in their contest with Megara for the possession of Salamis, a law was enacted that no one in future should speak in public in favour of renewing the contest. Solon, indignant, feigned to be mad & caused a report of his madness to be spread – then rushed into the agora & taking his stand on the herald's stone recited a poem (elegiac) of 100 lines urging the Athenians to recover the lovely island.[4]

1 The reference to Richard Morris, editor, *Dan Michel's Ayenbite of Inwit, or Remorse of Conscience, in the Kentish Dialect, 1340 AD* (London: Trübner for the Early English Text Society, 1866), may be from Tylor, *Primitive Culture*, I, 411, or Alexander John Ellis, *Early English Pronunciation*, I, 409n. For other notes from Ellis, see Pf 707 14; for Tylor, see B 183 and Pf 711 64, 65, and 70.
2 The source of these notes on mysticism has not been traced.
3 Source not traced: perhaps connected to the previous reference to the mediaeval mystic Levi ben Gerson or Gersonides (1288–1344).
4 Charles Peter Mason, 'Solon' in Smith's *Dictionary of Greek and Roman Biography and Mythology*, III, 858. This is the occasion that 'brought Solon prominently forward as an actor on the political stage'.

Palestrina

Pf 707 4, 5, 6, 7, 8, 9

GE's source for the following notes on music is 'Palestrina' in François Joseph Fétis, *Biographie universelle des musiciens et bibliographie générale de la musique,* 2nd edition, 8 vols. (Paris: Firmin-Didot, 1868–70), VI, 428–36. Fétis is also the source of notes in the Beinecke Notebook (entries 236 to 239 and 249 to 256). A coda to this long note on the intelligibility of sacred texts set to music may be found in DD ch. 32. In the synagogue at Frankfurt, Deronda 'gave himself up to the strongest effect of chanted liturgies which is independent of detailed verbal meaning – like the effect of ... a Palestrina's *Magnificat*' (339). Later in the chapter, Mirah sings a Hebrew hymn with lisped syllables like those she remembers her mother singing. Deronda asserts that the real words would not have more expression for him: 'the lisped syllables are very full of meaning', and to support his assertion cites his experience in the synagogue: 'the service impressed me just as much as if I had followed the words – perhaps more' (346).

The connection between Deronda's first experience of Jewish liturgy and GE's transcription from Fétis is noted by Beryl Gray, who finds it 'ironic' that 'the very effect stressed by George Eliot' contradicts the requirements prescribed by the Council of Trent, the Papal commission, and the Cardinals Vitelozzi and Borromeo: 'music still dominates the word'.[1] GE's carefully prepared analogy has a larger purpose than irony, however. In her dramatic presentation of this topic, the sacred and the profane, like the liturgical and the familial, are intimately mingled. Domination by one part over another is not of concern to her. Indeed, it may be noted that before Palestrina, the melody and fugal counterpart did not dominate either 'the lascivious and gross' or the sacred words. But GE is concerned to show that part-singing in several voices is uniquely capable of expressing individual participation in 'the sense of communion', 'a yearning to escape from the limitations of our own weakness ... or else a self-oblivious lifting up of gladness'. It is only 'with the cessation of the devotional sounds' that Deronda is chilled by the (mistaken) 'frigid idea that he had probably been alone in his feeling, and

1 *George Eliot and Music* (London: Macmillan, 1989), pp. 113–15.

perhaps the only person in the congregation for whom the service was more than a dull routine' (DD ch. 32: 340).

The central image of GE's lyric, 'O May I Join the Choir Invisible', is the experience of general participation in choir song, in which the 'discords' of the self may be 'quenched by meeting harmonies' and 'die in the large and charitable air' (*Poems*, p. 49). The hymn was incorporated into at least one Positivist New Year's Day service, but in June 1877 GE wrote to Frederic Harrison, declining to contribute to 'a liturgy' (as she called it) for a Religion of Humanity. He had in mind 'some equivalent for family prayer', but she had a much higher conception of liturgical composition: 'That form of contribution would hardly lie within my powers' (GEL VI, 387–8).

/4/

Palestrina (Joh. Pier Luigi) date of birth uncertain, but probably b. 1524 & d. 1594 . Improperii, Magnificats, Motets, Madrigals
Pergolesi (Giov. Baptist Jesi) b. 1707. Stabat, Salve Regina, Cantata of Orpheus, Operas, Serva Padrona [VI, 484–9]
Allegri, 1580–1652. Scarlatti, b. 1659 (Alessandro)[1].

L'usage de composer des messes entières & des motets sur le chant d'une antienne ou sur la mélodie d'une chanson profane s'était introduit dans la musique d'église dès le treizième siècle, ainsi qu'on peut le voir dans les motets à trois voix du trouvère Adam de la Hale. Pendant que trois ou quatre voix chantaient en contrepoint fugué Kyrie-Eleison, ou Gloria in Excelsis, ou Credo, la partie qui chantait la mélodie disait ou les paroles de l'antienne ou même celles de la chanson italienne ou française, quelquefois lascives et grossières.[2]

1 Fétis gives the date 1649. The source here may be Hullah, p, 113: see Pf 707 50.
2 For the following pages, the source is Fétis, VI, 429–31. Translation:
The practice of composing whole masses and motets on the antiphonal chant or on the melody of a profane song was introduced in church music as early as the 13th century, as one can see in the three-part motets of the *trouvere* Adam de la Hale. While three or four voices in fugal counterpoint sang the Kyrie Eleison, or the Gloria in Excelsis, or the Credo, the part which sang the melody said either the words of the anthem or even those of the Italian or French song, sometimes lascivious and coarse.

L'indécente et /5/ ridicule conception du mélange du profane et du sacré dans la musique de l'église, fut l'objet des censures du concile de Bâle, puis de celui de Trente. Les sessions de celui-ci ayant été closes au mois de décembre 1563, le pape Pie IV nomma pour exécuter les décrets de cette assemblée les cardinaux Vitelozzi et Borromée, qui s'adjoignirent, pour ce qui concernait la musique, une commission de huit membres, choisie en grande partie parmi les chapelains-chantres de la chapelle pontificale. Dès la première réunion de cette commission, il fut décidé: 1° qu'on ne chanterait plus à l'avenir les messes et motets où des paroles différentes étaient mêlées; 2° que les messes composées sur des thèmes de /6/ chansons profanes seraient bannies à jamais. Cependant, à l'exception des messes des anciens compositeurs appelées *sine nomine,* parce que les auteurs en avaient imaginé les thêmes, il n'existait pas de modèles pour la réforme qu'on voulait opérer. Ces messes *sine nomine* étaient d'ailleurs surchargées de toutes les puériles recherches de contrepoints conditionnels qui ne permettaient point de saisir le sens des textes sacrés.[1]

Les cardinaux ... insistaient sur la nécessité de rendre ces textes intelligibles dans l'audition de la musique; ils citaient comme des modèles à suivre le Te Deum de Constant Festa, et surtout les Improperii composés par Palestrina; mais les chantres de la chapelle pontificale répondaient que ces /7/ morceaux de peu d'étendue ne décidaient pas la question pour des messes, d'où l'on ne pouvait bannir le contrepoint fugué ni les canons. La discussion

1 Translation:

The indecent and ridiculous idea of mixing together the profane and the sacred in the music of the church was the object of censures by the Council of Basle and then the Council of Trent. The sessions of the latter having closed in December 1563, Pope Pius IV nominated, to put into effect the decrees of the Council, Cardinals Vitelozzi and Borromeo, who appointed, for matters concerning music, a committee of eight members, chosen for the most part from the chaplain-choristers of the pontifical chapel. At the first meeting of this committee it was decided: 1° that in future, masses and motets where different words were mixed together would no longer be sung; 2° that masses composed on the themes of profane songs would be banned for ever. However, with the exception of masses by the early composers called *sine nomine* [without name], because the authors had invented their themes, no models existed for the reform they were trying to effect. Besides, the *sine nomine* masses were overburdened with all the trivial pursuits of conditional counterpoints, which did not permit the meaning of the sacred texts to be grasped.

ne fut terminé que par une résolution bien honorable pour P. de Palestrina – qu'on inviterait ce maître à composer une messe qui pût concilier et la majesté du service divin et les exigences de l'art, telles qu'elles étaient conçues à cette époque. S'il atteignait le but proposé, la musique devait être conservée à l'Eglise; dans le cas contraire, il devait être pris une résolution qui aurait vraisembablement ramené toute la musique religieuse au simple *faux bourdon.*[1] Palestrina ne fut point /8/ effrayé de la responsabilité imposée à son génie: ému d'un saint enthousiasme, il composa *trois* messes à six voix qui furent entendues chez le cardinal Vitelozzi: les deux premières furent trouvées belles, mais la troisième excita la plus vive admiration, et fut considérée comme une des plus belles inspirations de l'esprit humain.[2]

Dès lors il fut décidé que la musique serait conservée dans la chapelle pontificale et dans les églises du culte catholique, apostolique et romain; et que les messes de Palestrina deviendraient les modèles de toutes les compositions du même genre.[3]

1 Translation:

The cardinals ... insisted on the need to render these texts intelligible to those hearing the music; they cited, as models to follow, Costanzo Festa's Te Deum, and above all Palestrina's Improperii; but the choristers of the pontifical chapel answered that these not very extensive pieces did not resolve the question for the masses, where fugal counterpoint or canons could not be banned. The discussion was ended only by a resolution of considerable honour for P. de Palestrina – that they would invite this master to compose a mass which would reconcile the majesty of the divine service and the requirements of art, as conceived at that time. If he attained the proposed objective, music would be preserved in the Church; in the contrary case, a resolution would have to be taken which would probably have brought all religious music back to the simple *faux bourdon.*

For GE's note on *faux bourdon,* see Pf 707 53.

2 Translation:

Palestrina was not daunted by the responsibility imposed on his genius; moved by a holy enthusiasm, he composed *three* masses for six voices, which were heard at Cardinal Vitelozzi's palace. The two first were thought beautiful, but the third excited the liveliest admiration, and was considered to be one of the most beautiful inspirations of the human spirit.

3 Translation:

From that time, it was settled that music would be kept in the pontifical chapel and the churches of the Catholic, Apostolic and Roman ritual; and that Palestrina 's masses would become the models for all compositions of the same kind.

/9/

Four sacred cities: Jerusalem, Hebron, Safet, Tiberius[1]

Birkenhead - ship going down - boats filled with women & passengers: soldiers ordered to draw up in file ready to sink with the ship. They obeyed & not one of them shrank.[2]
Troop of Lascars in the second Sikh war riding into a ditch in the Punjaub, knowing that they must fill it with themselves & their horses that their comrades might pass over them as a bridge.[3]

1 Salomon Munk, *Palestine. Description géographique, historique et archéologique* (Paris: Firmin-Didot, 1845), p. 35. GE's copy, in DWL, is included in the 'Books Wanted' list on Pf 711 21.

2 Charles Kingsley refers to the shipwreck of the *Birkenhead* in 'Heroism', *Cornhill Magazine* 27 (1873): 32, and recommends to his readers' attention his source for this and other episodes: *A Book of Golden Deeds of All Times and All Lands,* by Charlotte Mary Yonge, first published in 1864. In October 1873 GE wrote to Alexander Macmillan,

> A little while ago we inquired for Miss Yonge's *Book of Noble Deeds,* and it was out of print. I hope it is to be reproduced. (GEL V, 444)

It was reprinted by Macmillan in 1873 (and later editions). GE's copy was listed in Mrs Ouvry's inventory (*Libraries*, p. 121). Yonge includes the men of the Birkenhead in her chapter on 'Discipline' (pp. 427–9 in the 1888 edition; the present editor has not seen the 1873 edition).

In DD ch. 64, Sir Hugo, thinking of men whose heirs are not well provided for, puts another view of selfless heroism:

> 'I like that story of the fellows in the Crimean war, who were ready to go to the bottom of the sea, if their widows were provided for.' (704)

3 Neither Kingsley nor Yonge include the Lascars. Kingsley's article was a reprint of a lecture, during which he may have mentioned this act of self-sacrifice.

Celtic names

Pf 707 10, 11, 12, 13, 14, 15, 16, 26, 27

The major source for these pages of notes is Volume II of Charlotte Mary Yonge, *History of Christian Names,* 2 vols. (London: Parker, Son, and Bourne, 1863). GE was quite aware of implicit ironies in the derivation of modern 'Christian' names from those of ancient pagan goddesses. Gwendolen Harleth's Christian name has an ambivalent British history. Her role as 'a beauty of Arthur's Court' (Pf 707 11) is covertly present in the question raised in 'the make-believe of a beginning' of the novel: 'Was she beautiful or not beautiful?' As 'the British Venus', she may be morning star or evening star: 'Was the good or evil genius dominant in those beams?' (DD ch. 1: 3). Her namesake's eminence as 'the Lady of the bow' (Pf 707 10) is latent in the ironies of GE's account of the Brackenshaw Archery Meeting:

> Who can deny that bows and arrows are among the prettiest weapons in the world for feminine forms to play with? ... The time-honoured British resource of 'killing something' is no longer carried on with bow and quiver ... (DD ch. 10: 90)

Included in this section are references to publications of the Early English Text Society. GE's copies of twenty-five of these publications are in DWL. The note on the EETS edition of Havelock the Dane (Pf 707 14) may reflect GE's memory of the 'Story of Havelock the Dane' as summarized in her earlier note on Folger 13 9:

> Grim the fisherman, finds a child floating on the waters; he grows up a hero, & after various adventures turns out to be the son of a Danish King, & marries the daughter of a king of England. The foster father, with his aid, builds Grimsby.

The stories of Havelock and Arthur suggest some parallels with the story of Deronda.

/10/

Gwen is used in Welsh in the double sense of the colour white & of a woman, perhaps for the same reason that 'the fair' so often stands for a lady in poetry. *Gwen*, the feminine of *Gwyn*, white, becomes wen in composition.

Gwen is considered as the British Venus. The planet is Seren-Wener as a morning star, Gweno as an evening star; nay, it is highly probable that Venus herself may be but a Cymric Gwen.

Gwendolen, or the Lady of the bow, or perhaps from Gwendal, white browed, was, it seems, an ancient British goddess, probably the moon.

Gwendolen is made by Brut, & by Geoffrey of Monmouth, the daughter of Corineus, /11/ Duke of Cornwall, & wife of Locrine, son of the original Brutus. He deserted her for Estrild, a fair German captive, & she made war upon him, in the course of which he was killed, & Estrild & her daughter Sabre, or Avern, were made prisoners; whereupon the jealous & revengeful queen caused both to be drowned in the river, thenceforth called Sabrina or Severn, in Welsh, Havern.

The Welsh Saints give us St Gwendolen or Gwen as the mother of Caradoc Vreichfras, the excellent Sir Cradocke of the Round Table. In the Triads & the Mabinogian Gwendolen is a beauty of Arthur's Court, & in the bardic enumeration of the thirteen wonders of Britain appears the gold chess board of Gwendolen. [pp. 130–1]

/12/

Will without substratum – a doctrine of the Motazalites[1]

Marauder, in the Thirty Years' War from the lawless band of C[oun]t Merode. [p. 8]

Alma, all-good, a real old Erse name
Lassarina, flame or blush of wine
Vevina, the melodious woman [p. 22]
Buddug = Bonduca = Boadicea [p. 30]

Taliessin, radiant brow [p. 33]

1 Salomon Munk, *Mélanges de philosophie juive et arabe*, p. 325n. The context is his discussion of the concept of the will of God. For another note from Munk on the Motazalites, see Pf 707 32.

Lear = Lir, the sea in all Celtic tongues, also called Lwyd, grey or extended. [pp. 34, 36]

(In Scandinavian myth the name of the sea-storm is Œgir – hence the *Eager*, the great flood-tide in the Trent) [p. 34] [1]

Bri (root) force or strength: hence the Celtic words for King
Irish Behon, Cornish Bren or Brennyn – (Brennus) [pp. 41, 42]

/13/

In the Triads one of the three fatal disclosures is when Arthur reveals the spot where Bran's head is buried (supposed to be a spell against invasion) because he scorned to keep the kingdom except by his own might. [p. 43]

Cunobelinus = Cûn, lord, Bel god of light & war [p. 45]

Cara, friend, was sometimes prefixed to a saint's name by the Xtian Gael, as Cara Michel, friend of St Michael, whence such a name as Carmichael. [p. 47]

Bran, the dog of Fingal [p. 48]

Brigh – strength – Brighid (or Bride) daughter of the fire-god, Erse goddess of wisdom & poetry [p. 50]

Vercingetorix may be rendered into Fear-cuin-cedo-righ = man who is chief of a hundred heads
Gadhaelic, man = fear, pl. fir
Cymric – gwr, pl. wyr. [pp. 53–4]

/14/

Mr Keightley derives Parcival from the Arabic Parse or Parschfal, poor dummling, who appears to have been the hero of an Eastern tale of a wonderful cup, whence arose the mysterious allegory of the Holy Greal. The Welsh legend of Peredur in the Mabinogian is almost identical. The story of Mervyn Lez Breiz, stirred to chivalry by the sight of the knight whom he took for an angel, is repeated of Parcival. (Lez Breiz means support of Britain.) [pp. 151, 157]

Pelagius = Morgwn = dweller by the sea [p. 156]

1 See also Pf 707 73.

Celtic names Pf 707 14 15

Cuckoo Song } XIIIth century (*Ellis, Pronn of Eng*)[1]
Prisoner's Prayer

Merlin pub. by English Text Society[2]

Havelock the Dane 10/–[3]

like = lic. German *lich*
less = leas or loose – *los*
ship = shape. *schaft*[4]

/15/

The Feen or Fenians are a band of heroes claimed both by Ireland & Scotland. Last survivor of the band said to be converted by St Patrick, end of 4th century, – Oisean or Ossian: taken into a monastery, impatient of his life there, praying on his deathbed that his dear Fenians may be with him at the last day. 'Ossian after the Feen' is in Scotland a proverb for dreariness. [pp. 64, 66–7]

Macbeth, son of life [p. 100]

Bancu, white chief or white dog [p. 101]

Winifred = Welsh, Gwenfrewi [p. 102]

Gallowglass = giolla eachaid = Horse-servant
Gilla or Giolla – servant
Culdee is explained as *Giolla De*.
Giolla Iosa (Gillies) servant of Jesus [pp. 113, 114]

1 Alexander John Ellis, *Early English Pronunciation,* 3 parts (London: Trübner for the Early English Text Society, 1867– 9) II, 417 and 437. The note on 'Ayenbite of Inwit' on Pf 707 2 may also be from the EETS series.

2 Henry Benjamin Wheatley, editor, *The Romance of Merlin,* 3 parts (London: Trübner for EETS, 1865–69).

3 Walter William Skeat, editor, *The Lay of Havelock the Dane* (London: Trübner for EETS, 1868); published at 10 shillings.

4 Source: either Ellis, I, 387 and II, 474, or William Dwight Whitney, *Language and its Study* (London: Trübner, 1874), pp. 58, 59, 60. 'Whitney Lectures on Language' was read on 12 and 24 November 1874 (GHL Diary). GE added the German words. See the headnote to the 'Language' section, Pf 711 73 to 75.

/16/

From St Columba, Maelcolum = Malcolm, servant of Columb [p. 116]

Cam, the crooked [p. 122]

Arthur, Ard or Arth means high or noble [p. 125]

Pendragon [p. 129]

Ga gag, Celtic for stammering [p. 137]

'Great benefactors of mankind, Deliverers' Paradise Regained, III, 82[1]

Ten virtues constituting duty in the Law of Menu:
Resignation, the action of rendering good for evil, temperance, probity, purity, the repression of sensuality, the knowledge of the Sostras, that of the Supreme Soul, truth, & freedom from anger.[2]

Herod. II. 42. Hercules entreating Ammon to become visible, the god at last consented to show himself enveloped in the skin of a ram.[3]

1 This line from Milton's *Paradise Regained* is quoted as Deronda asks himself whether Mordecai, as one of 'the heirs of enthusiasm', is a true benefactor and deliverer of mankind, or only one of 'the devotees of phantasmal discovery' (DD ch. 41: 475).

2 Source not traced. On Folger 13 46, from another source, reference is made to the 'Laws of Manu' and the 'Sastra or Shasters, law-books, codes'.

3 According to David Grene's translation of Herodotus II, 42:

> But in the end, because Hercules was so insistent, Zeus made a contrivance of flaying a ram, taking off the ram's head and using it as a mask, and entering the fleece of the sheep and so displaying himself to Hercules.

'Herodotus Book II, On Egypt', included in a list of books 'Read since September [1872]' on Pf 711 11, is also the source of notes on Pf 711 14 and 23.

/26/

Rowena, in Kymric Rhonwen = white skirt [p. 57]

The isle of Erin has been supposed to be named from Eri, the West, but of late philologists have traced it to the same root as the other names indicating a branch of the Aryans or ploughing race. It seems according to its own historians to have been peopled by various immigrations from the East,[1] the most important of whom were the Tuath de Danan, whom they trace from Bœotia, & who brought the stone of destiny said to have been Jacob's pillow at Bethel, to which was attached the belief that the whole country would devolve on the line of chiefs who sat on it to be crowned. After these followed a tribe who by unvarying report are said to have come direct from Spain & to have been termed Scots. From their leader Milidh, they are known as Mic Milidh or Milesians, & theirs is considered the noblest blood in Ireland. [p. 7]

The favourite legends start this famous colony from the East ***/27/*** where Phenius, the head of the family, was supposed to have taught the Phoenicians letters & to have left them his name! His son Niul named the Nile, having been sent on an embassy to Egypt where he married Pharoah's daughter – whether named Scota or not authorities are not agreed – but either Niul or his son migrated to Spain. It is from this Niul or Neill that all Neales are descended. The name from *niadh*, champion. [pp. 59–60]

1 Yonge has 'West', but GE corrects this to 'East'. Compare Yonge II, 9: 'the tradition of the whole people points to a migration from the East'.

Kabbalah (from Ginsburg)

Pf 707 17, 18, 19, 20, 21, 22, 23, 24, 25

Christian David Ginsburg's account of *The Kabbalah: Its Doctrines, Development and Literature* (London: Longmans, Green, Reader, and Dyer, 1865) informs GE's use of Kabbalistic doctrine in her characterization of Mordecai.[1] The excerpt from Ginsburg on Pf 707 20–21 is similar to her exposition of the doctrine in the novel, as an image of Mordecai's relation to Deronda. In DD ch. 43, Mordecai articulates 'the doctrine of the Cabbala' to his new friend:

> '... souls are born again and again in new bodies till they are perfected and purified, and a soul liberated from a worn-out body may join the fellow-soul that needs it, that they may be perfected together, and their earthly work accomplished ... When my long-wandering soul is liberated from this weary body, it will join yours, and its work will be perfected.' (501–2)

Deronda feels at this time some resistance to this appeal, which has earlier been explained as the product of Mordecai's visionary 'imagination [which] had constructed'

> ... another man who would be something more ample than the second soul bestowed, according to the notion of the Cabbalists, to help out the insufficient first – who would be a blooming human life, ready to incorporate all that was worthiest in an existence whose visible, palpable part was burning itself fast away. His inward need for the conception of this expanded, prolonged self was reflected as an outward necessity. (DD ch. 38: 441)

1 For other notes on the Kabbalah, see B 136, 150, 168, 168v, 169, and 174. Baker has discussed GE's reading of Ginsburg in 'The Kabbalah, Mordecai, and George Eliot's Religion of Humanity', *Yearbook of English Studies* 3 (1973): 216–21, and *George Eliot and Judaism*, pp. 160–6.

In DD ch. 63, Mordecai, now known to be Ezra, declares,

> 'It has begun already – the marriage of our souls. It waits but the passing away of this body, and then they who are betrothed shall unite in a stricter bond, and what is mine shall be thine.' (698)

GE deliberately has Deronda reveal his double betrothal to Gwendolen in a single scene. He tells her he has become

> 'intimate with a very remarkable Jew, whose ideas have attracted me so much that I think of devoting the best part of my life to some effort at giving them effect ... I am resolved to begin it, however feebly. I am resolved to devote my life to it ... Yes ... I am going to marry.' (DD ch. 69: 746, 747, 749)

GE notes from Ginsburg that the advent of the Messiah

> ... is retarded by the few new souls that enter the world – so many old ones having to be born over again, & the soul of the Messiah cannot be born till all the rest have been born. Then the great Jubilee will begin when all souls will return into the bosom of the Infinite Source. (Pf 707 21)

As Mordecai tells Deronda in so many similar words,

> 'Then they will depart from the mortal region, and leave place for new souls to be born out of the store in the eternal bosom. It is the lingering imperfection of the souls already born into the mortal region that hinders the birth of new souls and the preparation for the Messianic time.' (DD ch. 43: 501)

The great Jubilee will begin with the reunion of all souls in 'the bosom of the Infinite Source – in the Palace of Love, where the Heavenly King is united with all souls by a kiss' (Pf 707 21). This image is incorporated into the novel's final chapter, which includes both Deronda's wedding to Mirah, 'their mutual pledge', and her brother's dying pledge. The strong paradox of his last words reflects the latent paradoxes in the doctrine of androgynous souls (Pf 707 20) marrying and mothering earlier-born souls.

> 'Death is coming to me as the divine kiss which is both parting and reunion – which takes me from your bodily eyes and gives me full presence in your soul ... Is it not begun? Have I not breathed my soul into you? We shall live together.' (DD ch. 70: 754)

Kabbalah (from Ginsburg) Pf 707 17 18

/17/

J'invoque et je célèbre le créateur Ahura-Mazda, lumineux, resplendissant, très grand et très bon, très parfait et très énergique, très intelligent et très beau, éminent en pureté, qui possède la bonne science, source de plaisirs, lui qui nous a créés, qui nous a formés, qui nous a nourris, lui le plus accompli des êtres intelligents.[1]

The Persian was forbidden to pray for himself says Herodotus – only for the prosperity of his country & king. [I, 132][2]

Moses commands not to harness together a horse & an ass – two animals of unequal strength.[3]

Chwolson, Treatise on the Remnants of the ancient Babylonian Literature in Arabic translations. Gutami, author of the Agricultura Nabat, 1400 BC
[Ginsburg, p. 76][4]

/18/

Kabbalah, receptio
Massorah, traditio [p. 4]
Sephiroth, emanations, or intelligences [p. 7]

1 This French translation of Yaçna 1, 1 of the *Avesta* differs from that in Charles de Harlez, *Avesta: Livre sacré des sectateurs de Zoroastre,* II, 61 (see Pf 707 1). Translations of the attributes of Ahura Mazda in this invocation are (perhaps necessarily) approximate and imprecise:

> I invoke and celebrate the Creator Ahura Mazda, radiant, glorious, greatest and best, most perfect and most full of energy, most intelligent and most beautiful, eminent in purity, who possesses good understanding, source of pleasures, he who has made us, who has formed us, who has nourished us, he who is the most accomplished of intelligent beings.

For an introduction to the relation between Zoroastrianism and Judaism, see Mary Boyce's lecture to the Friends of Dr. Williams's Library, reprinted as *Zoroastrianism: A Shadowy but Powerful Presence in the Judaeo-Christian World* (London: Dr. Williams's Trust, 1987).

2 In her copy of *Herodotus Graece et Latine* in DWL, GE pencilled in an index note on the endpapers of Volume I: 'Persian not permitted to pray for the private good, 196'.

3 Deuteronomy xxii, 10: 'Thou shalt not plow with an ox and an ass together'.

4 For other references to Chwolson's treatise, see Pf 711 92a, Pf 710 32, and Pf 707 23.

Kabbalah (from Ginsburg) Pf 707 18 19

Kabbalah derived from Neo-Platonism. The very expression *En Soph* (אין סוף) which the Kabbalah uses to designate the Incomprehensible One, is foreign, & is evidently an imitation of the Greek ἄπειρος. The speculations about the En Soph, that he is superior to actual being, thinking & knowing, are thoroughly Neo-Platonic (ἐπέκεινα οὐσίας, ἐνεργίας, νοῦ χαὶ νοήσεως); & R. Azariel whose work (Commentary on the Ten Sephiroth) is the first Cabbalistic production tells us that in viewing the Deity as purely negative, & divesting him of all attributes, he followed the opinion of the philosophers. He uses nearly the words of Proclus who tells us that 'although he is generally called the unity (τὸ ἕν) it would be better if no name were given him; for there is no word which can depict his nature – he is ἀῤῥητος, αγνωστὸς, the inexpressible, the unknown. Again, the Kabbalah says the En Soph made his existence **/19/** known in the creation of the world by the Sephiroth, emanations. So Neo-Platonism. The Sephiroth are divided into a trinity of triads denominated, 1° the intellectual world, 2° the sensuous world, 3° the material world, which exactly corresponds to the three triads of Neo-Platonism, νοῦς, ψύχη, φύσις ... Even the comparison between the emanation of the Sephiroth from the En Soph, & the rays proceeding from light to describe the immanency & perfect unity of the two, is the same as the Neo-Platonic figure employed to illustrate the emanations from one principium – οἱον ἐκ φωτὸς τὴν ἐξ αὑτοῦ περίλαμψιν. [pp. 105–6]

Ophanim (angels) wheels [p. 159][1]

Sephiroth

Intellectual triad, Crown, Wisdom, Intelligence
Moral or Sensuous, Love, Justice, Beauty
Material triad, firmness, Splendour, Foundation [pp. 8–10]

Many primordial worlds destroyed, not containing the human form until the present world was created [pp. 21–2]

1 This note is from the Glossary: 'אופנים ... translated *wheels* in the English version (Ezek. i, 20), is taken by the Jewish Rabbis to denote *a distinct order of angels,* just as the Cherubim and Seraphim.' See GE's note on *Angel,* Pf 710 5. For other notes on angels, see B 118 and 118v.

/20/

4 Worlds. 1. The *Atzilatic,* or world of emanations, most intimately allied with the En Soph, perfect & immutable. 2. The Briatic world, further removed – its ten Sephiroth of less potency but of purest nature without admixture of matter. 3. The Jetziratic World, called the world of formation, & of Angels. It is in this world where those intelligent & incorporeal beings reside who are wrapped in a luminous garment, & who assume a sensuous form when they appear to man. 4. The Assiatic World called the world of action & the world of *matter*. [p. 24–5]

Pre-existence of human souls. (This was believed in by the Jews before the Kabbalah came into vogue, v. B. of Wisdom viii, 20.[1] Josephus ascribes it to the Essenes, & Philo has it.) [p. 31n]

In its original state each soul is androgynous – separated into male & female when it descends on earth. [p. 32]

It is the destiny of the soul to return to the Infinite Source after developing the germs of perfection implanted in it. And since one term of life is not always enough for this another term or terms is allowed i.e. the soul reinhabits a body again & again – but only 3 times. If two souls in their 3d residence are still too weak they are both united or sent into one body, so that they may be /21/ able conjointly to learn that which they were too feeble to do separately. It sometimes however happens that it is the isolation of the soul which is the source of her weakness, & she requires help to pass thro her probation. In that case she chooses a companion soul of better fortune or more strength. The stronger of the two then becomes as it were the mother; she carries the sickly one in her bosom & nurses her as a woman her child. [pp. 42–3]

Entire restoration. Even the archangel of wickedness Samäel will be restored to his angelic nature. This will only take place at the advent of Messiah. Which advent however is retarded by the few new souls that enter the world – so many old ones having to be born over again, & the soul of the Messiah cannot be born till all the rest have been born. Then the great Jubilee will begin when all souls will return into the bosom of the Infinite Source – in the Palace of Love, where the Heavenly King is united with all souls by a kiss. Then hell

1 The AV translation (revised 1894) of the Apocryphal book of The Wisdom of Solomon vii, 20–21: 'Now I was a child of parts, and a good soul fell to my lot; nay rather, being good, I came into a body undefiled.'

shall disappear. In that state the creature will not be distinguished from the Creator. The same idea will illuminate both. [pp. 44–5]

/22/

Modes of interpretation

1	Gematria –	equivalence of letters & numbers
2	Notariken –	each letter of a word an initial
3		Initials & finals taken to form words
4		Two words in same verse joined into one
5	Themora, or permutation – one letter stands for another according to various arrangements – as for example in drapers' marks. (Also called Ziruph) [pp. 49–50, 156, 163]	

Yeçira or Jetzira. This pretends to be a monologue of the patriarch Abraham & premises that the contemplations it contains are those which led the father of the Hebrews to abandon the worship of the stars & embrace the faith of the true God. – The doctrines are delivered in the style of aphorisms or theorems. The design is to exhibit a system whereby the universe may be viewed methodically in connection with the truths given in the Bible, showing from the gradual & systematic development of the Creation, & from the harmony which prevails in all its parts that One God produced it & that he is over all. The alphabet is used as a key to mystical meanings, along with the numbers which it also stands for. – Nothing in common with the cardinal doctrines of Kabbalah. Zunz holds that it belongs to the period of the Gaonim, about the IXth century – suggested by a mention in the Talmud of some Treatises on the Creation (Sepher Jezira) **/23/** 'which R. Chanina & R. Oshaja studied every Friday, whereby they produced a calf 3 years old & ate it'. – Indeed Dr. Chwolson in his treatise 'on the Remnants of the ancient Babylonian Literature in Arabic translations' has shown that the ancient Babylonians laid it down as a maxim that if a man were minutely & carefully to observe the process of nature, he would be able to imitate nature & produce sundry creatures. Gutami, author of the Agricultura Nabat, devoted a long chapter to these artificial productions.[1] The ancient sorcerer Ankebuta declares in his work on artificial productions, that he created a man & shows how he did it; but he confesses that the man was without reason, could not eat but simply

1 For other references to Chwolson, see Pf 711 92a, Pf 710 32 and Pf 707 17.

opened & closed his eyes.[1] The book Jetzira mentioned in the Talmud was most probably a Babylonian document. [pp. 65–6, 75–7]

(Cassel's German version of Khozari with learned annotations)[2]

The Sohar contains

1 Tosephta & Mathanithan, or small additional pieces, scattered in different places – as supplementary discussions, &c.

/24/

2 Hechaloth. The mansions & abodes

3 Sithre Tora, Mysteries of the Pentateuch

4 Midrash-ha-Neelam, Hidden Secret (mystical exegesis of Scriptures)

5 Raja Mehemna, Faithful Shepherd (Moses – conferences with Elias & S[imon] b. Jochai)

6 Raze Derazin, Secret of Secrets

7 Saba Demishpatim, Discourse of the Aged in Mishpatim (the Aged is Elias)

8 Siphra Detzniutha, Book of Secrets – chiefly on Emanation & Creation

9 Idra Rabba, or Great Assembly

10 Januka, or discourse of the young man

11 Idra Sutra, small assembly

Not a systematic treatise – promiscuously & reiteratedly dilates on the diverse doctrines of the Kabbalah [pp. 78–83]

Author, Moses de Leon, 13th century [p. 90]

Commentary on the Ten Sephiroth by R. Azariel b[en] Menachem, b. 1160, pupil of Isaac the Blind, regarded as originator of the Kabbalah. Azariel died 1238. [p. 94]

1 Little Jacob Cohen, the false receiver of Mordecai's confidence in 'the notion of the Cabbalists', takes up 'this fascinating game of imitating unintelligible words' with results that may be seen as a childish imitation of the so-called 'practical Kabbala' (see B 136): 'Jacob's sense of power was increased and his time enlivened by a store of magical articulation with which he made the baby crow, or drove the large cat into a dark corner ...' (DD ch. 38: 445).

2 Ginsburg's reference (p. 77n) is to David Cassel, translator and editor, *Das Buch Kusari Jehuda-ha-Levi* (Leipzig: Colditz, 1853). For GE's note on Jehuda Halevy's *Chozari*, see B 166–166v.

Kabbalah (from Ginsburg) Pf 707 24 25

Raymond Lully made the Kabbalah known among Xtians, 1236–1315. Doctor Illuminatus [p. 117][1]

/25/

Midrash in its restricted sense is used to denote the collection of expositions on the Pentateuch & five Megilloth called Midrasch Rabba. Each of the books composing this collection is also quoted by its separate name,
e.g. the Commentary on Genesis is called Bereshith Rabba
- on Exodus, Shemoth Rabba
- on Leviticus, Va-Ikra Rabba
- on Numbers, Bamidbar Rabba
- Deuteronomy, Debarim Rabba

(The Kabbalah, by Ginsburg) [p. 161][2]

Parness, Gemeindevorsteher [Pf 710 31][3]

Geen ketter sonder letter: Dutch proverb
No heretic without a text[4]

Man's life like the shadow of a bird that flieth. Talmudic[5]

1 For another note on Raymond Lully, see Pf 711 96.
2 For other notes on *Midrash*, see B 106, 115, 115v, 123, 141 to 143, and 149v.
3 Source not traced. Translation: 'head of the congregation'.
4 Source not traced. Copied again on Folger 14 56.
5 Source not found in Levi's collection of Talmudic sayings.

Talmudic sayings

Pf 707 27, 28, 29, 30, 32, 33, 34

Mixed together with some miscellaneous notes from various sources on Jewish topics are a number of 'Talmudic Sayings' (Pf 707 28, 29, 32), extracted from Giuseppi Raffaele Levi, *Parabeln, Legenden und Gedanken aus Thalmud und Midrasch,* translated into German from the original Italian by Ludwig Seligmann (Leipzig, 1863). GE's annotated copy is in DWL. Levi is also the source of notes on B 158–9, which seem to be drawn from the original Italian text. These pithy sayings should be compared with the 'Rabbinical sayings' on Pf 708 98 and 99, which are copied from Deutsch's famous essay on the Talmud, published in the *Quarterly Review* in October 1867.

Several passages on Pf 707 32 and 33 are excerpted from Salomon Munk, *Mélanges de philosophie juive et arabe* (Paris: A. Franck, 1857), which is also the source of notes on Pf 707 12 and Pf 710 20, 23, 28, and 41. Munk's exploration of the intricately mingled connections between Jewish and Muslim-Arabian schools of philosophy apparently contradicts the comment from Heine, to whom Judaea seemed to be a distinct 'fragment of the West that had lost itself in the East'.

/27/

'Judäa erschien mir immer ein Stück Occident, das sich mitten in den Orient verloren.' Heine, *Bekenntnisse* et seq. [Graetz 11, 403]
Worth quoting on the contrast between Israel & the other Oriental nations.[1]

1 The passage, copied again on GE's Blotter (Waley, p. 10), is actually from Heine's *Geständnisse*, read by GE shortly after its publication in 1854, and a basis for her 1856 article, 'German Wit: Heinrich Heine' (*Essays*, pp. 216–54). William Stigand, in *The Life, Work, and Opinions of Heinrich Heine,* 2 vols. (London: Longmans, Green, 1875), translates this as 'Judaea always appeared to me like a fragment of the West that had lost itself in the East' (I, 91). 'Stigand: Life of Heine' was read from 21 to 23 December 1875 (GHL Diary), but GHL thought Stigand a 'blockhead and blunderer' (GEL VI, 201).

Middoth = rules, order of a writing
Jalkut, extracts(?)
Setarim, secrets[1]

/28/

'Therefore night shall be unto you that ye shall not have a vision; & it shall be dark unto you that ye shall not divine; & the sun shall go down over the prophets, & the day shall be dark over them.' [Micah iii, 6][2]

Usury. Deut. 23: 19, 20[3]

'Hebrewess', Jeremiah, 34: 9[4]

Robbery of man is worse than robbery of God. *Kiduschin* [Levi, p. 24][5]

1 The source of these notes may be Steinschneider's 'Jüdische Literatur', pp. 376 and 381. For other extracts from Steinschneider, see B 141 to 150.

2 Although Mordecai tells Deronda that he had to journey from the bright sun of Trieste into 'a night in exposure to cold and snow ... the beginning of this slow death' (DD ch. 43: 503), he has not suffered the mental darkness prophesied by Micah. GE does not endorse the severity of that prophet's rebuke or the determinism of his predicted punishment for 'the sins of the house of Israel' (Micah i, 5). Thus, although Mordecai says, 'Mine was the lot of Israel. For the sin of the father my soul must go into exile', his next thought is that his mother's spirit 'and the spirit of her fathers, who had worthy Jewish hearts, moved within me, and drew me.' The consequences of the sins of the fathers cannot be evaded, but at least there are other fathers to choose from and to emulate.

3 'Thou shalt not lend upon usury to thy brother; usury of money, usury of victuals, usury of anything that is leant upon usury: Unto a stranger thou mayest lend upon usury; but unto thy brother thou shalt not lend upon usury'. See also Pf 711 101 and B 167v.

4 'That every man should let his manservant, and every man his maidservant, being an Hebrew or an Hebrewess, go free'.

5 *Kiduschin* is a tractate of the Talmud, on betrothals, dealing incidentally with the laws concerning Hebrew manservants and maidservants. In GE's copy of Levi in DWL, her pencilled notes include an index on the back end-paper: 'offences against man no greater than against God, 24'. The 'no' is an inadvertent error. In DD ch. 42, Mordecai correctly states that 'the Masters have said, an offence against man is worse than an offence against God.' (498)

When Israel lives in peace & love, even the guilt of Idolatry is forgiven. [p. 24]

Serve God without thinking of reward. P. Aboth [p. 25][1]

Distrust thyself even to the day of thy death. Ibid. [p. 26]

He who wears the yoke of religion is a freeman: He who shakes off the yoke of religion is a slave of society & the great. ib. [p. 26]

He who makes himself beloved by men is beloved by God; – he is not beloved by God who makes himself disliked by men. ib. [p. 27]

/29/

Israel is dear to God, because he is called a Son; dear is every man to God, for he is the image of God. [p. 27]

The mighty man & the man of war, the judge & the prophet & the prudent & the ancient, the captain of fifty, & the honourable man, & the counsellor & the cunning artificer & the eloquent orator.[2]

=[3]

/30/

Allusions to the Mosaic History
In Isaiah x, 26, xi, 15, 16[4]
Frequent to Sodom & Gomorrah[5]

1 GE copied other extracts from Pirke Avot on B 152 and Pf 708 98 to 99.

2 Isaiah's prophecy of the Captivity, the removal of able community leaders – the men listed here – to Babylon: 'babes shall rule over' the remnant in Jerusalem, 'and the people shall be oppressed, every one by another, and every one by his neighbour' (Isaiah iii, 2–5). Deronda has early on 'shut the door' on 'the option of the army'. Isaiah's list of options in public life is perhaps broader than the views of Sir Hugo (DD ch. 16: 160).

3 Matthew Arnold's translation of the Hymn of St. Francis follows here.

4 Isaiah x, 26 includes a reference to Moses' rod: 'and as his rod was upon the sea, so shall he lift it up after the manner of Egypt'. Isaiah xi, 15, 16, refers to the destruction of 'the tongue of the Egyptian sea': 'men [shall] go over dryshod ... like as it was to Israel in the day that he came up out of the land of Egypt'.

5 Isaiah alludes once to the destruction of Sodom and Gomorrah: 'And Babylon, the glory of kingdoms, the beauty of the Chaldees' excellency, shall be as when God overthrew Sodom and Gomorrah' (xiii, 19).

Though he be not gentle born
Thou maiest well seine this in sooth,
That he is gentle because he doth
As longeth to a gentleman.

Chaucer, Romaunt of the Rose [ll. 2194–7] [1]

'And if thou have nought, spend the lesse' [l. 2274]

Who loveth true hath no fatnesse. [l. 2686]

Chaucer uses 'jolly' in the sense of agreeable.
Also 'jollily' in the sense of 'full well'. Romaunt of the Rose

/32/

Der süsseste Tod ist der Tod gegeben vom göttlichen Kusse. Die Seele löst sich vom Körper, wie man ein Haar aus der Milch zieht.

Talmud, Berachoth [Levi, p. 72][2]

Metempsychosis – hebr. *guilgoul hanneschamot* [Graetz 9, 441–2][3]

History of Oriental studies – Hyde, Pococke, d'Herbelot[4]

1 The edition read by GE may have been *The Poetical Works of Geoffrey Chaucer*, edited by Thomas Tyrwhitt (London: Edward Moxon, 1843 and later editions); see pp. 227 and 230. Line references are indicated within square brackets.

2 Translation: 'The sweetest death is the death given by a divine kiss. The soul is freed from the body, just as one draws out a hair from the milk.' In 'The Death of Moses', GE elaborates upon this mysterious, evocative image:

God spake to Gabriel, the messenger
Of mildest death that draws the parting life
Gently, as when a little rosy child
Lifts up its lips from off the bowl of milk
And so draws forth a curl that dipped its gold
In the soft white—thus Gabriel draws the soul. (ll. 17–22)

3 GE has transliterated the Hebrew. Compare her notes from Ginsburg on souls reinhabiting bodies 'again and again', Pf 707 20–21.

4 The seventeenth-century Orientalists Thomas Hyde, Edward Pocock, and Barthélemy d'Herbelot were major sources for Gibbon's *History of the Decline and Fall of the Roman Empire*; see Pf 707 41.

Motécallemin, en hébreu Medabberim = dialecticians, parleurs
[Munk, *Mélanges*, p. 320; Pf 710 28]

Scolastiques arabes, deux principales sectes, les Motazales et les Ascharites (from Aschar, their founder) [Munk, *Mélanges*, p. 324] [1]

Minhag, ceremonial, rite [2]
Dayan (judge) minor rabbi
Hatanim, bridegrooms of the law
Thebah, reading-desk

/33/

– my varied life
Drifts by me; I am young, old, happy, sad,
Hoping, desponding, acting, taking rest,
And all at once: that is, those past conditions
float back at once on me. Browning [*Paracelsus*, V, 487–91] [3]

Karaim = textuaires, ou partisans du texte [Munk, *Mélanges*, p. 472] [4]

Calâm, science de la parole [Munk, *Mélanges*, p. 312] [5]

1 Translation: 'Mutakallimun, in Hebrew Medabberim = dialecticians, discoursers. Arab scholastics, two principal sects, the Motazalites and the Ascharites'. A note on Pf 707 12, '*Will* without substratum – a doctrine of the Motazalites' is also from Munk. See also Pf 710 28 and compare B 193v.

2 This and the following definitions of Hebrew words are written in ink over erased pencil. Their source has not been traced.

3 The poem dramatizing the life and death of Paracelsus was the first published under Robert Browning's name (in 1835). These lines are spoken from Paracelsus' death-bed: 'I am dying. Festus, / And now that fast the storm of life subsides, / I first perceive how great the whirl has been' (V, 471–3). The lines chosen for the epigraph for DD ch. 50 speak of potential energies held in suspense: as 'If some mortal, born too soon, / Were laid away in some great trance' (I, 434–40). The role of the watching angelic spirit in the poem is shared in GE's novel by Deronda's various father-figures.

4 *Karaim* means 'partisans for, or advocates of, the bare text of the scriptures'. The Rabbanites were partisans of the Talmud (p. 477). According to Munk, Karaite theologians adopted the name of Motécallemîn, after the Muslim scholastics (p. 473). See also Pf 710 23 and Pf 711 55, where GE notes that the Karaites are a 'sect of Jewish puritans', whose 'Dogmas' include 'adherence solely to the written text'.

5 Kalam, 'the science of the word' in Muslim theology, is the etymological root of Mutakallimun.

Saadia in his book on Job denies the existence of a Satan or rebel angel.
[Munk, *Mélanges*, p. 478][1]

Ahi, ahi, ma conoscuito il mondo
Non cresce, anzi si scema, e assai piu vasto
L'etra sonante e l'alma terra, e il mare
Al fanciullin, che non al saggio, appare. Leopardi[2]

One monad fastens on a plant & sucks the chlorophyl first from that one cell then from another: a feebler monad, unable to make a hole in the cell-wall, thrusts long processes of its body into the hole already made: a third monad leads a predatory life, falling upon other monads **/34/** that have filled themselves with food.[3]

=[4]

1 According to Munk, Saadia shows that in the Book of Job, both Satan and the son of God are men, 'a bold opinion for that epoch'. The tenth-century Gaon Saadia ben Joseph led a counterattack against the Karaites. GE's note on Pf 711 55 refers to Saadia as the 'founder of biblical criticism'. For an excerpt from his philosophical and polemical *Book of Beliefs and Opinions,* see Pf 711 80. GE's copy of Julian Fürst's translation of this work, *Emunot we-dëot oder Glaubenslehre und Philosophie* (Leipzig: Otto Wigand, 1845), is in DWL.

2 Count Giacomo Leopardi, *Canti*, II: 'Ad Angelo Mai quand' ebbe trovato i libri de Cicerone *Della Republica*' (To Angelo Mai Upon his discovery of the manuscript of Cicero's *De Republica*), ll. 87–90. Translation by Geoffrey L. Bickersteth from *The Poems of Leopardi* (Cambridge: Cambridge University Press, 1923), p. 160:

Ah, but the world, when known,
Grows not, but rather shrinks, the more we learn.
Ocean, rich earth, the sounding atmosphere
To boys far vaster than to the sage appear.

Another of Leopardi's *Canti*, 'All' Italia', is the 'grand Ode to Italy' sung by Mirah (DD ch. 39: 451-2). Chapter 40 was completed on 10 February 1876 and the proofs for Book V were read 'again' on 25 February (GHL Diary).

3 GHL, *Problems of Life and Mind, Second Series: The Physical Basis of Mind* (London: Trübner, 1877), pp. 38–9. GE's and GHL's annotated copy is in DWL.

4 This page continues with excerpts from the 'Yule's *Marco Polo*' section.

Hymn of St. Francis

Pf 707 29

This English translation by Matthew Arnold of the 'Canticle of the Sun, Canticle of the Creatures – the poem goes by both names' is from his essay on 'Pagan and Mediaeval Religious Sentiment', reprinted in *Essays in Criticism*, 3rd revised edition (London: Macmillan, 1875), pp. 246–7. GE read *Essays in Criticism* from 19 to 24 January 1876 (GHL Diary). She copied a French translation of the 'Fioretti di San Francisco' on Folger 14 72 and the original Italian on Folger 14 79.

/29/

Hymn of St. Francis
(Translated from the Italian by Matthew Arnold)

O most high, almighty, good Lord God, to thee belong praise, glory, honour,
& all blessing!
Praised be my Lord God with all his creatures; & specially our brother the sun
who brings us the day, & who brings us the light; fair is he,
& shining with a very great splendour: O Lord, he signifies
to us thee!
Praised be my Lord for our sister the moon, & the stars, which he has set clear
& lovely in heaven.
– for our brother the wind &c.
– for our sister water, who is very serviceable unto us,
& humble & precious & clean.
– for our brother fire, through whom thou givest us light in the
darkness; & he is bright, & pleasant & very mighty & strong.
– for our mother the earth, the which doth sustain us
& keep us &c.
– for all those who pardon one another &c.
– for our sister, the death of the body, from which no man
escapeth. &c. &c.

Demosthenes

Pf 707 31

The source of this excerpt is Demosthenes, *De Corona*, §§ 263 and 264, in *The Orations of Demosthenes and Aeschines on the Crown*, edited by George Augustus Simcox and William Henry Simcox (Oxford: Clarendon Press, 1874), p. 212. The editors were the elder brothers of GE's friend Edith Simcox. GE's copy in DWL was withdrawn by Charles Lee Lewes.

Demosthenes urges the men of Athens to live up to the historical honour of their nation:

> But it cannot, it cannot be that you made a mistake, men of Athens, in taking upon yourselves the burden of danger for the freedom and security of all; I swear it by your ancestors in the front lines at Marathon, by those who stood at Plataia, by your naval men at Salamis and Artemisium and by many others who lie in public tombs, good men, all of them, whom the city buried because it thought them worthy of the same honor, not only those of them who were successful and victorious. And justly so.[1]

Mordecai alludes to *De Corona* when he denounces the 'rational Jew' who rejects the Jewish nation:

> 'Yet let his child learn by rote the speech of the Greek, where he adjures his fellow-citizens by the bravery of those who fought foremost at Marathon – let him learn to say, that was noble in the Greek, that is the spirit of an immortal nation! But the Jew has no memories that bind him to action; let him laugh that his nation is degraded from a nation...' (DD ch. 42: 491)

In an essay, 'A Fine Excess. Feeling is Energy', GE discusses grand instances of 'determining energy in human sympathy, which even in particular cases, where it has only a magnificent futility, is more adorable, or as we say divine, than ... a prudent calculation of results'.

1 Translation by John J. Keaney in James J. Murphy, editor, *Demosthenes' On the Crown* (New York: Random House, 1967), pp. 99–100.

> *V*. what Demosthenes says (De Coronâ) about Athens pursuing the same course, though she had known from the beginning that her heroic resistance would be in vain.[1]

This is the passage from Demosthenes copied on GE's Blotter:

> If the event had been manifest to the whole world beforehand, not even then ought Athens to have forsaken this course, if Athens had any regard for her glory, or for her past, or for the ages to come.
>
> *Demosthenes*, de Corona (Waley, p. 9)

On Folger 13 13 the 'Oath in Demosthenes de Coronâ' is quoted in part from a note in George Grote's *History of Greece*, which GE was reading in July 1869: 'οὐ μὰ τους εν Μαραθῶνι προκινδυνεύσαντας των προγωνων &c &c'.[2]

/31/

ἀλλ' οὐκ ἔστιν, οὐκ ἔστιν ὅπως ἡμάρτετε, ἄνδρες 'Αθηναῖοι,
τὸν ὑπὲρ τῆς ἀπάντων ἐλεθερίας καὶ σωτηρίας κίνδυνον ἀράμενοι,
μὰ τοὺς Μαραθῶνι προκινδυνεύσαντας τῶν προγόνων καὶ τοὺς ἐν
Πλαταιαῖς παραταξαμένους καὶ τοὺς ἐν Σαλαμῖνι ναυμαχήσαντας
καὶ τοὺς ἐπ' 'Αρτεμισίῳ καὶ πολλοὺς ἑτέρους τοὺς ἐν τοῖς δημοσίοις
μνήμασι κειμένους ἀγαθοὺς ἄνδρας, οὓς ἅπαντας ὁμοίως ἡ πόλις τῆς
αὐτῆς ἀξιώσασα τιμῆς ἔθαψεν, Αἰσχίνη, οὐχὶ τοὺς κατορθώσαντας
αὐτῶν οὐδὲ τοὺς κρατήσαντας μόνους. δικαίως.

1 Published posthumously in an edition by Charles Lee Lewes, *Essays and Leaves from a Notebook* (Edinburgh: Blackwood, 1884), p. 381n. Reprinted in *Essays*, p. 451.

2 Pratt and Neufeldt, pp. 102, 282.

Yule's *Marco Polo*

Pf 707 34, 35, 36, 37, 38, 39, 40, 42, 43, 44, 45

The following eleven pages (excepting Pf 707 41) are taken from *The Book of Ser Marco Polo the Venetian concerning the Kingdoms of the East,* 'newly done into English' by Henry Yule, 2nd edition, 2 vols. (London: John Murray, 1874). Yule is the source of the story of the life of Siddartha or Sakya-Muni or the Buddha (Pf 707 34–39), as well as numerous miscellaneous bits of information, many of which are copied again in the alphabetized notebook, Pf 710, which GE titled 'Oriental Memoranda'. In these pages her enduring interest in the Middle East and Mediterranean world begins to connect with the neighbouring cultures on the other side, the 'far east'.

/34/

Rook in chess taken from Rukh (roc) the huge bird of legend [Yule II, 412]

Brazil named from the dye so called – but doubts upon this, because there is an island of Brazil in legend [Yule II, 369]

The history of Barlaam & Josaphat, for several centuries one of the most popular books of Christendom, translated into all the chief European languages, its episodes & apologues used by poets & story tellers of diverse ages – Boccacio, Gower, compiler of the Gesta Romanorum, Shakspeare, &c,[1] has for its basis the story of Siddhárta or Sakya-Muni.[2]

The story first appears in Greek among the writings of John Damascenus, in the 8th cent[ury], who before he devoted himself to divinity had held high /35/ office at the court of the Khalif Abu Jáfar Almansúr. The outline of the story is as follows:

St Thomas had converted the people of India. Then a powerful pagan king, by name Abenner, arose & persecuted the Xtians, especially the ascetics. After

1 The story of the three caskets is adapted in *The Merchant of Venice.* GE's note on a German edition of *Gesta Romanorum* is on Pf 711 114.

2 GE adds 'or Sakya Muni'; see also Pf 710 34.

this king had long been childless, a son, greatly desired, is born to him, a boy of matchless beauty. The child is named Josaphat, & the astrologers foretell for him unexampled glory & prosperity – all but one, who assents to this, adds that the scene of this glory will not be his father's kingdom, & that the son will adopt the Xtian faith. Hence his father imprisoned him among delights in a splendid palace, where no knowledge of life's miseries can reach him so that he should have no inducement to think of another life, & never hear of Xt & his religion. He grows up in all accomplishments, & then occur the three encounters with the blind man, the sick, & the aged – as in the history of Siddharta. **/36/** Then comes Barlaam, a monk of great sanctity, in the disguise of a merchant & gains access to Josaphat, unfolds the Xtn doctrine & the blessedness of the monastic life. Suspicion is raised against Barlaam, & he departs. Then the King sends for a magician, Theudas, who removes the Prince's attendants & substitutes seductive girls, but all their blandishments are resisted through prayer. The King gives up his attempts at resistance & associates his son in the government. The Prince uses his power to promote religion & everything prospers in his hand. King Abenner dies after being drawn to the truth. Then Josaphat surrenders the kingdom to his friend Barachias & goes into the wilderness seeking Barlaam, wandering about & much buffeted by demons. He finds Barlaam, who dies in peace. Josaphat was 25 when he left his realm & led the life of a hermit 35 years; after which he died in peace & was buried by the side of Barlaam. King Barachias afterwards arrives & carries the bodies of the two friends to India. – From the Greek **/37/** church the history of the two saints passed into the Latin & they found a place in the Roman Martyrology under the 27th November. Their history occupies a large space in the *Speculum Historiale* of Vincent de Beauvais & is set forth in the Golden Legend. They are recognized by Baronius.

[Yule II, 305–8]

The *Pâtra* or alms-pot was the most valued legacy of Buddha. It had served the three previous Buddhas of this world-period, & was destined to serve the future one, Maitreya. The great Asoka sent it to Ceylon. Thence it was transferred to India by a Tamul chief in the 1st Century, but brought back, & is still shown in the Malagawa Vihara at Kandy. As usual, there were rival reliques, for Fahian found the alms-pot preserved at Peshawar. Hwen T'sang says in his time it was no longer there, but in Persia. And indeed the Pâtra from Peshawar according to Sir Henry Rawlinson **/38/** is still preserved at Kandahár, under the name of Kashkul or the Begging Pot. Sir H. R. conjectures that the deportation of the vessel, the palladium of the true

Gandhara (Peshawar) was accompanied by a popular emigration, & thus accounts for the transfer of that name to the chief city of Arachosia.

(v. Koeppen)[1]

Sir J. Tennent obtained the following Chinese extract referring to Ceylon & written in 1350: 'In front of the image of Buddha there is a sacred bowl, which is neither made of jade, nor copper, nor iron; it is of a purple colour, & glossy, & when struck it sounds like glass. At the commencement of the Yuen dynasty (i.e. under Kublai) three separate envoys were sent to obtain it' ... Fa-hian writes of the alms-pot at Pesháwar, that poor people could fill it with a few flowers whilst a rich man should not be able to do so with a 100, nay with a 1000 [grains], or 1000 bushels of rice. [Yule II, 310–12]

/39/

This Pâtra is the Holy Grail of Buddhism. German scholars have traced in the romances of the Grail remarkable indications of Oriental origin. It is not impossible that the alms-pot of Buddha was the prime source of them. Read the prophetic history of the Pâtra as Fa-hian heard it in India; its mysterious wanderings over Asia till it was taken up into the heaven of Tushita, where Maitreya the future Buddha dwells. When it has disappeared from Earth the Law gradually perishes, & violence & wickedness more & more prevail.

Yule's Marco Polo. vol II. 313

Prester John. First mention of him in the History of Otto bishop of Friesingen: 'We saw also there (at Rome 1145) **/40/** the ... B[isho]p of Gabala, from Syria – heard him bewailing with tears the peril of the Church beyond sea – also telling us how, not many years before, one John, King & Priest, who dwells in the extreme Orient beyond Persia & Armenia, & is (with his people) a Christian, but a Nestorian, had waged war against the brother Kings of the Persians & Medes &c ... At last Presbyter John (for so they are wont to style him) came forth victor – was advancing to fight in aid of the Church at Jerusalem; but when he had arrived at the Tigris & found there was no possible means of transport for his army, he turned northward ... This personage is said to be of the ancient race of those Magi who are mentioned in the Gospel, & to rule the same nations that they did, & to have such glory & wealth that he uses (they say) only an emerald sceptre. It was (they say) from

1 A reference to Karl Friedrich Köppen, *Die Religion des Buddha und ihre Entstehung*, 2 vols. (Berlin: Ferdinand Schneider, 1857–9), which is also mentioned on Pf 711 34, Pf 707 124, and Folger 13 63.

his being fired by the example of his fathers, who came to adore Xt in the cradle, that he was proposing to go to Jerusalem.' ib: 540 [Yule II, 539–40]

/42/

Om mani padme houm – formula of Bouddhist prayer:
O the perfection or jewel in the lotus – Amen [Yule II, 560; Pf 710 7]

'And kiss the lips of unacquainted change' King John [III, iv, 166][1]

Egyptian Cinderella

Rhodopis was bathing. An eagle carried off one of her sandals, & flying with it to Memphis, let it fall in the lap of the King, who was pronouncing judgment in the open air. Wondering at the smallness & beauty of the sandal, the King caused the owner to be searched for. And thus Rhodopis became his Queen.
(Strabo, p. 808)[2]

Apis = Hapi = Nile

Gr[eek]:	Eg[yptian]:	hier[oglyphic]:	signi[ficance]:
Phoenix =	bennu =	palm =	year or period[3]

Christ's College designed for the 'virtuous upbringing of miserable youths'[4]

'Ay, ay, cast that seed on the wind.'
Our talk is a casting of seed on the wind.[5]

/43/

Cairo was commonly called Babylon – Bambellonia d'Egitto in the middle ages. Babylon of Egypt is mentioned by Diodorus, Strabo & Ptolemy.
[Yule I, 24; Pf 710 7]

1 In Shakespeare's image, voiced by Cardinal Pandulph, the people turn away from young Prince Arthur and welcome innovation of which they know nothing.

2 Source: Smith's *Dictionary of Greek and Roman Biography and Mythology*, III, 652. The reference is to *Strabonis Geographica*, edited by Isaac Casaubon (1587), p. 808. On Pf 711 4, GE notes 'Greek story of Cinderella connected with Psammetichus (Rhodopis)'.

3 Perhaps from the trilingual inscription on the tablet of Canopus; see Pf 710 12

4 Reference not traced. Christ's Hospital, the 'Blue-coat School', was also founded for such a purpose.

5 Source not traced.

The Uighur character, introduced into Turkestan by Nestorian missionaries. The Uighur language is a branch of Oriental Turkish. [Yule I, 29; Pf 710 37]

Story of Alexander. How he drove a number of impure cannibal nations within a mountain barrier; & prayed that they might be shut up therein. The mountains drew together within a few cubits & Alexander then built up the gorge & closed it with gates of ivory. These nations afterwards said to be Gog & Magog who would come forth at the day of Antichrist. [Yule I, 56]

/44/

Zu'lkarnain, the two-horned, is an Arabic epithet of Alexander, with which legends have been connected, but which probably arose from the horned portrait on his coins. The term appears in Chaucer in the sense of *nonplus*: 'At *dulcarnon*, right at my wittes end'. This use is said to have arisen from the Arabic application of the term to the 47th Prop[osition] of Euclid. [Yule I, 169; Pf 710 40]

Baldacchino, from the rich silk & gold brocade so-called, of which canopies were made. [Yule I, 67]

Cramoisy – Kermes – crimson velvet originally [Yule I, 67]

Legend of the Three Kings in Marco Polo. One form was **/45/** that they were buried at Hadramaut in Arabia. Carried thence by order of the Empress Helena to Constantinople, thence to Milan, & thence by Frederic Barbarossa to Cologne. [Yule I, 84]

Old Man of the Mountain. He & his followers adherents of Ali (Shiites) – Ismailites established by Hassan in the mountains of N. Persia about 1090. De Sacy seems to have proved that they were called Hashishiya or Hashishin, from their use of the preparation of hemp called Hashish. [Yule I, 146–7]

The 'bombastical dissimulation of garments'
Anthropometamorphosis [Yule I, 172n][1]

Tacwin, Arabic name for an almanach (Early used by the Italians) [Yule I, 434; Pf 710 36]

1 Yule quotes from John Bulwer's work, *Anthropometamorphosis*, subtitled 'The Artificial Changeling' (1650): 'If they be not corpulent [they] counterfeit [corpulence] by the bombastical dissimulation of garments' (xix, 195). This note is copied again on Folger 14 56.

Gibbon's *History* and Huc's *Travels*

Pf 707 41, 46, 47, 48

Notes from Marco Polo's travels 'in the Kingdoms of the East' merge in these notebook pages with excerpts from *Souvenirs d'un voyage dans la Tartarie, le Thibet, et la Chine pendant les années 1844, 1845 et 1846*, 2 vols. (Paris: Adrien le Clerc, 1850) by Evariste Régis Huc, a missionary priest of the congregation of Saint-Lazare, and Edward Gibbon's *History of the Decline and Fall of the Roman Empire.* Many excerpts from Huc and Gibbon, like those from Yule, are copied again in Pf 710, GE's notebook of 'Oriental Memoranda'.

References to Gibbon, supplied within brackets, are to an 1872 reprint of an edition by Henry Hart Milman, with notes by Milman and François Guizot, revised by William Smith, 8 vols. (London: John Murray, 1854–5). GE's only precise citation does not, unfortunately, conform to the 1872 printing. An 8-volume set edited by 'W. Smith' is in Mrs Ouvry's inventory (*Libraries*, p. 72).

'Huc Voyage en Tartarie' was read on 17 November and from 10 to 30 December 1876 (GHL Diary). A year later, in November 1877, GHL recommended 'Huc: Voyage à Thibet (*Very* good – old)' (GEL VI, 429). Although an English translation by William Hazlitt, *Huc's Travels in Tartary*, was published in 1852, GE's notes are from the original.

/41/

Two kings among the Asiatic tribes fighting with each other – forsaken by their armies, who ran away in panic – left opposite each other on the plain attended only by their guards. v. Gibbon vi, 172 et seq. [ch. xlii][1]

Janizaries – Yengi cheri, new soldiers – Sclavonian captives converted into troops by the Turks [Gibbon viii, 29; ch. lxiv; Pf 710 22]

1 Gibbon's account, found in v, 167 of the 1872 edition, is of a battle in the Roman provinces south of the Danube, between the Lombards and the Gepidae.

Mamluc, pl. Mamalic, defined by Pococke & d'Herbelot, servum emptitium, seu qui pretio numerato in domini possessionem cedit. They frequently occur in the wars of Saladin, & it was only the Bahartie Mamalukes that were first introduced into Egypt by his descendants.

Note in Gibbon [vii, 252n; ch. lix; Pf 710 28][1]

/46/

Dekangestime?[2]

Minstrels among the Chinese, Tartars & Thibetans, singing national stories (Huc) [I, 88–92]

Barber's poisoned wheat sold to destroy birds. Dr Rutherford made experiments on rabbits to try & discover an antidote to the Picrotine or whatever was the poison used in the case, & he discovered that chloral was an effectual antidote.

Outcry against Rutherford – not against Barber & his customers[3]

Abydenus. Alexander Polyhistor[4]

Shekel = what is weighed, weight [Pf 710 34][5]

Zingis Khan 1206–1227. The meaning of Zingis is 'the most great', *Zin* being great & *gis* the sign of the superlative. [Gibbon viii, 3n; ch. lxiv; Pf 710 40]

Harran–Charrae, not far from the Euphrates. Socotra, from the Skrt – Dvipa Sukhatara – glückseliger Land [Yule II, 398–400][6]

1 Gibbon's reference is to Pocock, *Prolegomena ad Abulpharagius,* p. 7, and d' Herbelot, *Bibliothèque Orientale* (1697), p. 545. Translation: 'a bought slave, or one who goes for a price into the possession of a master'. The mercenary Mameluke soldiers, originally Caucasian slaves, became the rulers of Egypt in 1254 and continued to form the ruling class until they were massacred in 1811, after the French war.

2 Reference not traced.

3 Source not traced. GE added the last sentence later. According to the *DNB*, William Rutherford, physiologist and M.D. (1839–99), was 'extremely sensitive to criticism'.

4 Smith's *Dictionary of Greek and Roman Biography and Mythology,* I, 4 and 115. Also cited in Gibbon.

5 John Gardner Wilkinson, *A Popular Account of the Ancient Egyptians,* 2 vols. (London: John Murray, 1854) II, 148. For other notes from this source, see Pf 711 8 and B 97v.

6 GE added the German translation, not found in Yule, for the Sanskrit words: 'the fortunate, happy land'.

/47/

The Arabians, says Herodotus, have two gods only: Urotal (Dionysus) & Alilat (Aphrodite – Urania)[1]

'In the battle of Lignitz the Tartars (1235) defeated the dukes of Silesia, the Polish palatines & the grand master of the Teutonic order, & filled nine sacks with the right ears of the slain.' Gibbon [viii, 14; ch. lxiv]

Afterwards at Gran or Strigonium, after a promiscuous massacre 300 noble matrons were slain in the presence of the Khan. [Gibbon viii, 15; ch. lxiv]

The Western Khans – of Kipzak & Russia, Transoxiana & Persia – became independent of Zingis's descendants the Mogul emperors of the West & they & their people adopted Mohammedanism, '& while they adopted as their brethren the Arabs & Persians, they renounced all intercourse with the ancient Moguls, the idolaters of China.' [Gibbon viii, 18–19; ch. lxiv]

It was in the year 1299 that Othman (properly Osman) invaded the territory of Nicomedia. [Gibbon viii, 21–22; ch. lxiv]

/48/

Timour or Demir means *iron*. Beg, lord or prince. By the change of a letter or accent this is turned into Lenc, & the two words have been confounded in Tamerlane. [Gibbon viii, 40n; ch. lxv; Pf 710 36]

Timour erected on the ruins of Bagdad a pyramid of ninety thousand heads. Gibbon [viii, 53; ch. lxv]

(Huc's travels). Tree that grew from the hair of the Reformer Tsong Kaba actually standing at the 'Lamaserie' of Kounboum, with 'Thibetan' characters on each leaf & on the inner bark. [Huc, *Voyage dans le Thibet*, II, 113–15]

Sending horses to Travellers. Prayers are made, while horses drawn on paper are sent upon the winds, with the understanding that Bouddha will turn them into real horses. [Huc, II, 136–7]

1 The reference is to Herodotus III, 8, which is also the source of notes on B 150v and Pf 711 29, on Arabian pledges. These are sealed by marking seven stones with the blood of the contracting persons, while calling upon Dionysus and the Heavenly Aphrodite.

Peloponnesian War

Pf 707 49

These notes may be compared to the 'Sicilian Chron[ology]', from 878 to 336 BCE, on B 22v–23, which was copied from Folger 13 18. Pratt and Neufeldt (pp. 106–7 and 251) suggest that the basic table came from the 'Chronological Tables of Greek History' in Smith's *Dictionary of Greek and Roman Biography and Mythology*, III, 1337–1347. The sources of the following notes on the Ligurians, the beginning of the Roman provinces, and the Amazons, have not been traced.

/49/

Pelop[onnesia]n War 431
Battle of Syracuse 415
Aigos Potamos. Athen[ia]ns beaten by Lysander 405
Peace of Antalkidas, 387 (Sparta, Ages Laws)
Great cities given up to Persia in Asia Minor
Spartans driven out of Thebes by Pelop[onnesian]s & Span[iard]s 379
Beaten at Leuktra, 371
Battle of Cheronaea 338
Alexander set out for Asia 334. d. 323
Lamian War
Achaeian League begun 280

Ligurians including inhab[itan]ts of Corsica & Sardinia: probably akin to Basques

Beginning of Roman provinces with possession of Sicily by Rome at end of the first Punic War

Amazons – originated in the Hierodoulai of the goddess of Cumana – armed Virgins

(Cappadocia)

History of music (Hullah)

Pf 707 50, 51, 52, 53, 54, 55, 56, 57, 58, 59, 60, 61, 62

The source of these notes is John Pyke Hullah's *History of Modern Music,* 2nd edition (London: Longmans, Green, 1875). GE's copy is in Mrs Ouvry's inventory (*Libraries,* p. 79). Hullah was a 'singing-teacher, music historian, lecturer, and the composer of a successfully mounted opera on a libretto by Dickens (of which all the music was destroyed by fire during its run in Edinburgh)'.[1] His *History* began as a series of public lectures.

As Beryl Gray points out, GE's extracts from Hullah provided her with 'the full evolutionary background to Fétis's essay' (see Pf 707 4–8). Hullah divides his *History* into four periods:

> The first of these ('a period rather of preparation for music than of music itself, in our sense of the word') is deemed to have ended about 1400. The second takes him to around 1600; the third to about 1750; and the fourth to the time in which both he and George Eliot lived. Eleven of George Eliot's thirteen pages of notes are taken almost exclusively from the lectures on the first and second periods: that is, from the stretch of history that produced (at the end of the fourth century) St Ambrose – whom Hullah designates 'the Father of Music of the Western Church' (because his selection and establishment of scales meant that a proper repertory of church music could be rescued from the confusion it was then in); Pope Gregory (elected 590), whose name became virtually synonymous with plainsong; and Guido Aretino (c. 995–1050), whose important innovation was a movable-doh system for the teaching of sight-singing.

Gray finds it 'perhaps surprising' that, in GE's representation of Deronda's experience in the Frankfurt synagogue (DD ch. 32: 339), 'Palestrina and Allegri are evoked, rather than medieval plain-chant', which is more directly linked to its precursor in Jewish liturgical tradition. She concludes that Victorian readers would have agreed with Hullah's lack of sympathy with plainchant as 'strange, dull uncouth sort of stuff' whose performance is 'a lost

1 Beryl Gray, *George Eliot and Music* (New York: St Martin's Press, 1989), p. 126n. Subsequent references to this work are from pp. 115 and 116.

art' (Hullah, p. 32). The later composers' works, although foreign, were more generally perceived as harmonious and 'enchanting to the ear'.

/50/

Ut queant laxis
*Re*sonare fibris
*Mi*ra gestorum
*Fa*muli tuorum
*Sol*ve polluti
*La*bii reatum
Sancte Johannes[1]

Council of Laodicea, 315, forbade the laity to sing in church. In the same cent[ury] Pope Sylvester founded a singing school in Rome. Herein were formalized the 'authentic modes' – a set of scales or portions of scales beginning severally on D, E, F, G. Tradition ascribes their choice & even arrangement to Ambrose, created Bishop of Milan, 374, & his name they still bear: antiphonal singing was then first sanctioned in Europe. [p. 12]

The tetrachord, the basis of all melody, consists of four sounds separated by 2 tones & 1 semitone; it admits therefore of only 3 varieties, afforded by the position of this 1 semitone. The Greek tetrachord, that in which the semitone occupies the lowest place, includes both the modern 7th or leading note which **/51/** designates the key, & the *third* sound which designates the 'mode' of that key:

1 The first syllables in each line of this hymn to St John the Baptist, as GE notes on Pf 707 54, form a mnemonic device which enabled Guido Aretino's pupils to know the sounds of each degree of the six-tone scale: Ut, Re, Mi, Fa, Sol, La. GE may have copied the hymn from the preface by Fétis to his *Bibliographie universelle des musiciens*, p. xxii; see other notes from this source on Pf 707 4–8. The hymn is also copied from Fétis in the Beinecke Notebook, pp. 102 and 203. The source here, however, is probably Hullah, p. 24.

E is the leading note & A is the 3d of the key of F; the first tetrachord is therefore in F. B is the leading note & E the third of C; the second tetrachord is therefore in C. The 'diabolus in musica' of the middle ages is a tritone or succession of 3 tones. Monotone 'quantity' was carefully observed in Ambrosian chanting; & everything we should call melody was reserved for the endings of strains. [pp. 14–15]

Gregory began his reform by gathering together what remained of the Ambrosian & other labours & forming them into an antiphonary. (He was elected Pope in 590.) Then he added to four scales, which were now distinguished by the epithet authentic, four other scales called 'plagal'. From this time not only have the chants for the Psalms borne the name of Gregory **/52/** but every variety of ecclesiastical melody, nay the square notes, not invented till 600 years later & even then not used for plain song till after another 200 years, are called Gregorian.

Music of the 6th to 12th century written in *neumata* – a name given by Ducange with whom to 'neume' or 'neumaticize' is to note.

Isidore of Seville, contemp. of Gregory, in his Sententiae de Musica, makes the first known mention of harmony, which he divides into 'symphony' & 'diaphony'; by the former he would seem to mean a combination of consonant & by the latter of dissonant, intervals. In the 4 centuries between Gregory & Guido Aretino, there is only one name worthy of special mention – Hucbald a monk of St Armand in the diocese of Tournay in Belgic Gaul (author of a poem in praise of Baldness dedicated to Charles the Bald). **/53/** Hucbald died 932. Harmony inevitably arose from such an instrument as the *Crwth*, which being flat, shewing six strings, necessarily gave out several sounds at once when the bow was drawn across it. [pp. 16–19]

Faux Bourdon (*bourdon,* drone, unalterable pitch) an improved kind of diaphony. Hucbald gives examples of diaphony or organum. There were several kinds, & hideous as most of them may be to our ears, some of the worst are theoretically justifiable by the now well-ascertained & universally acknowledged laws of physical science, to the judicious observance of which the *organ* owes its peculiarities & pre-eminence. In Hucbald's treatise a melody to be harmonized is called *vox principalis,* or *principalis*, simply; & the part added, *vox organalis.* A principalis could be accompanied: – with the 8th above or below; with the 5th above; with the 4th above; with the 4th above & the 5th below, & vice versa.

Some discredit the possibility **/54/** of such sounds being borne, but, says Hullah, we must not imagine them performed as we play them on the piano; but so as to produce something of the effect of the 'mixtures' on the organ which are only made endurable by their different intensity. A similar disposition of voices may have been common in the Middle Ages; the mass of the congregation singing the *principalis* & a few voices only the organalis.

[pp. 21–3]

Of Guido Aretino we hear first early in the eleventh century as resident in the Benedictine monastery of Pomposa between Ferrara & Ravenna. What Guido did was to enable pupils to *hear with the eye* – to know the sound of a musical passage by the sight of the characters that represent it & conversely, by the sound to be able to write it. He chose the hymn 'Ut queant &c' because the first syllable of each verse or line is sung to a note one degree higher than the first syllable of the foregoing – the several first sounds formed a scale. Guido's use of this melody **/55/** was attended with consequences he never dreamed of – the practice of solmisation by 'hexachords' or scales of six sounds only; a practice only abandoned in this century; which consists in the adoption of each note of the hexachord of the said six syllables. Si, a modern addition, completes the modern septenary. [pp. 23–5]

In the Middle Ages as in our own time there was sacred & secular music. But the modern of both kinds is a cantus mensurabilis – it is always 'in time'. But there existed in the Middle Ages a species of music that was absolutely timeless; & up to a somewhat late period no other was heard in the church. Of such melody a great deal has come down to us in the service books of the Latin church; & the attention of every traveller who has entered a continental church must often have been called to certain strains, coarsely uttered, perhaps, but which being unlike anything heard out of church, extort a kind of respect... But it seems to be admitted among **/56/** those who have studied this music most closely that the performance of it is a lost art. This is *plain-song* as distinguished from the cantus mensurabilis. [pp. 25–7]

Was this the only music of the earlier Middle Ages? – It is true that before the XIth cent[ury] there is no mention by any scientific writer, of time or even of secular music; but not to say that theory is a result, not a cause, of practice & that art is always ahead of science, it is as unreasonable to assume a period when all music was without time as a period when men did not walk. Not to mention dancing, much 'national melody' is of high antiquity. There are M.S. melodies of the IXth century. [pp. 30–1]

History of Music (Hullah) Pf 707 56 57 58 59

Within 50 years of the death of Guido, (about the end of the eleventh cent.) appeared a music which was characterised by the combination of sounds of unequal lengths – two or more sounds succeeding each other while one equal to them in length was sustained. This was called *descantus* or 'descant'. Descant would **/57/** argue the existence of musical proportion among sounds of different lengths, & written descant some means of distinguishing such sounds. We hear of both inventions in the middle of the XIIth century, when the first treatise on the cantus mensurabilis, by Franco of Cologne, was made known, when notes appear to have been first used & signs to represent the raising & depressing of sounds – flats & sharps. [p. 34]

Second Period

Adam de la Hale, b. 1240, surnamed 'le Bossu d'Arras', was the author of some three-part songs & of the first comic opera, 'Li Gieus de Robin et de Marion'. In the next century (14th) appears the word counterpoint, first used in lieu of descant by Jean de Muris. The middle of the cent[ury] gives us the first example of music of 4 parts in a mass performed at the coronation of Charles the fifth of France, 1360, & composed by Guillaume de Machault, better known as one of the earliest French **/58/** poets. The organ must have reached some degree of mechanical reputation for we find a Francesco Landini sometimes called F. dei Organi distinguishing himself on the instrument in 1364. Recent research has shown that there was always a secular music differing widely from church music, & that this secular music was the *fons et origo* of the church music of the second period. [pp. 40–3]

The Flemings chief originators of modern music. William Dufay, Binchois &c – predecessors of Ockenheim & his pupils, who are called the 'masters of the new Belgian school'. Among his pupils was Josquin Deprès, usually called Del Prato, with whose name the last years of the XVth & the first of the XVIth century are associated in musical history. The praises of his contemporaries might fill a small volume. Luther said, 'other musicians do what they can with **/59/** notes, Josquin does what he will with them.' – Nothing but Gallo-Belgians as chief musicians everywhere in the latter days of the XVth & in the XVIth century.

No regular music school in Rome till 1540. Constanzo Festa, who died 1545, was one of the creators of the madrigal, & a Te Deum of his has been sung on the election of every Pope since his time. Giovanni & Paulo Animucci, florentine by birth but Roman by education, had also attained great reputation. The former, through his connection with San Filippo Neri, helped to originate the *Oratorio*. [pp. 44–56]

The Roman music school was opened by Claude Goudimel, of Besançon, b. 1510. Set to music the hymns of Clement Marot. Died in the Massacre of St. Bartholomew. His greatest pupil was *Palestrina* b. 1524–1594. [pp. 57–9]

The Italians now surpassed & eclipsed the Belgian school, **/60/** but first came Roland de Lattre called *Orlando di Lasso,* born 4 years before Palestrina. [p. 64]

From 1587 to 1609 books or sets of madrigals by Luca Marenzio alone were published in Venice. Luca is said to have composed 1000. In the 16th century the English musicians held a high place as original composers – Tallis, Farrant, Byrd, Bevin, in sacred music; Morley, Ward, Wilbye & Weelkes in madrigal; Bull in performance as well as composition; Dowland in part song; & Orlando Gibbons in all styles. [pp. 68–70]

Music in the IId Period (to about 1600) only vocal – actual music both vocal & instrumental, the latter in a high degree. (The piano a new instrument in 1767.) In the vocal music of the great masters of the Second Period there are no solos. [p. 76]

/61/

Monteverde, after 1600
Carissimi, born 1582 at Padua – educated at Venice – said to have been still living at Rome in 1672. The earliest great master of the Sacred Cantata. His oratorios, 'Jephtha', Judgment of Solomon, Jonah, Belshazzar. 'His recitative, in point of musical construction, accent & fitness for the voice, as near perfection as can be.' For his Orfeo an orchestra of 36 performers was employed, instrumental music having begun its development. But the instruments were used only two or three at once. [pp. 104–8]

Violin & fiddle the same word. Anglo-Sax. fithele. Anglo-Norm. fielle – vielle, viola &c. The organ may be said to have been perfected about the end of the 15th century.

Corelli, in 1683 published in Rome his first work. [pp. 109–12]

/62/

Carissimi said to be the master of Alessandro Scarlatti,
who was born 1659, in Sicily
J. B. Lully, born in Florence, 1633
Purcell lived from 1658–95
Handel born 1685 at Halle. d. 1759
Sebastian Bach, his contemporary
Haydn b. 1732
Mozart born 1754
Beethoven b. 1770. d. 1827
Schumann
Schubert b. 1797. d. 1828
Weber, b. 1786. d. 1826
Gluck born 1710. His Iphigenia performed at Paris in 1774
Cherubini b. 1760–1842[1]

During the most tremendous excesses of the French Revolution, the theatres were never closed & never empty for a single night. [p. 202]

1 The list of composers and dates is drawn from Hullah, pp. 112 to 201. The name Schumann was cancelled by GE. Her notes from Hullah have no direct connection to the music performed by Mirah, Gwendolen, Catherine Arrowpoint, or even Herr Klesmer – who will, according to Catherine, 'rank with Schubert and Mendelssohn' (DD ch. 22: 224).

Duncker

Pf 707 63, 64

Notes on these pages from Maximilian Wolfgang Duncker, *Geschichte des Alterthums*, Vol. I, *Aegypter und die Volker Westasiens bis auf die Zeiten des Kyros (550 v. Chr.)*, 3rd edition, (Berlin: Duncker and Humblot, 1863), are copied again in GE's alphabetized 'Oriental Memoranda' notebook, Pf 710.

/63/

– 'of a liberality of genius above bearing down an opinion merely because it wants friends.' Tristram Shandy[1]

(Duncker)

Naama i.e. – *die Holde* [p. 357; Pf 710 29][2]

Astoreth Karnaim, the horned Ashtoreth [p. 352; Pf 710 6]

Jubal = Beauty of Baal [p. 355; Pf 710 21]

Adonis = Tammuz i.e. der Geschiedene [pp. 355–6; Pf 710 36]

Baal – El – Eljon – Adonis – Tammuz – (in Damascus) Hadad – Rimmon. The centre of the Adonis cult was Byblos, 'the sacred city of Adonis'. The river, swollen with red earth from the mountains in autumn 'ran purple to the sea'. His grave was there & this *Trauerfest* was kept in the caves of Lebanon – the women cutting their hair & crying 'Ailanu!' It was this which led the Greeks to represent the body of Osiris as being driven to Byblos: & from the 'Ailanu' was derived the Linus-song. [p. 355–7][3]

1 Lawrence Sterne, *The Life and Opinions of Tristram Shandy,* Bk I, ch. 19. 'Tristram Shandy' was read again on 14 January 1877 (GHL Diary).

2 Naama, 'the beloved', is the name of Solomon's wife; see I Kings xix, 21, 31.

3 Tammuz' means 'the severed or separated'. *Trauerfest* may be translated as 'ceremony of mourning', and 'Ailanu!' as 'Woe to us!'

Anna = die Anmuthige [p. 357; Pf 710 6] [1]

/64/

Palgrave. Alf-Leyl-w-Leylah - Thousand & one nights (Arabic)[2]

Sahhabah, personal companions of the prophet [Palgrave I, 384; Pf 710 34]

The Phoenicians also gave a tithe to their gods.[3]

Kabirim, the strong ones [Duncker I, 363; Pf 710 23]

A name which all Englishmen ought to hold in honour is that of John Cornwall, master of grammar, who first began the change in the grammar schools of teaching in English.

English displaced French in the pleadings in Courts in Law in 1363.[4]

1 Translation: 'the graceful one'.

2 William Gifford Palgrave, in the Preface to his *Narrative of a Year's Journey through Central and Eastern Asia (1862–63)*, 2nd edition, 2 vols. (London: Macmillan, 1865), I, x, lists amongst his sources, 'the famous Alf-Leyl-w-Leylah, or Thousand-and-One Nights (a book in which often "more is meant than meets the ear")'. 'Palgrave's Central Arabia', was read from 16 to 29 January 1877 (GHL Diary). For notes from *The Arabian Nights*, see Pf 711 63 and 107.

3 The source, probably in Duncker, has not been traced.

4 Edward Augustus Freeman, *The History of the Norman Conquest of England, its Causes and its Results,* 5 vols. (Oxford: Clarendon Press, 1867–76), V, 536. A 3rd edition in 2 volumes was published in 1877. On 20 February 1877 GE and GHL read 'Freeman's Norman Conquest aloud' (GHL Diary). These notes are from chapter xxv, 'The Effects of the Norman Conquest on Language and Literature', in which Freeman deplores the influence of Norman French on the English language. The heading for the pages from which GE quotes is 'Final Victory of English'.

Egyptian pantheon

Pf 707 65, 66, 67, 68, 69, 70

The source of these notes is 'The Egyptian Pantheon', Appendix II in Amelia Blandford Edwards, *A Thousand Miles up the Nile,* 2 vols. (London: Longmans, Green, 1877), pp. 723–6. 'Miss Edwards' 1000 Miles up the Nile' was read from 22 February to 25 March 1877 (GHL Diary). The map of the Nile drawn on Pf 707 99 is not from Edwards; its source has not been traced. The brief historical notes on Pf 707 100 are from Duncker (see Pf 710 15–16). Besides Herodotus, Duncker, and Wilkinson's *Manners and Customs of the Ancient Egyptians,* GE read many other works on Egyptian history and religion. She may also have contemplated travelling in Egypt.[1]

In DD ch. 32, Deronda becomes conscious that he has 'fallen into a meditative numbness':

> Yet how distinguish what our will may wisely save in its completeness, from the heaping of cat-mummies and the expensive cult of enshrined putrefactions? (337)

The reader of GE's Notebooks, who has thus far followed GE in her studies of Judaism as a religion 'still throbbing in human lives', and not – as Deronda had supposed – 'a sort of eccentric fossilized form, which an accomplished man might dispense with studying' (DD ch. 32: 334), may be surprised to find her, at this late date, studying the worship of cat-mummies. Following her research, we may have come to perceive Judaism as a faith that has evolved from its early origins in the cult-worship of stones, planets, and fertility goddesses, to a higher form of life, and has in the course of its evolution formed two other major living religions, Islam and Christianity. What are we to we make, then, of an ibis-headed man-formed god with the pen and palette of a scribe, or (in the next section) a god whose ship 'has always a fair wind for any course, & can be packed in the pocket' (Pf 707 72)?

The religions of the Egyptians and Norsemen, long dead and buried, were nevertheless soon to partake of a curious afterlife. Miss Edwards's book admirably demonstrates how an 'expensive cult of enshrined putrefactions'

1 See GEL VI, 319n.

has been transformed into an expensive tourist attraction, and the gods of the ancient Egyptian pantheon have been saved to become acquisitions for nineteenth-century Europeans.

/65/

Egyptian Pantheon

The first or highest order of Gods comprised 8, who were different at Memphis & Thebes.

Memphis	*Thebes*	
Ptah	Amen-Ra	
Shu	Mentu	
Tefnu	Atum	
Seb	Shu & Tefnu	
Nut	Seb	
Osiris	Osiris	
Isis & Horus	Set & Nephthys	
Athor	Horus & Athor	(Birch)[1]

The Gods most commonly represented upon the monuments are Ptah, Kneph, Ra, Ammon-Ra, Khem, Osiris, Nefer Atum or Tum, Thoth, Seb, Seti, Khons, Horus, Maut, Neith, Isis, Nut, Hathor, Pasht.

Ptah: in form a mummy, holding the emblem called by some the Nilometer, by others the emblem of stability.

/66/

Kneph, Knoum, or *Knouphis*: Ram-headed. Called the Maker of Gods & men; the soul of the Gods. Chief Deity of Elephantine & the Cataracts

Ra: Hawk-headed, & crowned with the sun-disk encircled by an asp.
The divine disposer & organiser of the world.
Adored throughout Egypt

1 Edwards's source is Samuel Birch, *Guide to the First and Second Egyptian Rooms* (London: British Museum, 1874).

Amen-Ra: Of human form, crowned with a flat-topped cap & two long straight plumes; clothed in the *schenti*; his flesh sometimes painted blue. There are various forms of this god, but he is most generally described as King of the Gods. Chief deity of Thebes

Khem: Of human form, mummified; wears head-dress of Amen-Ra;
his right hand uplifted, holding the flail
The God of productiveness – generation

Osiris: Of human form, mummified, crowned with a mitre, & holding the flail & crook. **/67/** Called the Good; the Lord above all;
the one Lord. Was the God of the lower world; Judge of the dead;
& representative of the sun below the horizon
Adored throughout Egypt. Local Deity of Abydos

Nefer Atum: Human-headed, & crowned with the pschent
This God represented the nocturnal sun. Heliopolis

Thoth: In form a man, ibis-headed; generally depicted with the pen
& palette of a scribe. God of the moon & of letters.
Sesoon or Hermopolis

Seb: The Father of the Gods & deity of terrestrial vegetation.
In form a man with a goose upon his head

Set: Represented by a symbolic animal, with a muzzle & ears like a jackal, the body of an ass, & an upright tail, like the tail of a lion. Was originally a warlike god, & became in later times the **/68/** symbol of evil & the enemy of Osiris.

Khons: Hawk-headed, crowned with the sun disk & horns.
Is represented sometimes as a youth with the side-lock, standing on
a crocodile.

Horus: Appears variously as Horus, Horus Aroëris & Horus Harpakhrat or
the child. Is represented under the first two forms as
a man, hawk-headed, wearing the double crown of Egypt; in the
latter as a child with the side-lock.
Local deity of Edfoo (Apollinopolis Magna)

Maut: A woman draped & crowned with the pschent; generally with a cap below the pschent representing a vulture. Adored at Thebes

Neith: A woman holding sometimes a bow & arrows, crowned with the crown of Lower Egypt. Presided over war & the loom. Thebes

/69/

Isis: A woman crowned with the sun-disk surmounted by a throne, & sometimes enclosed between horns. Adored at Abydos
Her soul resided in Sothis, or the Dog Star.

Nut: A woman curved so as to touch the ground with her fingers
She represents the vault of heaven & is the mother of the Gods.

Hathor: Cow-headed, & crowned with the disk & plumes
Deity of Amenti, or the Egyptian Hades. Denderah

Pasht or *Bast*. As Bast, with a lion's head, the disk & urœus;
as Pasht, she is cat-headed & holds a sistrum.

'In the beginnings of formation, says Empedocles, many heads sprouted up without necks & naked arms went wandering forlorn of shoulders, & solitary eyes were straying **/70/** destitute of foreheads ... When element with element more fully mixed, these members fell together by haphazard ... Many came forth with double faces & two breasts, some shaped like oxen with a human front, others, again, of human race, with a bull's head; & some were mixed of male & female parts.' In connection with this last idea he gives forth the idea of separation & longing for reunion afterwards developed by Plato in the Banquet.[1]

Vide Plutarch, Cleomenes, for heroic wifehood[2]

1 Source not traced.

2 Leonidas II (not the heroic Leonidas, but a king of Sparta who reigned circa 256 to 244 and 240 to 236 BCE), having had Agis IV (king from 244 to 240) put to death, forced the widow Agiatis, who had just given birth to Agis's child, to marry Leonidas's son Cleomenes. Although she tried to escape the forced marriage, 'when she was married to Cleomenes, she made him a good and affectionate wife, though she hated his father.' Cleomenes 'would often ask her for the history of that unfortunate prince [Agis], and listen with great affection to her account of his sentiments and designs' for the restoration of the constitution and the regeneration of the Spartan character; see John and William Langhorne, translators, *Plutarch's Lives of Illustrious Men* (1770), new edition, 2 vols. (London: Henry G. Bohn, 1853), II, 856–7. A six-volume set of the Langhornes' Plutarch (1823) was sold at auction in 1923 (*Catalogue*, p. 231).

Northern mythology

Pf 707 71, 72, 73

The source of these notes is the first volume of Benjamin Thorpe's *Northern Mythology, comprising the Principal Popular Traditions and Superstitions of Scandinavia, North Germany, and the Netherlands*, 3 vols. (London: Edward Lumley, 1851–2).

/71/

N[orthern] M[ythology]

Allfadur = Surtur, the Dark
Ginnungagap, the gaping chasm = Space
Muspellheim, Light-world
Niflheim, Night-world [p. 3]

Ymir, the first Giant, from whom came the other Giants
& Frost Giants or Hrimthursen

Audumbla, the cow, the world mother [p. 4]
Midgard, the dwelling of men– between Muspellheim & Niflheim [p. 5]

Ragnarök, Götterdämmerung or destruction of the Gods [p. 8]
Asgard, abode of Gods

Yggdrasil, the ash-tree, the world-wide Life-tree, with three roots – one reaching to the Frost-giants (Hrymthursen) where was Ginnungagap, one to Niflheim where is Hvergelmir, the ancient Wellspring of the Urwelt, where Nidhöggr the giant snake gnaws at the root; the other to the Aesir or Gods. With the Frost giants in Mimir's well, where Odin came for a drink, & had to give up his eye before he could get it. With the Aesir by Urda's well, where the Gods hold their judgement seat, are the Nornen. [pp. 11–12]

Gladsheim, Odin's palace [p. 11]
Einherier, warriors, heroes, in Odin's burg [p. 15]

/72/

Hugin & Munin, Odin's ravens, understanding & memory [p. 19]
Gullinkambi, the golden-combed,
the Sun who wakes the Einherier & Valkyrien
Gungnir, Odin's spear [p. 39]
Draupnir, his ring (the moon) [p. 38]
Sleipnir, his eight-legged horse [p. 36]

Vili = Hœnir = Verstund = moon } Odin's brothers [p. 146]
Ve = Lodur = Force

Loki = fire = enemy [pp. 180–1]

Odin's sons: Baldur & Thor; their mother, Frigga, the Earth [p. 167]
Breidablik, Baldur's dwelling [p. 186]
Nanna (the Maiden), Baldur's wife who was laid on her husband's funeral pile, set fire to on Baldur's ship & driven into the open sea. [p. 75]

Thor & Freya – search for the Hammer (Alcestis & Hercules) [pp. 54–6]

Tyr [p. 28]
Bragi, wisdom & eloquence
Bragur, poesy [p. 189]

Vanir – Geschlecht, between Gods & men [p. 14]
Niord, father of Freyr & his sister Freya (the moon) [p. 25]
Freyr = Froh, diffuser of the sun-light; rides on Gold-bristles [p. 26]
Gullinbursti, the sun. His ship is Skidbladnir, which has always a fair wind for any course, & can be packed in the pocket. [p. 39]

Freya has two cats harnessed to her chariot. Born from the sea or foam.
One of her names, Ostara, Eastre, /73/ suggests Astarte – an old northern Astara. [p. 227]
Logi, fire
Kari, air
Œgir, the ocean [p. 27][1]
Nixies, alfs or dwarfs, & giants [pp. 246, 147]
Utgard, the entrance, eastern region [p. 10]

1 On Pf 707 12 the Œgir is said to be the name of a sea-storm.

Bibliographical index

George Eliot's sources

Works mentioned in the notebooks, but not sources of notes, are indicated by an asterisk. Editions known to have been owned by GE are indicated by one of three notes: 'in DWL', 'in Mrs Ouvry's inventory', or 'sold at auction'.

Annual Register: or a View of the History and Politics of the Year 1861. London: J. and R. Rivington, 1862. **Pf 711 71**

Annual Register: a Review of Public Events at Home and Abroad, for the Year 1865. London: Rivingtons, 1866. **Pf 711 95a**

Annual Register: a Review of Public Events at Home and Abroad, for the Year 1866. London: Rivingtons, 1867. **Pf 711 96a**

Annual Register: a Review of Public Events at Home and Abroad, for the Year 1867. London: Rivingtons, 1868. **Pf 711 97a**

Aristotle. *Rhetoric.* In *Werke.* Edited by Karl von Prantl et al. 3 vols. Leipzig, 1854, 1857, 1860. In DWL. **Pf 711 34***

Arnold, Matthew. *Literature and Dogma: An Essay towards a Better Apprehension of the Bible.* London: Smith, Elder, 1873. **Pf 711 14, 65**

'God and the Bible: A Review of Objections to "Literature and Dogma"'. Part III. *Contemporary Review* 25 (1875): 279–304. **Pf 711 79**

Bibliographical index

Arnold, Matthew. 'Pagan and Mediaeval Religious Sentiment'. In *Essays in Criticism.* 3rd rev. ed. London: Macmillan, 1875. **Pf 707 29**

Ascensio Isaiae Aethiopice et Latinae. Edited by August Dillmann. Leipzig: Brockhaus, 1877. In DWL. **Pf 711 30*, 93a*; Pf 710 20***

Bacon, Francis. *Bacon's Essays and Colours of Good and Evil.* Edited by William Aldis Wright. London: Macmillan, 1862. **Pf 711 62, 66, 67**

Bain, Alexander. *Logic.* 2 vols. London: Longmans, Green, Reader and Dyer, 1870. In DWL. **Pf 711 3**

Baring-Gould, Sabine. *The Book of Were Wolves.* London: Smith, Elder, 1865. **Pf 711 10***

Legends of Old Testament Characters from the Talmud and Other Sources. 2 vols. London: Macmillan, 1871. **B 135v*, 183v; Pf 711 92a, 93a; Pf 710 14, 20**

Bäumlein, Wilhelm von. *Commentatio de Homero ejusque carminibus.* Leipzig: Tauchnitz, 1854. **Pf 711 15***

Beaumont, Francis, and John Fletcher. *The Faithful Shepherdess. In The Works of Beaumont and Fletcher.* Edited by George Darley. 2 vols. London: Edward Moxon, 1840. Sold at auction. **Pf 711 41**

Becker, Bernhard. *Enthüllungen über das tragische Lebensende Ferdinand Lassalle's: auf Grund authentischer Belege.* Schleiz: Hugo Heyn, 1868. **Pf 711 35–37**

Bédarride, Jassuda. *Les Juifs en France, en Italie et en Espagne.* 3rd ed. Paris: Michel Lévy frères, 1867. **Pf 710 1***

Benfey, Theodor. *Pantschatantra: Funf Bücher indischer Fabeln, Märchen und Erzähkungen, aus den Sanskrit übersetzt.* 2 vols. Leipzig: Brockhaus, 1859. **Pf 711 10***

Benisch, Abraham. *Judaism Surveyed; Being a Sketch of the Rise and Development of Judaism from Moses to our Days.* London: Longmans, Green, 1874. **Pf 711 94***

Bergk, Wilhelm Theodor, ed. *Poetae Lyrici Graeci.* Leipzig: Reichenbach, 1843. In DWL. **B 92v–97; Pf 711 11***

Bibliographical index

Bibliographical index

Malachi iv, 4: **Pf 710 27***

John vii, 49: **Pf 711 30**

Bleek, Johannes Friedrich. *Einleitung in das alte Testament.* 3rd ed. Berlin: Georg Reimer, 1870. In DWL. **Pf 711 21*, 30–33**

Bonitz, Hermann. *Über den Ursprung der homerischen Gedichte.* 3rd ed. Vienna: Carl Gerold's Sohn, 1860. **Pf 711 15 , 16**

Bosworth Smith, Reginald. *Mohammed and Mohammedanism.* London: Smith, Elder, 1874. **Pf 711 51 ; Pf 710 7, 38**

Bristed, Charles Astor. *Five Years in an English University.* 2 vols. New York: Putnam, 1852. **Pf 711 86–93, 91a**

Browning, Robert. 'Waring'. **Pf 711 107**

Paracelsus. Pf 707 33

Brugsch-Bey, Heinrich Karl. *Histoire d'Egypte.* Leipzig: J. C. Hinrichs, 1859. **Pf 711 21***

Aus dem Orient. 2 vols. Berlin: Grosse, 1864, **Pf 711 44***

Buckle, Henry Thomas. *History of Civilization in England.* 2 vols. London: J. W. Parker and Sons, 1857–61. In DWL. **Pf 711 11***

Burke, John Bernard. *The General Armory of England, Scotland, Ireland and Wales: Comprising a Registry of Armorial Bearings from the Earliest to the Present Time.* London: Harrison, 1878. GE consulted an earlier edition. **Pf 711 81–85**

Burnouf, Emile Louis. *La Science des religions.* Paris: Maisonneuve, 1872. **Pf 711 11***

Burnouf, Eugène. *Introduction à l'histoire du buddhisme indien.* Introduction by J. Barthélemy Saint-Hilaire. 2nd ed. Paris: Maisonneuve, 1876. **Pf 711 34***

Buxtorf, Johann, ed. *Lexicon chaldaicum, talmudicum et rabbinicum* (1607). New ed. Edited by Bernard Fischer. Leipzig: Schaefer, 1875. **Pf 711 68***

Cairnes, John Elliott. *Some Leading Principles of Political Economy Newly Expounded.* London: Macmillan, 1874. In DWL. **Pf 711 114***

Bibliographical index

Cairnes, John Elliott. *The Character and Logical Method of Political Economy.* 2nd ed. New York: Harper, 1875. **Pf 711 114***

Cassel, David. 'Chisdai, the Son of Isaac'. In *Miscellany of Hebrew Literature.* Edited by Albert Löwy, I. 73–91. London: Trübner for the Society of Hebrew Literature, 1872. In DWL. **B 159v–161; Pf 711 75, 76**

Chabas, François Joseph. *Le plus ancien livre du monde. Etude sur le papyrus Prisse.* Paris, 1858. **Pf 710 31 ***

Chaucer, Geoffrey. *The Poetical Works of Geoffrey Chaucer.* Edited by Thomas Tyrwhitt. London: Edward Moxon, 1843 and later editions. **Pf 707 30**

Chwolson, Daniel Abramovich. *Über Tammûz und die Menschenverehrung bei den alten Babylonien.* St Petersburg, 1860. **Pf 711 92a *; Pf 710 32* ; Pf 707 17*, 23***

Coleridge, Hartley. Introduction to *The Dramatic Works of Massinger and Ford.* London: Edward Moxon, 1839 [1840]. Sold at auction. **Pf 711 39, 47**

Colvin, Sidney. 'Piero della Francesca' and 'Luca Signorelli'. *Cornhill Magazine* 31 (1875): 167–83, 457–66, 578–96. **Pf 711 95a**

Comte, Auguste. *Catéchisme Positiviste, ou Sommaire Exposition de la religion universelle.* Paris: the author, 1852. In DWL. **Pf 711 11***

The Positive Philosophy of Auguste Comte. 'Freely translated and condensed' by Harriet Martineau. 2 vols. London: John Chapman, 1853. 2nd ed. London: Trübner, 1875. **B 101v**

Positivist Calendar. In *System of Positive Polity, or Treatise on Sociology, Instituting the Religion of HUMANITY.* 4 vols. Volume I, *Containing the General View of Positivism and Introductory Principles.* Translated by John Henry Bridges. London: Longmans, Green, 1875.
B 175, 175v, 176, 176v, 177, 177v, 178, 178v, 179, 179v, 180, 180v, 181

Conversations-Lexicon zum Handgebrauch oder encyklopädisches Realwörterbuch aller Wissenschaften, Künste und Gewerbe. 4th ed. Leipzig: August Weichardt, 1846. In DWL. **Pf 707 1 ***

Curtius, Ernst. *Peloponnesos: Eine historisch-geographische Beschreibung der Halbinsel.* 2 vols. Gotha: Justus Perthes, 1851–2. **Pf 711 12, 13**

Bibliographical index

Darwin, Charles. *The Expression of the Emotions in Man and Animals.* London: John Murray, 1872. Sold at auction. **Pf711 6**

Das Innere Leben des Modernum Judenthums. Translated from English 'in R. Hirschfeld'. Publication not traced.
B 124, 125, 126, 123v, 124v, 125v, 126v, 127, 127v, 128, 129, 128v

de Sola, David Aaron, and Morris J. Raphall, transl. *Eighteen Treatises from the Mishna.* 2nd ed. London: Sherwood, Gilbert, and Piper, 1845.
B 110, 110v, 111; Pf711 21*

Delitzsch, Franz Julius. *Zur Geschichte der jüdischen Poësie vom Abschluss der heiligen Schriften Alten Bundes bis auf die neueste Zeit.* Leipzig: Karl Tauchnitz, 1836.
In DWL. **B 123, 140, 193v; Pf711 21*, 59**

Demosthenes. *The Orations of Demosthenes and Aeschines on the Crown.* Edited by George Augustus Simcox and William Henry Simcox. Oxford: Clarendon Press, 1874. **Pf 707 31**

Depping, Georges Bernard. *Les Juifs dans le moyen âge.* Paris: L'Imprimerie royale, 1834. **Pf711 21***

Derenbourg, Joseph. *Essai sur l'histoire et la géographie de la Palestine d'après les Thalmuds et les autres sources rabbiniques.* Paris: L'Imprimerie impériale, 1867.
Pf710 1*

Deutsch, Emanuel Oscar Menahem. 'Ein Stück jüdischer Volkspoesie, aus dem Midrasch der Klagelieder'. *Westermann's illustrirte deutsche Monatshefte fur das gesammte geistige Leben der Gegenwart.* Brunschweig 6, No. 35 (1859): 540–6.
B 115–117v, 123

'The Talmud'. *Quarterly Review* 123 (1867): 417–64. **B 106, 114, 149**

Literary Remains of the Late Emanuel Deutsch. Edited with a memoir by Lady Strangford. London: John Murray, 1874. In DWL. **Pf711 43, 44, 50, 51, 62; Pf710 23, 27; Pf 707 2**

Disraeli, Benjamin. *Tancred: or The New Crusade.* 3 vols. London: Henry Colburn, 1847. **Pf711 39, 40**

D'Israeli, Isaac. *The Genius of Judaism.* London: Edward Moxon, 1833. **711 91a***

Bibliographical index

Doeleke, Wilhelm Heinrich. *Kleine hebräische Grammatik.* Leipzig: Hahn, 1822. **Pf 710 1***

Dozy, Reinhart Pieter Anne. *De Israëliten te Mekka na Davids tijd tot in de vijfde eeuw onzer tijdrekening.* Haarlem, 1864. **Pf 710 35***

Die Israeliten zu Mekka von Davids Zeit bis in's fünfte Jahrhundert unserer Zeitrechnung. Leipzig: Engelmann, 1864. **Pf 711 103***

Draper, John William. *A History of the Intellectual Development of Europe.* 2 vols. London: Sampson Low, 1863. **Pf 711 63***

Duncker, Maximilian Wolfgang. *Geschichte des Alterthums.* Vol. I: *Aegypter und die Volker Westasiens bis auf die Zeiten des Kyros (550 v. Chr.).* 3rd ed. Berlin: Duncker and Humblot, 1863. **Pf 710 6, 15–16, 21, 23, 29, 36; Pf 707 63, 64**

Dyce, Alexander, ed. 'Some Account of the Life of Shakespeare'. In *The Works of William Shakespeare.* 3rd ed. Edited by John Forster. London, 1874. **Pf 711 47–49**

Edwards, Amelia Blandford. *A Thousand Miles up the Nile.* 2 vols. London: Longmans, Green, 1877. **Pf 707 65–70**

Eisenmenger, Johann Andreas. *Entdecktes Judenthum.* 2 vols. Königsberg, 1711. **B 112 v, 118, 119, 118v, 119v, 121; Pf 711 21***

Ellis, Alexander John. *Early English Pronunciation.* 3 parts. London: Trübner for the Early English Text Society, 1867– 9. **Pf 707 2, 14**

Ewald, Georg Heinrich August von. *Geschichte des Volkes Israel bis Christus.* 3 vols. Göttingen: Dieterich, 1843–8. **Pf 711 21***

Hebräische Sprachlehre für Anfänger. 2nd ed. Leipzig: Hahn, 1855. **Pf 710 1*, 32**

The History of Israel. Translated by Russell Martineau and J. Estlin Carpenter. 4 vols. London: Longmans, Green, 1867–71. In DWL. **Pf 711 21*, 53, 63**

Fäsi, Johann Ulrich. Introduction to his *Homers Odyssee.* 2 vols. Leipzig, 1849. **Pf 711 15***

Fawcett, Henry. *Manual of Political Economy.* 3rd ed. London: Macmillan, 1869. 4th ed. (1874) in DWL. **Pf 711 11***

Fétis, François Joseph. *Biographie universelle des musiciens et bibliographie générale de la musique.* 2nd ed. 8 vols. Paris: Firmin-Didot, 1868–70. **Pf 707 4–8**

Fiske, John. *Myths and Mythmakers: Old Tales and Superstitions Interpreted by Comparative Mythology.* Boston: James R. Osgood, 1873. In Mrs Ouvry's inventory. **Pf 711 10, 111**

Fitzgerald, Edward. *Rubáiyát of Omar Kháyyám, the Astronomer Poet of Persia. Translated into English Verse.* London: Bernard Quaritch, 1859. **Pf 711 42, 110–109**

Fontenelle, Bernard le Bovier de. *Entretiens sur la pluralité des mondes.* Paris: Dubuisson, 1866. In DWL. **Pf 711 17, 18**

Franck, Adolphe. *Philosophie et religion.* 2nd ed. Paris: Didier, 1869. In DWL. **Pf 710 7***

Frankl, Ludwig August. *Libanon: Ein Poetisches Familienbuch.* Vienna, 1855. **Pf 711 101***

Freeman, Edward Augustus. *The History of the Norman Conquest of England, its Causes and its Results.* 5 vols. Oxford: Clarendon Press, 1867–76. **Pf 707 64**

Old English History for Children. London: Macmillan, 1869. In Mrs Ouvry's inventory. **Pf 711 10, 11***

Frey, Joseph Samuel. *A Hebrew Grammar in the English Language.* London: Gale, Curtis and Fenner, 1823. **Pf 710 1***

Freytag, Gustav. *Die Technik des Dramas.* Leipzig: S. Hirzel, 1863. **Pf 711 11***

Friedländer, Ludwig. 'Die Homerische Kritik von Wolf bis Grote'. Dissertation. 1853. **Pf 711 15***

Galton, Francis. *Hereditary Genius: An Inquiry into its Law and Consequences.* London: Macmillan, 1869. **Pf 711 6***

Bibliographical index

Geiger, Abraham. *Das Judenthum und seine Geschichte.* 3 parts. Breslau: H. Skutsch, 1865–71. **Pf710 1***

Judaism and its History. Translated by Maurice Mayer. New York: Thalmessinger, 1865.
B 136v, 138v, 139, 149v, 150v, 154v, 193v, 194; Pf711 56–59; Pf710 39

Salomo Gabirol und seine Dichtungen. Leipzig: Oskar Leiner, 1867.
B 164v*

Geiger, Lazarus. *Ursprung und Entwickelung der menschlichen Sprache und Vernunft.* 2 vols. Stuttgart: Cotta, 1868–72. **Pf711 4, 11***

Geiger, Ludwig. *Johann Reuchlin, sein Leben und seine Werke.* Leipzig: Duncker und Humblot, 1871. **B 150: Pf711 95–98; Pf710 15, 29, 36**

Gibbon, Edward. *The History of the Decline and Fall of the Roman Empire.* Edited by Henry Hart Milman. New ed. by William Smith. 8 vols. London: John Murray, 1872. In Mrs Ouvry's inventory.
B 154v* ; Pf710 22, 28, 36, 39; Pf707 32, 41, 46–48

Gibbs, Joseph Willard. *A Manual Hebrew and English Lexicon including the Biblical Chaldee.* London: J.R. Priestley, 1833. **Pf710 1***

Ginsburg, Christian David. *The Kabbalah: Its Doctrines, Development and Literature.* London: Longmans, Green, Reader, and Dyer, 1865. **Pf707 17–25**

Gladstone, John Hall. *Michael Faraday.* London: Macmillan, 1872. **Pf711 4**

Gobineau, Joseph Arthur de. *Les Religions et les philosophies dans l'Asie centrale.* Paris: Didier, 1865. **Pf711 51*; Pf710 7***

Goethe, Johann Wolfgang von. 'Neue Liebe, neues Leben', 'Wonne der Wehmut'. **Pf711 106**

Graetz, Heinrich Hirsch. *Geschichte der Juden von den ältesten Zeiten bis auf die Gegenwart.* Mixed set of 1st and 2nd ed. 11 vols. Leipzig: Oskar Leiner, 1863–76. In DWL. **Pf711 21***

Graetz 2. *Geschichte der Juden vom Tode des königs Salomo (um 977 vorchr. Zeit) bis zum Tode Juda Makkabi 160.* 2 vols. in one. 1875–6. **Pf710 26**

Bibliographical index

Hamburger, Jacob. *Real-Encyclopädie des Judenthums. Wörterbuch für Gemeinde, Schule und Haus.* Strelitz, 1874. A reprint of *Real-Encyclopädie für Bible und Talmud* ... Vol. I, *Die Biblischen Artikel.* Strelitz, 1870. In DWL. **Pf 711 114*; Pf 710 5, 28, 29**

Real-Encyclopädie für Bibel und Talmud. Wörterbuch zum Handgebrauch für Bibelfreunde, Theologen, Juristen, Gemeinde- und Schulvorsteher, Lehrer, etc., Vol. II, *Die Talmudischen Artikel,* Part I (A - Essäer), Part II (Essäer - Haftarah). NeuStrelitz, 1874, 1875. In DWL. **Pf 711 114*; Pf 710 2–4, 6, 12, 15, 17, 18, 19, 23**

Hammer-Purgstall, Baron Joseph, von, transl. and ed. *O Kind! Die berühmte ethische Abhandlung Ghasalis, Arabisch und Deutsch.* Vienna: Strauss, 1838. **Pf 710 41* ; Pf 707 1***

Hardy, Robert Spence. *The Legends and Theories of the Buddhists, compared with history and science: with introductory notices of the life and system of Gotama Buddha.* London: Williams and Norgate, 1866. **Pf 711 34***

Harlez, Charles de, transl. and ed. *Avesta: Livre sacré des sectateurs de Zoroastre.* 3 vols. Paris: Firmin-Didot / Maisonneuve, 1875–7. **Pf 710 1* ; Pf 707 1***

Hartmann, Anton Theodor. *Die Hebräerin am Putztische und als Braut.* 3 vols. Amsterdam: Kunst- und Industrie Comptoir, 1809–10. **Pf 711 114***

Haug, Martin. *Essays on the Sacred Language, Writings and Religion of the Parsis.* 2nd ed. Edited by Edward William West. London: Trübner, 1878. **Pf 710 1*; Pf 707 1***

Haxthausen, Baron August von. *The Tribes of the Caucasus: with an Account of Schamyl and the Murids.* Translated by John Edward Taylor. London: Chapman and Hall, 1855. **Pf 711 51***

Heine, Heinrich. *Geständnisse.* **Pf 707 27**

Henderson, William. *Notes on the Folk Lore of the Northern Counties of England and the Borders.* London: Longmans, Green, 1866. **Pf 711 10***

Héricault, Charles de Ricault d'. *Essai sur l'origine de l'épopée française et sur son histoire au moyen âge.* Paris: A. Franck, 1859. **Pf 711 15***

Bibliographical index

Hermann, Johann Gottfried Jakob. *De Interpolationibus Homeri dissertatio.* Leipzig, 1832. **Pf 711 15***

Herodotus. *Herodotus Graece and Latine ex editionibus Wesselingii et Reizii.* Edited by George Dunbar. 7 vols. Edinburgh: William Laing, 1806. In DWL. **B 102*, 104*, 150v; Pf 711 2, 11*, 14, 23, 29, 39 ; Pf 707 16, 47**

Hertzberg, Gustav Friedrich. *Geschichte Griechenlands seit dem Absterben des antiken Lebens bis zur Gegenwart.* 4 vols. Gotha: F. A. Perthes, 1876–9. **Pf 707 1***

Hirschfeld, R. *Das innere Leben des modernum Judenthums.* Not traced. **B 124, 125, 126, 123v, 124v, 125v, 126v, 127, 127v, 128, 129, 128v**

Homer. *Ilias, Graece et Latine.* Edited by S. Clark. 16th ed. 2 vols. 1810–15. In DWL. **Pf 711 11***

Odyssey. **Pf 711 11***

Huc, Evariste Régis. *Souvenirs d'un voyage dans la Tartarie, le Thibet, et la Chine pendant les années 1844, 1845 et 1846.* 2 vols. Paris: Adrien le Clerc, 1850. **Pf 707 46, 48**

Hullah, John Pyke. *The History of Modern Music.* 2nd ed. London: Longmans, Green, 1875. **Pf 707 50–62**

Isaacs, Hyam. *Ceremonies, Customs, Rites and Traditions of the Jews.* London: William Buck, 1830. **B 129v–135v, 138, 150v; Pf 711 53–56; Pf 710 1***

Jacob, August. *Ueber die Entstehung der Ilias und der Odyssee.* Berlin: G. Reimer, 1856. **Pf 711 15***

Jellinek, Hermann, ed. *Uriel Acosta's Leben und Lehre.* Zerbst: Kummer, 1847. In DWL. **Pf 711 101* ; Pf 710 41***

Jerome, Saint. *Les Lettres de S. Jérôme.* Translated by Jean Petit. 2nd ed. Paris: Frédéric Léonard, 1679. In DWL. **B 193v* ; Pf 711 59***

Jewish Chronicle n. s. 6 (5635/1874–5). **B 193v; Pf 711 94, 95, 91a**

Johnson, Samuel. 'Life of Milton'. *Lives of the English Poets.* **Pf 711 2**

Bibliographical index

Joseph ben Joshua ben Meir. *The Chronicles of Rabbi Joseph ben Joshua ben Meir, the Sphardi.* Translated and edited by Christoph Heinrich Friedrich Bialloblotzky. 2 vols. London: Richard Bentley for the Oriental Translation Fund of Great Britain and Ireland, 1835–6. **B 193v; Pf 711 59–61**

Jost, Isaac Marcus. *Geschichte der Israeliten seit der Zeit der Maccabäer.* 10 vols. Berlin: Schlesinger, 1820–47. **Pf 711 21*; Pf 710 1***

Geschichte des Judenthums und seiner Secten. 3 vols. Leipzig: Dorffling, 1857–9. **Pf 711 21* ; Pf 710 1***

Kalisch, Ludwig. *Bilder aus meiner Knabenzeit.* Leipzig: Ernst Keil, 1872. **B 121, 137, 138, 182**

Karpeles, Gustav. *Die Frauen der jüdischen Literatur.* Berlin, 1871. **B 138***

Keats, John. 'Hyperion', 'Isabella; or, the Pot of Basil', and 'Ode on a Grecian Urn'. In *Lamia, Isabella, The Eve of St Agnes, and Other Poems.* London: Taylor and Hessey, 1820. **Pf 711 3, 11*, 113, 112**

Keble, John. *The Christian Year: Thoughts in Verse for the Sundays and Holy Days throughout the Year.* 1827 and many later editions. **Pf 711 108**

Kelly, Walter Keating. *Curiosities of Indo-European Tradition and Folklore.* London: Chapman and Hall, 1863. **Pf 711 10***

Kinglake, Alexander William. *The Invasion of the Crimea: its Origin, and an Account of its Progress down to the Death of Lord Raglan.* Vol. V. *The Battle of Inkerman.* Edinburgh: William Blackwood and Sons, 1875. **Pf 711 94**

Kingsley, Charles. 'Heroism' in the *Cornhill Magazine* 27 (1873): 32. **Pf 707 9**

Kirchhoff, Adolf. *Die Composition der Odyssee.* Berlin: W. Hertz, 1869. **Pf 711 15***

Kompert, Leopold. *Aus dem Ghetto.* Leipzig: Grunow, 1848. **Pf 711 11***

Köppen, Carl Friedrich. *Die Religion des Buddha und ihre Entstehung.* 2 vols. Berlin: Ferdinand Schneider, 1857–9. **Pf 711 34* ; Pf 707 38***

Bibliographical index

Kuenen, Abraham. *The Religion of Israel to the Fall of the Jewish State.* Translated by Alfred Heath May from the Dutch edition of 1869–70. 3 vols. London: Williams and Norgate, 1874–5.
Pf 710 6, 11, 12, 14, 15, 18, 19, 21, 22, 23, 27, 29, 30, 31, 35, 35a

Lachmann, Karl Konrad Friedrich Wilhelm. *Betrachtungen über Homers Ilias.* Berlin, 1847. In DWL. **Pf 711 15***

La Fontaine, Jean de. *Fables.* **Pf 707 2**

Lampronti, Isaak. [Talmudic Encyclopaedia]. 10 vols. Berlin: A. Berliner, 1864–88. **Pf 711 101***

Lane, Edward William, transl. *The Thousand and One Nights, commonly called, in England, The Arabian Nights' Entertainments.* New ed. 3 vols. London: Charles Knight, 1859. In Mrs Ouvry's inventory. **Pf 711 63*, 107**

La Roche, Jakob. 'Über die Enstehung der Homerischen Gedichte'. In *Zeitschrift für die österreichischen Gymnasien.* Vienna, 1863. pp. 161–202. **Pf 711 15***

Lenormant, François. *La Magie chez les chaldéens et les origines accadiennes.* Paris: Maisonneuve, 1874. In DWL. **Pf 711 43***

Leopardi, Count Giacomo. *Canti.* **Pf 707 33**

Levi, David, transl. *The Festival Prayers, According to the Custom of the German and Polish Jews.* 6 vols. London: Abrahams and Son, 5620/1859 to 5633/1873. **B 118, 184, 185, 185v, 186v, 187, 187v, 188, 188v, 189, 189v, 190, 194 ; Pf 711 105, 104**

Levi, Giuseppi Raffaele. *Parabeln, Legenden und Gedanken aus Thalmud und Midrasch.* Translated by Ludwig Seligmann. Leipzig: Institut zur Förderung der israelitischen Literatur, 1863. In DWL.
B 135v*, 158, 159 ; Pf 710 15*; Pf 707 28, 29, 32

Lewes, George Henry. *Problems of Life and Mind. First Series. Foundations of a Creed.* Vol. II. London: Trübner, 1875. In DWL. **Pf 711 3, 67**

Problems of Life and Mind. Second Series. The Physical Basis of Mind. London: Trübner, 1877. In DWL. **Pf 707 33–34**

Bibliographical index

Lewysohn, Ludwig. *Sechzig Epitaphien von Grabsteinen des israelitischen Friedhofes zu Worms.* Frankfurt: J. Baer, 1855. **B 138***

Littré, Maximilien Paul Emile. *Médecine et médecins.* Paris: Didier, 1872. In DWL. **Pf711 2**

La Science au point de vue philosophique. Paris: Didier, 1873. In DWL. **Pf711 2**

Löwy, Albert. 'Translator's Introduction to the Writings of Dr. Zunz'. In *Miscellany of Hebrew Literature.* Edited by Albert Löwy. I, 151–66. London: Trübner for the Society of Hebrew Literature, 1872. In DWL. **B 193v; Pf711 76**

Lübke, Wilhelm. 'Die Gothische Styl und die Nationalitäten'. Not traced. **Pf711 6**

Lyly, John. *Euphues, The Anatomy of Wit* (1579) and *Euphues and his England* (1580). Edited by Edward Arber. London: Alex Murray, 1868. **Pf711 51, 52**

Maimonides, or Moise ben Maimoun. *Le Guide des égarés.* Translated with a commentary by Salomon Munk. 3 vols. Paris: A. Franck, 1856–66. **B 112, 112v; Pf711 21***

Maimon, Salomon. *Salomon Maimons Lebensgeschichte von ihm selbst geschrieben.* Edited by K.P. Moritz. Berlin: Friedrich Vieweg, 1792. **B 136**

Maine, Henry James Sumner. *Village Communities in the East and West.* 2nd ed. London: John Murray, 1872. In DWL. **Pf711 11***

Lectures on the Early History of Institutions. London: John Murray, 1875. In DWL. **Pf711 81**

Malory, Thomas. *La Mort d' Arthure. The History of King Arthur and of the Knights of the Round Table.* Edited by Thomas Wright. 2nd ed. 3 vols. London: John Russell Smith, 1866. **Pf711 7, 8, 11***

Mandeville, John. 'The Book of Sir John Maundeville'. In Thomas Wright, ed. *Early Travels in Palestine.* London: Bohn, 1848. **B 99**

Martial. *Epigrams.* **Pf711 112**

Bibliographical index

Marx, Adolf Bernhard. *Ludwig van Beethoven. Leben und Schaffen.* 2nd ed. 2 vols. Berlin: Otto Janke, 1863. **Pf 711 5, 11***

Maxwell, James Clerk. 'Molecules': Presidential Address to the British Association for the Advancement of Science. *Nature* 2 (1870): 419–22. **B 100–101; Pf 711 67**

Mendelssohn, Moses. *Jerusalem: oder über religiöse Macht und Judenthum.* 2 vols. Berlin: Friedrich Maurer, 1783. **Pf 711 21***

Meres, Francis. *Palladis Tamia.* 1598. **Pf 711 47***

Mill, John Stuart. *Principles of Political Economy.* London: J. W. Parker, 1848 and later eds. **Pf 711 11***

Milman, Henry Hart. *The History of the Jews from the Earliest Period Down to Modern Times.* 4th ed. 3 vols. London: John Murray, 1866. In DWL.
B 106, 112v, 151, 153a, 154v, 155 ; Pf 711 8, 21*

Milton, John. *Paradise Regained.* **Pf 707 16**

Minckwitz, Johannes. *Vorschule zum Homer.* Stuttgart, 1863. **Pf 711 15***

Mimnermus. In Wilhelm Theodor Bergk, editor. *Poetae Lyrici Graeci.* Leipzig: Reichenbach, 1843. In DWL. **Pf 711 11***

Mivart, St George. 'Contemporary Evolution: Part IV'. *Contemporary Review* 23 (1874): 362–5. **Pf 711 62**

Mommsen, Theodor. *Römische Geschichte.* 2 vols. Berlin: Weidmann, 1854–5. **Pf 710 22***

Monro, David Binning. 'The Homeric Question'. *Quarterly Review* 125 (1868): 444. **B 105v**

Morley, John. 'Carlyle'. *Fortnightly Review* 8 n.s. (1870): 16. **Pf 711 4**

Morris, Richard, ed. *Dan Michel's Ayenbite of Inwit, or Remorse of Conscience, in the Kentish Dialect, 1340 AD.* London: Trübner for the Early English Text Society, 1866. **Pf 707 2***

Bibliographical index

Müller, Friedrich Max. *Introduction to the Science of Religion.* London: Longmans, 1873. In Mrs Ouvry's inventory. **Pf 710 15**

Müller, Karl Ottfried. *History of the Literature of Ancient Greece.* London: Baldwin and Cradock, 1840. In DWL. **Pf 711 112**

Munk, Salomon. *Palestine. Description géographique, historique et archéologique.* Paris: Firmin-Didot, 1845. In DWL. **B 150, 173 ; Pf 711 21*; Pf 710 33; Pf 707 9**

Mélanges de philosophie juive et arabe. Paris: A. Franck, 1857. **Pf 710 20, 23, 28, 41 ; Pf 707 1, 12, 32, 33**

Nitzsch, Gregor Wilhelm. *Die Sagenpoesie der Griechen, kritisch dargestellt.* 2 vols. Braunschweig: C. A. Schwetschke, 1852. **Pf 711 15***

Nöldeke, Theodor. *Untersuchungen zur Kritik des Alten Testaments.* Kiel: Schwers, 1869. **Pf 710 1***

Nordheimer, Isaac. *A Critical Grammar of the Hebrew Language.* New York: Wiley and Putnam, 1842. **Pf 710 1***

'Notes on Travel'. *Academy* 25 April 1874: 460. **Pf 711 45, 46**

Nutzhorn, Friedrich. *Die Enstehungsweise der homerischen Gedichte.* Leipzig: Teubner, 1869. **Pf 711 15***

Oppenheim, Moritz, and Leopold Stein. *Bilder aus dem altjüdischen Familienleben.* Frankfurt, 1866 [also 1868, 1872]. **B 123; Pf 711 53, 54**

Ovid. *The Metamorphoses ... and minor works of Ovid.* Edited and translated by H. T. Riley. 3 vols. Bohn's Classical Library, 1851–2. In DWL. **Pf 911 91a**

Paget, Sir James. *Clinical Lectures and Essays* . Edited by Howard Marsh. London: Longmans, Green, 1875. In DWL. **Pf 711 94a**

Paley, Frederick Apthorp. 'On the Comparatively Late Date and Composite Character of our Iliad and Odyssey'. *Transactions of the Cambridge Philosophical Society* 11 (1871), Part II: 360–86. **B 102–105**

'The Odyssey of Homer'. *British Quarterly Review* 58 (1873): 414–45. **B 91, 92, 105v**

Bibliographical index

Palgrave, William Gifford. *Narrative of a Year's Journey through Central and Eastern Asia (1862–63).* 2 vols. London: Macmillan, 1865. **Pf 710 34; Pf 707 64**

Essays on Eastern Questions. London: Macmillan, 1872. **Pf 711 51***

Paracelsus. *Nach seinem Leben und seinen Lehren dargestellt aus seinen eigen Schriften.* Sulzbach, 1819. In DWL. **B 99**

Paris, John Ayrton. *Pharmacologia.* 9th ed. London: Samuel Highley, 1843. **B 97v**

Paris, Paulin, ed. *Les Romans de la table ronde mis en nouveau langage.* 5 vols. Paris: Léon Techener, 1868–72. In DWL. **Pf 711 11***

Pascheles, Wolf, ed. *Sippurim, eine Sammlung jüdischer Volkssagen, Erzählungen, Mythen, Chroniken, Denkwürdigkeiten und Biographien berühmter Juden aller Jahrhunderte, insbesondere des Mittelalters,* Vol. III. Prague: Pascheles, 1854. In DWL. **B 137v; Pf 711 68, 114***

Persius. *Satires.* **B 120–122v; Pf 711 43**

Picciotto. James. *Sketches of Anglo-Jewish History.* London: Trübner, 1875. In DWL. **Pf 711 24, 94***

'Introduction to Sketches of Anglo-Jewish History'. *Jewish Chronicle* n. s. 6 (5635/1874–5): 638. **B 193v**

Pindar. In Wilhelm Theodor Bergk, ed. *Poetae Lyrici Graeci.* Leipzig: Reichenbach, 1843. In DWL . **B 92v–97; Pf 711 23**

Plato. *Phaedo.* In *Dialogie Graece et Latine.* 5 vols. Berolini, 1816–23. In DWL. **Pf 711 11***

The Dialogues of Plato translated into English with Analyses and Introductions. Translated by Benjamin Jowett. 2nd ed. 5 vols. Oxford: Clarendon Press, 1875. In DWL. **Pf 711 9, 11 ***

Pleyte, Willem. *Etudes égyptologiques.* Leiden: E. J. Brill, 1866–8. **Pf 710 31**

Plutarch's Lives of Illustrious Men. Translated by John and William Langhorne (1770). 6 vols. London: 1823. Sold at auction. **Pf 707 69**

Proctor, Richard Anthony. 'Gambling Superstitions'. *Cornhill Magazine* 25 (1872): 704–17. **Pf 711 40, 41**

Quintilian. *De Institutio Oratoria.* **Pf 707 2**

Rabbinowicz, Israel Jehiel Michael. *Hebräische Grammatik.* Grünberg: Levysohn, 1851. **Pf 710 1***

Hebräische Schulgrammatik. Breslau: 1853. **Pf 710 1***

Rabelais, François. *Les Oeuvres de François Rabelais.* 5 vols. Paris: Bibliothèque Nationale Collection, 1870–3. In DWL. **Pf 711 72, 85**

Religionsgebräuche, die abergläubischen und sehr beschwerlichen, den talmudischen Juden von ihren Rabbinen vorgeschrieben. Bern: Jenni, 1874. **B 182**

Renan, Ernest. *Le Livre de Job.* Paris: Michel Lévy frères, 1859. **Pf 710 1***

Histoire générale et système comparé des langues sémitiques. 3rd ed. Paris: Michel Lévy frères, 1863. In DWL. **B 184v; Pf 710 23**

Rio, Alexis François. *Les Quatre martyrs.* Paris: A. Bray, 1856. **Pf 711 101 ***

Rothschild, David. *Der synagogal-Cultus in historisch-kritischer Entwicklung populär dargestellt.* Vol. I. *Die synagogalen Gebete.* Alzey: Joseph Weiss, 1870. In DWL. **Pf 711 114***

Rousseau, Jean-Jacques. *Du Contrat social, ou principes du droit politique* (1762). New ed. Paris, 1866. Formerly in DWL. **Pf 711 19**

Sachs, Michael Jehiel. *Die religiöse Poesie der Juden in Spanien.* Berlin: Veit, 1845. **B 108*; Pf 711 21*; Pf 710 20***

Saigey, Emile. *Les Sciences au XVIIIe siècle, la physique de Voltaire.* Paris: G. Baillière, 1873. In DWL. **B 99; Pf 711 9**

Saint-Hilaire, J. Barthélemy. *Le Bouddha et sa religion.* 3rd ed. Paris: Didier, 1866. In DWL. **Pf 710 10, 34, 35**

Sale, George, transl. and ed. *The Koran, Commonly called the Alcoran of Mohammed.* New ed. London: Chandos Classics, 1876. In DWL. **Pf 707 1 ***

Salvador, Joseph. *Paris, Rome, Jérusalem: ou la question religieuse au XIXe siècle.* 2 vols. Paris: Michel Lévy frères, 1860. **Pf 711 21***

Histoire des institutions de Moïse et du peuple hébreu. 3rd ed. 2 vols. Paris: Michel Lévy frères, 1862. **Pf 711 21***

Sappho. In Wilhelm Theodor Bergk, editor. *Poetae Lyrici Graeci.* Leipzig: Reichenbach, 1843. In DWL. **Pf 711 11***

Sayce, Archibald Henry. *Babylonian Literature: Lectures Delivered at the Royal Institution.* London: Samuel Bagster, 1877. **Pf 710 1 ***

Schopenhauer, Arthur. *Die Welt als Wille und Vorstellung* (1818). 3rd ed. Leipzig: F. A. Brockhaus, 1859. **Pf 711 11***

Schudt, Johann Jacob. *Jüdische Merckwürdigkeiten vorstellende was sich curieuses und denkwürdiges in den neuern Zeiten bei einigen Jahrhunderten mit denen in alle IV Theil der Welt, sonderlich durch Teutschland, zerstreuten Juden zugetragen.* 2 vols. Frankfurt and Leipzig: S. T. Nocker, 1715–18. In DWL. **Pf 711 100*, 101***

Sengebusch, Maximilian. *Homerica dissertatio prior et posterior.* Leipzig, 1855–6. **Pf 711 15***

Shakespeare, William. *The Works of William Shakespeare.* Edited by Alexander Dyce and revised by John Forster. 3rd ed. London, 1874. **Pf 711 47, 48**

Hamlet **Pf 711 26**

1 Henry IV **Pf 711 107**

2 Henry VI **Pf 711 107**

Othello **Pf 711 106, 105**

Taming of the Shrew **Pf 711 63**

Troilus and Cressida **Pf 711 107**

Winter's Tale **Pf 711 63**

Skeat, Walter William, ed. *Reprinted Glossaries.* London: Trübner for the English Dialect Society, 1873–9, Series B, Nos. 1, 5, 6, and 23. In DWL. **Pf 711 13**

Tendlau, Abraham Moses. *Das Buch der Sagen und Legenden jüdischer Vorzeit.* 2nd ed. Stuttgart, 1845. **Pf 711 93a***

Sprichwörter und Redensarten deutsch-jüdischer Vorzeit. Als Beitrag zur Volks- Sprach- und Sprichwörter-Kunde. Frankfurt: Heinrich Keller, 1860. In Mrs Ouvry's inventory. **Pf 711 97a, 98a, 101–104, 114* ; Pf 710 7, 25, 27**

Tennyson, Alfred. *Idylls of the King.* **Pf 711 113**

'Sea-dreams' and 'Tithonus'. **Pf 711 112**

Thorpe, Benjamin. *Northern Mythology, Comprising the Principal Popular Traditions and Superstitions of Scandinavia, North Germany, and the Netherlands.* 3 vols. London: Edward Lumley, 1851–2. **Pf 707 71–73**

Tiedge, Christoph August. 'Macht der Gewohnheit'. **Pf 711 100***

Tillier, Anton von. *Geschichte der europäischen Menschheit im Mittelalter.* 4 vols. Frankfurt: Schmerber, 1829-30. In DWL. **Pf 711 3**

Tylor, Edward Burnett. *Researches into the Early History of Mankind and the Development of Civilization.* London: John Murray, 1865. **B 99; Pf 711 62, 63**

Primitive Culture: Researches into the Development of Mythology, Philosophy, Religion, Art and Custom. 2 vols. London: John Murray, 1871. In Mrs Ouvry's inventory. **Pf 711 64, 65, 70**

Tyndall, John. 'On the Scientific Use of the Imagination'. In *Fragments of Science for Unscientific People.* London: Longmans, Green, 1871. **B 101**

Six Lectures on Light, Delivered in America in 1872–1873. London: Longmans, Green, 1873. **B 97v, 99**

Inaugural Address as President of the British Association for the Advancement of Science, in Belfast on 19 August 1874. *Nature* 10 (1874): 308–19. **Pf 711 63**

Varro, Marcus Terentius. *De Lingua Latina.* **Pf 711 41**

Virchow, Rudolf L. C., and Franz von Holzendorff-Vietmansdorf, eds. *Sammlung gemeinverständlicher wissenschaftlicher Vorträge,* series VI. Berlin, 1871: 'Die Umwandlungsprocess im Mineralreich' (pp. 545–84); 'Ueber des hieroglyphische Schriftsystem' (pp. 363–98); 'Alte und neuere Astrologie' (pp. 710–40). **Pf 711 11***

Virgil. *Aeneid.* **Pf 711 11*, 112**

Wagenseil, Johann Christoph. *Johann Christof Wagenseils Belehrung der jüdisch-teutschen Red- und Schreibart.* 2 parts. Königsberg: P.F. Rhode, 1699. **B 183, 193v* ; Pf 711 54*; Pf 710 41***

Wallace, Alfred Russel. *The Malay Archipelago: The Land of the Orang-utan and the Bird of Paradise, a Narrative of Travel with Studies of Man and Nature.* 2 vols. London: Macmillan, 1869. **Pf 711 4**

Weinhold, Karl. *Die deutschen Frauen in dem Mittelalter.* Vienna: C. Gerold, 1851. **B 138***

Welcker, Friedrich Gottlieb. *Der epische Cyclus oder die homerischen Dichter.* Bonn: E. Weber, 1835. **Pf 711 15***

Wheatley, Henry Benjamin, ed. *The Romance of Merlin.* 3 parts. London: Trübner for the Early English Text Society, 1865, 1866, 1869. **Pf 707 14***

Whitney, William Dwight. *Language and its Study.* London: Trübner, 1874. **Pf 707 14**

Wilkinson, John Gardner. *A Popular Account of the Ancient Egyptians.* 2 vols. London: John Murray, 1854 . In Mrs Ouvry's inventory. Abridged from *The Private Life, Manners and Customs of the Ancient Egyptians.* 3 vols. London: John Murray, 1847. **B 97v; Pf 711 8, 11* ; Pf 710 34 ; Pf 707 46**

Williams, Joshua. *Principles of the Law of Real Property, Intended as a First Book for the Use of Students in Conveyancing.* 7th ed. London: H. Sweet, 1865. In DWL. **Pf 711 77, 78**

Wither, George. 'Faire-Virtue: or, The Mistresse of Phil'arete' (1622). Reprinted in *Juvenilia.* Manchester: Spenser Society, 1871. **Pf 711 4**

Wordsworth, William. *Prelude.* **Pf 711 111, 110**

'A Narrow Girdle of Rough Stones and Crags'. **Pf 711 8**

Subject Index

This index to particular persons, terms, and subjects is meant to supplement the preceding bibliographical index of George Eliot's sources. Information more directly accessible there is excluded here. In addition, George Eliot's own Index for the Berg Notebook (pp. 210–213) and her lists of the 'Chief Contents' of Pforzheimer 711 (p. 234) and Pforzheimer 707 (p. 437) serve as primary guides to the general subjects most significant to her. As noted in the Preface, most of the section titles listed in the table of Contents (pp. ix to xiii) derive from her index and 'contents' entries. For the alphabetically arranged Pforzheimer 710, a summary of its contents is provided on pp. 390–391.

Subject index

Subject index

Subject index

Subject index

Subject index

Subject index

Subject index

Printed in the United Kingdom
by Lightning Source UK Ltd.
135258UK00001B/167/P

9 780521 087971